Date: 9/2/21

**780.9 MUS V.1
Music around the world.
a global encyclopedia /**

Music around the World

Music around the World

A Global Encyclopedia

VOLUME I: A–G
Andrew R. Martin and
Matthew Mihalka, Editors

ABC-CLIO®

An Imprint of ABC-CLIO, LLC
Santa Barbara, California • Denver, Colorado

Copyright © 2020 by ABC-CLIO, LLC

All rights reserved. No part of this publication may be reproduced, stored in a retrieval system, or transmitted, in any form or by any means, electronic, mechanical, photocopying, recording, or otherwise, except for the inclusion of brief quotations in a review, without prior permission in writing from the publisher.

Library of Congress Cataloging-in-Publication Data

Names: Martin, Andrew R., editor. | Mihalka, Matthew, editor.
Title: Music around the world : a global encyclopedia / Andrew R. Martin and Matthew Mihalka, editors.
Description: 1st edition. | Santa Barbara : ABC-CLIO, 2020. | Includes bibliographical references and index.
Identifiers: LCCN 2019042635 (print) | LCCN 2019042636 (ebook) | ISBN 9781440846366 (v. 1 ; cloth) | ISBN 9781440846373 (v. 2 ; cloth) | ISBN 9781440846380 (v. 3 ; cloth) | ISBN 9781610694988 (cloth) | ISBN 9781610694995 (ebook)
Subjects: LCSH: World music—Encyclopedias.
Classification: LCC ML100 .M894 2020 (print) | LCC ML100 (ebook) | DDC 780.9—dc23
LC record available at https://lccn.loc.gov/2019042635
LC ebook record available at https://lccn.loc.gov/2019042636

ISBN: 978-1-61069-498-8 (set)
    978-1-4408-4636-6 (vol. 1)
    978-1-4408-4637-3 (vol. 2)
    978-1-4408-4638-0 (vol. 3)
    978-1-61069-499-5 (ebook)

24 23 22 21 20   1 2 3 4 5

This book is also available as an eBook.

ABC-CLIO
An Imprint of ABC-CLIO, LLC

ABC-CLIO, LLC
147 Castilian Drive
Santa Barbara, California 93117
www.abc-clio.com

This book is printed on acid-free paper ∞

Manufactured in the United States of America

Contents

Alphabetical List of Entries   vii

Preface   xiii

Introduction   xv

Entries: A–Z   1

About the Editors   965

Contributors   967

Index   973

Alphabetical List of Entries

VOLUME ONE
Acadian Music
Accordion (Americas)
Accordion, Types of
Adé, "King" Sunny
African Spirituals
Afrobeat (Afropop)
Afro-Cuban Jazz
Ahmad, Fadzil
Amadinda
Amish Hymns (*Ausbund*, *Gesangbuch*)
Andalusian Music
Andean Region, Music of the
Arab Classical Music
Armenian Music
Armstrong, Louis
Ashkenazi Jews, Music of
Astatke, Mulatu
Austro-German Dances
Bağlama
Bagpipes
Bandoneón
Banjo
Bariu, Laver
Bartók, Béla
Bashir Brothers (Munir and Jamil)
Basque, Music of the
Batá Drums
Beatles, The
Bebop
Bedouin Music
Bélé
Belly Dance
Berimbau
Björk
Bluegrass
Blues
Bol
Bolivia, Music of
Bollywood Music
Bomba, Ecuador
Bomba, Puerto Rico
Bones (Britain and Ireland)
Brazil, Music of
Buena Vista Social Club
Bunraku
Cajun Music
Calypso
Candomblé
Cantopop
Caribbean Art Music
Carmody, Kevin Daniel "Kev"
Carnival, Music of
Carter Family, The

Alphabetical List of Entries

Čechomor
Celtic Music
Chamarrita
Chanson (Urban/Modern)
Chinese Pop
Chopi People, Music of the
Chutney
Chutney Soca
Classical Music, European
Claves and Clave Rhythm
Cohan, George M.
Colometry/Colometric
Coltrane, John
Concerto
Congo Square
Conjunto
Conjunto (Norteños)
Corrido
Cossacks, Music of
Country Music
Cretan Lyra
Cruz, Celia
Cuatro
Cumbia
Dancehall
Darbuka
Dastgah
Davis, Miles (Dewey, III)
Densmore, Frances
Dhol
Dhrupad
Didgeridoo
Dixieland
Djembe
Dmitri Pokrovsky Ensemble
Dorsey, Thomas A.
Duduk
Dulcimer
Dylan, Bob
Eastern Woodland Native American Music
Emmett, Dan (Daniel Decatur)
Enka Music
Erhu
Eurovision Song Contest
Fado
Fairuz
Fiddle
Field Hollers
Flamenco Music
Folkways Records
Foster, Stephen Collins
French Folk Dances
Fujara
Funk
Gagaku
Gamelan Orchestra (Balinese)
Gamelan Orchestra (Javanese)
Ganga
Ganga Singing
Gender Wayang
Gimbri
Gospel Music
Greek Popular Music
Gregorian Chant
Griot
Guitarrón Mexicano
Gumba
Guoyue
Guthrie, Woody
Guzheng
Gyil

Alphabetical List of Entries

VOLUME TWO

Handy, W. C.
Harana and Kundiman
Hardanger Fiddle (Hardingfele)
Harmonium
Hawaii, Music of
Highlife
Hōgaku
Hornbostel, Erich Moritz von
Huayno
Huqin
Icelandic Ballads
Indian Folk Songs
Indonesian Pop Music
Iranian Classical Music
Irish American Vocal Music
Irish Dance Music
Irish Step Dancing
Italian Folk Music (Various Regions)
Jackson, Mahalia
Jali
Janggu
Japan, Music of
Jazz
Jehan, Noor
Jingju (Beijing Opera)
Johnson, Robert
Joik
Joplin, Scott
J-Pop
Kabuki
Kalthoum, Umm
Kamancheh
Karnatic Music
Kayokyoku
Kebyar
Kecak
Kendang
Khaled, Cheb
Khan, Nusrat Fateh Ali
Khayal
Khene
Kidjo, Angelique
Klezmer
Kodály, Zoltán
Kora
Koto
K-Pop (Korean Pop)
Kulintang
Kuti, Fela
Ladysmith Black Mambazo
Ländler
Launeddas
Lead Belly
Lenya, Lotte
Lithuanian Music
Lomax, Alan and John
Madrigal
Makam
Makeba, Miriam
Malay Music
Malhūn
Malouf
Mambo
Mande Music
Manu Chao
Mariachi
Marimba
Marley, Bob
Marshall Islands, Music of
Masakela, Hugh
Mbalax
Mbila
Mbube

McPhee, Colin
Medieval Secular Song
Mento
Merengue
Mestizo Music
Mexican Regional Music
Mikagura
Min'yô
Moravian Music
Morin Khuur
Mridangam
Musafir
Musicals
Native American Church Music
Native American Flute
Native American Music
Native American Popular Music
Navajo, Music of
Ney
Nisiotika
Nô Theater
Nongak
Nordic Jazz
North Korea, Music of
Norwegian Folk Music
Nueva Canción
Nyckelharpa
Olatunji, Babatunde
Opera
Original Dixieland Jazz Band
Ottoman Classical Music
Oud
Owiyo, Suzanna
Pakistan, Music of
Pansori (P'ansori)
Parker, Charlie
Pashto Music

Philippines, Music of the
Piazzolla, Astor
Pimba
Pipa
Piphat
Polish National Dances
Polka
Polynesia, Music of
Polynesian Hymns
Presley, Elvis
Psaltery
Puente, Tito

VOLUME THREE
Qānūn
Qin (Guqin)
Qraqeb
Quadrille
Quelbe
Race Records
Raga
Ragtime
Rai
Rainey, Ma
Rakha, Alla
Rancho Folclórico
Rap/Hip-Hop
Rap/Hip-Hop in Africa and the Middle East
Rara
Rebab
Redzepova, Esma
Reggae
Reggaetón
Rímur
Riq
Rock and Roll

Alphabetical List of Entries

Rodgers, Jimmie
Rodrigues, Amália
Romani Music
Rumba
Runo Song
Russian Orthodox Church Music
Salsa
Samba Instruments
Samba Music
Sanjo
Schlager
Schottische
Schrammelmusik
Scotch Snap
Seeger, Peter
Sephardic Music
Shajarian, Mohammed-Reza
Shakuhachi
Shamanic Music in Mongolia and Inner Asia
Shamisen
Shankar, Ravi
Shape-Note Singing
Shômyô
Singspiel
Sitar
Ska
Smith, Bessie
Soca
Soul
Steel Guitar
Steelpan
Sufism, Music of
Swing
Symphonic Poem
Symphony
Tabla
Tagore, Rabindranath
Taiko
Taiwanese Opera
Taiwanese Traditional and Popular Music
Tala
Tamboo Bamboo
Tango
Taqsīm
Tar
Tassa Drumming
Tejano Music
Thumri
Tibetan Buddhist Chant
Tibetan Singing Bowls
Tin Pan Alley
Tin/Pennywhistle
Tombak
Touré, Ali Farka
Turbo-Folk
Tuvan Popular Bands
Tuvan Throat Singing
Ukulele
Vaudeville
Veena
Villa-Lobos, Heitor
Virginia Minstrels
Vocables
Waltz
Wayang Kulit
Xalam
Yodeling
Yuman Music
Zajal
Ziegfeld, Florenz, Jr.
Zither
Zouk
Zydeco

Preface

Music around the World: A Global Encyclopedia covers a wide array of music, music cultures, and musical instruments from cultures spanning the inhabited world. This three-volume work explores the study of what is commonly referred to as "world music," a term that broadly encompasses a variety of musical styles, traditions, and genres, including art music, popular music, vernacular music, and indigenous music, among others. Our aim is to highlight the diversity of music produced throughout the world, celebrating the originality and uniqueness of these individual musical cultures while also exploring their connections to regional and global forces.

Globalization has had far-reaching impacts on music and migration as empires rise and fall and regional economic centers change the dissemination and formation of unique and localized music genres. Music and society are direct reflections of one another and with each of these changes to the global order so, too, does the music of homelands and diasporas change. *Music around the World* explores music in its various contexts, be it homelands, diaspora, or local scenes within specified regional areas. This includes subject entries on individual music genres, music cultures, musical instruments, important performers or practitioners, and scholars.

Rather than organize the three volumes into geographic regions, the entries are arranged in A-Z format to demonstrate the interconnectedness of many musical cultures from disparate locations. The Punjabi Indian traditional folk music genre *bhangra* has, for example, evolved into a new, but still related, form in the United Kingdom. Indeed, migration, colonialism, and economic mobility both voluntary and forced (slavery) have all contributed to the dissemination and continued development of many music cultures. *Music around the World* lends equal credence to diaspora studies, and many subject entries such as "Rap" have separate, but related, entries listed consecutively rather than separated via regional locations.

The entries in *Music around the World* are encyclopedic essays written by expert contributing authors, themselves spanning the globe and hailing from dozens of different countries across five continents. In addition to the essay, most entries include a "see also" cross-reference to related entries from throughout *Music around the World*'s three volumes, a further reading section with Web resources, and many feature short sidebars on interesting and/or related topics. Where variation or discrepancy between spellings of entries occurs, this work will defer to the most commonly understood spellings as noted by our team of expert authors.

Local, regional, and global music cultures and styles are products of the larger world that they inhabit. Because music and society are constantly evolving and developing anew, the three volumes of *Music around the World* are by no means exhaustive in their scope, as new music and changes in current musical genres are underway as you read these lines—a process of renewal that will continue into the future.

Introduction

Around 1987, executives for several major recording labels and their subsidiaries in the United States and the United Kingdom had a problem on their hands: What to do with the newly emerging and increasingly profitable market of non-Western musical genres? The popularity of artists such as Youssou N'Dour, Umm Kalthum, Ladysmith Black Mambazo, and Ravi Shankar was wide-ranging in Europe and the United States, yet these artists did not fit neatly into the established rock, pop, country, and classical paradigms that governed the music industry in the West. As sidemen for Western music icons the Beatles (Ravi Shankar) and Paul Simon (Ladysmith Black Mambazo), they enjoyed a global notoriety previously unheard of for non-Western musicians. This exposure sparked many curious listeners to seek out their respective work in traditional non-Western music genres as local practitioners, and it was here that, for the recording industry, the disconnect was occurring. In search of Fela Kuti at a record store (prior to the internet) one might find the African highlife superstar listed under "Afro-beat" or "Afro-pop" or "highlife" or other geographically specific markers such as "African" music or "Nigerian" music, and there was also the occasional (and aptly named) "other" category.

By midsummer, intrepid record executives realized that confusion was negatively affecting sales, and a meeting was called by several leading stakeholders (producers, executives, and artists' managers) to address the issue. The results of this labor were the formation and adoption of the category name "World Music" to be used in promotion and description for non-Western musical artists and genres, and this name has since remained the dominant semantic identifier for non-Western music genres in the recording industry (Anderson, 2000). The term has been adopted by many beyond the recording industry; it has become a widely used identifier in academia, primary education, and secondary education.

But what exactly is "world music"? How can we approach a study, such as this one, of music from both Western and non-Western societies? For example, salsa music is, for all intents and purposes, a Puerto Rican music genre created in New York City; this fact complicates the diverse study of non-Western music as we approach diaspora studies. Rap has a life of its own in Paris and *kechak* is an Indonesian music created anew out of the imagination of a Canadian composer to, in part, establish an imagined cultural identity and lure tourists to Indonesia. Whether appropriating, remaking, or creating anew any musical tradition, the tendency to label noncommercial or nonhegemonic music of the other as "world music" has plagued the study and consumption of non-Western music in the West for more than a century.

The roots of the term "world music" may only be approximately 40 years old; however, the engagement of the West with non-Western musical styles has a long history dating back to medieval Europe. From this time period, writings by French, Italian, German, and British aristocracy and ecclesiastical servants are full of accounts of roving Janissary music from the Ottoman/Turkish East, and the "exotic" music hailing from Moorish-controlled Spain has a well-documented history. Traders in Italy knew of many musical traditions from the Mediterranean region and incorporated these styles into local Italian folk and traditional styles. These intersections with non-Western musical styles had lasting effects on European music; however, during the European colonial exploration period (1400–1900 CE), the fascination with non-Western music styles moved to a new level. While Portuguese, Dutch, and English explorers were sending back stories to the European mainland chronicling the vast riches and amazing new peoples they had "discovered," these same explorers and missionaries also included tantalizing mentions of "new" and exotic musics performed by these newly encountered peoples during rituals, worships, and celebrations.

WORLD MUSIC IN SETTLER NATIONS AND MUSIC "SCENES"

Settler nation is a term generally applied to a country, such as the United States, in which indigenous people are replaced by "settlers" in a form of colonialism. At the turn of the 20th century, many settler nations sought labor from across the globe, often from various outposts of their colonial motherlands, and this influx of immigrants and cultures fueled the industrial revolution—but also brought with it a dearth of non-Western music traditions. The United States' ascendancy to global economic superpower status and role as a settler nation during the latter stages of the 19th and early 20th centuries served to create a rich and complex fabric of Western and non-Western music cultures. The United States has enjoyed a long history with world music, dating back to the country's inception some 300 years ago. However, the mass immigrations of the 19th century and post-World War II (1939–1945) era, coupled with this economic prowess, fueled exploration both domestically and international for exotic, regional, and remade non-Western music traditions.

By the 1920s, the recording industry in the United States that had begun only a few decades earlier was thriving, and regionally popular music from minority culture groups such as African Americans saw incredible gains. Industry executives, however, were under the impression that the American cultural mainstream—white American audiences—was more likely to buy jazz and other such "race records" if made by white musicians. An entire industry, with subsidiary record labels to boot, was created to market race records to a specific audience (African American, Irish, Polish, Jewish/Klezmer, etc.), and it had great success. Each new wave of immigrant labor meant an untapped market, and record labels competed to sign the best talent for what they perceived as the most appealing music cultures.

World War II signaled another major redistribution of peoples throughout the world, as the West and the East continued their codependent path of globalization. In industrialized nations such as the United States, Canada, the United Kingdom, and several others, once regionally isolated cultures relocated to large industrial cities (e.g., from the American South to the North) in search of work, and they brought along their unique music cultures. The crossover appeal of African American music styles and the Great Depression of the 1930s had long since ended the race record era. However, the overwhelming consumer abundance in post-war America was truly a dominant force that reached beyond economics and affected both social and cultural activities. By the early 1960s, Americans were spending upward of $300 billion annually on nonessential consumer products (Hurley, 2001, pp. 4–5). This increased spending correlated to increased interest in exotic music, often through nostalgic remembrances of experiences by American GIs from wartime outposts in the Far East. Non-Western music genres were *en vogue*, and the entertainment industry scrambled to capitalize on the deep pockets funding American consumers' penchant for escape.

At the same time as America's economic boom, Europe's postwar reconstruction was well underway, and one ancillary consequence was the shedding of their respective colonial tethers by several European colonies in the Caribbean, African, and Far East. Expanded routes and route agreements by major airline companies meant that travel to those exotic destinations increased tenfold; for example, the recently emancipated nations of the Caribbean and South America became travel hot spots for Americans. The stability of these fledgling governments now offered solid political constancy which simultaneously soothed and emboldened foreign travelers. A three-hour flight to from New York to Florida was outdone by a four-hour flight to St. Thomas, Jamaica, or Antigua. Reaching out with opens arms to the pocketbooks of eager American tourists meant offering the exotic, whether locally authentic, traditional, or imagined, and many foreign locals were eager to cater to American and European tourists' tastes and perceived notions of the "other." Often combining traditional cultural practices with newly imagined ones, regions such as the Leeward Islands and Lesser Antilles (which created an entire calendar of individual Carnival celebrations during the summer months to promote tourism during off-peak seasons) banded together in recreating (or newly creating) specific cultural and musical practices.

The exotica movement would see its peak in the late 1950s, but its embers still burned in the late 1960s when the Beatles recorded music with Indian musician Ravi Shankar. By the 1970s, scholars of non-Western music had begun exploring the work of non-Western music cultures in the diaspora. When a music style or music culture, diaspora included, creates anew a space for performance or regional acceptance, this area is referred to in *Music around the World* as a musical "scene." We use the term "scene" here in reference to the theories and work of ethnomusicologist Mark Slobin's concept of specifically located regional areas of musical activity. This is drawn from Slobin's landmark work *Subcultural Sounds: Microcosms of the West*, and the term and concept have been widely adopted throughout the field of ethnomusicology and musicology (Slobin, 1993). In his landmark publication in 1960, ethnomusicologist Mantle Hood argued that scholars needed the ability to balance two distinct cultural traditions—their own and another—in what he termed "bi-musicality" (Hood, 1960, 55–59). Hood's theory is apt in describing the heavy lifting necessary for any music culture to survive in scenes throughout the globe; however, given the continued globalization of the planet, one could argue that today's non-Western music cultures and performers practice a form of omni-musicality, thus reflecting the reality of today's digital interconnectedness.

MUSICAL INSTRUMENTS AND CLASSIFICATION

In the late 1870s and early 1880s, interdisciplinary scholars Eric Von Hornbostel and Curt Sachs developed a classification system for musical instruments for the purpose of cataloging instruments in the collections of museums and libraries. Their theories of organology and classification of musical instruments dominated the ethnomusicological world during the early 1900s and are a dominant method of categorizing musical instruments to this day. Many contributing authors of *Music around the World* make use of the Sachs-Hornbostel classification system, the terminology of which appears throughout in various entries.

According to the Sachs and Hornbostel system, the classification of musical instruments is done per a systematic arrangement of musical instruments based on a four-class system that, rather than basing categories on material construction (those made of metal, wood, bamboo, stone, etc.), is based on the means of sound production. The four categories of the Hornbostel and Sachs classification system are:

Idiophones—instrument itself sounds via striking, plucking, or by friction.

Membranophones—instrument has a stretched membrane that is struck, plucked, or sounded by friction.

Chordophones—instrument has strings that sound.

Aerophones—instrument uses air to sound.

Hornbostel used this new classification system to pioneer the field of comparative musicology, which itself became an integral element in the formation of ethnomusicology some 50 years thereafter. Hornbostel himself used this system of musical instrument classification to analyze traditional music styles of Asia, Africa, the Americas, and Europe. Many authors in *Music around the World* have referenced Hornbostel and Sachs or utilized their classification system in their individual subject entries in terms of musical instrument classification, rather than a methodology for comparative musicology.

WORLD MUSIC AND MUSICAL ANALYSIS

By simplifying their classification system to be guided by sound production, Sachs and Hornbostel avoided the complicated matter of applying sociological and anthropological elements to the analysis of musical instrument and non-Western musical genres. The theory of Cantometrics developed by Alan Lomax in the 1950s, for example, is one such well-known—though not widely adopted—classification theory that attempts to correlate music structure, social structure, and musical instrument construction. Lomax applied a series of analysis factors to a study group of 1,800 representative songs from music cultures across the globe. The recommendations of the study's results identify three main results, including a series of regional music types, correlations among musical components, and correlations between musical and social elements (Lomax, 1968).

In his landmark study of postcolonial attitudes in Europe, Edward Said redefined the term "orientalism" to mean the prejudices, false assumptions, and stereotypes that define Eurocentric attitudes toward the Far and Middle East. At some point, the European fascination with and study of Asia and the East during the previous century became, at times, fetishized to the point of fantasy; that is, the East became an imagined recreation of reality (Said, 2003). Said's study brings to light the impact and implications of colonialism as well as racial and ethnic condescension and fear. Most newly undertaken studies of music (whether contemporary or historical) have roots in orientalism, due in large part to the current climate of globalization and the digital interconnectedness of most world cultures.

In the case of world music writ large, a type of orientalism is at work, which expands and adjusts this perspective to reflect the prejudices, false assumptions, and stereotypes that define Western attitudes toward non-Western music and culture. This encyclopedia explores the impact of this modified brand of orientalism throughout the collection of various individual entries. Whenever pertinent, the authors aim to analyze the musical components and styles used to create non-Western music genres and styles, including in many cases an analysis of the contemporary and traditional cultural components that historically are represented by these musical identifiers. On nearly every level of construction, the sound design of many non-Western music genres elicits a musical balance between the familiar and the exotic, allowing the listener the maximum amount of leeway for applying and imprinting meaning.

Whereas Said's theory of orientalism was, and continues to be, widely celebrated, Lomax's Cantometrics system was widely criticized upon its introduction in the late 1950s, in part because of its reductivism and ethnocentrism. Cantometrics remains a cautionary tale for those embarking on the study of world music; however, its cultural imperialism aside, the study provides insight into various musical cultures.

In his groundbreaking 1963 study of ethnomusicology, Bruno Nettl tackled head-on perhaps the biggest problem and misconception plaguing the study of world music. Nettle noted that for centuries scholars have had a desire to understand all human music (that of animals or involuntary music aside) as part of a larger study of anthropology. The biggest success of this approach was the realization that the only common element in music of non-Western cultures was its "strangeness in relation to Western civilization" (Nettl, 1964, p. 2). The understanding of non-Western music in relation to Western music—a comparative musicology of sorts—is perhaps best clarified by Michael Bakan in his widely used textbook for college music courses. There Bakan aptly points out that music is not a universal language and that in fact many non-Western cultures do not have a word for music or describe it as such. He uses an example of the Qur'anic recitation and its intentions as prayer rather than music (Bakan, 2007).

Given the vastly different ways in which people view and engage with music throughout the world, Bakan offers a way forward by establishing five propositions for guiding the exploration of world music. These basic concepts boil down to: the basic property of music is sound; these sounds are organized in some way; the sounds are organized by people; the resulting music is a product of human intention; and the term (not conceptualization) "music" is "inescapably tied to Western culture and assumptions" (Bakan, 2007, pp. 2–7). To apply Bakan's assertions to this encyclopedia, the first four propositions are easily transferred and an apt way to describe the various entries selected for the project. Bakan's fifth proposition, too, applies as a guiding principle for this encyclopedia, as one could argue that that the lens by which the music cultures of the world are viewed is now, in 2019, filtered by the cultural dominance of the West and the shadow it casts throughout the world. Though written by authors from across the globe and dozens of cultures, *Music around the World* is inescapably tied to Western cultural perspectives. Despite this fact, every effort has been made throughout the work to provide insider and outsider perspectives of non-Western music cultures and genres.

Working in concert with Bakan's concept of a perspective filter through a Western lens, the global impact and development of any specific music culture or genre is perhaps best understood as a type of heritage (even in short individual studies such as those offered in this encyclopedia). Barbara Kirshenblatt-Gimblett suggests that theorizing heritage is a three-part concept in which heritage is a mode of cultural production in the present that has recourse to the past, heritage is a "value added" industry, and heritage produces the local for export (Kirshenblatt-Gimblett, 1995, pp. 367–380). Many of the individual entries in this encyclopedia are presented as heritage; that is, heritage in both a local and global understanding.

The application of Kirshenblatt-Gimblett's concept of heritage to the study of world music genres and performers should not, however, negate the musical proficiency and high artistic merit of non-Western music cultures and musicians. As Harvard ethnomusicologist Kay Shelemay has rightly pointed out in her past work, one issue plaguing the study of non-Western music is the reluctance of scholars working in the field to acknowledge virtuosic performers of a given genre. Such scholars have thus (intentionally or unintentionally) relegated the accomplishments of talented performers and complex, rich musical traditions to second-class status. There are, not doubt, many non-Western music traditions practiced by various cultures for various reasons that do not require virtuosity or complexity in order to serve their utilitarian cultural heritage and purpose. However, this encyclopedia has attempted, whenever applicable, to identify and celebrate non-Western music traditions found throughout the world (such as the steelband tradition in Trinidad and Tobago) that are full of "great men": iconic composers and/or performers who dominate the genre and capture the imagination of participants and audiences alike. Thus, here we celebrate the great achievers, developers, and iconic performers of non-Western music genres as well as the specific music cultures themselves. Contrary to firmly held Western misconceptions, not all non-Western music cultures are quaint folk practices. This encyclopedia aims to describe their depth and nuance whenever possible.

MUSIC AROUND THE WORLD: AN OVERVIEW

Music around the World is our attempt to chronicle many of the world's music cultures and genres in context. Our contributing authors span the globe and hail from dozens of different countries on five continents. Our approach to this work assumes that in many cases the best way to learn about elements of a specific local music style or genre is from a local expert, and many of our entries are written from this insider perspective. The three volumes are arranged from A to Z. The volumes take into account the various diasporas of any given culture, and users will find separate entries for certain music genres or cultures depending on the development of its music within its diaspora. An example is one entry on rap/hip-hop that focuses on Europe and another that focuses on the Americas.

Andrew R. Martin and Matthew Mihalka

FURTHER READING

Anderson, Ian. 2000. "World Music History." *fRoots* 201 (March). https://frootsmag.com/world-music-history.

Bakan, Michael. 2007. *World Music: Traditions and Transformations*, 2nd ed. New York: McGraw Hill.

Dudley, Shannon. 2008. *Music from Behind the Bridge: Steelband Aesthetics and Politics in Trinidad and Tobago*. New York: Oxford University Press.

Hood, Mantle. 1960. "The Challenge of 'Bi-Musicality.'" *Ethnomusicology* 4(2) (May), 55–59.

Hurley, Andrew. 2001. *Diners, Bowling Alleys and Trailer Parks: Chasing the American Dream in the Postwar Consumer Culture*. New York: Basic Books.

Kirshenblatt-Gimblett, Barbara. 1995. "Theorizing Heritage," *Ethnomusicology* 39(3) (Autumn), 367–380.

Lomax, Alan. 1968. *Folk Song Style and Culture*. Washington, DC: American Association for the Advancement of Science.

Nettl, Bruno. 1964. *Theory and Method in Ethnomusicology*. London: Free Press.

Said, Edward. 2003. *Orientalism*. London: Penguin.

Shelemay, Kay. 1987. "Response to Rice." *Ethnomusicology* 31(3) (Autumn), 489–490.

Slobin, Mark. 1993. *Subcultural Sounds: Microcosms of the West*. Middleton, CT: Wesleyan University Press.

Acadian Music

Acadian music dates back to the 1860s and has always played an important role in the Acadian culture. The earliest songs in the Acadian tradition were ballads with subject matter that focused on life difficulties and the oppression and suffering of the Acadian people. Shortly thereafter, Acadian music began to borrow from other immigrant music traditions—mainly Scottish-Irish and Native American. Much of the Acadians' early music involved *reels á bouche*, or music that is created with the mouth by humming or singing, with rhythmic clapping and foot stamping.

Acadia was founded as the first French colony in the New World in 1604, after Samuel de Champlain landed in Nova Scotia, Canada. Most of those settling in this area were from western France. When conflict arose between France and England over who would control North America's fur trade, the Acadians lost their lands and were forcibly removed. This scattered the Acadian people throughout North America and they eventually founded new settlements in New England, Louisiana, and Haiti in the diaspora. In their new homes in Louisiana, the Acadians became known as Cajuns.

When Acadians first came to Canada from France, they brought with them many of the older French songs, mostly originating in the Poitou region, the home region of most of the immigrants who relocated to the New World. The music from this area was largely comprised of ballads, lyrical songs with complicated texts, and instrumental ensemble playing on fiddles and wind instruments.

Early instruments incorporated into Acadian music include violins and fiddles (usually two, with one playing the rhythm and one playing the melody), triangles (called "'tit fer"), and accordions. In approximately 1928, Acadian bands began using guitars to accompany the fiddles, triangles, and accordions. The rub board also became popular during this time. In the 1930s, drums and electric amplification were introduced to the music, as were the harmonica and pedal steel guitar.

Among the first to record Acadian music were Joseph Falcon and his wife, Cleoma. The song was "Let's Go to Lafayette," recorded in 1928. The first national Acadian music hit was recorded by Harry Choates. The song was "Jolie Blonde," recorded in 1946. Since then, there have been a number of influential Acadian artists, including Dennis McGee, Luderin Darbonne and the Hackberry Ramblers, Iry LeJeune, Lawrence Walker, and Aldus Roger. The Pine Grove Boys became quite popular during the 1950s, and although their leader Nathan Abshire has passed on, the other original members of the band have regrouped and still play music today.

Acadian music played an active role in influencing swamp pop, a 1950s style of music inspired by Chuck Berry and Fats Domino that blends rock-and-roll sounds with the more traditional music. Acadian and Cajun music continue to be recorded today and festivals continue to celebrate this musical heritage.

Ronda L. Bowen

See also: Armstrong, Louis; Congo Square; Dixieland; Jazz; Rara

Further Reading

Broven, John. 1987. *South to Louisiana: The Music of the Cajun Bayous*. New York: Pelican.

Comeau, Paul-Emile. 2014. *Acadian Driftwood: The Roots of Acadian and Cajun Music*. Kingston, Ontario: Fox Music Books.

Accordion (Americas)

A cousin to the concertina, the accordion is classified as a reed instrument in which the sound is produced by air from a bellows controlled by the player. Often called a "squeezebox," the instrument has traditionally been used in folk or ethnic music, though it can be heard in mainstream popular styles as well as classical and operatic music. The familiar "piano-key" accordion, developed in Europe, gained widespread popularity in America during the 20th century. The accordion has been popularized through the music of such disparate artists as Clifton Chenier, Dick Contino, Myron Floren, Pee Wee King, Flaco Jimenez, Frankie Yankovic, and "Weird Al" Yankovic.

The word *accordion* is derived from the German "akkord," or "agreement," as in the concord of treble and bass. An early incarnation with chord buttons on both sides of the instrument originated around 1844 in England. It was often used by Irish and Irish-American musicians as a dance-music instrument as well as to accompany singing. Use of the accordion was broadened by the European "polka craze" which began in the mid-1840s.

The version of the accordion most familiar to Americans today was developed in Paris and Vienna. It boasted a row of piano keys on the right side along with bass chord buttons on the left. Usually called a "piano accordion," the instrument was frequently brought to the United States by immigrants who re-created and adapted the familiar music of their homeland. Although the accordion was known to be enjoyed by some of the aristocracy, it was often referred to as the "poor man's piano."

The accordion's portability made it easily utilized by a "one-man band" by playing the chord buttons with one hand and the melody with the other, and thus became a favorite among musicians. The player could also sing along and even stamp a foot on the floor or on the accordion case to keep the beat. It was loud enough to be heard in crowded taverns or dances, was ready to play without tuning, and lent itself to a variety of styles and traditional ethnic melodies. Given this versatility, the accordion played a role in the musical heritage of numerous countries across the globe. With immigrants coming to the melting pot of America in the 19th and 20th centuries, musical styles of different nations often blended with the accordion in a central role.

By the time of the American Civil War (1861–1865), German settlers had brought the accordion to much of the United States, using it to accompany polka music. Civil War soldiers in the armies of both the North and South entertained themselves with accordion music. It could be played by itself, or along with a banjo and fiddle, serving as an integral part of musical ensembles. After the war, folk musicians, particularly in the hard-hit South, played the accordion on street corners or train stations as buskers (performers who play in public hoping for gratuities).

The early 20th century is sometimes called the "Golden Age of the Accordion" in the United States. Italian immigrants Pietro Frosini (1885–1951), Guido Deiro (1886–1950), and Pietro Deiro (1888–1954) were popular vaudeville accordion acts, becoming nationwide celebrities. New recording technology allowed them to make records which could be played at home. In 1916, accordionist Frosini's record of "New York Blues" made him one of the first recording stars of the era.

Popular musical groups of the 1920s and 1930s, such as the Paul Whiteman Orchestra, prominently featured accordionists. Because of its ability to produce a myriad of sounds, the instrument was especially popular for playing George Gershwin's "Rhapsody in Blue" (1924), either by itself or with a large band.

During the 1930s and 1940s, many accordionists were performing on American radio, the mass entertainment medium of the era. Charles Magnante (1905–1986), one of the most popular accordionists of the time, is said to have played up to 30 live radio shows each week. Magnante earned further fame as an arranger of accordion music and by devising a method of accordion instruction. Another top entertainer in mid–20th-century America was Dick Contino (1930–), billed as the "World's Greatest Accordion Player."

One of the most popular radio programs of the 1930s and 1940s was broadcast from the Grand Ole Opry in Nashville, Tennessee, where a member of today's Country Music Hall of Fame emerged as a star. Frank Julius Anthony Kuczynski came from a German-Polish family in Wisconsin, where he played the accordion in his father's polka band. After changing his name to Pee Wee King (1914–2000), he found steady work as an accordionist, including as back-up for Gene Autry. For 10 years beginning in 1937, he was a regular at the Grand Ole Opry, where he won fame for his accordion playing on such songs as "The Tennessee Waltz." He is credited with breaking new ground in country music by bringing accordion-driven polkas to the mainstream.

During the 1940s, radio continued broadcasting popular music, including that of the accordion, to the American people. The instrument even found a place in the American military of World War II (1939–1945), with some accordionists entertaining their fellow soldiers with the portable and adaptable instrument. After the war, the accordion achieved a hugely popular niche on television beginning in the 1950s. Accordionist and big band leader Lawrence Welk (1903–1992) hosted a popular TV show of *Champagne Music* from 1955 through 1982. It not only featured Welk himself playing at least one accordion solo each week, but also introduced accordionist Myron Floren (1919–2005), who became enormously popular with the show's viewers as well as the record-buying public. Rebroadcasts of the show can still be seen in some areas of the United States.

The 1950s and 1960s brought forth a revolution in youth-oriented popular music. Rock and roll became the dominant force, with accordion music declining in popularity. Young people preferred to learn the guitar rather than the accordion which was considered "square," a relic of their parents' generation. However, in ethnic enclaves around the nation, the accordion not only held onto its popularity but also expanded into new types of music. As large numbers of German, Polish, and Czech immigrants settled in central and southern Texas, their traditional accordion melodies of polkas, schottisches, and waltzes merged with the Latin-flavored music of the local Hispanic population. This produced Tejano or "Tex-Mex" (short for "Texan-Mexican") music, sometimes said to have evolved yet again into the closely related musical style known as *conjunto* (translated as "group"). There have been many successful accordionists in this genre, with one of the best known being multiple-Grammy Award winner Flaco Jimenez (1939–), who worked with the Hohner company to create the Flaco Jimenez Signature Series of accordions.

Cajun music (the word being derived from "Acadian") began when the French-speaking Acadians were expelled from Canada by the English in the mid-1700s, bringing with them lightweight instruments such as fiddles. Experts believe that German-Jewish merchants who were familiar with European accordions imported the instruments to sell in Louisiana where many Acadians lived. Cajun musicians found that the accordion's tones were particularly compatible with the fiddle, producing an extremely pleasing musical sound on their old and new tunes. When traditional music from Louisiana's African American population joined the mix, a form which came to be known as *zydeco* evolved. Both zydeco and Cajun music rely heavily on the accordion. Some leading accordionists in these genres include Nathan Abshire (1913–1981) and Clifton Chenier (1925–1987).

Polka music never lost its popularity in the middle-American "Polka Belt," where descendants of Czech, German, Polish, and Slovenian immigrants celebrate the music their forebears brought from their homelands. A leading luminary was accordionist Frankie Yankovic (1915–1998), who won the first Grammy Award in the polka category and was known as "America's Polka King."

Probably the best known accordionist in contemporary popular music is also named Yankovic, but is no relation to Frankie. Albert "Weird Al" Yankovic (1959–) is a Grammy-winning accordionist who is generally considered to be the leading satirist/parodist of American popular music. Early in his career, he accompanied his own singing on the accordion, with no other musicians. His first band member, a percussionist, began his career with Yankovic by pounding on the singer's accordion case to provide a steady beat. In addition to song parodies of contemporary hits, Yankovic's concerts and albums almost always include a crowd-pleasing interpretation of rock tunes in an accordion-based polka medley, thus bringing the accordion full circle in American popular music.

Nancy Hendricks

See also: Accordion, Types of; Bluegrass; Cajun Music; Polka; Zydeco

Further Reading
Flynn, Ronald, Edwin Davison, and Edward Chavez. 1992. *The Golden Age of the Accordion.* Schertz, TX: Flynn Publications.

Howard, Robert. 2005. *An A to Z of the Accordion and Related Instruments*. Stockport, UK: Robaccord.

Jacobson, Marion. 2012. *Squeeze This! A Cultural History of the Accordion in America* (Folklore Studies in Multicultural World series). Urbana: University of Illinois Press.

Simonett, Helena, ed. 2012. *The Accordion in the Americas: Klezmer, Polka, Tango, Zydeco, and More!* (Music in American Life series). Urbana: University of Illinois Press.

Accordion, Types of

The accordion is a free-reed instrument consisting of pairs of pre-tuned steel reeds riveted to aluminum alloy plates. The plates are glued into a long reed-box projecting into the bellows, and reeds vibrate when air flows first over the reed, then through the slot on the plate. Air flowing in the opposite direction merely bends the reeds without vibrating them. Most modern accordions also have leather or plastic flaps over the air slots to prevent loss of pressure.

Pairs of reeds can be duplicated and combined to create special effects such as octave doubling, tremolos, and "beating" of two closely tuned pitches. Register knobs and tabs on the outside move slides to engage or close additional ranks of reeds; these may be marked by a code of two horizontal lines with a dot signifying normal pitch or octave displacement, depending on its position.

The instrument is held between the hands and played by drawing and compressing the bellows with the left hand. The left hand provides bass notes and chords, while the right provides melody and additional accompaniment. Earlier forms of the accordion were inspired by the introduction of the Chinese free-reed *sheng* into Europe by Père Amiot (1777). Haeckel's "Physharmonika" and Buschmann's mouthblown "Aura" or "Handaeoline" were patented in Vienna in 1821.

The name, from the German word *Akkord* (chord), first appears in an 1829 Viennese patent by Cyrillus Demian (1772–1847). Demian's description emphasized the "new" aspect of playing whole chords on one side of the instrument (one or two keys in early models), in contrast to older concertina construction (with melody buttons on each side of the bellows, and no chordal keys). By the 1830s to 1840s, the most successful manufacturers of the diatonic accordion were Charles Buffet (Belgium), Napoleon Fourneaux (France), and M. Busson (France). They produced instruments of lasting visual beauty and quiet, mellow tone, with ivory and mother-or-pearl inlays in rosewood, brass reeds, and 10 to 12 treble keys balanced by two bass buttons.

Single-action instruments include the melodeon and the British chromatic accordion. Each melody button controls a pair of reeds (usually adjacent notes of a scale), so a scale can be accomplished with only four buttons (C, E, G on the press and D, F, A, B on the draw). This is the original action of the earliest accordions, and is similar to that of mouth-blown harmonicas.

Double-action instruments such as the piano accordion and the Continental chromatic accordion favor music with a more complex, sweeping character, as the reeds within each pair give the same note, regardless of the way the bellows move.

Shortly after clockmaker Matthias Hohner established his harmonica firm in 1857, he shipped some to American relatives. Hohner pioneered the use of machine-punched reed covers and mass-produced wooden combs. Harmonicas (free-reed adaptations of the accordion-reed plate system) became popular on both sides of the Atlantic. President Abraham Lincoln carried a harmonica in his pocket, and the instrument was played by Civil War soldiers and by frontiersmen such as Wyatt Earp and Billy the Kid. Hohner also produced steel reeds for accordions and helped to champion uniform tone through push-action bellows. Stimulated by players' demands, the chromatic instrument with uniform tone became standard. By the beginning of the 20th century, the bass keyboard had gradually developed to provide accompaniments in all keys, but it remained essentially a folk instrument, heard in cafés, dance halls, and music halls all over the world.

W. C. Handy recalled hearing train imitations played on the harmonica and accordion in the 1870s, and the Hohner Marine Band diatonic (in multiple keys) became one of the defining sounds of early blues style. It was usually played in second position, a fifth above the normal tuning (also called "cross harp" due to the dominant seventh chords generated). Wood-combed harmonicas were often dipped in water to improve the tone and "bendability" of notes in this style. By the 1920s, the accordion and harmonica industry produced more than 50 million instruments a year. The 1925 White House Christmas tree was decorated with 50 harmonicas, and *The Hohner Harmony Hour* radio show debuted on Friday nights at 8:30 pm.

A music school for accordion teachers was established in Trossingen, Germany, in 1931; it became an official state academy in 1948 under the principalship of Hugo Herrmann (1896–1967), whose collection *Sieben neue Spielmusiken* (1927) was the first important musical composition for the solo accordion. The British College of Accordionists was founded in 1936 and provides a syllabus of accordion examinations still used today.

American design innovations have made the instrument more versatile: reeds were usually riveted, bolted, or screwed in place, but All-American models from the 1940s were held in place by tension. The United States experienced an accordion and harmonica shortage during World War II because most manufacturers were based in Germany and Japan. Wood and metal were in short supply due to military demand, so Finn Magnus, a Dutch-American entrepreneur, developed molded-plastic versions.

A large repertory of educational music exists for the accordion. Sonatas, concertos, and other concert works have been created by Robert Russell Bennett, Paul Creston, David Diamond, Roy Harris, William Grant Still, and Virgil Thomson. The accordion has been featured in many modernist masterworks, including Alban Berg's opera *Wozzeck* and Sergei Prokofiev's *Cantata for the 20th Anniversary of the October Revolution* (op. 74).

Accordions were introduced to Latin America in the 19th century by German immigrants. Accordion-family instruments can be found in many South American traditions, including Brazil (*sanfona*), Colombia (*valenato*), and Argentina (*bandoneón*). In Mexico and the United States, the *acordeón de botón* (button accordion without keyboard for the right hand) is commonly used in *tejano* and *norteño* music. Together with the *bajo sexto*, the *acordeón de botón* forms the backbone of the *norteño* conjunto. Two early pioneers on the instrument were brothers Narcisco Martínez and Raul "El Ruco" Martínez. Modern mariachis and *banda* groups include brass instruments, clarinets, saxophones, accordions, and even electric instruments.

Huapano tamaulipeco (*haupango norteño*, one of the main indigenous Mexican forms to be incorporated into *música tejana*), features the accordion and strengthens the music's ethnic identity; Tex-Mex repertoire consists equally of these regional folk dances and of European forms like the waltz, polka, and schottische, all of which call for accordion.

The most common kind of bass-button accordion layout is the Stradella bass system (now called the Standard bass system). It uses columns of buttons arranged in a circle of fifths; this places the principal chords of a key (I, IV, and V) in three adjacent columns. Each column contains, in order, the major third above the root; the root; the major triad; the minor triad; the dominant seventh chord (without the fifth on modern instruments); and the diminished seventh chord (without the fifth on modern instruments). The *bayan* is a type of chromatic button accordion invented in Russia in 1907 and named after the 11th-century bard Boyan. Although only mentioned in one epic source, the folklorist Alexander Afanasyev (1826–1871) considered Boyan to be a precursor of professional Ukrainian *kobzar* string bands. The *bayan* has broad, rectangular reeds (rather than European trapezoidal reeds) tuned without tremolo. Some register switches may be operated by the chin, and converter switches that move from standard preset chords to free bass (individual notes) are now common on larger instruments. The diminished seventh chord row is shifted, so that the diminished seventh G chord is where one would expect the diminished seventh C chord in the Stradella bass system.

The Cajun accordion, also called a *squeezebox*, is a single-row diatonic button accordion developed from ones brought to Acadiana in the 1890s. They add a distinctive sound to both Cajun and Zydeco music, and they differ from the multiple-row instruments more common to Irish, Italian, and polka bands. Since the mid-20th century, there has been a surge in the number of small Cajun accordion makers in Louisiana and Texas. Sidney Brown was a prominent early maker of Cajun accordions, using multiple reeds for every button and four "stops" or knobs controlling the number of reeds sounding.

The *bandoneón* (also spelled *bandonion*), so named for the German instrument dealer Heinrich Band (1821–1860) was originally intended as an accompanying instrument for small-group religious and popular music, in contrast to the folk concertina in Germany. Around 1870, the instrument appeared in Argentina, and was adopted into *milonga* and *tango* musics. By 1910, they were produced expressly for the Argentine and Uruguayan markets, with 25,000 shipping to Argentina in 1930 alone. The instrument is also popular in Lithuanian folk music. Aníbal Troilo and Astor Piazzolla wrote extensively for the bandoneón in the 1930s and 1940s; the disruption of German manufacturing during World War II led to a rapid decline in the manufacture of bandoneóns, accordions, and harmonicas.

Laura Stanfield Prichard

See also: Accordion (Americas); Austro-German Dances; Irish Dance Music; Polka

Further Reading

Clark, W. A. 2002. *From Tejano to Tango: Latin American Popular Music.* London: Routledge.

Häffner, Martin, and C. Wagner. 1993. *Made in Germany, Played in the USA.* Trossingen, Germany: Harmonikamuseum Trossingen.

van der Merwe, Peter. 1992. *Origins of the Popular Style: The Antecedents of Twentieth-Century Popular Music.* Oxford: Oxford University Press.

Adé, "King" Sunny (1946–)

Guitarist, bandleader, and juju superstar King Sunny Adé is one of the only Nigerian musicians to be widely known and internationally successful. Adé was born Sunny Adeniyi in Ondo, Nigeria, in 1946. He began his career as a percussionist, first working as a professional musician in 1963. He formed the Green Spot Band in Lagos in 1966 and achieved his first hit in 1967 with the praise song "Challenge Cup." Adé then switched to guitar and developed a reputation for technological innovation and technical proficiency, which he demonstrated on the 1968 45-rpm record *Alujonu Onigita* (*Wizard of the Guitar*). In 1972, Adé changed his band name to The African Beats and, in 1974, formed his own record label called Sunny Alade Records. *Synchro System Movement* (1967) shows the influence of American soul music and Fela Kuti's Afrobeat style in its slower tempos, ambiguous tonality, and languorous bass lines. This record was one of the first long-playing records to include an uninterrupted performance on one side, a traditional aspect of Yoruba music typically avoided because of the influence of Western popular music recording practices.

Nigerian musician King Sunny Adé performing live in 1988. Adé was prominent in the genre of juju, where he integrated elements of Yoruban culture, such as talking drums and lyrics drawn from Yoruban traditions. (Frans Schellekens/Redferns)

By 1979, Adé's ensemble had grown to include four guitars (one rhythm, one lap steel, and two lead), electric bass, two talking drums, synthesizer, drum set, and a bevy of auxiliary voices and percussion instruments. He also began incorporating rhythms from contemporary

African American music. Critics argued that Adé's stylistic shifts in the early 1980s diluted traditional elements in his music. These changes, however, reflect larger trends in juju music since the 1930s that blended new and old material and were intended to introduce him to a larger audience. Island Records signed Adé in 1982, and *Juju Music* was released in the West to both critical and commercial success. Despite this, 1983's *Syncro System* (re-released as *Synchro System* in 1990) was not as well received. Adé failed to meet the label's desires for filling the "world music" niche left by Bob Marley's death, and Island dropped Adé in 1984. A 1987 live concert release revived his career in the West, leading to 1995's *E Dide* and the 1998 release of *Odu*, an album of traditional Yoruba music recorded in Louisiana. While his fortunes have waxed and waned with ebbs and flows of world music's popularity in the West, he has released more than 100 albums in Nigeria. He has invested much of his wealth in Nigeria, with several concerns in both entertainment and other industries, and he established the King Sunny Adé Foundation to support underprivileged musicians and promulgate music education.

Adé's style is marked by extensive use of studio effects and by large ensembles that blend African and Western instruments. These forces were often augmented or overdubbed on records designed for international audiences, resulting in dense textures with multiple interlocking parts. His recordings for Western audiences typically feature shorter track lengths than those intended for African audiences. Adé sings in a "slightly nasalized, high-tessitura vocal style." His lyrics are in Yoruba and are typically derived from "a loosely-linked series of exhortations, proverbs, and catch phrases" (Waterman, 1990, pp. 132, 135). These texts begin with no real connection to one another but are linked through their associations and juxtaposition in Adé's songs (Waterman, 1990, p. 135).

John Hausmann

See also: Afrobeat (Afropop); Highlife; Kuti, Fela

Further Reading

Adé, King Sunny and His African Beats. 1982. *Juju Music.* Island Records 204 770.

Adé, King Sunny and His African Beats. 1983. *Synchro System.* Island Records 12 IS 122.

Adé, King Sunny and His African Beats. 2003. *Best of the Classic Years.* Shanachie SH 66034.

Stone, Ruth M. 1997. *"Africa."* In Ruth Stone (ed.), *The Garland Encyclopedia of World,* vol. 1. New York: Routledge.

Waterman, Christopher Alan. 1990. *Juju: A Social History and Ethnography of an African Popular Music.* Chicago: University of Chicago Press.

African Spirituals

The term *spiritual* comes from the biblical "spiritual songs," a term used in early publications to differentiate the texts from metrical psalms and hymns of traditional church usage. As defined by W.E.B. Du Bois, *spirituals* are songs of affirmation and sublime religious faith—a definition that defies geographical boundaries. Likewise, James Weldon Johnson's 1925 writings indicate that slave spirituals owe much to African influence and fundamental musical practices, such as rhythmic vitality, and to African song form and structure.

Historically, African spirituals have been used to dramatize the condition of the oppressed and their desire for freedom. In the same way that a caged bird yearns for freedom, the slaves cried in anguish under their captivity, and the spirituals were born from those cries. The spirituals became a bloodline, bringing the vital flow of hope and faith to the emotional and spiritual heart of the slave. Influenced by the presence of missionaries in Africa in the 1700s during the British Overseas Expansion and inspired by traditional African music, sacred songs known as African spirituals originated as a result of the co-opting of Anglican hymnody and indigenous musical and religious song practices. African performers incorporate dance, drama, language, and visual arts into their music. Taught by oral tradition and rote and influenced by the cultural environment, music and religion in Africa act as a singular enterprise. Between the two, there is no separation of sacred, secular, music, vocals, or instruments. Often, religious music incorporates call-and-response patterns as well as improvisation. The use of repetition, tag lines, and refrains provides opportunities for participation in performances between leader and people. The most popular forms consist of four-line arrangements of AAAB and the couplet with tag line, A (tag) B (tag). Spirit possession commonly occurs during a sacred song; at the same time, dancing becomes trance-like. Drums play a central role in both the song and the dance. Music reflects the beliefs of the community, sends prayers to particular gods of worship, and calls on spirits to influence personal actions. Religion establishes a code of African ethics to define the community and its actions.

The roots of African spirituals can be found in Tiv songs and are exemplified by the work of ethnomusicologist Charles Keil. Tiv oral poetry is composed mainly for praising, or begging, or settling personal scores: the poet fosters his career by "attacking in a series of songs someone who he feels has done him wrong" (Keil, 1979, p. 28). There are, of course, several approaches to the study of oral transmission of narratives and customs, the most well-known of which is Keil's, dealing with the function that oral art forms perform.

Tiv song, storytelling, and dance represent cultural beliefs and values in Tivland and serve as a strong collective antidote to the negative or individualistic aspects of Tsav. Tiv composers and their assistants serve as a cultural barometer through their songs by praising, condemning, advising, and blessing deeds and actions within the cultural matrix. The intense focus on song, stories, and dance is a reciprocal function of the worst forces in Tiv culture, and facilitate the society's function.

Tiv oral poetry consists of songs, chants, incantations, proverbs, and riddles. Delivery can be compared to recitative (half-spoken/half-sung) and aria (sung). Within these delivery methods, subcategories (such as sacred or curative), might be chanted, whereas sung portions may be concerned with love, praise, and laments. The terms for songs are *Imo* and *Icham*. *Icham* refers to religious hymns and is based on the content, function, and context of the songs such as during church services, funerals, storytelling sessions, and Kwaghir puppet performances. Most Tiv songs praise or satirize people, because all poets describe their art as either begging or crying due to their immediate experiences in society. As a result, most Tiv songs are multithematic and consist of many forms. Tiv songs are typically improvised and categorized into seven main groups: (1) Genyi, primarily dirges that can be either nonspecialized and spontaneous or specialized formal songs; (2) Biamegh song, the oldest known to the Tiv, which inculcates moral and cultural values into the younger generation; (3) Girinya, war songs that did not originate in Tivland, but were borrowed from Kwa-speaking peoples of Ogoja, used to mobilize troops; (4) Iyor-gbeer, elegiac songs concerned with death; (5) Akerangu, multithematic political songs; (6) Swange, modern praise song that includes pop and rock music; and (7) religio-medicinal songs.

In African societies music is used for worship, rituals, entertainment, comfort, and many other purposes. Young children use music in their games; boys and girls use music as a source of entertainment; and young adults may listen to or participate in a music-making session for entertainment reasons or to join in a group to foster solidarity and unity. In the life of an African child, music plays an important role in several life stages. These include birthright performances that introduce the child to the community; and song games during childhood, which serve the purpose of educating young children about appropriate social manners, the human body, gender roles, the surrounding environment and animals, and relationships. Further, music plays an important role in puberty rites and death rites.

A number of African musical songs and dances were and are still transmitted from one generation or group to another by word of mouth. Traditional music and dance in Africa are media that have remained immunized to the Western notational debates. They are largely taught and transmitted from one person to another orally. Modeling is one widely used method for teaching others. Dance troupes that visit different countries perform difficult, complex, multirhythmic and melodic phrases and movement through oral practices that have been perfected over the centuries. Stone argues that music, dance, and human lives in Africa and African performance are a tightly wrapped bundle of arts that is sometimes difficult to separate (Stone, 1998). African music has evolved over many years to accommodate external influences while preserving its essential elements such as rhythmic patterns and idioms.

Most African songs have been orally passed through a number of generations. The oral communication method has facilitated the changing of the original version of the song to a point where there is no one who is able to claim an "authentic" version of a song. This process of preserving music through oral traditions has propelled African communities to be creative, as each of their songs can be modified to suit a particular occasion. Consequently, African people can enjoy music of the 19th and 20th centuries now in the 21st century, while creating new music to address contemporary issues. It has been established that the music of ancient traditions has some intrinsic power, but by itself is not enough to induce the fullest transcendental experience. *Transcendence* is the transformation of the ordinary mental state, with its daily, mundane concerns, into an expansive, more cosmic mind in which the sense of infinity and eternity begin to replace the preoccupation with worldly circumstances. It occurs in degrees. The fullest degree is the complete immersion of awareness in the eternal and infinite Being. One such method is found in a form we now call ancient Eastern sacred music, in which the master has to inculcate in the pupil not just the technique of an instrument and the repertoire of traditional melodies, but also the very state of mind that the music is there to induce: a transformation from the mundane to the miraculous. The power of the master to elevate the pupil's state of mind is partly dependent on lineage, but it also depends on other external factors that include hardships, trials, and tribulations, voluntarily undertaken for the sake of learning.

Eldonna L. May and Morgen Chawawa

See also: Blues; Jazz; Vocables

Further Reading

Impey, Angela. 1998. "Popular Music in Africa." In Ruth Stone (ed.), *The Garland Encyclopedia of World Music*. New York: Garland.

Jones, A. M. 1978. *Studies in African Music*. London: Oxford University Press.

Keil, Charles. 1979. *Tiv Song*. Chicago: University of Chicago Press.

Nketia, J. H. Kwabena. 1974. *The Music of Africa*. New York: Norton.

Stone, Ruth. 1998. "Africa." In Ruth Stone (ed.), *The Garland Encyclopedia of World Music*. New York: Garland.

Afrobeat (Afropop)

Afrobeat is a hybrid style of West African popular music whose name was coined by one of its most important innovators, Fela Kuti (1938–1997). This music is marked by hypnotic, repetitive rhythms, supplied by percussion, drum set, electric guitars, and bass. Many Afrobeat tracks also include a brass section comprised of trumpet, saxophones, and trombone. Depending on the artist, the songs sometimes have a small amount of vocals (they are mostly instrumental tracks); when they do have lyrics, they can be quite political and critical of authority.

There are many types of African popular music from the various regions and countries of the continent, and Afrobeat is a combination of some of the styles that were popular in West Africa in the mid-20th century. Popular music scholar Peter Manuel sees two general trends in African popular music: (1) songs played by small groups with emphasis on electric guitars and social commentary, and (2) the dance-band model with lots of brass instruments and less focus on vocals (and therefore text). Afrobeat can be regarded as a combination of these two trends.

Nigerian Fela Kuti grew up playing saxophone and trumpet in highlife bands, which he continued to do while attending college in London. "Highlife" was the old style of mid–20th-century dance-band music which used instruments similar to an American big band. It was originally designed to entertain wealthy hotel guests in grand ballrooms. The theory is that the term *highlife* was coined by lower-class observers, peering in at the grand hotels and imitating the American- and British-style big bands. Highlife has its origins in Ghana, where it was popularized by E. T. Mensah (1919–1996), who sang in the vernacular languages of Ghanaians.

Another type of music that was played near and around hotels and tourist sites (in Nigeria and Ghana) was "palm-wine music" (sometimes called "palm-wine highlife"). This acoustic style was commonly performed by one voice and a guitar, or a small ensemble that consisted of only an acoustic guitar, drums (such as djembes or congas), handheld percussion, bottle percussion (for the "timeline"), and upright bass. These songs were sung, as many African performances are, by informal pick-up ensembles; passers-by may join in or leave at any time. The style received its name from palm-wine stands (basically outdoor bars), in which people (and the musicians themselves) passed the time by playing music and drinking wine.

Two other Nigerian styles predate Afrobeat, and have indirectly contributed to the style. *Juju* is a style that was popular beginning in the late 1950s, predominantly in the Yoruba-speaking southwest of the country. This music featured talking drums, accordion, and electric guitars, and significantly did not include brass instruments. It is generally associated with Christian Nigerians, and its most prominent artists were I. K. Dairo (1930–1996, the inventor of the style); Ebenezer Obey (1942–); and his rival, King Sunny Adé (1946–). Obey has, in more recent years, turned to playing exclusively gospel music. Adé is more well-known among Western world music fans, as he released several albums in the 1980s on Island Records.

Fuji is another Nigerian style, one that is generally associated with the Muslim population of the country. Its musical profile is based on Islamic chanting and calls to prayer, accompanied only by percussion instruments (talking drums, shakers, and other larger drums). Sikiru Ayinde (1948–2010) was one of the originators of this style, with his band The Supreme Fuji Commanders having released several hit albums since the late 1960s. Gradually, more melodic instruments were added over the years, but not many, and the style is still dominated by vocals and percussion.

As for the Afrobeat style itself, it is best described as halfway between jazz and funk, plus African drumming. It has a repetitive component from the funk styles of James Brown and Sly & the Family Stone, but it also includes several lengthy episodes of improvised solos (in Fela Kuti's case, on saxophone or keyboards; he also played the trumpet), and occasional vocal components. A rhythmic hallmark of Afrobeat is layered polyrhythm, where one instrument or group of instruments may begin a pattern based on four beats, and the next instrument that enters will have a pattern of six beats, the next a pattern of seven, and so on. This idea stems from West African drumming traditions, and not from highlife itself. Highlife influences can be heard in the extensive use of brass instruments, as well as in the dance-based aesthetic of Afrobeat.

Fela Kuti coined the term *Afrobeat* in 1967, after spending some time in Ghana under the influence of Afro-soul singer Geraldo Pino (1938–2008). Sometimes called the "godfather of Afrobeat," Pino and his band The Heartbeats imported American R & B and soul sounds into African pop styles. It is easy to hear the influence of James Brown and Stevie Wonder in his 1970 hit "Power to the People." Both Fela and Pino sang in English (or Pidgin English), which allowed many Africans all over the continent to understand the messages in the lyrics.

Fela Kuti's life was one of constant struggle with Nigerian authorities. While touring the United States with his band in 1969, he came into contact with members of the Black Power movement (including Sandra Smith), and was inspired to improve the lives of African people everywhere. When he returned to Nigeria in 1970, after the end of the Nigerian Civil War and after running afoul of the American Immigration and Naturalization Service, he named his band "Africa 70," and shortly thereafter established a commune/independent "nation" that he named the

Kalakuta Republic. It was here that he recorded many albums critical of the government, and kept some 15 to 27 wives, many of whom were in his band as backup singers and dancers. The most strident (and successful) of these records was 1976's *Zombie*, which prompted the Nigerian regime's assault on Kuti's compound, resulting in the murder of his mother and the destruction of his house and studio. Kuti was severely beaten in this attack, but nevertheless he continued to tour and record polemical albums, including *Unknown Soldier* (1981), and *Army Arrangement* (1985). In 1984, during one of the several Nigerian dictatorships of its recent history, Kuti was jailed for supposedly smuggling foreign currency. He was freed after a year and a half following an international outcry and pressure from Amnesty International. Kuti died in 1998 as a result of complications from AIDS.

The legacy of Fela includes the further explorations of Afrobeat by his son, Femi Kuti (1962–). Femi is somewhat less politically charged in his lyrical content (although still critical of the Nigerian government), and has found success in Europe and America. Femi plays the saxophone and has collaborated with R & B and hip-hop artists such as Common and Macy Gray, and jazz trumpeter Roy Hargrove. A main difference between his father's style and Femi's is that his tracks are generally shorter (in the six- to seven-minute range), rather than the 15- to 20-minute songs by Fela. Notable albums include *Shoki Shoki* (1998) and *Africa for Africa* (2011).

Tony Allen (1940–), the main drummer of Fela's band, has also carried on the legacy of his former collaborator and mentor into the 21st century. Allen is highly respected in the drumming community, and has recorded tracks with many leading contemporary artists.

Fela!, a musical based on the biography *Fela: This Bitch of a Life* by Carlos Moore, opened off Broadway in 2008, and was presented on Broadway from 2009 to 2011, after which it was nominated for several Tony Awards. It also was presented in London's West End in 2010, and was revived on Broadway in 2012. *Finding Fela* was a 2014 documentary film, directed by Alex Gibney, which was featured at the Sundance Film Festival.

Afrobeat was a major source of inspiration for David Byrne's band Talking Heads, especially in the late 1970s. Albums such as *Fear of Music* (1979) and *Remain in Light* (1980) exemplify this style in the group's output. Other groups that have been influenced by Afrobeat, either directly or indirectly, are King Crimson, Antibalas, Vampire Weekend, and the collaborations between Byrne and Brian Eno. More recently, a band from Chile called Newen Afrobeat has revived the style and has found success in using the music as a way to fight for indigenous rights in that country.

Christopher Gable

See also: Djembe; Highlife; Kuti, Fela

Further Reading

Broughton, Simon, et al., eds. 2006. *The Rough Guide to World Music; Vol. 1: Africa and Middle East,* 3rd ed. London: Rough Guides.

Haydon, Geoffrey, and Dennis Marks, eds. 1985. *Repercussions: A Celebration of African-American Music.* London: Century Publishing.

Manuel, Peter. 1990. *Popular Musics of the Non-Western World.* New York: Oxford University Press.

Moore, Carlos. 2009. *Fela: This Bitch of a Life.* Chicago: Lawrence Hill Books.

Veal, Michael. 2000. *Fela: The Life and Times of an African Musical Icon.* Philadelphia, PA: Temple University Press.

Afro-Cuban Jazz

Afro-Cuban jazz is a 1940s jazz style resulting from the combination of bebop and traditional Cuban musical elements. Dizzy Gillespie is the principal progenitor of the style. It is distinguishable from Latin jazz by its reliance upon Cuban dance, folk, and popular music, notably *son,* which combines African rhythms and percussion, Spanish canción, and Spanish guitar style elements.

The earliest use of Cuban elements is traceable to Alberto Socarras and Mario Bauzá in the late 1930s. Bauzá envisioned the creation of a dream band—a collective of jazz musicians who were able both to improvise and to perform harmonically sophisticated arrangements—with the core of the music driven by the complex polyrhythms of his native Cuba. His brother-in-law Frank Grillo (Machito) became the orchestra's vocalist and frontman. In 1940, Bauzá became musical director and chief arranger of the Machito Afro-Cubans. By the mid 1940s, the Machito Afro-Cubans broke new ground. As the first "fusion band," Bauzá brought together two old branches (jazz and Afro-Cuban music) of an ancient African tree. His band was the first group to use the triumvirate of conga, bongo, and timbales simultaneously. It also was the first ensemble to use the term "Afro," actively raising the consciousness of African Americans in the United States to the African elements in this music and its ancestral ties. The Machito Afro-Cubans were the first multiracial band, employing African American, Latinos, and Anglos. More important, the Afro-Cubans set a standard of professionalism and musical sophistication that gave Latinos in the 1940s pride in their multiracial culture. However, Afro-Cuban jazz became a clearly defined style and acquired an international following when Gillespie, who had been influenced by Bauzá, began to collaborate with the outstanding Cuban percussionist Chano Pozo. For Gillespie, Bauzá, and others, the main impulse for the Afro-Cuban movements came from their feeling that American jazz of the 1930s and 1940s, being essentially monorhythmic, needed the kind of enrichment that an infusion of Afro-Cuban polyrhythms would provide.

The trumpeter Dizzy Gillespie was one of the first major jazz figures to adopt the style, producing several classic recordings in 1947–1948 featuring the Cuban percussionist Chano Pozo (e.g., *Afro-Cuban Suite,* 1948). This collaboration is credited with activating a distinct lineage of Pan-African music-making and stands as a seminal moment in the history of intercultural music in the 20th century. Pozo and Gillespie were bebopping to African rhythms while simultaneously creating musical jazz to the rhythm of Cuban and African drums. Their work demonstrated a shared African cultural memory that resonated with the concept of the New World Negro. At the same time, Stan Kenton was popularizing the music in the big-band field with Latin-inspired recordings such as

Peanut Vendor and *Machito* (1947). Tadd Dameron, Charlie Parker, and Bud Powell were others who dabbled in the style.

In the decades leading to 1940, Latin American melodies and dance rhythms made their way farther northward into the United States via Latin band leaders such as Xavier Cugat (1931 Waldorf Astoria "house band") and Desi Arnaz (*Babalou*, 1939), along with calypso singers including Wilmoth Houdini (*Black But Sweet*, 1931). Simultaneously, the sounds of American jazz spread through the Caribbean and Central and South America, enabling musicians and dancers across the entire region to become familiar with both musical languages; the large swing orchestras of the Big Band era expanded their musical offerings to include Afro-Cuban dance music such as rumba, habanera, tango, and conga. These events contributed to the fusion of jazz and Cuban music, a process inaugurated in New York in 1940 with the launch of the Machito and the Afro-Cubans orchestra, directed by the Cuban trumpet virtuoso Mario Bauzá. Bauzá's *Tangá* (African word for marijuana) is considered to be the first true example of Latin jazz. When trumpeter Howard McGhee soloed with Machito's orchestra at the Apollo Theatre in August 1948, his ad-libs to *Tangá* resulted in another spin-off composition: *Cu-Bop City*, a tune recorded by Roost Records months later. The jam sessions occurring at New York's Royal Roots, Bop City, and Birdland between 1948 and 1949, when McGhee, tenor saxophonist Brew Moore, Charlie Parker, and Dizzy Gillespie sat in with the Machito orchestra, were unrehearsed, uninhibited, never-before-heard performances which master of ceremonies Symphony Sid named Afro-Cuban jazz.

The Gillespie-Pozo collaboration produced several important recordings of Pozo's compositions in the 1940s, including *Manteca* (1947), *Afro-Cuban Suite* (1948), and *Guarachi Guaro* (1948). These works, featuring Pozo's unique style of conga drumming, mark the first examples of the genre that effectively combine authentic Afro-Cuban polyrhythms with bebop riffs. The impact of these works not only influenced jazz luminaries such as Kenton and Dameron, but also Charlie Parker and Bud Powell. Gillespie's ensemble performed Afro-Cuban jazz during the 1950s and enabled other talented Cuban percussionists, such as Armando Perza and Mongo Santamaria, to rise to prominence in the field. In December 1950, the Machito orchestra recorded its *Afro-Cuban Jazz Suite* under the aegis of producer Norman Granz. It featured Charlie Parker (alto saxophone), Buddy Rich (drums), Flip Phillips (tenor saxophone), and Harry ("Sweets") Edison (trumpet), with arrangements by Arturo ("Chico") O'Farrill. Similarly, Cuban musicians, led by pianists Frank Emilio Flynn and Ramón ("Bebo") Valdés, contributed to the development of this new style. Valdés released *Con Poco Coco* in 1952, which was hailed as the first spontaneously improvised recorded Afro-Cuban jam session. As a result of changing audience preferences and fewer available economic incentives for musicians in the 1950s, big bands began to dissolve. Afro-Cuban jazz became known as Latin jazz, primarily for marketing purposes, and the music began to be performed by smaller ensembles. This trend was spearheaded by the pianist George Shearing and drummer Cal Tjader on the west coast of the United States.

This important musical legacy in American popular culture continues today. It resonates in the music of James Brown, Frank Sinatra, Santana, Celia Cruz,

Tower of Power, Lauren Hill, Tito Puente, Duke Ellington, and Frank Zappa, to name only a few.

Eldonna L. May and Morgen Chawawa

See also: African Spirituals; Bebop; Blues; Jazz

Further Reading

García, David. 2011. "'We Both Speak African': A Dialogic Study of Afro-Cuban Jazz." *Journal of the Society for American Music* 5, 195–233.

Loza, Steven. 2002. "Poncho Sánchez, Latin Jazz, and the Cuban Son: A Stylistic and Social Analysis." In Lise Waxer (ed.), *Situating Salsa: Global Markets and Local Meanings in Latin Popular Music*, 301–317. New York: Routledge.

Maggin, Donald L. 2005. "Cubop: Dizzy Gillespie, Chano Pozo and the Afro-Cuban Jazz Revolution." *Jazz Times* (Washington) (0272-572X), 35(3), 36.

Moreno, Jairo. 2004. "Bauza-Gillespie-Latin/Jazz: Difference, Modernity, and the Black Caribbean." *South Atlantic Quarterly* 103(1), 81–99.

Roberts, John Storm. 1999. *The Latin Tinge: The Impact of Latin American Music on the United States,* 2nd ed. New York: Oxford University Press.

Washburne, Christopher. 1997. "The Clave of Jazz: A Caribbean Contribution to the Rhythmic Foundation of an African-American Music." *Black Music Research Journal* 17(1), 59–80.

Washburne, Christopher. 2002. "Latin Jazz: The Other Jazz." *Current Musicology* 71–73, 409–26.

Ahmad, Fadzil (1941–)

A recognized master musician in Malaysia, Fadzil Ahmad is a well-known singer and *gambus* player who was a cultural coach at the Malaysian Ministry of Culture, Arts, and Tourism to the Ministry of Culture from 1976 to 1997. His most famous compositions are "Joget Cik Siti" (Siti Dance) and "Dia Datang" (She Is Coming), and his playing had a beautifully refined tone redolent of intimate, domestic music-making.

Born in Muar, Johor, a center of *ghazal* singing in Malaysia, Ahmad was taken to *bangsawan* performances by his musician father from age seven, performing as a singer and gambus player with ghazal quartets in Muar from 1958. He studied music theory, *maqaam*, and *taqsīm* with Arabic musicians, took private gambus lessons with four teachers, and contributed to 14 extended-play and 11 long-playing records with the Sri Maharani Ghazal Group (led by Ahmad Jusoh) from 1967 to 1974. Shifting from administration to teaching, he worked, until his retirement in early 2006, as gambus instructor at the National Academy of Arts Culture & Heritage (ASWARA). He taught music on a part-time basis at the nine-year-old Academy in Kuala Lumpur.

The gambus is a six-stringed lute originating from the Middle Eastern ud (oud), and is related to the rebab. The first four nylon strings are paired to facilitate plucking of melodies, as this instrument plays fast, repeated notes in ghazal. The fifth and sixth strings are made of metal, are not paired, and are used to play the lower bass notes. In terms of musical texture, gambus playing combines Malay linear elements (playing variations on the singer's melody) with Western triads (formed by guitars, harmonium, and gambus).

The gambus is commonly used to accompany singers of a sentimental form of syncretized folk pop derived from Indian ghazals, the poetic love songs of Indian light classical music. Two types of ghazal exist in Malaysia: one in the northern states (*ghazal parti* in Penang, Kedah, and Perlis) and one in the southern state of Johor (a typical part of wedding music). Ghazal groups also perform *asli, joget, keroncong,* and pop pieces. The gambus also appears as a member of instrumental ensembles accompanying dance.

In addition to being a highly successful gambus musician, Ahmad has also done some acting and directing. He has built up a small collection of musical instruments of the oud family, acquiring these in Iraq, Saudi Arabia, Turkey, and Egypt. His own preference is for the smaller and lighter Turkish gambus, because a musician can play it while standing.

As a singer and player, Ahmad visited more than 40 countries and assisted in the formation of cultural groups dedicated to preserving Malay-Arabic music, including a ghazal group in Parit Bakar, Muar, Johor (1958) and Setia Marahani Ghazal. Early ghazal groups were male quartets featuring harmonium, tabla, violin, and gambus. With the participation of Annis Es, S Fauziah (Fauziah Samsuri, his longtime duet partner), and using several songs created by Atan Penambang, he toured Malaysia and was featured on the radio. He remarked in 1998, "Most of the contemporary ghazals and gambus performances as well as those in electronic media are my creations" (Ahmad, 2018).

In the 1990s, he led the Ghazal Gambus Kuala Lumpur Group (Kumpulan Ghazal Gambus Kuala Lumpur) and recorded an album distributed by Amband Klasik. His second album, *Fadzil Ahmad—Raja Gambus* (King of the Gambus), featured Jamie Chik (ghazal singer) and Syed Ahmad Baagil (from Egypt); it contains a wide range of old and new songs and instrumentals, including "Malam Pegantim" (Bride Night), "Di Pantai Hiburan" (Beach Party), and "Di Lembah Sungai Nil" (Nile River Valley).

Ahmad has been a source for research on the history of the gambus in Malaysia. Scholars have documented his claims that the gambus replaced the *saragi* in ghazal ensembles and that the oud was introduced mainly in Johor in 1897. He has also corresponded with musicians who suggest that the gambus Hadhramaut has only been used since the 1950s.

Laura Stanfield Prichard

See also: Gamelan Orchestra (Javanese); Kalthoum, Umm; Karnatic Music; Wayang Kulit

Further Reading

Ahmad, Fadzil. 2018.Facebook post. https://m.facebook.com/profile.php?v=info&expand=1&id=12104575769. Accessed February 8, 2018.

Dewan budaya [Cultural Hall], 27: 6–12. *Dewan Bahasa dan Pustaka*, 2005.

Matusky, Patricia, and Tan Sooi Beng. 2017. *The Music of Malaysia: The Classical, Folk and Syncretic Traditions.* London: Routledge.

Meddegoda, Chinthaka Prageeth, and Gisa Jähnichen. 2016. *Hindustani Traces in Malay Ghazal: 'A Song, So Old and Yet Still Famous.'* Cambridge: Cambridge Scholars.

Razak, Rozi Abdul. 1998, April 28. "*Fadzil Ahmad: gambus khazanah bernilai* [Fadzil Ahmad: Valuable gambus treasures]." *Hiburan Magazine: Utusan online.* utusan.com.my.

Zakaria, Badrul Kamal. 2017, February 18. "*Raja Gambus Malaysia dari pandangan S Fauziah* [The king of gambus according to S Fauziah]." *BHOnline.* https://www.bharian.com.my/node/249698.

Amadinda

The *amadinda*, an idiophone with 12 keys from the xylophone family, is native to Uganda. The origin of the xylophone in Africa is not known, but sources indicate that it was around as early as the 12th century and found in various regions of Africa. The amadinda was connected to the royal courts and palaces of Uganda such as in the Kingdom of Buganda, the former court of Kabaka, where it was known as the *entaala*. It accompanied the singing griots in the royal court and was also used to entertain royalty. The amadinda has different names depending on the region of Uganda. It is related to the Ugandan *akadinda*, a log xylophone usually of 17 keys but sometimes 22 keys; and the *embaire*, a log xylophone of 15 keys that is popular in the Busoga region of Uganda.

The amadinda belongs to the free type of log xylophone instead of the fixed type, which is more permanent in construction and has fixed keys. It is built from tuned logs or thin strips of wood that form the keys. These are affixed to a wooden foundation such as two tree trunks (the banana tree trunk is a favorite). The trunks are separated by two slender strips of wood. Twelve small identical openings are drilled into the logs and slender pieces of wood are then placed into the openings for each of the tuned keys. With very small openings at each end, the 12 keys are strapped to tree trunks or another foundation with cords or strands from plants such as the banana tree. They are attached in such a manner that they easily vibrate when struck. Long slender sticks are used to separate the keys so they do not touch each other. The amadinda, which usually rests on some type of mat when played, can be as long as 30 inches and as wide as 6 inches. These are sometimes quite portable instruments that are constructed and pieced together for each performance (Anderson, 1967).

The amadinda lacks resonators and therefore produces a sound that is more rich and dark rather than sonorous and vibrant. It has a powerful punch and carrying power at its loudest intensity: one cannot miss hearing it even at a distance. To produce sound on the instrument, the rims of the keys are struck with slender sticks or mallets.

Music in Uganda has a strong rhythmic element. Influenced by the different regions and tribes, many of the rhythms and meters are complex. These elements are all used to capture the meaning of the text. Most of the music for the amadinda, which has been passed down orally, is usually performed in fast duple meter. The modal system is frequently used and a great majority of the melodies are pentatonic, including music for the amadinda. Although pentatonic tuning and scales are the norm, other scales exist and are also used, such as heptatonic and hexatonic. The instrumental tuning influences the music, especially the songs, and the tuning of the amadinda is achieved by making the ends or centers of the keys thinner. Tones that are too low are raised by thinning out the ends of the keys. Tuned to an octave are the first and sixth tones of the amadinda, with the intervals and pitches of the other tones varied.

The number of players on the instrument varies: one to two may sit across from each other while a third plays the two highest tones. There can be as many as five players and as few as a single player on the instrument. Due to the construction of the amadinda, a high level of specialized skill and coordination is demanded from the players, especially when there are numerous musicians on one instrument. Each performer is assigned his own part and together they play interlocking lines. Therefore, they must maintain a strong sense of ensemble cohesiveness. Creating intricate music, the performance usually commences with the prominent player beginning the tune, then joined by the second and third players one after the other. The third player sometimes uses a combination of tones and rhythms taken from the first and second players.

The amadinda is an important instrument in Ugandan instrumental ensembles. Often accompanied by drums, it is also used in social functions as an accompaniment to song and dance. In addition to being used to accompany other xylophones, it is also played solo.

Music and dance have always played an important role in the lives of the people of Africa, including Uganda. It is an important means for people to express themselves. The various tribes in Uganda have distinct dances and music and the amadinda is very popular in social gatherings, including religious, marital, and funeral rites and ceremonies, as well as entertainment.

Barbara Bonous-Smit

See also: African Spirituals

Further Reading

Anderson, Lois. 1967. "The African Xylophone." *African Arts* 1(1) (Autumn), 46–49, 66, 68–69.

Cooke, Peter. 1970. "Ganda Xylophone Music: Another Approach." *African Music* 4(4), 62–80, 95.

Cooke, Peter. 1990. *Play Amadinda: Xylophone Music from Uganda.* Edinburgh: K & C Productions.

Kubik, Gerhard. 1960. "The Structure of Kiganda Xylophone Music." *African Music* 2(3), 6–30.

Kubik, Gerhard. 1964. "Xylophone Playing in Southern Uganda." *Journal of the Royal Anthropological Institute of Great Britain and Ireland* 94(2) (July-December), 138–159.

Kubik, Gerhard. 2010. *Theory of African Music.* Chicago: University of Chicago Press.

Muyinda, Evalisto. 1991. *Traditional Music of Baganda as Formerly Played at the Court of the Kabaka of Buganda* (CD booklet notes). PAN Records.

Wegner, Ulrich. 1993. "Cognitive Aspects of Amadinda Xylophone: Music from Buganda: Inherent Patterns Reconsidered." *Ethnomusicology* 37(2) (Spring-Summer), 201–241.

Amish Hymns (*Ausbund, Gesangbuch*)

First published in 1564, the *Ausbund* is the oldest Protestant Christian hymnbook (German: *Gesangbuch*) in continuous use up to the present day, with the Old Order Amish still employing its songs in their services. Created in prison as a result of religious persecution in the 1530s, the *Ausbund* made its way to North America when the descendants of various Anabaptist groups fled more religious persecution in the 18th century. Since then, the old hymns have inspired generations of Anabaptist, and specifically Amish, Christians to stay true to their Lord in the midst of hardship.

The story of the *Ausbund* begins with the religious, political, and social tumult arising from the Protestant Reformation in the 16th century. Protestant leaders such as Martin Luther (1483–1546), Ulrich Zwingli (1484–1531), and John Calvin (1509–1564) criticized the supreme authority of the Catholic Pope to decide spiritual matters for Christians and instead asserted that the Bible was the Christians' sole authority. Such ideas shattered the unity that had prevailed in Western Christianity for more than a thousand years.

Some groups of Protestants went further with reforming the Christian Church than did Luther, Zwingli, and Calvin. A variety of groups called Anabaptists (meaning re-baptizers) thought that Catholics and Protestant leaders were mistaken in requiring infants to be baptized, thus simultaneously making them political citizens *and* a part of the church. They sought to separate church and state by baptizing and making church members only adults who could make a conscious decision to follow Christ. Catholic and Protestant authorities viewed the rebaptism of those who had already been baptized as infants as treason and imprisoned, tortured, and killed many Anabaptists throughout Europe.

In 1535, Catholic authorities arrested roughly 60 Anabaptists and put them into a dungeon in the southeastern German city of Passau to change their views. They remained imprisoned for their faith for five years, and some of them died. While in prison, they composed 53 songs, which became the core of the *Ausbund*. Many songs expressed fear and loneliness over their hardship but also hope and faith in Jesus Christ in the midst of their trials. Some of the major prison songwriters included Michael Schneider, the group's leader; Bernard Schneider; and Hans Betz. They likely did not have any paper, so the prisoners sang the songs repeatedly to memorize them. After their release in 1540, the Anabaptist prisoners wrote down their songs and published them in Switzerland in 1564. The hymnbook acquired the name *Ausbund* (likely meaning "selection") for the first time in a much-expanded edition of 131 hymns that was published in 1583.

Authorities continued to persecute various groups of Anabaptists in the 17th and 18th centuries. In response, some Anabaptist groups, such as the Mennonites and the Amish, followers of Jakob Ammann (1644–ca. 1730), moved to Pennsylvania because its founder, William Penn, had promised freedom of religion and the right to own land. Thus, they and a diverse number of German-speaking peoples immigrated to Pennsylvania in the 18th century. The Anabaptists took their beloved *Ausbund* with them and printed more copies in 1742 for worship in their new land.

By 1800, Mennonite use of the *Ausbund* declined when other hymnbooks became more popular, but some Amish communities (later called "Old Order" Amish) still use the book today. Next to learning the Bible, singing from the *Ausbund* is the most important activity that the Amish do in their biweekly worship services. Because the hymns are quite long (many have at least 25 stanzas), the *Vorsingers* (song leaders) select just some of the verses from a few of the hymns. Most Old Order communities sing hymn 131, *Das Loblied* (praise song), second in the service.

Perhaps most striking about the *Ausbund*'s hymns is that they contain no musical notes. The *Ausbund* does suggest some tunes to which the songs may be sung; some of these tunes came from various European folk melodies present in the 16th century. The sound of these tunes has been passed down through the centuries and varies from community to community. The *Vorsingers* help the congregation to identify the tune by singing out the first note. Also, the more traditional the community, the slower the singing will be. For instance, with *Das Loblied,* a song that contains four stanzas of seven lines, it may take up to 20 minutes to finish the song. For the Amish, the focus is on the meaning of the words and not the liveliness of the tune.

Jacob Hicks

See also: Gospel Music; Moravian Music; Native American Church Music

Further Reading

Blank, Benuel S. 2001. *The Amazing Story of the Ausbund: The Oldest Hymnal in the World Known to Still Be in Continuous Use.* Narvon, PA: B. S. Blank.

Kraybill, Donald B., Karen Johnson-Weiner, and Steven M. Nolt. 2013. *The Amish.* Baltimore, MD: Johns Hopkins University Press.

Nolt, Steven M. 1992. *A History of the Amish.* Intercourse, PA: Good Books.

Yoder, Paul M. 1964. *Four Hundred Years with the Ausbund.* Scottdale, PA: Herald Press.

Andalusian Music

The repertoire of Andalusian music is derived from a singular period of cultural history that can only be described as legendary. Like the "one brief shining moment that was known as Camelot," al-Andalus, or Muslim-controlled Spain, was a locale that Amnon Shiloah deems "the scene of one of the most fascinating examples of cultural exchange" in history, lasting nearly eight centuries, from 711 to 1492 (Shiloah, 1995, p. 73). What began as a nearly "vandalized" landscape under waves of invasion was transformed into a highly developed civilization that parlayed Eastern knowledge transmitted from the House of Wisdom (*Bayt al-Hikma*) in Baghdad into quantum advances in agriculture, civil engineering, medicine, astronomy, and the arts. Estimates of the holdings of the library in Córdoba, Spain, range from 40,000 to 400,000 items. Muslims, Christians, and Jews coexisted in a state of *convivencia,* leading to such contributions to scholarship as the philosophical, theological, and medical works of Moshe ben Maimon (Maimonides).

A pivotal development in music history occurred around 822, when the musician known as Ziryāb emigrated from Baghdad to the Umayyad caliphate of Córdoba, bringing musical instruments and founding the first conservatory of music on the European continent. Two signature poetical/musical genres emerged from the culture of al-Andalus: the *muwashshah* and *zajal*, which flourished for centuries and spread to the Maghreb, Levant, and Europe following the Reconquista. Andalusian musical culture tangibly influenced the Provençal troubadour tradition as well as the cantigas of Christian Iberia under Alfonso X, with Arab instrumentation adapted in Europe: the 'ūd (al-'ūd), for instance, morphed into the lute. The process of transmitting Andalusian culture indicates the interfaith character of the time, as the monastic system was a key node for disseminating knowledge. R. W. Southern captures the spirit of al-Andalus in *The Making of the Middle Ages*, describing the "one-way traffic of ideas" from East to West which began in the 11th century and subsequently brought monks and scholars from England, France, and Italy to centers in Spain and Sicily "in search of knowledge" (Southern, 1961, p. 66).

Mahmoud Guettat refers to an "Afro-Eastern tradition" as well as the "indigenous tradition of Gregorian and Visigothic-Mozarabic liturgical chant" around 800 CE (Guettat, 2002, p. 442). Ahmad al-Tifāshī's early-13th-century publication *Muta'at al-Asmā' fī 'ilm al-samā'* ("Pleasure to the Ears, on the Art of Music") quotes local sources who documented that "the songs of the people of Andalus were, in ancient times, either in the style of the Christians, or in the style of the Arab camel drivers [hudā'] . . . until the establishment of the Umayyad dynasty" (Liu and Monroe, 1989, p. 42). Al-Tifāshī credits Ziryāb as the linchpin in changing the landscape of musical expression; Guettat lauds him for establishing a "specifically Andalusian musical school in the great classical tradition of Baghdad" and introducing "all the instruments used in the Islamic East" (Guettat, 2002, p. 445). Al-Tifāshī enumerates some of the nearly 40 musical instruments imported by Ziryāb: the *'ūd* (lute), nāy (reed), *duff* (tambourine), *sīz* (castanets), *rabāb* (rebec), and *būq* (horn), which "emits . . . rare and magnificent melodies producing the greatest rapture and astonishment" (Liu and Monroe, 1989, p. 44). Shiloah observes that by Ziryāb's death in 857, "art music in al-Andalus had reached its peak and on the whole had divested itself of the bonds of Oriental models" (Shiloah, 1995, p. 74).

This infusion of new instrumentation into Iberia affected the cultural climate of al-Andalus, and later Europe. Along with new instrumentation, new musical genres emerged—among them the muwashshah and zajal, which exemplified the Arab-Andalusian aesthetic. Guettat refers to the "great poets of the time" who contributed to the "golden age" of these genres: Ibn Bājja (Avempace), Ibn Zuhr (Avenzohar), and Ibn Rushd (Averroes). Zajal is a poetic form written in colloquial, conversational language; in contrast, the lyrics in a muwashshah are expressed in classical Arabic as opposed to colloquial or regional Arabic. The strophic muwashshah differs from the *qasīdah*, an ancient poetic genre common in the Arab world, in its varied rhyme scheme, yet both genres are similar in their use of classical Arabic.

Córdoban poet Muqaddam ibn Mu'āfa is generally credited with the invention of the muwashshah around the turn of the 10th century, although this assertion is subject to scholarly debate. Shiloah attributes its origin to the Arabic word *wishāh*, a "belt ornamented with pearls and rubies" (Shiloah, 1995, p. 76).

The typical muwashshah opens with a prelude of two lines followed by a strophe, or stanza, which shares a common rhyme and concludes with a short refrain, repeating one or two of the opening lines and returning to the original rhyme scheme. Subsequent strophic sections introduce new rhyme schemes, and the entire muwashshah ends with a short section that may incorporate other stylistic elements. Lois Ibsen al Faruqi contextualizes the settings, language, and imagery of muwashshahāt within the abstract qualities of Islamic art (al Faruqi, 1975, p. 4). Poetic themes include satire, nature, courage, and lamentation, with love a pervasive motif; however, expressions of romantic love are usually addressed to the male gender, avoiding specific references to the female beloved, and are often conflated with the love of God. The range of imagery in the medieval Andalusian texts translated by Benjamin Liu and James Monroe encompasses wine and intoxication; natural scenes such as the full or crescent moon, willow branches, a breeze, birds, a rose, and gazelles; and physical references to a burning or inflamed heart and the beloved's facial features (eyelids, cheeks, and mouth).

This excerpt in Liu and Monroe's book is a mid–13th-century zajal by Sufi poet al-Shushtarī; the three indented lines of the strophe share a common rhyme scheme (AA bbb AA) in the original Arabic. Although technically a zajal, the rhyme scheme conforms to the muwashshah model. Al-Shushtarī is noted for his role in the transmission of Andalusian culture to the Maghreb via his *tarīqa* ("way") along with the successor Shādhiliyya tarīqa.

Following the expulsion of the Moors and Jews from the Iberian peninsula as the Reconquista reached its apogee in the late 15th century, the traditions of Andalusian music found new expressions across the Mediterranean Sea in North Africa. Moroccan, Algerian, Tunisian, and Libyan cultures incorporated this music, each adding its distinctive national flavor: resulting in *al-'alā al-andalusiyah* in Morocco and *ma'lūf* (*mūsīqā andalusiyya*) in Algeria, Tunisia, and Libya. *Tarab al-gharnātī*, with roots in Granada, migrated to Morocco and Algeria. Syrians incorporated the muwashshah into the *wasla*, or musical suite. The glory of al-Andalus would remain a compelling motif throughout the Arab world, with modern Egyptian and Levantine composers and performers reviving the muwashshah in the 20th century. The importance of the genre extends beyond artistry; Michael Frishkopf underscores the political significance of al-Andalus in the contemporary Egyptian imagination due to its "inversion" of the "power relations between the Arabs and the West," and the factor of "constituting proof that Western modernity is indebted to the Arabs" (Frishkopf, 2003, p. 152).

Hicham Chami

See also: Zajal

Further Reading

al Faruqi, Lois Ibsen. 1975. "Muwashshah: A Vocal Form in Islamic Culture." *Ethnomusicology* 19, 1–29.

Frishkopf, Michael. 2003. "Some Meanings of the Spanish Tinge in Contemporary Egyptian Music." In Goffredo Plastino (ed.), *Mediterranean Mosaic: Popular Music and Global Sounds*, 143–178. New York: Routledge.

Guettat, Mahmoud. 2002. "The Andalusian Musical Heritage." In Virginia Danielson, Dwight Reynolds, and Scott Marcus (eds.), *The Garland Encyclopedia of World Music; Vol. 6: The Middle East*, 441–454. New York: Routledge.

Liu, Benjamin M., and James T. Monroe. 1989. *Ten Hispano-Arabic Strophic Poems in Modern Oral Tradition: Music and Texts*. Berkeley: University of California Press.

Menocal, María Rosa. 2002. *The Ornament of the World: How Muslims, Jews, and Christians Created a Culture of Tolerance in Medieval Spain*. Boston: Little, Brown.

Shannon, Jonathan H. 2007. "Performing al-Andalus, Remembering al-Andalus: Mediterranean Soundings from Mashriq to Maghrib." *Journal of American Folklore* 120, 308–334.

Shiloah, Amnon. 1995. *Music in the World of Islam: A Socio-Cultural Study*. Detroit, MI: Wayne State University Press.

Southern, R. W. 1961. *The Making of the Middle Ages*. New Haven, CT: Yale University Press.

Touma, Habib Hassan. 2002. "Andalusian Nūba in Morocco." In Virginia Danielson, Dwight Reynolds, and Scott Marcus (eds.), *The Garland Encyclopedia of World Music; Vol. 6: The Middle East*, , 455–464. New York: Routledge.

Andean Region, Music of the

Although the Andes mountain range stretches the entire length of South America's western coast, from southernmost Chile to Venezuela, most scholarship dealing with the culture of the Andean region discusses the highland areas of Ecuador, Bolivia, or Peru. The territory now encompassed by these nations formed the core of the former Inca Empire, which extended into northern Chile and northwestern Argentina, as well as a sliver of southwestern Colombia. Despite the spread of Incan cultural elements, such as the Quechua language, throughout much of this area, groups subjugated by the Incas retained many of their distinctive musical practices. Spanish colonists arriving in the early 16th century imposed certain performance contexts related to Christian worship, and particular European musical genres and instruments, across a wide swath of the Andes. Nevertheless, indigenous communities adapted these musical customs in countless ways, and in many cases they have continued to foster significant aspects of their preconquest musical traditions through to the present day. African slaves who were brought to the Andes region during the colonial period have also contributed to the remarkable diversity of its music cultures.

Starting in the mid-1960s, a type of folkloric ensemble emerged, first in Bolivia and Chile, and later in Peru and Ecuador, that transformed the sound of rural traditional music into one that was accessible to urban audiences. The assemblage of instruments, genres, and overall aesthetics taken up by these urban folkloric groups is what has come to be known as "Andean music" for most international audiences. Commercial popular music styles based on indigenous or mestizo (of mixed Amerindian and European background) regional traditions also arose in the main cities of the Andean region at various junctures of the 20th century. As the 21st century dawned, the transnational Latin genre *cumbia* was one of the most widespread popular music genres in the Andes region.

ARGENTINA, CHILE, AND BOLIVIA

The northwestern reaches of Argentina's and Chile's northern zone have long been linked culturally to the Andean regions of Bolivia and Peru to the north. These areas have been inhabited by indigenous peoples from the same linguistic groups, were subject to common governance by the Inca Empire, and fell under the same administrative territories for much of the colonial period. More recently, they have been connected by economically driven cross-border migration. This shared history means that musical practices associated with the Bolivian and Peruvian Andes can also be found in northwestern Argentina and northern Chile. One important legacy of Andean indigenous culture in these areas is that musical performance remained closely linked to the agrarian cycle into the 20th century. Similarly, central Andean instruments such as the panpipes, *kena* and *tarka* flutes, and the *charango* (small guitar) also have a distinct presence in the music cultures of northwestern Argentina and northern Chile. Song and dance genres like *wayñu*, *carnavalito*, *bailecito*, and *cueca* are considered to be part of the local musical heritage on both sides of the Argentina-Bolivia border; the northern Chilean version of wayñu is called *trote*, and the cueca is likewise danced in this area.

In the Bolivian Andes, one of the primary modes of traditional music-making in indigenous communities is ensembles in which all participants play the same wind instrument. The main instruments used in these groups are different kinds of panpipes and several types of flutes, the most prevalent being *kenas*, *pinkillus*, and *tarkas*. Communal ensembles play different wind instruments depending on whether it is the rainy or dry season, and they usually accompany them with large drums such as the *wankara* and *bombo*, or the *caja* snare drum.

The panpipes (*zampoñas* in Spanish), kena, and bombo were integrated into a type of ensemble called *conjunto* that performed folkloric Andean music and gained popularity in Bolivian cities in the late 1960s. Two string instruments rounded out the conjunto's instrumentation: the *charango*—a small guitar variant developed in the Andes during the colonial era—and its ancestor, the Spanish guitar. Many conjuntos took names in Quechua or Aymara (the second most widely spoken native language in the Andes, after Quechua) and musicians often donned some kind of indigenous dress on stage. However, most musicians in this scene are in fact mestizo or white, and the style in which these groups performed was originally oriented toward cosmopolitan audiences. Since the 1980s, the most popular of these Bolivian folkloric ensembles has been Los Kjarkas, a group formed by three brothers from the Cochabamba region who were fluent in Quechua and Spanish. The name *Kjarkas* refers to a type of fortress built by the Inca, and their logo is made up of symbols drawn from Tiwanaku, a pre-Hispanic archeological site. Like other conjuntos, Los Kjarkas composed songs based musically on various Bolivian traditional genres but performed them all using the standard instrumentation just described.

One style for which Los Kjarkas was particularly well known was the *saya*, a genre that originated in Bolivia's small community of African descendants and is typified by its bass drum pattern in which the first two beats in successive triplets are accented. The saya's important role in Bolivian folkloric music was enhanced when it became the main accompaniment for the *caporales* dance that opens the large carnival and fiesta parades in the cities of La Paz, Oruro, and Cochabamba. In these boisterous settings, the music is provided by large brass bands, which also accompany other popular festival dances such as *morenadas* and *diabladas*.

PERU

Flute ensembles similar to those found in Bolivia are also common in the indigenous villages of southern Peru. In the Lake Titicaca region that straddles the border of the two countries, one particular type of panpipe, called *siku*, is the most popular. Sikus are played using a distinctive technique that was developed in pre-Hispanic times: each ensemble member plays one rank (row of tubes) of a two-rank panpipe, each with a different set of notes; to perform a complete melody, players of the two complementary ranks of the single instrument must alternate playing of their notes in tight coordination—music scholars call this procedure playing in hocket.

Indigenous communities in Peru have also adopted instruments brought to the Andes by Europeans. Harps and violins can be found, often together, in numerous traditional ensembles. A basic harp-violin duo accompanies the legendary scissors dance in central-southern Peru, in which dancers compete against each other while contributing to the rhythm with metal "scissors." Both instruments also appear alongside a large number of saxophones and clarinets in the typical orchestra of the central highlands. In this region, the violin is combined with another instrument resulting from colonization: indigenous groups used the horns of cattle, which were introduced to South America by Europeans, to make trumpets called *wakrapuku* (or *pututu* in Bolivia). Wakrapuku is played for cattle-branding rituals along with the violin, the indigenous *tinya* drum, and a singer. As in Bolivia, brass bands modeled on European military bands have been performing at festivals small and large throughout the Peruvian Andes for at least a century.

Many of the ensemble types mentioned here are likely to count several numbers in the *wayno* genre in their repertoire. The wayno evolved as a dance music type during the colonial period and has become one of the most widespread Andean genres. Wayno (sometimes spelled *wayñu*) substyles vary by region, and they typically sound different in Amerindian versus mestizo settings. Traditionally, indigenous performers in Peru have sung waynos in Quechua and preferred high-pitched women's voices and faster tempos, whereas mestizo waynos were sung at a lower pitch, slower tempo, and in Spanish (though sometimes mixed with Quechua). Most forms share a characteristic long-short-short accompaniment rhythm and mostly pentatonic melodies (based on five-note scales). Following dramatic migration from the rural highlands to the coastal capital, Lima, in the mid-20th century, wayno became the popular music of choice for the new city dwellers anxious to maintain ties with their home provinces. Several performers from different Andean regions had tremendous success through live performances and record sales. The performers El Picaflor de los Andes (The Hummingbird of the Andes) and La Pastorita Huaracina (The Shepherdess of Huaraz) were two of the biggest stars in this commercial wayno style.

ECUADOR AND COLOMBIA

The Quichua people who reside in the northern Ecuadorean province of Imbabura perform the *sanjuán*, whose duple meter resembles that of the wayno but most often with short-long-short rhythm. Quichua sanjuán often employs ballad-like texts sung in the Quichua language, with accompaniment frequently provided by a small harp. One ritual setting in which sanjuán has traditionally been performed is wakes for deceased infants, where it serves to promote dancing. Sanjuán and *pareja* (another type of dance music also performed at children's wakes) have influenced the music of highland African-Ecuadoreans in Imbabura's Chota Valley. This group's most important genre, *bomba*, also displays African-derived characteristics, including the performance technique for its signature bomba drum, which is held between the knees and played with the hands.

Paradoxically, it was the mestizo adaptation of sanjuán, named *sanjuanito*, which became an emblem of Ecuadorean indigenous culture in the late 20th century. Though both sanjuán and sanjuanito are typically performed by several types of ensembles, sanjuanito renditions by folkloric groups from the Otavalo area are perhaps the most widely known of the region. These groups feature instrumentation similar to the Bolivian conjuntos, sometimes with the addition of the Ecuadorean *rondador* panpipe and the violin. Participants at festivals of indigenous culture in Ecuador regularly dance to sanjuanitos composed by one such Otavaleño ensemble, the nationally and internationally renowned Ñanda Mañachi.

By the mid-20th century, the waltz-derived *pasillo* was the centerpiece of a musical category in Ecuador simply called "national music." The pasillo's national symbolism stemmed from the perception that it encapsulated the sentimental character of Ecuadoreans: pasillo lyrics often take a melancholic approach to love or express a nostalgic local pride. The sung form is commonly performed with duet voices accompanied by guitar and *requinto* (a small, high-pitched guitar). In the late 1970s, a working-class pasillo style became a component of *rocolera* music, which gets its name from the *rocolas* (jukeboxes) found in cantinas in lower-class neighborhoods. Because these venues and the activities that take place in them figured prominently in the pasillos, *valses*, and boleros that made up the rocolera category, the music was stigmatized by the middle classes for its associations with drunkenness, infidelity, and violence.

The Páez of the southwestern Colombian highlands perform in ensembles made up of flutes and drums; however, the style known as "Colombian Andean music" is executed primarily using various string instruments such as the guitar, *bandola* (a mandolin-like instrument), and the *tiple* (a small guitar type considered to be a national cultural symbol). Duos, trios, and larger groups called *estudiantinas* employ these instruments to perform the song genres that are identified with the interior region's predominantly mestizo population, such as *bambuco* and the Colombian pasillo. In the early and middle 20th century, Colombian Andean music constituted the major popular music in the country, as circulated in the recordings of famous duos such as Garzón y Collazos.

CUMBIA

While transnational popular music trends such as Latin jazz, salsa, pop ballads, and rock have exerted influences on Andean music in recent decades, the adoption of *cumbia* throughout the Andes since the 1960s has been one of the region's most significant musical developments. Originating during the 19th century as a traditional dance music cultivated by blacks in Colombia's and Panama's Atlantic coast region—with cultural input from Amerindian groups—cumbia later formed the core of the early 20th-century phenomenon known as *música tropical* (tropical music). Based on Afro-Colombian forms, but influenced by Afro-Cuban music and performed with jazz band instrumentation, by the 1950s música tropical had overtaken highland forms as the popular music of Colombia's Andean interior.

A simplified version of cumbia that was performed in smaller, more electrified groups and was popular in Colombia in the 1960s also had a major effect in Peru, Ecuador, and Bolivia. In Peru, cumbia was especially popular among the offspring of Andean migrants in Lima, who sought to identify with a cosmopolitan style befitting their status as residents of a modern city. Cumbia subsequently served as the basis for a new hybrid style known as *cumbia andina*, or *chicha* (the name of an Andean fermented corn drink), which involved adapting popular waynos to cumbia rhythms; this process was facilitated by the striking resemblance in the underlying rhythmic pattern of the two forms. A type of cumbia that flourished in Peru's Amazon region was a huge hit throughout the country during the 1990s. Labeled *technocumbia* because of the predominance of electronic instruments, this variant had cast off the Andean musical influences that were integral to chicha.

Peruvian technocumbia celebrity Rossy War had a successful tour in Ecuador in 1999, subsequently sparking a musical boom in the area. At a time when Ecuadoreans were leaving the country in droves due to economic crisis, many identified with technocumbia's typical lyrics about long-distance relationships and breakups. Upper- and middle-class Ecuadoreans disparaged technocumbia as an unsophisticated copy of Peruvian music, although some Ecuadorean-composed songs have incorporated elements from sanjuanito. The upper echelons of Bolivian society have expressed similar concern over the foreign origins of cumbia, which was the most popular dance music in that country during the early 2000s.

Joshua Katz-Rosene

See also: Bolivia, Music of; Cumbia; Nueva Canción

Further Reading

Céspedes, Gilka Wara. 1993. "Wayñu, Saya, and Chuntunqui: Bolivian Identity in the Music of 'Los Kjarkas.'" *Latin American Music Review* 14(1), 52–101.

Fernández L'Hoeste, Héctor, and Pablo Vila, eds. 2013. *Cumbia!: Scenes of a Migrant Latin American Music Genre.* Durham, NC: Duke University Press.

Meisch, Lynn A. 2002. *Andean Entrepreneurs: Otavalo Merchants and Musicians in the Global Arena.* Austin: University of Texas Press.

Ritter, Jonathan. 2012. "Peru and the Andes." In Robin Moore and Walter Aaron Clark (eds.), *Musics of Latin America*, 325–370. New York: W.W. Norton.

Romero, Raúl R. 2001. *Debating the Past: Music, Memory, and Identity in the Andes.* New York: Oxford University Press.

Schechter, John M., ed. 1999. *Music in Latin American Culture: Regional Traditions.* New York: Schirmer Books.

Turino, Thomas. 1993. *Moving Away from Silence: Music of the Peruvian Altiplano and the Experiment of Urban Migration.* Chicago: University of Chicago Press.

Wong, Ketty. 2012. *Whose National Music?: Identity, Mestizaje, and Migration in Ecuador.* Philadelphia, PA: Temple University Press.

Arab Classical Music

The vast repertoire of folk, religious, classical, and popular songs and instrumental works collectively known as Arab music encompasses traditions from 22 countries and territories comprising the Arab world. The Arab musical tradition (*turāth*), reflecting a shared cultural aesthetic, is simultaneously country-/tribal-specific, regionally based, and pan-Arab; it also incorporates significant cultural influences from neighboring regions as well as from the West. As with any geo-cultural region, the musics of the Arab world are both distinctive from other indigenous traditions and identifiable as Arab.

CONCEPTUAL FRAMEWORK

It is inevitable that musics of the Arab world sound different than those of Western traditions—but also different than other non-Western traditions. Singling out the particularities of Arab music makes it easier to compare and contrast within these frameworks. A central concept that operates in Arab culture is that of oral tradition. This concept affects everything from notation (specifically, the absence thereof) to pedagogy to performance practice. Musical instruction in the Arab world revolves around the relationship between teacher and student, with imitation a key tool in acquiring mastery of the instrument or voice; Christian Poché observes that "systematic teaching manuals" in the Arab world first emerged only in 1903 (Wright et al., 2001). Because of this strong teacher-student bond, along with the factor of regional variations, ensemble rehearsals can be tricky, with each musician advocating for his or her own teacher's interpretation of the work. Without notated scores, uniformity is impossible.

Yet this very flexibility plays a critical role in the performance of Arab music: *taqsīm* (instrumental improvisation) and *layālī* (vocal improvisation) showcase musician virtuosity in tandem with the dynamic of audience response. Herein is another major divider between East and West: a silent Arab audience is unheard of; instead, listeners applaud and call out their approval with phrases such as "yā salām" or "Allah!" The interaction between musicians and listeners (*sammi'ah*) not only determines the course of the performance in terms of repetitions and ornamentations by a vocalist or instrumentalist, but also inspires the quintessential element of *tarab*, a state of ecstasy or enchantment. Habib Hassan Touma refers to the "mosaic-like stringing together of musical form elements . . . within the framework of a tonal-spacial model" (Touma, 1996, p. xx), which helps maintain the artistic balance between predictability and spontaneity. The *maqām* (modal) system provides the underpinnings for the modulations that occur during taqsīm. Audiences consider skillful modulation from one maqām to another to be highly desirable, with the mastery of technique and execution contributing to the experience of tarab during performance.

Arab culture venerates the concept of beauty; the Hadith (a collection of narrations concerning the words and deeds of the Prophet Muhammad) contains the phrase "Allah is beautiful and loves beauty." This phrase connotes the honor and respect due to the Creation, and translates into a highly developed aesthetic encompassing visual, literary, and performing arts in the Arab world—interwoven with many other technical aspects of musical practice. In contrast to the diatonic scales in Western music, for instance, Arab music incorporates quarter-tones that convey an "Oriental" flavor. The principle of heterophony governs instrumental embellishments of melodic phrases. Song lyrics are rarely or never sung in harmony, but rather in unison. A parallel can be seen with the Western transition from monophony to polyphony in the late Middle Ages/Renaissance, with unison singing of Gregorian chant in the monastic setting suggesting the likelihood of mutual influences during the European medieval period concurrent with the flourishing of Moorish culture in al-Andalus on the Iberian Peninsula.

Another definitive artistic preference in Arab music culture is the importance of the vocalist, perhaps stemming from the real or perceived Islamic prohibition of music throughout Arab music history, coupled with the status of the voice as the primary vehicle for religious expression (indeed, vocal genres such as Qur'anic recitation, *tajwid*, or the call to prayer, *adhān*, are not termed "music" at all). Amnon Shiloah writes that music came under attack by jurists as early as the ninth century, with instruments condemned as "reprehensible digressions from a life of devoted piety" (Shiloah, 1995, p. 63). In discussing hierarchical schemes for instrumentation, Margaret Kartomi observes that 10th-century philosopher and music theoretician al-Fārābī "had followed the practice of giving supremacy to the human vocal instrument and to instruments producing sounds resembling it" (Kartomi, 1990, p. 128). The primacy of the vocalist has been translated into a performance model that regulates the scope and proportion of instrumental accompaniment. Until late in the 20th century, the traditional *takht*—the small ensemble providing instrumental support for the vocalist—was the norm for musical performance in Egypt and the Levant, but not the Maghreb (North Africa) or al-Andalus. The takht is comprised of violin or kamanjah, *qānūn* (a plucked-stringed instrument similar to the zither), *'ūd* (a short-necked, fretless predecessor of the lute), *nāy* (a reed instrument originally made of bamboo), and *riqq* (a tambourine-like percussion instrument); Touma includes the *darbuka* in the percussion roster.

The texts of Arabic songs conform to the Arab aesthetic; in addition to the classical poetry that forms the basis for the monorhymed and monometered qasīdah, which originated in pre-Islamic Arabia, the Andalusian *muwashshah* uses stylized poetic metaphor, in keeping with the Arab preference for subtlety and indirectness in love poetry. A. J. Racy notes the influence of the Ottoman ghazal tradition and the prevalence of nature-related imagery for the beloved, including roses, willow branches, and the moon. An excerpt from a 19th-century anthology compiled by Shihāb al-Dīn illustrates this technique (the gazelle was a recognized "emblem" for desire):

> Oh, my gazelle how they distanced you from me.
> They caused our separation and made you accustomed to abandoning me.
> (Racy, 2003, p. 151)

Quite simply, the Arab world does not always make clear-cut distinctions among folk, religious, classical/art, and popular forms; numerous crossovers exist (*cf.* the infusion of folk themes into classical compositions by Bartók, Glinka, and Vaughan Williams). The qasīdah serves as the basis for the texts of the Moroccan folk genre *malhūn*, although colloquial/dialectal language is used. Nonetheless, malhūn enjoys a prestigious designation in Morocco, along with Andalusian music.

Poet Ahmad Shawqi revived the qasīdah in writing lyrics to songs composed by Riyād al-Sunbātī for the legendary Egyptian vocalist Umm Kulthūm (1898–1975), reinforcing her connection to the *turāth*. It was Ibrahim Nagi, however, who wrote the lyrics for al-Sunbātī's composition "al-Atlāl" which, according to Virginia Danielson, served as a powerful political statement in light of Egypt's 1967 defeat: "Give me my freedom/Set loose my chains . . ." (Danielson, 1997, p. 179). Earlier, Umm Kulthūm's 1956 film *Sallāma*, in which she played the title character, includes a qasīdah in addition to a muwashshah and *mawwāl*, an improvisatory genre. Scott Marcus notes that Sayyed Darweesh (1892–1923), who mentored al-Sunbātī, composer of Egypt's national anthem, "Biladi" ("My Homeland"), included the muwashshah in his repertoire, which was rich in folkloric references and accessible to the common man (Darweesh once worked as a bricklayer).

HISTORICAL CONTEXT

A survey of the research reveals that 20th-century scholars have attempted to codify the history and development of Arab music, in the absence of an accepted periodization schema, in a way comparable to that for Western classical music (Baroque, Romantic, etc.). The schemas of Henry George Farmer, Hans Hickman, Alexis Chottin, and Simon Jargy stop before the current time frame; two comprehensive models are those of Touma and Peter Crossley-Holland. The starting point for each is the *Jāhiliyya*, or pre-Islamic period (the Arabic word means "age of ignorance").

THE SOUND OF ARAB MUSIC

The distinctive, instantly recognizable Arabic sound is produced by instruments and vocals that follow established patterns and melody through a system of modes, or *maqāmāt* (sing., *maqām*), that incorporate quarter-tones and varied intervals; and rhythms (*īqā'āt*; sing., *īqā'*). The landmark Congress of Cairo in 1932 adopted the use of the term *maqām*; the modes were "classified in terms of the seven degrees of the scale" (Wright et al., 2001). The Congress determined a system of tetrachords termed *ajnās* (sing., *jins*), of which two to four would constitute each mode. Examples of maqāmāt are *bayātī*, *farahfaza*, *hijāz*, and *rāst*, most of which have quarter-tones (half-flats are indicated by a diagonal slash across the top of the flat symbol).

Varied rhythmic patterns, played on hand drums, complement the melody and evoke kinesthetic responses. The Congress compiled a list of Arab rhythms, "articulated as a series of strong or weak beats determining the accentuation" (Wright et al., 2001). Percussionists use the term *dum* to indicate the lower sound produced by striking the center of the drumhead and *tak* the higher sound produced at its edge. Racy refers to dum as "deep sounding, emphatic" and tak as "light, crisp" (Racy, 2003, p. 113). *Ess* indicates the silence or rest. The īqā'āt are associated with specific genres: the 10-beat *Samā'ī Thaqīl* is used for the classical *samā'ī*, while the faster and livelier *maksūm* and *masmūdi* accompany belly dance.

The takht—an ensemble comprised of violin, qānūn, 'ūd, nāy, and riqq—is at the heart of authentic performance of classical Arab music. The characteristics of the instruments provide the balance and variety necessary for the vocal genres *dawr*, qasīdah, and muwashshah; and for the solely instrumental genres *bashraf*, *samā'ī*, *longah*, *tahmīlah*, and *dūlāb*. Beyond the melodic components, the riqq is essential in maintaining rhythmic integrity. In fact, the musician who plays the riqq is not considered merely a percussionist but is called *dhābit al-īqā'*, "officer of the rhythm." During performance, each instrumentalist has the opportunity to exhibit virtuosity and respond to audience reaction during improvisation, or taqsīm. Touma explains the evolution of instrumentation: initially, the *firqah* expanded the takht, including eight instruments or more. Later, the Europeanized "big Arabian orchestra" incorporated multiple violins, cellos, contrabasses, clarinets, oboes, trumpets, accordion, electric, synthesizer, timpani, and glockenspiel—resulting in a "huge racket." Touma laments the effect of Western instruments: "They have ... destroyed the principles of the Arabian tone system and, for all practical purposes, have eliminated the traditional takht ensemble and its intimate sound character." The vocal aspect has also been altered, with a "singer who croons a pop song into the microphone" (Touma, 1996, p. 141). Contrast this with Danielson's description of traditional vocal improvisation: "In a song the first task was the clear and skillful delivery of the initial segment. . . . Depending on audience response, the singer would then repeat that section, introducing variations, or go on to the next section of the piece . . ." (Danielson, 1997, p. 94). It is this audience response which inspires tarab.

POINT/COUNTERPOINT

Academic controversies surround the legacy of Andalusian music. Shiloah details the "furious polemics" of a 1921 debate between Julián Ribera y Tarragó and Higinio Anglès concerning Arab influence on the Cantigas de Santa María and the Troubadour repertoire. Farmer (Shiloah's own mentor) would side with Ribera, who presented evidence of similarities in rhyme scheme and performance practice between the zajal and cantigas. Four years later, Farmer expanded on Ribera's hypothesis with a groundbreaking article, "Clues for the Arabian Influence on

European Musical Theory" (which would spawn an ongoing publishing battle with Kathleen Schlesinger). Farmer cited specific instrumentation as well as the muwashshah and zajal genres, pointing out their "affinities with the Cantigas" and concluding that "many of the song forms and dance forms of the minstrelsy of Medieval Europe can be traced to the Arabs" (Shiloah, 1995, p. 81). The origins of the Andalusian tradition provide another source of dissent. Touma writes that "the Andalusians—that is, the medieval Spanish Muslims—first developed this repertoire, preserved it, and then introduced it into North Africa" (Touma, 2002, p. 455). Mahmoud Guettat reverses this assertion, claiming instead that "Andalusian-North African music began in North Africa" (Guettat, 2002, p. 441).

Perhaps the most critical controversy within the last century is not an academic one, but an artistic rivalry played out in the postcolonial milieu of mid–20th-century Egypt by Umm Kulthūm and Muhammad 'Abd al-Wahhāb (1902–1991). Although these two musicians had similar backgrounds, and incorporated patriotic themes in the music they composed and performed, they diverged widely in their receptiveness to Western influence: Umm Kulthūm steadfastly maintained the traditional Arab repertoire and instrumentation and 'Abd al-Wahhāb continually strove toward innovation and modernity. Urged to engage in a creative collaboration by President Nasser, who advocated this partnership as a tangible demonstration of Arab unity, the two finally shared a stage on February 6, 1964, with vocalist Umm Kulthūm performing 'Abd al-Wahhāb's composition "Inta 'Omri"—heard by 80 million people that night via the live radio broadcast. It would become Egypt's best-selling song of all time.

The inclusion of Western instruments in 'Abd al-Wahhāb's orchestra not only resulted in a "huge racket," echoing Touma's diatribe, but the modernist's carefully timed compositions (to conform to radio slots) also eliminated the possibility of improvisation. In the face of rapid cultural evolution in Egypt, the collaboration between Umm Kulthūm and 'Abd al-Wahhāb can be seen as a critical turning point: the exact moment when classical Arab music started dying. It is worth noting that not only did Umm Kulthūm perform 'Abd al-Wahhāb's songs until the end of her career—so that she is more likely to be remembered for "Inta 'Omri" than "al-Atlāl"—but also that 'Abd al-Wahhāb outlived Umm Kulthūm by 16 years, thus solidifying his influence with a new generation of listeners. The impulse toward fusion, particularly by high-profile Arab musicians in the diaspora, is testament to this continuing deterioration of the turāth.

Hicham Chami

See also: Andalusian Music; Bashir Brothers (Munir and Jamil); Kalthoum, Umm; Malhūn; Malouf; Ney; Oud; Qānūn; Rebab; Riq; Sufism, Music of; Taqsīm; Tar; Zajal

Further Reading

Chami, Hicham. 2011. "'Inta 'Omri': A Precious Yet Painful Collaboration; A Merging of Western Influence and Eastern Tradition in Egyptian Music." Paper presented at the Conference of the Society for Ethnomusicology-Niagara chapter, Eastman School of Music, Rochester, NY, March 5, 2011.

Danielson, Virginia. 1997. *The Voice of Egypt: Umm Kulthūm, Arabic Song, and Egyptian Song in the Twentieth Century.* Chicago: University of Chicago Press.

Farmer, Henry George. 1925. "Clues for the Arabian Influence on European Musical Theory." *Journal of the Royal Asiatic Society* 57(1), 61–80.

Guettat, Mahmoud. 2002. "The Andalusian Musical Heritage." In Virginia Danielson, Dwight Reynolds, and Scott Marcus (eds.), *Garland Encyclopedia of World Music; Vol. 6, The Middle East,* 441–454. New York: Routledge.

Kartomi, Margaret J. 1990. *On Concepts and Classifications of Musical Instruments.* Chicago: University of Chicago Press.

Marcus, Scott L. 2007. *Music in Egypt.* New York: Oxford University Press.

Racy, A. J. 2003. *Making Music in the Arab World: The Culture and Artistry of Tarab.* Cambridge: Cambridge University Press.

Robertson, Ale, and Denis Stevens, eds. 1960. *The Pelican History of Music; Vol. 1: Ancient Forms to Polyphony.* London: Penguin.

Shiloah, Amnon. 1995. *Music in the World of Islam: A Socio-Cultural Study.* Detroit, MI: Wayne State University Press.

Touma, Habib Hassan. 1996. *The Music of the Arabs,* trans. Laurie Schwartz. Portland, OR: Amadeus Press.

Touma, Habib Hassan. 2002. "Andalusian Nūba in Morocco." In Virginia Danielson, Dwight Reynolds, and Scott Marcus (eds.), *Garland Encyclopedia of World Music; Vol. 6, The Middle East,* 455–464. New York: Routledge.

Wright, Owen, et al. 2001. "Arab Music." *Grove Music Online.* www.oxfordmusiconline.com.

Armenian Music

Armenia is an ancient land located in the southern Caucasus borderlands straddling Asia and Europe. It has been aptly noted that Armenia historically has "demonstrated a fierce cultural independence over the centuries even as it was dominated politically by various outside powers and crisscrossed by Occidental and Oriental influences" (Rockwell, 1981). This tendency is evident in all forms of Armenian cultural expression, in none more so than its music.

Armenia was originally called Hayk and, later, Hayastan, names that are still used in reference to Armenian culture, including music. Armenian music itself is ancient, but now encompasses multiple genres: ballet, contemporary popular music (e.g., hip-hop, jazz, rock, and various fusions), hymns, opera, and symphonies, in addition to the vast corpus of traditional folk songs, many of which are believed to have originated hundreds of centuries before the Common Era. Armenian music is distinctive, but inflected with influences from neighboring countries in the Near East, the Middle East, Russia, and the many nations around the world in which the large Armenian Diaspora population has settled. To the untrained ear, Armenian music sounds Middle Eastern or Russian, which is one reason Armenian musical instruments, such as the *duduk*, are sometimes used in film soundtracks to evoke exotic aural images of the Middle and Near East, as is exemplified by Peter Gabriel's score for *The Last Temptation of Christ* (1988).

Present-day Armenia is a small, landlocked, mountainous nation situated between the Black and Caspian Seas. Its current area of approximately 11,500 square miles, which is about the same size as the U.S. state of Maryland or the

European country of Belgium, is greatly attenuated from its maximum territorial expanse, with much of the historic Armenian highlands today constituting the eastern third of Turkey (what Armenians regard as Western Armenia). It is surrounded by the neighboring countries of Georgia, Azerbaijan, Iran, and Turkey.

From 1922 until 1991, Armenia was one of the 15 Soviet socialist republics of the Union of Soviet Socialist Republics (USSR) or Soviet Union. In 1991, with the dissolution of the Soviet Union, Armenia declared its independence and reestablished national sovereignty as the Republic of Armenia. Today, Armenia has an ethnically homogeneous population of some 3 million people, more than 90 percent of whom are ethnic Armenians.

Armenians have suffered severe persecution and subjugation throughout much of their history, including forced deportations from their traditional homelands, resulting in a large diaspora population. More Armenians reside beyond the borders of the Republic of Armenia than within. An estimated 6 to 7 million Armenians are dispersed worldwide. Countries with sizeable Armenian populations include Russia, the United States, France, Iran, Argentina, Lebanon, and Syria. In the United States, the state of California has the largest Armenian population, with most Armenian-Americans residing in the greater Los Angeles area. The Armenian Diaspora, while in most respects fully assimilated into their host nations, endeavors to preserve a distinctive transnational cultural identity, and music is one of its means of doing so.

Two events have profoundly and irrevocably shaped Armenian cultural consciousness. The first is the establishment of Christianity as the national religion in 301 CE. The second is the Armenian genocide beginning at the end of the 19th century, intensifying in the first two decades of the 20th century, and culminating in the deaths of an estimated 1 to 2 million victims and the deportation of millions more from Near East areas historically claimed and occupied by Armenians.

LITURGICAL MUSIC

According to Armenian tradition, the first-generation Christian disciples Bartholomew and Jude (a.k.a. Thaddeus) evangelized Armenia in the first century CE. Bartholomew was martyred there, apparently in retribution for his role in converting a member of the royal family. The state church, the Armenian Apostolic Church, recognizes both disciples as patron saints.

When the disciples arrived, music was deeply entrenched in the culture, having emerged as a cultural practice hundreds of years earlier. Less than two centuries later, in 301 CE, according to tradition, Armenia became the first nation to declare Christianity its official national religion after Gregory the Illuminator (ca. 257–ca. 332) converted King Tiridates or Trdat III; thus, it is conceivable that the establishment of sacred music traditions soon would follow, as indeed did happen.

The earliest Armenian liturgical chants or hymns—*sharagan* or *sharakan*—are attributed to Mesrop Mashtots (362–440 CE), a theologian who is regarded as a national hero for having invented Armenia's written language, which, in turn, led to one of the earliest translations of the Bible from its original languages as well as the creation of many other Armenian theological texts. Mashtots's musical works include several hymns of repentance, such as "Ankanim Aadgi Qo." Many early church leaders or *catholicoi* also were hymnists, including Catholicos Sahak I a.k.a. Isaac the Great (348–439), Catholicos Hovhannes Mandakuni (?–490), Catholicos Sahak III Dzoraporetsi (?–703), Gregory of Narek (950–1010), and Catholicos Nerses IV a.k.a. Nerses Shnorhali (1102–1173). The official Armenian Church hymnal, *The Sharakan* or *Sharagnots*, contains a cycle of more than 1,000 hymns, "prayers in song" (Kerovpyan 2013a), which are characterized by simple, beautiful melodies and deeply emotional and spiritual lyrics.

For many centuries, Armenian chants or hymns were transcribed using a unique and complicated neumatic notation system called *khaz*. Neumatic notation uses neumes, symbols placed above words in sung texts to indicate, imprecisely, changes in pitch and rhythm. The Armenian composer Hampartzoum Limondjian (1768–1839) invented a modified notational system based on similar principles that the Armenian Church still uses.

CLASSICAL MUSIC

Armenia has produced many outstanding classical musicians. Tigran Chukhajian or Tchouhadjian (1837–1898) composed the first Armenian opera, *Arshak II* (1868). Armen Tigranian (1879–1950) infused elements of Armenian folk music into his masterpiece opera *Anoush* (1912), which is ranked among the greatest Armenian cultural achievements. Tigranian's contemporary, Alexander Spendiaryan (1871–1928), a student of the Russian composer Nikolai Rimsky-Korsakov, is regarded as the father of Armenian symphonic music. The Armenian classical musician who is best known internationally is Aram Khachaturian (1903–1978). A prolific composer, his best known work is "Sabre Dance" from his ballet *Gayane* (1942), which became very popular in the United States in the late 1940s.

As with Tigranian's *Anoush*, much of Armenian classical music is built on Armenian folk music traditions, reflecting a self-consciously nationalist aesthetic. The Armenian-American composer Alan Hovhaness (1911–2000) is perhaps foremost among contemporary classical diaspora musicians in this regard, although his prolific output is by no means restricted to a solitary ethnic influence.

FOLK MUSIC

Armenian folk music predates the culture's liturgical and classical music. Armenian culture is preternaturally musical, with music accompanying all types of social occasions.

As noted earlier, Armenian music has much in common with other musical traditions of the surrounding region and, because of a long history of cross-cultural contact, differentiating it from regional variants can be difficult. One way to do so is to listen for instrumentation that, often, is uniquely Armenian, as is especially the case with Armenia's national instrument, the *duduk*, a double-reed wind instrument that is sometimes called the Armenian oboe. Other musical instruments that help to define the sound of Armenian music are the *oud* (lute), *kanun* (harp), *zurna* (oboe), *kemenche* (violin), and *dhal* (drum).

Two persons are especially esteemed in the history of Armenian folk music. One is Harutyun Sayakian or Sayat Nova (King of Song) (1712–1795), an 18th-century *ashough* or troubadour who is known to have composed hundreds of folk songs, and possibly many more, in addition to lyric poems. Although ethnically Armenian, the multilingual Sayat Nova became famous throughout the Caucasus, and has come to epitomize the art of the troubadour. During a Muslim invasion, he was martyred for refusing to renounce his Christian faith, defiantly declaring himself Armenian and Christian.

The other is the classical musician, gifted singer, and priest Soghomon Soghomonian or, simply, Komitas (1869–1935) who, in addition to composing his own classical and liturgical works, collected more than 3,000 folk songs and hymns during a critical moment in Armenian history. As an ethnomusicologist, he is Armenia's counterpart to America's Alan Lomax. More importantly, his compulsive song collecting was timely in preserving Armenian folk music traditions that otherwise might have been lost forever during the years of genocide in the early 20th century, when Armenian culture was nearly eradicated. Michael Church wrote: "For Armenians, music is memory. And whenever they gather to honour their dead, the songs they sing are by the composer who speaks for the soul of their nation, Komitas Vardapet" (1869–1935) (Church, 2011).

CONTEMPORARY POPULAR MUSIC

Armenian culture, both domestic and diaspora, also has a vibrant contemporary music scene that typically fuses Armenian and Western musical styles, and uses modern recording techniques. Popular musicians and singers include Eileen Khatchadourian, Hayk Margaryan (HT Hayko), Sako Balasanyan (Super Sako), Sonya Varoujian, and Nune Yesayan. Well-known bands include The Bambir and System of a Down, a multiple Grammy-nominated Armenian-American hard rock group. Some Armenian pop musicians, notably Khatchadourian and Karnig Sarkissian, are exponents of Armenian culture and politics whose artistry embraces cultural motifs and serves as a platform for political agitation. Other ethnic Armenian pop musicians make no pretense of representing Armenian cultural consciousness; for instance, the legendary pop singer and actress Cher (born Cherilyn Sarkisian), and children's singer-songwriter Raffi (Cavoukian), who in ways are apparently culturally unselfconscious, carry on the tradition of Armenian troubadours.

Greg A. Phelps

See also: Duduk

Further Reading

At'Ayan, Robert. 2013. *The Armenian Neume System of Notation: Study and Analysis,* trans. V. N. Nersessian. New York: Routledge.

Church, Michael. 2011. "Komitas Vardapet, Forgotten Folk Hero." *The Guardian*, April 21, 2011. http://www.theguardian.com/music/2011/apr/21/komitas-vardapet-folk-music-armenia.

Fortescue, Adrian. 2014. "Gregory the Illuminator." *The Catholic Encyclopedia*, vol. 7. New York: Robert Appleton, 1910. http://www.newadvent.org/cathen/07023a.htm.

Hacikyan, Agop, et al., eds. 2000. *The Heritage of Armenian Literature: From the Oral Tradition to the Golden Age*, vol. 1. Detroit, MI: Wayne State University Press.

Kerovpyan, Aram. 2013a. "Prayer in Song: A Brief History of Armenian Liturgical Chant." http://akn-chant.org/en/chant.

Kerovpyan, Aram. 2013b. "The Sharagan." http://akn-chant.org/en/charakan.

Rockwell, John. 1981. "Opera: 'Anoush,' Classic of Armenia, in Detroit." *New York Times*, November 2. http://www.nytimes.com/1981/11/02/arts/opera-anoush-classic-of-armenia-in-detroit.html.

Shirodkar, Marco. n.d. "Alan Hovhaness Biographical Summary." *The Alan Hovhaness Web Site*. http://www.hovhaness.com/hovhaness-biography.html.

Armstrong, Louis (1901–1971)

Louis Armstrong (a.k.a. Pops, Satchelmouth, Satchmo, or Satch), along with pianist Jelly Roll Morton (1890–1941) and cornet player Joe "King" Oliver (1881–1938), was one of the dominant figures of early and mid–20th-century jazz. After World War I, Armstrong became a leading proponent of jazz, which developed in New Orleans, Louisiana, before spreading to Chicago and then the rest of America in the 1920s. Armstrong's unique musical style, as both a trumpeter and a singer, led him to be considered one of the most famous and important jazz musicians of the 20th century, and his influence upon musicians worldwide is significant.

Armstrong was born on August 4, 1901, in New Orleans and raised by his grandmother, Josephine Armstrong. Louis lived in one of the most deprived neighborhoods in New Orleans and his grandmother took him to church frequently. Armstrong later recalled that "[i]n church and Sunday school I did a whole lot of singing. That, I guess, is how I acquired my singing tactics" (Stein, 2012, p. 49). Growing up in New Orleans, Armstrong was exposed to the wealth of music that passed through the city in the form of parades and marching bands, and he quickly became a fan of cornet player Joe Oliver. Inspired, Armstrong bought a cornet and he later established a barbershop quartet with friends, in which he sang tenor.

In 1913, Armstrong was sent to the Colored Waif's Home for Boys—a type of young offenders' institute for African American boys—following a minor offense for vagrancy. The home also had a 15-piece brass band (a brass band which also included clarinets and saxophones) and a choir, and Armstrong began singing lessons there. He then joined the band, which later made him its leader; as its leader, Armstrong took the Colored Waif's Home band parading around his old neighborhood. Armstrong left the Home after two years, and it was around this time that Joe Oliver became a more significant influence on his musical life. In 1918, Oliver left New Orleans for work in Chicago, and Kid Ory, a trombonist and leader of the

Louis Armstrong was one of the 20th century's most important jazz innovators and performers. (Library of Congress)

band in which Oliver had played, asked Armstrong to take Oliver's place. As well as playing with this band, Armstrong worked in parades with Papa Celestin's Tuxedo Brass Band and performed in Fate Marable's orchestra on board Streckfus Line steamboats as they took day cruises up the Mississippi River. It was while performing on the steamboats that Armstrong developed his skills at music theory and reading notation. With numerous performances under his belt, a wealth of musical contacts, and an improving theoretical knowledge of music, Armstrong soon became a popular and well-known musician up and down the river.

By 1921, Armstrong had grown tired of life on the river and returned to New Orleans, working there with numerous bands and clubs. The following year Joe Oliver invited Armstrong to Chicago to join his Creole Jazz Band, and in 1923 the band began touring and making records. Armstrong quit Oliver's band in 1924 in order to join Fletcher Henderson's Orchestra in New York. This move sparked a series of recordings with numerous jazz musicians, perhaps the most famous of which was the blues singer Bessie Smith. In 1925, after moving back to Chicago, Armstrong began making his first recordings as band leader with what is now known as his most famous band: the Hot Five. With this band, Armstrong recorded some of his most popular pieces of music including "Heebie Jeebies," "King of the Zulus," and "West End Blues." Armstrong's work led both musicians and audiences to consider him one of the leading jazz musicians of the time, and this status led to numerous recordings, performances, and tours with different bands and musicians both nationally and internationally. This included collaborations with big names such as Ella Fitzgerald and Billie Holiday, with Armstrong performing as both a singer and a trumpeter. Armstrong was a keen writer and during his career he also wrote several books. The first, *Swing That Music* (1936), was his first autobiography and was one of the first books on the history of jazz music.

Starting in 1959, Armstrong suffered a number of heart attacks. It was perhaps his eagerness to return to work—for he never spent long in hospital following a collapse—that caused him to never make a full recovery. In March 1971, Armstrong suffered a heart attack that forced him into an intensive care unit. He returned home at the beginning of May but two months later, on July 6, 1971, he died in his sleep at his home in New York. Spanning five decades, Louis Armstrong's career was varied and hugely successful and he remains a globally popular, admired, and important musical figure.

C. M. Gregory-Thomas

See also: Blues; Davis, Miles; Jazz; Smith, Bessie

Further Reading
Bergreen, L. 1998. *Louis Armstrong: An Extravagant Life*. London: Harper Collins.
Bradbury, D. 2003. *Armstrong*. London: Haus.
Pinfold, M. 1988. *Louis Armstrong: His Life and Times*. London: Omnibus Press.
Stein, D. 2012. *Music Is My Life: Louis Armstrong, Autobiography, and American Jazz*. Ann Arbor: University of Michigan Press.

Ashkenazi Jews, Music of

The term *Ashkenazim* derives from the medieval Hebrew name for Germany (*ashkenaz*). Originally it referred only to the Jews of Germany, but it now denotes all Jews of Eastern European descent. The Ashkenazim trace their cultural origins to the Jewish settlements established on the banks of the Rhine in the Middle Ages. Liturgical chants were spread by itinerant cantors, and some absorbed elements of Slavic music. Psalmodic structures are still used to chant medieval poetic verses, such as the *Akdamut* by the 11th-century poet Rabbi Meir ben Isaac Nehorai of Worms. The biblical *shofar* (now commonly made of ram or kudu horn) was present in early European rituals; its blasts are featured in High Holy Days services.

Traditional Ashkenazi chants consist of five elements: psalmody and early centonized chants (called *niguim* in Hebrew, *alte Weise* in German, and *nusah* in eastern Europe); cantillation of sacred scripture; *mi-sinai* melodies (also known as *skarbove nigunim*, or "tunes of the treasure"); seasonal melodies mostly adapted from non-Jewish sources; and cantorial improvisations based on modal structures known as *shteyger* (documented since the 18th century).

By the late 13th century, Jewish communities flourished in southern Germany, Austria, Switzerland, northern Italy, northern and central France, the Low Countries, and England. Seasonal melodies included well-known liturgical poetry (*piyyutim*) in Aramaic or Hebrew from Pilgrimage festivals; they have become musical symbols and even leitmotifs for those seasons (the Hanukkah anthem

"Ma'oz tsur," the Pesach *hagadah* song "Adir hu," and the Tish'ah be'av lamentation "Eli Zion").

Ashkenazim developed cantillation systems for liturgical reading of biblical texts. The systems adhere to the *te'amei ha-miqra* (the Masoretic accents as classified in the 10th century by the Tiberias school of Masoretes). The *Sefer hasidim* (*Book of the Pious*) is an important source on cantillation practice from this period. As early as 1159, Torah scrolls were decorated with *rimonim* bells (named after the pomegranate shapes of Torah stave knobs) made of silver and gold.

Ashkenazi Hebrew (which some scholars argue has ancient roots) is the pronunciation system appropriate for Ashkenazi liturgical use. It survives today as a separate religious dialect alongside Modern Hebrew; Modern Hebrew as spoken in Israel was intended to be based on Mishnaic spelling and Sephardic Hebrew pronunciation, but has adapted seven aspects of Ashkenazi pronunciation. The unique sound of Ashkenazi liturgical song comes from vowel shifts and the use of "s" instead of "t" for the letter "tav," as in "Shabbos," rather than the Sephardic "Shabbat."

Due to persecution in the 14th century, many Ashkenazim migrated to northern Germany, Bohemia, and eventually to Hungary, Poland, Lithuania, and Russia. Yiddish, a modified version of Middle High German notated with Hebrew characters, became the most common Jewish vernacular in central Europe, and local liturgical traditions gradually gave way to those of the Ashkenazim through oral tradition. *Mi-sinai* melodies show influences of French mourning song, Gregorian chant, and German *Minnesang*; they were preferred by *hazzanim* (cantors) for High Holy Days services. Until the 20th century, the mi-sinai were erroneously attributed to the person who first popularized them (Rabbi Jacob Levy Segal Mölin, ca. 1365–1427). The most famous mi-sinai tune is the early 16th-century "Kol nidrei" (Aramaic for "all vows"), sung just before the Yom Kippur evening service.

During the Renaissance, western Ashkenazim were heavily influenced by German culture, whereas those in the east adopted Slavic and Ottoman characteristics. The German Ashkenazim employ five modally-specific musical systems for biblical cantillation: the Torah (for weekly readings), portions of the Pentateuch (read on Rosh Hashanah and Yom Kippur), *hoftarah* (the Prophetic portions read after the Pentateuch on the Sabbath and Holy Days), Esther, and Lamentations. Eastern Europeans also recognized a sixth system: they include a grouping of three later biblical chapters (the Song of Songs, Ruth, and Ecclesiastes). Western hazzanim used natural minor and mixolydian modes, whereas those in the East focused on scales with an augmented second. Leading scholars have documented the 500-year development of Torah cantillation (Avenary, 1978) and the different types of *shteyger* modes (Idelsohn, 1929).

Jewish composer Salamone Rossi (1570–1630) was court composer in Mantua; he made crucial contributions to the Baroque trio sonata form and composed a Hebrew choral cycle based on the Song of Songs. Klezmer (from the Hebrew *klei zemer*, instruments of song) began to develop in the 15th century as a secular tradition of Yiddish song, now influenced by jazz (in Europe and America) and brass bands (in eastern Europe). Although each Jewish community developed its own diasporic dance traditions, the names of *shtetl* dances corresponded closely to the kind of klezmer music being played.

Rabbinical literature and sacred music were shared across great distances. This heritage encouraged close cultural ties that grew stronger during Jewish emigrations of the 18th and 19th centuries. No examples of Ashkenazi music written before the 16th century survive: the earliest publications include Johannes Boeschenstein's musical appendix to Johannes Reuchlin's *De accentibus, et orthographia, linguae Hebraicae* (Hagenau, 1518) and Sebastian Muenster's notation of the Pentateuch cantillation in his *Institutiones grammaticae in Hebraeam linguam* (Basle, 1524). Chants of this period exhibit specific motifs for beginning, continuation, partial closure, preconclusion, and final cadence. The modality of these chants is determined by the texts, by the liturgical function, and by the type of service.

However, during the Baroque period, rabbinical writings begin to criticize cantorial virtuosity and showmanship (influenced by contemporary trends in Italian opera). Some cantors elaborated mi-sinai melodies into long choral fantasias; they interpolated secular, non-Jewish Rococo melodies, *meshorerim* (trio and choral accompaniments), extensive improvisations, and instrumental music (in Prague and southern Germany) into synagogue worship. Meshorerim singers sometimes imitated instrumental sounds and even used choreographed facial and hand gestures to enhance their contributions (this style survives in East European practice but was generally replaced by temple choirs in the West). Throughout Europe, hazzanim made their livelihoods by wandering with their choristers from one *shtetl* (a small town with a predominantly Jewish population) to another.

In the Classical period, there was a gradual increase in demand in Germany for East European cantors, who were noted for their sweet voices. Florid recitatives and prayer chants began to be notated. The earliest extant notation for a melismatic *Kol nidrei* chant dates from this period (by Berlin *hazzan* Aron Beer, ca. 1765). Regarded as a musical symbol of Jewish suffering and hope for redemption, this melody was considered most sacred and was therefore highly embellished by cantors. Non-Jewish musicians also arranged it as concert works (such as Max Bruch's score for cello and orchestra, published in 1881).

Nineteenth-century cantorial manuals and rabbinical texts provide examples of music, liturgy, and performance practice; they include new fashionable tunes in binary forms such as minuets, sicilianas, and Waldhorns (brass fanfares) intended to be sung to nonsense syllables or to rhyming *piyyutim* (such as "Lekha dodi" on Friday night, "Melekh 'elyon" at Rosh Hashanah, "Yigdal," and "Adon Olam"). Polish, Russian, and Baltic Ashkenazim preferred hazzanim with high lyric voices who could perform fast, florid coloratura and *zogekhts* (Yiddish for modal patterns); cantors eschewed songs of praise in favor of highly emotional and melismatic recitatives.

Unlike the Sephardim, the Ashkenazim have a limited repertory of psalmodic melodies with narrow ranges (less than an octave), as they usually recited their psalms individually and silently. Cantors chant short psalmodic formulas for the last verses of each psalm or prayer in the *pesuqei de-zimra* (*zemirot*) section of the morning service in order to encourage the congregational heterophonic murmur so typical of Ashkenazi synagogues. *Zemirot* are hymns typically sung at table during Shabbas and special meals (usually in Aramaic or Hebrew and occasionally in

Ladino or Yiddish). *Nigunim* are simple combinations of melodic formulae that may be sung by a *ba'al tefillah* (nonprofessional cantor). These wordless melodies are a form of vocalized instrumental music; popular contemporary melodies include the "Erev Shabbas Nigum" and Rebbe Nachman's "Lecha Dodi."

For the past 200 years, East European liturgical music has been enriched by the musical creativity of the *hasidim*. The Hasidic movement was founded by the Rabbi Israel Baal Shem Tov (1698–1760); he sought to blend kabbalistic mysticism with "redeemed" melodies to bring communal salvation through enthusiastic song and dance. Hasidic music was enriched with Polish mazurkas, Russian kozatchocks, Ukrainian hopaks, Romanian shepherd songs, marches, and waltzes. Nineteenth-century hasidic leaders (Yiddish *rebbes* or *tsadakim*) established courts that became musical centers. Some rebbes were professional musicians, and others employed *menagenim* (court musicians); there was a premium on new compositions; and most texts (in Yiddish, Ukrainian, and other Eastern European languages) were transmitted by oral tradition rather than by notation. The Hasidic movement has been particularly successful in Israel and the United States, where the most significant types of Yiddish tunes are the *nigunei dvéikus* (slow songs designed to raise the soul to its divine source) and the *hopkelekh* (repeated dances).

The gradual emancipation of European Jews in the 18th and 19th centuries encouraged new philosophical approaches such as the writings of Moses Mendelssohn (1729–1786, grandfather of the composer Felix). The Reform movement, led by Israel Jacobsen (1728–1828) in Westphalia and David Friedländer (1750–1834) in Berlin, introduced the organ and congregational chorale singing into the synagogue, reduced the role of the cantor, replaced traditional Hebrew prayers in the *siddur* (daily prayer book) with new German texts, and abolished traditional chanting of the Scriptures according to the *te'amim* marks. This led to many previously sung texts being declaimed and led to bitter controversy among rabbis and scholars. New *Synagogenorderungen* (regulations) discouraged older practices, replaced the meshorerim with choirs, and replaced the traditional apprenticeships of hazzanim with regulated study in teachers' seminaries.

The most influential of the Moderate Reform synagogues was the Seitenstettengasse Temple in Vienna (dedicated in 1826 for the third largest Jewish community in Europe) where Salomon Sulzer (1804–1890) introduced new liturgical music, trained cantors from all over Europe, published musical collections (*Shir Tsiyyon*), and conducted a four-part *a cappella* choir of men and boys. Sulzer commissioned new choral works in Hebrew such as Franz Schubert's *Psalm xcii* (D. 942). The London synagogues followed suit under Asher, Mombach, and Hast, and their innovations were sung throughout the British Empire.

At the Paris Synagogue, Samuel Naumbourg (1815–1880) published complete Hebrew services for hazzan and male choir influenced by French opera and southern German chants (*Zemiroth Yisrael*, 1847–1864). For the three volumes of *Zemiroth Yisrael*, Naumbourg commissioned other Jewish composers, such as Giacomo Meyerbeer (1791–1864) and Fromental Halévy (1799–1862, famous for his opera *La Juive* [1835]) to contribute liturgical music. Jacques Offenbach (1819–1880), the leading composer of French Romantic operetta, was the son of an Ashkenazi cantor, and also grew up steeped in Jewish traditional music.

During the 1870s, the Neue Synagoge on Oranjenburger Strasse in Berlin (dedicated in 1866) became the new center of the Moderate Reform movement. Louis Lewandowski (1821–1894), considered to be the leading Romantic composer of Ashkenazic liturgical music, led a large choir of men and boys, and published *Kol rinnah u't'fillah* (an 1871 hazzanic manual with music for two-part choir) and *Todah w'simrah* (works dating from 1876 to 1882 for hazzan, choir, and optional organ accompaniment). Many of these compositions were also sung in Reform and Orthodox settings. Eastern composers such as Nissan Blumenthal (1805–1903), David Nowakowsky (1848–1921, Odessa) and Eliezer Gerovitsch (1844–1913, Rostov na Donu) combined these innovations in German harmony and counterpoint with Eastern modality and embellishments. The design of the Grand Choral Synagogue of St. Petersburg (consecrated in 1893) was partially inspired by Berlin's Neue Synagoge.

American Reform congregations, such as those in Charleston (established in 1824) and Baltimore (established 1842) adopted the practices of the Hamburg Reform Temple. Students of Sulzer, such as Fränkel and Goldstein, published new liturgical collections (*Zimrat yah*, 1871–1886) and served Moderate Reform congregations where the hazzan was often replaced by an organist and choir. Other influential American emigré composers include Sigmund Schlessinger in Mobile, Alabama (1835–1906) and Max Janowski in Chicago, Illinois (1902–1991).

At the end of the 19th century, composers from the St. Petersburg Society for Jewish Folkmusic made thousands of transcriptions of Yiddish folksongs. Composers such as Joel Engel, Bloch, and Shostakovich combined the *kretschen* (moaning) melodies of shtetls with modern harmonies. Mahler used klezmer-influenced melodies in the third movement of his first symphony, Milhaud wrote about being influenced by the Provençal Jewish community, and Castelnuovo-Tedesco wrote songs in Ladino and choral cantatas based on Jewish melodies (*Naomi and Ruth* and *Queen of Sheba*).

Although European Ashkenazim and the shtetls in which they lived were two of the main targets of the Holocaust during World War II, century-old communities survived in North and South America, South Africa, Australia, and Palestine. As the *minhag ashkenaz* (the original German Jewish tradition) came under attack, many aspects of its traditional music were lost. After the war, Ashkenazim communities were re-established in eastern Europe, although those who lived under Communist regimes encountered religious and cultural suppression. Arnold Schoenberg (1874–1951) composed several Jewish choral works (*Kol Nidre*, *A Survivor from Warsaw*, *Psalm 130*, *Prelude to Genesis Suite*, and the 1932 opera *Moses und Aron*). Leonard Bernstein incorporated Jewish materials and Hebrew liturgical texts into symphonies and choral works; he first conducted in Israel in 1947, and maintained a lifelong association with its orchestras.

Laura Stanfield Prichard

See also: Austro-German Dances; Klezmer; Polish National Dances; Schrammelmusik

Further Reading

Adler, Israel. 1840. *Hebrew Notated Manuscript Sources up to Circa 1840*. Munich: G. Henle Verlag.

Avenary, Hanoch. 1978. *The Ashkenazi Tradition of Biblical Chant between 1500 and 1900: Documentation and Musical Analysis.* Tel Aviv, Israel: Tel Aviv University.

Idelsohn, Abraham Zevi. 1929. *Jewish Music: Its Historical Development.* New York: Dover.

Strom, Yale. 2011. *The Book of the Klezmer: The History, the Music, the Folklore.* Chicago: Chicago Review Press.

Astatke, Mulatu (1943–)

Composer, vibraphonist, and keyboardist Mulatu Astatke (French spelling: Astatqé) is a key figure of the Ethio-jazz style and one of the few Ethiopian musicians with a global reputation. Astatke combined his interest in jazz, Latin, and traditional Ethiopian musics into a new style termed *Ethio-jazz*. This music combined five-note Ethiopian modes with the twelve-tone Western scale and fused these collections with African and Latin rhythms.

Born in Jimma, Ethiopia, Astatke studied music in Wales and London before becoming the first African musician to study at Boston's Berklee College of Music, in 1958. His work in the 1960s in New York City was contemporaneous with that of two other future leaders of African music, Fela Kuti and Hugh Masekela. Returning to Ethiopia in the early 1970s, Astatke arrived in the heyday of "Swinging Addis," a booming music scene in the capital Addis Ababa. During this time, he

Ethiopian musician Mulatu Astatke performing at the Royal Festival Hall in London in 2014. Astatke combined traditional Ethiopian music with elements of jazz and Latin American styles. (Edu Hawkins/Redferns via Getty Images)

made several recordings and collaborated with Duke Ellington when Ellington's band toured Ethiopia (1973).

After the Derg, a Soviet-supported military junta, came to power, political changes caused the collapse of Addis Ababa's nightlife and recording scene by 1975. Since that time, Astatke has performed and recorded globally. He has also worked to develop a culture of music appreciation in Ethiopia, which lacks a tradition of school music education. His efforts to educate audiences have included a long-running radio program that programs Western, Latin, and African music in a variety of musical styles.

Astatke was little known outside Africa until recently. His music did not circulate widely until record label Buda Musique's *Éthiopiques* series devoted a full release to his music in 1998. Further interest was spurred by Jim Jarmusch's movie *Broken Flowers* (2005), which used seven Astatke pieces. His music has been sampled by hip-hop musicians (including K'naan and Nas) and he has collaborated with the Either/Orchestra and the Heliocentrics. Growing international recognition led to a Harvard Radcliffe Institute Fellowship in 2008, where he completed *The Yared Opera*, a work based on the legend of St. Jared, the creator of the Ethiopian Orthodox Church's sacred music tradition. This electronic composition for string quartet and two electronic synthesizers features a characteristic blending of old and new and includes traditional chant texts in Ge'ez, the Ethiopian liturgical language (Shelemay and Kimberlin, 2013).

He has continued writing and recording, producing two albums, *Mulatu Steps Ahead* (2010) and *Sketches of Ethiopia* (2013), and has collaborated with musicians from Mali and Brazil. He has also been experimenting with techniques for amplifying and recording indigenous African instruments and for blending those sounds into his music. Astatke takes his role of cultural ambassador seriously, and has worked for decades to raise global understanding of Ethiopia's rich cultural legacies.

In contrast to much Ethiopian music, which is vocal, Astatke's music is largely instrumental. His compositions typically blend previously written and improvised music for ensembles featuring European acoustic and electric instruments. He uses combinations of the four different Ethiopian modes (all pentatonic collections) as well as the Western twelve-note scale and extended jazz harmonies. Astatke mixes Ethiopian and Latin rhythms and percussion instruments to create dense rhythmic grooves that frequently use polymeter or asymmetric phrase groupings. He prefers playing vibraphone (an instrument he helped popularize in Ethiopia) because of its similarities to the *balafon*, an African percussion idiophone made of wood.

John Hausmann

See also: Afrobeat; Kuti, Fela

Further Reading

Astatke, Mulatu. 1972. *Mulatu of Ethiopia.* Worthy Records (2) W-1020.

Astatke, Mulatu. 2007. "Interview by Monk One, Red Bull Music Academy." http://www.redbullmusicacademy.com/lectures/mulatu-astatke-ethiopian-knight.

Astatqé, Mulatu. 1998. *Éthiopiques 4: Ethio Jazz & Musique Instrumentale 1969–1974.* Buda Musique 82964–2.

Astatqé, Mulatu, and The Heliocentrics. 2009. *Inspiration Information, Vol. 3*. Strut—STRUT040LP.

Shelemay, Kay Kaufman, and Cynthia Tse Kimberlin. 2013, July 25. "Ethiopia, Federal Democratic Republic of." *Grove Music Online*. http://www.oxfordmusiconline.com.

Ausbund (see Amish Hymns)

Austro-German Dances

Alpine dances, such as the waltz, ländler, zwiefacher, deutscher dreher, polka, and Germanic versions of the schottische, are all turning couples dances. Except for the *Schuhplattler*, they are danced in the easy-flowing, smooth, grounded Alpine social style and can be seen in Alsace, the Black Forest, Swabia, Switzerland, Bavaria, Bohemia, and Upper Austria.

The Schuhplattler, mentioned in Latin writings as early as 1,000 CE, came from the Tyrolian region in southern Bavaria. It was part of a distinctive group of "show clapping" dances in which the body was hit percussively to create highly syncopated rhythms. Dancers slapped (*platteln*) their feet, knees, thighs, buttocks, and cheeks, and men hit their traditional *Lederhosen* (leather pants). Some Austrian male dancers also hit each other to create unique sounds. Dance scholars claim these movements imitate the mating and fighting behavior of the capercaille (a native Bavarian black grouse). There are two versions of the Schuhplattler: a duo performed by two men (symbolizing a bird fight, and usually seen in the context of a *Trachten* society folk performance); and the more common partnered version, in which the man struts around the woman to woo her.

The couple dance version of the Schuhplattler has four sections: *Nachsteigen* or *Vorspiel, Einlaufer, Plattler*, and *Ländler*. In the Nachsteigen section, the man hisses, clicks his tongue, and claps (*paschen*) his hands as he leaps (and sometimes somersaults) around the woman; both dancers swing their arms forward and backward in four-beat patterns. The man's body is held in an exaggeratedly erect position so that the knees and feet must be lifted very high in order to be slapped by the winglike movements of the arms and hands. For the Einlaufer, the right hand slaps the right knee, followed by the left pairing. This is repeated at least once, and is followed by the right hand hitting either foot (once or more), and the left hand hitting the left foot. The woman spins in place until the man has fallen to his knees in a concluding pose (*Schlussfigur*). During the Plattler, the woman spins around the man while he slaps his body continuously.

The Ländler, a gliding and turning dance that includes a love pantomime and kissing one's partner, developed from the final section of the Schuhplattler into its own dance form. Curt Sachs reported in *World History of the Dance* (1935) that some early versions of the Ländler portion of the Schuhplattler dance involved competitions requiring the balancing of beakers filled with liquid on the dancers' heads. The earliest written reference to such a German courtship dance (*Balztanz*) dates from an 11th-century Latin poem entitled *Ruodlieb*. This depicts a medieval

German knight as he plays the harp to accompany song and dance. The poem describes courting a woman through dance, mimicking the movements of birds ("He is like a falcon, and she glides like a swallow. No sooner are they near each other than they are already parted").

The Ländler (also called *Länderer, Länderli,* and *Länderische Tanz*) is one of several alpine turning dances popular in Germany, Bavaria, Austria, and Bohemia. These couples dances, all including a close embrace while rotating, were usually grouped together under the term *Deutsche Tänze* (throughout the Alps) or *Volkstanz* (in Austria). Melodies developed from rhythmic work songs relating to reaping, sowing, and other types of manual labor, such as that done by blacksmiths and hunters (cleaning their catch). Each type was identified either by an aspect of the movement such as *dreher* (spinning top), *weller* (wool cloth seller), *spinner,* or *schleifer* (sliding); or by a geographical location such as *Steirer* (Styria, Austria) or *Ländler* (*Das Landl/Landl ob der Enns,* i.e., upper Austria). Some scholars believe the Ländler is the direct forerunner of the waltz, but the terms exist simultaneously for more than 100 years.

During the Ländler, couples glide together at a moderate tempo in triple time. The most typical rhythm for the dance consists of two quarter notes followed by a dotted eighth-note and sixteenth-note pair. The alpine Ländler is accompanied by singing or yodeling, the Styrian harmonica (an accordion), fiddle, clarinet, harp, flute, and brass band (sometimes supported by contrabass or guitar, but never percussion). Its lilting melodies and wide leaping intervals encouraged deep swinging movements and lifts. The climax of the folk version of the Ländler involved the man tossing the woman vigorously in the air (like the contemporaneous Italian *volta*), before bringing her gently back down at the end of the dance. Some scholars of ancient dancers have tied this movement to fertility rites, in which the height (when tossed in the air) of the woman's skirt would determine the height of the crops.

Katherina Breuer has traced the Ländler from its origins as a medieval round dance to a "pair dance in which the man leads the girl with complicated turns and twists to the final reunion of the pair in slow Waltz step" (1948, p. 25). Early figures include the spinning of the woman on the upraised hand of her stamping partner, simultaneous spinning of both dancers with hands clasped above their heads, gliding past a partner beneath the arm, changing of sides by passing back to back, and a final turn in close embrace. According to a fresco by Benozzo Gozzoli in the Camp Santo at Pisa (before 1485), the same type of spinning was also common in Renaissance Italy. The folk term in the Italian and Austrian Alps for this type of figured turning dance is *Schaim,* and it has been largely replaced by the simple waltz. Ernst Hamza described seeing an early form of the old processional alternating with the figure pantomime: "In dancing the *Ländler,* the man frequently lets go of his partner (purposely!) and claps his hands in time to the music. The other men react to this, begin likewise to clap, and all stand together, in a circle with their faces touching. The girls walk around the outside. This is kept up as long as it amuses the boys—*die Buam gfreut.* Then each one takes his partner again and the dance goes on before" (1914).

As with the volta, German Renaissance folk dances, especially those employing rapid turns (exposing the limbs), were a source of controversy. The dance required the man's hands to be placed on the woman's waist and the woman's hands on his shoulders. In Ulm (1404), a ban was imposed on dancers to prevent "intimate contact": this resulted in dances being adapted to single files. In 1494, Sebastian Brant commented on the immoral nature of turning dances in his satirical poem *Das Narrenschiff*: "There dance priests and monks and laymen . . . they run and whirl about, so that one sees their naked legs." As the Protestant Reformation swept Europe, condemnations included clergyman Melchior Ambach's 1543 characterization of dance as "a surrender to lust, a consent to vice, an encouragement to unchastity"; and a writing from the pastor at Schellenwalde, Florian Daule von Fürstenberg, noting "scandalous, shameless swinging, throwing, turning and allurements of the dance devils . . . that the skirts . . . sometimes fly above their girdles or even over their heads" (1567). The *weller* variation of the Ländler was sung about in 1525 by prizewinning Nürnberg meistersinger Kunz Has: "When they have weddings now, they dance no more as years ago, when dancing was discreet and slow . . . Now they dance the wild *weller*, the *dreher* (spinner)."

Vienna passed a legal ordinance in 1572 stating, "Male persons are to refrain from whirling and other such frivolities," lest they be "brought to jail." However, Martin Luther participated in turning dances; he wrote that modest dancing should be permissible, and that dancing was not inherently sinful unless it brought out the "disorderly appetites of the dancers." As late as 1760, attempts were made to ban the Ländler. Stern warnings were issued from German-speaking pulpits against doing any "German waltzing dances" in the streets, and the bishops of Würzburg and Fulda issued decrees prohibiting "gliding and waltzing." In this context the German word *waltz* took on the additional meaning of "rolling," rather than simple turning, and demanded more extensive traveling (while turning) around the dance floor.

German-speaking aristocratic society appropriated folk music and dance in court entertainment through the Renaissance, Baroque, and Classical periods. The Emperor Ferdinand (1637–1657) preferred German dancing to French, and Leopold I (1658–1705) flatly forbade French court ballet. During the reign of Charles VI (1711–1740), the duchesses were allowed to participate in German dances, including turning and spinning figures, although the emperor and empress merely observed.

The old Hapsburg monarchy was a feudal state, so there was constant contact between the upper and lower classes. Seventeenth-century Austrian entertainments included the Emperor and his family dressed in folk garb, acting out scenes of peasant life, and dancing the Ländler (although wearing satin slippers on a polished drawing room floor). The waltz gradually replaced the Ländler and its predecessors during the 1700s. In 1765, the young Johann Wolfgang von Goethe learned the Ländler (while a student in Strassburg), "for without knowledge of this dance, it was impossible to enter the highest social circles." The Ländler became so popular that a journalist remarked in 1797 that turning "is as common and contagious as a cold in the head." The Viennese Court opened the Palace Ballrooms to the public, to dance the waltz, from 1772 onward. The Prussian Court never allowed the waltz to be danced by anyone, right down to the end in 1918. Several Romantic composers included Ländler rhythms in their music, including Beethoven, Schubert, Bruckner, Mahler, and Berg. The Broadway musical *The Sound of Music* included an artificial (newly choreographed) Ländler in duple time, which resembled a polka.

The *Deutscher Dreher* is present throughout German and Scandinavian areas, consisting of a procession and slow waltz pattern. It evolved from the *Drehtanz* (turning dance) and was shown in Heinrich Aldgrever's beautifully engraved *The Wedding Dancers* (1538) and described by visitors to the house of the Fuggers in Augsburg (1580s). Dancers placed hands firmly on the partner's back, and turned as a couple, sometimes touching cheeks. The Bohemian *husička* is a variation of this idea, alternating 16 polka beats with a threatening pantomime, framed with a slow procession. This dance is also referred to as the *Dreischritt Dreher* (the three-part turn), and Nordic variations (present only after 1600) are called the *Hambo* (with a three-beat turn), *Snoa* (with a two-beat turn), *Trava, Kora*, and *Snurrebocken*. The Dreher could be an ill-behaved dance, but it occupies a central position in the history of southern German and Austrian folk movement. Phases of this dance are illustrated in Jost Amman's eight Swiss woodcuts entitled *Ehebrecherbrücke des Konigs Artus* (Adulterer's bridge of King Arthur, ca. 1570) and especially in the detailed etchings of Virgil Solis (ca. 1550).

The *Zwiefacher*, or *Zweifache*, is a southern German folk dance with a quick tempo and changing beat patterns (from three to two), danced primarily in central Bavaria. The oldest description of a Zwiefache dates from 1740, in the Black Forest region of southern Germany. The Zwiefache, like English Morris dancing, may have a Moorish connection, as it turns but does not travel. In variations, dancers may choose to turn as much or as little (or not at all) as they choose; they follow the changing meter by alternating three-beat Ländler or waltz steps with two-beat dreher or pivot steps. Dance scholar Felix Hörburger collected more than 112 Zwiefacher tunes with 474 different names in the 1950s.

Zwiefach (with the first syllable pronounced "tsvi") means "of dual kind," or "double": "Fach" is German for "kind, type, or category," and "Zwie-" is the equivalent of English "twi-" as in twilight or twin. (To say Zweifach (tsvai-) instead of Zwiefach (tsvi-) is like saying "two-light" instead of "twilight.") The name (in 18th-century Bavaria) indicates two time signatures that alternate during the dance, and (in 19th-century Austria) refers to the couple themselves, being tightly wound against each other. Related folk forms include the *Schliefer* (slide), *übern Fuaß* ("over the foot" from Swabia), *Grad und Ungrad* ("pass/fail"), *Eisenkeilnest* (Kingfisher's nest, from Austria), and *Bairischer* (meaning "Farmer Dance," but not to be confused with the faster, duple-time Bavarian polka). Classical composers Carl Orff (in his *Carmina Burana*) and Bedrich Smetana (in the "Furiant" in act 2 of his opera *The Bartered Bride*) both wrote in the Zwiefach form.

Sprachinseltänze (literally "language island dances") are those Austrian dances danced by German-speaking minority groups outside Austria (such as in Transylvania). An example of this type of dance is the *Rediwaire*.

Laura Stanfield Prichard

See also: Schottische; Yodeling

Further Reading

Ambach, Melchior. 1543. *Von Tantzen, Vrtheil ausz heiler Schrifft.* Publisher unknown.

Breuer, Katherina. 1948. *Dances of Austria.* New York: Chanticleer.

Deutch, Walter. 1998. *Der Landler: Volksmusik in Oberösterreich.* Vienna: Bühlau.

Hamza, Ernst. 1914. *Zeitschrift des Deutschen und Österreichischen Alpenvereins.* Vienna: Carl Gerold's Sohn.

Sachs, Curt. 1935. *World History of the Dance.* New York: Norton.

von Fürstenberg, Florian Daule. 1567. *Tantzteuffel.*

B

Bağlama

The *bağlama* is a long-necked, plucked lute with movable frets and a bowl-shaped body. The most popular instrument in Turkey, it is played by both professional and amateur musicians in urban and rural settings, and is important to religious groups like the Alevis. Long-necked plucked lutes were mentioned in Central Asian epic tales as early as the 14th century, and have appeared in various forms in the Turkic world. Since the 20th century, the bağlama has played a central role in reconstructing Turkish folk music practice and theory, and "has come to represent the very soul (*gönül*) of the musician" (Stokes, 1992, p. 70).

The bağlama is part of a family of different-sized plucked lutes, collectively called *saz*. Its name comes from the Turkish verb *bağlamak* (to tie), as the frets are wound onto the neck with thin cord and tied by hand. Measuring between 32 and 36 inches long, the bağlama has seven metal strings in three courses; two, two, and three strings, respectively, from top to bottom, when held in playing position (Stokes, 1992, p. 72). A plectrum of soft plastic is used for strumming and plucking, and an older technique of playing only with the fingers, called *şelpe*, has been revived and developed to a high art by urban professional musicians.

Folk music played an important role in establishing a new, nationalist vision for the modern, secular Republic of Turkey. In the 1920s, Mustafa Kemal Atatürk (father of the Turks) and his associates instituted reforms to create an integrated society combining Turkish values and elements of Western civilization. Folk music helped promote an identity based on Central Asian Turkic heritage, replacing ties to the former Ottoman Empire (1300s–early 1900s) and its legacy of Arab- and Persian-influenced classical music. The state organized widespread projects to collect folk music, which was then transcribed and archived by European-trained Turkish composers and musicologists. The music of Turkey's many regions, once played only in insular, rural communities, was popularized through live radio broadcasts and state-supported education institutions called *Halk Evleri* (People's Houses). Turkish folk music historian and archivist Muzaffer Sarisözen (1899–1963) was instrumental in the success of the radio initiative. He arranged folk melodies for vocal and instrumental ensembles, selected and trained talented regional performers, and conducted the live broadcasts. The bağlama was prominently featured in recordings and performing ensembles on radio and later, on television, with the result that it came to be regarded as Turkey's national instrument.

The bağlama is a powerful symbol of group identity for Turkish Alevis, the country's largest minority. The physical parts of the instrument are said to represent different aspects of the Alevi creed. Musicians in the *cem* (worship service) perform a sacred repertory of hymns and sung poetry on the bağlama. Alevi poet-minstrels compose and perform songs as their predecessors in Muslim mystical brotherhoods did from the 12th century onward. The bağlama is also central to the *muhabbet*, a social music-making event in which instruments are passed around the room for all participants to play.

Melanie T. Pinkert

See also: Arab Classical Music

Further Reading

Bates, Eliot. 2011. *Music in Turkey: Experiencing Music, Expressing Culture.* New York: Oxford University Press.

Bates, Eliot. 2012. "The Social Life of Musical Instruments." *Ethnomusicology* 56(3), 363–395.

Markoff, Irene. 1986. "The Role of Expressive Culture in the Demystification of a Secret Sect of Islam." *The World of Music* 28(3), 42–56.

Markoff, Irene. 1990. "The Ideology of Musical Practice and the Professional Turkish Folk Musician: Tempering the Creative Impulse." *Asian Music* 22(1), 129–145.

Picken, Laurence. 1975. *Folk Musical Instruments of Turkey.* London: Oxford University Press.

Stokes, Marvin. 1992. *The Arabesk Debate.* Oxford: Clarendon Press.

Turkish Music Portal. 2018. "Turkish Folk Music." http://www.turkishmusicportal.org/en/types-of-turkish-music/turkish-folk-music-history.

Bagpipes

The bagpipe is the collective name for a group of instruments that all have some sort of hollow flexible cavity (the bag) that provides a constant supply of sound-producing air. Even though the sound quality and design vary somewhat in examples of instruments all over the world, the basic functionality is consistent across many disparate cultures. The bag is traditionally made of animal skin, and is in most cases held under the arm. This supplies the constant air flow, which comes out of various pipes which are either "chanters," which are fingered by both hands of the player and are used to play melodies, or out of "drones," which do not change pitch and have no finger holes. The bag is inflated by blowing into it either via a blowpipe, or through a small bellows mechanism that squeezes sufficient air into the instrument to keep a constant sound. Because the pipes themselves are nowhere near the player's mouth (with the exception of the blowpipe), the most effective method of sound production is via a reed. Depending on the region and the style of the instrument, these are either single- or double-reed pipes. Thus, the instrument is classified as a reed aerophone.

Bagpipes have been discovered in archaeological sites dating back to Roman times (the first century CE), but most of the evidence regarding the existence of these instruments has come through the written word or surviving artworks. Images of pipes have been found on ancient stone carvings in Ireland dating from the eighth or ninth centuries. Instruments that are essentially bagpipes have been developed in India, Africa, the Middle East, Europe, and the Americas.

The most common and well-known (and what most people think of when they hear the name "bagpipes") are the Great Highland Bagpipes from Scotland, which have three drone pipes, a chanter, and a blowpipe. Because this relatively modern instrument is essentially incapable of silence (because of the one-way valve at the end of the blowpipe: the only way for the air to come out is through the sounding pipes), the music is ideally suited to constant physical activity, such as marching or dancing. Most of the repertoire for this instrument comes from the folk and oral tradition; melodies have been handed down for generations. Some traditions have developed a rich collection of melodic ornaments (such as grace notes, "shakes," and "throws") that provide variety and articulation to the otherwise overwhelming stream of sound.

The typical Scottish Highland-type bagpipe is an incredibly loud instrument, designed to be heard over miles of Scottish landscape, and historically for leading troops into battle. Today they are often played as part of a pipe band, which retains its military association in its participation in parades and other state functions in many English-speaking countries around the world. The Scottish Highland bagpipes are played at funerals of people of Scotch-Irish descent. They are often featured at commemoration events of wars or other moments of national sorrow, such as tributes to the victims of the September 11, 2001, terrorist attacks.

The Scottish Highland bagpipe typically has a bass drone pipe and two tenor drones. These are nominally pitched on the note A (and sometimes on the fifth above, at E), but the actual pitch that comes out is closer to B-flat. The chanter has seven finger holes (as well as a thumb hole on the back, like a recorder). The Highland

Scottish highlander wearing a kilt and playing bagpipes. Bagpipes can be found in many cultures throughout the world and typically consist of some type of air supply, a bag that serves as an air reservoir, a chanter used to play the melody, and at least one drone that sounds a constant pitch. (Odemll/Dreamstime.com)

bagpipe chanter has a fairly limited range of only nine notes: from the G above middle C up to the A a ninth above the bottom note. However, the pitches within this scale are not equal-tempered, and even though they generally sound like the notes of a D-major scale (with two sharps), they are not quite the same intonation as the notes on a piano keyboard. The ascending notes produced are ostensibly G-A-B-C#-D-E-F#-G-A, but there is a great deal of variation from the "correct" tuning of equal temperament. Bagpipe students also use a practice chanter to work on fingering; this is a small oboe-like pipe, independent of the main instrument.

Other bagpipes used in the British Isles are: the Lowland bagpipes, which feature a detachable bellows mechanism to provide the air, and is played while seated; the Northumbrian smallpipes (similar to the Lowland pipes); and the *uilleann* pipes (also known as the Irish union pipe). This instrument features metal keys installed on the chanter pipe, which allows for more note possibilities and extends the range. The uilleann pipes are a popular instrument in Celtic folk groups (such as The Chieftains) and folk-rock bands (like the Afro-Celt Sound System).

Across the English Channel, in Brittany, the *biniou* is still played by that region's Breton people. This instrument is relatively small, only has one drone pipe, and is often accompanied by the *bombarde*, a double-reed instrument that resembles a small oboe. The biniou is also part of a particular type of Breton marching band known as the *bagdad*. This ensemble consists of, in addition to the biniou, the bombarde, various sizes of marching drums, and the *biniou bras* (the "large biniou"), which is essentially the same instrument as the Scottish Highland bagpipes. The bagdad plays in parades and town celebrations in Brittany.

In the 17th and 18th centuries, another type of bagpipe was popular in France. The *musette* was a small instrument with two parallel chanters (the second one for higher-register notes), and one or two drone pipes. The drone pipes had multiple reeds inside of them, so that the player could choose which pitches would sustain as drones. The musette's bag was inflated by a bellows, operated with the elbow. Unlike many other bagpipe-type instruments in history, the musette was favored by upper-class aristocrats and monarchs. Thus, the surviving specimens are decorated with embroidery and include pipes made from ivory. The musette (and its associated dance) was also an influence on several composers: J. S. Bach wrote a gavotte in the style of a musette in his English Suite No. 3 (for keyboard), and in the 20th century Béla Bartók included a musette-inspired piece for piano in his *Mikrokosmos*.

In contrast to the high volume of the Highland bagpipes, other cultures have used the same concept of construction for a more pastoral instrument. The *gaita* of Spain, the *duda* or *dudy* of central Europe, and the *zampogna* of central and southern Italy were all used in the herding of sheep and cows. Therefore, they do not produce an extremely high volume; one does not startle farm animals if one wants to control them. Still, such instruments must be heard across a large field. These smaller bagpipe styles sometimes have only one or two drone pipes; they are also sometimes used as an accompaniment instrument to a player who may also sing when not blowing into the chanter.

The zampogna of Italy is unique in that it has two chanters, one for each hand. This allows players to alternate which pipe will have the melody, or, alternatively, they can play two melodies at once. These are in addition to any drone pipes that may be present (specimens vary by region: from zero drones to up to three). The zampogna is traditionally played in pairs with a smaller double-reed instrument, the *piffero*. Traditionally, these two instruments are used to serenade Nativity scenes during Christmastime. This tradition has echoes in some classical Christmas compositions of the "pastoral" variety: the sinfonias in J. S. Bach's *Christmas Oratorio* and Handel's *Messiah*.

In Germany and Scandinavia, bagpipes were used for pastoral purposes, but also for dance accompaniment. A popular one that has survived into the 21st century is the Swedish *Säckpipa*. Some of the more northern instrument makers use seal skin as the material for the bag.

The *duda* of Hungary has many local variants, but most of the central European bagpipes include a curved bell (made from a cow horn) on the end of each pipe, so that the sound points up. Also, the chanter pipe(s) often are carved into the shape of an animal head, such as a goat's head.

In Spain, bagpipes are known as *gaita, cornamusa,* or *zampoña*. Historically, they were mostly used in the extreme northwest regions of Galicia and Asturias, although the cornamusa was played in the Catalonia region surrounding Barcelona. All of the instruments in Spain are mouth-blown and have a single drone. In the 20th century, the traditional instrument in Galicia, the gaita, experienced a resurgence of interest.

In the Middle East, many types of bagpipes do not include drone pipes, but the general physics of the instrument are similar to those of the instruments of Eastern Europe. Some of them (for example, the *mizwad* of Tunisia) have double chanters. In India, most bagpipes used today are modified Scottish Highland models, but they are generally called *mashak*.

Bagpipes in some form are still used in many parts of the world in the context of popular music. The most common instrument in this field is of course the Scottish Highland bagpipes, because of its loud volume that can compete with amplified guitars and drums. Some notable examples of Highland bagpipes in rock music are AC/DC's "It's a Long Way to the Top (If You Wanna Rock 'n' Roll)" from 1976, and Korn's "Shoots and Ladders" from 1994. Sting has used uilleann pipes and Northumbrian smallpipes frequently in his folk-derived songs, such as smallpipes player Kathryn Tickell's contributions to his *The Soul Cages* album (1991), and in his 2013 musical *The Last Ship*. In the 1990s and early 2000s the *Säckpipa* was part of the resurgence of interest in Scandinavian folk-based rock, particularly in the Swedish band Hedningarna.

Christopher Gable

See also: Celtic Music; Irish American Vocal Music; Irish Dance Music; Irish Step Dancing; Scotch Snap

Further Reading

Baines, Anthony. 1960. *Bagpipes*. Oxford: Pitt Rivers Museum, University of Oxford.

Cannon, Roderick D. 2008. *The Highland Bagpipe and Its Music,* rev. ed. Edinburgh: Birlinn.

Cheape, Hugh. 1999. *The Book of the Bagpipe*. Belfast: Appletree Press.

Bandoneón

The *bandoneón*, which is part of the accordion family of instruments, is a bellows-driven portable free-reed aerophone. Although today it is most commonly associated with Latin America (Central and South America) and referred to as the bandoneón (Spanish), it is of German origin and was originally called a *bandonion* (German). Like other instruments in the accordion family, bellows are operated manually and sound is produced by pushing air past flexible reeds within a frame. The bandoneón is a square-built concertina and features buttons rather than keys. Today the bandoneón is most commonly associated with tango in the Rio de la Plata region of Argentina and Uruguay.

HISTORY

The bandonion emerged from the Chemnitz concertina, a German diatonic concertina created by Carl Friedrich Uhlig in Chemnitz, Germany, in the 1830s. This early version of the bandonion was square in shape and produced single notes instead of chords on the bass side. Chemnitz concertinas were manufactured by Carl Friedrich Zimmerman in the 1840s and distributed throughout Germany, including to Heinrich Band. Heinrich Band, a musician, teacher, and instrument seller, ordered a Chemnitz concertina with 88 pitches. After receiving the concertina, Band retuned some of those 88 pitches and called the new instrument the bandonion, naming the instrument after himself. The name first appeared in 1856 and became widely popular as a result of Band's persistent marketing of the instrument through teaching, as well as the production and sale of sheet music.

The bandonion gained additional popularity through its exportation to Latin America in the mid-19th century, where it was renamed the bandoneón. It was particularly popular in the Rio de la Plata region (Argentina and Uruguay) and in Brazil. As early as the 1850s, German immigrants in northeastern Argentina and Southern Brazil introduced the bandoneón and other varieties of the accordion to the region through genres such as the polka and mazurka. As a result, the bandoneón was integrated into regional Argentine folk genres such as the *chamamé*, where it was performed alongside guitar and violin. By the 1880s, Argentine music catalogues included bandoneóns imported from Germany. As the largest port city in South America, Buenos Aires saw a large influx of immigrants from Europe in the 19th century. This immigration, coupled with rural to urban migration from the pampas to Buenos Aires in the 1880s, was highly influential on the early tango. The popularity of the German accordion among immigrant communities and rural migrants resulted in the incorporation of the bandoneón in milonga and tango ensembles as early as 1890. The bandoneón was quickly incorporated as a lead instrument in the genre and has since become the iconic voice of the tango in Argentina and Uruguay. It is associated today with virtuoso performers such as Argentine musician Astor Piazzolla (1921–1992).

CONSTRUCTION

The earliest version of the bandoneón was diatonic and included two sets of reed banks with two metal reeds per pitch tuned to a perfect octave. Like other diatonic button accordions, the bandoneón employs bi-sonor sound production in the treble keys. Bi-sonor sound production is created when each button is associated with two reeds tuned to different pitches, resulting in the sounding of different notes depending on if the bellows are being pushed or pulled. Unlike other diatonic button accordions, however, the bass keys of the bandoneón do not produce chords, but rather single pitches. Additionally, unlike other diatonic accordions, the bandoneón does not include *shifts*, switches used to create tremolo or changes in timbre and dynamics. Early bandoneóns featured 32 bi-sonor buttons, but as the bandoneón evolved it began to include 53, 65, or 71 buttons. Of these, the 71-button bandoneón is the most popular in Latin America; it includes 38 buttons for the upper register and 33 for the lower. Because each button is bi-sonor, the common 71-button bandoneón can produce a total of 142 notes.

The gradual addition of buttons over time resulted in a seemingly illogical placement of the buttons, making the instrument difficult to learn. An attempt to standardize the order and arrangement of buttons occurred in the 1920s in Germany (resulting in the *Einheitsbandoneon* or "Unity bandoneón"). Additionally, a chromatic uni-sonor variant of the bandoneón was created in 1921. Both the Einheitsbandoneon and the chromatic uni-sonor bandoneón failed to gain popularity among tango musicians, the leading performer-users of the instrument today. Currently, bandoneóns are manufactured in Argentina by Bandoneones Mariani and in Germany by Hohner Gutjahr II Bandoneon.

Emily Rose McManus

See also: Accordion, Types of; Tango

Further Reading

Azzi, Marí Susana. 2012. "'A Hellish Instrument': The Story of the Tango Bandoneon." In Helena Simonett (ed.), *The Accordion in the Americas: Klezmer, Polka, Tango, Zydeco, and More!*, 233–248. Urbana: University of Illinois Press.

Azzi, Marí Susana, and Simon Collier. 2000. *Le Grand Tango: The Life and Music of Astor Piazzolla*. Oxford: Oxford University Press.

Baim, Jo. 2007. *Tango: Creation of a Cultural Icon*. Bloomington: Indiana University Press.

Jacobson, Marion. 2012. *Squeeze This!: A Cultural History of the Accordion in America*. Urbana: University of Illinois Press.

Penón, Arturo, Javier García Méndez, and Tim Barnard. 1988. *The Bandonion: A Tango History*. London: Nightwood Editions.

Simonett, Helena, ed. 2012. *The Accordion in the Americas: Klezmer, Polka, Tango, Zydeco, and More!* Urbana: University of Illinois Press.

Banjo

Of West African origin, the banjo was brought to the Americas by slaves during the 17th century. In the New World it has been used in many types of music, including slave songs, minstrel songs, string band, jazz, country, bluegrass, newgrass, and classical. The modern banjo is an instrument in the lute family consisting of five strings stretched over a sounding body and an extension called a neck. It has four long strings and one short string, called the thumbstring or drone string because it is struck by the thumb and usually sounds only one note. Today the five strings are most commonly tuned g-C-G-B-D. Certain pieces and traditions, commonly found in the southern United States, utilize alternative tunings. Extending from folk practices of the 19th century and possibly earlier, these tunings include g-D-G-B-D and G-d-g-c-d.

The banjo is played in two distinct styles. The oldest, called "clawhammer," likely evolved from African traditions. In this style, downward strokes are made by the right thumb while the index and middle fingers together make downward strokes on the longer strings. In fingerpicking style, downward strokes of the right thumb are combined with upward strokes of individual fingers. In both styles, the left hand depresses strings, plucks, and slides on the neck to change the pitch and create different effects.

HISTORY

Of the thousands of plucked lutes that exist in the Senegambian region of West Africa today, scholars believe that the two most closely resembling the modern banjo are representative of the instruments from which the American banjo evolved. One consists of a round stick fastened to a bisected gourd or calabash with animal skin stretched across the opening of the body. The strings—most often two long and one short—are attached to the stick. The Jola people refer to the instrument as the *ekonting*, the Manjago community calls it a *bunchundo*, and the Papel call it a *busunde*. The other instrument resembling the modern banjo possesses a wooden body and a short drone string. In Mali, the Bamana refer to this instrument as *ngoni*, and in Senegal the Wolof call it a *xalam*. Playing styles differ throughout West Africa, but some methods resemble the clawhammer style of New World banjo playing.

Throughout the 17th century, reports of African slaves playing the banjo in the West Indies were frequent, though the instrument was usually referred to as the *banza*. By the end of the century, the instrument was common in the Caribbean, and visitors often recorded that they had encountered blacks playing it. For example, Hans Sloane traveled throughout the region between 1687 and 1689. In his reflections, published as *A Voyage to the Islands of Madeira, Barbados, Nieves, S. Christopher and Jamaica* (1707), he described instruments that consisted of "small Gourds fitted with Neck, strung with Horse hairs, or the peeled stalks of climbing Plants or Withs. These instruments are sometimes made of hollow'd Timber covered with Parchment or other Skin wetted, having a Bow for its Neck, the Strings ty'd longer or shorter, as they would alter their sounds" (Sabatella, 2018). Sloane also included an illustration which shows that the instrument had adopted some of the characteristics of European lutes, including a flat neck and pegs around which the strings were wound. By the early 1700s, this instrument was referred to as a *banjo*, but this term was not universal until the mid-19th century.

Although it is not known how or when the banjo was first introduced to the North American continent, numerous records indicate that African slaves played the instrument there throughout the 18th century. Many diaries and journals mention slave music featuring the banjo, and advertisements for runaway slaves commonly listed banjo playing as an identifying characteristic. Famously, Thomas Jefferson claimed, in his *Notes on the State of Virginia* (1785), "The instrument proper to [blacks] is the Banjer, which they brought hither from Africa" ("The Banjo," 2001). Around the time Jefferson wrote these words, an anonymous artist painted the earliest image of banjo playing on the continent. The watercolor, called "The Old Plantation," is currently housed at the Abby Aldrich Rockefeller Folk Art Museum in Williamsburg, Virginia. It depicts slaves dancing while a black musician plays a banjo that resembles the four-stringed instrument in Sloane's illustration.

The 1820s witnessed the emergence of minstrelsy, in which white actors blackened their faces and performed songs and routines in character as slaves. In the 1830s, white performers such as Joel Walker Sweeney and Bill Whitlock, who were taught to play the banjo by black mentors, began to play the instrument in minstrel shows. As minstrelsy spread across the country, more whites learned to play the banjo, and they in turn taught other whites. For example, black mentors taught the artist known as Ferguson, and he taught Dan Emmett, who became one of the most important early minstrel performers and composers. Because minstrel shows were intended to represent black slave life, the syncopations found in minstrel banjo music, like the many jigs by Emmett, are believed to derive from black banjo playing styles. The absence of notated black banjo music from the period makes this difficult to prove, but it is a logical explanation for why banjo songs for minstrel shows departed from the Irish rhythms characteristic of other American folk-music traditions.

Through minstrelsy, the banjo became more popular among white musicians and audiences. In the 1840s William Boucher began to mass-produce the instrument in Baltimore, and others soon followed. Mass production caused the gourd banjo to give way to the wooden-framed banjo. Moreover, Sweeney popularized the five-string banjo, which became the instrument most commonly mass-produced. In the 1850s, the banjo joined the guitar, fiddle, and mandolin as a common instrument in the string bands that accompanied dancing in the southern United States, and it also joined the piano as an instrument commonly played to entertain in white homes. It appears that a fingerpicking technique utilizing the thumb and first two fingers emerged as white guitar players began to learn to play the banjo. This technique was first discussed in *Briggs' Banjo Instructor* in 1855. While the banjo continued to be associated with folk music, the fingerpicking style allowed it to be treated as a melodic instrument capable of being played in a style resembling classical guitar. Instrument makers worked to position the banjo as a genteel instrument, distancing it from its associations with black culture by making elaborate and beautiful banjos. They also made banjos of different sizes and tunings, and by the end of the 19th century, banjo orchestras that utilized these instruments had appeared in many white communities.

Alongside these developments, the banjo continued to be a part of both black culture and white representations of black culture. The popularity of minstrelsy

An African American man plays a banjo on his front porch in 1902. The banjo has its roots in West Africa. (Bettmann/Getty Images)

persisted throughout the 19th century—especially in the South—and sheet music publishers frequently featured images of black banjo players on the covers of songs related to slavery. After the Civil War (1861–1865), many songs took on a sentimental quality, and the image of the black banjo player was associated with nostalgia for the Old South. For example, Stephen Foster's "Old Folks at Home," written from the imagined perspective of an old slave, explicitly concerns "longing for de old plantation." The protagonist wonders, "When will I hear de banjo tumming / Down in my good old home?" By the end of the 19th century, the syncopated rhythms that had characterized minstrelsy's banjo music became the defining characteristic of a new genre called *ragtime*, which was widely considered to be a style of black origins. Though the current popularity of Scott Joplin's rags has caused ragtime to be seen as a genre of piano music, many early recordings of ragtime dating to the 1890s feature the banjo. Furthermore, in the 1910s and 1920s, banjoists like "Black Face" Eddie Ross, Fred Van Eps, and Vess Ossman issued commercial recordings of ragtime music. Even sheet music for rags not written for the banjo—like the famous song "Hello! My Baby"—featured the image of black banjo players on their covers. In addition to these commercial musics, black folk traditions continued throughout the 20th century, witnessed in the recordings of North Carolinians such as Dink Roberts and John Snipes, and the Mississippi delta-blues style recordings of Gus Cannon and Lucius Smith.

In the 1920s, the banjo became an important component of jazz and dance orchestras. In this setting it was primarily a rhythm instrument that supplied chord changes. This new role necessitated modifications to the instrument. To facilitate strumming, the drone string was eliminated, resulting in a new type of four-stringed banjo. Furthermore, to be heard over the orchestra, a resonator was added to the body of the instrument, and to produce a louder sound, players began to replace catgut strings with steel strings, which they played with a plectrum (a pick) rather than their fingers. While many four-stringed banjos simply dropped the drone string, the tenor banjo, with strings tuned C-G-D-A, was also popular. One of the first popular tenor banjo players was Harry Reser, who rose to fame in the 1920s playing novelty music with various white dance bands.

By 1940, the banjo had been largely displaced in blues and jazz by the guitar, but its resurgence began after World War II (1939–1945) when it became one of the definitive instruments of a new style of music known as *bluegrass*. Pioneered by mandolinist Bill Monroe and banjoist Earl Scruggs, bluegrass was a subset of country music, or "hillbilly" as it was referred to in the music industry at the time. It featured mandolin, banjo, and fiddle as melodic instruments accompanied by guitar and double bass. Scruggs was integral to the development of the bluegrass banjo, combining the resonator of the jazz-band banjo with the short fifth string of earlier instruments. Scruggs also pioneered the fast-paced fingerpicking style of bluegrass banjo playing that required use of the thumb and three fingers. Folk musician Pete Seeger was another champion of the banjo at the time, and he described the bluegrass technique in *How to Play the 5-String Banjo* (1948). The banjo remains a common but not essential instrument in country music.

The postwar folk revival influenced the folk-rock musicians of the 1960s. Although musicians such as Bob Dylan, Joni Mitchell, and Simon and Garfunkel preferred the accompaniment of the acoustic guitar, the banjo featured prominently in progressive bluegrass music, also known as *newgrass*. In this style, bluegrass instruments were combined with procedures from rock music, like jamming, as exhibited in the music of the bands the Dillards and Seldom Scene. The band New Grass Revival became known for recording with studio effects associated with rock music, and recording rock-and-roll songs such as "Great Balls of Fire." The banjo continues to be an important newgrass instrument, played by Béla Fleck in the band Béla Fleck and the Flecktones, and Noam Pikelny, who plays with the band Punch Brothers.

In addition to newgrass, the banjo is heard in many genres today. Jazz bands like the Preservation Hall Jazz Band and bluegrass bands like Hot Rize continue to keep older traditions alive, and more recently Mumford and Sons introduced the banjo to a new generation of pop music listeners. In indie music circles, Sufjan Stevens has become a popular banjoist, and the banjo is also used in classical music. Béla Fleck recorded an album of famous classical pieces arranged for the instrument (*Perpetual Motion*) in 2001, and several current composers regularly color their music with the banjo. Mark Sylvester featured it in an album of chamber music called *New Music for Banjo* (2009), and the Jake Schepps Quintet—a traditional string band of banjo, mandolin, violin, guitar, and bass—commissions classical composers to write extended pieces for the ensemble. In 2015 they released an album called *Entwined*, which features the music of Marc Mellits and Matt McBane.

Christopher Lynch

See also: Bluegrass; Country Music; Dylan, Bob; Emmett, Dan; Fiddle; Foster, Stephen Collins; Irish American Vocal Music; Jazz; Joplin, Scott; Ragtime; Rock and Roll; Seeger, Peter; Virginia Minstrels

Further Reading

"The Banjo." 2001. *American Roots Music: Instruments and Innovations*, Public Broadcasting Service. https://www.pbs.org/americanrootsmusic/pbs_arm_ii_banjo.html.

Conway, Cecelia. 1995. *African Banjo Echoes in Appalachia: A Study of Folk Traditions.* Knoxville: University of Tennessee Press.

Epstein, Dena. 1975. "The Folk Banjo: A Documentary History." *Ethnomusicology* 19(3) (September), 347–371.

Epstein, Dena. 1977. *Sinful Tunes and Spirituals: Black Folk Music to the Civil War.* Urbana: University of Illinois Press.

Floyd, Jr., Samuel A., and Marsha T. Reisser. 1984. "The Sources and Resources of Classic Ragtime Music." *Black Music Research Journal* 4, 22–59.

Linn, Karen. 1991. *That Half-Barbaric Twang: The Banjo in American Popular Culture.* Urbana: University of Illinois Press.

Nathan, Hans. 1956. "Early Banjo Tunes and American Syncopation." *Musical Quarterly* 42(4) (October), 455–472.

Sabatella, Matthew. 2018. "Banjo Roots and Branches: Into the New World—Caribbean Developments." *Ballad of America, American Heritage Music.* https://www.balladofamerica.org/banjo-roots-and-branches-2/.

Bariu, Laver (1929–2014)

Laver Bariu was a prominent figure in Albanian folk music. With his group, Permet Sats, Laver was well known both in his own country and abroad. An uncontested clarinet master, Laver cultivated hobbies like astronomy and parapsychology (Broughton, Ellingham, and Trillo, 1999).

The son of a singer and lute player, Laver was born on May 2, 1929, to in Permet, Albania. He was first inspired by the music played by his father and attempted to play the *gajde*, a sort of bagpipe. His family's inability to afford an instrument led him to build his own instruments from tree branches or wheat canes. His father taught him to play the lute. Bariu's musical progress was influenced by the German invasion of Albania in 1939, by which time Bariu had left his family and was living in Korca. During this period a Greek clarinetist moved to Laver's hometown: he recruited the young Bariu to play drums in his group, which had started performing in local clubs. That experience had a profound influence on Bariu's music, as he became increasingly fascinated by the clarinet and an accomplished self-taught clarinetist.

In 1944, Bariu moved back to Permet, where he worked with local musicians and organized his own group. With this group he participated at the first National Folk Festival in Tirana in 1952, where he was awarded the first prize as a popular instrumentalist. He started recording his own music in 1954.

Over time, Bariu's group underwent a radical structural reorganization: from more traditional instruments, in 1951, to a mix of traditional and classical instruments in 1976. Most of his music could be conceived of as a musical sage preserving the ancient polyphonic singing tradition of southern Albania in a multi-instrumental dialectic.

In March 2001, Bariu was named "Citizen of Honor" of Permet. He died at the age of 86 after a severe illness.

Antonella Di Giulio

See also: Klezmer; Romani Music

Further Reading
Broughton, Simon, Mark Ellingham, and Richard Trillo. 1999. *World Music; Vol. 1: Africa, Europe and Middle East*. London: Rough Guides.
Emerson, June. 1994. *The Music of Albania*. Ampleforth, UK: Emerson.

Bartók, Béla (1881–1945)

The Hungarian composer, pianist, and music ethnologist Béla Bartók is one of the most important composers of classical music of the 20th century. Folk music from Hungary became the central source for his musical style and influenced him throughout his whole career. Until 1918, he did more than 30 excursions into far-reaching areas. In 1918, his archive, partly recorded with a phonograph, contained around 10,000 folksong melodies: more than 1,800 from Hungarian sources; around 3,500 from Rumanian sources; more than 3,200 from Slovakian sources; smaller collections from Ruthenian, Serbian, and Bulgarian cultures; and around 100 melodies from Arab and Berber folk music recorded with a phonograph during an excursion to Algeria in 1913.

Bartók first came into contact with the native music of his country in 1904, when he visited a village in northern Hungary and heard peasant music. In 1905, he met the coeval Zoltán Kodály (1882–1967), who had published an article about Hungarian folk songs, and who had studied at the Budapest conservatory in the same composition class. The two became friends and collaborated on many ethnological music projects. From then on, collecting, transcribing, and classifying native folk songs took the central role in Bartók's life and work. In 1907, he settled in Budapest, where he got a professorship for piano at the conservatory and stayed until 1940. During that time he had a fixed salary, and in addition to teaching and composing, enough time for field investigation during vacations.

At that time, Hungary was much bigger than it is today, encompassing what is now Slovakia and Croatia (without Dalmatia), the Vojvodina (the northern part of Serbia), a huge part of Romania (mostly Transylvania), and small parts of Poland and the Ukraine. In 1920, with the signing of the Treaty of Versailles, Hungary lost parts of its country, which made it impossible for Bartók to visit these regions any longer. In the mid-1920s, he finished several articles and books

---

Béla Bartók in the United States

In the midst of a world-class career as a composer, Béla Bartók was forced to flee Hungary in 1940 to escape the Nazi occupation of that country. Bartók, a noted dissident against the Nazi cause, opposed Hungary's siding with the German forces. In the autumn of 1940, Bartók and his wife left Lisbon and arrived in New York City, where he would reside until his death of leukemia in 1945. Despite his status as an elite composer of Western art music, Bartók found Americans unreceptive to his music, and he spent a majority of his time in the United States working as an ethnomusicologist for Columbia University, curating and editing a large collection of Serbian and Croatian folk songs held in the university's library collection.

about Hungarian folk music. Beginning in 1934, his teaching duties were reduced, so, together with Kodály, he became the editor of a complete edition of Hungarian folk songs that included more than 14,000 melodies. In 1936, he made his last excursion to Anatolia, Turkey. After the annexation of Austria to Adolf Hitler's Germany in 1938, Bartók moved to the United States, arriving in 1940, where he obtained a job at Columbia University to transcribe Serbo-Croatian folk songs from the Milman Parry collection of Harvard University. (Parry was a music ethnologist and, between 1933 and 1935, had done research in the former Yugoslavia.) In 1943–1944, Bartók finished several books about Hungarian folk songs.

Bartók was not interested in writing progressive "world music"; instead, he wanted to build up a Hungarian national art. Because he did not regard Hungarian music from the 19th century as being valuable, he had to scent out another tradition, which he saw in peasant music. This music helped him to free himself from the major-minor tonality. During the years 1908 to 1911, he developed his own musical style, influenced by Claude Debussy and peasant music. This led to quartal chords, pentatonic clusters, bimodality, and scales outside of major and minor. He adopted elements of melody and rhythm from Hungarian native music, such as changing meters and a recitative-like vocal style, basing the latter on the *parlando* of folk songs.

There were collectors of Hungarian folklore during the 19th century, but they differed from Bartók in two respects: First, they were more interested in the text than in the music, often printing the folk songs without the music; second, they uncritically mixed popular tunes, patriotic songs, and folk songs. These concepts were strengthened by the popularity of *verbunkos*, a recruiting dance, played by Gypsies, who mixed folk tunes with ornamentation and stereotypical cadence formulae, which developed it from dance music to a musical style, and from there to the *csárdas*. Its popular tunes overshadowed folk tradition (most famous are Johannes Brahms's 21 *Hungarian Dances* for four-handed piano, published 1869 and 1880), which was pointed out by Bartók (and Kodály)—whose musical mother tongue was this music from the 19th century—at the beginning of the 20th century.

Hungarian composer and ethnomusicologist Béla Bartók (1881–1947). Bartók collected and researched folk music, frequently including folk elements in his compositions. (Bettmann/Getty Images)

Bartók's kind of transcription can be roughly divided into

three phases: first, at the beginning, his notation is a little bit schematic and sketchy; second, using the phonograph, the transcriptions became more differentiated even in the slightest ornamentations; third, during the 1930s, working on the complete edition of Hungarian folk songs, he revised the whole material. Still, in 1907, he used symbols for quarter tones, but did not mark smaller intervals. For his transcriptions of Arabic melodies, he used the plus-and-minus system, developed by the music ethnologists Erich von Hornbostel and Otto Abrahm in 1910, to mark microtonality. Concerning tempo, at first he did not add metronome numbers or the common Italian expression marks. Later, he did, but emphasized that the tempo of a melody is variable, so it is more important to name the character of the music. Here Bartók differentiated between rate of speech and dancing step. His transformation of the influence from folk songs can also be divided into three parts: first, transcription of arrangements of peasant music; second, simulation of such melodies; third, creating art music that uses the same idiom as the peasant music.

Lampert (2008) analyzed 34 of Bartók's music editions between 1904 (*Székely Folksong*) and 1945 (*The Husband's Lament*) and found 313 arranged melodies, recorded at 138 different places: 159 Hungarian melodies, 81 Slovak, 66 Romanian, 5 Ruthenian, 1 Serbian, and 1 Arabic.

Jörg Jewanski

See also: Kodály, Zoltán

Further Reading
Antokoletz, Elliott. 1988. *Béla Bartók. A Guide to Research*. New York: Garland.
Erdely, Stephen. 2001. "Bartók and Folk Music." In Amanda Bayley (ed.), *The Cambridge Companion to Bartók*, 24–42. Cambridge: Cambridge University Press.
Gillies, Malcom, 2001. "Béla Bartók." In Stanley Sadie (ed.), *The New Grove Dictionary of Music and Musicians,* vol. 2, 2nd ed., 787–818. London: Macmillan.
Lampert, Vera. 2008. *Folk Music in Bartók's Compositions: A Source Catalogue. Arab, Hungarian, Romanion, Ruthenian, Serbian, and Slovak Melodies*. Budapest: Helikon/ Munich, Germany: Henle.
Parker, Sylvia B. 2008. "Béla Bartók's Arab Music Research and Composition." *Studia Musicologica* 49, 407–458.
Somfai, László. 1996. *Béla Bartók: Composition, Concepts, and Autograph Sources*. Berkeley: University of California Press.
Suchoff, Benjamin. 1987. "Ethnomusicological Roots of Béla Bartók's Musical Language." *World of Music* 29(1), 43–65.
Suchoff, Benjamin, ed. 1997. *Béla Bartók's Studies in Ethnomusicology*. Lincoln: University of Nebraska Press.
Suchoff, Benjamin. 2001. *Béla Bartók: Life and Work*. Lanham, MD: Scarecrow.

Bashir Brothers (Munir and Jamil)

Iraqi brothers Munir and Jamil Bashir were noted for their study and performance of the *'ūd*, a fretless stringed instrument popular throughout the Middle East; it was Munir, however, who would attain international prominence through his virtuosity in performance and improvisation (*taqsīm*). The Bashirs' repertoire included elements of the classical Arab tradition and the indigenous *al-maqam al-'Iraqi*, a poetically based suite, with Munir known for incorporating eclectic musical expressions.

The Bashir brothers—Jamil (1921–1977) and Munir (1930–1997)—were born in the Iraqi city of Mosul, also known as al-Mawsil, a locale important in the transmission of knowledge from Baghdad to al-Andalus (Muslim-controlled Spain) during the medieval period. The robust musical culture which had produced the influential musician and educator Ziryāb more than a millennium earlier provided the brothers with their initial 'ūd instruction. Jamil and Munir began learning the 'ūd from their father, 'Abd al-Aziz, who was an 'ūd player and instrument maker; they later studied at the Institute of Fine Arts in Baghdad with Turkish-trained 'ūd player Sharīf Muhyī al-Dīn Haydar. Jamil remained in Iraq, teaching 'ūd at the Institute, performing on 'ūd and violin, composing instrumental works, and later heading the Baghdad Radio Orchestra and Music Department. He wrote a book entitled *Ud—Ways and Methods of Teaching* in 1961, and in 1974 issued a solo recording in Jean-Claude Chabrier's "Arabesques" series, *Luth Traditionnel en Iraq*.

In contrast, Munir Bashir's professional life extended beyond Iraq to the Levant, Europe, and North America. In 1953, he relocated to Beirut, where he accompanied the vocal diva Fairūz. Following his first European concert tour, Munir studied with Zoltán Kodály at the Franz Liszt Conservatory in Budapest and received a doctorate in musicology in 1965. Fellow musicologists Simon Jargy and Poul Rovsing Olsen convinced Munir to focus on solo improvisation in performance, a practice he adopted in his concerts and recordings.

Munir Bashir's style of playing the 'ūd has been described as mystical, highly lyrical, meditative, and healing (the musician received inspiration from a Sufi conference in the United States while on tour). He pushed the boundaries of the taqsīm beyond its customary time frame, requiring what Ali Jihad Racy terms "quiet concentration" from listeners (Racy, 2000, p. 313). Christian Poché cites the "religious silence" that Munir imposed on audiences in order to reach the state of ecstasy known as *tarab* (Poché, 2002, p. 594). Racy also notes that Munir's *taqāsīm* typically remained within the same *maqām*, or melodic mode, rather than modulating to other modes; and that his "seamless" style resulted in an absence of "clear cut qaflāt," the concluding cadences of a taqsīm (Racy, 2000, p. 313).

Munir Bashir left a rich recording legacy; his 1974 recording, in the same "Arabesques" series as Jamil's, is entitled *Luth Classique en Iraq*. Subsequent recordings include *Babylon Mood*; live concerts in Geneva, Paris, and Budapest; the folk-inspired *Oud Around the Arab World*; and *Flamenco Roots*. He recorded *Duo de 'Ud* with his son Omar in 1994; the Indian-infused *Ragâ Roots* was released after his death. Poché expands on Munir's legacy as "restoring nobility" to the 'ud and rejecting its role as "mere accompaniment to the voice" (Poché, 2002, p. 593). On a technical level, Poché describes Munir's development of a "new sonority" for the 'ūd: combining the "sinewy plucking" of Arab practice with the Egyptian method of striking the plectrum and the vibrato of the Turkish school to enhance the "beauty of the note itself" (Poché, 2002, p. 594). Beyond artistry, Munir himself upheld Arab heritage: "[I]t is traditional music which expresses not only our cultural and human but also national and progressive identity" (Bachir, 1978, p. 77).

Hicham Chami

See also: Arab Classical Music; Oud; Taqsīm

Further Reading

Asmar, Sami W., and Kathleen Hood. 2001. "Modern Arab Music: Portraits of Enchantment from the Middle Generation." In Sherifa Zuhur (ed.), *Colors of Enchantment: Theater, Dance, Music, and the Visual Arts of the Middle East,* 297–320. Cairo, Egypt: American University in Cairo Press.

Bachir, Mounir. 1978. "Musical Planning in a Developing Country: Iraq and the Preservation of Musical Identity." *The World of Music* 20, 74–77.

Hassan, Scheherazade Qassim. 2001. "Bashir, Djamil." *Grove Music Online.* https://www.oxfordmusiconline.com.

Hassan, Scheherazade Qassim. 2001. "Bashir, Munir." *Grove Music Online.* https://www.oxfordmusiconline.com.

Poché, Christian. 2002. "Snapshot: Munir Bashir." In Virginia Danielson, Dwight Reynolds, and Scott Marcus (eds.), *Garland Encyclopedia of World Music; Vol. 6, The Middle East,* 593–595. New York: Routledge.

Racy, Ali Jihad. 2000. "The Many Faces of Improvisation: The Arab Taqāsīm as a Musical Symbol." *Ethnomusicology* 44, 302–320.

Touma, Habib Hassan. 1996. *The Music of the Arabs,* trans. Laurie Schwartz. Portland, OR: Amadeus Press.

Basque, Music of the

The Basque live on both sides of the western Pyrenees Mountains, in an area encompassing the southwest of France (referred to as Northern Basque Country or *Iparralde* in the Basque language) and the north of Spain (Southern Basque Country or *Hegoalde*) around the Bay of Biscay. Basque culture is thus cross-national. The French denomination *Pays Basque* comprises both regions, whereas the Spanish *País Vasco* and the Basque term *Euskadi* refer to the autonomous community of northern Spain; in English, "Basque Country" is applied to both areas. In the Spanish region, both Spanish and Basque are official languages, whereas in the French area only French has been granted such official status. The Basque language comprises six dialects—Biscayan, Gipuzkoan, Upper Navarrese, Lower Navarrese, Lapurdian and Souletin—which approximately coincide with administrative borders.

The territory inhabited by the Basque had been populated for centuries before the term "Basque" was applied to them. It is therefore important to recognize the nuances in the numerous identity connotations of the word "Basque" within the context of the so-called Basque Renaissance (*Euskal Pizkundea*), which developed between 1876 and 1936, in parallel to similar cultural movements in other Spanish territories such as Catalonia and Galicia. The founding during this period of the Royal Academy of the Basque Language (the *Euskaltzaindia*, in 1918) established the process to unify the different dialects, which led to the consolidation of a standardized version of the language (*Batua*) in the 1970s. Batua is used by the administration as well as in education and mass media; it has eased communication among regions and is most widely used in cities, whereas old-day dialects are still the vernacular tongue in rural areas and smaller towns. The historiography of Basque music has thus been closely linked to the study and preservation of the Basque language, on the one hand, and of its national identity on the other.

Ethnographers and folklorists began to collect and print Basque popular songs in the early 19th century. One of the earliest examples of Basque songs and dances is Juan Ignacio de Iztueta's (1767–1845) *Guipuzcoaco dantza gogoangarrien condaira edo historia* (1824), followed by Jean Dominique Julien Sallaberry's (1837–1903) *Chants Populaires du Pays Basque* (1870) and Charles Bordes's (1863–1909) *Douze Chansons Amoureuses du Pays Basque Français* (1898), to note but a few. Among the most prominent 19th-century composers are Irish descendant Rufino Lacy (1795–1847) and Juan Crisóstomo de Arriaga (1806–1826), followed as the turn of the century approached by Maurice Ravel (1875–1937), Secundino Esnaola (1878–1929), Emma Chacón (1886–1972), Emiliana Zubeldia (1888–1987), and Pablo Sorozábal (1897–1988); and in the 20th century by Francisco Escudero (1912–2002), Carmelo Bernaola (1929–2002), Luis de Pablo (1930–), Ramón Lazkano (1968–), and Idoia Azurmendi (1971–).

The new political context of the 20th century encouraged a second generation of musicologists to approach Basque popular music from a nationalist perspective, also offering piano arrangements and ethnological information on the sources and localization of each piece and its variations. This nationalist perspective subscribed to a bucolic and idealized vision of the countryside and the rural which had to be protected from exotic influences, namely those coming from cities in Spain, France, and Italy. In 1925, Resurrección María de Azkue (1864–1951) published his *Cancionero popular vasco*. This, along with the *Euskal Eres-Sorta* (1921) of José Gonzalo Zulaika (1886–1956, better known as Aita Donostia), established the grounds for the development of a Basque nationalist music, as exemplified in the works of Jesús Guridi (1886–1961) and Aita Donostia himself.

Basque culture has developed a series of native musical instruments of all families that are commonly used to play traditional dance music and which also contribute to the sound of current pop bands. One of the most widely played instruments is the *txistu*, a three-hole flute, which is often played in conjunction with a small drum. The *alboka*, a double clarinet made of a middle wooden body and two horns (usually ox horns), with one of the horns functioning as a drone, is played using the circular breathing technique. Also belonging to the family of wind instruments is the *trikitrixa*, a small diatonic accordion; and the *dultzaina*, a regional variation of the bagpipe. Among percussion instruments, the *txalaparta* stands out: it is an idiophone consisting of a pair or more of wooden boards held horizontally in front of the (more often than not) two performers, who strike the instrument with two wooden sticks each.

Vocal music holds a particularly important status in Basque culture. *Bertsolaris* are oral popular poets who improvise verses in the Basque language on current political, cultural, or social issues following a set of metric and rhythmic rules. Though a traditionally male-based activity, it is nowadays usual to listen to *bertsos* sung by women in the numerous contests that are held throughout the country dedicated to this kind of improvised cross between literature and music. Choral music is also an important element of Basque musical identity. The Sociedad Coral de Bilbao was founded in 1886, followed by the inauguration of the Orfeón Donostiarra in the city of San Sebastian in 1897. On a smaller scale, the *ochote* or *oxote*, a choral ensemble of eight bass voices, emerged in festive contexts in the 1930s and has persisted up to the present moment as a very popular form of music-making.

In the southern Basque country, Francisco Franco's dictatorship (1939–1975) imposed severe censorship on all forms of Basque culture, with many of its public expressions being prohibited and remaining thus inextricably contained to the domestic sphere. The inspiration for 1960s protest music against Francoism came from the Northern Basque Country and the key figure Michel Labéguerie (1921–1980), the father of the "nouvelle chanson basque" or "Euskal kantagintza berria." Soon thereafter, modernist artist Jorge Oteiza (1908–2003) gave name to Ez Dok Amairu, an avant-garde group that included songwriters and singers such as Benito Lertxundi (1942), Lourdes Iriondo (1935–2005), and Mikel Laboa (1934–2008), among others.

Since the ratification of the statute of autonomy in 1979, the Basque government in Spain has been making a clear effort to preserve and promote Basque culture both within and beyond the Basque territory. To this end, activities dealing with Basque popular culture are eligible to receive important funding from the government. The Eusko Jaularitza (as the government is known in Basque) gives such support to activities fostering the use of the Basque language, as well as to institutions aiming to disseminate the culture of the Basque Country. Consequently, an archive for Basque music was created in 1974, called Eresbil and located in the Gipuzkoan town of Errenteria, which houses a vast collection of Basque music scores, audio and video recordings, and concert programs, together with an array of miscellaneous documents and objects.

The 1980s saw the advent of a new genre of socially engaged music known as Basque Radikal Rock (*rock radikal vasco*). The music of Hertzainak, Potato, Eskorbuto, and Kortatu, for example, was inspired by punk and underground countercultural movements. Among the most successful and popular bands and musicians of today are Mikel Erentxun, Ken Zazpi, Oskorri, Kepa Junkera, Niko Etxart, Su Ta Gar and Kuraia (in the Basque language); and Duncan Dhu, Doctor Deseo, Delorean, Sidonie, Lehendakaris Muertos, Fito y los Fitipaldis, Alex Ubago, and La Oreja de Van Gogh (in Spanish).

At present, a vast number of differing musical expressions coexist in the Basque Country. As a cross-national culture, its musical venues and events span more than one identity group, and different musical practices can all be gathered under the common denomination "Basque." Numerous traditional music festivals are held throughout the Basque territory, such as the Txalaparta Festa in the Guipuzkoan village of Hernani, the itinerant Udaberriko Bertso Saioak, and the Euskal Herria Zuzenean festival, which also changes location with each new season.

The main cities of the region also offer a wide musical agenda. San Sebastián, for instance, hosts a series of annual and well-established events, including the jazz festival, Jazzaldia, has been taking place since 1966; and the Quincena Musical, one of the oldest classic music festivals in Europe, established in 1939. Basque audiences also benefit from a number of popular music festivals that bring together some of the most widely acclaimed international pop bands, such as the Azkena Rock Festival (Vitoria) and the BBK Live festival (Bilbao). The Guggenheim Museum (Bilbao) also presents several programs of contemporary and electronic music.

Lola San Martín Arbide

See also: Accordion, Types of; Bagpipes

Further Reading

Arana Martija, J. A. 1985. *Basque Music*, trans. Michael E. Morris. Bilbao: Basque Government.

Aulestia, G. 1995. *Improvisational Poetry from the Basque Country*, trans. Lisa Corcostegui and Linda White. Reno: University of Nevada Press.

Khteian-Keeton, T. 2000. *Guide to Basque Music*. Boise: Idaho Arts Archives & Research Center.

López, E. 2011. *Historia del rock vasco. Edozein herriko jaixetan.* Vitoria: Aianai Kultur Elkartea.

Morel Borotra, N. 2003. *L'opéra basque, 1884–1937.* Saint-Étienne-de-Baïgorry: Izpegui.

Batá Drums

Batá drums are a set of three double-headed, hourglass-shaped drums, with one side being larger than the other in size and surface area. It is important to note that the word *batá* can refer to any single drum in the set or to the whole set as an ensemble.

Played with the hands, the double-headed batá drum has a large lower-pitched head called the *enú* and a smaller higher-pitched head called the *chachá*. These sides are sometime referred to as the "mouth" and "butt," respectively. Batá drums are constructed using several methods and materials; traditional batá are carved from a single piece of wood, whereas most North American drums are constructed from small slats of wood. Commercialized drums are also available in alternative materials such as fiberglass. Traditionally, animal skin heads are mounted on a hoop with rope and/or leather used to provide tension on the head of the batá. Most commercially available modern batá drums utilize metal lugs and bolts to provide proper tension on a processed animal skin or synthetic head.

The most popular and best-known form of the batá drum is from Cuba. However, the Cuban set of drums can be traced back to West Africa, specifically the areas in and around Nigeria. Batá drums were brought to Cuba by the Yorùbá people of the region sometimes referred to as Yorùbáland, which encompasses southwestern Nigeria and extends west to Benin and Togo.

In the Cuban tradition, the drums from largest to smallest are *iyá, itótele*, and *okónkolo* (also referred to as the *omelé*). The lowest pitched drum or iyá is also considered the mother drum. The iyá is the lead drum played by the most experienced drummer and thus has the most complicated part, with much freedom for musical interpretation by the performer. In Cuba, the enú (large head) of the iyá has a ring of clay, called *idá* or *fardela*, that helps lower the fundamental pitch of the drum and reduce higher overtones. Rather than a clay ring, a dot of paste, also called idá, is used for tuning in Nigeria (Villepastour, 2019, p. 24).

During religious use in Cuba, large sleigh bells called *chaguoro* are present on the iyá (Amira and Cornelius, 1999, p. 125). The smaller, brass bells on the *ìyáàlù* are called *ṣaworo* in Nigeria (Villepastour, 2019, p. 24). The middle pitched drum, the itótele, is often played by the next most experienced drummer. The itótele drummer is allowed some variation and keeps regular conversation with the iyá. The okónkolo, which the highest-pitched drum, plays a stagnant rhythm to support the ensemble. Returning to the origin of the batá ensemble in Yorùbáland, the names of the three primary drums are *ìyáàlù, omele abo,* and *omelet akọ* from largest and lead drum to smallest drum. In Nigeria a *bílálà*, a flexible rawhide beater, is used to strike the small side head of the batá and both hands use bílálà on the omele akọ (Villepastour, 2010, p. 24).

Although in recent years there has been development and use of unconsecrated batá in commercial and secular music, the batá ensemble is primarily used in a ceremonial and religious context. *Lucumí* is the term used to identify enslaved Yorùbán people and their language in Cuba. Historically, the religion was often called Santería; currently, practitioners also call their religion Lucumí. The batá ensemble is played at religious parties or events, called *bembé*, which are held to honor an *orisha*, one of the deities of Lucumí and traditional Yorùbá religion (Amira and Cornelius, 1999, p. 126). Playing techniques of batá will vary upon usage (consecrated/ceremonial vs. secular use).

In the Cuban tradition, drummers sit while they play and use a strap called an *olori* that wraps around the thighs and holds the batá drum in place on the performer's lap. In Nigeria, batá drummers use a strap called an *apá* to hold the drum over the shoulder, as they typically play standing up. Many hand and finger gestures are utilized to strike batá, resulting in various sounds referred to as tones. Some of the tones commonly utilized are slaps, open, and muted. These gestures are used in combinations and toque (rhythms) to create a variety of patterns. These patterns become a series of complex, syncopated rhythms that are part of a larger structure. *Oru* is the sequence of religious batá toques and songs that are part of events like the bembé. Each drum and praise rhythm has its own unique character and adds to these events in specific ways.

Joshua Watkins

See also: Calypso; Rara; Reggae; Salsa; Tassa Drumming; Zouk

Further Reading

Amira, John, and Steven Cornelius. 1999. *The Music of Santeria: Traditional Rhythms of the Batá Drums.* Reno, NV: White Cliffs Media.

Harvard University Pluralism Project. "'Santería,' The Lucumí Way." http://pluralism.org/religions/afro-caribbean/afro-caribbean-traditions/santeria-the-lucumi-way.

Klein, Debra. 2007. *Yoruba Batá Goes Global: Artists, Culture, and Fans.* Chicago: University of Chicago Press.

Schweitzer, Kenneth. 2013. *The Artistry of Afro-Cuban Batá Drumming: Aesthetics, Transmission, Bonding, and Creativity* (Caribbean Studies Series). Oxford, MS: University Press of Mississippi.

Villepastour, Amanda. 2019. *Ancient Text Messages of the Yoruba Batá Drum: Cracking the Code.* Abington, UK: Routledge.

Beatles, The

More than any other famous bands of the 1960s, the Beatles, a British pop-rock band, who had 27 number-one hits on the UK and/or U.S. charts, and up to today have sold more than 1 billion records, opened their musical language to world music, and did it in their songs with different influences in different ways.

The Beatles had no change in their basic lineup since August 1962, with John Lennon (1940–1980, guitar), Paul McCartney (1942–, bass, guitar), George Harrison (1943–2001, guitar), and Ringo Starr (1940–, drums). However, they also invited guest musicians from pop-rock, classical, and world music. George Martin, who had a degree from the Guildhall School of Music in London, became their producer, musical advisor, and arranger (none of the Beatles could read music), and sometimes played keyboard, too. He and the sound engineer Geoff Emerick realized the sound experiments of the band in the studio. The Beatles ended their live concerts in August 1966. Starting in 1965 (with the album *Rubber Soul*), their music became more experimental and turned dance music into an art form. They recorded until 1970, and thereafter separated to pursue their solo careers.

INFLUENCES FROM NORTH AMERICA

The band started with a mixture of skiffle, blues, country, and rock and roll. Initially, their style was oriented toward guitars, mostly had a quick tempo in 4/4-meter and catchy melodies. Rock and roll—a danceable mixture of blues and country, two native American music styles—became popular during the 1950s. During their first years, mainly until 1964, the Beatles covered many songs, some of which were even recorded several times: songs by Chuck Berry, Carl Perkins, Little Richard, Buddy Holly, Elvis Presley, Larry Williams, and other rockabilly songs by other artists. With the Beatles, rock and roll came to Britain. They not only covered rock and roll songs, but also borrowed stylistic elements, like Presley's expressive vocal embellishments, Berry's bass ostinati, Little Richard's vocal

---

The Beatles and Ska

Well-known for their incorporation of non-Western musical influences, the Beatles sampled and adapted music from a variety of music cultures based on the various interests of the individual band members. Their 1968 hit "Ob-La-Di, Ob-La-Da" stems, in particular, from the band's interest in Caribbean music: calypso song (from Trinidad and Tobago) and Ska dance rhythms from Jamaica. The Beatles' proximity to these music cultures stems not from their travels to the region, but from the strong Jamaican and Trinidadian expatriate populations that settled in London's west side beginning in the 1950s and robustly expanding in the 1960s. Many of the world's most famous calypsonians (such as Aldwyn Lord Kitchener) and Ska Jamaican reggae/ska bands (such as Byron Lee & the Dragonaires) were based in London or spent significant time performing in the city during this time. The Beatles also collaborated with Trinidadian Harold "Lord Woodbine" Phillips during their formative years in Liverpool.

falsetto, and Jerry Lee Lewis's keyboard pounding (witness Lennon's playing the electric organ in "I'm Down," 1965).

Fingerpicking on an acoustic guitar harks back to a special tradition of folk, blues, and country; it was used by musicians such as The Byrds and Bob Dylan, but also by the Beatles: "I've Just Seen a Face" (1965) with three acoustic steel-string guitars, one of them a twelve-string guitar, is typical for country music. The whole song is played unplugged and is the first authentic country-western tune by the Beatles—not very typical for British pop music of that year. Another example of this style is "What Goes On" (1965). Both songs show the Beatles' idea of combining pop-rock music with folk or country elements. "Yer Blues" (1968) is a parody of the blues boom in the UK during the 1960s. In the same year, 1968, for "Dear Prudence," "Rocky Raccoon" (with a piano part in the barrelhouse style, a simple style of playing piano, transferring blues playing from a guitar), and "Blackbird," the Beatles used fingerpicking. "Blackbird" was a solo by McCartney, accompanied only by his acoustic guitar.

INFLUENCES FROM GREAT BRITAIN

Next to American folk music, the influence of the Beatles' home folk music can be heard. At the end of "All You Need Is Love" (1967), the folk tune "Greensleeves" from the 16th century incorporated. This influence also appears in their frequent use of modal scales, which is typical for British folk tunes: for example, in "Norwegian Wood" (1965) and "Eleanor Rigby" (1966). "Maggie Mae" (1970) is an arrangement of a traditional Liverpool folk song.

LATIN AMERICAN INFLUENCES

Another influence came from Latin America. During the late 1950s and early 1960s, Latin American music influenced much of Britain's popular music. The Beatles included Latin styles in even their early recordings: with "Bésame Mucho" (1962), an often recorded rumba ballade, the Beatles started their first recording session at the Abbey Road studios. Latin influences can be heard in several songs, such as "Till There Was You" (1963), with bongos (an Afro-Cuban percussion instrument consisting of a pair of drums, played with the hands), and "And I Love Her" (1964), with bongos, and claves (a Cuban percussion instrument consisting of two dowels). "Twist and Shout" (1963) is a cover version of Richie Valens's *La bamba*, an adaption of a Mexican folk song. "Ob-La-Di, Ob-La-Da" (1968) uses a calypso rhythm (a synthesis of African and Indian folk music, danced and sung mainly in Trinidad and Tobago). Bongos, congas (the big version of the bongos), and maracas (a native instrument of Latin America, consisting of a pair of small gourds filled with rice or beans) appear in many Beatles songs. Influences from bossa nova (a mixture of Brazilian samba and elements of cool jazz), integrated in fast pop music, can be heard in "No Reply" (1964) and "The Night Before" (1965) with their 3+3+2 rhythm.

INFLUENCES FROM INDIA

Latin American rhythm gave new accents to popular music, but Indian music was much more complicated. Its influence in the Beatles' music and also in song texts (Indian philosophy) ran parallel to their experiments with mind-expanding drugs like LSD between 1965 and 1968. During the 1960s, Indian music, with its repetitive rhythms in irregular meters, which made one lose the feeling of time, became a background sound for drug experiments and were said to enhance psychedelic and spiritual experiences. Altogether, there are 21 Beatles songs that relate to India (Reck 1985); most of those, which integrate elements of Indian music, were composed by Harrison.

He got in contact with the sitar, an Indian plucked stringed instrument, during the making of the Beatles' *Help!* (1965), a film in which the band is on the run from a fictive Indian cult, and someone from this cult played a sitar. Afterward, Harrison bought an instrument, and at that point his lifelong interest in Hindu philosophy began. In "Norwegian Wood," Harrison played a sitar as a kind of an "exotic guitar" in a simple way, and only doubled the melody without the instrument's characteristic sympathetic strings; nevertheless, with its weird timbre, it perfectly underlined the ironic text of the song.

With the release of the album *Rubber Soul* (in December 1965), the sitar began its presence in pop, rock, jazz, and fusion music. "Love You To" (recorded in

George Harrison of the Beatles receiving musical instruction on the sitar while other members of the band look on. The Beatles were particularly interested in the music of India and included the sitar in such songs as "Norwegian Wood" and "Love You To." (Bettmann/Getty Images)

April 1966) starts with a 35-second improvised solo (in Indian music, it is the opening section, which introduces a *raga*, a melodic mode of classical Indian music) on the sitar, which dominates the whole song, supported by *tabla* (a pair of hand drums) and *tampura* (a plucked instrument, similar to the sitar, but without frets). Its melody is based on a Dorian scale; there are several metrical changes; Western band instruments (guitar and tambourine) are hardly audible and only in the background; and the piece ends by speeding up with improvisation on sitar and tabla, a typical end for Indian music. This is first time that a Western pop song was based almost entirely on Indian classical music—only the text remained in the Western sphere.

In June 1966, Harrison attended a concert of the sitar virtuoso Ravi Shankar in London and, from then on, took lessons from Shankar in Britain and India (the first music lessons he had ever taken). In "Getting Better" (recorded March 1967), the *bourdon* sound of a *tampura*, only at the beginning of the third verse, mixes with the plucked strings of a piano-like instrument, played by Martin. In "Within You Without You" (recorded in March/April 1967), again Indian musicians add to Harrison's voice and sitar playing (he is the only Beatle playing in this recording) with the Indian instruments *dilruba* (string instrument, related to the plucked sitar), *svarmandal* (zither), tabla, and tampura. There is no guitar, and no other percussion instrument in this song, only an additional ensemble of classical string players. This song, with its contrast of rhythmical groove, given by the tabla player, and the slow-flowing melody, sung by Harrison, replaced the band with an Indian ensemble and showed a strong development in comparison to "Norwegian Wood." In Mumbai, India, in January 1968, Harrison recorded "The Inner Light" with Indian musicians, who played the traditional instruments *shehnai* (a double-reed oboe), *sarod* (a lutelike stringed instrument with a neck becoming broader toward the corpus), *pakavaj* (a barrel-shaped, two-headed drum), and tabla.

Beside these integrations of Indian instruments and musicians, influences from structures of Indian music can also be heard in songs which were recorded with Western instruments. With long-sounding bourdons and exotic melismas in the choir voices, "Rain" (1966) clearly shows the influence of Indian music. "Blue Jay Way" (1967) is based on an Indian raga (g-a#-b-c#'-d'-e'-f#'-g'); the opening motif fluctuates between a minor and a major third, and the melodic is raga-like. After their disappointing stay in Rishikesh, India, and Harrison's acceptance of his limited sitar-playing ability, he ended the integration of Indian instruments in the Beatles' music. Although most of the songs of their next album, *The White Album* (1968), were written in India, there is almost no orientalism in the music itself. Only in "Helter Skelter" is the typical Indian bourdon sound included. The electric guitars are so strongly struck that the pitch swings into a quarter tone above the normal pitch. With this effect, the sound of a sitar with its rich overtones is imitated. In the next album, *Abbey Road* (1969), there is no trace of orientalism with the exception of "Here Comes the Sun," which often uses a melodic-rhythmic pattern at the end of a phrase with a 3 + 3+3 + 3+4 structure, which relates to a special Indian pattern marking cadences. The Beatles' last album, *Let It Be* (1970), contained "Across the Universe," written in

1967 during a phase of meditation, which spawned the text. Next to Harrison playing the sitar, a Sanskrit phrase appears in the lyrics: "Jai Guru Deva Om," which means "Victory to Guru-God" and ends with "Om," the holy sound that represents the universe.

Jörg Jewanski

See also: Brazil, Music of; Country Music; Raga; Rock and Roll; Shankar, Ravi; Sitar; Tabla

Further Reading

Brocken, Michael, and Melissa Davis. 2012. *The Beatles Bibliography: A New Guide to the Literature.* Manitou Springs, CO: Beatle Works.

Cunningham, Trent. 2011. *Psychedelic Orientalism: Representations of India in the Music of the Beatles.* Undergraduate thesis, University of Pittsburgh, PA. http://d-scholarship.pitt.edu/10746.

Everett, Walter. 1999. *The Beatles as Musicians: "Revolver" through "The Anthology."* Oxford: Oxford University Press.

Everett, Walter. 2001. *The Beatles as Musicians: "The Quarry Men" through "Rubber Soul."* Oxford: Oxford University Press.

Hertsgaard, Mark. 1995. *A Day in the Life. The Music and Artistry of the Beatles.* New York: Delacorte.

Lavezzoli, Peter. 2009/10. "Structural Elements of George Harrison's 'Love You To.'" *Journal of the Indian Musicological Society* 40, 76–83.

Lee, Pedro van der. 1998. "Sitars and Bossas: World Music Influences." *Popular Music* 17(1), 45–70.

MacDonald, Ian. 1994/2005. *Revolution in the Head. The Beatles' Records and the Sixties.* London: Fourth Estate (1994); 2nd rev. ed., London: Pimlico (2005).

O'Grady, Terence J. 1979. "Rubber Soul and the Social Dance Tradition." *Ethnomusicology* 23(1), 87–94.

Price, Charles Gower. 1997. "Sources of American Styles in the Music of the Beatles." *American Music* 15(2), 208–232.

Reck, David. 1985. "Beatles Orientalis: Influences from Asia in a Popular Song Tradition." *Asian Music* 16(1), 83–149.

Reck, David. 2008. "The Beatles and Indian Music." In Olivier Julien (ed.), *Sgt. Pepper and the Beatles. It Was Forty Years Ago Today*, 63–73. Aldershot, UK: Ashgate.

Bebop

By 1945, the term "bebop" had come to denote a style of jazz that departed from many of the practices of swing, the most popular style of music in the early 1940s. To begin, whereas swing is performed by big bands consisting of a rhythm section (drums, bass, and piano) and sections of trombonists, trumpet players, and woodwind players, bebop typically features a small combo of bass, drums, and piano with solo trumpet and saxophone on melody. Further, whereas big band music depends on arrangements, bebop emphasizes improvisation over composition. The only precomposed music in a bebop performance is the chorus, also known as the "head," which is played at the beginning and end. In between these sections, soloists alternate improvising over the chords of the chorus. Also unlike big band music, bebop is intentionally difficult to dance to; the blistering fast pace, unequal musical phrases, emphasis of weak beats, and highly syncopated rhythms are too rhythmically complex. Similarly, the composed and improvised melodies are often unsingable by nonprofessionals due to the abundance of chromatic alterations and awkward leaps, and the emphasis of notes a distant 9th, 11th, or 13th above the root of any individual chord.

Although bebop is most easily described by the ways in which it departed from swing, it was not arrived at through an instantaneous revolution of musical practices. Rather, it steadily and quickly grew out of procedures associated with big band music. For one, bebop generally adopted the 4/4 beat of the Kansas City big band style associated with the Count Basie Orchestra. Moreover, many bebop pieces are contrafacts—pieces that borrow chord progressions from other works—of music from the big band repertoire. For example, Charlie Parker borrowed the chord progression of "Ko-Ko" from "Cherokee," which both Count Basie and Duke Ellington frequently performed with their orchestras. As "Ko-Ko" exemplifies, bebop melodies tend to be much more chromatic and disjointed than the typical swing melody. Nevertheless, consistencies between the styles exist. Count Basie's guitarist Charley Christian improvised phrases of unusual length, and his band mate Lester Young tended to emphasize 9ths, 11ths, and 13ths in his improvisations on tenor saxophone. Such approaches to melody were bequeathed to the younger boppers at late-night jam sessions at Harlem establishments such as Minton's Playhouse and Monroe's Uptown House, where jazz musicians gathered to practice and show off their virtuosity in improvisation competitions called "cutting contests." Bebop was born in this after-hours atmosphere, where artists were free from the need to please an audience. There the likes of alto saxophonist Parker, trumpeter Dizzy Gillespie, and Minton's house pianist Thelonious Monk practiced and competed with their predecessors, including both Christian and Young, eventually arriving at a level of rhythmic and melodic complexity previously unseen in jazz.

Racial politics greatly shaped the development of bebop. The style appealed to many black performers because it offered them work at a time when their options were limited. For others, the music itself was political: it was exclusively black, deliberately designed as something that white audiences would not understand, and that white record producers would not record. It is easy to see why white audiences were slow to embrace bebop, but this gradually changed as they became increasingly acquainted with the music at clubs located just a short walk from New York's theater district on 52nd Street between 5th and 7th Avenues. Although most white critics initially dismissed the music, critics Barry Ulanov and Leonard Feather encouraged their readers to attend performances, which became increasingly easy for the public to find. Beginning in 1945, producers Monte Kay and Mal Braveman booked artists such as Parker and Gillespie at white concert venues, including New York's Town Hall, and disc jockey Symphony Sid promoted bebop on his radio shows. The music's growing radio popularity led major record producers such as Norman Granz to turn to artists like Parker. Granz further made bebop accessible to a wide audience by having his artists record well-known standards. By 1949, bebop had evolved from a little known and after-hours type of jazz to a genre that ranked with rhythm and blues (R & B) as the most popular musical style among both white and black listeners.

Recordings from the era preserve 1940s bebop. Jerry Newman was among the many jazz fans who made amateur recordings of early bebop jam sessions. Some of Newman's recordings of Gillespie, Parker, Christian, and others at Minton's and Monroe's have been commercially released. They reveal that in the early 1940s the music at these jam sessions was still very much in a swing style. The earliest commercial recordings of bebop, made by small labels such as Guild, Manor, and Savoy, display how rapidly the style developed. A February 1945 recording of Gillespie's "Groovin' High" contains all of the definitive features of bebop, as well as the mature bop-style soloing of Gillespie and Parker. Other famous bebop recordings from the period include "Salt Peanuts" and "Hot House," recorded in May 1945 with Gillespie, Parker, Al Haig on piano, Curley Russell on bass, and Sid Catlett on drums. While Gillespie experimented with small combos, he also continued to lead larger ensembles, and his big bands began to show the influence of bebop. A famous example is the Cuban-influenced "Manteca," first recorded in 1947, which features bebop-style solos by Gillespie and others. Parker's recordings for the Dial label, made in 1946 and 1947, include what are generally considered his best bebop recordings, such as the classic takes of "Moose the Mooch" and "Ornithology." By 1948, Parker was recording user-friendly standards under Granz's direction. Some of these sessions featured the stark contrast of Parker's modernistic improvisations with a Hollywood-style string orchestra.

Perhaps bebop's greatest legacy was popularizing a preference for the most progressive jazz styles available. Of course, this new taste led artists and audiences to move on from bebop once it became popular. By the late 1940s, even Parker's protégé Miles Davis moved in new directions, embracing a style that came to be known as cool jazz. However, even as other approaches to jazz emerged, such as fusion and free jazz in the 1960s, bebop never completely disappeared, and its best tunes, including the pieces mentioned here, have become standards in the jazz repertoire.

Christopher Lynch

See also: Afro-Cuban Jazz; Davis, Miles; Jazz; Parker, Charlie; Swing

Further Reading

Deveaux, Scott. 1997. *The Birth of Bebop: A Social and Musical History*. Berkeley: University of California Press.
Gabbard, Krin, ed. 1995. *Jazz Among the Discourses*. Durham, NC: Duke University Press.
Gillespie, Dizzy. 1995. *The Complete RCA Victor Recordings* (2-CD set). RCA Victor.
Myers, Marc. 2013. *Why Jazz Happened*. Berkeley: University of California Press.
Owens, Thomas. 1995. *Bebop: The Music and Its Players*. New York: Oxford University Press.
Parker, Charlie. 2009. *The Complete Savoy and Dial Studio Recordings, 1944–1948* (8-CD boxed set). Savoy.

Bedouin Music

Bedouin music is mainly vocal and is dominated by poetic types, mainly of the Nabati and the Samri styles. Such recitations are accompanied by a single horsehair stringed instrument called a *rabab* or *rababah*; because this instrument frequently is used along with sung or chanted poetry, it is called *rabab al-Sha'ir*, meaning the poet's rabab. It is the Bedouin ancestor of the three-stringed rabab used in classical Arabic music and by urban coffee-house recitations of major classical epic poems, called *qasidah*, that tell of the adventures of the Bedouin hero Abu Zayd al-Hilali or the Mamluk Sultan Baybars. Bedouin poems relate similar tales of tribal heroes or relate genealogies of the tribe for guests at the tent of the *shaykh*. The rababah is found in the shakykh's tent and is always present when he entertains guests. His poet is an honored member of the shaykh's household for keeping family lineages known through his poetry (Jargy, 1996, p. 21). Bedouin music is not the same throughout the Arab world, with influences from Africa, Iran, and India depending on where the tribes live. Thus tribes in Yemen, Oman, and the Gulf show strong African influences; those in northern Arabia, Syria, and Iraq have urban Arab, Iranian, and Turkish influences; and those in North Africa have African influences. Music of the Hijaz in modern Saudi Arabia formed the base for Arab classical musical scales (*maqamat*), along with Persian and Byzantine pentatonic (five-note) scales, but Bedouin music remains free of the framework imposed by urban composers.

Along the Red Sea coast and up the Nile, in Egypt, Sudan, and Yemen the rababah is replaced with the *tanburah* or *simsimiyyah*, a five-stringed lyre (Lagrange, 1996, p. 26). The simsimiyyah is strummed rather than plucked and thus the tune tends to be simple. It is played by Bedouin in Upper Egypt and Sudan as well as by fishermen from Port Said, where it gained in popularity with folklore groups in the Canal Zone in the second half of the 20th century (Lagrange, 1996, p. 26). It is also used in the Arabian Gulf area by both seafaring peoples and Bedouin. Because Bedouin men would often seek seasonal employment on pearling ships, the transfer of both instruments and songs was a common occurrence. The rababah is thought to be of African origins (Jargy, 1996, p. 20). Jargy notes that in the peninsula, there are a number of cross-cultural traditions where African, Iranian, Indian, and Arab instruments or poetic compositions intermingle (Jargy, 1996, p. 20).

In general, Bedouin make use of the large, single-headed frame drum called a *tar* or a *daff* and the hourglass-shaped single-headed drum called a *darbukah*. These accompany the songs and dances of the Bedouin, with the tar the most used. The inside of the tar has numerous small rings of metal that add to the sound when the drum is struck with the hand. Many tar, used in the Bedouin dance called the *'ardhah* or the war dance, are large and mounted on a handle so that they can be swung up and down and back and forth to the beat (Shoup, 2009, p. 315). In central Saudi Arabia, these drums are double faced and are decorated with woolen tassels that add to the color and display as the drummers form a line between two lines of dancers bearing swords or guns. As the dance proceeds, the drums with their tassels are swung up and down to the beat. Occasionally, they are held up above the heads of the drummers for a beat or two before being swung back down toward the ground again as they are struck with a stick. The wooden stick adds to the cracking sound of the drum beat, while the metal rings give it a rattle similar to the sound of a snare drum. As noted earlier, this is done in central Saudi Arabia in the region of Najd; today, the dance is often called *al-'Ardhah al-Najdiyyah*, but it is also called *al-'Ayalah* or *al-Razif* in the Emirates (Shoup, 2009, p. 314; Jargy, 1996, p. 20; Dubai Municipality, 1996, p. 27).

Bedouin poetry requires both a quick mind to make up lines in classical Arabic and a good memory to remember what was said by the leader of line to the others to repeat in a particular rhythm. This often ends when one side is unable to keep up with the poetry and, in the *'ayalah* or *razif*, bows out and ceremonially surrenders to the side that can keep going. Surrender is indicated by bowing deeply to the winning side and placing the swords or camel sticks pointed end down into the ground. Other line dances include the Syrian/Jordanian *debkah* and the Iraqi *chobe* that make use of a *mizmar*, a simple reed or metal flute called a *ney*, a *daff* or two, and a darbukah, and generally the words are not in classical Arabic, but in dialect. The poetry form is like the classical form of *nabati*, which is a common form in Arabic. Nabati is called "Bedouin poetry" and supposedly takes its name from the Nabateans, an Arab people who lived in Petra (southern Jordan) in pre-Islamic times (Jargy, 1996, p. 22). There are three main types of nabati poetry with different themes: *hjini* related to the sung poetry by camel drivers based on the rhythm of a camel's pace, the *ardhah* or war songs, and the *sammari* or love songs that today serve as the basis for more sophisticated songs performed by settled Bedouin in places like the UAE and Saudi Arabia (Jargy, 1996, p. 23).

The shaykh's tent is also where he has coffee prepared for guests. The preparation of coffee included roasting the beans, cooling them off, and then pounding them into powder for the final boiling in a brass coffee pot. Each step in the process is accompanied by songs/poems, and the pounding is done in a *mihbaj*, a wooden mortar with a wooden pestle that uses a special beat. When the beat is heard in the nearby tents, all of the males come to the shaykh's tent to receive some of the hospitality and generosity that is being prepared for his guest. This custom still persists in settlements, towns, and villages, but it is no longer possible to hear the preparation unless the shaykh retains his tent to entertain guests (as many do).

Other instruments include a number of African drums, such as the large single-headed *musund* that must sit on a tripod or be made with feet, and the double-headed *shaqwa* and *kaser* that are played with hands, one on each of the two faces. They are suspended over the shoulders of the players, thus allowing them to walk up and down the rows of dancers (Dubai Municipality, 1996, p. 33). These are used in dances such as the *'ardhah* and the *'ayalah*, which are the war dances of the Peninsula, Syrian Desert, and Gulf regions. In Saudi Arabia, the 'ardhah, and in the Emirates, the 'ayalah, are done for honored state guests such as visiting presidents (such as Donald Trump), and those guests are often asked to join in and dance with the princes of the country. Although the dance is not hard, the beats seem to be "off" for most Westerners and such displays are often unintentionally hilarious (as with Donald Trump). The poetry sung or chanted at that time tell the history and bravery of the ruling family, their lineage, and the tribes they belong to (Dubai Municipality, 1996, p. 27).

In more recent years; the 'ayalah and the similar razif have been adopted for wedding parties, and more professional groups have started what is called *firqat al-Harbiyyah*: literally, war groups that sing love songs but are accompanied by dance groups using camel sticks, swords, and sometimes wooden guns doing the movements of the original dances. They have adapted instruments such as various reed pipes/flutes, the mizmar, *arghul* (which has a drone pipe in addition to the one producing the melody), and the *hubban* (a bagpipe that has only the chanter and no drones). Frequently these are replaced by an electric organ that can produce similar reed sounds. The reed instruments are more common among the settled people along the Gulf, and the habban is also used on the Iranian side as much as on the Arab side. It is the major instrument in Iranian *bandari* music. The habban or *hubban* is made from the skin of a goat, and the mouthpiece is placed where one of the legs was and the two back legs are tied off to make it secure. The fourth hole is where the other front leg had been, and this is where the chanter is attached. The neck is tied off to secure the body for the collection of air.

The Bedouin have developed the *taghrudah*, which is a poetry contest between two people or two groups. The product is a new poem as each side builds the composition around the previous line recited. The taghrudah is based on the life of the Bedouin and celebrates being able to get by under the harsh conditions of the desert (Dubai Municipality, 1996, p. 13). These contests used to be a normal part of a wedding ceremony, but they have been abandoned in recent years, as Bedouin lifestyle has greatly changed. In the northern Peninsula and in the Syrian Desert, this sort of contest is called *zajal* and it is shared with settled peoples. In Jordan, several men of well-known ability in poetry were employed on the television station to use zajal to teach people such things as how to properly answer the telephone. In Saudi Arabia, these contests are also televised and there are prizes for the winners. Bedouin music has changed with the times in the Middle East and in the Arabian Peninsula in particular. Life conditions have changed and the music, like many other aspects of Bedouin life, has now been relegated to heritage. In the United Arab Emirates, Kuwait, and Saudi Arabia, the younger generations learn about Bedouin music in specific cultural heritage centers (museums) where they also encounter Bedouin weaving and other such activities.

Samirah Tawfiq (1935–) is a "Bedouin" singer who was born in Syria and raised in Lebanon, but is identified with Jordan for her use of Bedouin dialect in her songs and movies. She became famous while living in Jordan and she took lessons in the Bedouin dialect so that she would sound authentic. Her songs have a strong Bedouin character to them, both in how they sound and in the themes they deal with. Her career began in the 1960s and 1970s and her films frequently pitched her as the innocent country girl (*Badawyyah*) against the plotting of urban dwellers (*Hadar*) and showed the virtue of the Bedouin over city people that matched the nationalism being built in Jordan (*Badw/Hadar* is the traditional division of Arab society). Most of Tawfiq's films are Syrian, and though the Syrian government was building a different concept of nationalism, policies did favor rural over urban. Her use of the Bedouin dialect set her apart from other artists of her time; her popularity in Jordan was such that among her fans was King Hussein. She sings very little today and others have emerged using the Bedouin dialect, but they cannot match her popularity.

'Umar Sulayman is another Syrian Bedouin singer (1966–) who comes from northern Syria. He began his career in the 1990s as a wedding singer, and he brought electronic versions of Bedouin songs when he joined the opposition to the Bashar al-Asad regime. His songs were supposed to criticize the Asad government, but one of his best known song is *"Ya Bashar Habib al-Sh'ab"* (O Bashar Beloved of the People), which is a *mawal* in praise of Bashar al-Asad. He moved to Turkey in 2011 and has performed at concerts in Europe and the United States in support of rebels in Syria.

John A. Shoup

See also: Arab Classical Music; Darbuka; Makam; Ney; Rebab; Riq; Tar; Zajal

Further Reading

Dubai Municipality. 1996. *Folk Songs and Dances: The United Arab Emirates.* Dubai: Government of Dubai.

Jargy, Simon. 1996. Booklet notes to CD. *Sung Poetry of the Bedouin. Anthologie Musicale de la Péninsule Arabique,* vol. 1. Geneva: Archives internationales de music populaire.

Lagrange, Frédéric. 1996. *Musiques d'Egypte.* Paris: Cité de la Musique/Actes Sud.

Shoup, John A. 2009. "Music: Traditional and Contemporary." In Sebastian Maisel and John A. Shoup (eds.), *Saudi Arabia and the Gulf States Today,* 315–317. Westport, CT: Greenwood Press.

Suleiman, Omar. 2011. *Ya Bashar Habib al-Sh'ab.* September 25. https://www.youtube.com/watch?v=35wg74Ufwr8.

Bélé

Bélé is a vibrant type of musical expression found in various types of traditional Creole folk dance and musical styles. This often highly passionate music is rooted in the various traditions of countries such as Haiti, Martinique, Dominica, Guadeloupe, and Saint Lucia. Historically, bélé was associated with fertility dances in Africa, but the music has since expanded to become included in several rituals such as full moons and funeral wakes.

The etymology of the name "bélé" is unclear; however, given its prominence in Creole-speaking countries, the name is likely based on the French term *belle aire* meaning "lovely song." It has, however, also been speculated that the name bélé was derived from a colonial interpretation of the term referring to the hip movements which are prominent in the dance.

The instrumentation of bélé performances is primarily percussion instruments and traditionally, bélé percussionists use drums made of goatskin fastened over a tree trunk. This drum is known as the *tambour bélé*. In Martinique-style bélé, for example, the tambour bélé is accompanied by maracas and *tibwa*, which are wooden sticks played on a piece of bamboo for additional rhythms. In general, bélé drummers lead dancers by guiding the dance via drum calls for each step of a specific dance. Dancers align their feet to move with the changing patterns and rhythms of the drums, with the tambour and other percussion adding emphasis to the bélé ritual. Bélé is typically performed with bare feet.

Also notable in bélé music are the vocalists, who typically function in the African *orisha*-style of call–and-response with a lead vocalist and a chorus. The lead vocalist is known as the *chantwèl* and the chorus is known as the *lavwa*. The chantwèl will deliver exuberant and exciting vocals while the lavwa respond in harmony, creating a conversation of sorts between the chantwèl and the lavwa.

Bélé performances are visual as well as musical affairs. This is nowhere more evident than in the fertility-rites dance style of bélé, which traditionally involves a dramatization of a romantic play between two prospective lovers. The two dancers, known as the cavalier and the dam, take turns dancing as a means of seducing one another. In the final and liveliest part of this dance, the cavalier and the dam unite and dance together. The dramatic action is supported by the lavwa, which functions as a chorus for and a commentator on the courtship between the cavalier and the dam. While this concept provides a basic framework for bélé, different countries have different ways of performing the ritual. Most bélé dancers feature more than two dancers, allowing dancers to show off their performance styles and add further individuality to the entire routine.

Another important aspect of bélé is the costuming, which features flamboyant and stylish outfits. Women will wear colorful skirts of varying lengths, while men will wear a shirt and pants. In Martinique bélé, male dancers will sometimes wear uniquely colored scarves associated with energy; colors often seen in bélé dance costuming include yellow, white, blue, red, green, purple, and orange. Some bélé performers wear skirts with solid patterns, while others have more eclectic designs.

Bélé is a long-standing tradition in Creole culture, and it brings together many elements of artistic expression, including dancing, singing, playing of musical instruments, and storytelling.

Broderick Kenny

See also: Batá Drums; Rara; Steelpan; Tassa Drumming

Further Reading

Guilbault, Jocelyne. 1993. *Zouk: World Music in the West Indies*. Chicago: University of Chicago Press.

Herskovits, Melville. 1990. *The Myth of the Negro Past*. New York: Beacon Reprint Press.

Pearse, Andrew. 1956. "Carnival in Nineteenth Century Trinidad." *Caribbean Quarterly* 4(1), 175–193.

Waterman, Richard. 1943. "African Patterns in Trinidad Negro Music." PhD diss., Northwestern University.

Belly Dance

Typically performed solo with improvised and often sensual movements of the hips, pelvis, stomach, legs, head, arms, and hands, belly dancing appears to have originated centuries ago in an area that encompasses North Africa, the Middle East, and Central Asia. It is known in Arabic as *raqs sharqi* (or dance of the East) and in Turkish as *çifte telli* (or double-stringed, referring to the musical instrument that often accompanies the dance). French speakers call it *la danse du ventre* (dance of the stomach), which was translated into English as "belly dance" in 1893 at the World's Columbian Exposition (or World's Fair) in Chicago. Due to its sexual suggestiveness—particularly as performed by young women on the Midway Plaisance of the Chicago World's Fair—belly dancing became a popular sensation in the early 20th century.

Belly dancing even enjoyed a renaissance among women in the United States—most of whom had no connection to the Middle East—during the 1970s and 1980s, thanks in part to feminist thought that regarded the dance as symbolic of personal and sexual liberation. Conversely, more conservative groups in the United States regard belly dancing as unsavory and disreputable. In either case, belly dancing is regarded as *exotic* in both senses of the word: (1) coming from another part of the world, and (2) sensually erotic, even to the point of striptease. Although belly dancing is primarily a female activity in the United States, male dancers perform in many areas of the Middle East, such as Egypt, Iran, Lebanon, and Syria.

Because of its varied origins and improvisational methods, belly dancing is not uniform everywhere it exists, but rather is a complex of dances that differ according to region or by rural versus urban environments. Similarly, the forms of music that accompany belly dancing exhibit great variety. Just as much of belly dancing may be improvisational, so too is much of the music that accompanies the dance. In the best cases, the dance may visually represent the melodic and rhythmic intricacy of the music.

Throughout the Middle East and the Arab diaspora, belly dancing is closely associated with Arabic music that is modern classical—also known as *al-jadid* (or *al-gadid*), meaning "new." Al-jadid music is celebrated for its power to transform both listener and performer; this makes it a perfect accompaniment for a type of performance (such as belly dancing) in which inner emotions are made manifest through body movements.

When Roma people (sometimes known as Gypsies) perform belly dancing, the music may combine Arabic, Greek, and Turkish melodies. The tempo may vary from a 7/8 beat, in which the movements of the torso predominate, to a 9/8 beat, which incorporates faster footwork. A clarinet and violin are the instruments most typically used to accompany Roma belly dancing—sometimes to blend with each other and sometimes to provide musical counterpoint. If more plaintive sounds are desired, the musicians may add a *bouzouki* (a mandolin-like stringed instrument).

Starting in the 1950s, Middle Eastern nightclubs and cabarets that featured belly dancing began appearing in the United States. These venues tended to stereotype or exoticize the culture of the Middle East as a form of representation that scholars call *Orientalism*. By the 1990s, the Orientalist romanticization had waned, due in part to increased immigration from the Arab world and in part to increased solidarity among Arab Americans. However, nightclubs and cabarets with Middle Eastern belly dancing still exist. When belly dancers perform in such environments, the music often follows a distinct rhythmic pattern in which the dancer uses finger cymbals to accompany the beat of a drum. A typical dance performance may include an entrance piece to demonstrate the dancer's versatility and expertise; a slow piece that may include more sensual movements, such as shimmies, slides, and "floor work"; a drum solo for playful, rhythmic articulations of the torso, such as hip bumps; and a lively, quick-paced finale.

James I. Deutsch

See also: Bedouin Music; Romani Music

Further Reading
Athounasiou, Anestos. 1971. *Music for Belly Dancing: Instrumentals from the Near East*. Monitor Records 740. http://www.folkways.si.edu/anestos-athounasiou/music-for-belly-dancing-instrumentals-from-the-near-east/world/music/album/smithsonian.
Carlton, Donna. 1994. *Looking for Little Egypt*. Bloomington, IN: International Dance Discovery Books.
McDonald, Caitlin E., and Barbara Sellers-Young, eds. 2013. *Belly Dance around the World: New Communities, Performance and Identity*. Jefferson, NC: McFarland.
Richards, Tazz, ed. 2000. *The Belly Dance Book: Rediscovering the Oldest Dance*. Concord, CA: Backbeat Press.
Shay, Anthony. 2008. *Dancing across Borders: The American Fascination with Exotic Dance Forms*. Jefferson, NC: McFarland.
Shay, Anthony, and Barbara Sellers-Young, eds. 2005. *Belly Dance: Orientalism, Transnationalism, and Harem Fantasy*. Costa Mesa, CA: Mazda Publishers.

Berimbau

Berimbau is a general term to describe the Afro-Brazilian musical bow that is most intimately connected with the complex Brazilian martial art capoeira. Commonly known as the *berimbau de barriga* ("berimbau of the belly"), with origins linked to Kongo/Angolan musical bows, today the berimbau is an instrument that has found its way into many dimensions of Brazilian culture, and has emerged as an important symbol of Brazilian nationalism.

The berimbau consists of a wooden bow (*verga*) ranging from 50 to 60 inches in height and made from the *gobiraba* tree, with a dried hollowed-out gourd attached called a *cabaça*. Made from steel wire taken from the lining of automobile tires, the string (*arame de aço*) is attached to the wooden bow and is struck by the player using a stick (*baqueta*) also made from wood. To change pitch on the instrument, the performer uses a coin (*dobrão*) or stone (*pedra*) that is pressed against the string. Held in the same hand as the baqueta is the *caxixi* shaker, in the form of a wicker basket filled with seashells or tictum seeds that is shaken at the same time. Three types of berimbau are used in Brazil: *berimbau de barriga*—the gourd-resonated bow most commonly used in capoeira; *berimbau de boca*—referring to types of berimbau in the form of either a mouth-bow or a Jew's harp; *berimbau de boca*—a type of berimbau that uses a bottle as a slider to change the pitch, and which is played seated with the instrument in a vertical position like a string bass.

Berimbau is typically played standing, with the second and third fingers of the left hand holding the instrument while the dobrão is fixed between the index finger and thumb. In the right hand the performer holds the baqueta and caxixi that is looped through the musician's middle fingers. For the berimbau de barriga, the player uses the cabaça provides that characteristic "wha-wha" sound by either pressing the gourd into the stomach or lifting it off to manipulate the sound of the instrument.

Between striking the string with the baqueta and altering the tone of it with the dobrão, the musician can achieve three distinct sounds or tones, commonly referred to as an open string or low open note sound achieved by simply striking the string, a higher pitched tone which is determined by the amount of strength one uses to press the dobrão onto the string, and the buzzing tone which is achieved by holding the dobrão lightly on the string. The caxixi in the right hand can either be shaken alone or can add an additional level of pulsation when shaken on each beat in the right hand.

The contemporary berimbau has existed in many manifestations and experienced many refinements since being introduced to modern-day Brazil through enslaved Africans during the period of the trans-Atlantic slave trade. Scholarship suggests that the instrument is of Kongo/Angolan origin, with two African bows in particular being most influential—the *hungu* of Luanda and the *mbulumbumba* of southwestern Angola. The origin of the caxixi rattle attached to the berimbau has been a topic of debate, with some suggesting that it is of Nigerian/Cameroonian origins and others suggesting that it too can be traced back to Kongo/Angola. In Brazil, there have been many technological changes and performance technique innovations that have made the contemporary berimbau quite distinct from its African predecessors, such as the use of thicker and denser strings, and the addition of the dobrão and caxixi rattle that increase the complexity of the playing style.

The most common performance context for the berimbau is in connection with the complex Brazilian art of capoeira, which combines elements of dance, folklore, martial art, sport, ritual, and training for unarmed (and sometimes armed) fighting. In capoeira performances, three types of berimbau of different sizes and pitches are commonly used: gunga, the lowest-pitched instrument which leads the ensemble; medio, the medium-pitched instrument; and viola, the highest-pitched instrument that improvises during performances. During capoeira events called "games," the berimbau serves many important functions, such as directing the pace of the interactions between individuals, providing signals to participants on when to stop or to control overly aggressive players, and dictating the style of interactions between participants.

During the early 1970s, the berimbau began to emerge as a solo instrument connected with several genres of Brazilian popular music, thereby expanding the instrument's use outside of "traditional" forms of music expression closely associated with capoeira. Three musicians in particular—Naná Vasconcelos (1944–), Dinho Nascimento (1951–), and Ramiro Musotto (1963–)—are among the most prominent musical figures in Brazil who have expanded the boundaries and use of the berimbau within the realm of Brazilian popular music.

Vasconcelos has established himself as an internationally renowned berimbau musician, working with many top jazz artists such as Don Cherry and Pat Metheny, and who despite his unique approach to berimbau performance, and little connection with capoeira, is well respected by *capoeiristas* (practitioners of capoeira). Nascimento is a *capoeirista* from Salvador in Bahia, Brazil, who is a formally trained musician and the creator of the electric berimbau. He is particularly noted for his fusion of berimbau performance with the blues through playing the instrument with a glass slide in a manner similar to that used to play slide guitar. The Argentinian-born but Brazil-based Musotto is the youngest of the three, who also spent significant time studying the instrument within the tradition of capoeira. His musical fusions with the berimbau include compositions featuring arrangements for multiple berimbaus and experimentation with electronic music and sampling. These musicians, along with the growing popularity of the instrument globally, have significantly broadened the performance contexts of the berimbau beyond its historically fixed context of capoeira.

Gavin Webb

See also: Brazil, Music of

Further Reading

Downey, Greg. 2002. "Listening to Capoeira: Phenomenology, Embodiment, and the Materiality of Music." *Ethnomusicology* 46(3) (Autumn), 487–509.

Galm, Eric. 2011. "Tension and 'Tradition': Explorations of the Brazilian Berimbau by Naná Vasconcelos, Dinho Nascimento and Ramiro Musotto." *Luso-Brazilian Review* 48(1), 79–99.

Graham, Richard. 1991. "Technology and Culture Change: The Development of the Berimbau in Colonial Brazil." *Latin American Music Review* 12(1) (Spring/Summer), 1–20.

Kubik, Gerhard. 1979. *Angolan Traits in Black Music, Games and Dances of Brazil: A Study of African Cultural Extensions Overseas*. Lisbon: Junta de Investigações Científicas do Ultramar.

Björk (1965–)

Björk Guðmundsdottir is a singer, producer, and instrumentalist from Iceland, who has received critical praise not only for her solo musical efforts, but also for her career as an award-winning film actress in *Dancer in the Dark* (2000); albums of jazz standards (*Gling-Gló* 1990); and her work with the music of composers John Tavener, Meredith Monk, and Arnold Schoenberg. Her music draws influences from electronic, pop, rock, classical, jazz, and the *avant-garde*. With fourteen Grammy nominations, two Golden Globe awards, and one Academy Award, she has maintained a constant presence since her inception into the popular music world, and continues to remain relevant today through collaborative efforts with other popular musicians.

Born to Guðmundur Gunnarsson, an electrician, and Hildur Hauksdóttir, a political activist, Björk was raised in Reykjavík, Iceland. Her parents divorced when she was three, and she was raised in alternating households. She emphasized this difference, pointing out the ultraconservative and ultraliberal particularities of her union-worker father and "hippie" mother (Broughton, 1994, p. 30). Her mother remarried, to Icelandic musician Sævar Árnason, and they lived in a communal household with other musicians; thus Björk was surrounded by music at an incredibly early age. Björk attended the Barnamúsikskóli Reykjavíkur (Reykjavík Music School) from the age of five until she was 15. One of Björk's teachers recorded her singing Tina Charles's "I Love to Love (But My Baby Loves to Dance)," and sent it to Iceland's national broadcasting service, Ríkisútvarpið. The recording made it to the ears of a *Fálkinn* record-label representative, and her debut album, *Björk*, was recorded in 1977.

Björk was influenced by punk throughout her teens, and formed several bands throughout her years in music school. She formed Tappi Tíkarrass in 1981. The group remained active for only two years, though it made a significant contribution to the growing punk scene in Iceland. In 1983, the owner of Gramm Records, Ásmundur Jónsson, put together a supergroup comprised of members of Tappi Tíkarrass and other Icelandic bands, for the radio show *Áfangar*. *Kukl* ("sorcery") blended elements of punk, no-wave, free jazz, and experimental idioms. Kukl is the first musical project in which Björk started to use her characteristic wide, dynamic vocal range. The band signed with Crass Records and was managed by the English anarcho-punk outfit Crass. Kukl spent a considerable amount of time touring Europe in a van, living off of "bread and cheese" and sleeping at squats (Hjálmarsson, 2010).

Kukl dissolved in 1986, with several members creating the label *Smekkleysa* ("Bad Taste"), and other members performing with the Sugarcubes. Björk cites the day she gave birth to her son, Sirindi, on the same day that the Sugarcubes formed. John Peel, radio presenter for the British Broadcasting Channel, named "Birthday" (from Smekkleysa's 1988 *Life's Too Good*) as his number-one song in his annual "Festive Fifty" best songs list. This publicity aided in the Sugarcubes' rush of popularity in Europe and the United States. They signed with One Little Indian

Icelandic musician Björk performing in 2007. Björk is known for drawing from multiple genres and styles in her music. (Edd Westmacott/Photoshot/Getty Images)

Records, with which Björk remained associated until 2011. *Life's Too Good* reached international fame with the help of a distribution deal from Elektra Records. The band released a remarkably large discography before breaking up in 1992.

After the Sugarcubes, Björk pursued a solo career in London. Her (second) debut album, aptly titled *Debut*, went platinum. The album featured an eclectic mix of songwriting, with a heavy dance-music emphasis. The subsequent album, *Post* (1995), was certified platinum in the United States. The album also featured the contribution of numerous producers and incorporated elements of electronica. These albums set the stage for *Homogenic* (1997). During the time of *Post*'s release, Björk experienced overwhelming commercial success. This popularity came with its downsides: in 1996, obsessed fan Ricardo López mailed an acid bomb to Björk's London residence in a failed murder-suicide attempt. The matter left Björk emotionally traumatized, and she cites the event as the critical factor in her leaving the UK scene, moving to Spain to escape the publicity and to work on *Homogenic* (Dibben, 2009, p. 18). Certified gold in 2001 and the first record of Björk's to be a true concept album, *Homogenic* was also the first of her discography to break away from the naïve, pixie image for which she was known. The album was "much more consistent in sonic and thematic content; gone are the jazz covers, and instead the songs are much darker in mood" (Dibben, 2009, p. 19). Dibben cites Björk's enculturation of Icelandic nationalism, and the dichotomous relationship between technology and nature, as the dominant forces behind the juxtaposition of sonic and visual imagery in works such as *Jóga*. "With this song, I really had a sort of Icelandic national anthem in mind . . . Not the national anthem [itself] but certain classic Icelandic songs—very romantic, very proud, very patriotic. Mountains, glaciers, that kind of thing" (Björk, quoted in Pytlik, 2003, p. 185).

Vespertine (2001) is considered her most introverted studio album to date. The album features instrumentation comprised of found sounds. Björk cites her acquisition of a laptop computer as the inspiration for her desire to "miniaturize" sounds—to record, deconstruct, and sample found sounds (Dibben, 2009, p. 20). "*Homogenic* was a record for scaling mountains; *Vespertine* was made for peeking out at them through the warmth of your bedroom window" (Pytlik, 2003, p. 159). *Vespertine* is Björk's most personal album, the term "vespertine" referring to blossoming or emergence in the late evening. Drawing inspiration from the album's title, Björk found the inspiration for the album's most popular track, *Cocoon*, in the late hours of the night "in a sudden rush" (Pytlik, 2003, p. 162). For the album artwork and publicity, Björk donned a dress decorated to resemble a dead swan draped around her body, with its neck wrung around her own. She wore the same dress to the 2001 Oscar awards, strategically dropping "swan eggs" from under her skirt as she walked up the red carpet "in a theatrical statement reminiscent of Bad Taste's (*Smekkleysa's*) earlier pranksterism" (Dibben, 2009, p. 20). Concurrent with the release of *Vespertine*, Björk began working on the Grammy-nominated film *Dancer in the Dark* with filmmaker Lars von Trier. Called the saddest film in the world, the film starred Björk as Selma, a blind musical factory worker. In 2001, Björk met her current partner, Matthew Barney, at his Guggenheim Museum exhibit in New York City. She gave birth to their daughter, Isadora, in 2002.

Working with Faith No More's Mike Patton, hip-hop beatboxer Rahzel, and Inuk (Canadian) throat-singer Tanya "Tagaq" Gillis, *Medúlla* (2004) featured soundscapes of manipulated percussive, melodic, and harmonic *a cappella* vocals. Immediately succeeding *Medúlla*, Björk became more politically active, after observing the current international political climate. After *Medúlla*, Björk released *Volta* (2007), collaborating with Timbaland, Antony Hegarty (of Antony and the Johnsons), Toumani Diabaté (Malian kora player), and others.

In 2010, Björk wrote an open letter in Reykjavík's *Grapevine*, asking the Icelandic government to revoke all power from Magma Energy, a Canadian corporation with interests in Icelandic resources (Guðmundsdottir, 2010). Björk released *Biophilia* in 2011, with an interactive iOS application that featured songs from the album. *Biophilia* was released "to encourage scientific awareness through technological innovation." *Biophilia* is the first since Björk's beginnings as a solo artist to *not* be released by One Little Indian Records; the album was released both by National Geographic and Nonesuch Records.

John Forrestal

See also: Classical Music, European; Icelandic Ballads; Jazz; Kora; Rap/Hip-Hop; Rímur; Rock and Roll; Tuvan Throat Singing

Further Reading

Associated Press. 2004. "Björk, Tiesto Help Ring in Olympics." *Billboard,* August 14. http://www.billboard.com/articles/news/66903/bjork-tiesto-help-ring-in-olympics.

Branigan, Tania. 2013. "Björk's Tibet Protest Offends Chinese Fans." *The Guardian,* March 15. http://www.theguardian.com/world/2008/mar/05/china.musicnews.

Broughton, Frank. 1994. "Björk's Big Night Out." *I-D,* April 1.

Dibben, Nicola. 2009. *Björk*. Bloomington: Indiana University Press.

Godfrey, Alex. 2013. "Björk: The History and Style of a Music Maverick." *Noisey: Music by Vice,* July 16. http://noisey.vice.com/en_au/blog/bjrk-the-history-and-style-of-a-music-maverick.

Guðmundsdottir, Björk. 2010. "Björk on Magma Energy." *The Reykjavík Grapevine,* May 21. http://grapevine.is/Features/ReadArticle/Letter-From-Bjork-About-Magma-Energy.

Hjálmarsson, Gunnar (Dr. Gunni). 2010. "The Rise and Fall of Kukl." *The Reykjavík Grapevine,* August 13. http://www.grapevine.is/Music/ReadArticle/The-Rise-And-Fall-Of-Kukl.

Lynskey, Dorian. 2005. "Björk, Army of Me: Remixes and Covers." *The Guardian,* April 29. http://www.theguardian.com/music/2005/apr/29/popandrock.shopping6.

McDonnell, Evelyn. 2001. *Army of She: Icelandic, Iconoclastic, Irrepressible Björk*. New York: Random Press.

Pytlik, Mark. 2003. *Björk: Wow and Flutter.* Toronto, Canada: ECW Press.

Bluegrass

A subgenre of country music, bluegrass music emerged during the mid-1940s as several musicians blended elements of the blues, ragtime, and jazz with a variety of early country music styles. A typical bluegrass band includes banjo, mandolin, fiddle, guitar, and bass, though some bands also feature a resonator guitar (or Dobro) player. Although a wide array of singers have contributed to the style, bluegrass vocals frequently embody what has been described as "the high, lonesome sound," with high, straining tenor voices accompanied by another singer in close harmony. A predominantly song-based style, bluegrass instrumentalists typically perform short quasi-improvisational solos, called "breaks," in between the verses of a song. During the vocals, however, instrumentalists play a supportive role, marking the meter and adding brief fills in between the vocal phrases.

Invention of the style is often attributed to Bill Monroe (1911–1996), a mandolinist and Grand Ole Opry star whose band, the Blue Grass Boys, first made the music popular and provided it with a name that pays homage to Monroe's Kentucky heritage. In 1945, the Blue Grass Boys featured two young instrumentalists whose approaches would come to define bluegrass: banjoist Earl Scruggs (1924–2012) and guitarist and singer Lester Flatt (1914–1979). As heard in such songs as "Blue Grass Breakdown" (Columbia 1947), Scruggs, a native of the North Carolina Piedmont, developed a distinctive picking style that allowed him to play quick passages in a ragtime rhythm, while Flatt's hard-driving rhythm guitar playing and trademark "G-run" added energy to the ensemble. Combined with Monroe's powerful falsetto vocals, the sound of this iteration of the Blue Grass Boys quickly came to define the genre as, in the words of folklorist Alan Lomax, "Folk Music with Over Drive" (Lomax, 1959, p. 108).

Joining Monroe and the Blue Grass Boys in the early days of bluegrass were Flatt and Scruggs and the Foggy Mountain Boys (formed after both musicians left the Blue Grass Boys in 1948) and the Stanley Brothers (Carter [1925–1966] and Ralph [1927-]), forming what bluegrass historian Fred Bartenstein (2005) has described as the second generation of bluegrass bands. Flatt and Scruggs took the music to national prominence through their work with the Grand Ole Opry, heard on the radio and through syndicated television broadcasts sponsored at one time by the Martha White Flour Company, and their performance of the theme song to the *Beverly Hillbillies*, a situation comedy broadcast on the CBS television network from 1962 to 1971. The Stanley Brothers, from southwestern Virginia, emulated some components of the classic Blue Grass Boys style, especially in Ralph Stanley's adoption of the three-finger Scruggs style of banjo playing, but they also maintained a strong connection to the old-time string band traditions of central Appalachia, especially in songs such as "Pretty Polly" (Columbia 1950) and "Angel Band" (Mercury 1955).

By the middle of the 1950s, bluegrass was a thriving style of commercial country music throughout the American South and in Northeastern and Midwestern cities that played home to Appalachian residents who traveled there in search of factory work. At the same time, bluegrass music also began to draw the attention of a younger generation of folk revivalist musicians and folk music enthusiasts in New York and several college and university towns throughout the country. Groups such as the New Lost City Ramblers emulated Monroe's style as well as the sounds of early recorded string band music, while organizations such as the Friends of Old Time Music in New York hosted Monroe, Stanley, and guitar virtuoso Doc Watson, among many others, during the early 1960s.

During the 1960s and 1970s, bluegrass musicians increasingly began to expand the bluegrass repertoire by drawing from other strains of popular music. In Washington, D.C., for instance, the Country Gentlemen—a group known for their intricate vocal harmonies—and the Seldom Scene explored the work of such contemporary singer-songwriters as Bob Dylan, James Taylor, Steve Goodman, and John Prine, among others. By the early 1970s, "progressive bluegrass" or "newgrass" musicians such as Bluegrass Alliance and the New Grass Revival began performing cover versions of early rock-and-roll songs, while singer-songwriter and multi-instrumentalist John Hartford (1937–2001) experimented with contemporary rock production techniques in his acclaimed *Steam Powered Aereo-Plain* (Warner Brothers 1971). Although the developments around newgrass or progressive bluegrass were not always widely celebrated by the bluegrass community, they were responsible for cultivating a younger audience for the genre that continued to support bluegrass in the following decades.

The 1960s also witnessed the establishment of a fan culture that persists with only slight changes to the present day. The first periodical publications to be devoted exclusively to the genre, including most notably *Bluegrass Unlimited* (July 1966–present) and *Muleskinner News* (1969–1977), began to appear on newsstands and offered news about current recording releases, album reviews, and concert advertisements, among other features on bluegrass artists. Around the same time, the festival culture that continues to support many of the national and regional touring bands began to emerge. The first multi-day bluegrass festival was organized by Carlton Haney and held in Roanoke, Virginia, in September 1965; by the 1970s, bluegrass festivals could be found throughout the United States. Perhaps the most significant festival is the Bean Blossom Bluegrass Festival established by Bill Monroe, held in Indiana each June. Festivals remain the lifeblood of bluegrass culture in the United States, providing much-needed performance opportunities for touring acts and local and regional bands, as well as creating important spaces for the development of fan communities and a bluegrass-based economy.

By the 1980s, bluegrass music was no longer part of the country music mainstream, yet journalist and bluegrass historian Thomas A. Goldsmith has characterized the last two decades of the 20th century as part of "another roots revival" (Goldsmith, 2004, p. x). Groups such as the Johnson Mountain Boys, Doyle Lawson (1944–) and Quicksilver, the Nashville Bluegrass Band, and the Bluegrass Album Band mined the sounds of first-generation bluegrass in their recordings of traditional bluegrass songs and new compositions. In the late 1980s and 1990s, groups such as the Lonesome River Band, Alison Krauss (1971–) and Union Station, and Nickel Creek continued the exploration of pop songwriting practices developed by the newgrass pioneers of the 1970s.

The new millennium witnessed an increased national interest in bluegrass music following the success of the soundtrack to the Coen Brothers' film *O Brother, Where Art Thou* (2000), which included performances by Stanley, Krauss, Hartford, Norman Blake (1938–), and the Whites, among others. As had been the case during the folk revival of the 1950s and 1960s, bluegrass music has come to be viewed as a significant American vernacular music in the past two decades, with such figures as Ralph Stanley continuing to tour into his eighth decade and being celebrated as a national folk hero and former Blue Grass Boy and bandleader Del McCoury (1939–) receiving a National Endowment for the Arts National Heritage Fellowship in 2010. At the same time, progressive bluegrass musicians continue to expand the genre's possibilities. Most notably, mandolinist Chris Thile (1981–), working with the bands Nickel Creek and the Punch Brothers and as a solo artist, has achieved great acclaim in the national consciousness for his efforts to blend bluegrass, jazz, and classical styles; he received a MacArthur Foundation "genius" grant for his work in 2012. More recently, bluegrass styles have also been incorporated into a wide variety of mainstream popular musics, particularly through the efforts of Mumford and Sons and the Avett Brothers to include the banjo as a lead instrument.

Although bluegrass music continues to thrive in the present day as a commercial popular music played by professional musicians and supported by professional organizations and music industry infrastructure, it has another life as a form of amateur music-making: what bluegrass scholar Robert Cantwell has called "'back-porch' bluegrass" (Cantwell, 1984, p. 147). Many communities throughout the United States and Canada boast local jam sessions, and the many bluegrass festivals that proliferate in North America each summer play host to informal jams in the parking lots and campgrounds surrounding the festival grounds. Yet, unlike their colleagues in many other fields of popular music, professional bluegrass musicians often join amateurs in these informal gatherings, using them as an opportunity to meet and mentor aspiring musicians and to stretch their musicianship in new ways.

Like many other forms of American popular music, bluegrass music has enjoyed a particularly rich history outside of the United States as well. Throughout the 1970s, Japan developed a rich bluegrass community that resulted in landmark Japanese tours by Ralph Stanley and the Clinch Mountain Boys and J. D. Crowe and the New South, as well as festival appearances by the Japanese group Bluegrass 45. Similarly, as ethnomusicologist Lee Bidgood has demonstrated, the Czech Republic has also boasted a thriving bluegrass scene for many years (Bidgood, 2011). In both instances, bluegrass musicians have adopted a core repertory of songs from the catalogues of Monroe and Flatt & Scruggs, while also incorporating stylistic elements (including lyrical themes) of early American bluegrass artists in the creation of new bluegrass songs, both in English and in their native languages.

Travis D. Stimeling

See also: Banjo; Country Music; Fiddle

Further Reading

Adler, Thomas A. 2011. *Bean Blossom: The Brown County Jamboree and Bill Monroe's Bluegrass Festivals.* Urbana: University of Illinois Press.

Allen, Ray. 2010. *The New Lost City Ramblers & The Folk Music Revival.* Urbana: University of Illinois Press.

Bartenstein, Fred. 2005. "Summary Characteristics of Bluegrass Generations." *Bartenstein & Bluegrass,* December 19. http://www.fredbartenstein.com/bggensum.html.

Bidgood, Lee. 2011. "'America Is All Around Here': An Ethnography of Bluegrass Music in the Contemporary Czech Republic." PhD diss., University of Virginia.

Cantwell, Robert. 1984. *Bluegrass Breakdown: The Making of the Old Southern Sound.* Urbana: University of Illinois Press.

Goldsmith, Thomas A. 2004. *The Bluegrass Reader.* Urbana: University of Illinois Press.

Lomax, Alan. 1959. "Bluegrass Background: Folk Music with Overdrive." *Esquire* 52 (October), 108.

Rosenberg, Neil V. 1985. *Bluegrass: A History.* Urbana: University of Illinois Press.

Blues

Blues music is an African American musical genre that has transcended and influenced most American musical styles and genres well into the 21st century. Initially, the blues was a highly localized music that served African Americans in the aforementioned areas as a means of expressing, and possibly curtailing, their "blue" feelings, as well as a mode of protest against their social marginalization during the most restrictive period of Jim Crow laws. Eventually, the blues would revolutionize American music, inspiring commercial forms of the blues and fundamentally influencing such 20th-century popular music genres as jazz, country music, rhythm and blues, and rock and roll.

During the 1890s, a new form of secular African American folk music—blues music—emerged among African Americans in the rural areas and small towns of the Deep South, particularly on large plantations and at industrial sites in the Mississippi River valley. The originators of blues music were African Americans born shortly after emancipation. Many first-generation blues musicians had left small, family-owned, agriculturally underproducing plots of land to take temporary jobs as paid laborers on large cotton farms or as industrial workers.

To express their feelings of alienation and frustration from living an insecure, nomadic existence, these musicians wrote lyrics that reflected the everyday experiences of African Americans in the South, exploring such themes as the vagaries of interpersonal relationships and the predicament of being socially marginalized (i.e., as outcasts and outlaws). Incorporating musical elements from traditional African American music genres (especially from field hollers and spirituals), blues music was performed informally in public settings (e.g., on the street for tip money from passersby or at neighborhood gatherings) or more formally as entertainment in more exclusive social gatherings (for instance, in small clubs known as "juke joints" or at private parties).

Before World War I, African Americans traveling across the South usually performed the blues as solo musicians, singing their interpretations of locally traditional or self-composed blues lyrics to variations of the blues tune form; such performances were generally self-accompanied on one of several instruments—initially on the fiddle, the banjo, or the one-stringed diddley bow (an Africa-derived instrument) and, with increasing frequency by the World War I years, on the piano, the harmonica, and especially the guitar.

With its flexibility and portability, the guitar by the 1920s became the instrument most commonly associated with the blues. Guitar techniques utilized by blues players included fingerpicking the strings in various tunings (often minor-keyed with unfretted "drone" strings); "bending" strings to produce blue notes; and using a slide (usually a bottleneck or a knife) on the strings to create a whining sound. The instrumental part on the blues guitar was often performed to sound like a second vocal.

In the early 20th century, blues musicians migrating across the Deep South transported the genre to new settings, ultimately yielding several subregional traditions of rural blues (later termed "country blues" by scholars). In east Texas, for instance, blues performed on guitar combined accentuated notes on the bass strings with floating, improvised note patterns on the high strings, whereas the blues that proliferated in the piedmont areas of Georgia, South Carolina, North Carolina, and Virginia emphasized a highly syncopated, intricate fingerpicking style on the guitar and a more upbeat and harmonic approach to singing than found elsewhere in the South.

By World War I, several professional African American musicians in the South had begun to compose new songs influenced by the blues. The most noteworthy among such musicians was bandleader and composer W. C. Handy, a native of Florence, Alabama, who achieved considerable commercial success through publishing his original blues compositions. After World War I, rural blues began to be overshadowed by the more sophisticated approach to blues associated with African Americans who had migrated to urban areas.

At various venues (such as theaters and places selling liquor) in southern and northern cities, musicians performed commercial blues songs containing self-consciously urbane lyrics set to standardized rhythmic structures (especially in the popular 12-bar blues form, which incorporated the three-line A-A-B rhyme pattern). Blues singers at such venues tended to be women, several of whom—such as Bessie Smith, Ida Cox, and Ma Rainey—committed part of their blues repertoire for release on commercial records during the first half of the 1920s, attracting new audiences to the blues, including white listeners who would not otherwise have had the opportunity to hear the blues.

By the late 1920s, numerous rural blues performers were likewise making records, including "Mississippi" John Hurt, Nehemiah "Skip" James, Charlie Patton, Henry Thomas, Furry Lewis, Blind Lemon Jefferson, Blind Blake, and Thomas A. "Georgia Tom" Dorsey. Records featuring rural blues at this time rarely sold as widely as overtly commercial urban blues records, and most of the aforementioned musicians ceased performing blues by the 1930s (some—including Patton and Jefferson—died young; others—Hurt and James—gave up music entirely for decades, only to be "rediscovered" by white blues fans in the 1960s; Dorsey gravitated toward sacred music, inventing black gospel music).

During the Depression, both urban and rural blues fell out of favor. Testament to the music's comparative obscurity during the 1930s was the fact that Robert Johnson—who today is arguably the most acclaimed rural blues musician of all time—recorded in the mid-1930s for a major label (Columbia), and his biggest hit record then sold only a few thousand copies. The sound and feeling of the blues remained alive and widely heard, however, during the Depression within another black music genre, as jazz musicians—including such acclaimed instrumentalists as Louis Armstrong, Charlie Christian, Coleman Hawkins, and Charlie Parker and such jazz composers/arrangers as Duke Ellington—turned to the blues for inspiration and thus kept the genre at the forefront of musical experimentation within the United States.

Similarly, the blues had a profound impact in the 1920s and 1930s on classical music composers (such as George Gershwin and Aaron Copland). Several white musicians in 1930s-era country music—particularly Jimmie Rodgers, the Delmore Brothers, and Bob Wills—incorporated into their recordings stylistic techniques and song themes freely interpreted from the blues. Although the blues had fallen into public neglect nationally, several blues musicians of future importance within the music genre (including Son House, McKinley "Muddy Waters" Morganfield, and Huddie "Leadbelly" Ledbetter) were "discovered" by—and made their first recordings for—folklorist Alan Lomax, who traveled through the rural South to make "field" recordings of various traditional musicians in their home locales.

In the late 1940s and early 1950s, the blues experienced a surge in popularity, as a number of recording companies (primarily small labels, such as Chess, Sun, and King) released singles and albums by various practitioners of the new urban blues then being performed in cities in the North. Important urban centers included Chicago, the adopted home of such musicians as Muddy Waters and Howlin' Wolf (Chester Burnett); and Detroit, where John Lee Hooker was first based. In the South, Memphis was principally represented, and was the home of Riley "B. B." King, along with Houston, the home location of Sam "Lightnin" Hopkins. In the West, Oakland, was significant for being the base for Lowell Fulson.

During the 1940s and 1950s, the blues served as a significant influence on three other emerging American musical genres: gospel, rhythm and blues, and rock and roll. In the early 1960s, the rural blues received a major revival when young white music fans embraced the recordings of an older generation of black blues musicians (such as the forgotten recordings by Robert Johnson), and white entrepreneurs located several still-living rural blues musicians (including Hurt, James, House, and "Mississippi" Fred McDowell) and brought them into the international spotlight. Other black blues musicians soon became widely popular among young whites: urban blues musicians such as B. B. King, Albert King, and Junior Wells and acoustic rural blues acts such as the duo Brownie McGhee and Sonny Terry.

As a result of this new popularity, a generation of rock musicians—including such American acts as Jimi Hendrix, the Lovin' Spoonful, and the Doors and British acts such as Eric Clapton, the Rolling Stones, and Van Morrison—cited the blues as their favorite genre of music and lauded blues musicians as their main sources of inspiration. Meanwhile, emerging to considerable popularity at this time were numerous white blues interpreters: such American musicians as John Hammond Jr., Paul Butterfield, and Johnny Winter and such British musicians as Alexis Korner and John Mayall. Although the presence of the blues on the world music scene diminished somewhat in the 1970s and 1980s, a number of popular musicians—such black musicians as Taj Mahal and Robert Cray and such white musicians as Duane and Gregg Allman, Bonnie Raitt, and Stevie Ray Vaughan—continued to incorporate into their repertoires both blues compositions and blues feeling.

The 1980s and 1990s saw the blues reach new audiences. Older black performers (B. B. King, Buddy Guy, Albert Collins, Ruth Brown, and Koko Taylor, among others) and new blues interpreters (whites such as Rory Block, Roy Book Binder, and Paul Geremia and blacks such as Keb' Mo', Corey Harris, Shemekia Copeland, and Alvin Youngblood Hart) performed blues music to older as well as younger music fans. Recording companies (for instance, Alligator Records and Bullseye Blues) and magazines (most notably, *Living Blues*) were established during this period to showcase the lives and music of both living and deceased blues acts and to promote the blues as a vital, enduring art form. Visibility of the blues increased with the arrival of the new century, with the music genre serving as the subject of several major documentary productions (including *The Blues—A Musical Journey*, a 2003 series of films, with a range of accompanying CD soundtracks, produced by filmmaker Martin Scorsese). The blues as an African American music tradition was also portrayed in *O Brother, Where Art Thou?* (2000), a popular movie and best-selling soundtrack.

Uninitiated listeners have sometimes characterized blues music as possessing a predictable, simple structure, yet the genre is in fact subtly complex; performances of the blues generally balance musical articulation that is both improvisational and idiosyncratic with lyrics that exhibit a high degree of verbal creativity, individuality, emotional directness, and realism. Historically, an important component of blues music was the "blue note" (a musical note expressed with a slight deviation from its standard temperament), a distinctive musical element that would have a profound impact on virtually every genre of American music, whether traditional, popular, or classical.

Ted Olson

See also: Jazz; Kora; Tin Pan Alley; Vaudeville

Further Reading

Evans, David. 1982. *Big Road Blues: Tradition and Creativity in the Folk Blues*. Berkeley: University of California Press.

Ferris, William R. 1978. *Blues from the Delta*. Garden City, NY: Anchor Press.

Levine, Lawrence W. 1977. *Black Culture and Black Consciousness: Afro-American Folk Thought from Slavery to Freedom*. New York: Oxford University Press.

Palmer, Robert. 1981. *Deep Blues: A Musical and Cultural History of the Mississippi Delta*. New York: Viking Penguin.

Titon, Jeff Todd. 1977. *Early Downhome Blues: A Musical and Cultural Analysis*. Urbana: University of Illinois Press.

Bol

Bol, from the Sanskrit word *bolna* meaning "to speak," is the mnemonic system for oral transmission of rhythm in Hindustani (primarily North Indian) classical music. *Bols* are mnemonic patterns used by Indian drummers and dancers to memorize the musical content of a composition, including tone color, articulation, and ornamentation.

The concept of bol relates specifically to the oral transmission of Hindustani drumming, so it excludes several similar oral mnemonic systems of South Asia. While many melodic instrumentalists and singers in South Asia use *sargam* "sa-re-ga-ma-pa-dha-ni-sa" syllables to memorize pitch, sargam is not rhythmically based, so it is not a part of bol. In Carnatic music of South India, a similar rhythmic recitation is referred to as *solkattu* or *khonakol* (from the Tamil word for "bound together"). Hindustani melodic instruments such as the sitar use bol to a limited degree to illuminate plucking technique, but this is also beyond the scope of this article.

Bol is the key to Indian rhythm. It helps the performer remember patterns of playing technique (*theka*), and to learn *tihai*, the technique that repeats a pattern three times as a way to emphasize the first beat of a *tala* cycle. Playing the same pattern three times and arriving at the first beat of the tala requires thinking about math aided by bol. It also helps players understand the subtleties of rhythmic cycle. Bol are also integral to oral transmission in Hindustani music. In the practice of transmission, students are expected to spend many hours learning the bol before playing drums. Bol provides a foundation of knowledge that informs playing technique. While traditionally there was no written music, students can write down bol as a convenient way to remember theka patterns.

Tala is the rhythmic cycle of Indian music. A tala has a definite number of beats or *matras* that are grouped into sections called *anga* (bar divisions). The first matra, called *sam*, is the most important matra, having the strongest accent in the cycle. To counterbalance sam, in a tala cycle there is a *khali* unaccented beat. The most important factor in a tala cycle is the theka, consisting of certain standard and fixed syllables—bols—which symbolically represent the tala.

Bol techniques vary depending on *gharana* playing style and musical context; however, the bol for basic sounds of *tabla dayan* are: 1) *ta* or *na*—lightly tap outer edge (*kinar*) with index finger; 2) *ti* or *tin*—lightly tap the area between *gab* and kinar (*luv*); 3) *tun*—lightly tap the gab to create a resonant sound; 4) *te*—tap the gab with middle, ring, and pinkie fingers making a dampened (closed) sound; 5) *re/te*—tap center of gab with index finger making a closed sound. The sounds of *bayan* are: 6) *ghe, ge, ghi,* or *ga*—with heel of hand on luv, lightly tap opposite side of lab with middle or index finger, adjusting pitch by applying pressure with heel of hand; and 7) *kat*—with heel of hand on *lub*, drop closed hand onto opposite side of bayan, making a closed sound. There are many possible combinations of these basic sounds.

Musicians combine all of these sounds together in order to make a tala or composition. For instance, the most popular tala in India is named *Tintal*, with 16 beats divided as 4|4|4|4 with three claps called *tali* marks and a no-clap wave called *khali*. The first beat of the tala is called *sam* (+), the fifth beat is second clap, the ninth beat is wave khali, and the thirteenth beat is the third clap. Bols clarify the accented beats (including the primary beat sam) and nonaccented beats (khali or wave beats). They help musicians keep track of where they are in the cycle.

South India uses a similar mnemonic system called *solkattu*. In other Indian artistic representations, such as *kathak* dance, it is common for the dancer and drummer to use bol to communicate in rehearsal as well as on stage. After the dancer or drummer speaks bol, they express the content with dance and/or drumming.

Abdur Rahman

See also: Dhrupad; Harmonium; Indian Folk Songs; Rahka, Alla; Sitar; Tabla

Further Reading
Lavezzoli, Peter. 2007. *The Dawn of Indian Music in the West.* New York: Continuum.
Nelson, David P. 2008. *Solkattu Manual.* Middletown, CT: Wesleyan University Press.

Bolivia, Music of

Bolivia is a multiethnic country in South America whose large number of cultures has provided a wide diversity in its musical fabric. The geography of Bolivia can be divided into three large regions: the Andean region or altiplano (high plain), located in the southwest part of the territory; the sub-Andean region or valleys, located in the center and south of the country; and the llanos (plain) region, in the north and east parts of the country, containing flat lands and extensive rainforests. Although the different cultures present in the country present very different and particular cultural, social, and historical characteristics, they all suffered an imposition of Western culture after European colonization. Thus, for better comprehension, the music of Bolivia is divided into two categories: music before European colonization and music after European colonization.

BEFORE EUROPEAN COLONIZATION

The largest language groups of the Andes are the *Quechua*, from the Inca Empire, and the *Aymara*, a language which experts affirm comes from the *Tiahuanaco* pre-Incan ritual site near Lake Titicaca. Apart from these large groups, there are other small groups of Amerindians in the Andean region, such as the *Chipayas, Urus,* and *Kallawayas,* among others.

Andean music primarily utilizes wind instruments, with some drums in a smaller scale. No stringed instrument was known in this region before Europeans arrived. These wind instruments can be divided into three basic categories: *sikus* (panpipes), *quenas* (notched flutes), and *pinkillos* (duct flutes), all of which were found in different sizes and pitches. In the Andes region, dance, music, text, and ritual are intimately intertwined. This intermeshing is certainly not exclusive to Andean music, but the extremely ritual Andean culture, with profound veneration of deities such as the *Pachamana* (mother earth), make it impossible to conceive of or understand sounds, text, and movement outside of their ritual context.

Most music in the Altiplano is based on the anhemitonic (no semitones) pentatonic scale. With the influence of European music, however, the use of major and minor scales became common. Rhythmically, a binary character predominates in pre-Columbian Bolivian music, as in the case of the *huayno,* today considered one of the most important music and dance expressions from the Andes region.

Unlike the case of the Incas in the Andes, there were no large empires on the other side of the country, the Llanos. However, more than 30 ethnic groups were found in the region. Some of these groups are the *Ayoreos, Chiquitanos, Chiriguanos, Guarayús, Itonamas, Izozeños, Matacos, Morés, Moxos, Sirionós,* and *Tacanas.* Some of the instruments found in this region, prior to the Spanish colonization,

> **Saya (Afro-Bolivians)**
>
> During the 18th and 19th centuries, many enslaved Africans were brought to South America to work in various capacities. In Bolivia, Africans were favored by the ruling class for their abilities to work in the silver mines of the mountainous region. Silver mines were very dangerous and Afro-Bolivians suffered high mortality rates. The situation resulted in the loss of most Afro-Bolivian cultural practices that had formerly been passed down from generation to generation. One tradition that has remained and since flourished is Saya music. Saya combines Aymara and Afro-Bolivian cultural elements and consists of a call-and-response leading voice improvising verses and repeated by communal singing responses—very much in the African tradition. The singing is accompanied by drums playing African-inspired polyrhythms, along with Aymara-influenced bells (usually attached to the body) and dancing. The unique confluence of styles is a classic example of the interconnectedness of cultures and peoples in Latin America.

were the *sibibire* (transverse flute), *yopeque* (bone flute), *jerure* (panpipes), *matraca* and *cascabel* (rattles), among others. A rare example of a pre-Columbian South American instrument, the *mapuip*, a two-string mouthbow, was also found amongst the *Morés*, a community located in the region of Beni.

Music has always been associated with different rituals and there are many examples of this in Bolivia. The *Hibera*, a song sung by a *Sirionó* hunter before dawn, is improvised and sung individually, calling for luck in the hunt. Another example is the microtonally-structured songs of the *Ayoreos*, sung for their healing power. Despite the enormous variety of music and dance expressions, there has been little ethnomusicological research in the region, and today very few of these musical practices survive.

AFTER COLONIZATION

With European colonization came the hybridization of the three main cultures present in the colonial period: the Native American, the African, and the European. This syncretism spawned important new music genres and dances. The music resulting from this mixture is usually called *mestizo* music. With the arrival of vihuelas, lutes, bandurrias, and guitars, plucked string instruments were incorporated in the regional music, and new instruments, such as the *charango*, emerged. Bowed string instruments, specially the violin, were also widely adopted throughout Bolivia.

Although a 2/4 time was predominant before the Europeans, toward the end of the 18th century many Bolivian music genres and dances adopted a 6/8 time, usually altering to 3/4 in cadences, or combining both time signatures, with the melody in 6/8 and the bass in 3/4. A most representative example of this is the *cueca*, a dance and musical style present in Bolivia, Peru, Chile, Argentina, and Ecuador. In Bolivia the cueca has the status of national dance. In fact, the country's most famous cueca, "Viva mi patria Bolivia," composed in 1939 by Apolinar Camacho (1917–2002), is considered to be the second national anthem.

Other examples of mestizo music and dance are the *bailecito* and *carnavalito*, as well as pre-Columbian music that has been adapted and taken to urban areas, such as the *huayno, kacharpaya, kaluyo, taquirari, tinku*, and *yaraví*. The presence of the Jesuits, who had missions in a considerable area of the Bolivian Llanos in the 17th and 18th centuries, had broad effects on the culture and music of the region. The Moxos and Chiquitanos received music instruction from the Jesuits for almost 100 years. They were taught to compose and play European secular and sacred music and to build Western instruments. Many traditional dances and rituals had to "adapt" to Christianity to be allowed to continue being performed. Since 1996, a music festival (Festival Internacional de Música Renacentista y Barroca Americana—Misiones Jesuíticas de Chiquitos) is held every two years in the different cities and communities where the Jesuits had their missions, with the purpose of preserving and divulging this music. As important as this event is, it is also important to observe that no such effort is made to preserve the music practices present in this region before European influence.

Another important postcolonial influence in the music of Bolivia comes from the region of *Yungas*, a transitional zone between the Altiplano and the Llano, in the department of La Paz. Historically, large numbers of Africans were brought to Bolivia as slaves to help the natives work the silver mines. Some managed to escape to the Yungas, a region not far from the city of La Paz, but with warm and humid weather. In the beginning of the 19th century, after the end of slavery, most Bolivians of African ancestry, called Afro-Bolivians, relocated to the Yungas. This region was mostly inhabited by some Aymara people, who were receptive to the Afro-Bolivians. In fact, Afro-Bolivians intermarried with the Aymara people, adopted some of their cultural elements such as their clothing, and even adopted the Aymara language.

Although many elements of their culture were lost, such as language and spiritual beliefs, Afro-Bolivians also had great influence in the Bolivian culture, perhaps the most notorious being *Saya* music. Saya is performed by large groups of the community. It usually consists of a leading voice improvising verses, which are repeated by communal singing. The singing is accompanied by drums playing polyrhythms, some bells usually attached to the singer's body, and dancing. Afro-Bolivians have found in the saya a strong tool to struggle for a place and visibility within Bolivian society.

During the first half of the 20th century, traditional Bolivian music was greatly discriminated against in urban areas, but this changed in later years. In the second half of the century, urban mestizo music gathered large numbers of people at festivities such as the *Fiesta del Gran Poder* in La Paz, and the *Carnaval de Oruro*, which present different dances such as *caporales, diablada, doctorcitos, kullawada, llamerada, morenada, tobas, toritos*, and others. With traditional Bolivian music gaining popularity in urban society, musicians such as Alfredo Domínguez, Ernesto Cavour, Gilberto Favre, Mauro Núñez, and Armando Terceros, who initiated new forms of mestizo music, soon obtained national recognition. Among the groups that gained high levels of popularity were Kalamarca, Khanata, Los Kjarkas, Los Masis, Paja Brava, Savia Andina, and Wara, which brought further changes in form, structure, and instrumentation. In a somewhat different direction, female singer Luzmila Carpio and the group *Grupo Aymara* gained international praise for performing pre-Columbian Andean music, although none closed the doors to experimentation.

In 1983, a new musical movement called *Nueva Canción* was formed in Bolivia. This movement, which had political and social roots, followed traditional Bolivian genres such as the cueca and huayno, but also adopted elements of foreign music. Some of the most important figures in politically oriented Bolivian music are Luis Rico, Nilo Soruco, Matilde Casazola, Jenny Cárdenas, Emma Junaro, and the group *Savia Nueva*, among others.

At the end of the 19th century, Bolivia experienced a period of musical nationalism, in which composers combined the written music of the European tradition—so-called "art music"—with elements of indigenous and mestizo Bolivian music. One of the most important composers in this area was José María Velasco Maidana (1896–1989), whose extensive work include *Cuento Brujo, Los Khusillos*, the ballet *Amerindia, Estampas de mi Tierra*, the symphony *María Asunsolo*, and *Suite Andina*. Other important composers of Bolivian nationalism were Simeón Roncal (1870–1953), Miguel Ángel Valda (1885–1957), Adrián Patiño (1895–1951), Humberto Viscarra Monje (1898–1971), Eduardo Caba (1890–1943), Antonio González Bravo (1885–1961), and Teófilo Vargas Candia (1886–1961).

In the second half of the 20th century, composers brought new aesthetic contributions to Bolivian music. One of the leading composers of this period is Alberto Villalpando (1940–), who has greatly influenced the contemporary musical language of the country. Other important composers of this period are Atiliano Auza (1928–), Gustavo Navarre (1931–), Florencio Pozadas Cordero (1939–1968), and Marvin Sandi (1938–1968).

One of the most famous composers of the past few decades is Cergio Prudencia (1955–). He created the *Orquesta Experimental de Instrumentos Nativos*, merging Andean music with a contemporary musical language.

Felix Eid

See also: Andean Region, Music of the; Native American Music

Further Reading

Auza, Atiliano L. 1996. *Historia de la música boliviana*. La Paz/Cochabamba: Los Amigos del Libro.

Candia, Antonio Paredes. 1991. *La danza folclórica en Bolivia*. La Paz: Librería Editorial Popular.

Claure, Willy. 2005. *Matrimonio y cueca en el valle de Punata*. Santa Cruz de la Sierra, Bolivia: Editorial el País.

Grove. 2001. *The New Grove Dictionary of Music and Musicians*. London: Macmillan.

Leichtman, Ellen. 1989. "Musical Interaction: A Bolivian Mestizo Perspective." *Latin American Music Review* 10(1), 29–52.

Pekkola, Sari. 1996. *Magical Flutes: Music Culture and Music Groups in a Changing Bolivia*. Lund, Sweden: Lund University Publications.

Wara Céspedes, Gilka. 1984. "New Currents in *música folklórica* in La Paz, Bolivia." *Latin American Music Review* 5(2), 217–242.

Bollywood Music

Bollywood is a term that generally refers to the Hindi film industry in India. The term is a combination of *Bombay* (the former name of Mumbai, India) and *Hollywood*. The name was not used until the late 20th century, although it is now used to describe Indian film in general. Originally, there was the term "Tollywood," which referred to the Bengali film industry based in Tollygunge, Kolkata (Calcutta). The name "Bollywood" derives from that earlier name. There are smaller centers of film production in the region, such as "Lollywood," which is a nickname for Punjabi films that originate in Lahore, Pakistan. "Bollywood" has also come to mean the style of film song from this film industry, as well as the style of complex and colorful musical numbers. Bollywood is the largest film industry in the world; the films produced in Bollywood number approximately 800 per year, and they constitute a multimillion-dollar industry.

Bollywood films are known for their escapist thematic style and frequent use of music and dance sequences. The often-elaborate choreography and cinematography are reminiscent of American director Busby Berkeley's production numbers of the 1930s. Whereas the Hollywood industry would call this type of film a "musical," in a Bollywood film musical numbers are included as a matter of course. The general trend over the Indian film industry's history is that of an ever-expanding number of singers, dancers, and instruments used in the soundtrack; this is not to mention the increasing number of musical sequences per film (although the standard is between six and ten songs). Bollywood songs as a genre are generally called *filmi*, especially when considered as a soundtrack to a film.

A typical Bollywood film length is around three hours, which includes an intermission. A showing of a film in India may include audience interactions such as cheering, clapping, dancing in the aisles, and throwing things at the screen. It is a major social event.

The history of Indian cinema is complicated by many factors. Primary among them is the fact that the country was a British colony until 1947, at which time it was then split into two countries during the "Partition": Pakistan and India. In addition, there are several languages that are spoken in various regions of the country—the major ones being Hindi, Bengali, Tamil, Teluju, and English—and these are

---

Bollywood

Despite being named after its predecessor in the United States, Bollywood far surpasses Hollywood in the number of films produced. In fact, by number of viewers the Indian film industry is nearly twice as large as the American film industry. In 2012, for example, Bollywood produced more than 1,600 films, compared to China, which produced 750, and, in a distant third place, Hollywood with 476. In that same year, Bollywood logged some 2.76 billion tickets sold at the box office, compared to Hollywood's 1.36 billion. Bollywood does, however, lag behind Hollywood in total gross revenue, which in 2012 was $10.8 billion U.S. in comparison to Bollywood's $1.6 billion.

inherently tied to ethnic identity. Some early and mid–20th-century Indian films were actually produced in multiple versions in multiple languages. Most current Bollywood films use a combination of Hindi and Urdu called "Hindustani" (with lots of English phrases mixed in, usually for comedic effect).

The first Indian films were silent, as in the West, but they were accompanied by live Indian classical musicians. These accompanists used traditional classical instruments, such as the *tabla* and harmonium, to accentuate the drama or action on the screen. The first film with sound, *Alam Ara* (1931), was essentially a filmed theatrical performance, which included traditional musicians. Many of the early films were based on mythological subjects, such as *Gopal Krishna* (1938, a sound remake of an earlier silent film), which depicted Lord Krishna (a major deity in Hinduism) as an oppressed cowherder who foils a plot by the king to kill him.

After independence from the United Kingdom in 1947, the Indian film industry increased by leaps and bounds. Production budgets increased, filming and recording technology improved, and the general quality of the films was raised. Indian filmmakers and writers were asserting their cultural identity as Indians, after centuries of living under British rule. Garnering more attention from the West, films such as *Mother India* (1957) attracted expatriates living in England and elsewhere. This film was the first Indian production to be nominated for an Academy Award. An important trilogy of films, the *Apu Trilogy*, was released between 1955 and 1959. Although these were technically not "Bollywood" films, as they were directed by Bengali director Satyajit Ray, they featured music by sitarist Ravi Shankar, and had a great deal of influence on the soundtracks of future Bollywood movies. Other important films by Ray were *Awaara* (1951), *Jalsaghar* ("The Music Room," 1958), and *Paper Flowers* (1959). During the 1950s, soundtracks to Bollywood films included more folk-inspired songs and imitations of Western popular music, such as swing and jazz. It was also during this decade that the role of "music director" (really, a composer) rose in prominence, to such an extent that this person would have almost equal billing with the film director. Unlike in the West, a Bollywood movie's soundtrack is released well before the film itself, so that the songs themselves are used as promotion for the film.

The 1960s are normally considered the "Golden Age" of the Bollywood musical. Pictures were usually filmed in widescreen formats, in full color and with high production values. Many of the films were either romanticized historical features, or "social" stories set in the present day. The Indian censors were very powerful in this period, and thus no adult themes were portrayed on screen (not even kissing). It is considered normal that the actors in the films do not actually sing the songs for the soundtrack. Rather, they are sung by "playback singers," some of whom are just as famous as the screen actors. Probably the best-known playback singer in all of Indian cinema is Lata Mangeshkar (1929–). Her voice is so beloved and recognizable that Indian film fans do not mind hearing her voice coming out of various actors' mouths over the years. Among her many singing roles was that of the female lead in *Sargam* (1979), which is about a mute dancer who only "speaks" through song. Recently, she was the singing voice of the matriarch in the family drama *Kabhi Khushi Kabhie Gham* ("Through Laughter, Through Tears," 2001). A famous male playback singer was Mukesh (1923–1976), who sang in *Sangam*

(1964), and *Kabhi Kabhie* (1976), among many others. Although moviegoers may only be familiar with their voices, the playback singers are often as beloved and recognized as the screen actors themselves.

In the 1970s, there was a general trend that favored crime and action films. These still included song and dance numbers, but not as many, and the musical sequences felt a bit more incongruous. The following decade saw a return to more romanticized musicals, and during the 1980s there was a renewed focus on the pan-Indian market, so that the films could be enjoyed by everyone, no matter the ethnicity or class of the viewer. In the 1990s and continuing to the present, most Bollywood films are in the preferred genre of *Masala* film, which denotes a "mixture" (the word *Masala* means a spice mixture) of plot points: switching rapidly from comedy to drama to family to action-thriller.

From the 1990s forward, the industry entered the "New Bollywood" era. Films now are much freer with subject matter and content, and many of them reflect the lived experiences of modern-day Indians, including films which explore the lives of immigrants in the Indian diaspora. For example, the blockbuster from 1995, *Dilwale Dulhania Le Jayenge*, concerns two "non-resident Indians" who fall in love while on a trip through Europe. *Kabhi Khushi Kabhie Gham*, mentioned earlier, is about the reconciling of a family after the oldest son moves away from India to London. Other notable films from the more recent period are *Asoka* (2001), *Everybody Says I'm Fine* (notably, entirely in English, 2001), *Lagaan: Once Upon a Time in India* (with music by leading composer A. R. Rahman, 2001), *Never Say Goodbye* (set in New York City, 2006), and *My Name Is Khan* (2010).

The success of Bollywood films has reverberated around the world. Several Western-produced films have found success while incorporating Bollywood-inspired musical numbers, including the Oscar-winning film of 2008, *Slumdog Millionaire* (again with music by A. R. Rahman), and the charming retelling of the Snow White story, *Mirror Mirror* (2012); there is even a *Simpsons* episode with an homage to Bollywood. Director Baz Luhrmann has said that his *Moulin Rouge!* (2001) was directly influenced by Bollywood musical numbers. Some expatriate Indian directors have found success in the United States and England, including Mira Nair, who created compelling stories of the Indian diaspora in films such as *Mississippi Masala* (1991) and *Monsoon Wedding* (2001).

Bollywood does not refer to "film music" in the same way that the Western film industry does. In Bollywood, "film music" simply means the songs from the film, not the incidental music that underscores scenes or provides transitions between them. In contrast, the Western film industry considers film music to include not only the songs on the soundtrack, but also incidental music, the title theme music, and the end credits. The instrumental ensembles that accompanied the songs in Bollywood films grew throughout the 20th century, eventually reaching the size of a modern classical orchestra (akin to, say, an orchestral film score by John Williams, like *Star Wars* or *Harry Potter and the Sorcerer's Stone*). In a Bollywood film, traditional Indian classical instruments such as the sitar, *tabla, sruti* box, or *sarod* may be added. More recent films include instruments from the Western pop and rock worlds (electric guitars, bass, drum set, synthesizers, and the like). *Filmi* songs were, for most of the 20th century, the dominant genre of Indian popular music.

The spread of the easy-to-use and easy-to-duplicate cassette put a dent in the sales of film songs, but they still remain popular today. Film composers have shown great resilience and have adapted new styles and sounds into what is essentially a conservative art form.

Another interesting transcultural phenomenon that appears in Bollywood soundtracks is the deliberate referencing, translation, or outright entire performance of Western pop songs in the film. One example of this is again from *Kabhi Khushi Kabhie Gham*, in which an attractive, flirty female character suddenly breaks into The Weather Girls' 1982 hit "It's Raining Men." The producers of the film were subsequently sued by the copyright holder of the song for unauthorized use.

Most Bollywood songs follow a standard format of refrain-verse. After an orchestral introduction, the main singer/character sings the refrain in a relatively low vocal register. After the first verse, the refrain is heard again, but in a higher octave. After each subsequent refrain, there is an orchestral interlude. This form is of course expanded for longer dance sequences. This format allows the composer great flexibility in terms of the length a director or choreographer requires for the musical number.

From a film theory point of view, the cinematography of Bollywood songs is usually full of quick edits and cross-cutting. Lines of text are sung in completely different rooms of a house, for example, but there is of course no break between the musical phrases. Things that are impossible in the real world become quite natural in the musical world.

Christopher Gable

See also: Karnatic Music; Khan, Nusrat Fateh Al; Sufism, Music of; Tabla

Further Reading

Cooke, Mervyn. 2008. *A History of Film Music.* Cambridge: Cambridge University Press.

Dwyer, Rachel. 2014. *Bollywood's India: Hindi Cinema as a Guide to Contemporary India.* London: Reaktion Books.

Ganti, Tejaswini. 2013. *Bollywood: A Guidebook to Popular Hindi Cinema,* 2nd ed. London: Routledge.

Kavoori, Anandam P., and Aswin Punathambekar, eds. 2008. *Global Bollywood.* New York: New York University Press.

Mehta, Rini Bhattacharya, and Rajeshwari V. Pandharipande, eds. 2011. *Bollywood and Globalization: Indian Popular Cinema, Nation, and Diaspora.* London: Anthem Press.

Bomba, Ecuador

Bomba refers to a drum, rhythm, and genre of music and dance from the Chota-Mira valley of Ecuador. Located in the northern highland provinces of Imbabura and Carchi, this region is populated by the descendants of enslaved Africans brought to labor on local sugarcane plantations during the 18th and 19th centuries. A hybrid genre, *bomba* is today celebrated as a symbol of highland Afro-Ecuadorian identity and culture.

As an oral tradition, bomba's origins and development up through the mid-20th century are little known. It is believed that the genre emerged sometime during the colonial period (1563–1822 CE) among the region's enslaved African and Afro-descendant population. The first known written reference to the bomba (drum), likely of African origin, appears in a 19th-century travelogue. Instruments known to accompany the bomba include an orange leaf (buzzed across the lips), a donkey-jaw bone (*cumbamba*), a hollowed-gourd trumpet-like instrument (*puro*), and possibly the guitar. Socioreligious occasions, such as saint-feast days, the sacraments, Christmas, Carnival, and Holy Week, provided the predominant performance opportunities context for bomba during this time.

Today, bomba is associated with the bomba drum and its characteristic rhythm. The double-headed drum is made entirely of materials found in nature and is believed to symbolize matrimony in its use of male and female goat hides. The bomba rhythm is comprised of two complementary rhythmic patterns, respectively referred to as *sol* and *tierra* (sun and earth) or *cielo* and *suelo* (sky/heaven and ground), and may be played in either simple- or compound-duple meter (2/4 or 6/8). The compound-duple meter version of the bomba rhythm produces a two against three feel. In addition to the bomba (drum), a typical bomba ensemble consists of a shaker or scraper; bass, rhythm, and lead guitars (typically played on a *requinto*); and lead and harmonizing vocals. The bomba ensemble reinforces and supports the basic bomba rhythm while the lead guitar or requinto mimics, embellishes, and responds to the vocal melody.

Besides the drum, bomba is also characterized by its song texts and associated dance. Song texts are typically set in paired couplets known as *coplas*, a poetic form of Iberian origin, and often reference local events, places, people, and sayings. Though bomba may be danced individually, it typically features a male dancing in circles around a female who balances a wine or liquor bottle on the top of her head. Whether danced alone or with a partner, the dance is characterized by strong hip movements as well as a stepping or shuffling motion of the feet, which follows the bomba rhythm.

Since 1980, bomba has proliferated as a commercial popular music genre and is today heard performed live or mediated in a variety of contexts throughout Ecuador. As a result, it continues to develop as new genres and rhythms are increasingly incorporated into the genre. Prominent bomba groups include Milton Tadeo and Los Hermanos Congo, Grupo Juventud de Carpuela, Los Hermanos Lastra, Neri Padilla, Oro Negro, Los Genuinos del Ritmo, Grupo Marabu, Poder Negro, and Sol Naciente.

Francisco D. Lara

See also: Bolivia, Music of; Bomba, Puerto Rico

Further Reading

Bueno, Julio J. 1991. "La Bomba en la Cuenca del Chota-Mira: Sincretismo o nueva realidad." *Sarance* 15, 171–193.

Coba-Andade, Carlos Alberto. 1980. *Literatura popular afroecuatoriana*. Otavalo, Ecuador: Instituto Otavaleño de Antropología.

Hassaurek, Friedrich. 1868. *Four Years among Spanish-Americans*. London: Sampson Low.

Schechter, John. 1992. "Latin America/Ecuador." In Jeff Todd Titon (ed.), *Worlds of Music: An Introduction to the Music of the World's Peoples*, 2nd ed., 376–428. New York: Schirmer Books.

Schechter, John. 1994. "Los Hermanos Congo y Milton Tadeo Ten Years Later: Evolution of an African-Ecuadorian Traditions of the Valle del Chota, Highland Ecuador." In Gerard H. Béhague (ed.), *Music and Black Ethnicity: The Caribbean and South America*, 285–305. Miami: University of Miami.

Schechter, John. 2001. "Ecuador." In Stanley Sadie (ed.), *The New Grove Dictionary of Music and Musicians*, 2nd ed., 871–879. London: Macmillan.

Bomba, Puerto Rico

Bomba is a music type indigenous to Puerto Rico and an example of the African retentions or articulations in Puerto Rican music. Developed as a fusion of multiple traditions by enslaved Africans during the Spanish Colonial period (1508–1898), bomba performances typically encompass singing, drumming, speech, and dancing.

The earliest documented examples of bomba music date back to 1797, when bomba celebrations were organized by enslaved Africans who came together to sing, dance, or even organize formal rebellions. To the enslaved African populations, bomba was a source of political and spiritual expression, with lyrics rooted in their sense of frustration and anger about their plight. At times these songs would serve as a catalyst for rebellion or uprising. Bomba was also an important recreational music genre that gave enslaved Africans a chance to express themselves, celebrate, and create a sense of community and shared identity as African people.

Although the first recordings of bomba date back to the early 1900s (by Columbia and Victor Record labels), up until the middle part of the 20th century bomba performances were for the most part confined to working-class neighborhoods made up of Afro-Puerto Ricans, and as a performance genre bomba was in decline as local youth drifted toward imported styles of dance-band music in favor of what they perceived to be an archaic art form. The 1950s saw a resurgence in bomba's popularity that resulted from the concerted efforts of individuals such as Castor Ayala and Rafael Cepeda, who transformed bomba performances for the stage; and Rafael Cortijo (1928–1982), who joined forces with Ismael Rivera to form *Cortijo y su Combo con Ismael Rivera* and arrange bomba music for a dance-band orchestra format. By the 1960s, the Institute of Puerto Rican Culture (ICP) sought to institutionalize and standardize bomba in order to maintain its "authenticity" and integrity, establishing certain performance standards designed to promote an "authentic" style of bomba. This performance style was to adhere to certain rhyme and rhythmic specifications, use the correct instrumentation, limit the range of subject matter dealt with in song texts, and standardize costume dress. Bomba's impact has also been felt outside the island, as seen with several examples of fusions with salsa by people such as Hector Lavoe, or the significant bomba scene in New York housing internationally renowned groups such as Viento de Auga, marking its international profile as a performance genre.

In addition to the solo lead singer and the chorus, typical bomba performances include a small number of drums and idiophones. These include the *cuá*, a long piece of bamboo mounted on a stand that is struck with two sticks; *maraca*, a shaken gourd rattle filled with seeds or small stones that is mounted on a handle; and *barriles* or *bulas*, a wooden barrel drum covered by a goatskin. Within an ensemble, a minimum of two drums of different sizes are used, with the smaller drum functioning as the lead (*primo*) and the larger drum playing the support (*buleador*) part. Depending on the tradition, drums are played either positioned vertically with the performer seated in a chair, or positioned horizontally with the performed seated on top of the instrument.

Reflecting its African roots, singing in bomba is based around call-and-response structures between the lead singer and a chorus that responds at appropriate times in unison. Song texts are typically in French Creole or Spanish, with the occasional word of West African origin inserted.

Because of differences in opinion on what constitutes a separate style and what could be categorized as a substyle, there are conflicting accounts as to the number of rhythms or substyles that together make up the genre of bomba, with numbers ranging from 10 to 52. Each style is connected with a particular tempo, rhythm, and style of dance. There are 10 distinct styles of bomba: Sicá, Cunyá, Belén, Calindá, Cuembé or Güemb, Seis Corrido, Yubá, Holandés, Clave Tres, and Mariandá.

Dancing is an integral feature of the community performance contexts called *bombazos*. A common form for the dance sequences includes an introductory walking style of movement (*paseo*), followed by a sharp jerk (*ponche*), which is then followed by a series of sharp improvised dance movements called *piquetes* that are responded to by the drummer rhythmically. This interaction or "challenge" between the lead drummer and dancer is a characteristic feature of bomba performances. Female dancers dress in European-style skirts made of white materials, with their heads covered with colorful head wraps. Male dancers are also typically dressed in white, with a rimmed panama hat. Dancers perform in a circle in front of the drummers called a *soberao*, and one by one come out from the circle in front of the drummers to improvise for the drummers to follow.

Gavin Webb

See also: Bomba, Ecuador

Further Reading

Alam-Pastrana, Carlos. 2009. "*Con el Eco de los Barriles*: Race, Gender and the *Bomba* Imaginary in Puerto Rico." *Identities: Global Studies in Culture and Power* 16(5), 573–600. https://www.tandfonline.com/doi/abs/10.1080/10702890903172736.

Diaz Diaz, Edgardo. "Bomba." Center for Puerto Rican Studies, Hunter College. https://centropr.hunter.cuny.edu/centrovoices/arts-culture/bomba-and-plena-old-steps-new-paths.

Ferreras, Salvadore E. 2005. "Solo Drumming in the Puerto Rican Bomba: An Analysis of Musical Processes and Improvisational Strategies." PhD diss., The University of British Columbia, Canada.

Bones (Britain and Ireland)

A common British folk instrument, the bones are a pair of directly struck idiophones required for 19th-century minstrelsy and found in traditional music of the British Isles as an accompanying percussion instrument.

Though originally constructed of two cow or sheep ribs (roughly six inches long and one inch wide), modern variants of curved wood (especially maple) and plastic are common. The bones are played by holding a pair on either side of the middle finger in one hand in a loose fist, convex surfaces facing in. The distinctive "clacking" sound is obtained by shaking the wrist side-to-side to create a clapper effect through momentum. Advanced players learn to achieve a triple-click or "clickety" sound. Because bones playing is so individualized, and is not notated, an infinite variety of rhythmic and tonal combinations are possible.

More than half of the length of the bones must extend beyond the palm, with the fingers curved gently around the instrument. Most players hold the bone further from the thumb against the palm, while the one closer to the thumb moves freely, but the reverse is possible.

The playing of two clappers in a single hand was recorded in ancient Babylon, China, and the Mediterranean. A cylinder seal from Ur (2800 BCE), near the Euphrates River, depicts a small animal playing a pair of short clappers. Fourteen centuries later, similar clappers appear on Egyptian reliefs in the New Kingdom. Shakespeare's character Bottom in *A Midsummer Night's Dream* remarked, "I have a reasonable good ear in music. Let's have the tongs and the bones." Modern varieties include the egg-clappers and spoons in England, ivory castanets in France, wooden castanets in Spain, their larger relatives the *castanyoles* of the Balearic Islands, and the Indian *kartâl*.

According to folk legend, the bones were brought to Ireland through traveling minstrel shows from the United States in the 19th century. The minstrel show as a theatrical form originated in 1839 when four Anglo-Irish performers, led by fiddler Daniel Emmett, presented an entire evening of blackface songs, patter, jokes, dances, and sketches in New York City. The Virginia Minstrels (also billed as Ethiopian delineators), as this group of white performers called themselves, played mainly lightly syncopated variants of English/Scots/Irish fiddle tunes. They created new "American" songs rooted in African American folklore and stereotypes. The original bones player for the Virginia Minstrels was Frank Brower, who stomped around the stage while playing *fortissimo* patterns with his right hand. This group introduced the combination of the banjo, tambourine, and bones to English and Irish audiences in 1843. The tambourine and bones were played by the two comedians Mr. Tambo and Mr. Bones, who sat at the ends of a semicircle (the "endmen"). They always appeared in blackface, even after the other performers ceased to do so.

In the same year, banjo player Edwin P. Christy founded the Christy Minstrels in Buffalo, New York, featuring bones player (and drag performer) George Harrington (Christy). Versions of the company were in residence in London and Dublin from 1857 to 1904. This became America's leading cultural export to Europe, and an 1861 German newspaper commented, "Henry James? Herman Melville? Feh! . . . *Wir möchten gern Herrn. Bones und Tambo länger gehören* (We'd rather hear more of Misters Bones and Tambo)." According to *Dwight's Journal* (Boston, 1861), a virtuosic bones player named Pell created intricate patterns on his "primitive rattle . . . with the most fantastic contortions" producing "something entirely without precedent."

The high-stepping minstrel dances combined elements of English clogging, African dance, and Irish jigs; this led directly to the creation of tap dancing, accompanied by bones until the 20th century.

Because so much of Irish music was originally intended to accompany dance, dancers' feet supplied most of the percussive rhythms. However, two percussion instruments are present both in Irish traditional music meant for the stage (since the founding of Ceoltóirí Chualann by Séan Ó Riada in 1960) and music of the Irish diaspora: bones (or spoons) and the *bodhrán* drum. Ronnie McShane was the first bones player for Ceoltóirí Chualann, and bodhrán player Peader Mercier brought both instruments to the Chieftains.

Much of what is known as Appalachian rhythm is actually of Irish derivation. This intermingling of folk influences led to there being many instruments in common (like the bones) in bluegrass, zydeco, French-Canadian, Nova Scotian, and Irish folk music. Some early records of the Acadian and Cajun *frottoir* (washboard) compare it to the sound of bones over a ribcage. Bones (more often in two pairs outside of the British Isles) can even be found accompanying some types of blues.

Laura Stanfield Prichard

See also: Irish American Vocal Music; Irish Dance Music; Irish Step Dancing

Further Reading

Cantwell, Robert. 2002. *Bluegrass Breakdown: The Making of the Old Southern Sound.* Urbana: University of Illinois Press.

Vallely, Fintan. 1999. *The Companion to Traditional Irish Music.* New York: New York University Press.

Brazil, Music of

The music of Brazil comprises a diverse corpus of styles across folk, art, and popular traditions. Occupying much of South America's eastern Atlantic coast, Brazil has been a converging point for peoples across the globe throughout much of the country's history, and its music emerges especially out of a historic confluence of cultures from Latin America, Europe, and Africa. Today, Brazil's musical legacy continues to express many unique fusions between these cultural groups—from Heitor Villa-Lobos's cherished classical works infused with Brazilian popular and indigenous melodies to the infectious Afro-Brazilian pulse of *samba* that flows through the streets of Rio de Janeiro during the city's legendary Carnival celebration each year.

INDIGENOUS MUSIC

Long before the arrival of Portuguese explorer Pedro Álvares Cabral to Brazilian territory in 1500, indigenous peoples populated the Brazilian coastal territory.

Though virtually no musical sources remain from the pre-colonial period, some native Indian populations of Brazil have remained largely without contact with other cultural groups and have thus retained autonomous musical traditions. Nonetheless, the music of many tribes—which are today drastically reduced following centuries of disease and devastation—has never had any comprehensive study due to the linguistic and geographical barriers that isolate them from Western society.

The few existing studies reveal that the music of Brazil's indigenous populations largely comprises song and dance genres based on the rituals of daily social and religious life. The Suyá Indians of the Brazilian state Mato Grosso, for instance, produce song genres extensively in the establishment and maintenance of social identity within the community. Use of instruments beyond basic idiophones (rattles) is rare in the Suyá tradition, although elsewhere in the Amazon, native populations utilize more extensive instrumental music, including wind and percussion instruments and a variety of drums as an accompaniment to ritual dance. The Nambicuara Indians in Brazil's southernmost region, for instance, utilize several types of flutes in ritual and social music making.

Throughout the country's history, the spread of Western culture and industry to Brazil's interior—especially through the exploitation of the Amazon's natural resources—has increasingly drawn Brazil's indigenous cultures into contact with the Western world, and the musical traditions of indigenous peoples in Brazil continue both to resist and to assimilate new influences from these interactions. Moreover, the music of Brazil's indigenous tribes has increasingly attracted attention from Western musicians. Brazilian composer Heitor Villa-Lobos (1887–1959), for instance, drew on indigenous music and the Amazon soundscape in his 1917 ballets, *Amazonas* and *Uirapurú*. Though Villa-Lobos sought to incorporate indigenous music as an expression of early 20th-century Brazilian national identity, more recently engagement with such music by Brazilian and global popular musicians has served as an expression of solidarity against rainforest devastation and social injustice against Brazilian indigenous populations. In the 1980s, British pop artist Sting famously collaborated with the Brazilian Kayapó chief Raoni to raise global awareness of Amazon deforestation.

EUROPEAN MUSIC IN THE COLONY

At the same time that indigenous traditions subsisted and evolved during the colonial period, Portuguese colonizers imported European art and popular music traditions to Brazil. Jesuit missionaries introduced European music largely for the purposes of education from about 1550, though little evidence regarding the exact nature of that music exists from before the 18th century. Among the compositions that proliferated in Brazil during the latter part of the 18th century—especially around the flourishing economic states of São Paulo, Bahia, Rio de Janeiro, and Minas Gerais—most were sacred liturgical works to Latin texts, which utilized primarily choral singing and light orchestral accompaniment.

Unlike in Europe, many of the Brazilian composers and musicians that produced European style music by the mid-18th century in the colony were of mixed racial (mulatto) backgrounds. As Portuguese colonizers organized the extensive importation of West African slaves (especially from Angola and Benin) during the country's long period of slavery, which began shortly after colonization and endured through 1889, they also created a large mulatto population by producing frequent offspring with black female slaves. So long as such offspring maintained closer ties to white, European society in the colony, they were able to find success as musicians. Numerous biracial composers and performers achieved considerable success in Brazil as chapel masters in major cathedrals, such as mulatto composer Luiz Álvares Pinto (1719–1789). Brazilian mulattos also forged successful music careers in the colony's capital in Europe (Lisbon, Portugal), including the guitarist and composer Domingos Caldas Barbosa (ca. 1739–1800) and the soprano singer Joaquina Lapinha (ca. late 19th–early 19th century).

AFRICAN INFLUENCES

Although many mulatto Brazilians assimilated European musical styles and culture, in other contexts the musical roots of slaves brought to the colony from Africa also remained strong. In such contexts, African musical traditions helped to mediate the new circumstances in the colony and to maintain an abstracted diasporic connection to the African native land through religious, social, and cultural rituals. Many African-derived musical practices remain important facets of Afro-Brazilian identity today in Brazil, especially in the northeastern states of Bahia and Pernambuco, where the population contains a much higher concentration of African descendants.

Among the most important vestiges of African religious ritual in Brazil is the widely practiced northeastern tradition of *candomblé*. Derived from Yoruba, Fon, and Bantu belief systems in West Africa, candomblé constitutes a complex ritual system in which music and dance serve numerous ceremonial functions, the most important of which is the facilitation of spirit possession by African deities called *orixás*. A secular manifestation of candomblé called *afoxé* utilizes roughly the same styles of music but is practiced largely outside religious ritual by organized associations of Carnival musicians in northeastern Brazil. Other vestiges of African religious heritage can be found in the practice of *maracatu*, a type of religious and musical procession that depicts characters and ceremonies from African folklore during Carnival. The procession features especially the dancing of the *caboclo de lança*, a male warrior figure who wields a lance, holds a white flower between his lips, and displays a distinctive headdress made of multicolor metallic streamers and a large beaded cape draped over a square frame.

Beyond religious ritual, African slaves in Brazil also sought to maintain a connection to their heritage through social and physical play. Disguised as a gamelike dance with musical accompaniment, *capoeira* developed as a synthesis of African and Brazilian street fighting styles practiced by slaves to refine their capacity for physical defense against slave owners. Though the exact origins of the term and form of early practice are difficult to determine, in its contemporary form, music accompanies the organized play of participants (called *capoeiritsas*) in a circle (*roda*). *Mestres* (master teachers) lead accompanimental songs (also called *cantigas*), while other capoeiristas perform accompaniment on percussion and *berimbau*, a stringed percussion instrument. Capoeira has grown in popularity since the early 20th century under the leadership of renowned mestres, who have largely promoted capoeira as an organized system of martial arts.

ART MUSIC AFTER THE COLONIAL PERIOD

From the 19th century onward, art music gained in importance in Brazil, especially following the transfer of the Portuguese royal court from Portugal to Rio de Janeiro in 1808. Fleeing French invasions in Portugal, the Portuguese monarchy brought many of the musicians and the royal music library from Europe on the transatlantic journey, but named Brazilian biracial composer and keyboardist José Maurício Nunes Garcia (1767–1830) master of the new Portuguese royal chapel in Rio de Janeiro. Garcia achieved a considerable reputation under the patronage of the Portuguese court, and his existing music (mostly sacred liturgical works) reveals his advanced compositional skill. Alongside native Brazilians, European composers and musicians also increasingly migrated to and achieved success in Brazil during this period, largely under the patronage of the court, as was the case with Portuguese composer Marcos Portugal (1762–1830) and Austrian composer Sigismund Neukomm (1778–1858).

Following Brazilian independence in 1822, the Brazilian art music scene continued to revolve around the political center of Rio de Janeiro, where contemporary Italian operas were the main musical productions. Antônio Carlos Gomes (1836–1896) was among the first Brazilian composers to produce a native opera with his *A noite do castelo* (The Night of the Castle) in 1861. He later produced the first New World opera to gain international fame, *Il Guarany* (The Guarany), which premiered to great acclaim at Milan's La Scala Theater in 1870. Based on the novel *O Guarani* by José de Alencar (1829–1877), the work featured a Brazilian Indian character as its protagonist and was closely aligned with the Romantic Brazilian *indianismo* movement, which sought authentic Brazilian national identity in the heritage of its indigenous cultures.

During the late 19th and early 20th centuries, Brazilian composers became increasingly interested in establishing a national art music that drew European genres together with more distinctive Brazilian musical traditions. The Brazilian musical nationalist movement culminated during the period under dictator Getúlio Vargas (1930–1945) in the works of Heitor Villa-Lobos, who remains one of the most popular and influential Latin American composers to date. Villa-Lobos immersed himself deeply in Brazilian music of all sorts in his search for a Brazilian national style. He traveled to Brazil's interior to study indigenous music, played in Brazilian street bands in Rio de Janeiro, and later established a professional career as a classical cellist. He also developed a widely practiced system of musical education in Brazil called *canto orfeônico* (Orpheonic singing), which taught musical pitches through a system of syllables and hand symbols. The most popular of Villa-Lobos's classical works remain his series of chamber suites entitled "Bachianas brasileiras" (Brazilian *Bachianas,* or pieces in the style of Bach), written between 1930 and 1945, which demonstrate his careful blend of European and Brazilian styles. In these works, Villa-Lobos attempted not to simply incorporate Brazilian tunes and styles into a larger European musical genre, but rather sought to fully merge the two by adapting and applying the harmonic and melodic style of Johann Sebastian Bach to Brazilian traditional music (Béhague, 1994). Villa-Lobos also based compositions on Brazilian popular music: his series of chamber works *Chôros* (1920–1929) drew inspiration from the late 19th-century Brazilian instrumental genre *choro*, which popularized short, improvisatory, jazz-like pieces for guitar, *cavaquinho* (Brazilian ukelele), solo wind instrument (flute/clarinet), and *pandeiro* (tambourine).

Throughout the development of Brazilian art music, non-Brazilian composers have also contributed to and engaged with the unique repertoire of Brazilian sounds. French composer Darius Milhaud (1892–1974), for instance, spent a period of several years in Brazil during the early 20th century and wrote several compositions that drew on Brazilian sounds and styles. His ballet *Le Boeuf sur le Toit* (The Ox on the Roof, 1920), for instance, juxtaposes a recurring theme of Milhaud's invention with a collage of more than 20 contemporary Brazilian popular tunes. Subsequent generations of Brazilian and international composers have continued to integrate Brazilian styles into larger trends in contemporary art music, and since the 1960s have especially fostered the use of experimental and electro-acoustic techniques in music.

EARLY POPULAR MUSIC, SAMBA, AND THE EMERGENCE OF CARNIVAL CULTURE

As early as the 19th century, Brazilian music entered into the developmental phases of what would become one of the most robust and diverse centers of global popular music. From the 18th century, urban (largely white) elites organized musical salons—not unlike those in contemporary Europe—for the social performance and enjoyment of popular song and dance. Short, romantic, sentimental songs in Portuguese, called *modinhas* (diminutive of *moda* or "song"), and European and Brazilian couple dances, such as *lundus* (a dance of Afro-Brazilian heritage), polkas, and waltzes, served as common repertoire by the mid-1800s. Merging such genres with the increasingly popular *habanera* rhythm out of Cuba, new Brazilian genres emerged: the *tango brasileiro* and *maxixe*, both popular dance genres in late 19th-century Rio de Janeiro, combined elements of the European polka with the *habanera* rhythm and later gave way to the choro instrumental mentioned above.

When choro began to fall out of fashion in the early 20th century, a new genre emerged that would come to dominate Brazilian popular music to the present day: the *samba*. The term had previously designated various sorts of dance genres of African origin called *rural samba*, yet by the 1920s, a newer urban genre by the same name arose in Rio de Janeiro at the hands of the same black artists still producing choro, such as the saxophonist and composer Pixinguinha (Alfreda da Rocha Viana, Jr., 1897–1973). The new urban samba featured short songs with light, driving percussion, sentimental lyrics, and instrumental accompaniment in the character of stylized ballroom or nightclub dance. Donga's (Ernesto Joaquim dos

Santos, 1890–1974) "Pelo Telefone" (By the Telephone, 1917) is credited as the first recorded urban samba, and subsequent generations of artists, including Sinhô (José Barbosa da Silva, 1888–1930), Noel Rosa (1910–1937), and Ari Barroso (1903–1964) continued to contribute new sambas to the repertoire. Carmen Miranda (1909–1955) later popularized a more melodramatic version of the urban samba style abroad through her work as a singer and actress in a series of highly successful North American movie-musicals, which nonetheless presented Brazilian (and Latin American culture more generally) in a highly exaggerated and often exoticized manner.

At the same time, samba took on another role in the materializing culture of Brazilian Carnival (carnival, a pre-Lenten Catholic festival). From the 1920s, musicians in Rio de Janeiro incorporated samba into the parade performances of percussion ensembles (called *baterias*) during carnival celebrations, especially in the city's slum districts (*favelas*). Soon thereafter musicians began to establish *escolas de samba* (samba schools) as organizational structures for distinct groups of Carnival performers. Through the 21st century, Rio's Carnival tradition has grown to include an elaborate system of parade floats and costumes, as well, and female samba dancers in large feather headdresses and sequined costumes performing fast-paced samba choreography are today iconic of the tradition. The main carnival parade today takes place at Rio's *Sambódromo* (Sambadrome), a long, alley-like stadium designed especially to accommodate such performances.

Carnival celebrations in Brazil's northeastern regions have assumed a character distinct from the more popular Rio festival. Leaving aside the elaborate costumes and parade designs, carnival in Salvador, Bahia, assumes the character of a more informal street festival in which *trios eléctricos* (large trucks equipped with sound systems and rooftop stages) serve as moving performance stages amid the crowded streets. Popular Bahian performers, such as Ivete Sangalo (1972–), provide musical performances atop the *trios eléctricos* in typical northeastern genres, such as *axé* (popular music incorporating a variety of Afro-Brazilian and pop styles), *frevo* (fast dance music derived from capoeira movements), and *forró* (a popular dance style, more commonly associated with June saint celebrations in northeast Brazil). Northeastern carnival celebrations have also provided a major platform for the development of Brazil's Afro-Brazilian musical identity with the establishment of *blocos afros* (samba schools exclusive to performers of African descent) in the 1970s. Blocos afros such as Ilê Aiyê and Olodum continue to promote and uphold African identity in Brazil through lyrical, visual, and musical references to the country's African heritage and the African diaspora.

BOSSA NOVA, MPB, AND TROPICALIA

Urban samba endured as Brazil's most prevalent style of popular music through the advent of *bossa nova* in the late 1950s. Enjoying a period of relative prosperity and political stability under President Juscelino Kubitschek (in office 1956–1961), Rio de Janeiro's privileged youth class nevertheless sought a new form of Brazilian artistic expression, which would leave behind the musically overblown and stereotyped depictions of Carmen Miranda-era samba for a higher level of cultural sophistication. Working within a large circle of poets and musicians, three artists—Antônio Carlos (Tom) Jobim (1927–1994), Vinícius de Moraes (1913–1980), and João Gilberto (1931–)—formulated and popularized a new style called *bossa nova*, which drew together voice and accompaniment in an intricate web of relaxed but highly syncopated music, complex harmonic structures, and elaborate poetry. Gilberto's 1960 album *O amor, o sorriso, e a flor* (The love, the smile, and the flower) reflects the movement's carefree, apolitical aesthetic, and its tracks—many now classic bossa nova songs—demonstrate the music's careful interaction with the poetry, as well as the complex interweaving of Gilberto's guitar in syncopation with soft, nasal vocals and muted percussion. Gilberto's later collaboration with American saxophonist Stan Getz on the 1964 bossa nova album *Getz/Gilberto* helped to advance the genre's popularity around the world, and the album's premier track "The Girl from Ipanema" remains a characteristic and well-known example of the bossa nova style.

The period of political comfort that gave rise to the bossa nova drew to a quick close in 1964 following a Brazilian military coup that deposed the leftist government and established a military regime that would hold power until 1985. As musicians struggled to find their place in the new order, their works adopted more strongly charged political undertones and saw a renewed engagement with Brazilian musical authenticity. By the late 1960s, artists such as Elis Regina (1945–1982), Chico Buarque (1944–), and Milton Nascimento (1942–)—many of whom had participated in the bossa nova movement and continued to produce bossa nova-style works—headed the emerging *Música Popular Brasileira* (Brazilian Popular Music, MPB) movement, which sought Brazil's musical roots in samba and folk music styles and folded political dissent (often veiled poetically) into its lyrics. Aside from the political bent of its lyrics, Música Popular Brasileira lacks a single defining aesthetic style, favoring instead the incorporation of a wide variety of regional musical traditions.

Though similar in the political focus of its lyrics, a roughly simultaneous movement known as *tropicália* sought to develop a new Brazilian musical aesthetic by merging Brazilian musical styles with international popular music and new electronic sounds—an aesthetic of complete artistic consumption termed "cultural cannibalism" by Brazilian writer Oswald de Andrade in 1928. The movement transpired largely in São Paulo through the work of two artists of Bahian descent, Caetano Veloso (1942–) and Gilberto Gil (1942–). Their new aesthetic ideas crystallized into a veritable musical manifesto with the album *Tropicália: ou Panis et Circenses* (Tropicalia: or Bread and Circuses, 1968), which featured the contributions of a tropicalist collective of artists, including Veloso, Gil, and Os Mutantes. Though tropicália (like Música Popular Brasileira) lacks a centrally defined musical aesthetic, much of the music produced by tropicalist artists adopts the psychedelic and experimental tones of broader global pop and rock that emerged during the 1970s. The movement proliferated for only two years (1967–1969) before Veloso and Gil were both arrested and exiled to London, though the effects of the movement were long-lasting. It remains one of the most influential aesthetic movements in Brazilian popular music history, and artists from both Música Popular Brasileira and tropicália traditions continue to contribute to Brazil's popular music today.

BRAZILIAN MUSIC TODAY

Since the end of the military regime in the 1980s, Brazilian music has continued to engage with both distinctively Brazilian musical styles and foreign international styles, creating new characteristics blends such as *samba-reggae* and promoting Brazilian artists in all facets of global pop music. Though less commonly discussed for its lack of political or musical progressiveness, *música sertaneja*—Brazil's "country music"—has drawn significant audiences to its pop-like, accordion-driven sound in recent years, and *sertaneja* artists such as Michel Teló (1981–) have achieved significant international success. Other artists, such as Marisa Monte (1967–) continue to produce widely acclaimed MPB-style works, while others such as BNegão (1973–) and Sepultura contribute to the Brazilian music scene through international genres from hip-hop to heavy metal. With Brazil gaining ground on the international stage as host to high-profile cultural events like the 2014 FIFA World Cup and the 2016 Summer Olympics, the country's rich legacy of musical traditions continues to reach and captivate new international audiences.

Danielle M. Kuntz

See also: Berimbau; Candomblé; Carnival, Music of; Samba Instruments; Samba Music

Further Reading

Avelar, Idelbar, and Christopher Dunn, eds. 2011. *Brazilian Popular Music and Citizenship*. Durham, NC: Duke University Press.

Béhague, Gerard. 1984. "Patterns of Candomblé Music Performance: An Afro-Brazilian Religious Setting." In Gerard Béhague (ed.), *Performance Practice: Ethnomusicological Perspectives,* 222–254. Westport, CT: Greenwood Press.

Fryer, Peter. 2000. *Rhythms of Resistance: African Musical Heritage in Brazil*. Middletown, CT: Wesleyan University Press.

Goldschmitt, Kariann. 2011. "Doing the Bossa Nova: The Curious Life of a Social Dance in 1960s North America." *Luso-Brazilian Review* 48(1); *New Perspectives on Brazilian Instrumental Music*, 61–78.

Hertzman, Marc A. 2013. *Making Samba: A New History of Race and Music in Brazil.* Durham, NC: Duke University Press.

Livingston-Isenhour, Tamara Elena, and Thomas George Caracas Garcia. 2005. *Choro: A Social History of a Brazilian Popular Music*. Bloomington: Indiana University Press.

Magaldi, Christina. 2004. *Music in Imperial Rio de Janeiro: European Culture in a Tropical Milieu*. Lanham, MD: Scarecrow Press.

Murphy, John. 2006. *Music in Brazil: Experiencing Music, Expressing Culture*. New York: Oxford University Press.

Perrone, Charles A., and Christopher Dunn, eds. 2001. *Brazilian Popular Music and Globalization*. Gainesville: University Press of Florida.

Reily, Suzel Ana. "Tom Jobim and the Bossa Nova Era." *Popular Music* 15(1), 1–16.

Veloso, Caetano. 2002. *Tropical Truth: A Story of Music and Revolution in Brazil*, ed. Barbara Einzig, trans. Isabel de Sena. New York: Alfred A. Knopf.

Vianna, Hermano. 1999. *The Mystery of Samba: Popular Music and National Identity in Brazil*. Chapel Hill: University of North Carolina Press.

Buena Vista Social Club

The Buena Vista Social Club originally derived its name from a popular dance club in Havana's district Buena Vista during the 1940s and 1950s. Initiated by the American guitarist Ry Cooder and the record promoter Nick Gold, the group consisted of contemporary musicians from Afro-Cuban All Stars, a Cuban band conducted by Juan de Marcos González, and altogether around 20 musicians (including Cooder and his son). They recorded an album with the same name in 1996 (released in 1997 by the English label World Circuit). This recording featured new arrangements of well-known Cuban songs, received a Grammy Award, and sold more than 8 million copies, becoming the biggest selling world music album of all time.

The history of the revitalization of authentic Cuban music did not start with this album, but in 1967 with González and his band Sierra Maestra. In 1994, they started their collaboration with World Circuit and the album ¡*Dundunbanz!*. González's idea of blending the experience of older members with the energy of the younger players led to three releases in 1997, which paid tribute to musicians of the 1950s: *Buena Vista Social Club, Introducing. . . . Rubén González*, and the Afro-Cuban All Stars's *A Toda Cuba Le Gusta*. These activities were supported by Gold, who ran the label until 1987. For the album *Buena Vista Social Club*, Gold, González, and Cooder (who produced it) worked together.

The track list (with musical forms in parentheses) of the *Buena Vista Social Club* album reflects diverse styles of Cuban traditional music popular in the Havana clubs during this time as well as influences from North America:

1. Chan Chan (son)
2. De camino a la vereda (son)
3. El cuatro de Tula (son)
4. Pueblo nuevo (danzón)
5. Dos gardenias (bolero)
6. ¿Y tú qué has hecho? (bolero)
7. Veinte años (bolero)
8. El carretero (guajira)
9. Candela (son/tumbao)
10. Amor de loca juventud (influenced by Americana/gospel/blues)
11. Orgullecida (influenced by Americana/jazz)
12. Murmullo (ballad)
13. Buena Vista Social Club (danzón)
14. La bayamesa (criolla)

Compay Segundo's 1987 song "Chan Chan" became the calling card of the Buena Vista Social Club. The texts of the songs are inseparably connected with everyday life and deal with questions of survival and love. Two traditional Cuban plucked instruments are used for the recording. An *armónico*, a mixture of a guitar and a *tres* with the tuning e-a-d'-g'g'-b-e', was developed by Segundo and played in "¿Y

> **Buena Vista Social Club *Album***
>
> Since its release in 1997, the *Bueno Vista Social Club* album by the group Buena Vista Social Club sparked a revival and continued interest in traditional Cuban music styles. As of 2015, the album had sold more than 12 million copies, millions more digital downloads, and tens of millions of YouTube plays. The album was meant to showcase and revive pre-revolutionary Cuban musical styles of the *trova* and *filin* tradition, which includes Cuban *son*, *bolero*, *guajiras*, and *danzón*. The uniqueness of these older and somewhat lesser known outside of Cuba styles is a large part of the album's appeal and continued popularity. Between 1997 and 2000, *Buena Vista Social Club* topped album charts in dozens of European countries as well as the United States. The album was, however, less commercially popular in Latin America, perhaps hinting at the complexities of cultural adoption in the European and American music industry.

tú qué has hecho?." The other instrument used is the *laúd* (*laoud*) or *laúd cubano*, which is a guitar with 12 metal strings in six double rows fixed via a peg at the edge of the body.

Although the Buena Vista Social Club was not a touring group, they gave two concerts in 1998, the first at the Carré Theatre, Amsterdam (which for most of the musicians was their European debut), and a second, as their United States debut, in July at Carnegie Hall, New York. (The latter concert was released as a live album in 2008 by World Circuit.) The German film director Wim Wenders recorded both concerts and took them as the basis of his award-winning documentary film with the same name (first released at the Berlin International Film Festival in 1999). The release of the film helped to fuel the overwhelming success of the Buena Vista Social Club.

In Europe and the United States, the success of both the album and the film led to renewed attention to Cuban traditional music and propelled the career of the Buena Vista Social Club musicians such as Ibrahim Ferrer (voice, 1927–2005), Rubén González (piano, 1919–2003), Omara Portuondo (voice, ?–1930) and Compay Segundo (voice, guitar and armónico, 1907–2003). Buena Vista Social Club became globally famous and became a registered trademark. Several albums by these musicians were published, among them Buena Vista Social Club *Presents Ibrahim Ferrer* (1999, selling more than 1.5 million copies), *Compay Segundo—Cien años de son* (1999), *Buena Vista Social Club Presents Omara Portuondo* (2000), González's *Chanchullo* (2000), and Ferrer's *Buenos Hermanos* (2003, Grammy Award). These musicians toured worldwide, won accolades, and became minor pop stars while helping fuel the global popularity of Cuban traditional music of the 1940s and 1950s. Despite the death of several band members, the ensemble, under the name *Orquestra Buena Vista Social Club*, still gives concerts to this day.

Its cold reception in Cuba aside, the success of the Buena Vista Social Club in Europe and the United States was due to several reasons which brought the music out of the circle of world music specialists and propagated a "Cubaphilia." First, contrary to other kinds of world music (traditional Chinese music, for example), the music of the Buena Vista Social Club mixes folkloric music with elements of Western pop and rock, is easy to listen to, and has danceable grooves—the song

The Cuban group Buena Vista Social Club performing live. Since 1996 they have recorded and performed a variety of Cuban musical styles and are among the most popular and successful Cuban musicians. (Rob Verhorst/Redferns)

"Chan Chan" especially has the quality of an earworm. Second, parallel to the increase of tourism at that time, people were fascinated by Cuban nostalgia and clichés, which are transferred via Wenders's film and his "postcard pictures" of Havana as "a city of grand, run-down buildings, industrial archaeology and exceptionally-gifted octogenarians." Cuba became "a 'paradise lost' for American tourism and a 'paradise found' for Europeans" (Wenders, 1999). Third, the celebration of elderly musicians with their charisma and movingly romantic stories gave a special atmosphere to both the album and the film.

The Buena Vista Social Club was not without detractors: many viewers were critical of the fact that Ry Cooder playing "Hawaiian" slide guitar and his son playing African instruments (such as the African *udu* or the Persian *dumbek*, none of which are common in Cuban music) were ubiquitously present throughout the film. For many people, though, the Buena Vista Social Club became a synonym for Cuban music. After its success, however, many younger generation Cuban musicians have struggled to move beyond the perception and mythological vision of the old Cuba created by the Buena Vista Social Club.

Jörg Jewanski

See also: Batá Drums; Puente, Tito

Further Reading

Barker, Hugh, and Yuval Taylor. 2007. "Y tú, qué has hecho? The Re-creation of Cultural Authenticity." In *Faking It: The Quest for Authenticity in Popular Music*, 297–317. New York: Norton.

Neustadt, Robert. 2002. "*Buena Vista Social Club* versus La Charanga Habanera: The Politics of Cuban Rhythm." *Journal of Popular Music Studies* 14, 139–162.

Perna, Vincenzo. 2005. "Marketing Nostalgia: The Rise of *Buena Vista Social Club*." In *Timba: The Sound of the Cuban Crisis*, 240–263. Aldershot, UK: Ashgate.

Roy, Maya. 2002. "By Way of a Provisional Epilogue: *Buena Vista Social Club* or *Timba cubana?*" In *Cuban Music*, 179–204. Princeton, NJ: Markus Wiener.

Wenders, Wim, dir. 1999. *Buena Vista Social Club* [DVD]. Amsterdam: PBS.

Bunraku

Bunraku is an elaborate Japanese puppet theater form that has captivated audiences since the late 16th century CE with its intricate combination of narrative storytelling, music, and complex puppetry. The narrative style, based on *jôruri*, an ancient and well-known narrative form, was combined with *shamisen* (a three-stringed, long-neck lute) accompaniment in the 1590s CE and later joined with puppetry to become *bunraku*. This form rose to prominence during the Edo Period (1603–1868 CE, also known as the Tokugawa Period) and despite a rapid decline after 1800 CE, enjoyed a revival after the Meiji restoration (1868 CE) (Harich-Schneider, 1973, p. 525). Although other folk theaters now include women, bunraku has been a male-only tradition since the mid-17th century CE.

The jôruri texts are not intended to be stand-alone texts, though some researchers have studied them as literary works; rather, they are intended to be narrated with the bunraku style of music, called *gidayû-bushi*. The texts fall into two categories: *jidaimono* "period pieces," and *sewamono* "contemporary pieces" (Yamada, 2008, pp. 202–203). Jidaimono are set prior to the Edo Period and usually center on *samurai*, the military class. They are typically set in five multiple-scene acts depicting grand exaggerated stories with complex expression. Sewamono, in contrast, center on the daily lives of commoners from the Edo Period and are typically shorter, less grand plays aimed at realism. These pieces are often in a faster-paced narrative style and are set into three (and sometimes two) acts. Nearly half of the approximately 150 bunraku plays are jidaimono (Yamada, 2008, pp. 202–203).

In most performances, just one *tayû*, or narrator, narrates all dramatic characters, from stern samurai to peasant women; he conveys their emotions, mental states, and actions all while working in concert with the shamisen player and puppeteers. He performs from a handwritten text and switches seamlessly from spoken recitation to sung melodies as the puppets interact with each other. Narrating the play is exhausting work and takes years to master. The tayû works closely with the shamisen player. To call the shamisen player simply an accompanist is misleading. A good gidayû-bushi musician "must [be able] to breathe with the *tayû* and express the text with him" (Yamada, 2008, p. 204) while providing a musical backdrop for the puppets' emotions and movements.

Bunraku employs a unique three-man manipulation system for the puppets that was initiated in the early 18th century CE. The lead puppeteer uses his left hand to manipulate the puppet's head from the inside and his right hand to manipulate the puppet's right arm. Two other puppeteers manipulate the puppet's left arm and legs. This teamed practice results in the puppets looking incredibly realistic.

The tayû and shamisen player sit at stage left and perform entirely in front of the audience. So that the puppets may take center stage, the puppeteers, who are seen by the audience, traditionally dress in black kimonos with black hoods to cover their faces. On occasion, a master lead puppeteer will forgo the headwear if the puppet is quite active in a performance (Yamada, 2008, p. 201).

Justin R. Hunter

See also: Kabuki; Nô Theater

Further Reading

Brandon, James R. 1997. *The Cambridge Guide to Asian Theatre.* Cambridge: Cambridge University Press.

Harich-Schneider, Eta. 1973. *A History of Japanese Music.* London: Oxford University Press.

Yamada, Tieko [Chieko]. 2001. "Theatrical Genres: Bunraku." In Robert Provine, Yosihiko Yokumaru, and Lawrence Witzleben (eds.), *Garland Encyclopedia of World Music; Vol. 7: China, Japan, and Korea,* 663–665. New York: Routledge.

Yamada, Chieko. 2008. "*Gidayū-bushi*: Music of the *Bunraku* Puppet Theatre." In Alison McQueen Tokita and David W. Hughes (eds.), *The Ashgate Research Companion to Japanese Music,* 197–228. Surrey, UK: Ashgate.

C

Cajun Music

The term "Cajun music," while enveloping a variety of styles, refers to a form of American music indigenous to southern Louisiana. Heavy on fiddles and accordions, it is often exuberant in character, though its themes can also embrace life's tragedies. Along with being extremely popular at dance halls, it is also played at funerals. Its roots lie in the Old World ballads of the French-speaking Acadians of eastern Canada. Cajun music is sometimes mentioned synonymously with zydeco. Though they share characteristics of their Louisiana heritage, the two are different musical forms in both instrumentation and cultural derivation. Cajun music has influenced country and western as well as American popular music, with some noted Cajun musicians including Cléoma Breaux, Joe Falcon, Dewey Balfa, and Doug Kershaw.

In the same manner that English-speaking Americans corrupted the word "Indians" to "Injuns," the Acadian exiles from Canada came to be called "Acajien," and ultimately "Cajun." Southern Louisiana was settled by French colonists as early as the 17th century, but the Cajuns evolved differently. They were French-speaking people who were forcibly expelled by the English from their home in the area of eastern Canada called Acadia, consisting largely of today's Nova Scotia, New Brunswick, and Prince Edward Island. As the countries of France and England entered the hostilities of the Seven Years' War (1756–1763), the position of the Canadian settlement became precarious. What came to be known as the Great Expulsion saw the exile of around 15,000 Acadians to British colonies around the Western Hemisphere. Historians estimate that about half died, either on the sea voyages or in the harsh conditions of the new lands where they found themselves. Those in Louisiana fared better than many, attracting more Acadian settlers to that area. Though some prospered, many became subsistence farmers, developing their own Cajun-French dialect along with a unique folk culture of music and cuisine.

When the bulk of Acadians came to Louisiana in 1764, they brought traditional ballads from France which formed the basis for their new musical form, which was layered with sad stories of losing their homes and loved ones. Often these songs were sung a capella (unaccompanied by musical instruments). Some musicians managed to bring, acquire, or make their own simple violins. By the late 19th century, accordions were introduced into Louisiana, and found to be perfect for both the music and the settings in which it was played.

The ballads, with frequent themes of death, loneliness, hardship, and lost love, were traditionally sung at weddings, funerals, or house parties (*bals de maison*) for a few friends and family members. The Cajuns soon found that they also liked to socialize with large groups. Dancing in public dance halls allowed them to mix with a variety of people, court potential mates, and generally enjoy life despite its hardships. Spirits flowed freely, and the accordion could distinctly be heard over the noisy party atmosphere. Additionally, singing Cajun music, in the worldwide oral storytelling tradition, allowed them to share and preserve their heritage in a semi-literate community.

The Cajuns were not as insular as many believed, but the popularity of their music was essentially regional until the recording technology of the early 20th century brought it to the world. Some of the earliest recordings of Cajun music were captured in the late 1920s by folklorist Alan Lomax. What is generally recognized as the first mass-market recording of a Cajun song appeared in 1928 with the release of "Allons à Lafayette" ("Let's Go to Lafayette") by Cléoma Breaux and Joe Falcon. Other noted Cajun musicians of that era include Amédé Ardoin, the Breaux Brothers, Segura Brothers, Leo Soileau with accordionist Mayuse Lafleur, and Dennis McGee with fiddlers Sady Courville or Ernest Frugé.

In the 1930s, the Great Depression resulted in migrations of large numbers of people and many left Louisiana to find work elsewhere, while others arrived from other parts of the country. As they mingled with other groups, Cajun musicians began singing more frequently in both French and English, so as to be understood. Listening to the radio, they were also able to borrow tunes and chord progressions from Texas swing and country music, which were popular.

When oil was discovered in southern Louisiana, new highways carried people from outside the state who brought their own musical styles. Some Cajuns moved to east Texas to find jobs in the oilfields and refineries there, and thus were exposed to different musical forms. Both factors led to the incorporation of country and western music into the Cajun format. New instruments, such as bass, drums, and steel guitar, were added to the mix. The dominance of the accordion in Cajun music waned for a while, but had a resurgence in the late 1940s due to the popularity of accordionists such as Iry LeJeune and Nathan Abshire. Many returning World War II veterans sought the familiarity of traditional sounds, and the accordion and fiddle once again became predominant.

In 1946, the Cajun song "Jole Blon" ("Jolie Blonde" or "Pretty Blonde") became a national hit record when it was performed by Harry Choates. Interest in Cajun music took a tremendous leap forward in 1952 when country star Hank Williams recorded "Jambalaya (On the Bayou)." The song was based on the Cajun melody "Grand Texas," which concerned a lost love. "Jambalaya," however, was upbeat and referenced the fun-loving side of Cajun life, including poling a pirogue (flat-bottomed boat) down the bayou to get married. At the feast afterward, the gathering goes "hog wild," as the attendees drink from fruit jars and eat Cajun delicacies. The song has been covered by everyone from the Carpenters to the Muppets, with hit international versions appearing in languages from Croatian to Mandarin Chinese.

In the 1960s, Cajun fiddler Doug Kershaw was a popular guest on network television and at rock venues such as the Fillmore East, further expanding the nationwide audience for Cajun music. In 1964, Cajun musician Dewey Balfa was acclaimed at the Newport Folk Festival, heralding what was known as the "Cajun Renaissance" which has lasted to the present. It demonstrates pride in the Cajun culture by preserving its French-Cajun language and unique traditions. In

1972, the Council for the Development of French in Louisiana started an annual festival that came to be known as Festivals Acadien et Creole. In 2007, a new Grammy category was announced for "Best Zydeco or Cajun Music Album" in its folk music field. Award recipients include Terrance Simien and the Zydeco Experience, BeauSoleil avec Michael Doucet, Chubby Carrier and the Bayou Swamp Band, and Buckwheat Zydeco. The category is now part of the larger Best Regional Roots Music category.

Today, Cajun music draws from its own tradition and local flavor as well as outside contemporary musical forms. Live music, which allows performers and audience to interact, remains its optimal experience. Many popular venues for live Cajun music can be found in the dance halls and restaurants of Lafayette and Breaux Bridge, Louisiana. Annual events like Festivals Acadien et Creole in Lafayette and the Breaux Bridge Crawfish Festival expose huge crowds to Cajun music.

Cajun fiddler Dewey Balfa in 1981. Balfa helped popularize Cajun music. (Philip Gould/Corbis via Getty Images)

Nancy Hendricks

See also: Accordion (Americas); Bluegrass; Fiddle; Jazz; Zydeco

Further Reading

Ancelet, Barry Jean. 1989. *Cajun Music: Its Origins and Development.* Lafayette: Center for Louisiana Studies, University of Southwestern Louisiana (currently University of Louisiana Lafayette).

Brasseaux, Ryan Andre. 2009. *Cajun Breakdown: The Emergence of an American-Made Music.* New York: Oxford University Press.

Broven, John. 1983. *South to Louisiana: The Music of the Cajun Bayous.* Gretna, LA: Pelican Publishing.

Gould, Philip. 1992. *Cajun Music and Zydeco.* Baton Rouge: Louisiana State University Press.

Calypso

Calypso (sometimes called *Kaiso*) is a Caribbean song style that originated in Trinidad and Tobago. Though calypso is popular throughout the Anglophone Caribbean and its diaspora, the people of Trinidad and Tobago claim calypso as a vital component of their national history and cultural identity. Most scholars agree that calypso first emerged in Trinidad, though it is clearly related to other West Indian genres of popular music that display West African-derived syncopations and emphasis on song texts of praise and derision.

The development of calypso is closely linked with the history of Trinidadian slavery. Christopher Columbus claimed the island for Spain in 1498, though it remained largely undeveloped until after 1783 when the *Cedula of Population* guaranteed free land to Roman Catholic settlers. Those who took advantage of the offer were mostly planters from neighboring French Antillean islands who brought their slaves along with them. By the time the British seized Trinidad in 1797, these new settlers largely accounted for the more than 10,000 slaves (a majority of the island's total population) working on sugar, coffee, cocoa, and cotton plantations. As production expanded, so did the importation of slaves, to the point that in 1808—one year after the end of the British slave trade—the number of Trinidadian slaves more than doubled to nearly 22,000. Slavery was finally abolished in 1838. The late introduction of the plantation economy, followed quickly by the end of the slave trade and the abolition of slavery, resulted in the preservation of African traditions to a greater degree in Trinidad than in other locales such as, for example, the United States, where a longer intervening period between the end of the slave trade (1807) and the abolition of slavery (1865) stopped significant infusions of native African culture into enslaved populations.

After emancipation, Afro-Trinidadians exerted profound cultural influence despite having their actions carefully controlled by colonial authorities. Most relevant for calypso was the creolization of Carnival, a pre-Lenten festival rooted in Catholic folk tradition that was brought to the Caribbean by Europeans but has remained largely the domain of Afro-Caribbeans since the late 1800s. Afro-Trinidadians began celebrating Carnival even before emancipation, though the practice gained widespread traction after 1838, especially in Port of Spain. Whereas Trinidadian planters and colonial elites conversed in a mixture of Spanish, French, and English, Creole—with a vocabulary comprised of French and African elements—became the lingua franca among slaves and remained so after emancipation until English ultimately took precedence in the early 20th century. Accounts of Carnival-time songs sung in Creole appear in newspaper reports from the late 19th century, but it was not until 1900 that the term *calypso* was first used in print to describe them. Though numerous theories have been proposed to explain the etymology of this term, it probably derives from an Anglicization of the Hausa word *kaicho* or *kaiso*, an exclamation of triumph or contempt. Today, calypso aficionados still use the word *kaiso* to describe music of calypsonians.

Calypso's foundations lay in the music of 19th-century *kalinda* bands comprised of singers and drummers who sang to encourage or demoralize combatants in Carnival stick-fighting competitions. Clashing bands usually offered a single fighter from each group; the rest would sing and drum to strengthen the will of their respective champions. Each band was led by a *chantwell*, a kind of singing musical director, who used boastful, challenging, and satirical language sung in call-and-response dialogue with the crowd. This call-and-response style of calypso was known as a *lavway* (from French *la voix*, "the voice") and later as a road march, this indicating its use in Carnival parades. After the use of drums was banned from Carnival in 1884, calypso was usually accompanied by *tamboo bamboo*. One of the earliest recorded examples of a tamboo bamboo-accompanied lavway is Jules Sims's "Bagai Sala Que Pocheray Moin," released in 1914 when the style was already regarded as old-fashioned. Of note on this recording is the Creole song text and long-breathed descending contour of the repetitive melodic phrases, the latter of which remains an important feature of calypso today.

By the 1920s, the songs of the chantwell were highly anticipated entertainment in the weeks leading up to Carnival. To meet public demand, entrepreneurial promoters organized pre-Carnival shows for paying customers to hear popular chantwells sing individually and with each other in *picong* style, an improvised kind of calypso in which singers alternately boast of their own prowess and insult their opponents. The music performed in these so-called calypso tents diverged from the road march most importantly in terms of musical accompaniment and song structure. Rather than tamboo bamboo, tent calypso was accompanied by a band of string and wind instruments—chief among them guitar, *cuatro*, clarinet, flute, trumpet, and violin—borrowed from popular Latin-derived genres such as *parang*. Despite a rather sparse accompaniment, the 1914 recordings of Julian Whiterose are the earliest preserved examples of tent calypso style, then in its infancy. The vocal for Whiterose's "Iron Duke in the Land" is self-confident, boastful, and accompanied in a minor key by cuatro and guitar. The song's structure features call-and-response sections reminiscent of the road march, but with eight-line verses built in rhyming couplets. "Iron Duke in the Land" also marks a shift from Creole to English song texts.

Calypso underwent significant development in the 1930s. Indicating the chantwell's shift from lavway leader to composer and stage performer, chantwells singing in calypso tents became calypsonians who continued to compose both road march and tent calypsos. By the end of the decade, road-march calypsos were most often arranged for steel orchestras rather than tamboo bamboo, with each song's distinctive melody not sung by the calypsonian himself, but instead played by the tenor steelpans. As bands paraded through the streets, crowds marched and sang alongside. Tent calypso instrumentation also shifted to reflect global pop music trends, with bands featuring fewer strings, more winds, and the addition of trap sets. Eight-line verses, harmonies built around I-IV-V chord progressions, and distinctive *habanera*-style bass lines became defining characteristics of the genre. "Rum and Coca Cola" by Lord Invader (born Rupert Grand [1914–1961]) is a good example of this tent calypso style.

"Rum and Coca Cola" also demonstrates how calypsonians used clever lyrical metaphors to draw attention to social issues. The song was written during the "American Invasion" of Trinidad, a period during and after World War II (1939–1945) when the United States maintained two military bases in Trinidad. In this calypso, Invader draws upon a metaphor of mixing rum, a typical Caribbean drink, with Coca-Cola, the quintessential American beverage, to draw his audience's attention to licentious sexual behavior between Trinidadian prostitutes and U.S. servicemen.

The Calypso Monarch competition was first organized in 1939 as a formalized calypso contest played out on a national stage. One of the most memorable Calypso King winners is Grenada-born Mighty Sparrow (born Slinger Francisco [1935–]) whose 1956 calypso "Jean and Dinah" celebrated the exit of the majority of United States servicemen from the island and simultaneously chastised those Trinidadians who had been dependent upon the revenue generated by their presence. Like Invader, Sparrow used the metaphor of prostitution to make his point.

"Jean and Dinah" is remarkable not only for its double entendre, but also for its tweaking of structural details. While maintaining the traditional eight-line verse and habanera bass line, Sparrow added a catchy refrain and used riff-based melodies throughout, all set to an upbeat, pop-inspired groove. Revelers enjoyed this fresh sound so much so that "Jean and Dinah" also won the Carnival Road March competition that same year—the first calypso to garner both titles simultaneously. The Road March winner is the song played most often as masquerade bands pass specified judging points along a designated Carnival parade route. In 1956, these songs were played exclusively by steelbands in lavway fashion. Although most calypsos tend to be forgotten as the excitement of Carnival fades away year after year, "Jean and Dinah" remains an important touchstone of Trinidadian musical and cultural memory, not only for its musical quality but also for the significance of the calypsonian's words. On one level, "Jean and Dinah" is a fun, danceable tune. But on another, Sparrow's lyrics continue to resonate with Trinidadians because of the playful juxtaposition of literal and figurative meanings that help intellectuals and laymen alike process complex social issues in an understandable way.

With the exception of a handful of calypsonians who traveled to New York and London for performances and recording sessions beginning in the 1930s, calypso largely remained a Caribbean phenomenon until 1945 when the Andrews Sisters recorded "Rum and Coca Cola." It became the group's biggest hit and introduced North American audiences to calypso, albeit with a jazzier sound and transformed lyrics that emphasized romantic love rather than Invader's critique of prostitution. This sanitization of calypso's social commentary would continue with Jamaican-American singer Harry Belafonte's phenomenally successful album *Calypso*, which was released in 1956, the same year as Sparrow's groundbreaking "Jean and Dinah." The first long-playing (LP) record in history to sell a million copies, *Calypso* sparked a craze for exotic sounds that threatened to overtake rock-and-roll's popularity. Of the 11 songs on the album, only two—"Brown Skin Girl" and "Man Smart (Woman Smarter)"—are Trinidadian calypsos, both composed by King Radio (Norman Span). The rest are arrangements of Caribbean folk songs and Jamaican-style *mento* tunes. Perhaps the most enduring of these is "Day-O," Belafonte's most memorable hit. The appeal of *Calypso* stemmed from Belafonte's expressive baritone voice, silky backing vocals, *mambo*-inspired Latin percussion accompaniment, and Belafonte's energetic, faux-West Indian accent. Though hints of American Invasion-era social commentary remain in King Radio's tunes, the social import of calypso so important in the work of Trinidadian calypsonians is noticeably absent in *Calypso*. Belafonte's success inspired numerous imitators.

Notable among them was Maya Angelou, future poet laureate of the United States, whose 1957 album *Miss Calypso* conflates Belafonte-style calypso with a litany of exotic, pan-African images.

The exotic image of the Caribbean presented in North American tropes of calypso did not diminish traditional practice in Trinidad. The 1960s and 1970s saw several musical and social changes affect the calypso. Perhaps most important during this era was the emergence of *soca*, today's dominant celebratory Carnival music style, the invention of which is widely credited to calypsonian Lord Shorty (born Garfield Blackman [1941–2000]). Shorty's 1973 song "Indrani" demonstrates this nascent style, which blends Indian-Trinidadian musical elements with calypso. Women also made inroads into the traditionally male-dominated calypso arena with the women-only Calypso Queen competition, first organized in the late 1960s. In its early years, Tobago-born Calypso Rose (born McArtha Lewis [1940–]) dominated this contest; then she made history by winning the 1977 Road March and later placing first in 1978's Calypso King competition, an event that prompted the competition to be renamed to the gender-neutral Calypso Monarch. Despite Rose's achievement, another woman would not be crowned Calypso Monarch until Singing Sandra in 1999.

Today, calypso remains a beacon of Trinidadian identity. Despite calypsonians' attempts to keep abreast with musical trends, however, young Trinidadians tend to regard calypso as old fashioned and largely prefer more recent soca, reggae, and North American pop for everyday listening. Nonetheless, virtually all Trinidadians become calypso fans during Carnival season. Veteran calypsonians like the popular road-march calypsonians, especially those who claim the Monarch title, are able to earn a living from performances throughout the Anglophone Caribbean and in the West Indian diaspora areas in North America and London where Trinidadian expatriates have cultivated an appreciation for the music of their homeland.

Christopher L. Ballengee

See also: Chutney Soca; Soca; Steelpan; Tassa Drumming

Further Reading
Crowley, Daniel J. 1959. "Toward a Definition of Calypso (Part 1)." *Ethnomusicology* 3(2), 61–62.
Guilbault, Jocelyne. 2007. *Governing Sound: The Cultural Politics of Trinidad's Carnival Musics*. Chicago: University of Chicago Press.
Hill, Eroll. 1967. "On the Origin of the Term Calypso." *Ethnomusicology* 11(3), 359–363.
Williams, Eric. 1962. *History of the People of Trinidad and Tobago*. Buffalo, NY: Eworld.

Candomblé

Candomblé is one of the four main religions of Brazil (with Catholicism, Protestantism, and native religions) and one of the four main Afro-Brazilian religions. The name is sometimes considered an umbrella term for the others (e.g., Candomblé, Tambor de Mina, Batuque, and Umbanda). A Brazilian census in 2000 found 140,000 Candomblé followers (0.08% of the population), although real numbers might differ because, as a long-stigmatized religion, many individuals have declared

Catholicism their "official" religion, even though they follow Candomblé as a primary or secondary faith.

As a word of dubious etymology, "Candomblé" may have originally come from the name of a dance of African origin as well as a Yoruba word for "prayer." Candomblé was developed by groups of African descendants, in large percentage from the Yoruba peoples of Western Africa. These groups initially settled in Salvador da Bahia, the first capital of Brazil. It is estimated that about 3 to 5 million Africans were chartered to Brazil starting in the 16th century. With them travelled ancient African traditions such as the worship of *Orixás*, deities often representing divinized clan ancestors, thus providing a strong link with the past. Orixás were thought of as individuals capable of manipulating the forces of nature for purposes of survival, and often taking human frames of mind such as vanity, jealousy, maternal instincts, and even sexual drives.

In Brazil, Candomblé operated as a cosmological fetishist practice of numerous African ethnic groups that were obliged to convert to and observe Catholicism—Brazil's official religion until the Constitution of 1891; these groups devised syncretic approaches that blended the two religious traditions. For example, they established parallels between African deities and Catholic saints, and observed feast days as well. Some freed or runaway slaves established rural settlements called *quilombo*, where they practiced *batuques* (nocturnal drumming sessions) that often involved spirit possession. Former slaves and slaves residing in urban areas and more closely subordinated to the Church also formed confraternities known as *Irmandades*, which consisted of social outreach organizations that contributed to the preservation of African cultural symbols and traditions, and whose members frequented Candomblé ceremonies. Hence, Candomblé is intricately mixed with Catholic rites. In Brazil, African culture likewise influenced Catholic traditions in various ways, including infiltrations into church music and sculpture where certain saints acquired African complexion and attire.

Candomblé is a matriarchal religion, led by women, and is noted as a religion with a high tolerance of homosexuals (*adés*), who often hold positions of leadership. Candomblé developed from various free or runaway slave groups that organized themselves in small tracts of land called *terreiros* (farmyards). The highly hierarchical schema of these groups presented many similarities with the Catholic structure. Like independent churches, the *terreiros* were (and still are) led by the *Ialorixá* (*Mãe-de-Santo*, a priestess, or *Babalorixá*, a male priest) whose members are named *Iaôs* (*filhos-de-santo*, daughters- and sons-of-saints) and *Abiãs* (initiates). The formation of *terreiros* helped displaced Africans to recreate a semblance of the family and ethnic ties lost during colonialism. As such, the *terreiros* combine a religious and social function. Ialorixás also act as healers and spiritual guides to their sons and daughters. *Terreiros* usually have a main house with several rooms (some for living persons and some for Orixás themselves), a room designated for private consultations, and a special ceremonial room with a marker at the center of the floor to indicate the sacred arena of Candomblé.

Similar to Catholicism, Candomblé followers believe in one supreme God, *Olorum*, who rules the world through several smaller deities, the Orixás, each associated with particular attributes (e.g., *Iemanjá* is the goddess of the ocean, *Xangô* the god of fire and thunder, etc.) and song/rhythmic calling. Being part of a gendered tradition, the Orixás are seen as male or female, yet frequently adopt human characteristics such as desire, jealousy, fear, surprise, and the like.

Music and dance are an integral part of Candomblé ceremonials. Prior to worship (usually Friday evenings, sometimes lasting through the night), the musicians' bandstand is purified with water and powdery substances. The ceremony also entails animal and food offerings (*despacho*), special dress for the participants, and opening gestures (e.g., kneeling three times at the entrance of the house). The *agogô* (bell-like metal instrument) is hit with a stick that provides the basic tempo summoning all to the start of the ceremony. This is followed by an *Orô*, groups of songs in specific sequences calling each of the Orixás, always starting with *Exú*. The extensive musical repertoire—often seven to 21 songs per Orixá—is performed by three main drummers. The lead and more experienced musician, *Alabê*, plays a larger drum calling the rhythms of each Orixá and intoning the texts, usually answered by the dancers (usually women) arranged in a circle at the center of the sacred arena. The songs are repetitive and intense, inducing a state of mental fatigue whose response is a hypnotic state. In a trancelike state, the individual "being possessed" communicates with the Orixá who is said to descend through the person's head to take human form. In such state, the individual may present violent body contortions, with moaning and screaming, which may last for several hours. Other audience members may also participate by either clapping or singing.

In this highly ritualistic scenario, musical instruments are considered living beings with the special function of inviting the Orixás to partake in the ceremony. The instruments become "sacred" after an initial baptism and are also fed offerings such as oils and flowers on an annual basis, to renew their "power." The main instrument is the *atabaque*, a long wooden drum covered by animal skin (head) that is tied to the drum by ropes in a ring form and adjusted with wooden wedges. Atabaques are also placed in a stand. Constructed in three different sizes (*rum, rumpi*, and *lê*), atabaques are generally played with hands or sticks (*agidavis*), by an ensemble of three male drummers.

Candomblé players also participate in numerous musical activities throughout the year, including Carnival and popular bands. African rhythms and influence have extended to cultural and touristic events in Salvador da Bahia and even abroad. Historically, Candomblé underwent further changes with its dispersal to different parts of the country. For example, after emancipation, thousands of slaves migrated south to metropolitan areas such as São Paulo and Rio de Janeiro, where Candomblé assumed a more urban and syncretic approach, called *Umbanda*. In Umbanda, the Orixás underwent a more dichotomous evolution, being divided into "good" or "bad" entities whose polarized features more closely resemble Christian dogma, particularly its division between heaven and hell. Because some of the "bad" Orixás were interpreted as representing evil beings, many Christians tended to marginalize not only this Afro-Brazilian religion but also its followers.

As an oral tradition, Candomblé has suffered significant challenges as it tries to remain competitive in the 21st-century religious market, with increasing reliance on high-tech capabilities and business models (e.g., rise of evangelical megachurches). As a complex system with closely guarded initiation practices, codes, and symbols that represent long-term kinships with African clan organizations, Candomblé by nature tends to veer away from highly visible and more impersonal vehicles of transmission, such as mass media and technology. It is likely that Candomblé will survive into the future, but with varying forms and modifications.

Silvia M. Lazo

See also: Carnival, Music of; Samba Instruments; Samba Music

Further Reading

Béhague, Gerard. 1982. "Ecuadorian, Peruvian and Brazilian Ethnomusicology: A General View." *Latin American Music Review* 3(1), 17–35.

Béhague, Gerard. 1984. "Patterns of *Candomblé* Music Performance: An Afro-Brazilian Religious Setting." In Gerard Béhague (ed.), *Performance Practice: Ethnomusicological Perspectives*, 222–254. Westport, CT: Greenwood Press.

Béhague, Gerard. 1986. "Musical Change: A Case Study from South America." *World of Music* 28(1), 16–25.

Henry, Clarence Bernard. 2000. "Religious and Musical Expressions of Candomblé in Salvador da Bahia, Brazil, and Los Angeles, California." PhD diss., UCLA.

Johnson, Paul Christopher. 2002. *Secrets, Gossips and Lies: The Transformation of Candomblé*. Oxford: Oxford University Press.

Lewis, J. Lowell. 1992. *Ring of Liberation: Deceptive Discourse in Brazilian Capoeira*. Chicago: University of Chicago Press.

Mendoza de Arce, Daniel. 1981. "A Structural Approach to the Rural Society and Music of the Río de la Plata and Southern Brazil." *Latin American Music Review* 2(1), 66–90.

Cantopop

Cantonese popular music (Cantopop) is a cultural product mainly produced in Hong Kong, but it is circulated worldwide. A primary dialect of Hong Kong, Canton (Guangdong) province, and its vicinity, Cantonese has nine tones and is preconstructed musically. Thus, writing Cantonese lyrics is particularly challenging. Since the 1970s, Hong Kong has been the main production site for Cantopop. It first spread to East and Southeast Asia in the 1970s, then to mainland China and overseas Chinese communities around the world following the Chinese diaspora and emigration waves in the 1980s. According to the International Federation of the Phonographic Industry (IFPI), the peak of Cantopop was in 1996, with U.S. $231.5 million in retail value sales.

Before Cantopop became popular, Cantonese opera, Mandarin Chinese popular music (Mandopop), and English popular music were the mainstream musics in Hong Kong. Cantonese opera was a popular form of entertainment for Hong Kong locals. Mandopop was mainly imported from Shanghai, and sometimes complemented movies in the early days. The Beatlemania in the 1960s and the Beatles' visit to Hong Kong in 1964 not only led to the increased popularity of English popular music, but also created a trend among Hong Kong youths to play music in a band setting.

The development of Cantopop was greatly influenced by the southward migration of musical talents, including lyricists, songwriters, and Mandopop producers, during the Japanese invasion and the Chinese Civil War from 1946 to 1949. The arrival of a large number of postwar, Cantonese-speaking migrants from mainland China provided manpower for the industrialization of Hong Kong. Following the 1967 riots, which originated as a labor dispute but later turned into a pro-communist demonstration, Hong Kong locals started to search for their own distinct identity. At that time, the working class made up a large portion of the Hong Kong population; more than one-third of the population was living in the government-built resettlement buildings. The development of the local free television (TV) industry, with the establishment of Television Broadcasts Ltd. (TVB) in 1967, provided a cheap form of entertainment for the working class. Therefore, locals started to build up their cultural identity through TV programs as well as the Cantopop songs attached to them. It is not surprising that the first popularized Cantopop song, "The Fatal Irony," was a TV drama theme song. Hong Kong music scholars agree that this song marks the beginning of the Cantopop era in 1974, as it altered the public's perception of Cantopop by merging Chinese traditional and Western musical styles. Sam Hui Kwun Kit's use of colloquial Cantonese in his music also contributed to the popularization of Cantopop in the same time period. TV dramas and Hong Kong-produced movies, along with using colloquial Cantonese in songs, facilitated the circulation of Cantopop locally as well as overseas.

During the 1970s, the structure of Cantopop songs became standardized. According to the renowned lyricist and songwriter Wong Jum Sum, Cantopop followed the basic format of AABA, which was modeled after American popular music and was adapted by popular music songwriters in Shanghai (Wong, 2003, pp. 35, 96–98). Western music labels, such as EMI, set up branch offices, recording studios, and a record manufacturing factory in Shanghai as early as 1914. There were three reasons for Cantopop to adapt to this format: the influence of Mandopop imported from Shanghai; the consequential relationship between the British colonial rule, compulsory English education, and musical taste; and the fact that songwriters such as Joseph Koo were educated in Western countries.

The golden age of Cantopop was between the 1980s and mid-1990s. During that time, album sales were high, and many outstanding Cantopop singers enjoyed great fame not only in Hong Kong, but also in East and Southeast Asia, because of the Chinese diaspora and the success of Hong Kong TV dramas and movies overseas. Some of these cross-continent Cantopop stars were Anita Mui Yim Fong, Leslie Cheung Kwok Wing, Alan Tam Wing Lun, and the "Four Heavenly Kings"—Jacky Cheung Hok Yau, Andy Lau Tak Wah, Leon Lai Ming, and Aaron Kwok Fu Shing. The deaths of Anita Mui and Leslie Cheung in 2003 were considered the end of the golden era of Cantopop by the media.

From 1982 to 1996, the New Talent Singing Awards, co-hosted by TVB and the local music label Capital Artists, fed new quality singers into the Cantopop industry. Many Cantopop stars were either the winners of or high-placing contestants in this competition, such as Anita Mui, Jacky Cheung, Hacken Lee Hak Kan, Leon Lai Ming, Andy Hui Chi On, Sammi Cheng Sau Man, Eason Chan Yik Shun, Miriam Yeung Chin Wah, and Denise Ho Wan Sze. The termination of the collaboration between TVB and Capital Artists, as well as the renaming of the competition, drastically reduced its influence in the industry.

Technological advances, such as piracy and digitalization of music, led to the decline of Cantopop. This decline was exacerbated by the industry's emphases on karaoke songs (K-song) and an infusion of poorly trained singers, which turned many musical talents away. K-song was first developed to accommodate the demand of the karaoke business, but later was simplified to match the skills of poorly trained singers. The term *K-song* sometimes carries a negative connotation. K-songs often share the theme of love, and are characterized by slow and catchy melodies, easy-to-remember and even highly repetitive lyrics, and narrow pitch ranges. Meanwhile, the mainland Chinese audience became less interested in Hong Kong-produced Cantopop, as Hong Kong lost its uniqueness after its sovereignty was returned to China in 1997. Competing with the high-quality music production of Japanese and Korean popular music (J-Pop and K-Pop), as well as Mandopop produced primarily in Taiwan, the market of Cantopop inevitably shrank. Since the 1980s, some Cantopop songs have been re-arrangements of J-Pop and K-Pop music, such as Leslie Cheung's "Monica" and Sammi Cheng's "Faith." In recent decades, Eason Chan and Joey Yung Cho Yee dominated the best male and female singer awards respectively, while Lin Xi and Wyman Wong Wai Man are the two main lyricists.

It was not until recently that political elements appeared in Cantopop, accompanied by the locals' increasing awareness of the relationship between popular music and politics. Prior to the repatriation of Hong Kong in 1997, some scholars argued that the link between Cantopop and local politics was weak, because (1) fans did not relate Cantopop songs to politics, and (2) political messages were not explicit in Cantopop, although others maintained that Cantopop lyrics embodied cultural (and political) ideologies. Lately, the media and audience have started to interpret Cantopop songs through political lenses. For example, "Boundless Oceans, Vast Skies," a song by the local rock band Beyond released in 1993, has the theme of pursuing one's dream without hesitation. Named as "the song of Hong Kong," protestors have been singing it since 2012 in various protest venues to demonstrate their determination. Nevertheless, controversies were generated about how the Hong Kong Dome Festival in 2013 and 2014 drew youth participants away from the annual July 1st protest. Two local bands, RubberBand and Mr., were being criticized by the locals for their participation in the festival in 2013. Both singers and lyricists convey their political stance in Cantopop songs, especially lyricists Lin Xi and Adrian Chow Pok Yin, and singers Denise Ho and Anthony Wong Yiu Ming, who are the co-founders of Big Love Alliance fighting for the rights of the LGBTQ community, as well as Kay Tse On Kei, whose songs advocate for the lower and working classes of Hong Kong.

Hei Ting (Hety) Wong

See also: Chinese Pop; J-Pop; K-Pop

Further Reading

Ho, Wai Chung. 2003. "Between Globalisation and Localisation: A Study of Hong Kong Popular Music." *Popular Music* 22(2), 143–157.

Tse, Ka Ho. 2012. "The Literature of Hong Kong Cantonese Popular Music and the Local Cultural Ideology." *Sinological Research of East Asia* 2, 275–281.

Witzleben, J. Lawrence. 1999. "Cantopop and Mandapop in Pre-Postcolonial Hong Kong: Identity Negotiation in the Performances of Anita Mui Yim-Fong." *Popular Music* 18(2), 241–258.

Wong, Chi Chung (Elvin). 1997. "Making and Using Pop Music in Hong Kong." MPhil thesis, The University of Hong Kong.

Wong, Jum Sum. 2003. "The Rise and Decline of Cantopop: A Study of Hong Kong Popular Music (1949–1997)." PhD diss., The University of Hong Kong.

Caribbean Art Music

The popular and folk musics of the Caribbean region have large international audiences and are widely studied worldwide. This music includes styles such as reggae, calypso, and merengue, and regional instruments such as the steelpan. The region's art music, though less widely known, is in no way less alive.

The distinction between art music and folk music is not always clear. Throughout history, composers of art music have drawn on folk themes, melodies, and rhythms, weaving them into formal works of classical structure. One major distinction remains between the two: folk music is typically an oral tradition. Art music, however, is a written tradition and focuses on the interpretation of, rather than the improvisation by, the performer. Western-style staff notation records the intention of the composer and directs the performer.

Caribbean art music is as varied as the island nations that comprise the region. The populations and cultures of those nations are the product of European colonialism. In pre-colonial times, many of the Caribbean islands had native populations, some of whom fiercely resisted colonization. But the natives were soon overwhelmed by two groups of newcomers: Europeans, who came either to earn fortunes to send home, or else to settle permanently; and slaves brought from Africa to provide labor for the plantation economies of the islands. The fusion of these two heritages, the European and the African, created the many unique "creole" cultures of the Caribbean. Colonizers came from many European nations, predominantly England, France, Spain, and the Netherlands, accounting for many of the social, cultural, and linguistic differences between colonies. Furthermore, control of individual islands often passed back and forth over the centuries, based on changing European political rivalries and alliances. Therefore, a Caribbean island may demonstrate cultural traditions derived from multiple European colonizers.

The slave newcomers, whose homelands were mainly in the widely diverse regions of West Africa, brought to the New World their own languages and cultural practices. These African practices, particularly music, dance, and drumming, were frequently suppressed. Missionaries and clergy condemned such traditions as indecent, and slave owners were quick to curtail any practice they feared could lead to slave uprisings. By adopting elements from European art music—the music of the colonizers—African musical traditions survived in hybrid, "creolized" forms.

Art music arrived and survived in the Caribbean through various means. Firstly, many colonizers were eager to maintain ties to their homelands and to recreate the lives of the European cultural elite. Musical parties and private balls were popular among the European upper classes and were imitated in the colonies. Composed dance music evolved from imported ballroom styles such as quadrille, contradance, and waltz, and many islands have unique local dance-music traditions: the Antillean waltz of Curaçao, the biguine of Martinique, the kwadril of St. Lucia, the danza of Puerto Rico, the méringue of Haiti. The islands of the former Netherlands Antilles are especially rich in creole dance music. Jan Gerard Palm (1857–1907), father of a musical dynasty, and Wim Statius Muller, both of Curaçao, composed waltzes, polkas, and mazurkas.

The Christian church provided another motivation and opportunity for art music in the Caribbean when missionaries brought Christianity to the islands. Music plays an important role in church services and funerals. At such events, musical choices—from hymn singing to drumming—vary by denomination. Cuban Esteban Salas y Castro (1725–1803), a priest and choirmaster at the cathedral of Santiago de Cuba, composed church music influenced by classical and Baroque styles.

Another source of art music in the Caribbean was the military. Music, especially drumming, has historically been an important aspect of military maneuvers, both battle and ceremonial. Military and police bands provided music for public events and, hence, performed music for all levels of society. Members of military and police bands could often play several different instruments and could read music. Such bands are still reliable sources of musical training in many Caribbean nations. Alton Adams (1889–1987), from the U.S. Virgin Islands, composed marches and waltzes for band, and was the United States Navy's first black bandmaster.

Art music also appeared on stages in the form of opera, ballet, and other theatrical performances. Theater companies from Europe often visited Caribbean islands during their long sea voyages between Europe and the United States. Many islands, in particular French Caribbean ones, regularly featured performances by such companies. Composers of the region include Joseph Bologne, the Chevalier de Saint Georges (ca. 1739–1799), often called "the Black Mozart," who was born in Guadeloupe but lived in France from a young age. His compositions are particularly European in style, and he composed a wealth of classical works, from sonatas to orchestral works to opera, in pre-Revolutionary France. Jamaican Samuel Felsted (1743–1802) composed *Jonah* (ca. 1775), the first oratorio written in the Americas.

More commonly, Caribbean art music is creole: Caribbean composers of art music blend the traditional musical forms, structures, and harmonies of European classical music with indigenous elements such as native rhythms, folk tunes, and local instruments. In Haiti, composers such as Werner Jaegerhuber (1900–1953) and Julio Racine (1945–) wove melodic, lyrical, and, most importantly, rhythmic elements of vodou ceremony into their compositions. Similarly, the piano works of Haitian composer Ludovic Lamothe (1882–1953) draw on melodies and rhythms from African dance and from vodou ritual. Cuban composer Amadeo Roldán (1900–1939) wrote a series of pieces based on the poems of Nicolás Guillén, whose poetry was inspired by the sounds and rhythms of Afro-Cuban music.

The sounds of indigenous instruments are also important in Caribbean art music. Trinidadian Dominique Le Gendre (1960–) makes use of local instruments such as steelpan and the conch shell in her chamber and music-theater works.

Christine Gangelhoff and Cathleen LeGrand

See also: Calypso; Soca; Steelpan; Tassa Drumming

Further Reading

Carpentier, Alejo. 2002. *Music in Cuba,* ed. Timothy Brennan, trans. Alan West-Durán. Minneapolis: University of Minnesota Press.

Gangelhoff, Christine, and Cathleen LeGrand. 2013. "Caribbean Art Music Bibliography, Vol. 2." *International Journal of Bahamian Studies* 19, 1–76.

Inanga, Glen. 2008. "Genre Theory, Western Classical Music, and the Caribbean Musical Arts." *Journal of the University College of the Cayman Islands* 2, 4–17.

Largey, Michael. 2006. *Vodou Nation: Haitian Art Music and Cultural Nationalism.* Chicago, IL: University of Chicago Press.

Manuel, Peter, with Kenneth Bilby and Michael Largey. 2006. *Caribbean Currents: Caribbean Music from Rumba to Reggae.* Philadelphia, PA: Temple University Press.

Mendoza de Arce, Daniel. 2006. *Music in North America and the West Indies from the Discovery to 1850: A Historical Survey.* Lanham, MD: Scarecrow Press.

Carmody, Kevin Daniel "Kev" (1946–)

A native of Queensland, Australia, singer-songwriter Kev Carmody is widely considered one of Australia's most important indigenous singers, songwriters, and storytellers. His work blends folk, rock, and other popular music genres to create a unique and widely accessible style. Carmody is a champion of aboriginal rights and culture in Australia and many of his songs and recordings call attention to the plight of Australia's aboriginal people.

Carmody was raised by his Irish father and indigenous Murri mother, who were cattle drovers on a station near Goranba. At the age of 10, he and his younger brother were forcibly removed from their parents and sent to a Catholic school in Toowoomba (per the government's assimilation policy). At age 16, Carmody left school and returned to his rural roots in agriculture (shearing, droving, welding, wool pressing, and loading). He credits his beginnings in traditional Aboriginal storytelling and song to "what my grandmother, my mother, father, aunty, and uncles told me. I'm just a conduit of stories" (Carmody, 1992).

His professional musical career was partially inspired by his university studies at the Darling Downs Institute of Advanced Education (now part of the University of Southern Queensland), from which he received a B.A., a Diploma in Education, and an honorary doctorate. While focusing on history and music there in his mid-30s, he submitted many assignments in a vocal format accompanied by guitar, in line with indigenous oral tradition.

Carmody signed a recording contract in 1987, and has released five studio albums and one live album in musical styles ranging from acoustic folk and country to reggae and rock. He was inducted into the Australian Recording Industry Association (ARIA) Hall of Fame and received a Queensland Greats Award in 2009.

His best-known song is "From Little Things Big Things Grow," recorded in 1991 with co-writer Paul Kelly (1955–). It is a historical account of the event that began the indigenous rights land movement: beginning in 1966, Aboriginal stockman Vincent Lingiari (1919–1988) led a successful eight-year strike of fellow Gurindji tribe drovers at Wave Hill Cattle Station in the Northern Territory. He became an important activist, leading his people and being named a Member of the Order of Australia after the passing of the Aboriginal Land Rights Act in 1976. In 2008, the song peaked at number four on the ARIA singles chart in a cover by the Get Up Mob, featuring the original songwriters with Urthboy and Missy Higgins. Carmody, commenting on the release, said: "This is the first step, a new beginning for Australia as a nation, to mature. Denial of the past makes the future a lie—through history the victors have written the history of the vanquished . . . this contemporized version of the song transforms us from a negative concept of the past to the positive possibilities of the future" (Edwards, 2008).

Carmody's first acoustic album, *Pillars of Society* (1988), focused on the oppression of indigenous Australians by British settlers in songs such as "Black Deaths in Custody" and the bitterly ironic "Thou Shall Not Steal." It was praised as "the best protest album ever made in Australia" by *Rolling Stone* and was nominated for an ARIA award. In 1990, Carmody released a collaborative album with Paul Kelly & The Messengers and the pioneering rock band Mixed Relations: *Eulogy (for a Black Person)* addressed social issues such as land rights, black deaths in custody, Aboriginal pride, alienation ("Blood Red Rose"), sex workers ("Elle"), and the David Gundy slaying.

In 1993, Carmody was the subject of a musical documentary by Rachel Perkins and Trevor Graham (director) entitled *Blood Brothers—From Little Things Big Things Grow*. In the same year, he released his third album, *Bloodlines*, featuring the popular singles "From Little Things Big Things Grow" and "On the Wire." After releasing a fourth album (*Images and Illusions*, 1995), he took a decade-long break from recording, but continued to perform live and on television and to speak to diverse audiences. He contributed music to the Australian film *One Night the Moon* (2001), which won an Australian Guild of Screen Composers "Screen Music Award" in 2002. His most recent recordings include a self-financed album (*Mirrors*, 2004), which combines social and political commentary with sounds recorded in the Australian bush; a retrospective tribute album (the 2007 double-CD *Cannot Buy My Soul—The Songs of Kev Carmody*); a live concert DVD (*Cannot Buy My Soul: Kev Carmody* [2008]); and the 2016 4-CD retrospective album *Recollections . . . Reflections . . . (A Journey)*.

Carmody has three sons with his first wife Helen, and has retired (due to arthritis) to live with his partner Beryl in southeast Queensland. Lyrics for his published songs and sheet music "for busking" are available through his personal website (http://www.kevcarmody.com.au). Fellow songwriter Paul Kelly has described Carmody's impact on Australian songwriting: "I first heard his music twenty years ago, and was drawn straight away to his blend of politics and prayer, poetry, anger, and pride. His body of work is one of our great cultural treasures" (Mengel, 2007).

Laura Stanfield Prichard

See also: Didgeridoo

Further Reading

Carmody, Kevin. 1992. *Address at the National Press Club on April 22, 1992, Canberra* [luncheon address]. Canberra: National Press Club Audiobook.

Carmody, Kevin. 2013. *Carmody-Groarke: Seven Years.* London: Carmody Groarke.

Carmody, Kevin, and Ned Lander. 2007. *Blood Brothers. Jardiwarnpa: A Warlpiri Fire Ceremony* [DVD]. Sydney: Film Australia.

Edwards, Anna. 2008. "Single Samples Rudd, Keating." *The Courier-Mail,* April 22, p. 10.

Graham, Trevor, and Rachel Perkins. 1993. "From Little Things Big Things Grow." Episode 3 of *Blood Brothers* [four-part film anthology]. Department for Education and Children's Services, SBS-TV. Australian Film Corp., Aboriginal Unit.

Mengel, Noel. 2007. "Why Kev Carmody Rules, OK." *The Courier-Mail*, February 17.

Roberts, Rhoda. 2004. *Kev Carmody Interviewed* [audiobook]. Sydney: Australian Broadcasting Corp.

Carnival, Music of

Carnival (sometimes called "Carnaval") is one of the oldest and largest musical spectacles of humanity, celebrated in the days immediately preceding the Catholic Lenten season. The Carnival of Rio de Janeiro, Brazil, is considered the largest in the world, with an audience of approximately 6 million people. For this reason, the city is considered the global epicenter of Carnival. The festival entails a large parade of Samba Schools (large bands of musicians with more than 3,000 members each) featuring large floats and music in a style called the *samba enredo* (annual musical theme). The music is performed by a singer with accompaniment of the *bateria*—a large percussion ensemble of approximately 300 drummers. Carnival is a one-of-a-kind multimedia show of vibrant colors, upbeat music, and groups of dancers drawing audiences from all over the globe.

HISTORY AND DEVELOPMENT

Some historians cite Carnival as the oldest known festivity of the agrarian cults of the Nomos—communities inhabiting the Nile region circa 4000 BCE. A subsequent celebration entailed the pagan cult to the god Dionysius, made official in

---

American Indian Elements in Mardi Gras

The Afro-Caribbean tradition, which brought steelbands to the world through the Caribbean and Samba Schools in Brazil, represents only part of the Carnival tradition in the United States. Mardi Gras tradition in New Orleans, the United States' best-known Carnival tradition, incorporates French/Acadian, creole, and American Indian elements in this cultural tradition. Typical creole elements such as ritual "showouts," various masking traditions, Indian songs, and the like are present, along with the French-inspired masquerade tradition, begging tradition, and parade float-building commonly found within Carnival tradition throughout the globe. Carnival (Mardi Gras) traditions throughout the world employ regional favorites in terms of thematic characters, which explains, for example, the popularity of Indians and parasols in New Orleans' Mardi Gras—which are less popular in Trinidad—and the popularity of burrokeets and bats in Trinidadian Carnival, which are less popular in New Orleans. Unlike Caribbean and South American Carnival traditions, Mardi Gras in New Orleans embraces several Native American themes and traditions within its Carnival celebration, making the Mardi Gras tradition in New Orleans a true amalgam of Native American, creole, African, and Francophile traditions.

Ancient Greece in the seventh century CE. In Greece, revelry in honor of Dionysus (also called Bacchus) involved processions filled with wine, music, dance, and drama. According to hieroglyphic sources, Dionysus was considered the god of metamorphosis, whose annual expulsion from Olympus led him to Greece in the spring.

In Rome, Roman Saturnalias, honoring the god Saturn (Chronos to the Greeks; god of agriculture to the Romans) provided a break from daily activities in that slaves were allowed time off, and schools and tribunals were temporarily closed (December 17–19). During the actual festivities, a conscious reversal of social roles permitted slaves to take to the streets celebrating equality and freedom, which sometimes meant tumultuous gatherings with rough playing.

Carnival eventually became a Christian festival when Pope Gregory I officially legitimized the event in 590 CE. Initially opposed by the Catholic Church, Carnival proved to be an unbeatable affair, and the church eventually acquiesced, adapting a pagan event to its Christian calendar. Since then Carnival has been formally celebrated on the seventh Sunday preceding Easter. In this sense, Carnival can be thought of as an event antithetic to Lent. This dichotomy has been signified by the French as *jours gras* (day of fat) and *jours maigres* (day of lean). Carnival is personified in the caricature of a chubby man whose boldness is associated with a lack of sexual or gastronomical inhibitions, after which the Lenten season begins—a time for recovery and restraint. Thus, Carnival is synonymous with an affirmation of the human, the carnal, and instant desires, thereby suggesting a thin line dividing freedom, liberality, and licentiousness.

Traditionally, Carnival involved the presence of parade floats (especially in Florence, Italy) in addition to various forms of popular entertainments such as competitions, dances, frolics, and theater. Furthermore, the performance of ritual satires and social inversions was quite common: men dressed as women and vice versa, novices simulating parody masses ridiculed and questioned the church, and people donned burlesque costumes representing politicians and historical characters. The use of masks was (and still is) a shared custom. Many scholars of Carnival interpret it as a collective ritualistic metamorphosis whereby masked individuals may become a subject "other," reversing roles and confronting political, moral, and social discrepancies.

Carnival was seen as a time when public streets were converted into stages for performance of relatively structured events that stretched across Europe. In Portugal it was called *Entrudo*, occurring mostly between groups of neighbors and family. Common "street riots" included throwing water, flour, and perfume on passersby. Circa 1900, following stricter genteel French customs, Carnival entailed a procession of carriages by persons representing elite clubs, who also held ancillary private balls with masks and luxurious costumes. Other customs considered "coarse and popular" lost their status, causing a social rift between wealthier and underprivileged classes.

Following Portuguese cultural practice, Carnival in 19th-century Brazil, called "Grande Carnival," adopted conservative European influences consisting of a parade of bourgeois vehicles (*marches*) cruising the central avenues of Rio de Janeiro. Parallel to the parades, *bailes de mascaras* (private masked balls) entertained upper-class revelers and tourists. When the Áurea law emancipated African slaves, causing a mass migration to the urban centers of the south, people from the suburban working classes gathered streamers and confetti left by the premier parade, creating a secondary assemblage (*ranches*) called "Carnival Popular."

SAMBA SCHOOLS

During the Vargas era (the presidency of Getúlio Vargas, 1930–1945), nationalist impulses promoted the status of samba schools or, formally speaking, recreational guilds (*Grêmios Recreativos*), representing several Afro-Brazilian slum communities. These "schools" were then able to join the premier parade at Rio Branco Avenue, promoting greater (albeit fleeting) interaction between the upper and lower classes. Carnival, continuously reported by mass media, started to gain momentum and bigger supporters. By 1960, a second wave of growth made samba schools beneficiaries of grants from the state and private companies, causing this popular manifestation to become increasingly more competitive, with luxurious floats and extravagant costumes. This second surge also caused ticket costs to rise, decreasing access by those in impoverished communities and re-establishing social divides.

Reinventing ancient traditions, Rio's Carnival involves games and competitions. Major samba schools, for example, compete for various rankings based on criteria such as rhythm (maintenance of the percussion ensemble's steady beat), lyrics, harmony, evolution (fluency and dynamism of sections), *enredo* (theme), ensemble (musical, rhythmic and visual unity), allegories of floats (sculptures, materials, and colors), costumes, front commission (chaperones of the samba school to the audience), and *Mestre-Sala/Porta Bandeira* (King and Flag Queen). Besides these elements, schools feature a section of Bahian women (*Ala das Baianas*) and an elders' section (*Velha Guarda*). The number of members of a school ranges between 3,000 and 5,000 people.

MUSICAL ENSEMBLES AND THE PARADE

The most important element of a samba school is the *samba enredo*—the musical theme chosen by the school, developed scenically and choreographically. This theme can embrace one of several topics: politics, sports, history, social debates of the moment, and so on. The first known *samba enredo* is "Sua Majestade o Samba" by Antonio da Silva Caetano. The bateria, the segment containing a group of percussionists, accompanies the vocals, giving rhythmic shape and sustenance. A bateria is divided into smaller instrumental sections, usually in the following order: *cuícas* (a small cylindrical drum with a stick fastened to the internal center of the drumhead, whose pull and friction provides a high-pitched sound), *agogôs* (usually two iron bells connected through a curved stem), *pandeiros* (a flat circular tambourine made of a goatskin head, held together by a brass or wood frame, the adjustable bars of which often hold small metal shakers), *chocalhos* (a multiply-lined shaker infused with tiny metal plates that produce a nice rattling sound), followed by a mixed group of *caixas* (lightweight drum with nylon heads), *repiques* (middle-size drum) and *surdos* (large-size drum). The samba theme is sung by an interpreter called the *puxador* (puller) who heads the procession with his or her vocals. A fast-tempo samba, usually in double meter (2/4) has an accent on the second beat. Between these two beats several layers of predetermined rhythms (polyrhythms) are added, some specific to each unique samba school.

Throughout the year, samba schools plan and organize the annual parade, allotting 80 minutes per school. The parade takes place at the Sambódromo (Sambadrome) located at Rua Marques de Sapucaí in downtown Rio de Janeiro, which seats 60,000 people. The samba schools are divided into two organizations: those belonging to the "Special Group" (*Grupo Especial*) constituents of the Independent League of Samba Schools, and those with a secondary, less prominent, affiliation to the Association of Samba Schools of Rio de Janeiro. The parade is most competitive among the schools of the Special Group.

Samba schools manufacture parade floats and costumes in large warehouses located in *Cidade do Samba* (Samba City), a suburb of Rio. They have developed ancillary organizations such as the Instituto do Carnaval (a center for professional studies), Casa da Memória (a museum), and *quadras* (open rehearsal spaces located near the shantytowns). Secondarily, samba schools function as social clubs, offering a variety of art classes for children as well as nightly and weekend gathering places for adults and families. This demonstrates that music and dance are an integral part of everyday life in Brazil. Perhaps for this reason, casual events seemingly never cease to appear. A good example is the renewed "Carnaval Popular," a spontaneous parade of common folk and modest bands that has, in recent times, reorganized around the streets of Rio de Janeiro, challenging the "commercial" Carnival of the Sambódromo.

OTHER BRAZILIAN CARNIVAL DESTINATIONS

Despite Rio's magnificent and lavish Carnival, many other Brazilian and international locations produce unique Carnival festivities. For example, the Carnival of Salvador da Bahia is another destination of great cultural significance. The city of Salvador (capital of the State of Bahia) was also the first capital of Brazil (1549–1763) and the site of the first slave market trade in the New World. Bahian Carnival is generally more relaxed and composed of blocs of people who follow the *trio elétrico* (trucks carrying an amplified band). The music style, called *axé*, is usually led by a singer and electric guitar evoking Caribbean rhythms. Other groups, called *Afroblocos* (e.g., Ilê Ayiê, Olodum, etc.), specifically promote African culture and pride.

In the northeastern city of Recife (Pernambuco State), a former Dutch colony, Carnival has a more folkloric tone, with *frevo* and *maracatu* bands predominating. The frevo ("fervor" or "fever") arose from folk musics of the 17th century at the confluence of military bands, dobrados, marches, and polkas with indigenous and African traditions. The frevo is predominantly played with brass instruments (clarinet, saxophone, trumpet, trombone, trumpets), surdo, pandeiro (tambourine), and electric keyboard. It has a fast tempo and an ABA form comprised of 16-bar form structures. The frevo dance resembles Russian *Trepak* and *capoeira* movements, in that dancers crouch near the ground and alternate extending the legs. Due to the instrumental arrangements and rhythmic virtuosity of the frevo, the music requires players with good sight-reading skills and rhythmic dexterity.

The *maracatu* is a peculiar tradition attached to the Congolese-African customs of crowning of kings and queens, princes and princesses, followed by a parade of dignitaries (wearing richly adorned garments and crowns) and musicians. It is secondarily associated with local Christian devotional worship of Our Lady of the Rosary, wherein processions of several "clans" stop at the entrance doors of local churches. This Carnival in many ways reenacts the social structure of African nations lost during colonization. Part of the fetish includes sacerdotal and theatrical choreographies honoring the black doll *Calunga*, which leads the parade and represents *Candomblé* (Afro-Brazilian religion). Musically the band is comprised of bombos, triangles, and shakers, played at a slow and measured pace. In Ceará, maracatu groups are even more exotic: participants often paint their faces black and men dress up as women (often as queens).

CARNIVAL INTERNATIONALLY

Internationally, the Carnivals of Venice, Rome, New Orleans, Belgium, Bonn (*Weiberfastnacht* or Women's Carnival), and Trinidad and Tobago are highly sought after destinations. In the United States, the best known Carnival is Mardi Gras ("Fat Tuesday"), which began when members of the traders' club "The Mystick Krewe of Comus" (1857) began to parade the streets of New Orleans with floats and musicians. Currently, Mardi Gras in New Orleans features approximately 50 groups.

Silvia M. Lazo

See also: Candomblé; Samba Instruments; Samba Music

Further Reading

Cavalcanti, Maria Laura. 2002. "Os Sentidos no Espetáculo [The senses in the show]." *Revista de Antropologia* 45(1), 37–78.

Costa, José Fabiano Serra, Bruno Barros da Silva, and Carolina Ramalho. 2010. "Critérios de Julgamento dos Quesitos das Escolas de Samba do Grupo Especial do Carnaval do Rio de Janeiro: Uma Análise Multicritério [Judgment criteria for the samba schools of the Rio de Janeiro Special Carnival Group: A multicriteria analysis]." *Pesquisa Operacional para o Desenvolvimento* 2(2) (May-August), 100–118.

Crowley, Donald. 1956. "The Traditional Masques of Carnival." *Caribbean Quarterly* 4, 194–223.

Dunn, Christopher. 1996. "O mistério do samba [The mystery of samba]." *Mana* 2(2), 208–211.

Hill, Errol. 1972. *The Trinidad Carnival: Mandate for a National Theatre.* Austin, TX: University of Texas Press.

Santos, Luiz Gustavo. 2012. "O Carnaval no Tempo e na Atualidade [Carnival of the past and today]." Seminário dos Alunos de Pós-Graduação em Comunicação Social [Seminar of graduate students in social communication], Rio de Janeiro, Pontificia Universidade Católica, November 7–9..

Carter Family, The

The Carter Family, which is called the "first family of country music," was one of the genre's first prominent acts. It blended Anglo-Celtic folk ballads and instrumental dance tunes with the harmonies of shape-note hymnody and rural gospel singing to effectively create the country genre.

The Carter Family was formed in Virginia and originally consisted of A.P. (Alvin Pleasant Delaney) Carter (1891–1960) and his wife Sara (Dougherty; 1898–1979). Both were involved in music throughout their lives, receiving most of their musical training through their families. A.P. learned to play the fiddle as a child and sang in a gospel quartet with two uncles and his sister when he was older. Sara played several instruments, including autoharp, guitar, and banjo. They married in 1915 and performed locally. In 1925, Maybelle Addington (1909–1978), Sara's first cousin and a proficient guitarist, began to perform with the group. The trio began to perform under the moniker "the Carter Family" after Maybelle married A.P.'s brother Ezra.

This group established the fledgling country style and also influenced generations of country, folk, and even rock musicians to come. Sara generally sang lead while accompanying on the guitar or autoharp. A.P. occasionally joined in the instrumental accompaniment, but most often restricted his contributions to singing in his baritone/bass voice. The uniqueness of the Carter sound was Maybelle's guitar accompaniments. Contrary to standard practice, she played the melody with her thumb on the bass strings and strummed chords on the treble strings. She also frequently downtuned her guitar to better suit the vocals.

In 1927, the Carter Family recorded six songs for Victor Records, and signed with the label in 1928. Over the next seven years, the Carter Family recorded many of its best-known songs, including "Wildwood Flower," "Wabash Cannonball," "Will the Circle (Be Unbroken)," and its signature song, "Keep on the Sunny Side." After A.P. learned the label would give him songwriting credit and additional royalties for adaptations of public-domain songs, he and Sara also travelled throughout the South to discover new songs to record.

Pioneering early country music group the Carter Family, ca. 1937. Pictured, from left: Maybelle Carter, A. P. Carter, and Sarah Carter. (Donaldson Collection/Getty Images)

By the end of the 1920s, the Carter Family was nationally known, but touring was not possible due to financial hardships caused by the Great Depression. The members of the group eventually had to leave their homes in Maces Spring, Virginia, in search of work in other places. A.P. relocated temporarily to Detroit, while Maybelle and Ezra moved to Washington, D.C. A.P. and Sara separated in 1932, and the members of the group saw each other only for recording sessions.

In 1936, the Carters signed with Decca, for which they recorded such hits as "Coal Miner Blues," "My Dixie Darling," and "Hello Stranger." They eventually signed a radio contract with station XERF in Del Rio, Texas, which led to additional contracts with stations in San Antonio, Texas, where the broadcasts were recorded and distributed to other stations along the Texas-Mexico border, and eventually Charlotte, North Carolina. These contracts enabled the Carters' music to be heard throughout the nation. By 1939, a new generation of Carters joined the act. A.P. and Sara's children, Janette (1923–2006) and Joe (1927–2005), and Maybelle's children, Helen (1927–1998), June (later June Carter Cash, 1929–2003), and Anita (1933–1999), began singing with the group.

The professional success of the Carter Family could not save A.P. and Sara's marriage, and the two divorced in 1938. Sara married A.P.'s cousin, Coy Bayes, in 1939 and moved to California in 1943. The group disbanded in 1944. Following the dissolution of the Carter Family, Maybelle began to perform with her daughters as "the Carter Sisters" or "Mother Maybelle and the Carter Sisters." The group sang many of the original Carter Family songs along with some pop and gospel songs. June, who struggled with pitch problems early on, began to interject her natural comedic talents into the act, particularly the popular "Aunt Polly" routine. The Carter Sisters first performed in the Richmond, Virginia, area. In 1946, they became regulars on the *Old Dominion Barn Dance* show airing on Richmond's WRVA. In 1948, Mother Maybelle and the Carter Sisters moved to Knoxville, Tennessee, where they began performing on WNOX's *Tennessee Barn Dance* and the *Mid-Day Merry-Go-Round*. While in Knoxville, they met a young guitarist named Chet Atkins (1924–2001), who played with them into the early 1950s.

The Carter Sisters, along with Atkins, released their first recordings in 1949 for RCA Victor. In 1950, the group was invited to perform at the Grand Ole Opry in Nashville, Tennessee. Over the next 10 years, they performed with stars such as Elvis Presley (1935–1977), Ernest Tubb (1914–1984), and Johnny Cash (1932–2003), and were inducted as members of the Opry.

After the death of A.P. in 1960, Maybelle officially renamed the group the Carter Family. The newly renamed group joined Johnny Cash on tour. They also recorded the song "Busted" with Cash for his *Blood, Sweat, and Tears* album. The song peaked at number 13 on *Billboard's* "Hot Country Songs" chart, the highest position of any song the group recorded (*Billboard* did not chart country songs until 1944, so the earliest Carter Family songs were not charted). June and Cash married in 1968. During this time, all four members of the group recorded as solo artists as well as with the group. Maybelle's albums featured instrumentals as well as vocal songs; Anita's albums were minor successes, with a total of three top-ten hits, while Helen and June struggled to achieve success on their own. June had a number of hit duets with Cash, including four top-ten songs.

In 1967, Sara and Maybelle reunited to record an album of old-time songs entitled *An Historic Reunion: Sara and Maybelle—The Original Carters*. The Carter Family announced that it was disbanding in 1969, but that did not actually happen; in fact, this incarnation of the Carter Family enjoyed its greatest successes during the early 1970s. The group appeared regularly on *The Johnny Cash Show* during this time period. Its 1972 album, *Travelin' Minstrel Band*, was its first to chart, reaching number 44, and the title track and "A Song to Mama" placed on the *Billboard* country chart. In 1973, the Carter Family won the American Music Award for "Favorite Country Vocal Group."

Maybelle's health declined in the mid-1970s, leading to her death in 1978, and Sara died the following year. After their mother's death, Maybelle's daughters continued to perform as the Carter Family through the late 1990s. Helen and Anita died in 1998 and 1999 respectively, and June died in 2003. In 2012, June and Johnny Cash's son, John Carter Cash, and his wife, Laura, joined with Dale Jett, son of A.P. and Sara's daughter Janette, to create "Carter Family III" and carry on the legacy of the Carter Family.

Eric S. Strother

See also: Bluegrass; Country Music; Rodgers, Jimmie

Further Reading

Dawidoff, Nicholas. 1998. *In the Country of Country: A Journey to the Roots of American Music*. New York: Vintage Books.

Malone, Bill C., and Jocelyn R. Neal. 2010. *Country Music, U.S.A.* Austin: University of Texas Press.

Zwonitzer, Mark, and Charles Hirshberg. 2002. *Will You Miss Me When I'm Gone?: The Carter Family and Their Legacy in American Music*. New York: Simon & Schuster.

Čechomor

Čechomor is a band hailing from the Czech Republic whose style has been variously categorized as world music, electronic folk, and folk music arranged like rock and roll. It is difficult to say which of these is the most accurate description, as the group draws on several musical styles—including folk, pop, jazz, and classical—and has explored several different approaches to integrating these styles through instrumentation, song selection, and production choices. Čechomor has been performing for more than 25 years and has produced more than 20 albums. They have a large following in their native country and have enjoyed immense international touring success as well. Their innovative approach to folk music has introduced many fans to the sounds of traditional Czech instruments and songs.

The band formed in 1988 under the name The First Czech-Moravian Independent Music Company, with Jiří Břenek and Antonín Svoboda on violin, František Černý on guitar and vocals, and Jiří Michálek on accordion. They played primarily at outdoor fairs, street markets, and other casual venues. In the early 1990s the band was ready make a change in their approach, and a new direction was inspired by a collection of Moravian folksongs compiled by the 19th-century song collector František Sušil. Moravian folk music is rich in cultural and dialectical differences, and the band utilized this variety to experiment with their sound. The group also experimented with their name and released their first two albums, *Dověcnosti* (*Into Eternity*) and *Mezi Horami* (*Among the Mountains*) as The First Czech-Moravian Independent Music Company and The Czech-Moravian Music Company, respectively. Throughout the 1990s the group continued to refine their sound, integrating electronic instrumentation and exploring rock-and-roll elements in their arranging. Their membership changed as well during this period, mostly through the addition of new performers, but also through the premature death of Jiří Břenek, who died of cancer in 1996. During this transitional period the band made a final modification to their name, which finally reached its current shortened version in the year 2000. At the beginning of the new millennium, Čechomor released a self-titled album and presented the public with the new sound they had been developing.

Throughout the early 2000s, Čechomor continued expanding their musical style, collaborating with Jaz Coleman and the Czech Philharmonic Collegium on an album with elements of classical music. The result of this collaborative project was their fourth release, *Proměny* (*Transformations*), which won several awards and sold more than 80,000 copies. This success ensured Čechomor's renown in the Czech Republic. During this period Čechomor pursued other collaborative relationships with film director Petr Zelenka, journalist Petr Dorůžka, and producer Ben Mandelson. The band released 11 more albums between 2001 and 2010, including some live recordings and a compilation album.

Near the end of the decade, Čechomor launched a recording project that revisited their folk roots. On their three-album recording *Písně z Hradů á Zamků* (*Songs of Castles and Palaces*), the band performs folk songs from Bohemia, Moravia, and Silesia related to legends of castles. The Czech version of this recording project features narration of these legends, while the international version forgoes the storytelling and features only the music. This creative approach demonstrated Čechomor's willingness to continue experimenting with their performance style.

Čechomor's most recent album at the time of this publication is a celebration of their 25th anniversary: *Čechomor 25 let Český Krumlov Live* (*Čechomor 25 Years, Live in Český Krumlov*). The album features several new takes on Čechomor hits, as well as several guest artists, including the Smíchovská Komorní Filharmonie symphony orchestra, the Kühnův Mixed Choir, and Japanese drummer and flutist Joji Hirota. Hirota has collaborated with Čechomor on other albums, and his contribution to Čechomor's discography is indicative of their broad take on folk music and their exploration of Eastern influences on Czech culture and music.

Today Čechomor has seven members: guitarist and singer František Černý, who has been with the group since its beginning and composes music and lyrics; violinist and singer Karel Holas, who joined Čechomor in 1994; trumpeter and accordionist Radek Pobořil, who first appeared with the band as a guest artist on the album *Dověcnosti*; cellist and bagpiper Michal Pavlík, who joined the group in

1994; violinist Taras Voloshchuk, who joined Čechomor in 2007; guitarist Michael Vašíček, who joined the band in 2011; and percussionist Patrik Sas, who has been a band member since 2012. Several members of the group have conservatory backgrounds, and many have performed with other bands or in other performance mediums.

Amelia Davidson

See also: Eurovision Song Contest; Moravian Music

Further Reading

Andress, Mark. 2001. "Emarcy Readies Czech Folk Act Cechomor for Export." *Billboard* 113(38) (September 22), 57.

Hunt, Ken. 2005. "Platinum Czechs." *Froots* 269 (November), 55–57.

Winick, Steve. 2007. "Bouncing Czechs: A Conversation with Cechomor." *Dirty Linen* 131 (August), 20–24.

Celtic Music

Unlike the origins of the Celtic languages still spoken in Europe to this day—the Brittonic and the Gaelic branches, both subdivisions of Insular Celtic—the origins of what today is termed "Celtic music" are extremely difficult to define in a systematic and methodical way, for lack of actual traces. We can only surmise that today's jigs, reels, or *gwerzioù* probably have very little to do with what the musicians of the early Middle Ages played in Ireland, Brittany, Scotland, or Wales, and even less with the kind of entertainment enjoyed by the first Celtic peoples 3,000 years ago in central Europe. Nevertheless, contrary to popular belief, the emergence of a common "Celtic" musical tradition goes back well beyond the 1970s.

The validity of the term "Celtic music" can thus be questioned, and should first be examined from an archaeological point of view, where modest evidence of common factors can be detected. The circulation of musicians and instruments during the Middle Ages and thereafter can also provide some information regarding the interconnections between the different Celtic nations, which after the 18th century led to a common determination to save ancient traditions and create new links based on assumed historical bonds and similar political situations. For reasons that remain to be fully explained, the expression "Celtic music" gained enormous popularity among the general public in the late 20th century, though with sometimes very different meanings from one community to another: having spread far beyond the respective diasporas of Ireland, Brittany, Wales, or Scotland, this plethora of meanings seems to confirm that identity in the 21st century is more and more often based on a choice, both personal and collective.

Seven almost complete *carnyxes* from the first century BCE, discovered in 2004 in Tintignac (France), seem to indicate that these war horns, undoubtedly played in groups and essentially intended to frighten the enemy during battle, were the first real common instruments of the Celtic tribes in continental Europe. Their use, as documented on the famous Gundestrup cauldron (ca. 200 BCE), does not seem to have gone beyond the second century of our era.

A 17-inch-high granite statuette, probably also dating back to the second century BCE and found in 1988 in Paule, Brittany—now on display in Rennes at the Musée de Bretagne—is the first known proof of the importance given by Celtic tribes to stringed instruments: a seated bard holds a seven-string instrument belonging to the family of lyres. In Ireland, the first representation in our possession of this family of instruments, a harp engraved on a granite cross near the small church of Carndonagh, on the Inishowen Peninsula, in County Donegal, dates back to the eighth or ninth century.

We also know that music played a key role for the Celts as early as 2,000 years ago or more, as evidenced by the many references in the mythological texts that have come down to us. Music is thus the main attribute of the Dagda, the main deity of Irish mythology, owner of the magic harp in which all the melodies are held.

In the Middle Ages, very few traces subsist in the archives of Brittany concerning the importance of musicians. One mention in the Cartulary of Landévennec (ninth century) probably refers to the musicians at the court of King Gradlon (la Borderie, 1888, p. 79), and a charter from the Cartulary of Quimperlé (12th century) mentions an enigmatic "Kadiou Citharista (Cadiou harper) in the service of Hoël II" (Maître and De Berthou, 1904, p. 189), although it is not clear whether this was meant as a nickname or as a function.

In contrast, Irish court musicians already enjoyed a favorable reputation in Europe, and there are a number of texts attesting to the admiration of European travelers. The most famous of these was written in the 12th century by a Welsh churchman named Giraldus Cambrensis (ca. 1146–ca. 1223). Although very critical of the Irish, he conceded, "I find in these people of laudable fervour only as regards the musical instruments, that they play incomparably better than any other nation of my acquaintance" (Cambrensis, 1867, p. 153). In due course, the importance of the harp and music in Ireland materialized in the 13th century outside the Celtic world, when the instrument appeared as the emblem of that country in the Armorial of Wijnbergen, one of the oldest armorials in Europe, compiled in continental Europe between 1270 and 1291 (Jéquier and Adam-Even, 1951–1954).

One of the main criticisms often made during the 19th and 20th centuries toward the grouping of Celtic peoples of the Antiquity and the Middle Ages was their lack of tangible unity, both politically and administratively. It would be detrimental, however, to forget the cultural unity that undeniably brought these peoples together in religious, linguistic, and artistic terms, three perspectives closely linked to music and singing. For instance, it remains to this day impossible to determine whether the famous 14th-century harp on display at the Trinity College Museum in Dublin—which has served as a model for the official emblems of Ireland since its independence in 1921, and is still today represented on all euro coins minted in Ireland—was made in Ireland or in Scotland. The same applies to its twin sisters, the Queen Marie harp and the Lamont harp, both dating back to the 15th century. It is also known that the harpers of the two countries very often rubbed shoulders: Scottish harper Ruaidhri Dall Morison (1656–1714) regularly travelled to Ireland, and his Irish counterparts Rory Dall Ó Catháin (1570–1650) and Denis Hempson (1695–1807) also extended their travel territory to Scotland in the 17th and 18th centuries.

Other evidence of a common culture of the harp between Ireland and Wales dates back to the 12th century, with harpers enjoying a special status in both countries, codified during the early Middle Ages—albeit very theoretically—by the Brehon law in Ireland (Atkinson, 1901), and during the 16th century in Wales for the Eisteddfod Festivals, between 1523 and 1567.

In Ireland in particular, the late arrival of the feudal system caused the disappearance of court harpers, who were then reduced to the status of itinerant musicians, and who all but vanished during the 17th and 18th centuries when the Gaelic Order gave way to a more centralized British social and political organization. As a response to this major cultural disruption, a large-scale movement emerged at the end of the 18th century (mainly among the aristocracy in Ireland and Brittany) to collect and safeguard this cultural heritage. Harp competitions were organized in the north of Ireland between 1783 and 1792, and served as pretexts for the collection of melodies from the 10 musicians who were present, while enthusiasts from Brittany and Wales decided to create a cross-border movement on the occasion of the Welsh Eisteddfod festival of 1838. Together with the publication in 1839 of the first edition of Hersart de La Villemarqué's *Barzaz Breiz*—a vast collection of Breton tunes and songs—this led to the first international Celtic Congress, held in Saint-Brieuc in 1867, and to the first panCeltic congress in Wales in 1899, with Irish, Breton, and Scottish delegates. Musically speaking, this period was mainly centered around exchanges between Wales and Brittany, whose languages are very still similar. This was notably exemplified through the adoption of the Welsh national anthem in 1904 by the Union Régionaliste Bretonne as the Breton anthem, renamed the *Bro gozh ma zadoù*.

After the interruption of interCeltic exchanges during the First World War, the 1920s and 1930s saw a rapid increase in new activity. Festivals were held mostly in Brittany, but were brought to a halt during World War II, which also saw the creation of the first Breton *bagadoù*—based on the Scottish pipebands—thanks to a new association, *Bodadeg ar Sonerien* ("the assembly of the pipers"). Dancing was an additional item on the agenda of many, as a federation of Breton associations (*Kendalc'h*) was created in 1950, mainly focused on the teaching and dissemination of Breton dances. Thanks in particular to Loeiz Ropars, it was followed in 1954 by the revival of the *fest-noz*, an evening of Breton dancing and singing, still widely practiced in Brittany today and which was included by UNESCO in the inventory of "Intangible Cultural Heritage of Humanity" in 2011. At about the same time in Ireland (1951), the *Comhaltas Ceoltóirí Éireann* (Association of Irish Musicians) was created to foster a new appreciation for traditional Irish music, dance, and song through an annual festival, *Fleadh Cheoil na hÉireann*, which was openly imitated in Brittany by Polig Montjarret (1920–2003) with the *Kan ar Bobl* festival in 1973.

The 1970s saw the emergence on the world stage of major musicians from the various Celtic nations. Of these, Alan Stivell (1944–) is by far the most famous, thanks to the sound of his bardic harp (built by his father), and to a keen sense of how to breathe new electric life into traditional music. The constant use of the word "Celtic" by Alan Stivell since his second album (*Renaissance of the Celtic Harp*, 1971) originally represented a deep conviction on his part, as well as being a stroke of genius in marketing terms. It was undeniably a masterstroke as well for the perpetuation of this traditional music, which might not have survived into the 21st century had it not adapted to new urban traditions.

Since the huge wave of renewal in the 1970s, and even more so since the second wave in the 1990s, a broad commercial category called "Celtic music" has invaded the record bins of music stores around the world (Thornton, 2000). In the United States, the phrase is sometimes synonymous with a subgenre of "New Age music" or (more often) associated with Irish music. Enya (1961–), a former singer and musician with the band Clannad, is one example that immediately comes to mind, notably since her first album was composed for the BBC documentary "The Celts" in 1987. But other forms have also been proposed, including the "*Héritage des Celtes*" show with prestigious artists from Brittany, Scotland, Ireland, Wales, the Isle of Man, and British Cornwall for a super-production organized by Dan Ar Braz (1949–, former Stivell guitarist in the 1970s), which premiered at the 70th Festival in Quimper, on July 24, 1993. The craze for "Celtic music" was such during the 1990s that it spread far beyond the Celtic nations: artists such as Nobuo Uematsu in Japan even called upon several Irish musicians in 1991 to compose the music for the Final Fantasy IV video game *Celtic Moon*.

Traditional Irish music performed in a pub on instruments such as the *bodhrán*, a frame drum. (James Fraher/Redferns)

For many musicians today, the sole purpose of this "Celtic" label is purely to attract the attention of the public in order to sell more records or concert tickets, and has the unfortunate effect of erasing the very tangible musical and cultural distinctions between the Celtic nations. In this sense, it is merely a very effective media concept. On the other hand, other musicians and cultural activists argue that a feeling of belonging remains very strong within a certain community, and that such a common perception can be as valid a reality, as embodied by events such as the Festival Interceltique de Lorient, created in 1971, the constant expansion of which confirms its cultural and economic relevance.

The multiplication of Celtic music festivals around the world also remains to be interpreted: in the United States of course, and for the most part in all regions of the world where Irish, Breton, or Scottish diasporas and populations are present, but also to a certain extent in Germany, Scandinavia, Poland, Italy, and elsewhere. But is it more incongruous to find a festival of Celtic music in Warsaw than a jazz festival in Vienna or a festival of Western classical music in Japan? Whatever the outcome, such an evolution bears witness once more to the crucial role played by the media and the economy during the 20th century in the constitution of a representative collective image of cultures from Ireland, Wales, Scotland, Brittany, Cornwall, the Isle of Man, Galicia, and Asturias.

Surprisingly, this musical effervescence has rarely led to scientific attempts to define "Celtic music," although the broad definitions that have been proposed generally tend to focus on three aspects: the use of a Celtic language, the use of instruments originating in one of the present-day Celtic regions, or personal conviction. Such is the case, for example, of Breton harpist Alan Stivell, whose attempts remain nonetheless far too vague for musicologists (Chartier, 2010, p. 546).

Another tendency, fortunately even rarer, is for some to consider Celtic music an extreme affirmation of European identity. Based on the musical theory of non-tempered scales used in many genres of traditional music in Europe, Celtic music has sometimes mistakenly been considered by some biased activists as a white European cultural expression that has remained pure and intact for millennia. With these contentions, however, they deny music its capacity for evolution and its capacity to adapt to the environment, which would undoubtedly have led to the disappearance of its social function and thus to the disappearance of the music itself, as has been the case for so many other genres of traditional music in the past 200 years.

More pragmatically, it seems that the expression "Celtic music" can now be seen as representing a simple solution to summarize—for the media and the general public—different musical realities from neighboring regions whose dance and song traditions are ultimately very disparate. It should, however, be noted that the same goes for the terms "Scottish music," "Welsh music," "Breton music," or "Irish music" which, in each case, cover a wide range of styles and techniques and are themselves quite discrete traditions.

All these facts could lead us to argue in favor of the nonexistence of actual Celtic music. This would, however, ignore one of the commonly accepted definitions of identity, which recognizes a "sense of belonging" as one of the relevant factors. Such a sense of coherence and unity, deliberately sought for more than a century and a half, testifies to this "will to live together" described by Ernest Renan in a famous lecture given in 1882 on the concept of "nation." Whether based on realities or symbols, Celtic music is a marker of identity as a deliberate choice: although it might be considered to some extent a historical fiction, it has proved to be quite effective and popular as a present economic reality. In this sense it can be regarded as an "invented tradition," as proposed by Hobsbawm and Ranger in 1983, or as an "imagined community," an extension of nationalism resulting from the industrial revolution, as proposed by Anderson (2016).

As regards the future, it seems it would be quite inadequate if the musicians of Ireland, Brittany, Scotland, or Wales claimed exclusive ownership of the term "Celtic music," thus replicating the monopoly on the term "music" too often exercised in certain circles.

Erick Falc'her-Poyroux

See also: Accordion, Types of; Bagpipes; Irish American Vocal Music; Irish Step Dancing

Further Reading

Anderson, Benedict. 2016. *Imagined Communities: Reflections on the Origin and Spread of Nationalism.* London: Verso.

Atkinson, Robert, ed. 1901. *Ancient Laws of Ireland,* vol. 5. Dublin: Alexander Thom.

Bévant, Yann. 2010. "Nations in Tune: The Influence of Irish Music on the Breton Musical Revival." *Proceedings of the 29th Celtic Colloquium of the University of Harvard, USA,* 30–44. Cambridge, MA: Harvard University Press.

Bohlman, Philip V., ed. 2003. *Celtic Modern: Music at the Global Fringe (Europea: Ethnomusicologies and Modernities).* Oxford: Scarecrow Press.

Cadden, Jerry A. 2005. *Celtic Music: Tradition and Transformation in Ireland, Scotland and Beyond* (World Music series). Santa Barbara, CA: ABC-CLIO.

Cambrensis, Giraldus. 1867. *Topographica Hiberniae. Complete Works,* vol. 5, ed., J. S. Brewer, J. F. Dimrock, and G. F. Warner. London: Longmans.

Chapman, Malcolm. 1992. *The Celts: The Construction of a Myth.* Basingstoke, UK: Palgrave Macmillan.

Chapman, Malcolm. 1994. "Thoughts on Celtic Music in Ethnicity, Identity and Music." In Martin Stokes, *Ethnicity, Identity and Music—The Musical Construction of Place,* 29–44. Oxford: Berg Publishers.

Chartier, Erwan. 2010. *La construction de l'interceltisme en Bretagne, des origines à nos jours: mise en perspective historique et idéologique* [The construction of interceltism in Brittany, from its origins to the present day: Historical and ideological perspective]. Rennes, France: Université Rennes 2-Haute-Bretagne.

de la Borderie, Arthur, ed. 1888. *Cartulaire de l'abbaye de Landevenec.* Rennes, France.

Hersart de la Villemarqué, Théodore. 1981. *Le Barzaz Breiz: Chants populaires de la Bretagne* [Le Barzaz Breiz: popular songs of Brittany]. Paris: La Découverte.

Hobsbawm, Erich, and Terence Ranger, eds. 1983. *The Invention of Tradition.* Cambridge: Cambridge University Press.

Jéquier, Léon, and Paul Adam-Even. 1951–1954. *Un Armorial Français du XIIIe Siècle: l'Armorial Wijnbergen* [A French armorial of the 13th century: The Wijnberger Armorial]. Lausanne, Switzerland: Archives héraldiques suisses.

Maître, Leon, and Paul De Berthou. 1904. *Cartulaire de l'abbaye de Sainte Croix de Quimperle.* 2nd ed. Paris: n.p.

Mathieson, Kenny, ed. 2001. *Celtic Music: Third Ear—The Essential Listening Companion.* San Francisco: Backbeat Books.

Renan, Ernest. 1882. *Qu'est-ce qu'une nation?* Lecture given at the Sorbonne, March 11, 1882. Paris: Calmann Lévy.

Stivell, Alan. 1971. *Renaissance de la Harpe Celtique.* Fontana 6325.302.

Thornton, Shannon. 2000. "Reading the Record Bins, the Commercial Construction of Celtic Music." In Amy Hale and Philip Payton (eds.), *New Directions in Celtic Studies,* 19–29. Exeter: University of Exeter Press.

Chamarrita

The *chamarrita* is a traditional dance from the Azores Islands (nine autonomous Portuguese islands situated in the North Atlantic Ocean). Couples perform the dance to the accompaniment of stringed instruments and one or more vocalists, who sing lyrics and direct the dance. Though the dance is native to the Azores, versions of the chamarrita (also called *chimarrita*) can be found in unique iterations in southern Brazil, Uruguay, and Argentina. The chamarrita, in its Azorean form, is still commonly performed in several varieties on the islands of the Azores, especially the western islands of Pico and Faial, as well as in Azorean-American communities along the U.S. East coast.

One of many folk dances native to the Azores, the chamarrita is characterized by a moderately paced, triple-meter feel to which paired dancers engage in cued dance choreography. Often taking the form of a square or round dance, dancers frequently shift between partners. Dancers sometimes embrace the partner, while at other times both dancers move with their hands above their heads, as if holding castanets. More professional performances—such as those by folklore dance and music troupes (*ranchos folclóricos*) at folk dance festivals and competitions—often feature complicated choreography. The dance may also be performed informally at social events and celebrations in simpler versions.

One or more vocalists (*mandadores*) direct the dance by calling out choreographic cues and singing traditional poetic lyrics. Less valued for refined vocal performance (i.e., skilled vocal production with advanced technique and tone quality), the singers focus on providing commanding vocal cues, often yelled out above the dancing. Moreover, the *mandadores* favor energetic, dynamic singing in loud, commanding chest voices that display the singer's personal style, intermixed with shouts and hollers. Songs are typically structured in verses that repeat the same music to various stanzas of poetic text, sometimes including a chorus that separates the stanzas; alternatively, callers will replace the chorus with additional dance cues.

The musical accompaniment of the chamarrita features a wide variety and number of instruments depending on performance context and musical resources. Most often, chamarrita performances include a violin or fiddle that provides a straightforward tune and several types of Portuguese strummed string instruments for harmonic accompaniment. Strummed string instruments typically include one or more *bandolim* (mandolin) and various types of *viola* (guitar), such as the *viola da terra*, a typical Azorean guitar that uses 12 metal strings in five courses and bears two distinctive heart-shaped sound holes. Ensembles sometimes also utilize accordion as accompaniment. Accompaniment ensembles display great variety: sometimes the ensemble is formed by a large group of instrumentalists, sometimes only guitarists, or sometimes just a solo violin.

Though chamarrita is danced across the Azores archipelago, two of the strongest traditions remain those associated with the islands of Pico and Faial. Within the broad family of dances called "chamarrita," Julio Andrade (1957) identifies four types common in the mid-20th century on Faial, each with distinct dance and musical elements: *chamarrita nova* (new chamarrita), *chamarrita de cima* (chamarrita "from above"), *chamarrita do caracol* ("snail" or "spiral" chamarrita), and the *chamarrita do meio* (chamarrita "from the center"). In the *chamarrita do caracol*, for instance, the partners begin by facing each other in two long rows (men in one row, women in the other) before executing turns and various choreographed movements to form a round dance. The dance in many ways mimics the poetry of the *chamarrita do caracol* text: "*A vida do caracol / È uma vida arrastada / Anda com a casa às costas / Onde quer faz a morada*" (The life of the snail / is a life dragged along / It goes with its house on its shoulders / Everywhere is its home) (Andrade, 1957, p. 104; my translation). Additionally, the singers will call out "*caracol*" as a dance cue, which causes the dancers to let go of their hands and dance in place, turning from left to right, until the caller yells "*salta*"—a command that prompts a circular dance, with men moving right and women moving left, interweaving with one another.

Outside the Azores, the chamarrita remains common in Portuguese-American communities in New England, where a large number of Azoreans emigrated in the late 19th and early-to-mid 20th centuries. A dance by the same name also exists in South America, though little evidence exists to link the tradition definitely to that of the Azores. Scholars believe that the dance likely traveled to Brazil with Portuguese colonizers and spread to other countries as a Brazilian folk dance through Brazil's southernmost region, Rio Grande do Sul. The chamarrita (more usually spelled "chimarrita" in South America) is common today in southern Brazil, Uruguay, and Argentina. The South American forms differ considerably in musical style and typical dance choreography, bearing greater resemblance to other popular Latin American dances such as the tango and fandango than the Azorean folk dance.

Danielle M. Kuntz

See also: Rancho Folclórico

Further Reading

Andrade, Júlio. 1957. "A chamarrita." *Boletim do núcleo cultural da horta* [Garden cultural center bulletin] 1–2, 97–106.

Hare, Maud Cuney. 1928. "Portuguese Folk-Songs, from Provincetown, Cape Cod, Mass." *The Musical Quarterly* 14(1), 35–53.

Chanson (Urban/Modern)

Le chanson (the song) is the pinnacle of French popular music; it has no equivalent in the English-speaking world, thus making it a phenomenon that is closely related to and truly significant for French cultural identity. With a history spanning more than eight centuries, chanson is a unique alloy of socially and emotionally charged poetry accompanied by lyrical music and passionate performance.

Jacques Brel, Georges Brassens, and Léo Ferré are the best representatives of postwar French popular music; they have frequently been associated with and described as the embodiment of chanson and of "Frenchness." Brel, Brassens, and Ferré have been called the trinity of chanson (Looseley, 2003), or "a triumvirate representing the *summum* of French *chanson*" (Poole, 2004, p. xv). Their lyrics and music were a big part of the development of national traditions that supported the cultural aspirations of postwar French society. Brel, Brassens, and Ferré were the epitome of the left-wing intellectual and of the true "Gaul" spirit (Cordier, 2014). They have also been called anarchists and anticlericals because of their lyrics and the inspiration of their songs.

Born in 1916, Léo Ferré enjoyed the career of a vibrant performer in France after World War II until his death in 1993. Forty albums of his music and most of the lyrics written and performed by the singer, as well as many singles, were released between 1960 and the mid-1970s. Some of his songs have become classics of the French chanson repertoire, including "Avec le temps," "C'est extra," "Jolie Môme," and "Paris canaille." Despite his fame and popularity among French-speaking audiences, his music is little known in the English-speaking world. Ferré's songwriting was extremely poetic yet famously highly attuned to the problems of the day. Often seen as the typical French protest singer, he broke free from traditional song, inventing and renovating his own dramatic performances by mixing opposites: rebellion and melancholy, lyricism and coarse language, verse and prose. Ferré became synonymous with the rebel of the times; a young man with a red open-neck shirt and tormented and tragic stage presence, he was called "a musical anarchist," and his repertoire included many "caustic" numbers. Ferré and Brassens were inevitably compared for their rebellious poetry, anarchic character, misanthropy, and fierce individualism (Cordier, 2014, p. 8).

Georges Brassens was born in 1921 in southern France and is considered one of France's most talented postwar poets. He started composing before World War II, but made a name for himself in 1952 when cabaret singer Patachou launched him onto the stage. With more than 20 albums and huge success in France, Brassens rarely performed abroad because of the difficulty of translating his lyrics (though attempts have been made). His songs often decried hypocrisy and self-righteousness in the conservative French society of the time. He often criticized the well-to-do, the clerics, and the people in power indirectly, focusing on the good deeds or the innocence of the poorer classes. His elegant use of language, dark humor, and lively melodies often gave a rather playful feel to even the most serious and somber lyrics. Brassens's music and poetry are considered the embodiment of "intangible French quintessence" (Poole, 2004, p. 9). Numerous international artists from Russia, Israel, the United States, Italy, and Spain have translated and covered Brassens's songs for years. However, being typically French in the contents and expression of their musical art, both Ferré and Brassens were not as widely known internationally as Jacques Brel, the third member of the triumvirate.

Jacques Brel was born in Belgium, in a suburb of Brussels, in 1929. As a young man, Jacques discovered his love for music and had started writing his first songs and performing them at family gatherings by his early twenties. Yet, he did not receive the support and encouragement of relatives and friends to pursue a singing career; what is more, some of his lyrics and his passionate performances were quite a shock to them. In 1953, the young crooner sang at La Rose Noire (The Black Rose), a cabaret in Brussels, and recorded his first single. Impressed by it, the Philips recording label artistic director Jacques Canetti invited Brel to Paris. There, Brel struggled long and hard to get his career off the ground. In 1954, Brel took part in the Grand Prix de la Chanson; he didn't win, but after hearing one of his songs, "Ça va le diable" ("Going to the Devil"), French star Juliette Gréco requested to sing it at the prestigious Olympia music hall. By the end of 1958, Brel had recorded two albums and returned to the Olympia, where he succeeded in captivating the audience with his deeply emotional performance. Three years later, there again, Brel won over the critics who proclaimed him the newest chanson star on the French horizon. Riding his newly found fame, Brel started a grueling world tour. In New York, the American press dubbed him the "Magnetic Hurricane" for his exceptional stage performance. Brel's best-known songs are still covered today by artists the world over. French singers Juliette Gréco, Julien Clerc, Yves Montand, Dalida, Sege Lama, and Isabelle Aubret have recorded numerous Brel classics. His songs have also been covered internationally: Nina Simone and Sting, "Ne me quitte pas" ("If You Go Away"); David Bowie, "Amsterdam"; and Céline Dion, "Quand on a que l'amour" ("When We Have Only Love").

The year 1961 marked the triumph of another pop star, Johnny Hallyday, and symbolized the arrival of rock and roll, or the yé-yé song, with its superficial and foreign lyrics, in France. It also marked the turning of artists such as Brel, Brassens, Ferré, Montand, and Aznavour into emblematic figures of French chanson. "In the era of records and transistors, what are French singers up to? There are still ten of them—ten big names. Chevalier the Parisian, Trenet the poet, Montand the commoner, Distel the nice guy, the dynamic Becaud, Brassens the anarchist, Aznavour the lost child, the passionate Brel and the fierce Ferré" (Cordier, 2014, p. 9).

Juliana Tzvetkova

See also: French Folk Dances

Further Reading

Cordier, Adeline. 2014. *Post War French Popular Music: Cultural Identity.* London: Ashgate.

Harrison, Kim. 2004. "Brassens: Chansons." *The Modern Language Review* 99(2), 503–505.

Looseley, David. 2003. *Popular Music in Contemporary France.* Oxford: Berg.

Poole, Sara. 2001. *Brassens: Chansons.* London: Grant & Cutler.

Poole, Sara. 2004. *Brel and Chansons: A Critical Appreciation.* Lanham, MD: University Press of America.

Chao, Manu (see Manu Chao)

Chinese Pop

Chinese pop music, or "C-Pop," is a fairly recent musical phenomenon that arose in the early 20th century. "Chinese pop music" is a loose umbrella term describing popular music from mainland China, Hong Kong, and Taiwan. Genres that fall under the category of C-Pop include not only pop in the Western sense of the word, but also Chinese rock, R & B, rap, and hip-hop. The term itself developed with the advent of American jazz music in Chinese nightclubs and dancehalls in the 1920s. There are currently two main regional genres of C-Pop: Mandopop and Cantopop. Today, C-Pop, though not as internationally known as other regional Asian popular musics (such as Korean K-Pop or Japanese J-Pop), is growing steadily in popularity both in and outside of China.

The first usage of the term "C-Pop" dates back to the early 1920s, in the circulation of Mandopop in the Shanghai Jazz scene. Extant sources link the arrival of Western musical instruments and theory in China as far back as 1601 (Jones, 2001, pp. 30–35). By the late 19th century, several Western countries established districts in Shanghai as part of international treaties, as with the 1842 Treaty of Nanking (Moskowitz, 2010, p. 16). These districts helped to establish an international presence in Shanghai, and define the city as a growing center of cosmopolitan wealth, sophistication, and progression. Jazz was seen as a reflection of this status, which Shanghai embraced, importing musicians from Japan and Europe to perform in nightclubs for both the Western expatriates and the wealthy Chinese elite.

Mandopop (Mandarin-language Chinese pop) was a byproduct of the musical efforts of pioneering, controversial musician and educator Li Jinhui. Known as *shidaiqu*, Jinhui fused Western traditions with Chinese folk instruments and musicality. Shidaiqu's popularity also blossomed as a result of the Shanghaiese silent film industry, and the commercial success of the gramophone and vinyl record. Jinhui's *Maomaoyu*, written in 1927, was incorporated into Cantonese opera, and is largely considered by many to be the first Chinese "pop" song (Siu and Ku, 2009, p. 60). Jinhui's Bright Moon Song and Dance Troupe was also formed in the 1920s as a music and live dance troupe, replete with "sing-song girls" (*xi sheng*), a term of questionable origin, possibly a reflection of the potential concubinage that sing-song girls might provide to wealthy Chinese men and expatriates.

Nie Er, one of Jinhui's musicians, was an incredibly talented violinist and musician who, in the wake of the Second Sino-Japanese War (1937–1945), consciously decided to pursue the creation of "a new music" for the *petit bourgeoisie* (Jones, 2010, p. 106). Er and Jinhui's collective musical efforts, perhaps because of their relation to the proletarianized music movement and the controversial history of the dance troupe, raised concerns for both the *Kuo Min Tang* (Chinese Nationalist Party or KMT) and the Communist Party of China (CPC). Both political parties labeled the music as "yellow music" (*huang se*)—a reference to the color yellow being associated with pornography. Jinhui's decision to partner with Lianhua Film Company in 1931 opened the doors for those who would become the Seven Great Singing Stars (*qī da gēxīng*) of the recording and film industry in the Shanghai shidaiqu era, whose efforts transformed the public image of the sing-song girl to stardom. When the Second Sino-Japanese War began, music productions shifted south to Hong Kong, which remained the center of popular music until the 1960s.

The China Record Corporation, established in 1949 with the People's Republic of China (PRC), produced only folk music, *guoyue* (artificial pan-Chinese music created for concert halls and televised performances), and patriotic music, in line with the political ideologies consistent with the PRC (Jones, in Ellingham, 2000, p. 34). Mao Zedong made it explicit in his Yan'an Conference that any alternative political or musical voice was to be silenced (Moskowitz, 2010, p. 18).

Much of the shidaiqu music at this time was in Mandarin, a language not understood by the majority of its Hong Kong listeners. By the mid and late 1950s in Hong Kong, shidaiqu and Shanghaiese popular music faced a sharp decline, replaced with the sounds of Cantopop (Cantonese popular music). Owing to Britain's occupation of Hong Kong after World War II, Hong Kong served as a political intermediary through which mainland Chinese could access and listen to Western music. Cantopop became the new sensation, with the new generation of musicians drawing influences from Western pop acts such as the Beatles; interest in earlier Cantonese genres, such as Cantonese opera, was considered old-fashioned (Ellingham, 2000, pp. 49–50). Cantopop and Western music was smuggled into the PRC, and labeled *gangtai*—a term derived from the two Chinese neighboring polities Xiang*gang* and *Tai*wan (Baranovitch, 2003, p. 10). Gangtai, or Cantopop, featured the feelings of loss or heartbreak once associated with shidaiqu, which had been replaced with patriotism and nationalism for the PRC. This music, featuring soft, slow accompaniment and brooding vocals, provided the emotional foundation that music under the PRC lacked (Baranovitch, 2003, p. 12).

Following Mao Zedong's death in 1976, the PRC cultivated a campaign against gangtai music, by embracing Westernized, cosmopolitan musical values. The PRC musical campaigns embraced current genres such as disco, but eschewed any lyric content or musical meanings that they deemed to constitute "spiritual pollution" (Baranovitch, 2003, p. 15). PRC songwriters embraced gangtai as what Mandopop should become (Jones, 2001, p. 67). With the expansion of gangtai into the Mainland Chinese consumer market, it became immensely more accessible to them simply because of the "shared linguistic [and] cultural traditions"; additionally, the PRC banned on European and American music, deeming it morally questionable (Moskowitz, 2010, p. 21). Gangtai simply had no Western competition in this market, and it overwhelmingly controlled the Chinese music market. In the 1980s, the PRC produced its own form of gangtai-style pop, replete with sociopolitical values. The 1980s and 1990s also saw the development of Music Television (MTV) and televised singing competitions, which attracted more than 700 million Chinese viewers.

Today, Cantopop is still considerably more popular than Mandopop. This can be attributed to China's political systems; Hong Kong, the birthplace of Cantopop, has had a considerably longer period of experience with a capitalist market, given its previous British affiliation (Moskowitz, 2010, p. 5). The Cantonese-speaking Chinese diaspora in Singapore also play a significant role in the discourse of contemporary C-Pop. Many Singaporeans identify themselves as ethnically Chinese, and when Singapore was decolonized from the United Kingdom and disassociated with Malaysia in the mid-1960s, efforts were made to encourage the multilingual background of the Singaporean community. By the 1980s, Cantopop circulated throughout Singapore, and Singaporean Cantopop also made its way into Hong Kong and mainland China.

Current popular trends reflect the global awareness of pan-Asian regional pop genres, such as boy- and girl-bands, solo artists, and super-groups. Korean pop made its way into Taiwan and mainland China in 1997 with the first broadcasts of Korean television. Chinese newspapers criticized Korean music's sudden popularity as "culturally odorless" (Iwabuchi, 1998), a remark made about K-Pop's Orientalized, Westernized qualities. Korean pop largely features interpolated English catchphrases in refrains; band names are made of English acronyms (2NE1, for example); and the music, albeit high quality in its aural and visual production, stems from Western popular music (Howard, 2006, p. 177). Musical shifts in Taiwan, Singapore, and Hong Kong reflect the influence of the "Korean *'hallyu'* wave," especially the visual and sonic aesthetics found in Korean pop (Howard, 2006).

John Forrestal

See also: Cantopop; J-Pop; K-Pop; Taiwanese Traditional and Popular Music

Further Reading

Baranovitch, Nimrod. 2003. *China's New Voices: Popular Music, Ethnicity, Gender, and Politics, 1978–1997.* Berkeley: University of California Press.

Chun, Allen, N. Rossiter, and B. Shoesmith, eds. 2004. *Refashioning Pop Music in Asia: Cosmopolitan Flows, Political Tempos, and Aesthetic Industries.* New York: Routledge Curzon.

Craig, Timothy J., and Richard King, eds. 2002. *Global Goes Local: Popular Culture in Asia.* Vancouver: University of British Columbia Press.

Ellingham, Mark. 2000. *World Music: The Rough Guide; Vol. 2: Latin and North America, Caribbean, India, Asia & Pacific.* New York: Rough Guides.

Howard, Keith, ed. 2006. *Korean Pop Music: Riding the Wave.* Kent, UK: Global Oriental.

Iwabuchi, Koichi. 1998. "Marketing 'Japan': Japanese Cultural Presence Under Global Gaze." *Japanese Studies* 18(2): 165–180.

Jones, Andrew F. 1992. *Like a Knife: Ideology and Genre in Contemporary Chinese Popular Music.* Ithaca, NY: Cornell East Asia University Press.

Jones, Andrew F. 2001. *Yellow Music: Media Culture and Colonial Modernity in the Chinese Jazz Age.* Durham, NC: Duke University Press.

Moeran, Brian, ed. 2001. *Asian Media Productions.* Richmond, UK: Routledge Curzon.

Moskowitz, Marc. 2010. *Cries of Joy, Songs of Sorrow: Chinese Pop Music and Its Cultural Connotations.* Honolulu: University of Hawaii Press.

Siu, Helen F., and Agnes S. Ku, eds. 2008. *Hong Kong Mobile: Making a Global Population.* Hong Kong: Hong Kong University Press.

Chopi People, Music of the

The Chopi people are an ethnic group of Mozambique. They are famous for their xylophone practice known as Timbila Orchestra. They have lived in a region extending from some 70 miles south-southwest of Inhambane province to the Inharrime River valley. They speak the Chopi language, which is a tonal language in the Bantu family.

The identity of the ethnic group as "Chopi" formed through a historical process. In the 19th century, a Gaza regiment (1824–1895) that was led by Soshangana (1790–1858) invaded and conquered the area of southern Mozambique, in a conflict that produced many refugees. Although many people between the Limpopo and the Sabi Rivers came directly under the control of the Gaza, and others came under the authority of the Portuguese authorities at Inhambane, those settled in a band of territory along the Inharrime valley were able to remain independent for several decades (Vail and White, 1991, p. 114). The mixture of refugees of diverse origins and the local population formed a culturally homogeneous ethnic group known as Chopi (Vail and White, 1991, p. 114). *Chopi* meant "the bowmen" or "the archers" in Northern Nguni. They protected their territory with large stockades and their considerable skill as archers.

Independence of the Chopi eroded after 1886, because of the reinvasion of Gaza. In 1891, troops of Gungunyana (1850–1906), a leader of the Gaza regime, massacred many of the Chopi people and enslaved some others. In 1895, a conflict between the Portuguese and the Gaza occurred, during which the Portuguese army captured Gungunyana. After that the Portuguese began to rule all areas in southern Africa, including the Chopi habitat. Portuguese control continued until Mozambique achieved independence in 1975. Many Chopi people were displaced and killed by the civil war that was fought throughout Inhambane district between the FRELIMO government and the Resistência Nacional Moçambique (RENAMO) guerilla movement.

The Chopi are renowned for their traditional music. The most famous music instrument is their xylophone *mbila* (pl. *timbila*). The keys (slats) of the mbila are made of *mwenje* (sneezewood) trees, and they are struck by drumsticks capped with rubber. The mbila xylophone is played in a large group which is often called a *timbila* orchestra; such an orchestra consists of 10 to 15 xylophones of five sizes covering a range of four octaves. They are accompanied by a single-headed drum and small idiophones. The timbila orchestra has a history of more than 500 years. It was first described in the writing of André Fernandes, a Portuguese visitor, in 1562 (Lutero, 1980, p. 39). In 2005 the Chopi timbila was recognized as a Masterpiece of Oral and Intangible Cultural Heritage of Humanity by UNESCO.

Other representative musical instruments of Chopi people are the *shitende* (or *chitende*), the *chizambi* (variously also known as *chivelane* or *shivelan*) and the *tsudi*. The *shitende* is a gourd-resonated bow, which is also played in the large part of southern Mozambique and neighboring countries. It consists of a wooden bow with a wire string and a dried bottle gourd attached to the bow which acts as a resonator. To play shitende, the player holds it with one hand, pressing the string with the fingers, and also holds a stick with the other hand to beat the string. The bottle gourd attached to the bow is pressed against the player's chest and lifted away to vary the sound. Usually shitende is played singly and accompanies the player's song. *Shivelan* is a mouth-resonated bow consisting of a wooden bow with notches and a string. The string is made of dried palm leaf. To play shivelan, the player holds the bow with one hand placing the string between the lips, and also holds a stick with the other hand to stroke the notched part. To change the pitch, the player fingers the string. Neighboring ethnic groups, the Thonga and Ndau, also play shivela. *Tsudi* is an instrument made of bamboo (or other type of wooden tube). Generally, young men play this instrument while dancing *chimveka* (or *xinveca*). They dance in the circle in the moonlight. About seven flutes are used for this dance. They use various sizes of reed pipes, each of which has a different tone. Sometimes they play a rattle at the same time with the other hand.

Though many dances and music instruments are common with the culture of other ethnic groups, *mbila* xylophone has been handed down only among the Chopi people. Traditionally, mbila xylophones are played in the *ngodo* (pl. *migodo*), which is a dance drama of Chopi. Ngodo dance dramas consist of choreographed dance,

Chopi musician from Mozambique playing a *mbila*, a type of xylophone. (Picture Post/Hulton Archive/Getty Images)

music of the timbila orchestra, and lyrics. Usually a dance drama lasts about 45 minutes. Each ngodo consists of between nine and 11 sections. Some sections are orchestral pieces, but others are dances with mbila music. New migodo are composed every two years or so.

One of the very obvious limitations of this genre was its male domination (Vail and White, 1991, p. 125). South African musicologist Hugh Tracey, who had been in Inhambane district between 1940 and 1943 to study the music of the Chopi, did not describe anything about women participants in ngodo. However, there are many female dancers and timbila players nowadays.

Ngodo plays a role as a forum for criticism. The topic of the lyrics is social problems or concerns. The themes of the ngodo have changed to reflect their Chopi people's social realities and their lives. Lyrics of ngodo written by a colonial administrator, Augusto Cabral, in the early 1900s were about historical warfare or complaint in the early years of colonial rule (Vail and White, 1991, p. 118). In the early 1940s, besides the complaint about the Portuguese colonial rule, social problems created by the migrant-labor system also became a primary theme of ngodo. Many Chopi men had to migrate to the gold mines of South Africa to pay taxes imposed by the Portuguese. Reduction of the male population due to the migrant-labor system threatened the handing down of the timbila. A change in the traditional chief's role brought about by colonial rule and the new government's policy of independent Mozambique also adversely affected the practice of ngodo. Traditionally, chiefs sponsored the Chopi timbila ensembles, but their diminishing power and authority in Mozambique has made them unable to financially support such ensembles, some of which have since turned to government agencies for sponsorship (Hogan, 2006, p. 6). Moreover, Mozambique's civil war (1977–1992) heavily damaged the society of Chopi and many timbila masters migrated to the capital Maputo.

Though many social changes weakened the practice of ngodo in the Chopi community in Mozambique, newly adapted ngodo have been composed in communities of migrant miners in South Africa. Migrant workers have formed musical communities in their mining towns, drawing diverse musical practices together in the performance of modified timbila music (Hogan, 2006, p. 6). Revival of timbila orchestras in Mozambique is mainly due to Venâncio Mbande (1930–), who was born in Inhambane and migrated to South Africa to work in the mines. He is a famous mbila player, as well as a composer and craftsman who formed timbila orchestras in a mine. After he returned to his home in Inhambane province, he started to train young musicians.

A cultural organization called AMIZAVA (Amigos de Zavala) was founded in 1994 to promote the culture in the Zavala district of Inhambane where Chopi people live. They organize a timbila festival called *M'saho* every year in Zavala.

Mayako Koja

See also: Mbila

Further Reading

Hogan, Brian. 2006. "Locating the Chopi Xylophone Ensembles of Southern Mozambique." *Pacific Review of Ethnomusicology* 11, 1–18.

Lutero, Martinho. 1980. "As Timbila." In Ganbinete de Organização do Festival da Canção e Música Tradicional (ed.), *Música tradicional em Moçambique*, 39–45. Maputo: Tipografia Académica.

Tracey, Hugh. 1948. *Chopi Musicians: Their Music, Poetry, and Instruments*. London: International African Institute.

Vali, Leroy, and Landeg White. 1991. *Power and the Praise Poem: Southern African Voices in History*. Charlottesville: University Press of Virginia.

Chutney

Chutney is a genre of Indian-Caribbean music popular in Trinidad and Tobago, Guyana, Suriname, and the Indian-Caribbean diaspora. Chutney is commonly programmed on Caribbean and diaspora radio stations, played for entertainment at nightclubs and parties, and sold at CD shops catering to Indo-Caribbeans; it has been slow to penetrate the digital distribution market. Chutney is best regarded as a conglomerate of styles loosely bound by a common instrumentation, at least marginal use of *Bhojpuri* (a dialect of Hindi) song texts, and typically upbeat tempos. The name "chutney" derives from the Hindi word *chatni*, referring to a mixture of hot spices and fruits. This term was borrowed for the musical genre to describe its risqué subject matter and the "hotness" of its syncopated rhythmic groove.

Indians began arriving in Trinidad in 1845 as indentured agricultural laborers. By 1917, nearly 150,000 had settled there permanently. As few were professional musicians, a unique Indian-Trinidadian musical system coalesced from fragments of Indian folk and classical music traditions. From an amalgam of Hindu devotional songs, popular melodies, and marginal borrowing from local European- and African-Trinidadian sources, Indian-Trinidadians created new forms distinct from those of their Indian forebears. Therefore, the stylistic foundation of chutney lay in a mix of Indian-derived musical sources, most importantly bawdy women's songs and local classical (*tan*) singing.

During indenture and much of the 20th century, Hindu life-cycle ceremonies provided ample opportunity for women's amateur music-making, often done by singing groups accompanying themselves with the small double-headed *dholak* drum and stick idiophone *dhantal* while singing *lachari* (bawdy Bhojpuri-language songs). The most important contexts for lachari were weddings and childbirth ceremonies. Repertoire for these gatherings featured a repetitive verse/refrain and syncopated percussive accompaniment with humorously sexual song texts. Given that these rites ultimately stemmed from fertility rituals, such songs were certainly vulgar, but not inappropriate. Women today continue to sing at similar ceremonies, though the repertoire has greatly declined as the number of Bhojpuri speakers has decreased.

Local classical singing is a broad category of song genres derived from Indian courtly singing and Hindu devotional and folk music. Coalescing in Trinidad and Tobago, Guyana, and Suriname in the early 20th century, local classical singing was done by men who exchanged musical ideas across political borders at annual competitions first organized in the 1920s. Indian-derived genres such as *thumri*, *dhrupad*, *tilana*, and others were sung in Indian-Caribbean style for competitions and in performance contexts such as weddings, *Ramayan* recitations, and community events. Unlike women's songs, local classical singing was perpetuated by specialists who developed a loose set of musical theoretical principles, a body of repertoire, and a cultivated performance practice passed from one generation to the next. From about 1940, instrumentation always included the small pump organ *harmonium*—never an essential part of women's singing in the contexts described earlier—in addition to dholak and dhantal.

By the 1970s, mostly male musicians with a background in local classical singing began performing lachari-style songs with faster tempos and Bhojpuri and English texts. This style used a core instrumentation of harmonium, dholak, and dhantal but sometimes added synthesizers, drum machine, guitar, bass, and a horn section. Sundar Popo (born Sunilal Popo Bahora; 1943–2000) was foremost among those who popularized this new style, which was eventually marketed as "chutney." Popo's father was a *tassa* drummer who played for weddings and his mother was a wedding singer. Popo learned the fundamental lachari-style repertoire by ear as he was taken along to weddings as a child. Popo's comfort with lachari and pop styles is apparent in his first hit "Nani and Nana" (1969), often regarded as the first pop chutney tune. The instrumentation of the original recording includes a synthesizer instead of harmonium, a tambourine instead of dhantal, dholak, and electric rhythm and lead guitars, with a liberal use of Bhojpuri words throughout the text.

Music of Anand and Rakesh Yankaran, sons of late local classical singer Isaac Yankaran (1932–1969) and each a chutney star in his own right, is illustrative of the current stylistic range of chutney. Whereas Anand generally maintains chutney's core instrumentation, his brother Rakesh's arrangements frequently feature additional instruments and pop rhythms, though each sings almost exclusively in Bhojpuri. Since the late 1980s, women have frequently succeeded as chutney stars. Drupatee Ramgoonai stirred controversy for her suggestive lyrics and crossover to chutney-soca in the early 1990s. More recently, Rasika Dindial has emerged among a new vanguard of chutney singers whose sound and image typify a conservative chutney style descending from local classical tradition.

Christopher L. Ballengee

See also: Calypso; Chutney Soca; Soca; Steelpan

Further Reading

Manuel, Peter. 2000. *Tān-singing, Chutney, and the Making of Indo-Caribbean Culture.* Philadelphia: Temple University Press.

Myers, Helen. 1998. *Music of Hindu Trinidad: Songs from the India Diaspora.* Chicago: University of Chicago Press.

Ramnarine, Tina K. 2001. *Creating Their Own Space: The Development of an Indian-Caribbean Musical Tradition.* Mona, Jamaica: University of the West Indies Press.

Chutney Soca

Chutney soca is a pop music genre of Trinidad and Tobago conceived as a fusion of two parent musical genres, chutney and soca. Elements drawn from chutney include Indian-derived melodic contours, a mixture of English and Bhojpuri or Hindi song texts, and inclusion (or at least electronic timbral evocation) of chutney instrumentation: the small double-headed drum *dholak*, the stick idiophone *dhantal*, and the small pump organ *harmonium*. Elements drawn from soca include fast tempos, a repetitive syncopated dance groove emphasizing strong bass tones on each beat, and synthesized instrumental timbres. Though the musical styles of chutney singer Sundar Popo and calypsonian Lord Shorty laid the groundwork for Indian/African-Trinidadian musical fusions in the early 1970s, the first unequivocal chutney soca superstar was Drupatee (born Drupatee Ramgoonai, 1945–) who burst onto the Carnival music scene in the late 1980s. Trained in local classical singing by James Ramsawak, Drupatee's 1987 album *Chatnee Soca* and subsequent megahit single "Mr. Bissesar (Roll Up de Tassa)" (1988) marked her transition to pop music and established a musical blueprint for an emerging new sound. "Mr. Bissessar" is particularly notable for its integration of *tassa* drumming, an important marker of Indian-Trinidadian culture, into a soca framework.

Drupatee ignited controversy as an assertive and sexy Indo-Trinidadian woman entering the arena of Carnival music, which up to that time had been dominated by African-Trinidadian men. While many praised her perspective as refreshing, others criticized her music as an unwelcome intrusion—this stemming from persistent racial divisions apparent in many facets of Trinidadian society. Moreover, her suggestive lyrics and sensual performances (aspects typical of both soca and the ribald women's songs from which chutney ultimately derives) drew criticism from conservative Indian-Trinidadians who saw chutney soca as a degradation of Indian culture by virtue of its mixing with Creole elements and regarded Drupatee's performances in particular as "immoral and disgusting." Proponents and fans of chutney soca, however, conceptualized her new sound as symbolic of the reality of a creolized (and therefore fundamentally fused and hybrid) Trinidadian society in which all people were free to mix as they chose, either musically or otherwise.

Chutney soca today is undoubtedly mainstream. With the advent of the Chutney Soca Monarch competition—first organized in 1996 and modeled on the venerable Calypso Monarch contest—chutney soca claimed a permanent place in Carnival, an annual festival central to Trinidadian national identity. Rikki Jai is currently the most successful Chutney Soca Monarch champion, having won the contest six times since its inception. Jai made headlines as the first nationally popular Indian-Trinidadian soca singer in the 1980s, but had largely transitioned into chutney soca by the early 1990s. "Mor Tor" (2005), a chutney soca arrangement of a song sung for *lawa* (women's rice-parching ritual at Hindu weddings), is indicative of his more recent work. Recorded in collaboration with soca phenom Machel Montano, Jai sings the melody in Hindi with Montano singing the refrain in English. The musical texture foregrounds synthesized dholak, dhantal, and harmonium timbres accentuated by a soca-style drum machine program.

Christopher L. Ballengee

See also: Calypso; Chutney; Soca; Steelpan

Further Reading

Chutney Soca. 2000. JMC Music Group JMC 1228.

Manuel, Peter. 2000. *Tān-singing, Chutney, and the Making of Indo-Caribbean Culture.* Philadelphia: Temple University Press.

Classical Music, European

The term "classical music" refers to so-called art music, which originated in Europe around the ninth century, and developed its most important features between the late Renaissance and the end of the 19th century. The same term also indicates a shorter period of European musical production which stretches from around 1730 to around 1830. The philosophical and theoretical roots of European classical music date back to ancient Greek and Latin culture.

ORIGINS

Pythagoras of Samos (ca. 570–ca. 495 BCE) discovered that musical notes could be translated into mathematical equations, and that individual tones of the scales were just the result of ratios. He created a tuning system (Pythagorean tuning) using the monochord. This musical instrument—a single string stretched over a sound box—has been used for centuries for didactic and study purposes. Severinus Boethius (ca. 480–ca. 525), in his *De institutione musica*, introduced a threefold classification of music: *musica mundana* (music of the spheres), *musica humana* (spiritual harmony, vocal music), and *musica instrumentalis* (instrumental music). This represented the foundation of musical philosophy until the late 18th century, when aesthetic theories began to prevail.

The Middle Ages saw the foundation of modern music theory. Most of the music surviving from this period is plainchant: monophonic music mostly connected to liturgy and influenced by local older traditions. It later developed into Gregorian chant, thanks to the joint action of Pepin the Younger (ca. 714–768) and Pope Gregory II (669–731), which unified local traditions and spread the new music for the Catholic liturgy all over Europe. Gregorian chant first used an adiastematic notation which gave no indication of the value of intervals between sounds, and no suggestion of rhythm. The Italian monk Guido d'Arezzo (ca. 995–after 1033) played a central role in the development of music theory. He not only introduced the modern names of notes (ut, re, mi, fa, sol, la), but also began to use staves in musical notation.

Starting from the early 1000s, Gregorian chant used four-line staves and black square neumes, giving a more precise indication of pitch. Music sources contain mostly monodies until the 12th century; however, early examples of polyphonic music date back even to the early 10th century, when the anonymous treatise *Musica enchiriadis* gave suggestions on how to improvise polyphony and recorded a first attempt to notate polyphony using the rare Daseian notation.

The School of Notre Dame (ca. 1160–ca. 1250), based in Paris, developed polyphony through new musical genres such as *organum*, *motet* (both borrowing material from Gregorian chant), and *conductus*, the first polyphonic genre to make use of only newly composed musical material. Composers such as Léonin and Pérotin are mentioned in a musical treatise written in the 13th century by an English student at Notre Dame, which is now considered the main theoretical source for the music of that period.

The 14th century saw the rise of a new practice (*Ars Nova*), of which the development of musical notation is considered one of the main achievements. Its main exponents were Guillame de Machaut (ca. 1300–1377) and Francesco Landini (ca. 1325–1397), the former from France, and the latter from Italian territories. Although their styles were different, both schools focused on secular music to a degree that none ever had before, exploiting genres such as motet, *ballade, lais, virelais, rondeau, caccia*, and madrigal.

The madrigal played a central role in musical development during the Renaissance. From the second half of the 16th century, it usually used five voices, and demonstrated a growing interest in the relationship between music and words, through its use of chromaticism, counterpoint, and timbre. In the early books of madrigals by Claudio Monteverdi (1567–1643), the first signs of modern tonality are already noticeable. The dramatic sensibility of his works for the theater foreshadows the baroque style. In *Orfeo* (1607) the new form of "melodrama" attains a perfect balance between action and lyricism. The later opera *L'incoronazione di Poppea* (1643) can be considered one of the milestones of musical theater.

Giovanni Luigi da Palestrina (1525–1594) is considered the sacred counterpart of Monteverdi, as he developed forms more related to the liturgy, such as masses and motets. His masterpiece is certainly the *Missa Papae Marcelli*, which makes use of a distinct homorhythm and no pre-existent musical material. It differs from many polyphonic masses of the 16th century in that the text of its voices never overlaps, in order to make the words clearly understandable by the audience.

BAROQUE

Baroque style is characterized by the extensive use of melodic ornamentation and variation, and the use of the *basso continuo*, which accompanies the music through the improvised elaboration of chords, following the lowest line of the score. Baroque music aimed to stupefy and amuse the audience; thus, sudden changes of rhythm and meter, virtuoso passages, and complex counterpoint were all used. All these features characterized the fugue, a form based on the elaboration of one or more thematic ideas, first stated and then reaffirmed several times over the piece, exploiting its expressive potential.

The fugue reached its peak with Johann Sebastian Bach (1685–1750), who in 1722 published *The Well-Tempered Clavier* (*Das Wohltemperierte Klavier*) comprised of 48 fugues, which became a turning point in modern tonality and counterpoint. The baroque era saw an acceptance of modern music theory; meanwhile, musical instruments themselves were acquiring their modern shapes. The rise of keyboard instruments such as the harpsichord and the spinet was accompanied by the development of the family of bowed strings, which were taking the forms generally seen today. The early orchestra evolved, together with the hegemony of string instruments; bassoon and harpsichord acted as basso continuo, contrasting with more melodic instruments such as flutes and oboes. *A cappella* vocal music progressively decayed, replaced by the choral music in opera and the new genre of oratorio. The latter was a paraliturgical musical performance inspired by religious narrative, in the form of recitatives and arias, accompanied by harpsichord and orchestra. In this sense it is similar to melodrama, but it was performed in oratories and churches rather than theaters.

In instrumental music, the baroque period saw the birth of other important forms such as the suite and *concerto grosso*. The former was a composition comprised of several pieces inspired by dances, among which were the *allemande, courante, sarabande, gigue, minuet, gavotte,* and *bourrée*. Important works in this form are the Six Cello Suites (1717–1723) by J. S. Bach, and *Water Music* (1717) and *Music for the Royal Fireworks* (1749) by G. F. Handel (1685–1759). Handel also played a noteworthy part in the production of *concerti grossi*, for instance with his Twelve *Concerti Grossi* (op. 6, 1739), where a *concertino* (smaller ensemble of soloists) of two violins and a cello was set off from the *ripieno* (bigger ensemble), made of a four-part string orchestra with basso continuo. A further significant example of the genre is Bach's Brandenburg Concertos (*Concerts avec plusieurs instruments*, 1721), a collection of six compositions dedicated to Christian Ludwig, Margrave of Brandenburg.

In the 18th century, the contrast between concertino and ripieno developed into a stronger distinction between whole orchestra and solo instruments, consequently giving birth to the new form of concerto for solo and orchestra. Initially concertos were composed for violin, trumpet, or oboe, by composers such as Torelli and Albinoni, but soon the range of solo instruments grew, as witnessed in Vivaldi's wide variety of solo compositions. These compositions formed the basis of a musical form that remained unchanged for centuries: a succession of three movements (fast-slow-fast), the middle movement in a different tonality from the initial and final movements. In the fast movements the soloist often displayed technical skills in an improvised passage known as a *cadenza*, which remained a standard element in music over the entire classical and romantic periods.

CLASSICISM

The Classical period, from about 1750 to the first decades of the 19th century, was characterized by the attempt to create a balance among the various parts of a composition. The most typical example of this is the introduction of the formal scheme known as sonata form. This structure was based on the dialectic between two themes, and articulated in three main sections: exposition, development, and recapitulation. It was used in several genres, including concerto and symphony. Wolfgang Amadeus Mozart (1756–1791) played a key role in the development of both these genres, writing masterpieces such as his renowned Piano Concerto no. 21 (1785), and Symphony no. 41 in C major (*Jupiter*; 1788).

Ludwig van Beethoven (1770–1827) is remembered mainly for his contribution to symphonic music. His Symphony no. 9 (op. 125, 1824), composed when he was totally deaf, was the first symphony to make use of vocal music and marked a crucial turning point in this genre. In the classical era the orchestra was modernized. The harpsichord progressively lost relevance, while the violin acquired its leading role. Even in chamber music the harpsichord was gradually replaced by the fortepiano and then the piano, where the player's control of dynamics allows for superior expression. Wind instruments such as the oboe and bassoon had already been standardized in the previous century, but instruments in the single-reed family (mostly clarinets and basset horn) were not widely used until Mozart developed their role in both the orchestra and chamber ensembles.

In the theater, several regional styles developed in Italy, France, and German-speaking lands. A singer's agency to improvise became more restricted, as composers aimed for perfect balance between music and drama. Mozart himself was quite prolific in writing music for the theater, with operas such as *Le nozze di Figaro* (1786), *Don Giovanni* (1787), *Così fan tutte* (1790), and *Die Zauberflöte* (1791).

Another form developed during the 18th century was the string quartet. Generally composed of two violins, one viola, and a cello, the string quartet is often considered one of the most important genres in chamber music. It was developed extensively by Joseph Haydn (1732–1809), whose wittiness marked the quartet no. 2, op. 33, *The Joke*. Nowadays, the tune of the second movement of his quartet no. 3. op. 76, constitutes the main theme of Germany's national anthem.

ROMANTICISM

During the 19th century, music tended to be composed according to principles of the romantic aesthetic. Romantic composers tried to express feelings and passions, refusing to obey the rigid formal rules of classicism. Consequently, concise freeforms such as *nocturne*, *lied*, *fantasia*, romance with no words, and prelude became quite common. Normally such compositions were privately performed, mostly for philanthropists, patrons, or wealthy families. Melody played a key role as a means of expression, along with more use of chromaticism. Dynamics became less regular, and more attention was paid to instrumental timbres with regard to orchestration. The variety of instruments in the orchestra expanded, especially the range of percussion (snare drum, bass drum, cymbals, triangle, tambourine, glockenspiel).

The introduction of rotary valves gave brass instruments the chance to play a wider range of notes, expanding their use in the orchestra. Such technical improvements boosted orchestras' capability and, together with a peculiarly romantic aesthetic, led to the composition of innovative symphonies like Berlioz's *Symphonie Fantastique* (op. 14, 1830). This kind of work, called either "symphonic poem" or more generically "program music," started the distinctive romantic fashion of writing compositions explicitly based on a given extra-musical idea. Further notable works of this sort were the *Ouverture 1812* by Tchaikovsky (1840–1893), and later *Finlandia* (op. 26, 1899) by the Finnish composer Jean Sibelius (1865–1957), which illustrated episodes from Finnish history. Indeed, in the early 19th century a nationalist musical movement emerged, first as support for regional political independence movements, then as a reaction against the dominance of a mainstream European classical tradition. It was characterized by the use of national musical elements (folk tunes or rhythms), as well as the adoption of nationalist subjects in operas and symphonic poems.

A distinctive folk idea is obvious in the mazurkas and polonaises by the Polish composer Frédéric Chopin (1810–1849), one of the first to incorporate nationalist elements into his works. The Czech Bedřich Smetana (1824–1884) wrote a symphonic cycle titled *Má Vlast* ("My Homeland," 1874–1879), in which he depicted some traditional traits of his country. Italians under the rule of the Austro-Hungarian Empire could recognize their political condition in the opera *Nabucodonosor* (1841), one of the most celebrated works by Giuseppe Verdi (1813–1910), which portrayed the Jews suffering under Babylonian rule.

CONTEMPORARY MUSIC

In the late 19th and early 20th centuries, composers started to reject musical characteristics which had traditionally been valued (tonality, melody, structure, and even instrumentation), developing brand new musical theories and techniques. The starting point for the modern disintegration of tonality can be considered the half-diminished seventh chord set by Richard Wagner (1813–1883) to the opening phrase of the opera *Tristan und Isolde* (1865). Although the chord itself was not unusual at that time, the audience considered it disorienting, due to its unfamiliar relationship to the implied tonality.

The earliest post-romantic composers were still born within the boundaries of the previous century, among them Gustav Mahler (1860–1911) and Richard Strauss (1864–1949). The former is remembered mainly for his contribution to the development of the symphonic form. His eighth symphony is often called *Symphony of a Thousand* (1906), as it requires enormous instrumental and vocal forces. It is one of the largest-scale choral works in the classical concert repertoire. Strauss is renowned for the conspicuous number of symphonic poems he wrote, and advances he made in the composition of programmatic music. Among them are *Till Eulenspiegels lustige Streiche* (op. 28, 1894), *Also sprach Zarathustra* (op. 30, 1896), and *Eine Alpensinfonie* (op. 64, 1915).

After the end of the Great War (World War I), music witnessed the birth of neo-classicism. Composers took inspiration from the Renaissance, baroque, and classical periods (e.g., *Le tombeau de Couperin*, 1914–1917, by Maurice Ravel). Regarding subjects for opera and ballets, many composers were drawn to ancient literary sources from Greek and Latin myths, as for *Oedipus Rex* (1927) by Igor Stravinsky (1882–1971). In the early 20th century, tonality was seen to have reached a point of breakdown. The continuous use of ambiguous chords and progressively sporadic melodic and rhythmic changes made clear that the syntax of traditional harmony had finally been loosened.

The Austrian Arnold Schönberg (1874–1951) was certainly the most influential composer of the early 20th century, especially through his contribution to the development of atonality (absence of tonality) and dodecaphonic technique, which manipulates an ordered series of all 12 notes in the chromatic scale. His music is often labeled "expressionist," as he valued the exasperated emotional side of reality rather than its perceived objectivity. His students include many significant composers, such as Alban Berg, Anton Webern, and later John Cage. It must be noted, however, that the 20th century also witnessed other musical currents not particularly involved in the dissolution of tonality.

Jacopo Mazzeo

See also: Concerto; Gregorian Chant; Medieval Secular Song; Opera; Polish National Dances; Polka; Psaltery; Singspiel; Symphonic Poem; Symphony; Waltz

Further Reading

Alwes, Chester Lee. 2014. *A History of Western Choral Music*. New York: Oxford University Press.

Atlas, Allan W. 1998. *Renaissance Music: Music in Western Europe, 1400–1600*. New York: Norton.

Burkholder, J. Peter, and Claude V. Palisca. 2010. *Norton Anthology of Western Music*. New York: W.W. Norton.

Everist, Mark. 2011. *The Cambridge Companion to Medieval Music*. Cambridge: Cambridge University Press.

Fassler, Margot Elsbeth. 2014. *Music in the Medieval West*. New York: W.W. Norton.

Gracyk, Theodore, and Andrew Kania. 2014. *The Routledge Companion to Philosophy and Music*. Abingdon, UK: Routledge.

Grout, Donald Jay, J. Peter Burkholder, and Claude V. Palisca. 2006. *A History of Western Music*. New York: W.W. Norton.

Haar, James. 2006. *European Music, 1520–1640*. Woodbridge, UK: Boydell Press.

Heller, Wendy. 2014. *Music in the Baroque*. New York: Norton.

Hill, John Walter. 2005. *Baroque Music: Music in Western Europe, 1580–1750*. New York: W.W. Norton.

Keefe, Simon P. 2005. *The Cambridge Companion to the Concerto*. Cambridge: Cambridge University Press.

Parker, Roger. 1994. *The Oxford Illustrated History of Opera*. New York: Oxford University Press.

Plantinga, Leon. 1999. *Beethoven's Concertos: History, Style, Performance*. New York: W.W. Norton.

Roand, Ellen, and Carl Anthon. 1985. *Renaissance Music*. New York: Garland.

Roeder, Michael Thomas. 1994. *A History of the Concerto*. Portland, OR: Amadeus Press.

Taruskin, Richard. 2005. *The Oxford History of Western Music*. New York: Oxford University Press.

Till, Nicholas. 2012. *The Cambridge Companion to Opera Studies*. Cambridge: Cambridge University Press.
White, Chappell. 1992. *From Vivaldi to Viotti: A History of the Early Classical Violin Concerto*. Philadelphia: Gordon and Breach.
Wright, Craig M., and Bryan R. Simms. 2006. *Music in Western Civilization*. Belmont, CA: Thomson Schirmer.

Claves and Clave Rhythm

The term "clave rhythm" describes the rhythmic and temporal organization foundational to many types of music in the Caribbean, Latin America, and Africa. In particular, Cuba, where the clave's musical impact may be most deeply felt, this rhythm is often played on a pair of wooden struck idiophones of the same name—*claves*—that provides the rhythmic framework for many styles of Afro-Cuban music.

CLAVES

Claves is the name given to the Cuban percussion instrument performed in many Afro-Cuban folk and popular music styles, and in ritual performance contexts. It is an instrument that can also be found in many other parts of Latin America. Claves consist of a pair of short sticks or cylindrical rods made from various types of hardwood such as rosewood, granadilla, or ebony. Traditionally the size of the claves may vary; however, typically they are between eight to eleven inches long and roughly one to two inches wide. Gender identities are ascribed to the claves that also impact their size relative to one another—a common feature of paired instruments in many parts of Africa and the diaspora. The *macho* is the male, and the *hembra* is the female, which is typically a half-inch shorter. Today one can find claves made of a special kind of fiberglass that gives the instrument more volume and is more durable.

The origins of the claves are linked to the development of Cuba's ship-building industry, which began in the late 16th century, particularly in the shipyards of Havana. During this period, ships were not constructed using nails, but wooden pegs called *clavijas* that were made of dense, hard wood that was able to resist the moist conditions of the sea. By the 17th century, Cuba became an important location for Spanish ship building, drawing largely on the high-quality hardwood forests that surrounded Havana and the labor of enslaved Africans, *negros curros* (Spanish black or mulattos), Spanish prisoners, and free *guajiros* (Cuban peasant class). It was during this time and in this context that the uses and function of the *clavijas* transformed and were modified to that of the contemporary claves.

Performers of claves achieve a sound by striking the two sticks together to produce a clear, piercing tone that cuts through the instrumental ensemble. Typically players use the stick in the right hand to strike the middle of the stick in the left. Sometimes players will cup the left hand while holding the stick to give the instrument a louder sound. In these instances the hand functions as a type of resonator that can be "tuned" by the performer through increasing or decreasing the depth of the cupped hand, thereby affecting the depth of the tone.

In Cuba, claves are used in popular styles like *son*, *danzon*, or *pachanga*. In the various forms of Afro-Cuban rumba, which also feature the claves, the *sonero* or lead singer typically plays the instrument. This is appropriate, since in the early days of the claves' development in Cuba they were connected with the singing activities of both black and white laborers in Havana's shipyards. Claves were used to keep time during such singing sessions when guitars and drums were prohibited.

CLAVE RHYTHM

As a prolific musical phenomenon encompassing only five notes, claves have received significant scholarly attention from ethnomusicologists and music enthusiasts seeking to uncover its origins, function, development, and theoretical implications. A reoccurring rhythmic ostinato pattern that serves as an important organizing principle in compositions, the origins of the clave pattern or rhythm are linked to West African musical practices in particular and the trans-Atlantic slave trade that forced large populations of enslaved Africans to the Caribbean and the Americas to fuel a number of European colonial economies. Although the term has taken on a deeper complexity over the years, the etymology of the word is Spanish, literally meaning "key," "code," "clef," or "keystone," underscoring its importance as a foundational and deeply meaningful musical concept.

The earliest recorded manifestations of the clave pattern date back to mid–13th-century Bagdad, in a manuscript written by the music scholar Safi al-Din who notated and named the rhythm "al-thaqil al-awwal." However, historical evidence from oral or written accounts in West Africa offer little evidence that the clave rhythmic pattern connected with Afro-Cuba or elsewhere in the African diaspora existed in Africa prior to the trans-Atlantic slave trade, despite the existence of binary musical types built off reoccurring timelines. Some scholars suggest that the clave pattern is derived from a similar five-note rhythm used in ternary music types found in West Africa, and was altered from this 12/8 construction to its current 4/4 type during the African diaspora. Others disagree, identifying music types in Africa built off the clave pattern. The flow of music between Africa and the African diaspora adds profound complexity to this debate, especially when considering the impact of Caribbean and Latin American music on many forms of music in Africa since the early 19th century.

In 4/4 time, the clave pattern is represented in transcriptions within a set of 16 pulses, and in staff notation is most commonly transcribed using 16th notes. Using the Time Unit Box System (TUBS) to represent the clave pattern, each box represents a pulse. An empty box indicates a period of rest for that interval, while an "X" inside the box represents a sounded note. Sixteen boxes therefore represent the 16th notes that one would use to transcribe the clave pattern in 4/4 time using staff notation. Clave can also be played, and therefore written, in triple meter as well.

It is common to hear musicians familiar with music built off the clave pattern to refer to different types, namely the standard "3:2" or "2:3" constructions. These terms describe the different ways the clave is organized temporally in a piece of music, and likely developed out of the Afro-Jazz era in the United States as a way for non-Cuban musicians to distinguish them from one another. Many folkloric and popular musicians from Cuba have insisted that the concept of 3:2 vs. 2:3 is foreign to Cuban musical discourses.

The 3:2 clave is sometimes referred to as the *son clave*, marking its close connection with Afro-Cuban forms of music. Manifestations of the clave in triple meter are commonly heard as well, particularly in a fast style of Cuban rumba called *Columbia*. This construction of the clave in 12/8 is the rhythm from Africa that some scholars suggest was the basis for the clave's development in Cuba, and is also the ternary manifestation of the 3:2 clave. As with some timeline structures in Africa, duple-pulse clave forms have their triple-pulse correlative. Note that it is also common to see the ternary constructions of the clave notated in 6/8, and therefore represented as a two-bar phrase.

The 2:3 clave is built on the same principle as the 3:2 clave, with the second half of the rhythm (beats 9–16) occurring first, followed by the first half (beats 1–8) of the standard 3:2 clave.

The 3:2 versus 2:3 opposition articulated by non-Cuban musicians was their way of identifying the underlying theoretical properties of the clave rhythm. The commonly used 3:2 clave is structured around two musical periods that give the rhythm its dynamic quality—one antecedent and one consequent. The first half, the antecedent, is built off three rhythmic onsets and is commonly described as the *tresillo*—the Spanish word for "triplet." This rhythmic period in the context of the entire rhythm gives a sense of tension to the listener. By contrast, the second half of the rhythm is the consequent, and is built off two onsets. Its execution gives listeners a sense of resolution or conclusion, particularly during the onset heard in cell 13, or the downbeat of beat four in 4/4 time.

The relationship between the antecedent and consequent should not be conceived of as conflicting parts, but in terms of balanced opposites that bear what one ethnomusicologist called the *rhythmic oddity property*, making the clave uniquely dynamic as a timeline. Many permutations of isochronal or nonisochronal rhythms can be realized from different combinations of five notes within a 16-pulse structure. But it is this particular asymmetrical relationship between the first and the second half of the pattern that achieves the right balance of unevenness to make the clave a widely popular musical rhythm.

Scholars have identified two notes within the clave structure that are afforded special status in Afro-Cuban music. *Bombo* (bass drum) is the name given to the note in cell four in the 3:2 clave structure. Anticipating the second downbeat in 4/4 time, it gives the pattern a sense of momentum and syncopation. Typically, in Afro-Cuban orchestras, the bass or a member of the percussion section would lock onto this part of the pattern throughout a performance. Similarly, *ponche* (punch) is the name given to the third note of the 3:2 clave. In performances it is often accented, or the point within the cycle where orchestras transition to new sections within a composition, particularly in salsa music. Both accents or important moments within the cycle are realized in the 2:3 clave as well.

The clave's theoretical implications, however, can be extended beyond its rhythmic properties or function as a timeline. Many scholars and connoisseurs of Afro-Cuban music suggest that the clave structure is deeply embedded in all dimensions of composition, including the form and melodic contour of a piece. In this sense the clave is always implied in composition and orchestration, so much so that even in the absence of an individual playing the clave pattern musicians would be able to determine the underlying clave structure of a given piece.

Further complicating the theoretical properties of clave is the distinction between clave *direction* and clave *alignment*. In order to determine where the clave begins, one must listen to the melody of the song. How it is phrased and where the accents lie within the melody will determine the clave structure or *clave direction*. However, styles such as Afro-Cuban jazz or salsa include compositional techniques whereby a song can pivot back and forth from one side of the clave to the other. This means that musicians will alter their orientation to the clave to ensure that they are properly aligned with it. Not being aligned properly with the clave is an offense among musicians, and would attract the accusation of being *cruzado* or "crossed." To put it more simply, the direction of the clave is relative to the composition, whereas the alignment with clave is absolute and critical to proper performance.

General guidelines by which one can determine if a musical phrase is properly aligned with the clave, or "in clave," include: (1) Accented notes correspond with one or all of the clave strokes; (2) no strong accents are played on a nonclave stroke beat if they are not balanced by equally strong accents on clave stroke beats; (3) the measures of the music alternate between an "on the beat" and a "syncopated beat" phrase or vice versa, similar to the clave pattern; and (4) a phrase may still be considered in clave if the rhythm starts out clashing but eventually resolves strongly on a clave beat, creating rhythmic tension and resolution.

The clave is a musical rhythm and concept that has profoundly shaped the development of Cuban music, but it has also had considerable impact on many global popular genres. For example, scholarship on the origins of jazz music in New Orleans demonstrates how, in addition to other Afro-Caribbean rhythms like the *cinquillo* and *tresillo*, the clave's presence has had a marked impact on the development of jazz, particularly up until the 1940s, and most explicitly with the development of "Cubop movement." The clave was often employed when composing rhythmic breaks in arrangements, as a basis for the "comping" patterns performed by the rhythm section in support of a soloist, horn "riff" arrangements, melodic organization, or phrasing. This use of the clave was distinct from Afro-Cuban performance norms, and reflected the performance and aesthetic qualities inherent in jazz, which privilege "individuality of expression, constant variation, sparing use of repetition, and patterns set up to be broken" (Washburne, 1997, p. 71).

Clave has also made its impact felt in American rock and roll and R & B since the 1950s, beginning with Bo Diddley's 1955 self-titled track featuring the "Bo Diddley Beat" that was based on the clave pattern. This beat made a lasting impression on American popular music, and went on to inspire other compositions by rock and R & B artists such as Johnny Otis, The Doobie Brothers, and Buddy Holly, all of whom drew on the clave pattern for their compositions.

The clave also made its way back to Africa to influence many styles of neotraditional and popular music. For example, the Congolese popular genre Soukous finds its roots in Cuban "rumba" (the music was actually Cuban *son*) that grew in popularity in places like Kinshasa, and many compositions drew on the clave pattern. Ghanaian highlife from the 1950s began to draw on Afro-Cuban and Afro-Caribbean music styles like Cuban son and Trinidadian calypso. ET Mensah and His Tempos band were known as pioneers in this regard, with the young Guy Warren (a/k/a Kofi Ghanaba) credited with introducing Afro-Cuban rhythms like the clave explicitly in the band's compositions. Neotraditional drumming and dancing styles, such as the Ga *kpanlogo* that developed in Accra in the late 1950s, also drew on the clave for its bell structure. Similarly, Ga folk groups such as Wulomei and others, whose compositions were labeled both "popular" and "traditional," often employed the clave as a foundation for their songs.

Gavin Webb

See also: Afro-Cuban Jazz; Rumba

Further Reading

Rodriguez, Arturo. 2003. *Traditional Afro–Cuban Concepts in Contemporary Music* (Ethnic Percussion series). Pacific, MO: Mel Bay Publications.

Toussaint, Godfried T. 2011. "The Rhythm That Conquered the World: What Makes a 'Good' Rhythm Good." *Percussive Notes* (November), 52–59.

Vurkaç, Mehmet. 2012. "A Cross-Cultural Grammar for Temporal Harmony in Afro-Latin Musics: Clave, Partido-Alto and Other Timelines." *Current Musicology* 94 (Fall), 37–65.

Washburne, Christopher. 1997. "The Clave of Jazz: A Caribbean Contribution to the Rhythmic Foundation of an African-American Music." *Black Music Research Journal* 17(1) (Spring): 55–90.

Cohan, George M. (1878–1942)

Although George M. Cohan called himself merely a "song-and-dance man," he was one of the most versatile figures in the history of the American musical theater. Being a singer, dancer, choreographer, playwright, actor, songwriter, lyricist, theater owner, and producer, Cohan was an entertainer in all domains.

According to his baptismal certificate, he was born on July 3, 1878, but he and his family insisted that George had been born on the fourth of July. His paternal grandfather emigrated to American from Ireland and his parents were travelling vaudevillians. Cohan started his career as a child performer at age eight, first on violin and then as a dancer. He was one of the members of the family vaudeville act called *The Four Cohans*, together with his parents and his sister. In 1891, the family scored a hit with the play *Peck's Bad Boy*, in which George reveled in the title role. The Four Cohans toured across the country from 1890 to 1901 and made their Manhattan debut in 1893. They became the most highly paid four-act in vaudeville, but the act disbanded when George left vaudeville for Broadway.

Cohan's first Broadway work, *The Governor's Son* (1901), did not go well. Poor Broadway reviews signaled its cancellation after 32 performances. His first breakout hit, *Little Johnny Jones*, came in 1904, which introduced his beloved tunes "Give My Regards to Broadway" and "The Yankee Doodle Boy" and helped to initiate his long career in Broadway. George wrote the script and the songs, produced, directed, and starred in the title role of *Little Johnny Jones*, and the show made two return trips to New York during its year-long tour. From 1904 to 1920, Cohan created and produced more than 50 musicals, plays, and revues on Broadway together with Sam Harris, a Broadway producer and theater owner, including *Little Johnny Jones*, *Seven Keys to Baldpate* (1913), *Going Up* (1917), and *The Royal Vagabond* (1919).

Actor, playwright, songwriter, and theatrical producer George M. Cohan was one of the foremost talents in American musical theater in the early 20th century. (Hulton Archive/Getty Images)

In 1899, Cohan married Ethel Levey, a musical comedy actress and dancer who joined The Four Cohans when his sister married. Cohan wrote *George Washington Jr.* (1906) for his wife: the play featured George as the son of a senator who refuses his father's proposition to marry him off to a titled English woman because he loves a Southern girl, played by Ethel. However, Ethel was too talented to stay in George's shadow for long, and because of the tensions between them, the couple divorced in 1907. George married Agnes Mary Nolan in 1908 and had two daughters and a son. The eldest daughter, Mary Cohan Ronkin, became a cabaret singer, and in 1968 she supervised the lyrics and music revision for *George M!*, a musical based on her father's stories.

As the actor-comedian William Collier commented, "George . . . is not the best actor or author or composer or dancer or playwright, but he can dance better than any other author, write better than any other actor, compose better than any other manager, and manage better than any playwright—and that makes him a very great man" (McCabe, 1973, pp. xi-xii). After a series of successes, Cohan was at the top of his profession. In an age without electronic mass media, he was a superstar of the American show business and his fame reached coast to coast. He became one of the leading Tin Pan Alley songwriters. He composed more than 500 songs and published more than 300 of them, such as "You're a Grand Old Flag," "Give My

Regards to Broadway," "The Yankee Doodle Boy," "So Long Mary," "There's Only One Little Girl," "That Haunting Melody," "There's Only One Little Girl for Me," "Mary's a Grand Old Name," "Harrigan," "That Haunting Melody," "I Want to Hear a Yankee Doodle Tune," "I'm Mighty Glad I'm Living, That's All," "Over There," and so on. Among these beloved tunes, "Over There" became the most popular patriotic song with U.S. soldiers in both world wars. Charles King, Enrico Caruso, Nora Bayes, Billy Murray, and Arthur Fields all recorded it, among others. In 1936, the United States Congress awarded Cohan the Congressional Gold Medal in recognition of the extraordinary role of "Over There" during World War I, but Cohan disliked ceremonies. Eventually, in 1940 he traveled to Washington, D.C. and accepted the medal personally from President Franklin Roosevelt. Cohan was the first person in any artistic field selected for this honor, which previously had gone only to military and political leaders, philanthropists, scientists, inventors, and explorers, such as Orville and Wilbur Wright, Thomas Edison, and Lincoln Ellsworth.

Cohan was one of the founding members of the American Society of Composers, Authors and Publishers (ASCAP) in 1914. In 1919, he unsuccessfully opposed a historic strike by the Actors' Equity Association. The 1919 Equity strike was especially significant because it helped to reshape the definition of "labor," and Cohan opposed the strike because in addition to being an actor, he was also a producer of the musical theater who set the terms and conditions of the actors' employment. During the strike, Cohan donated $100,000 to finance the Actors' Retirement Fund in Englewood Cliffs, New Jersey.

Besides Broadway, Cohan appeared in several Hollywood films. In the musical film, *The Phantom President* (1932; score by Richard Rodgers and Lorenz Hart and released by Paramount Pictures), Cohan starred in a dual role as a cold, corrupt politician and his charming, idealistic campaign double, a feat made possible by using split-screen technology in several scenes. After returning to New York, the illustrious Theater Guild persuaded him to create the role of Nat Miller, the good-natured father in Eugene O'Neill's nostalgic comedy *Ah Wilderness* (1933), which earned him acclaim as a serious actor. He also appeared in Rodgers and Hart's musical *I'd Rather Be Right* (1937), in which he played the role of a song-and-dance President Franklin Roosevelt instead of impersonating the wheelchair-bound president. He reunited with Harris in the same year to produce *Fulton of Oak Falls*, a play in which Cohan took the role of Ed Fulton. His final play, *The Return of the Vagabond* (1940), a sequel to his old hit *The Tavern* (1920), was his kind of show. However, the audience was not interested, and after a brief run of seven shows Cohan announced his retirement. He had been diagnosed with terminal stomach cancer, but kept the disease a secret, and never performed again.

In 1942, a musical film based on Cohan's life, *Yankee Doodle Dandy*, was released, and James Cagney won the Academy Award and the New York Drama Critics Award of Best Actor for playing the role of Cohan. This film was privately screened for Cohan as he battled his last stages of abdominal cancer. On November 5, 1942, Cohan died of cancer at the age of 64. In 1959, at the behest of lyricist Oscar Hammerstein II, a bronze statue of Cohan was dedicated in Times Square at Broadway and 46th Street in Manhattan, New York City.

Chloe Hsun Lin

See also: Lomax, Alan and John; Ragtime; Smith, Bessie

Further Reading

Cohan, George M. 1925. *Twenty Years on Broadway, and the Years It Took to Get There.* New York: Harper & Brothers.

Cullen, Frank. 2006. *Vaudeville, Old and New: An Encyclopedia of Variety Performers in America.* New York: Routledge.

McCabe, John. 1973. *George M. Cohan: The Man Who Owned Broadway.* New York: Doubleday.

Morehouse, Ward. 1971. *George M. Cohan, Prince of the American Theater.* Westport, CT: Greenwood.

Colometry/Colometric

Colometry is a term coined by ethnomusicologist Jaap Kunst to describe the hierarchical rhythmic and melodic structures used in Indonesian *gamelan* music. *Colometry* is often used interchangeably with *colotomy*—and *colometric* with *colotomic*. The term loosely applies to other Southeast Asian musics, insofar as dealing with types of hierarchical, cyclic rhythm; although it is most associated with gamelan music from Bali and Java, the term has also been applied to the Thai *piphat* ensemble, and to Japanese *gagaku* court music (in dealing with the cyclic gong and drum patterns), both by ethnomusicologist William Malm (Malm, 1977).

Several variations of terminology have surfaced within the discourse of ethnomusicology to help classify colotomy or colometry; ethnomusicologist Michael Tenzer refers to *colotomic* as being derived from Greek, meaning "arm, or limb" (Tenzer, 2011, p. 49). Patricia Matusky defines *colotomic structure* in *The Garland Handbook of Southeast Asian Music* as "periodic punctuation" (Miller and Williams, 2008, p. 332). Kunst himself uses the term to describe the "help[ing] of the gong . . . with the subdivision of the *nuclear* theme into regular periods" (Kunst, 1973, p. 149). Thus, the core melody—the very essence of the piece of gamelan music—is divided and demarcated by colometric musical "beats." These beats act as subdivisions, to help memorize a long, repetitious melody or elucidate the reasoning behind less apparent cyclic structures in gamelan music. In short, each colometric instrument—an instrument serving a purpose of subdividing the nuclear melody played by a small number of gamelan instruments—is helping the others, and functioning within the greater rhythmic, cyclic whole of the gamelan.

Colotomic structures in gamelan music help reflect the cyclic nature of the *balungan*, or core "nuclear" melody (Sumarsam, 2005, pp. 150–152). The term *colometry*, albeit similar to *colotomy* (related to "arm or limb"), stems from ancient Greek poetics, and is closely related to the Greek term *stichometry*. Initially, the purpose of stichometry was to help early Greek scribes appraise values for books, as this was before the advent of the printing press and handwritten texts were considered an expensive and valuable commodity. Stichometry also referred to the practice of dividing text, so as to assess the length of the book. Similar to stichometry, or the division of texts according to their stanzas or lines, colometry divides texts according to their inner rhythm into smaller subdivisions (*cola*), enabling a better understanding of textual inflections, pauses, and ultimately a text's meaning (Metzger, quoted in Lee and Scott, 2009, p. 136). This draws many similarities between textual or poetic colometry and that of music. Whereas colometry in text divides stanzas and passages into smaller, inflected subdivisions, colometric structures in music (here, specifically gamelan music) divide the core melody into structures that are based upon its natural inflections. Kunst also referred to these colometric instruments as "interpunctuating," again borrowing literary terminology to explicate the purpose of these instruments and their roles in their respective music.

In the gamelan orchestra, we can visually see the stratification of colometric instruments, rhythms, and structures in performance practice. In the case of the Balinese *gamelan gong kebyar* ensemble, the instruments outlining the colometric structure (from largest to smallest) are the one or two gongs (*gong ageng*); a suspended kettle-gong, *klentong*; the smaller suspended kettle-gong, *kempur*; and the *kempli*, a horizontally suspended kettle-gong. These instruments are also written here in order from the largest to the smallest cyclic value within the *gong* cycle, or *gongan*, which is the largest colotomic structure within gamelan music. For example, imagine that the gong ageng only plays once every 16 beats. To keep time, and for better clarity for the faster, interlocking 16th-note rhythms employed by the *gangsa* section (which plays an ornamented variation of the melody), the kempli plays every beat, acting as a metronome. Out of this 16-beat phrase, the kempur plays beats five and thirteen, and the klentong plays beat nine, exactly halfway through the 16-beat cycle.

Another analysis would argue that the gong ageng acts as one gongan cycle. The klentong subdivides the gongan into two halves by playing beat nine of the 16-beat phrase. The kempur then subdivides those two halves further, so that there are four equidistant phrases within the gongan. The kempli divides the 16-beat pulse into 16 separate beats; alternatively, the kempli simply keeps a distinct metronomic pulse—each pulse worth one beat. A third analysis and theoretical approach proposes that one should view colometric structures in gamelan as based upon ratios of cyclic and rhythmic value. From largest to smallest, this would interpret the gong ageng as having a ratio of 1:1; the klentong as 2:1; the kempur as 4:1; and the kempli as 16:1.

Colotomic structures are also realized within the pitched, melodic instruments of the gamelan. Take another example of the gamelan gong kebyar tradition. In gamelan gong kebyar, the ensemble is divided into two rough halves: the *pokok*, or instruments that play the nuclear melody; and the *gangsa*, which add interlocking rapid-fire ornamentation to an interpolation of the nuclear melody. In the pokok section, imagine that the *ugal*—a 15-keyed metallophone—plays a four-note melody in its entirety. The five- or seven-keyed *jublag* plays a variation of this melody, although it only strikes every other note—in a four-note passage, notes one and three, respectively. These notes are in unison with the ugal. Finally, the *jegogan*, a large five-keyed instrument tuned one octave lower than the jublag and ugal, plays the same melody, though it strikes the first of the four notes and in octave with the jublag and ugal. This example results in a stratified melodic texture, wherein the ugal plays four notes; the jublag plays two notes (notes one and three); and the jegogan only plays note one—although in theory it would play note five if the four-note motif repeats, or if the passage is longer than four notes.

Colotomic elements of Southeast Asian music, and gamelan in particular, later influenced such Western composers as Claude Debussy (1862–1918), Colin McPhee (1900–1964), Lou Harrison (1917–2003), Terry Riley (1935–), and Steve Reich (1936–). Debussy's *Pagodes*, from his *Estampes*, L. 100 (1903) is a quintessential example of works using colometry in a Western idiom, for solo piano (Parker, 2012).

John Forrestal

See also: Classical Music, European; Gagaku; Gamelan Orchestra (Balinese); Gamelan Orchestra (Javanese); Gender Wayang; Japan, Music of; Kebyar; Kecak; Kendang; Malay Music; McPhee, Colin; Piphat

Further Reading

Kunst, Jaap. 1973. *Music in Java: Its History, Its Theory and Its Technique.* The Hague: Martinus Nijhoff.

Lee, Margaret Ellen, and Bernard Brandon Scott. 2009. *Sound Mapping the New Testament.* Salem, OR: Polebridge Press.

Lindsay, Jennifer. 1992. *Javanese Gamelan.* New York: Oxford University Press.

Malm, William. 1977. *Music Cultures of the Pacific, The Near East, and Asia,* 2nd ed. Englewood Cliffs, New Jersey: Prentice-Hall.

Matusky, Patricia, and Tan Sooi Beng. 2004. *The Music of Malaysia: The Classical, Folk, and Syncretic Traditions.* Burlington, VT: Ashgate.

Miller, Terry E., and Sean Williams, eds. 1998. *The Garland Encyclopedia of World Music; Vol. 4: Southeast Asia.* New York: Garland.

Miller, Terry E., and Sean Williams, eds. 2008. *The Garland Handbook of Southeast Asian Music.* New York: Garland.

Parker, Sylvia. 2012. "Claude Debussy's Gamelan." *College Music Symposium*, August 27. http://symposium.music.org/index.php?option=com_k2&view=item&id=22:claude-debussys-gamelan&Itemid=124#twentyfour.

Sumarsam. 1995. *Gamelan: Cultural Interaction and Musical Development in Central Java.* Chicago: University of Chicago Press.

Tenzer, Michael. 2011. *Balinese Gamelan Music*, 3rd ed. Singapore: Tuttle Publishing.

Coltrane, John (1926–1967)

John William Coltrane was one of the leading figures in post-bop jazz. As a composer and saxophonist, Coltrane was a pioneer in modal jazz and free jazz; he also was a key figure in the introduction of world music into jazz. His later works were connected to a pantheistic spirituality and an increasingly unorthodox sound palette.

Coltrane was born September 23, 1926, in Hamlet, North Carolina, and grew up in High Point. After graduating from high school, he enlisted in the Navy and was stationed in Hawaii, where he joined the Navy jazz band as an alto saxophonist. After returning to civilian life, Coltrane began to study music theory and play tenor saxophone in Eddie "Cleanhead" Vinson's band. He also played in groups with Charlie Parker, Dizzy Gillespie, and Johnny Hodges in the late 1940s and early 1950s.

In 1955, Coltrane was invited by trumpeter Miles Davis to join Davis's new quintet. This group recorded several albums, including *Cookin' with the Miles Davis Quintet* and *'Round About Midnight*, before Coltrane was dismissed in April 1957 because of his increasing unreliability due to heroin addiction. Three months later, he joined pianist Thelonious Monk's quartet. His work with Monk, who was known for an unconventional approach to music, gave Coltrane an opportunity to experiment more with his techniques and philosophies, such as his signature "sheets of sound" style which featured rapid melodic runs that gave the impression of a harp glissando. Coltrane also recorded his first album as leader of his own group. *Blue Train* (1957) featured four original compositions and demonstrated some of the earliest experiments with thirds-related chord substitution patterns that would come to be known as "Coltrane changes."

John Coltrane was a pioneering jazz saxophonist and composer of the mid-20th century. (Library of Congress)

Coltrane rejoined Davis in 1958, coinciding with Davis's modal period. *Milestones* (1958) also marked Coltrane's first work with alto saxophonist Julian "Cannonball" Adderley. The culmination of this period was *Kind of Blue* (1959), which was constructed entirely around Davis's modal concepts. *Kind of Blue* was Coltrane's final collaboration with Davis.

Two weeks after finishing *Kind of Blue*, Coltrane was back in the studio to record his debut album for Atlantic Records, *Giant Steps*. On *Giant Steps*, Coltrane continued experimenting with thirds-related progressions and the sheets-of-sound technique. In 1960, he returned to the studio with the first version of the John Coltrane Quartet (with McCoy Tyner, piano; Steve Davis, bass; Elvin Jones, drums) to record *My Favorite Things*. This was the first album to feature Coltrane playing soprano saxophone, inspired by his admiration for clarinetist and soprano saxophonist Sidney Bechet. The title track, a jazz version of the Rodgers and Hammerstein classic, explored the modal jazz approach Coltrane had learned from Davis as well as his growing interest in Indian music.

In 1961, record executive Creed Taylor bought out Coltrane's contract with Atlantic Records and signed him to Taylor's new label, Impulse. Many of Coltrane's most celebrated recordings came during his Impulse years. *Impressions* (1963) was the first album to feature the "classic" quartet of Coltrane, Tyner, Jones, and bassist Reggie Workman. *Live in Birdland* (1964) is renowned for being the only album to contain the song "Alabama," which is Coltrane's tribute to the four children killed in the 16th Street Baptist Church bombing in Birmingham, Alabama, in September 1963.

Of all the albums Coltrane recorded for Impulse, none is more highly regarded than *A Love Supreme* (1965). The album describes a spiritual journey and was likely inspired by the events surrounding his overcoming of his heroin addiction in 1957, which Coltrane referenced in the liner notes to the album. From this point on, much of Coltrane's music was tied to spiritual matters. In 1963, Coltrane met pianist Alice McLeod. They married in 1966 after the births of their sons John, Jr. and Ravi and after Coltrane's divorce from his first wife Naima (Juanita Naima Grubbs) was finalized. Alice shared many of his spiritual beliefs.

The last few years of Coltrane's life were marked by an increasingly experimental approach to his music. He collaborated with fellow tenor saxophonist Pharoah Sanders, who influenced Coltrane's use of multiphonics and overblowing into the altissimo register. This culminated in the 1965 recording *Ascension*, a 40-minute continuous free-jazz performance.

Coltrane died from liver cancer on July 17, 1967, at Huntington Hospital in New York City. Free jazz groups led by Albert Ayler and Ornette Coleman played at his funeral. Coltrane was buried at Pinelawn Cemetery in Farmingdale, New York.

Eric S. Strother

See also: Bebop; Davis, Miles; Jazz; Parker, Charlie

Further Reading

Brown, Leonard. 2010. *John Coltrane and Black America's Quest for Freedom: Spirituality and the Music.* New York: Oxford University Press.

Cole, Bill. 2001. *John Coltrane.* New York: Da Capo Press.

Nisenson, Eric. 1995. *Ascension: John Coltrane and His Quest.* New York: Da Capo Press.

Porter, Lewis. 2000. *John Coltrane: His Life and Music.* Ann Arbor: University of Michigan Press.

Ratliff, Ben. 2008. *Coltrane: The Story of a Sound.* New York: Farrar, Straus and Giroux.

Concerto

A *concerto* is a composition for solo instrument and orchestra, typically in three movements. It represents one of the main genres for large ensembles in Western classical music. In its early use as a musical term, "concerto" stood for generic ensemble music. The noun comes from the Italian *concerto*, which denotes agreement on something, while its etymology comes from the Latin *conserere*: to tie, to interlace, or *concertare*: to contend, to dispute.

First created in the early 17th century, the word is first mentioned in *Concerti di Andrea, et di Giovanni Gabrieli*, by Giovanni Gabrieli (Venice, 1587), and *Cento concerti ecclesiastici* by Lodovico Grossi da Viadana (Venice, 1602). At the earliest point in its existence, however, the concerto was not solely an instrumental composition, as indeed proven by Claudio Monteverdi's seventh book of madrigals titled *Concerto* (Venice, 1619).

The purely instrumental concerto originated in the second half of the 17th century, when several Italian composers begun to exploit technical and textural contrasts between *solo* (soloist) and *tutti* (ensemble) in compositions for the orchestra. Maurizio Cazzati and Giuseppe Torelli (1658–1709) of the Bolognese school of San

Petronio were particularly influential through their pieces for trumpet, in which the contrapuntal peculiarity of the solo sonata is replaced by unexpected textural contrasts and thematic interchange. Torelli composed with violin concertos as well, making use of the dynamic style which already distinguished his trumpet compositions.

Whereas in the north of Italy the string orchestra alternated with the soloist (usually the first violin), in Rome the division was between the *ripieno* (full orchestra) and the *concertino* (a smaller ensemble of usually two violins, a cello, and the continuo). This practice led to the birth of the *concerto grosso*, of which Arcangelo Corelli (1653–1713) was the first main exponent. The Roman concerto spread all over Europe, quickly reaching Germany, where Georg Muffat's five sonatas in the *Armonico tributo* (Salzburg, 1682) denote the first appearance of this tradition in the area. Further composers inspired by the Roman school were Muffat's pupil Benedict Anton Aufschnaiter, who published the sonatas *Dulcis fidium harmonia symphoniis ecclesiasticis concinnata* op. 3 (Augsburg, 1703), and Heinrich Weissenburg, with his Concertos op. 7 (1705).

In the first decades of the *settecento*, a Venetian school flourished as well. While he was employed by Charles IV, Duke of Mantua, Tomaso Giovanni Albinoni (1671–1751) published a collection of instrumental works featuring concertos mostly intermediating two fast movements with a slower one. Another Venetian, Antonio Vivaldi (1678–1741), composed around 600 concertos, achieving a bright orchestral language through the use of memorable thematic ideas together with peculiar virtuoso solo parts. He first adopted the concept of *ritornello* in his *L'estro armonico* (Venice, 1711). The ritornello entailed one or more thematic ideas stated at the beginning of the movement, and then recurring several times; it interpolates solo parts in order to demarcate modulations throughout the piece.

Two-soloist or bigger-ensemble concertos were extant as well, though not as widespread as those for a single soloist. In pieces with two soloists, they were either playing the same melody in parallel at different intervals of a third or a fifth, one providing accompaniment for the other; or alternating with each other. Further techniques, such as imitation, were also contemplated.

Germany produced imitators of both Vivaldi and Corelli. Georg Philipp Telemann (1681–1767) wrote several combinations of concertos for solo and orchestra, composing for less common instruments such as chalumeau, bassoon, and horn. His *Concerto in G Major for Viola and String Orchestra* is the first known concerto for viola, and it is still regularly performed today.

Johann Sebastian Bach (1685–1750) played a fundamental role in the development of the genre, especially outside the Italian territories. His Vivaldian inspiration is clearly apparent from the inclusion of some concertos written by the Italian priest in Bach's keyboard transcriptions (ca. 1713). Likewise, he demonstrates a borrowing of the ritornello form in his *Third English Suite* (ca. 1715). His masterwork in the concerto field is undoubtedly the six so-called *Brandenburg Concertos* (*Concerts avec plusieurs instruments*, 1721) dedicated to Christian Ludwig, Margrave of Brandenburg. Bach exploited uncommon combinations of instruments, thus drifting away from the traditional *concerto grosso* form: the third Brandenburg concerto is for three string ensembles, while the fourth alternates a *concertino*, formed by violin and a couple of recorders, and a *tutti* with strings and basso continuo (i.e., the bass line). In England, George Friedrich Händel (1685–1759) took inspiration from Corelli in his *12 Concerti Grossi*, op. 6 (1739). Formerly performed as introductions to his oratorios, Händel's organ concertos (for instance, op. 4 [ca. 1738] and op. 7 [1761]) embody his most original contribution to the repertoire.

The solo concerto became established in the 18th century, when the contrast between concertino and ripieno developed into a stronger distinction between whole orchestra and soloist instrument. The architecture of this type of concerto can vary: generally a long main theme is predominant within a lengthy interchange between tutti sections and soloist. Usually a second theme comes in, although it is not elaborated extensively. It is usually formed of three movements (allegro-adagio-allegro), with or without adagios introducing the allegros. Four- or five-movement concertos were also composed.

Most of the solo concertos composed at the beginning of the second half of the 18th century were for violin or flute, but the piano increased in popularity during the last decades of the century. Among others, this development is accredited to Carl Philipp Emmanuel Bach (1714–1788), who composed almost 50 concertos for harpsichord in his life. The period of transition between the Vivaldian style and the classical concerto is represented by late baroque Italian composers, in particular Giuseppe Tartini (1692–1770), who strongly influenced the German Mannheimer School (ca. 1740–1778). In his *L'arte del violino* op. 3 (1733), he foreruns later solo concertos not only through the exploitation of long ritornellos, often featuring more than one theme, but also in the inclusion of a cadenza in the allegros.

Undoubtedly, the large set of concertos written by Wolfgang Amadeus Mozart (1756–1791) is considered the most relevant and influential works of the genre in the late 18th century. Mozart's union between orchestra and piano represents one of the peaks of the development of classical style. Although he mostly wrote for the keyboard, concertos for violin and wind instruments are extant as well. Overall, he wrote combinations for nearly 50 instruments and orchestra. His role as soloist for most of his piano concertos is shown in his autographs, where the solo part is seldom completely notated. More often it is just sketched in, so as to be mostly improvised on the stage, thus giving his composition an unprecedented lightness and natural touch. Mozart's great admirer, Ludwig van Beethoven (1770–1827) moved toward a more dramatic relationship between soloist and orchestra and a more complex symphonic language, as evident in his fourth and fifth piano concertos (1806 and 1809, respectively). After Mozart's and Beethoven's compositions, the soloist's virtuosity absolutely predominates, as in the works of Niccolò Paganini (1782–1840) for the violin, and Sigismond Thalberg (1812–1871) for the piano.

During the romantic era, solo concertos gradually became specifically designed to display virtuosos' ability, so much so that the concerto acquired a more exceptional role, and progressively lost relevance as a composition for the orchestra in favor of the symphony, which suddenly rose in popularity. The role of the virtuoso was so crucial that composers preferred to write music for specific performers, as in the cases of Johannes Brahms, who wrote for the violinist Joseph Joachim, abandoning the strong contrast between solo and orchestra in the name of a lyricism enriched with crepuscular shades and a meditative melancholy. Felix Mendelssohn wrote his *Violin Concerto in E minor* op. 64 (1844) for Ferdinand David; Robert Schuman composed the *Piano Concerto in A minor* op. 54 (1854) for his own wife, Clara. Franz Liszt had already revolutionized piano technique through his two early piano concertos (1849 and 1839, both reworked in a second version). Liszt's theatrical and passionate approach to performance helped to create the modern concept of celebrity, as no one else had done before.

Several 29th-century composers, such as Stravinsky, Hindemith, Bloch, Petrassi, Bartók, Tippett, Kodály, and Lutoslawski, tried to go back to the original meaning of the word "concerto," through their "concertos for orchestra," where individual members or sections of the orchestra played parts in a soloist fashion. A fair number of works can still be more or less ascribed to the romantic tradition: for instance, Sibelius's *Violin Concerto in D minor* op. 47 (1903) and Sergei Rachmaninoff's piano concertos op. 1, 18, and 30 (1891, 1901, and 1909). However, the 20th century also saw a rise in interest about musical instruments previously ignored, such as percussion or instruments from local folklore, thanks to the influence of popular and jazz music.

Jacopo Mazzeo

See also: Classical Music, European; Madrigal; Medieval Secular Song; Symphony

Further Reading

Heller, Wendy. 2014. *Music in the Baroque.* New York: Norton.

Hill, John Walter. 2005. *Baroque Music: Music in Western Europe, 1580–1750.* New York: W.W. Norton.

Hutchings, Arthur. 1973. *The Baroque Concerto.* London: Faber.

Hutchings, Arthur. 2005. *The Cambridge Companion to the Concerto.* Cambridge: Cambridge University Press.

Lang, Paul Henry. 1969. *The Concerto, 1800–1900: A Norton Music Anthology.* New York: W.W. Norton.

Layton, Robert. 1989. *A Companion to the Concerto.* New York: Schirmer Books.

Riepel, Joseph Eckert Stefan. 2013. *Violin Concertos.* Middleton, WI: A-R Editions.

Roeder, Michael Thomas. 1994. *A History of the Concerto.* Portland, OR: Amadeus Press.

Rowland, David. 2011. *The Cambridge Companion to the Piano.* Cambridge: Cambridge University Press.

Steinberg, Michael. 1998. *The Concerto: A Listener's Guide.* New York: Oxford University Press.

Taruskin, R. 2005. *The Oxford History of Western Music.* Oxford: Oxford University Press.

Congo Square

An historic landmark incorporated into the New Orleans Jazz National Historic Park, Congo Square is a place mentioned in many accounts of jazz history. Once a large field in New Orleans where African slaves were permitted to gather on Sunday to sing, dance, and play their drums in their traditional native manner, it is now an open space in the southern corner of Louis Armstrong Park. This 31-acre site is considered to be one of the birthplaces of jazz and blues music. The primary significance of Congo Square to the history of jazz is that it gave original African music a place to be heard where it could influence and be influenced by European music. When the famous dance of Congo Square began in 1817, the backgrounds of the participants produced a music that was often a cross between French and Spanish with African rhythmic patterns.

Originally a ceremonial site for Native Americans, Congo Square was incorporated into the city of Nouvelle-Orléans by French settlers and was chosen as a gathering place for slaves on Sundays, their usual day off from work. Also known as Place de Nègres, Place Publique, and Circus Square, it eventually became known as Congo Square. It was formally created by municipal ordinance in 1817 that essentially served to formally recognize its existence on the official map. Situated in the French Quarter across Rampart Street from the Vieux Carré, from about 1740 onward it was a marketplace where slaves, free blacks, and "colored" people met to trade and to socialize. Visitors to Congo Square sang songs, played music on homemade drums and stringed instruments, and nearly everyone danced. Plantation owners and townspeople would come to watch the hundreds of dancers wearing finery and exotic costumes perform versions of African dances brought from their homelands. Spanish colonizers continued the tradition, which dissipated in the 1880s as a result of the growing popularity of ragtime and jazz bands in venues farther uptown. Congo Square then became the location for brass-band concerts presented by the area's community of "creoles of color." Local voodoo practitioners continue to view Congo Square as a sacred site and occasionally meet there for religious rites incorporating song and trance dance.

Equally famous as the subject of musical compositions, Congo Square is memorialized by Louis Moreau Gottschalk's (1829–1869) *Bamboula*, op. 2; Henry F. Gilbert's (1868–1928) *The Dance in Place Congo*, and Wynton Marsalis (1961–) and Yacub Addy's (1931–2015) *Congo Square*. It continues to be a notable venue for music festivals, brass-band parades, protest marches, and drum circles to the present day.

Eldonna L. May

See also: Armstrong, Louis; Blues; Field Hollers; Jazz; Ragtime

Further Reading

Evans, Freddi Williams. 2011. *Congo Square: African Roots in New Orleans*. Lafayette: University of Louisiana at Lafayette Press.

Sublette, Ned. 2009. *The World that Made New Orleans: From Spanish Silver to Congo Square,* repr. ed. Chicago: Chicago Review Press.

Thorpe, Edward. 1990. *Black Dance*. Woodstock, NY: Overlook Hardcover.

Conjunto

A type of Tejano ("Texan") music, *conjunto* is an originally instrumental popular folk music genre. Its emergence in the mid-19th century was influenced by the conflicts between *tejanos* (Texans of Mexican descent) and *anglos* (Texans of European descent), specifically after the independence of Texas from Mexico in 1836. After the introduction of the button accordion by German immigrants in Texas during the mid-19th century, conjunto (Spanish for "group") evolved in an oral tradition to an ensemble with accordion as the melodic lead instrument, sometimes together with brass instruments for larger outdoor events, and the *bajo sexto* (a Mexican guitar with 12 steel strings), acoustic bass guitar or double bass, and drums as rhythm section. A drum set (with snare drum, bass drum, and cymbal) and an electric bass (replacing the acoustic bass) were added to the instrumentation in the 1940s and 1950s, respectively.

The European genres of polka, waltz, redowa, mazurka, and schottische influenced the initial evolution of, and were musically integrated into, conjunto as popular folk music, performed at Saturday dances, weddings, and other occasions. *Rancheras* (a Mexican song genre) became more and more important during the second half of the 20th century in conjunto. In addition to polkas and rancheras, the modern conjunto also relies more heavily on boleros, but less on redowa, mazurka, and schottische. The 20th century saw the emergence of Progressive Conjunto, which added pitos (a set of saxophones and/or trumpets) and keyboards (organ or synthesizer) to the ensemble. Other developments include the Norteño Conjunto as well as the fusion of conjunto with other popular music genres such as country, rock and roll, soul, funk, rock, and jazz.

Conjunto continues to thrive and to spread beyond Texas. Numerous Tejano record labels; festivals such as the annual *Tejano Conjunto Festival en San Antonio*; museums such as the Tejano R.O.O.T.S. Hall of Fame in Alice, Texas; and awards such as the Tejano Music Awards show the importance of Tejano music in general in the southern United States and beyond. As a subgenre of Tejano music, conjunto influenced the development of, and is closely related to, banda/orquesta and El Grupo. Leaders of notable conjunto groups include Bruno Villarreal (1901–1976), Pedro Ayala (1911–1990), Narciso Martínez (1911–1992), Santiago Jiménez Sr. (1913–1984), Valerio Longoria (1924–2000), Leonardo "Flaco" Jiménez (1939–), Paulino Bernal (1939–), Esteban "Steve" Jordan (1939–2010), Eva Ybarra (1945–), and Emilio Navaira III (1962–).

Nico Schüler

See also: Accordion (Americas); Conjunto (Norteños); Mexican Regional Music; Tejano Music

Further Reading

Burr, Ramiro. 1999. *The Billboard Guide to Tejano and Regional Mexican Music*. New York: Billboard Books.

Hartman, Gary. 2008. *The History of Texas Music*. College Station: Texas A&M University Press.

Koegel, John. 2002. "Crossing Borders: Mexicana, Tejana, and Chicana Musicians in the United States and Mexico." In Walter Aaron Clark (ed.), *From Tejano to Tango: Latin American Popular Music*, 97–125. New York: Routledge.

Peña, Manuel H. 1999. *Música Tejana: The Cultural Economy of Artistic Transformation*. College Station: Texas A&M University Press.

Reyna, José R. 2001. "Tejano Music." In Ellen Koskoff (ed.), *The Garland Encyclopedia of World Music; Vol. 3: The United States and Canada*, 770–782. New York: Garland.

San Miguel, Guadalupe, Jr. 2002. *Tejano Proud: Tex-Mex Music in the Twentieth-Century*. College Station: Texas A&M University Press.

Conjunto (Norteños)

Until the 1950s, *conjunto* and *norteña* were used interchangeably to refer to any ensemble featuring the accordion and the *bajo sexto* (12-string guitar). With the arrival of European immigrants to build railroads between Monterrey and south Texas in 1882, European social dances such as the polka, redowa, waltz, and schottische combined with local Mexican song forms to create a new hybrid style of *conjunto* (group) social dance music.

Norteña (northern Mexican) music is now considered to be the popular music vehicle for the traditional Mexican *corrido*, a topical narrative ballad sung, without a refrain, to a triple-time melody; modern norteña and conjunto performances prefer duple time, especially in songs influenced by European social dance forms. The text is organized into four quatrains of octosyllabic lines, usually in an a-b-c-d rhyme scheme. Though norteña is popular in Mexico, primarily among rural and working-class audiences, it is usually excluded from being considered "Mexican" popular music, because the bulk of its audience lies along the United States/Mexico border region, which has an historically estranged relationship with the government and cultural center of Mexico.

Norteña style was developed in tandem with the regionally specific *tejano* (Texas-Mexican) conjunto, a southern Texas variant of norteña with the same instrumentation that, beginning in the late 1940s, became associated with Texas-Mexicans and later with more assimilated Chicanos throughout the Southwest. Conjunto and norteña instrumentation both feature a three-row button accordion, a bajo sexto (a bass guitar with 12 strings in six double courses), an electric bass (*tololoche*), and drums (which can include a drum set, the homemade *redova,* or the *tarola* snare drum). Norteña music is rougher and simpler, with louder bass and faster tempi; many norteña groups also retain flute and violin as remnants of the elite *orquesta típica* groups of the 1880s–1930s. Tejano conjunto can be more refined and difficult to play, but is rhythmically steadier and has benefited from advances in audio technology more readily available in the United States.

In the early 1950s, second-generation Texas-Mexican Tony de la Rosa took over as the house accordionist at Ideal Records (based in Alice, Texas), and formed his own group in 1955. Born in Riviera, Texas, just south of Corpus Christi, he played with Texas swing bands and listened to a variety of folk music styles. He was the first accordionist to include drums and electric bass in recordings; the consistent rhythmic backbeat was slowed to a dance-hall glide, providing a solid pulse that emphasized offbeats. The addition of drums and the electrification of instruments slowed the tempo, especially on polkas, freeing the accordion and bajo sexto to explore new modes of articulation. Ideal Records featured sophisticated *orquesta tejana* ensembles and eventually was the main producer of conjunto recordings.

La Rosa established the conjunto "dance hall" sound for tejano ensembles in both Texas and northern Mexico. His popularity in the late 1950s finally demanded that a distinction be made between norteña and conjunto. Texas-Mexicans referred to La Rosa's sound as *conjunto*, a term probably taken from the group's name, Tony de la Rosa y Su Conjunto. This music also mirrored a desire among Tejanos to distinguish themselves from the migratory Mexican population while not completely assimilating into the Anglo-American population. Public dances and radio airplay of Texas-Mexican artists such as La Rosa and Longoria encouraged the development of a separate tejano music industry. Conjunto was performed in 1960s dance halls where upbeat dance rhythms like the *polca, chotíses, valse, redova,* and *huapango* were emphasized and fewer narrative *corridos* played.

However, ensembles located in the border region, where the bajo sexto and accordion accompanied the corrido and other song forms, maintained the name *norteña*. Avoiding the instrumental polkas, schottisches, and redovas of the conjunto groups, norteña groups focused on song forms—especially topical corridos and cancio-corridos that contained few repetitions. The norteña story-like narrative songs required fluency in Spanish and were filled with Mexican slang. Falcon Records, founded by Alnaldo Ramírez in 1947, was based in McClellan, Texas, and focused on norteña artists for the border-based migrant worker community. Ideal Records continued to market conjunto groups to the bilingual, and increasingly well-educated, sons and daughters of the Tejano community.

The folklorist and ethnomusicologist Manuel Peña's seminal research on conjunto music, which he describes as the working-class music of Mexican Americans in the Southwest, suggests that conjunto is a powerful expression of the modern Tejano or Chicano experience, which contributed to its emergence as a highly stylized North American regional music phenomenon. As this popular music became more assimilated, bilingual, and upwardly mobile, other more "Americanized" genres emerged from conjunto's core. *Orquesta tejana* evolved in the 1940s and 1950s in response to the expanding middle class of Texas-Mexicans. This genre merged with North American popular styles such as rock and roll, Mexican folk song forms such as rancheras and corridos, and popular Latin rhythms such as cumbia and salsa and elements of conjunto. This style is the predecessor to contemporary *música tejana*, or tejano, which evolved in the 1980s and 1990s.

Conjunto and norteña music are geared to a dancing public, and the lyrics deal with issues of love and celebrate Tejano/Chicano pride. The "folkloric" Texas-Mexican conjunto holds a deeply powerful role in the creation and strengthening of a distinct Texas-Mexican culture and identity. Conjunto provides a cultural platform for Texas-based Mexicans to recreate Mexican history and culture nostalgically. In the 1990s, the popular music journalist Sam Quiñones published articles about the popularity of narcocorridos among Mexican laborers in rural villages and municipalities throughout Mexico. He wrote biographies of narcocorrido composers such as Chalino Sánchez, who reinvigorated the norteña industry and the narcocorrido by writing songs that were more realistic and violent than those of Los Tigres. Influenced by gangsta rap in Los Angeles, Sánchez brought a younger audience to the corrido form.

In norteña, the bajo sexto player is often the bandleader and lead vocalist, as the focus is on the Spanish lyrics, and the accordionist acts as an accompanist, occasionally playing solos between stanzas. The norteña group Los Tigres del Norte—the most commercially successful band among Latinos in the United States—provides an excellent example of this style. They were featured in a 2009 PBS documentary entitled *Latino Music USA*, and use traditional norteña performance practices, including a lead singer who establishes the beat; a button accordion entering with a syncopated solo in parallel thirds over an oom-pah, oom-pah rhythmic bass provided by an electric bass playing on the downbeats; and a bajo sexto strumming chords on the upbeat with support from the drums. Their audiences clap, sing, and whistle along with the verses, which often deal with transnational issues of alienation and discrimination relevant to members of the Mexican diaspora.

In contrast, in tejano conjunto, the accordionist is always the bandleader and is expected to take solos and show off his virtuosity. Many popular tejano conjunto groups are known by their accordionist's names, such as Santiago Jiménez Jr. y Su Conjunto, Flaco Jiménez y Su Conjunto, Esteban Jordán y Su Conjunto, Mingo Saldívar y Sus Tremendos Cuatro Espadas (four tremendous swords), and Eva Ybarra y Su Conjunto.

Laura Stanfield Prichard

See also: Conjunto; Mariachi; Mexican Regional Music

Further Reading

Peña, Manuel. 1985. *The Texas-Mexican Conjunto: Music of a Working-Class People.* Austin: University of Texas.

Ragland, Cathy. 2009. *Musica Norteña: Mexican Migrants Creating a Nation between Nations.* Philadelphia: Temple University Press.

Corrido

From the Spanish *correr* (meaning "to run," plausibly indicating the "running" narrative of the form), the Mexican *corrido* is a style of popular song that tells a story, often through oral transmission. The topics presented in typical corridos convey historical events, such as famous heroes and tragic deaths, as well a certain social relevance, including oppression and the daily lives of the working class. Developed throughout Mexico in the 19th century, the corrido became particularly popular along the U.S.-Mexico border, contributing to its contemporary association with *música de la frontera* (border music). Similar to the English ballad and the Spanish *romance*, a ballad form developed during the Middle Ages and brought to the region by Spanish conquistadors, the corrido served as the media for the Mexican people, disseminating information throughout the countryside for a largely illiterate population before the advent of newspapers, radio, television, internet, and the like. In addition to its place in Mexican popular culture, the corrido was used during the Nicaraguan Revolutions of the 20th century and in recent years has further stimulated the *narcocorrido*, a Mexican and Columbian style glorifying contemporary drug culture. (The term *corrido* can also refer to a traditional form of Spanish dance music from the 19th and early 20th centuries, as well as a type of song popular in Brazilian *capoeira* traditions.)

Although Mexican corridos were traditionally performed in the Spanish language, modern practices often incorporate English or a mixture of the two languages, corresponding to the changing cultural orientations (and identification as Mexican American) along the U.S.-Mexico border. Using everyday language and relatively simple music, corridos introduced a story—either fictional or historical—to working-class listeners, especially in the days before radio, television, and other forms of mass media. However, songs lacking the narrative style but corresponding to other musical and structural aspects of the traditional form also generally retain the classification of corrido. The music is usually in a major key, and the singer employs a short (generally less than an octave) range corresponding to the most piercing part of the voice, thus enhancing consequent ability to clearly reach the audience (without recordings or amplification). With the primary emphasis on the words and the story, the same melody is sometimes used interchangeably for multiple sets of lyrics. A corrido uses fast waltz time or (more common in recent songs) a polka rhythm.

The historic form is most typically performed by men, accompanied by guitar or *bajo sexto*, a Spanish/Mexican bass-rhythm guitar with 12 strings in six double courses, tuned in fourths. While traditional corridos show some variation in the general structure, the most common form consists of 36 lines, divided into six stanzas of six lines each or nine stanzas of four lines each. Each line typically contains seven to ten syllables (eight is the most common), with lines sometimes repeated. The corrido usually begins with an introduction by the singer (setting up the story, including the date and place, as applicable), followed by the story itself, and ending with a conclusion/moral and farewell by the singer. Instrumental music usually provides an introduction to the song as well as interludes between individual stanzas. Traditionally, the corrido form does not include a refrain.

The first known corridos in Mexico come from versions of Spanish *romances*, with topics of love and religion. These early songs include "La Martina" (originally "La Esposa Infiel"), depicting an absent husband and his unfaithful wife; and "La Delgadina," describing a young woman's tragic death following her refusal to marry her father. Beginning with the Mexican War of Independence (1810–1821) and continuing throughout the Mexican-American War of the 1840s, the corrido was used to elucidate and distribute (and ultimately preserve) the stories of the war throughout a Mexican folk population. With the dictatorial rule of Mexican soldier and politician Porfirio Díaz (1830–1915) between 1876 and 1911 and the subsequent Mexican Revolution from 1910 to around 1920, the corrido became a popular outlet to convey a growing resistance by the people and to immortalize Mexican heroes such as Emiliano Zapata and Pancho Villa (portrayed in song as heroic revolutionaries who fought for the rights of the people). For example, the corrido "El Mayor de los Dorados" introduces the soldiers of Villa; likewise, the lyrics of the standard "La Cucaracha" were altered during this time to describe the political battle between Venustiano Carranza and the troops of Zapata and Villa. Sheet music of popular corridos was also distributed at this time via mass publications and passed out for free as propaganda. Following the Mexican Revolution, and largely corresponding to the rise of electronic forms of mass media, the corrido lost some of its popularity as a communicative form, with the role of the style shifting instead toward providing recognition and signification of working-class oppression, farmworkers' rights, and the growing culture of Mexican drug cartels. Of course, it also gave pure entertainment value throughout the United States and Mexico (although primarily among the Mexican American ethnic population).

During the 20th century, the corrido became a form of expression for working-class culture on both sides of the U.S.-Mexico border, depicting ethnic and socioeconomic injustices in contemporary society. For example, the popular song "Discriminación a un mártir," written by José Morante in 1949, describes the denial of funeral services for Félix Longoria, a Mexican American veteran of World War II (for more information, see Peña, 1999, pp. 77–80). Later corridos focused on migrant work, immigration, and the struggles of immigrant communities. By the middle of the century, corridos had become more commercialized and were distributed as recordings and via radio programming (this commercialization is also demonstrated by the attributable authorship of modern corridos, contrasting with the earlier anonymous nature of the tradition). The assassination of John F. Kennedy in 1963 also provided a new, heroic topic for contemporary corridos, and dozens of Texas-Mexican "Kennedy corridos" were produced during this time. After the mid-1960s, corridos began to be used as part of the Chicano movement in the United States. Ultimately, 20th-century corridos—in Mexico as well as Colombia—began to incorporate the modern practices of drug trafficking (including beheadings, shootings, and drug smuggling), creating a controversial form called the *narcocorrido* (the "drug" corrido). For example, "La Chacalosa" by popular artist Jenni Rivera (1969–2012) relates the tale of a young girl who inherits her family's drug business at the age of 15, learns to use a gun, and takes her place in that male-oriented community. Beyond this increased incorporation of drug culture, contemporary corridos have also been used to characterize the explosion of the space shuttle *Challenger* in 1986, the death of the popular singer Selena in 1995, and the 9/11 terrorist attacks in 2001. Moving beyond the earlier form of solo singer with guitar, modern corridos are often performed with larger bands (often *norteño/conjunto* ensembles, a style of music common along the Texas-Mexico border), various instruments (accordion, bajo sexto, drums, and saxophone, among others), and multiple vocalists. Contemporary recording artists who include corridos (and narcocorridos) within their typical repertories include Los Cadetes de Linares, Chalino Sánchez, Ramon Ayala, Roberto Tapia, and Los Tigres del Norte. Many of these later corridos incorporate elements of additional popular styles, such as electronica, rock, and hip-hop, as well as Latin American styles like the bolero and the cumbia.

Overall, and beyond a wide variety of actual sonic manifestations during the 19th, 20th, and 21st centuries, the corrido is, at its core, a contemporary expression of the Mexican and Mexican American (as well as, to a certain extent, Colombian) people. Promoting heroic stories, historical events, working-class experiences, farmworkers' rights, modern drug culture, and fictional accounts through the vernacular language and simple music, the corrido has functioned over the last two centuries as a form of communication—whether as basic news media, or as a form of ethnic identity and sociocultural resistance. From its origins in medieval Europe, through its early influence along the U.S.-Mexico border, to its eventual incorporation in modern society, the corrido tells a story and thus unites a people.

Erin E. Bauer

See also: Accordion (Americas); Conjunto; Conjunto (Norteños); Cumbia; Mexican Regional Music; Rap/Hip-Hop; Rock and Roll; Tejano Music

Further Reading

Chew Sánchez, Martha I. 2006. *Corridos in Migrant Memory*. Albuquerque: University of New Mexico Press.

"Corridos sin Fronteras." *Smithsonian Institution Traveling Exhibition Service*. https://www.museumsandtheweb.com/mw2003/papers/songer/songer.html.

Dickey, Dan W. 1978. *The Kennedy Corridos: A Study of the Ballads of a Mexican American Hero*. Austin: University of Texas Press.

Flores, Richard R. 1992. "The Corrido and the Emergence of Texas-Mexican Social Identity." *Journal of American Folklore* 105(416) (Spring), 166–182.

Herrera-Sobek, Maria. 1990. *The Mexican Corrido: A Feminist Analysis*. Bloomington: Indiana University Press.

Mendoza, Vicente T. 1954. *El Corrido Mexicano*. Mexico City: Fondo de Cultura Económica.

Paredes, Américo. 1958. *With His Pistol in His Hand: A Border Ballad and Its Hero*. Austin: University of Texas Press.

Peña, Manuel H. 1999. *Música Tejana: The Cultural Economy of Artistic Transformation*. College Station: Texas A&M University Press.

Simmons, Merle. 1957. *The Mexican Corrido as a Source of an Interpretive Study of Modern Mexico, 1870–1950*. Bloomington: University of Indiana Press.

Wald, Elijah. 2001. *Narcocorrido: A Journey into the Music of Drugs, Guns, and Guerillas*. New York: Rayo/Harper Collins.

Cossacks, Music of

The term *Cossacks* often refers to diverse historical and contemporary groups. Although the Cossacks are mainly linked to Russia and Ukraine, there are Cossack communities in North America, Asia, Australia, and elsewhere. Cossack music, mainly songs, reflects their history, records military and cultural experiences, and serves as the main basis for a Cossack cultural identity. Since the late 20th century, Cossack music culture has played an increasingly important role in folk revival movements in Russia and Ukraine.

The Cossacks originate from the steppe regions along the Dnieper and Don rivers. In the 15th and 16th centuries, the Zaporozhian and Don Cossacks (democratically run military nomadic communities) attracted runaway serfs and outlaws from the Polish–Lithuanian Commonwealth and the Grand Duchy of Moscow. The Cossacks allied with the Russian Tsar and gradually advanced to the Caucasus, the Urals, and Siberia. After the Zaporozhian host became subordinate in the middle of the 17th century, most of the Cossacks became Russian subjects, although some remained in the Polish–Lithuanian Commonwealth or resettled to the Ottoman Empire. By the early 19th century, the ethnically and culturally heterogeneous Cossacks were made into a semi-military legal estate which had to perform border guard service. During the 19th century, Cossack communities spread as far as Central Asia and the Pacific coast.

The Cossacks' great regional diversity and eventful history, which included the wars against the Ottoman Empire, the Patriotic War of 1812, the Caucasian War, the Russo-Japanese War, and the First World War, ensured the heterogeneity of Cossack music culture, which features a wide variety of songs. Slavic (mainly Ukrainian and Russian) folk songs and epic ballads, music of Caucasian and Siberian indigenous peoples, and authored compositions all influenced Cossack songwriting. Cossack songs emphasized their freedom and military prowess, narrated certain historical events, and described the landscapes where particular communities dwelled. After their transition from nomadic to sedentary life, home, love, and family became further topics of Cossack songs.

In the Ukraine, the Cossacks became an integral part of national culture. The first Ukrainian-language opera, *A Zaporozhian beyond the Danube* by Semen Hulak-Artemovsky (1813–1873), focused on the exiled Cossack experience in the Ottoman Empire. Mykola Lysenko (1842–1912), a major Ukrainian nationalist composer of Cossack origin, explored the Cossack roots of Ukraine in his opera *Taras Bulba* and symphonic fantasy *Shumka the Cossack*.

On the imperial scale, the Cossacks were united by their estate membership and military service. The Cossack host choirs performed secular songs and Russian Orthodox Church music. Although the patriotism, Christianity, and loyalty to the tsar which appeared in the Cossack songs contributed to the formation of a Russian Imperial identity, the Cossacks were not a homogenous group. They spoke different languages and professed different religions. Some Cossacks of the Transbaikal Cossack Host, for instance, were Buryat and Buddhist. Intermarriages between Cossacks and non-Cossacks further contributed to the transculturality of the estate.

The Kuban Cossack Choir performs in celebration of Russia's National Unity Day at the Arnold Kats State Concert Hall in Novosibirsk, November 4, 2017. The group is one of the leading folk ensembles of Russia. (Kirill Kukhmar/TASS via Getty Images)

The estates were abolished by the Bolsheviks in 1917. During the Russian Civil War (1917–1922), the Cossacks formed the backbone of the anti-Bolshevik forces in the southern and eastern parts of the former empire. Many Cossacks joined the Red Army. A group of Kuban Cossacks formed the Kuban People's Republic, which warred against both of the two main sides in the Civil War. The anthem of the republic was a Cossack song *You, Kuban, You Are Our Motherland*. It was written in 1914 and in post-Soviet Russia became the anthem of the Krasnodar Krai. Cossack songs pledging alliance to both the Reds and the Whites were written and performed. The Don Cossack song *Friends, Do Not Fear the Slander* became widely known as an anthem of the White Movement.

After the establishment of the Soviet regime, which initiated systematic repression against the Cossacks, many of them left Russia. Diaspora communities formed in China, the United States, Australia, and other countries. Some groups maintained a Cossack cultural identity in which the Russian and Orthodox elements played a major role. Cossack emigrants formed ensembles and performed Russian Orthodox Church music, Cossack songs, and Cossack dances. Concerts of the Terek Cossack Choir were popular in interwar Shanghai. The Don Cossack Choir, founded in 1921 by Serge Jaroff in a Turkish internment camp and later relocated to the United States, became known internationally.

In the 1930s, the Soviet authorities redefined the Cossacks as a subethnic group of the Russians and allowed their cultural expression. In 1936, the Kuban Cossack Choir was reestablished. During the Second World War, the Soviet government formed Cossack divisions, but they were disbanded after the war ended. In the postwar Soviet Union, music remained the only way to articulate and maintain a Cossack identity. Cossack songs and dances were frequently performed by Russian and Ukrainian folk ensembles; for example, the famous Alexandrov Ensemble performed them both in the Soviet Union and abroad. The masculinity and militancy of Cossack music helped attract boys into the numerous folklore ensembles across the Soviet Union. Two high-tempo dances of Cossack origin, *hopak* and *kazachok*, became central to many concert programs.

The performances of state-sponsored folk ensembles were criticized for the lack of authenticity in their polished and professionally choreographed performances. Also, the Cossack songs that did not make into their repertoires (especially those related to the outlawed traditional customs), gradually faded into oblivion. Some of them were recorded by enthusiasts like Alexander Listopadov (1873–1949), who collected five volumes of Don Cossack songs.

Things started to change in the 1960s when Vyacheslav Shchurov (1942–) and other ethnomusicologists started organizing performances of unedited folklore gathered during scientific expeditions. Shchurov's concerts inspired Dmitri Pokrovsky, another ethnomusicologist, to create an ensemble for performing Cossack and other Russian folklore. Through the Pokrovsky Ensemble, a different interpretation of Cossack music, featuring improvisations and complex polyphony, found its way to the global public. After Perestroika and the fall of the Soviet Union, a major revival of Cossack culture ensued. Ensembles such as the Cossack Circle and Krinitsa perform Cossack songs a capella or to the accompaniment of accordion, balalaika, hurdy-gurdy, and other instruments across Russia and abroad.

In post-Soviet Russia, Cossack music has become intermingled with politics. The masculinity, patriotism, pride, heritage, and Orthodox faith ascribed to the Cossack culture were reimagined as elements of a Russian identity. Descendants of the Cossacks and those interested in Cossack culture formed numerous associations, youth education centers, and other organizations. In 2005, Cossack paramilitary formations were officially established.

The people who claim to be Cossacks in contemporary Russia are very diverse and do not seem to agree on the nature of the Cossack revival. Some view Cossack culture as an alternative to Western culture, a necessary element in a new Russian identity. Others view the Cossacks as an ethnic group that has to be redefined in modern terms and separated from the image of archaic horsemen. In this respect, Cossack music finds itself in a situation similar to that of other indigenous cultures, which is to be preserved without denying their right to development.

Ivan Sablin

See also: Dmitri Pokrovsky Ensemble; Russian Orthodox Church Music

Further Reading

Boeck, Brian J. 2009. *Imperial Boundaries: Cossack Communities and Empire-Building in the Age of Peter the Great.* Cambridge: Cambridge University Press.

Derluguian, Georgi M., and Serge Cipko. 1997. "The Politics of Identity in a Russian Borderland Province: The Kuban Neo-Cossack Movement, 1989–1996." *Europe-Asia Studies* 49(8), 1485–1500.

Olson, Laura J. 2004. *Performing Russia: Folk Revival and Russian Identity.* New York: Routledge.

Toje, Hege. 2006. "Cossack Identity in the New Russia: Kuban Cossack Revival and Local Politics." *Europe-Asia Studies* 58(7), 1057–1077.

Country Music

The term "country music" describes a wide range of popular music styles, including old-time, honky-tonk, Nashville Sound, alternative country, and bluegrass, among others. Over the course of its nearly century-long history, this music has been known as "hillbilly music," "country & western," "C&W," and, most recently, "country music." First recorded during the 1920s, country music has been predominantly marketed to rural white audiences, and historically has had close associations with the culture of working-class whites in the American South. More recent scholarship has complicated this portrait by documenting the early appeal of country music in the American Midwest. Despite its origins in the United States, country music's popularity has been global in reach almost from the outset. A product of the commercial music industry, country music has both emulated and influenced the stylistic characteristics and topical concerns of other forms of American popular music, as well as popular musics from around the world.

Early country music—known in the 1920s by such monikers as "hillbilly music" or "Old Familiar Tunes"—has often been linked to the musical traditions of rural southern whites, particularly those living in Appalachia, the Piedmont region of North Carolina and South Carolina, and the American Southwest. The decision to hew so closely to an exclusively white image of country music was made by record industry executives who hoped to use a racialized marketing scheme to reach previously underperforming markets for commercial recordings. Close listening to hillbilly recordings from the 1920s, however, reveals the strong influence of African American, Mexican American, and Hawaiian styles, as well as the persistence of the 19th-century popular song repertory and minstrel stereotypes. A survey of early country recordings reveals a remarkably heterogeneous repertory, including traditional Anglo-American ballads, shape-note gospel compositions, new compositions about contemporary news stories, and a rich variety of dance tunes. For instance, Georgia native Fiddlin' John Carson (ca. 1868–1949), whose 1923 recording of the popular 19th-century minstrel song "Little Old Log Cabin in the Lane" is often credited with starting the craze for hillbilly music, not only recorded numerous songs from the traditional European American fiddle repertoire, but also blues numbers such as "Stockade Blues" (1934). Similarly, the Mississippi-born country entertainer Jimmie Rodgers (1897–1933), whose meteoric career spanned only six years from 1927 to his premature death in 1933, was internationally renowned for his trademark "Blue Yodels," which featured collaborations with Hawaiian musicians Joe Kaipo and Lani McIntire and jazz musicians Louis Armstrong and Lil Hardin. Even the Carter Family of southwestern Virginia—a group that is considered by many American music historians as the scions of Anglo-American vernacular music—recorded blues numbers ("Worried Man Blues" [1935], for example) and partnered with African American guitarist Lesley Riddle (1905–1980), who helped the group transcribe folk songs and original compositions for copyright purposes.

By the late 1920s, the early effects of the Great Depression were being felt in the communities that purchased hillbilly recordings, and record sales began to decline precipitously as a consequence. Radio—which, unlike phonograph recordings, required a one-time purchase and delivered free content thereafter—became the dominant medium for the transmission of country music. Although radio stations across the United States began broadcasting "barn dance" programs as early as 1923, the Great Depression ushered in a golden age of rural-themed programming that featured old-time string band music, cowboy songs, vaudeville-style comedy skits, and sentimental ballads. Chief among these programs were the *WLS Barn Dance* (later *The National Barn Dance*) from Chicago, WSM Nashville's *The Grand Ole Opry*, and *The Renfro Valley Barn Dance*, which was broadcast by Cincinnati station WLW. As numerous scholars have demonstrated, radio barn dances appealed broadly to long-time urban residents, recent migrants from the nation's rural communities, and émigrés from southern and eastern Europe. Although *The Grand Ole Opry* holds the record for the longest-running barn dance program, *The National Barn Dance* was far more influential during the 1930s and 1940s, launching the careers of such celebrated artists as Patsy Montana (Ruby Blevins, 1908–1996), Bradley Kincaid (1895–1989), and Gene Autry (1907–1998), among many others. Autry, who began his singing career as a Jimmie Rodgers impersonator, adopted the crooning vocal style made popular by Bing Crosby and Frank Sinatra and quickly found himself in demand in Hollywood Westerns, where, as a member of the Republic studio, he helped to bring the "singing cowboy" genre to national and international acclaim during the 1930s and solidified country music's Western iconography.

Also flourishing during the Great Depression was western swing, a country-jazz hybrid that was immensely popular among white audiences in Texas and Oklahoma. Western swing bands such as the Light Crust Doughboys, Milton Brown and His Musical Brownies, and Bob Wills and His Texas Playboys capitalized on the widespread national popularity of big band jazz (also known as "swing") and was strongly influenced by the classic blues of Bessie Smith and the "gypsy jazz" made popular by Belgian guitarist Django Reinhardt, French violinist Stéphane Grappelli, and the Quintette du Hot Club de France. To compete with the sounds of boisterous dancers in dance halls throughout Texas and Oklahoma, the western swing bands frequently augmented their string band core with horns (trumpets, trombones, and saxophones), electric guitar and steel guitar, piano, and drums. The repertoire of the western swing bands was remarkably diverse by most contemporary standards for country music, reflecting the multicultural nature of Texas music more generally. It was not uncommon to hear a tune played in a Tejano *conjunto* style immediately after a polka from Texas's German and Czech immigrants and a classic blues piece during a western swing band's performances, and their recorded outputs reveal similar tendencies. Moreover, western swing musicians frequently engaged in the common jazz practice of improvisation, the details of which may not have been captured well on recordings that required groups to adhere to a strict length. In fact, as musicologist Jean Boyd has documented, many western swing musicians did not see themselves as "country" or "hillbilly" musicians, but as jazz musicians. Western swing's hybrid nature and association with white working-class audiences have, unfortunately, led to its absence from the prevailing narratives of jazz history.

The audiences that originally supported western swing in Texas and Oklahoma were disproportionately affected by the simultaneous occurrence of the Great Depression and the Dust Bowl, forcing thousands of "Okies" to migrate to southern California in search of better economic opportunities. By the middle of World War II, western swing was thriving on the West Coast of the United States, as was a new style of country music known as honky-tonk. Honky-tonk lyrics were reflective of the broader class tensions arising from the Okie migration and the changing gender roles brought about by the war, and frequently discussed such topics as extramarital affairs, divorce, and substance abuse. Honky-tonk music, which also flourished in the petrochemical boom towns of Texas and Louisiana, embraced the electrified instruments of the western swing bands and was built around a core instrumentation of acoustic rhythm guitar, electric lead guitar, lap (and, later, pedal) steel guitar, fiddle, and string bass. Although the most celebrated honky-tonk musician—Hank Williams (1923–1953)—was male, several women, including Rose Lee Maddox (1925–1998) and Kitty Wells (born Muriel Deason, 1919–2012), contributed valuable female perspectives to the genre and commented on the gender and sexual politics of life in the honky-tonk. The California honky-tonk scene also gave birth to the "Bakersfield Sound," a more raucous honky-tonk style that reached the pinnacle of its popularity during the 1950s and 1960s. As heard in the music of Buck Owens (1929–2006) and Merle Haggard (1937–), Bakersfield Sound showcases the high-frequency sounds of Fender Telecaster guitars, bright steel guitar timbres, and close vocal harmonies. The Bakersfield Sound work of Buck Owens also enjoyed some popularity on *Billboard*'s "Hot 100" pop charts, reaching Top 40 radio listeners in the United States through Owens's recordings and cover versions by Ray Charles and the Beatles.

The 1940s also witnessed the development of bluegrass music, an approach to string band music that showcased exceptional instrumental virtuosity, "high lonesome" vocals, and songs about failed romantic love and longing for lost rural homes. Named after mandolinist Bill Monroe's (1911–1996) band, the Blue Grass Boys, most scholars and fans trace the origins of bluegrass to 1945, when banjoist Earl Scruggs (1924–2012) and guitarist and vocalist Lester Flatt (1914–1979) joined Monroe's group. Although Monroe initially sought to maintain proprietary control over the genre, numerous groups emerged in the late 1940s and 1950s to emulate and advance bluegrass music, including Flatt & Scruggs and the Foggy Mountain Boys, and the Stanley Brothers. Bluegrass spread rapidly during the 1950s and 1960s as college students across the United States became interested in American vernacular musics as part of a widespread folk music revival. Like the string band traditions from which it emerged, bluegrass music is remarkably heterogeneous and has given new life to many of the songs made famous by early hillbilly recording artists.

During the 1950s, Nashville—which had long been a major center for country music because of the Grand Ole Opry—became the leading center for the recording of country music. By the late 1950s, RCA Victor, Columbia, and Decca all owned or had established working relationships with recording studios in Nashville, and the city boasted a team of session musicians—known collectively as "the A team"—who supplied accompaniments to a wide range of singers in an equally diverse array of country music styles. Working in collaboration with producers Chet Atkins (1924–2001) and Owen Bradley (1915–1998), among others, session musicians such as guitarists Grady Martin (1929–2001), Velma Smith (1924–2014), Hank Garland (1930–2004); vocalist and arranger Anita Kerr (1927–); and pianist Floyd Cramer (1933–1997) helped to create the "Nashville Sound," a style of country music characterized by lush background vocals, string arrangements, and carefully recorded vocal and instrumental tracks. The style is heard most clearly in the work of Patsy Cline (born Virginia Hensley, 1932–1963) and Jim Reeves (1923–1964). The Nashville Sound era also witnessed the development of the first all-country radio stations, the Country Music Association, and the contemporary country music industry, and helped to secure Nashville's current status as the international center of country music production and distribution. By the late 1960s, the Nashville Sound had incorporated elements of the honky-tonk edge in both lyrical content and musical style, developing what many have described as a "countrypolitan" sound, as heard in the music of George Jones (1931–2013), Tammy Wynette (1942–1998), and Conway Twitty (1933–1993).

In response to the countercultural upheavals of the late 1960s and 1970s, several varieties of country-rock music emerged, including the California country-rock of the Byrds, the Flying Burrito Brothers, and the Eagles; the "progressive country" of such Texas-based musicians as Michael Murphey (1945–), Jerry Jeff Walker

(1942–), and Asleep at the Wheel; and the harder-edged Southern rock of such southeastern groups as the Allman Brothers Band, Lynyrd Skynyrd, and the Charlie Daniels Band. At the same time, bluegrass music also became more closely associated with the counterculture through the work of such "progressive bluegrass" and "newgrass" artists as John Hartford (1937–2001) and the New Grass Revival. Although each of these country-rock styles emphasized the "country" and "rock" elements of the hybrid in different proportions, they all spoke to the growing generational conflicts of the time and offered ways for young people to participate in country music culture at a time when mainstream country music was dealing with more adult themes. Furthermore, like the country styles that preceded them, country-rock approaches found their way into the genre's broader stylistic vocabulary and would later become key signifiers of country music tradition for subsequent generations of listeners.

Since the 1980s, country music has increasingly become a style of American popular music that draws freely upon a wide range of country music signifiers while also incorporating elements of mainstream popular music. During the early 1980s, for instance, mainstream country music was decidedly pop-oriented in the wake of the blockbuster film *Urban Cowboy*, which led to the establishment of Texas-style country dancehalls throughout the United States. But, by the middle of the decade, country radio began to turn away from country-pop in favor of a "neotraditional" approach that revived honky-tonk and bluegrass styles, as heard in the work of Randy Travis (1959–), Dwight Yoakam (1956–), and Reba McEntire (1955–), among others. By the early 1990s, neotraditionalist "hat acts" defined the core sound of country radio, culminating in the rise of Garth Brooks (1962–), an Oklahoma-born singer-songwriter who broke numerous album sales and concert attendance records with his arena-rock styled concerts and honky-tonk-oriented sound. The massive popularity of "hot new country" was countered by an emergent "alternative country" movement in the early 1990s, as groups such as Uncle Tupelo, Whiskeytown, and BR-549 blended punk rock's do-it-yourself ethos and country music styles to reach out to audiences that were disaffected by country music's mainstream popularity. Since the late 1990s, country music audiences have become increasingly fragmented, in part due to satellite and internet radio services that provide access to narrowly defined subgenres and the rise of the mp3, which allows listeners to eschew radio formats altogether.

Although country music is primarily a product of the popular music industry in the United States, it has enjoyed a significant global history almost since the genre's beginnings. During the 1920s and 1930s, radio broadcasts and recordings frequently traveled from the United States to the rest of North America and even to parts of Europe. During and after World War II, country music traveled to Europe and Asia with American servicemen who brought recordings with them and listened to radio broadcasts emanating from American military bases. As a consequence of these engagements, country music has come to thrive in Great Britain, Germany, and Japan, among other places. Australia, too, can claim a long independent country music history that dates to at least the 1930s; although they have thriving country music communities, few Australian artists in this genre have been successful in the United States. Numerous scholars have also demonstrated the significant role that country music has played in helping musicians in Brazil, Thailand, Canada, Zimbabwe, and the Czech Republic articulate key cultural issues through country music's rural, pastoral framework.

Travis D. Stimeling

See also: Bluegrass; Blues; Carter Family, The; Fiddle; Jazz; Rodgers, Jimmie

Further Reading

Bidgood, Lee. 2011. "'America Is All Around Here': An Ethnography of Bluegrass Music in the Contemporary Czech Republic." PhD diss., University of Virginia.

Boyd, Jean A. 1998. *The Jazz of the Southwest: An Oral History of Western Swing.* Austin: University of Texas Press.

Bufwack, Mary A., and Robert K. Oermann. 2003. *Finding Her Voice: Women in Country Music, 1800–2000.* Nashville, TN: Country Music Foundation Press and Vanderbilt University Press.

Cantwell, Robert. 1984. *Bluegrass Breakdown: The Making of the Old Southern Sound.* Urbana: University of Illinois Press.

Cohen, Sara. 2005. "Country at the Heart of the City: Music, Heritage, and Regeneration in Liverpool." *Ethnomusicology* 49(1) (Winter), 25–48.

Daniel, Wayne W. 1990. *Pickin' on Peachtree: A History of Country Music in Atlanta, Georgia.* Urbana: University of Illinois Press.

Dent, Alexander Sebastian. 2009. *River of Tears: Country Music, Memory, and Modernity in Brazil.* Durham, NC: Duke University Press.

Dueck, Byron. 2013. *Musical Intimacies & Indigenous Imaginaries: Aboriginal Music and Dance in Public Performance.* New York: Oxford University Press.

Ellison, Curtis W. 1995. *Country Music Culture: From Hard Times to Heaven.* Jackson: University Press of Mississippi.

Fox, Aaron A. 2004. *Real Country: Music and Language in Working-Class Culture.* Durham, NC: Duke University Press.

Fox, Pamela. 2009. *Natural Acts: Gender, Race, and Rusticity in Country Music.* Ann Arbor: University of Michigan Press.

Fox, Pamela, and Barbara Ching, eds. 2008. *Old Roots, New Routes: The Cultural Politics of Alt. Country Music.* Ann Arbor: University of Michigan Press.

Green, Douglas B. 2002. *Singing in the Saddle: The History of the Singing Cowboy.* Nashville, TN: Country Music Foundation Press and Vanderbilt University Press.

Huber, Patrick. 2008. *Linthead Stomp: The Creation of Country Music in the Piedmont South.* Chapel Hill: University of North Carolina Press.

Jensen, Joli. 1998. *The Nashville Sound: Authenticity, Commercialization, and Country Music.* Nashville, TN: Country Music Foundation and Vanderbilt University Press.

LaChapelle, Peter. 2007. *Proud to Be an Okie: Cultural Politics, Country Music, and Migration to Southern California.* Berkeley: University of California Press.

Malone, Bill C. 1993. *Singing Cowboys and Musical Mountaineers: Southern Culture and the Roots of Country Music.* Mercer University Lamar Memorial Lectures No. 34. Athens, GA: University of Georgia Press.

Malone, Bill C. 2002. *Don't Get Above Your Raisin': Country Music and the Southern Working Class.* Urbana: University of Illinois Press.

Malone, Bill C., and Jocelyn R. Neal. 2010. *Country Music, U.S.A.,* 3rd rev. ed. Austin: University of Texas Press.

McCusker, Kristine M. 2008. *Lonesome Cowgirls and Honky-Tonk Angels: The Women of Barn Dance Radio*. Urbana: University of Illinois Press.

Miller, Karl Hagstrom. 2010. *Segregating Sound: Inventing Folk and Pop Music in the Age of Jim Crow*. Durham, NC: Duke University Press.

Pecknold, Diane. 2007. *The Selling Sound: The Rise of the Country Music Industry*. Durham, NC: Duke University Press.

Pecknold, Diane, ed. 2013. *Hidden in the Mix: The African American Presence in Country Music*. Durham, NC: Duke University Press.

Peterson, Richard A. 1997. *Creating Country Music: Fabricating Authenticity*. Chicago: University of Chicago Press.

Rosenberg, Neil V. 1985. *Bluegrass: A History*. Urbana: University of Illinois Press.

Russell, Tony. 2007. *Country Music Originals: The Legends and the Lost*. New York: Oxford University Press.

Wolfe, Charles K. 2001. *Classic Country: Legends of Country Music*. New York: Routledge.

Cretan Lyra

The Cretan lyra (*lýra*) is a pear-form, bowed chordophone (typically with three strings) musical instrument of Greece, played mainly in Crete but also in other islands of the Aegean Sea. It is practically similar to the Byzantine *lyra*, the Renaissance *rebec*, the Western classical violin, the Afghan *rubab*, and the Turkish *kemençe*. Historically speaking, we can identify four kinds of Cretan lyras: (1) a small, primitive model of lyra with a sharp sound, called the *lyráki*; (2) the *vrontólyra*, which is a larger type of lyra for louder playing of bass tones, once used for lengthy open-space performances; (3) the *violólyra*, a nowadays rare, eight-shaped violin-lyra hybrid, usually with four strings, created during the interwar period; and (4) the standard Cretan lyra, which is a newer combination of the *lyráki* and the violin, common in all modern Cretan music.

Faithfully following the authentic local tradition, most lyras are entirely handmade. The main body of a characteristic Cretan lyra is carved together with its neck from a single piece of maple, ivy, oleander, walnut, or mulberry that is at least 10 to 15 years old. The cover of a lyra's soundboard is made of aged cedarwood, and has two similar hemispherical soundholes that define the particular timbre of the instrument. Another essential part of the lyra is the "soul" (also known as the "devil's wood-stick"), that is the soundpost, a small dowel which functions as a sound transmitter and critically affects the instrument's volume and its quality of sound. The strings of a lyra are tuned in fifths (G3-D4-A4). Older versions of lyras were tuned in fourths and fifths (D5-A4-D4 or A4-D4-A3), which was called *alla turca* tuning. The tuning of a lyra depends on the voice capabilities of the musician, along with the thickness of its cords. Its strings were formerly made of animal guts, but today they are constructed of steel or various synthetic materials. The bow of the lyra is a bent fiddlestick with 150–200 horsetail hairs, occasionally accompanied by a number of additional small round bells that mark the rhythm. All woods are carefully selected, so as to be unaffected by age or weather and bear no scratches or knots. Construction of a lyra requires seven to nine days.

> **Lyra and Minstrel**
>
> In its most basic sense, the idea of a minstrel simply envisions a musician with a stringed instrument who travels the land singing songs of love, loss, and social criticism. Minstrels have often been tasked historically with keeping and recounting oral histories. Minstrels have been present in a variety of cultures throughout the past millennia, including the Kora players of Africa Kora, the troubadours and trouveres of 13th- and 14th-century France, the meistersingers and minnesingers of 15th- and 16th-century Germany, the blackface minstrels of 19th- and early 20th-century America, and the folk singer/songwriters of the 1940s–1960s United States (such as Woody Guthrie and Bob Dylan). However, the roots of the minstrel in Western civilization trace to lyra players of the ancient Greeks, as evidenced by the writings of Plato, Aristotle, and other notables of the period.

Each lyra is independently adjusted to produce the desired sound (treble, middle, bass, etc.) and meet the requirements of its owner/user. The instruments are produced mostly by local manufacturers who are also professional music players.

Cretan lyra is a perfect instrument for performing speedy and vivid music as well as calm and expressive traditional melodies. Today, Cretan music is generally performed by a duo that consists of a *lyráris* (lyrist, the lyra player) accompanied by a *la(g)outiéris* (lutist, the lute player). The second musician plays the rhythm and the chords and occasionally improvises on the lyra's melodic line. Sometimes lyra is played unaccompanied. As a rule, the lyrist also acts as the vocalist who sings the traditional 15-syllable rhyming couplets of *mantinádes*, which is a widespread type of musical and poetical dialogical practice in Crete and other Mediterranean insular cultures.

The instrument's fingerboard has no frets at all. The lyrist employs an unusual way of fingering a lyra's string. Instead of pressing it with the fingertip like a violinist or a guitarist, he pushes against one side of the string with the top of his fingernail. In addition, the lyrist plays the lyra in an upright position rather than holding it between the jaw and the shoulder. If he is seated, he rests it on his knee; if he is standing, he puts his foot up on a chair and rests the lyra on his thigh to ensure its stability. These positions are very conducive to playing an ornamented, vibrant melody.

When performing a tune, the lyrist plays on the first (the highest) string. Although the second and third strings are seldom used for playing melodic phrases, the bow often rasps both the second and the first or the second and third strings together, thus accompanying the melody with rough drone tones that create a primal sound and mood.

Since the second half of the 20th century, the lyra has become a powerful local symbol of cultural identity. Despite the fact that in many other Greek regions the violin dominates musical performance, the lyra in Crete enhanced its popularity while imitating the form, timbre, and masterful techniques of violin. This resulted in the extension of the lyra's repertory; thus, modern lyras can be used to perform entirely new songs and dances in addition to the older ones. The most well-known tune played on lyra is the *syrtós*, a characteristic traditional Cretan dance, which is widely known and performed in the regional recording industry and connects contemporary music practices to their historical background influences—both Western and Eastern. Other major Cretan dances performed on lyra are *pentozáli(s)* (either slow or fast), *soústa*, and *maleviziόti(ko)s*. Lyra performance is also applied in *kontiliés*, which are small melodic riffs and musical motifs with limited variety, on which *mantinádes* are improvised.

Distinguished Cretan lyra performers are, among others, Charálambos Garganourákis, Giórgos Kalogrídis, Alékos Karavítis, Leonídas Kládos, Manólis Lagoudákis (Lagós), Kóstas Mountákis, Antónis Papadákis (Kareklás), Manólis Pasparákis (Stravós), Charílaos Piparákis, Antréas Rodinós, Thanásis Skordalós, Vasílis Skoulás, Antónis Xyloúris (Psarantónis), and the legendary Níkos Xyloúris. Ross Daly, an Irish artist who has been living in Crete for more than 35 years, specializes in the performance and study of Cretan lyra in the novel context of the global "world music" networks.

Although Cretan lyra is a musical instrument exclusively performed by men, Aspasía Papadáki (a famous female lyrist) has been interrelated with the persona of a woman playing the lyra. As the figure of the lyra is symbolically associated with a man's body, one can realize why "lyra music" is tightly connected with the values and beliefs of contemporary Cretan society by articulating a wide range of emotions experienced by sensitive, yet harsh, males and manipulating cultural tourism policies through the control of commercial production of traditional Cretan music.

Nick Poulakis

See also: Greek Popular Music; Nisiotika

Further Reading

Cooper, David, and Kevin Dawe, eds. 2005. *The Mediterranean in Music: Critical Perspectives, Common Concerns, Cultural Differences.* Lanham, MD: Scarecrow Press.

Dawe, Kevin. 2007. *Music and Musicians in Crete: Performance and Ethnography in a Mediterranean Island Society.* Lanham, MD: Scarecrow Press.

Hnaraki, Maria. 2007. *Cretan Music: Unfolding Ariadne's Thread.* Athens: Kerkyra Publications.

Kallimopoulou, Eleni. 2009. *Paradosiaká: Music, Meaning and Identity in Modern Greece.* Burlington, VT: Ashgate.

Cruz, Celia (1925–2003)

Celia Cruz (birth name Hilaria Celia Caridad Cruz Alfonso, though it is sometimes shown as Úrsula Hilaria Celia de la Caridad Cruz Alfonso de la Santísima Trinidad) was one of the most iconic and popular singers of salsa music. Her renown led her to be called the "Queen of Salsa" as well as the "Queen of Latin Music." Though the Cuban-born Cruz spent much of her career based in the United States, she is cited as the best known and most influential female performer in the history of Cuban music. Cruz became known for her trademark shout "*¡Azúcar!*" the Spanish word for "sugar."

Salsa, the type of music with which Cruz is identified, is the Spanish word for "sauce," the spicy, colorful dish popularized in Latin America and the Caribbean. Salsa music was a repackaging of traditional upbeat, rhythmic Cuban dance music, marketed to new audiences. The term "salsa music" was heavily promoted in New York City during the 1970s, but like the sauce for which it is named, it was a combination of many ingredients. Some of the forms represented in salsa music include Afro-Cuban percussion, Latin jazz, mambo, rhumba, and merengue, as well as elements of rock and roll, rhythm and blues, and funk, all added into a base of traditional Cuban music. With the political estrangement between the United States and Cuba, conditions favored christening salsa as a new musical form, and one of its most renowned performers was Cruz.

Celia Cruz was born in the Santos Suárez neighborhood of Havana, Cuba, on October 21, 1925. She was the second of four children born to homemaker Catalina "Ollita" Alfonso and Simon Cruz, a railroad worker. Cruz said the family lived in a poor section of Santos Suárez, a working-class area of diverse races and ethnicities where she could hear a variety of musical styles through the open windows. Behind their house lived a woman known as a "Santera" who practiced Santeria, a non-Christian form of worship whose roots are African. Cruz was captivated by the sound of the drums and tribal rhythms, which she said were expressive of her own African roots.

Cruz loved to hear her mother sing and her mother became Cruz's mentor. As Cruz grew older, she attended dances with her extended family where she was exposed to many types of Cuban music. She was assigned the duty of singing younger siblings to sleep. When she was a teenager, an aunt took Cruz to sing at local dances. In 1947, she won a radio talent show, "La Hora de Té," bringing her local fame. However, her father insisted that she concentrate on her studies, hoping she would have a respectable career as a teacher. One day a teacher told Celia that an entertainer could earn in one day what most Cuban teachers earned in a month; with this advice, Cruz left school to become a professional singer.

Cruz appeared first in amateur talent shows but was soon sought as a paid entertainer. She was noted for her unique singing style which incorporated the chants of street vendors. Enrolling at the local conservatory of music, she sought to refine her presentation by studying voice and learning music theory. After three years of study, her father accepted and approve of her attempting a professional singing career, though she went to performances chaperoned by a female relative.

In 1950, Cruz became the lead singer of the Sonora Matancera, said to be Cuba's most popular orchestra, which headlined at the world-famous Tropicana Casino nightclub. During the 15 years she was with that band, they traveled throughout Latin America. It was at this time that Cruz became known for her trademark shout of "¡Azúcar!" which started out as the punchline of a joke she often told at concerts about ordering café Cubano (Cuban coffee) in Miami, when she told the waiter one cannot drink Cuban coffee without it.

With Cruz as its lead singer, Sonora Matancera attained great fame in Cuba and made frequent international tours, adding to their celebrity with appearances on radio and in movies. When Fidel Castro took power in Cuba following the revolution in 1959, the band left the island by claiming to be embarking on yet another tour. In 1960 and 1961, they established a home base in Mexico, entertaining that country with their Cuban sound and publicly stating that they would not return to Cuba. In late 1961, they left for the United States, which would become Cruz's adopted homeland. The band accepted a long-term contract at the Hollywood Palladium in Los Angeles.

Cruz's first years in America were not fruitful, as many young Latinos preferred rock and roll to the brand of Cuban-inspired music that Cruz performed. On July 14, 1962, Cruz married trumpeter Pedro Knight Caraballo (1921–2007), who became her manager and musical director. With his help, her career in the United States began to take off. After moving to New York with Knight, Cruz recorded numerous albums, including collaborations with Johnny Pacheco and Tito Puente, two of the most influential figures in Latin music. Puente later said he first heard Cruz singing on Cuban radio and thought it was a man because her voice was so powerful and energetic.

Cuban American singer and salsa pioneer Celia Cruz (1925–2003), performing in 1987. (Frans Schellekens/Redferns)

By the early 1970s, Cruz was captivating new audiences, including young Latinos who had just discovered her music for the first time as well as those who cherished it as a reminder of their previous lives in Cuba. She was selected to sing the role of "Gracia Divina" in the opera *Hommy*, a Latin reworking of the Who's rock opera *Tommy* with an Afro-Caribbean beat. It was brought to the stage by bandleader-arranger Larry Harlow at New York's Carnegie Hall in 1973. Cruz's performance became legendary for its energy and power, which further spread her renown. She began to be called "salsa's most celebrated singer" as well as the preserver of "real salsa."

Critics and audiences often flocked to see Cruz in live performance to experience the full effect of her talent. Along with her powerful voice, she was celebrated for her magnetic stage presence and unpredictable performances, which sometimes lasted up to three hours. She was legendary for her exotic, extravagant costumes which usually included feathers, lace, and sequins along with many yards of brightly colored fabric. Sometimes her fashions virtually took up the entire stage, though they never inhibited her energetic performances, which featured signature leaps and dance moves. On July 16, 2003, with Knight at her side,

Cruz died of brain cancer at the age of 77 at her home in Fort Lee, New Jersey. She is buried at Woodlawn Cemetery in the Bronx, New York. An epilogue to her autobiography states that per her wishes, soil from a visit to Guantánamo Bay, Cuba, was used in her burial.

Nancy Hendricks

See also: Calypso; Claves and Clave Rhythm; Reggaetón; Salsa

Further Reading

Cartlidge, Cherese. 2010. *Celia Cruz* (The Great Hispanic Heritage series). New York: Chelsea House.

Cruz, Celia, and Ana Cristina Reymundo. 2004. *Celia: My Life*. New York: Rayo from HarperCollins.

Marceles, Eduardo. 2004. *Azucar! The New Biography of Celia Cruz*. Gainesville, GA: Reed Press.

Cuatro

The *cuatro* is an original four-stringed guitar-like instrument, played in the northern parts of Latin America. There are two main variants, one in Venezuela and one in Puerto Rico. Both are traditionally used for accompanying singers and dancers; however, since the second half of the 20th century, solo music has also been played on both instrument types. The music for this instrument is always folkloristic (in contrast to another four-stringed instrument: the ukulele).

In Latin America, with its distinctive tradition of folk music, many different types of guitars are in use, mainly for accompanying singers and dancers. These instruments have their roots in Spain and Portugal and were brought to Latin America by the conquistadores in the 16th century. Therefore, many similarities can be found in form, stringing, and tuning to Spanish guitars and *vihuelas*, as well as to the Portuguese four-coursed *cavaquinho* (something between a guitar and a mandolin).

In Venezuela, where it is the national instrument, the cuatro has four single strings (from which its name derives) and is made like a small guitar with a length of roughly 80 cm, a width measuring about 54 cm, and a depth of about 10 cm. (This type of instrument is also in use in the neighboring countries and in Mexico.) The nylon strings are tuned similar to the highest four strings of a guitar (d-g-b-e′, the same intervals as the four-course European Renaissance guitar from the 16th century), with two exceptions: first, the highest string is one octave deeper, so that it sounds only one whole tone higher than the fourth string; second, its tuning is a fifth higher than that of the guitar. This (a-d′-f#′-b) is similar to the tuning of a Hawaiian ukulele (a′-d′-f#′-b′). There are variants with five and six strings, which are named *cinco* and *seis* respectively.

The cuatro provides a rhythmic and harmonic base for most Venezuelan folk music and is part of *Joropo*, a dance and music form in Venezuela, which today is recognized as the national dance. The most famous cuatro player was Fredy Reyna (1917–2001), who started as a guitar player and switched in 1948 to the cuatro. He changed the traditional tuning to the one of a Renaissance guitar, with the first string as the highest: a-d´-f#´-b´ (although the absolute pitch was not fixed during the Renaissance). Reyna established the Venezuelan cuatro as a solo instrument, made many recordings, and gave concerts in Europe as well as Venezuela.

The cuatro in Puerto Rico also derived from the European Renaissance guitar and, at first, was a four-stringed instrument in the form of a keyhole, which existed until the middle of the 20th century. This instrument was brought to Hawaii by immigrants in 1901, where it remained until the middle 1930s and was replaced by the tenor guitar, a four-string guitar. Since the end of the 19th century, a louder variant was developed in Puerto Rico. Although it kept its ancient name, the instrument was modified to have five double metal strings (a fifth course was added below the original four) and the form of a violin. It has a length of about 34 inches, a circumference of 20 inches, and a depth of 3 inches; it is tuned in fourths (bB-e´e-a-d´d´-g´g´, like the Spanish *bandurria*, a mandolin-like instrument. A variant with six courses is called a *seiz*. Traditionally, it was played by mountain farmers, often during religious contexts or secular events. During the 19th century, it was played in salon orchestras in coastal cities and in country ensembles in the mountains (the *jíbaro* ensembles, which included a singer). Today it also can be heard accompanied by another cuatro or by a guitar. The most famous Puerto Rican cuatro player was Yomo Toro (1933–2012), who recorded many albums and opened "Latin-pop" to his instrument.

Jörg Jewanski

See also: Ukulele

Further Reading

Montanaro, Bruno. 1983. *Guitares hispano-américaines.* Aix-en-Provence, France: Édisud.

The Puerto Rican Cuatro Project. n.d. www.cuatro-pr.org.

Reyna, Fredy, and Jesús Rosas Marcano. 1988. *El mago del cuento.* Venezuela: Grostz.

Solís, Ted. 1995. "Jíbaro Image and the Ecology of Hawai'i Puerto Rican Musical Instruments." *Latin American Music Review/Revista de música latinoamericana* 16(2), 123–153.

Torres, Aquiles. 2008. "The Venezuelan Cuatro." *American Lutherie* 94, 42–49.

Cumbia

Cumbia is the most representative musical style from Colombia and its most important cultural influence in the world music scene. This musical genre is a mixture of Aborigine, African, and European rhythms. It has grown in popularity in Latin America since the mid-20th century, and today has reached an important level of recognition as a regional characteristic music style with variations that emerge in different countries across the Americas.

Cumbia is a combination of native South American, African, and Spanish musical styles, which were re-elaborated to form this particular rhythm. The word *cumbia* derives from the African expression *cumbe*, which means "dance party" and is shown in both the sounds and the dance movements between male and female dancers. This musical genre emerged sometime in the 18th century in land on the shores of the Magdalena River and the Colombian Caribbean coast. Despite the difficulty of determining the particular birthplace of this style, cities such as El Plato and Cienaga (in Magdalena), Soledad (Atlántico), Mompox, Santa Marta, and Barranquilla have been important epicenters for this musical genre, not only for its creation but also for its diffusion across the Caribbean region and Colombia.

Slaves from Africa who arrived to Colombia in the colonial period to work in the gold and silver mines mixed their own styles, supported by drums, with the sounds of local Native American instruments such as *gaitas* and *maracas* and European musical cadences to create this style. The rhythm evolved from a basic to a complex musical genre. Initially, cumbia was an instrumental style of the low-income classes on the Caribbean coast. Nevertheless, by the beginning of the 20th century, when it appeared in the Carnival de Barranquilla as a "happy dance," middle- and high-income classes adopted cumbia as a symbolic and representative genre. What began as an instrumental style was transformed into a complex musical genre that incorporated lyrics and more elaborate rhythms.

Between the 1940s and 1950s, cumbia was carried into the elegant dance halls, thanks to the indirect influence of bands in Colombia, and the particular musical arrangements of Lucho Bermudez, a prominent composer and music director. This development was paired with the emergence of the most important record labels in Colombia, particularly Discos Fuentes, which associated with RCA Victor. This combination allowed cumbia to spread to several places in the Americas from Mexico, passing throughout the Caribbean to Argentina. In this way, cumbia (and tango) became the most popular genres in the region in that time period.

Between the 1960s and the 1980s, cumbia attracted several Colombian and international followers and mixed with other local musical styles, thereby developing a particular rhythm called "Chucu Chucu," which was widely recognized and danced to in Latin America. Since the 1990s and into the first years of the 21st century, cumbia has appeared in different presentations from the old-school and classical styles to adapt to new style trends and formats that include electronic instruments. Perhaps the most important classical artists are Toto la Momposina; Leonor González Mina, "La Negra Grande de Colombia"; and Petrona Martinez, though at the same time new cumbia artists and bands have emerged to transform and reinvigorate cumbia rhythms, including La MiniTK del Miedo, Bomba Stereo, and Choquitown (among others).

Cumbia instruments vary widely. They include wind instruments native to South America, in particular a kind of long flutes with different numbers of orifice, called *gaitas* and made with local bamboo (*guadua*). A *Gaita macho"* (male gaita) has two orifices and produces a harmonic and rhythmic sound; a *Gaita hembra* (female gaita) has five orifices and produces a melodic sound. Other wind instruments used in cumbia include the *Flauta de Millo* (Flute of Millo), a small flute with four orifices and a reed in the top of the flute that generates a high-pitched sound. In terms of drums, there are three main types: the *tambor llamador* (calling drum), a small drum that carries the rhythm; the *tambora*, a medium-size drum that sounds like a bass drum played with sticks; and the *tambor hembra*, a long and tiny drum that generates multiple quick sounds. All of these instruments are made with wood and leather patches. Other important instruments include *maracas* and *guache*, which are percussion instruments full of small pieces from the inside of a dried pumpkin that create a rhythm sound when shaken. Finally, cumbia incorporates, on occasion, European wind instruments such as trumpet, tuba, and French horn.

Cumbia is considered one of the most emblematic Colombian musical styles. As with other traditional local rhythms, dance and clothing are very important, as cumbia is considered a national symbol for Colombians. Usually, the woman is the most important character in the dance performance: she wears a flowery vest with a strapless chemise, a long and ample skirt called a *pollera*, and commonly is barefoot. In her hand she carries a couple of candles, and on her head she wears a bunch of Colombian flowers. The male character wears white pants, a long-sleeved shirt, and a red scarf on the shoulders. The man also wears a *sombrero vueltiao* on the head and a *mochila* (artisan bag). However, depending on the Colombian region, clothing can vary.

Dance is another basic component of cumbia, taking the form of a kind of courtship ritual between woman and man. Basically, in this dance ritual the man tries to conquer the woman and she avoids him; after that, she takes her skirt and moves her hips and shoulders while the man follows her, moving his body and raising and lowering his sombrero vueltiao (traditional hat). Finally, the woman salutes him and invites him with body language to follow her cadence.

TYPES OF COLOMBIAN CUMBIA

There are four types of cumbia: classical cumbia, cumbiamba, cumbia sabanera, and cumbia vallenata. Classical cumbia uses a mixture of gaita and drum sounds; there is no singing or chorus expression. Usually this musical style is used to support traditional dancing in Carnival or other collective celebrations in small towns. *Cumbiamba* is a type of cumbia that uses the flauta de millo and accordion. Some experts point out that this type of cumbia differs significantly from the basic style, and believe it was the original expression of African slaves who arrived to Colombia and mixed their rhythms with indigenous ones. This style includes lyrics recounting the daily activities of African and aboriginal peoples, and it has different choreography which includes festive body movements.

Cumbia sabanera is a subgenre that uses several European wind metallic instruments. It is played by local bands called *bandas pelayeras*, which are from the inner regions of the Colombian Caribe coast (in particular, the shores of the Sinu and San Jorge Rivers). This style shows more explicitly European influence than others.

Cumbia vallenata is a particular style that mixes two of the most emblematic Caribbean musical genres of Colombia: cumbia and vallenato. Its distinguishing characteristic is the use of a vallenato accordion as a main instrument in addition to the classical cumbia ones. This subgenre includes singing and lyrics that tell stories about rural activities, love, coldness, and loyalty.

MAIN PERFORMERS

Francisco Galan (1906–1988), called "Pacho" Galan, was one of the pioneers of mixing of Colombian rhythms with big band and jazz styles in the 1940s. As a composer and musical director, he adapted Colombian tropical and Caribbean rhythms to big orchestras, so as to popularize the cumbia and merecumbe styles among the middle and higher social classes.

Lucho Bermudez (1912–1994) was a composer, musical director, and performer on clarinet and saxophone. Along with Pacho Galan, he revolutionized cumbia and Colombian tropical styles, adapting them to dancehall. Bermudez spread cumbia and other styles widely in the Americas by recording an album with RCA Victor in Buenos Aires in 1946. He also lived in Mexico and Cuba in the 1950s.

Toto la Momposina (1940–) is a Colombian folkloric singer and dancer and the most international of cumbia performers. Her art work and shows are well-known in several countries.

Petrona Martinez (1939–) is an Afro-Colombian singer and composer. She is part of a long tradition of female traditional singers from the Caribbean coast, known as *cantadoras*. Her singing style combines several styles from Afro-Colombian musical traditions, including cumbia in its purest traditional form. Her style is supported by drums, gaitas, clap sounds, and chorus.

Los Corraleros de Majagual is a Colombian traditional-music band widely known and respected in the United States and Latin America, and has been an important diffuser of cumbia in the Andean and Caribbean countries. Founded in 1962 by Isaac Villanueva, Calixto Ochoa, and Alfredo Gutiérrez, under the sponsorship of Discos Fuentes, the band began as a project that reunited musical traditions of the Colombian Caribbean coast.

Leonor Gonzalez Mina (1934–), known as "La Negra Grande de Colombia," is a Colombian singer, actress, and dancer. Best known as a TV actress, her singing style nevertheless has influenced several generations of young Colombians due to her musical proficiency.

LATIN AMERICA'S CUMBIA VARIATIONS

Cumbia reached several countries across the Americas, and in each country was adapted, transformed, and re-elaborated to accommodate local styles, feelings, and realities. Since the mid-20th century, this music style has been very popular as tropical and festivity music—more than any other rhythm in the region, until salsa competed for this role years later. Because of its regional interpretations, it is possible to find cumbia Mexicana, cumbia Argentina, and cumbia Chilena, among others.

The primary countries where cumbia was popular were Mexico and Peru. Cumbia Mexicana emerged in the mid-1960s through artists such as Carmen Rivero and Mike Laure, who played Colombian classical songs and adapted this style to Mexican sensibilities. They used other modern instruments to present and interpret this genre, such as electric guitar, electric bass, and keyboards. One of the main adaptations was cumbia sonidera, which appeared in the 1990s as an electronic adaptation of original cumbia. Peruvian cumbia also became a genre unto itself and achieved some popularity in other countries. Peruvian cumbia took Colombian cumbia and mixed it with Peruvian traditional rhythms such as *huayno*. This new type of cumbia spread to Bolivia and Argentina and was played with strident electric guitars and electronic sounds.

Other South American versions of the cumbia include cumbia Chilena, a style that took Colombian cumbia songs and mixed in other music styles (including rock, bolero, cueca, and reggae) to create a unique style that used electric instruments. One of the most important artists of cumbia Chilena is Chico Trujillo, a well-known performer of the "Nueva Cumbia Chilena" movement. Another version is cumbia Argentina, which has two specifically identifiable subgenres: cumbia Santafesina, a very close relative of cumbia Peruana style that includes accordion; and cumbia villera, a low-income musical movement from the outskirts of Buenos Aires that is played in a style similar to Peruvian cumbia, but includes portable keyboards and electric guitars.

Saul Mauricio Rodriguez-Hernandez

See also: Andean Region, Music of the

Further Reading

Convers, Leonor, and Ochoa Juan Sebastian. 2007. *Gaiteros y tamboleros: material para abordar el estudio de la música de gaitas de San Jacinto, Bolívar (Colombia)* [Pipers and drummers: Material to address the study of bagpipe music from San Jacinto, Bolívar (Colombia)]. Bogota, Colombia: Universidad Javeriana.

Fernández L'Hoeste, Héctor D., and Pablo Vila. 2013. *Cumbia!: Scenes of a Migrant Latin American Music Genre.* Durham, NC: Duke University Press.

Ocampo Lopez, Javier. 1990. *Musica y folclor de Colombia* [Music and folklore of Colombia]. Bogota, Colombia: Plaza y Janes Editores.

Peter, Wade. 2000. *Music, Race and Nation: Musica Tropical in Colombia.* Chicago: Chicago University Press.

Pombo Hernández, Gerardo. 1995. *Kumbia: Legado cultural de los indígenas del Caribe colombiano* [Cumbia: Cultural legacy of the Colombian-Caribbean indigenous peoples]. Bogota, Colombia: Editorial Antillas.

D

Dancehall

A musical genre, a style of clothing, a type of dance, and for many, a "living, breathing, organic part of Jamaican life," dancehall is a very popular form of Jamaican cultural expression (Hope, 2006). Dancehall, also known on the island as "Buggu Yagga" for its juxtaposition of heavy bass lines and high vocals, is a contemporary expression of the reggae tradition (Buggu Yagga, 2014).

Dancehall music was born in the 1980s as a reaction to decades of economic pressure and political upheaval that divided Jamaican society between the privileged and the underprivileged. In the Jamaican cities of Kingston and St. Andrew, going to a dance party at a dance hall in the 1980s became a popular escape from the poverty-stricken life of the slums for many. The kind of music that developed during that period at the dance parties took on the name of the location: dancehall. Because of this history, dancehall, as a musical genre, both reflects and communicates the political, economic, and social tensions of Jamaican society through its lyrics and expression (Hope, 2006). Dancehall is often noted for an intensely male-centered bravado that sexualizes women, celebrates violence, and promotes homophobia (Samponaro, 2009).

The musical style of dancehall draws upon the previous traditions of reggae, ska, mento, and dub music. The earliest form of the style featured disc jockeys (DJs) in the hall talking or singing over a popular, already established reggae rhythm, often making up the lyrics on the spot (Hope, 2006). This style followed a long-standing tradition of the *griot*—a singing, storytelling poet/musician/historian that was traditional in West Africa. Just as griot were understood in Africa to tell true stories and recognize reality, dancehall performers turned from the traditionally positive reggae themes of peace, black pride, and coexistence to name the problems and challenges that they faced in society, such as poverty, violence, and police brutality. Because of this, DJs in dancehall are still often referred to as griot and use slang from the ghettos in their lyrics (Hope, 2006). Continuing into the 21st century, dancehall remains a club-oriented, dance-party form of reggae that addresses difficult issues while using traditional reggae instrumentation and rhythms (Hoffman, 2009).

Although earlier figures such as U Roy helped define the position of the live DJ in dancehall music, one of the first DJs to turn his griot skill into an internationally successful career was King Yellowman. Yellowman was an albino from a poor background, which allowed him to speak directly to the social and economic problems of many Jamaicans. In the 1980s Yellowman became the model for the DJs who would follow him: products of the poor and ghetto lifestyle who could write lyrics that spoke directly to the lives and realities of young, struggling Jamaicans

(Hope, 2006). Yellowman, in particular, is also recognized for his inclusion of sexually explicit lyrics and themes in his songs, an element of dancehall music now known as "slack" or "slackness" ("King Yellowman Biography," 2014).

Other important dancehall superstar griot of the 21st century include Shaggy, Elephant Man, Beenie Man, Shaba, Mr. Vegas, and Popcaan. Though many dancehall artists continue to be hugely popular on the island, most remain unheard of in the United States, as it can be hard for Jamaican artists to find radio airplay in the United States or Europe (Kenner, 2014). One notable exception is the griot Sean Paul. Sean Paul became a crossover sensation in the early 21st century, becoming the first Jamaican artist ever to reach the number-one position on *Billboard*'s Rap Albums chart. Since his first album in 2000, Sean Paul has had a string of number-one pop hits and won a Grammy in 2002 for his album, *Dutty Rock* (Hoffman, 2009).

While it is very common to hear dancehall music on the radio, the most important location for experiencing dancehall continues to be in the hall itself. Going to the dance hall in Jamaica is as much about the music as it is about being seen going to the dance hall. The event is a type of public street theater, an opportunity to demonstrate wealth and attract attention, from the colorful and revealing clothing that people wear to the flashy motorcycles that they drive (Niaah and Niaah, 2006). One element of the display at a dancehall event is the "skin-out"—a tradition in which women in very revealing clothing strike sexual and erotic poses on the dance floor. These displays of erotic beauty often become contests in the dance hall, where women are judged on dance skills, stage presence, and sexual attractiveness. Although some researchers have identified this activity related to dancehall as a mark of women's sexual liberation, others have noted that this type of context continues to present women as objects subject to male judges' approval (Hope, 2006).

Dancehall is immensely popular but also is associated negatively with the poorer economic classes in Jamaica. As a society rigidly divided between the richer and poorer social classes, dancehall music and the type of clothing associated with the music mark a person for many as "lower class" (Hope, 2006). Many members of Jamaica's upper classes see dancehall as a vulgar threat to traditional values and culture and often blame it for everything from youth violence to children's poor grades in schools (Hope, 2006).

Elizabeth Gackstetter Nichols and Timothy R. Robbins

See also: Reggae; Reggaetón

Further Reading

Hoffman, Melody K. 2009. "Sean Paul's Dancehall Music Tops Rap Charts." *Jet* 116(10), 18.

Hope, Donna P. 2006. *Inna Di Dancehall: Popular Culture and the Politics of Identity in Jamaica*. Mona, Jamaica: University of the West Indies Press.

Kenner, Rob. 2014. "Dancehall's New King Takes His Shot." *Billboard* 126(20), 56.

Niaah, Jalani, and Sonjah Stanley Niaah. 2006. "'Ace' of the Dancehall Space: A Preliminary Look at U Roy's Version and Subversion in Sound." *Social & Economic Studies* 55(1/2), 167–189.

Nichols, Elizabeth Gackstetter, and Timothy R. Robbin. 2015. *Pop Culture in Latin America and the Caribbean*. Santa Barbara, CA: ABC-CLIO.

Samponaro, Philip. 2009. "'*Oye mi canto*' ('Listen to My Song'): The History and Politics of Reggaeton." *Popular Music & Society* 32(4), 489–506.

Darbuka

The *darbuka* (also spelled *darabukka, derbuka, derbuga,* and *derbukka*) is a single-headed, goblet-shaped hand drum used throughout the Middle East, Eastern Europe, and South Asia. The darbuka is also known as a *tabla* or *tablah* (Egypt), *dümbelek* (Turkey), *dunbak* (Iraq), and *tombak* (Iran). Grove attributes the etymology of the darbuka to the Arabic word *darba*, "to strike." The drum is made of pottery, wood, or metal and was originally covered with goat skin, but plastic is now an option; the base is open. The drum is held on the lap and over the knee, under the arm, or fastened with a strap while standing. Playing the darbuka is physically demanding for the percussionist, who uses the fingers of both hands to strike the center or edge of the drum head to produce deeper or higher pitches as well as a variety of ornamentations.

Orientalist Edward Lane's account describes the instrument as a *darábukkeh*, which, along with the *tár*, a tambourine 11 inches in diameter, was common in the mid–19th-century Cairene "hareem of a person of moderate wealth, and which the women often use[d] for their diversion." Lane documents the darábukkeh as being made of earth or wood, the latter adorned with mother-of-pearl and tortoiseshell. He notes its size as 15 inches long, with a covering of fishes' skin. Lane observed the instrument positioned in the left arm "suspended by a string that passes over the left shoulder," and "beaten with both hands" (Lane, 1860, pp. 77–78). Both percussion instruments would produce "different sounds when beaten near the edge and in the middle" (Lane, 1860, p. 78). The notation for these sounds is now referred to as *tak* and *dum*.

The darbuka is essential for maintaining the rhythm and tempo in performances of belly dance, also known as *raqs Sharqi*. North Africa darbuka ensembles include

Drum Shape

The hourglass shape of the *darbuka* is a unique characteristic of this drum found throughout the Middle East, Egypt, and eastern Europe. However, the drum has many closely related relatives in North Africa, such as the *doumbek*, stemming all the way west to Morocco. The darbuka and the doumbek are usually made of either clay or metal and feature a fish or animal skin as the playing surface. The *djembe* of Gold Coast West Africa, though much larger, has the same hourglass shape as the doumbek. Made with local materials such as wood from large trees and featuring a goatskin playing surface, the djembe likely derived its shape from instruments carried by Arab traders who travelled along the Silk Road trading routes, which began at the coast of West Africa and extended through the Mali kingdom of Saharan and sub-Saharan Africa before going east through the Middle East and reaching all the way to China in the Far East.

instruments of varying sizes. The darbuka is part of the North African *Andalusī* ensemble and the Iraqi *jālchī baghdādī* ensemble. Habib Hassan Touma includes the darbuka in the roster for the classical *takht* ensemble in Egypt and the Levant, along with the *'ūd, qānūn, kamanjah, nāy,* and *riqq.* The takht supports the vocalist in performing such genres as *dawr, qasīda, muwashshah, layālī,* and *mawwāl,* in addition to the solely instrumental genres *bashraf, samā'ī, tahmīlah,* and *dūlāb.* The traditional takht instruments are augmented by multiple violins, cellos, contrabasses, clarinets, oboes, trumpets, accordion, electric, synthesizer, timpani, and glockenspiel to comprise the "huge racket" of the modern Europeanized Arab orchestra.

Hicham Chami

See also: Belly Dance; Tabla

Further Reading

Conner, William J., Milfie Howell, and Tony Langlois. 2001. "Darabukka." *Grove Music Online.* https://www.oxfordmusiconline.com.

Hassan, Scheherazade Qassim. 2002. "Musical Instruments in the Arab World." In Virginia Danielson, Dwight Reynolds, and Scott Marcus (eds.), *Garland Encyclopedia of World Music; Vol. 6: The Middle East,* 401–424. New York: Routledge.

Lane, Edward William. 1860. *An Account of the Manners and Customs of the Modern Egyptians.* London: John Murray.

Touma, Habib Hassan. 1996. *The Music of the Arabs,* trans. Laurie Schwartz. Portland, OR: Amadeus Press.

Dastgah

Translated as "system" from Persian, *dastgah* is a hierarchical, highly detailed modal system that comprises the tradition of Persian art music, known as the *radif.* The dastgah was loosely standardized in the late 19th century chiefly by the *tar* and *setar* musician Mirza Abdollah Farahani (1843–1918), but was also influenced by master musicians such as tar musicians Mirza Hossein Gholi (1853–1916) and Darvish Khan (1872–1926), and setar musician Abolhasan Saba (1902–1957). Through the early 20th century, the dastgah remained dependent upon local music traditions and was taught orally from musician to musician. It was not until the mid-20th century that the system of modes became fully standardized, mostly due to the work of renowned tar player Ali-Naqi Vaziri (1887–1979), a student of Mirza Abdollah, who was the first to transcribe the *radif.*

The radif—the practice of Persian classical music—is primarily composed of 12 distinct dastgahs, which in turn consist of 365 individual *gushehs,* or melodies, which provide a modal framework for improvisatory performance. In actuality, there are more than 50 dastgahs, but particularly in modern-day classical music, the radif has been standardized to focus on a set of 12 dastgahs. The 12 principal dastgahs take their names from the corresponding dominant mode that is always introduced at the beginning of the performance: *shur, abu ata, dashti, bayat-e tork, afshari, segah, chahargah, homayun, bayat-e Esfahan, nava, mahur,* and *rast.* Often, the dastgahs are further divided into two main categories: seven of them are considered the main dominant dastgahs (*shur, segah, chahargah, homayun, nava, mahur,* and *rast*), while the other five are labeled *awaz*, a subordinate set of melodies (*abu ata, dashti, bayat-e tork, afshari,* and *bayat-e Esfahan*). Overall, the dastgah are defined by a set of pitches (*maqam*) and a specific melodic character (*mayeh*). Although there are 12 dastgahs, only six or seven scales are represented. Sometimes the differences between dastgahs can be structural: for example, featuring different transitions between sections, or different sequences of modulations.

The series of pieces within the dastgah groups can be manipulated and improvised upon. These pieces, individually known as *gusheh*, each carry their own specific names, as they represent different genres within the radif tradition. Each gusheh serves a specific function within a performance, whether it is introductory, conclusive, or transitory to introduce new sections of dance-like rhythms or new modulatory material. The number of gusheh varies between the dastgahs: some contain a large number and others only a few.

When the dastgah is performed, it begins with an introduction comprised of one or more sections, known as *daramad*. The daramad indicates the maqam and mayeh to follow. Typically, the daramad employs the lower registers of the performing instrument or voice. After the introduction, the gusheh are performed in parts, which are distinguished from the daramad by their melodic contour. Some gusheh may cross over from one dastgah to another, while others are exclusive to a particular dastgah. The gusheh gradually ascend into the higher registers of the instrument or voice, and continue to be manipulated and improvised upon through modulations and transpositions. This is followed by a *forud*, a rapid return to the original mode. A full performance of a dastgah can vary greatly in length, sometimes taking only a few minutes, and other times more than an hour.

The performance of a dastgah is highly dependent upon the organization of the gusheh and how they are presented and improvised upon in selected pieces. There is no concrete method for performing the dastgah and thus every performance will be different, even when centered upon the same dastgah. As a result, the training for the dastgah is arduous, taking many years to learn and master the musical tradition and its improvisatory nature.

The dastgah has traditionally been taught and learned orally and aurally, through gradual absorption of the modal process and its many gusheh. However, in the late 19th and 20th centuries, the tradition of performing dastgah became influenced by Western traditions, primarily due to the efforts of Ali-Naqi Vaziri, who introduced the elements of Western instrumentation, including the violin and the clarinet (tuned to Persian tuning standards), and Western notation. Today, the system of dastgah remains mostly the same as it has been since the late 19th century.

Theresa Steward

See also: Iranian Classical Music

Further Reading

Farhat, Hormoz. 1990. *The Dastgah Concept in Persian Music.* Cambridge: Cambridge University Press.

Nettl, Bruno. 1992. *The Radif of Persian Music: Studies of Structure and Cultural Context*. Champaign, IL: Elephant & Cat.

Zonis, Ella. 1973. *Classical Persian Music: An Introduction*. Cambridge, MA: Harvard University Press.

Davis, Miles (Dewey, III) (1926–1991)

American jazz trumpeter and bandleader Miles Davis was one of the most musically diverse musicians of his generation. A creative, expressive soloist and an exacting band leader, Davis championed cool jazz, hard bop, and fusion, with his final album combining jazz and hip-hop. While Davis's contemporaries, including Duke Ellington and Max Roach, endeavored to eclipse categorization that would position jazz below classical music, Davis was significantly more radical in his rejection of a partition between jazz and popular music. He was the most consistently innovative, outspoken musician in jazz on the relationships between the music industry, racism, artistic innovation, and commercial success from the late 1940s until the mid-1970s. Davis transformed jazz several times during his 46-year career, either by his own actions or by serving as a catalyst that enabled others to be musical pioneers. His musical development after his formative bebop years can be divided into three periods: cool (1949–1964), modal (1959–1968), and electric/fusion (after 1968).

Davis was born on May 26, 1926, in Alton, Illinois. Soon his family relocated to East St. Louis, Illinois, where his father, a dental surgeon, ensured that the family never suffered financial hardship. Determined that her children would be culturally aware, Davis's mother made sure that music lessons were an important part of family life. Upon Miles's 13th birthday, his father presented him with a trumpet—not a violin as his mother had envisioned—and lessons with local musician Elwood Buchanon, who can be credited with David's trademark sound. Davis compensated for his shortcomings in musical technique and finesse with determination and enthusiasm. By age 16, he was a regular performer with Randolph's Blue Devils. In 1944, when Billy Eckstine's orchestra came to town in need of a trumpet player, Davis substituted for three weeks, playing in the group with both Charlie Parker and Dizzy Gillespie, who were members of Eckstine's group at the time. Following his high school graduation Davis coerced his parents into sending him to New York where Parker and Gillespie were working. He had been accepted by the Julliard School of Music, but as soon as Davis arrived in New York, he sought out Charlie Parker. Although Davis attended Julliard for one semester, most of his true education occurred in the jazz clubs of New York, where he benefited from the coaching and encouragement of Thelonious Monk, Tadd Dameron, and Dizzy Gillespie.

In 1955, Davis appeared informally at the Newport Jazz Festival. Here, his astounding improvisations garnered extensive publicity and sufficient engagements to establish a quintet (1955–1957) with Red Garland (piano), Paul Chambers (double bass), Philly Joe Jones (drums), and John Coltrane. In May 1957, Davis made the first of several remarkable solo recordings on trumpet and flugelhorn against unusual jazz orchestrations by Gil Evans. In the autumn of 1957, he organized a quintet, later joined by Cannonball Adderley, that proved short-lived; in that same year he also wrote and recorded music in Paris for Louis Malle's film *Ascenseur pour l'échafaud* (*Elevator to the Gallows*; 1961). Upon his return to the United States, Davis reformed his original quintet of 1955 with Adderley as a sixth member. Inspired by Gil Evans and Bill Evans Davis, he adopted an emerging musical approach known as modal playing, but the inclusion of modality in Davis's *Milestones* (1958) and *Kind of Blue* (1959) proved less effective than his slackening of harmonic rhythm. Abandoning fast-moving, functional chord progressions, Davis instead relied upon diatonic ostinatos, drones, half-tone oscillation inherent in flamenco music, and tone-dominant alternation in the bass line. On the LP *Kind of Blue*, the Davis sextet offered a veritable renaissance of the nonet's cool affect from a decade earlier, exemplified by "Flamenco Sketches" and "Blue in Green" which primarily relied upon individual solos instead of pre-composed parts and offered musicians an opportunity to create solos using specific modes over profoundly simplified harmonic foundations. His modal exploits on *Kind of Blue* created a myriad of possibilities for musicians of the 1960s and these features formed the core components of Davis's playing throughout his career.

Jazz trumpeter Miles Davis at a recording session for his album *Quiet Nights* in 1962. During his long career, Davis was a leading innovator of jazz music. (Michael Ochs Archives/Getty Images)

In 1968–1969, Davis turned his attention to jazz-rock. The albums *In a Silent Way* and *Bitches Brew* (both 1969) combined acoustic and electronic instruments, and melodic jazz improvisations with freestyle rock accompaniment. From 1969 to 1975 these various groups utilized electronically altered trumpet, Indian *sitār* and *tablā*, and African and Brazilian percussion, as well as African American dance rhythms. Their music is best described by the term *fusion*, which incorporates a blend of musical elements broader than jazz-rock. Among his projects in his final years was an effort to unite jazz and rap music. New young members of Davis's groups included Branford Marsalis, the guitarist John Scofield, and the saxophonist Kenny Garrett.

During his final decade, Davis was proclaimed a "living legend" by the musical community—a title he despised because it ran counter to his desire to be associated with new popular music and energetic, youthful activities, but one that was certainly appropriate, because it acknowledged his iconic status. Among his many awards, Davis received an honorary doctorate from the New England Conservatory of Music in 1986 in recognition of his long-standing achievements.

Eldonna L. May

See also: Bebop; Jazz; Swing

Further Reading

Baker, David. 1991. *The Jazz Style of Miles Davis: A Musical and Historical Perspective.* Van Nuys, CA: Alfred Music.

Carr, Ian. 1982. *Miles Davis: A Critical Biography.* London: Morrow.

Davis, Miles, with Quincy Troupe. 1989; repr. 1990. *Miles: The Autobiography.* New York: Simon & Schuster.

Feather, Leonard. 1987. *From Satchmo to Miles.* New York: Da Capo Press.

McRae, Barry. 1988. *Miles Davis.* London: Apollo Press.

Naitho, Tadauki. 1981. *Miles.* Holsworthy, UK: Hidden Drive Publishing.

Densmore, Frances (1867–1957)

Frances Densmore, born in Red Wing, Minnesota, was a pioneering ethnomusicologist known for her extensive recordings and preservation of North American indigenous musics. She studied piano and organ as well as music theory at the Oberlin Conservatory of Music in Ohio. After working as a music teacher and organist, she took advanced piano training and further studies in counterpoint in Boston. While there, she began to develop an interest in Native American studies, with encouragement from her mentor, noted ethnologist Alice Cunningham Fletcher (1838–1923).

Densmore's first publication on Native American music came in 1901 and was based on songs of Sioux women near Red Wing. After observing the Chippewa at the White Earth Reservation in Minnesota, she made her first extensive field trip in 1905, to Grand Portage on the north shore of Lake Superior. Densmore was quite prolific in her studies, working with a wide variety of indigenous peoples from all over North America. Her collection includes thousands of recorded songs and more than 2,400 transcribed pieces ("Frances Densmore," 2005). Among ethnographers and ethnomusicologists, the extent of Densmore's cataloguing and publishing (on more than a dozen individual groups) well exceeds that of any other scholar. Much of this was thanks to her work as a collaborator with the Bureau of American Ethnology of the Smithsonian Institution in Washington, D.C., a partnership that lasted from 1907 until her death in 1957. The Bureau published 13 monographs on North American indigenous musics, five anthropological studies, and one paper in the bureau's Annual Report series (Rhodes, 2001, p. 218).

Despite her amassed works, scholars have scrutinized Densmore's transcriptions since the late 1950s. After working with Fletcher, Densmore grew less interested in theoretical work, instead choosing to develop her skills as an ethnographer and preferring isolated studies. Her isolation allowed her to hone her techniques for collection and transcription, as she attempted to stay unaffected by contemporary European and American ideas on the study of world music. This insulated approach became evident in her writing and especially in her transcriptions of indigenous musics. New generations denounced her use of Western key signatures, non-native forms of classification into major and minor keys, regulation of rhythms to accommodate Western time signatures, and disregard for repetition, variation, and beginning and ending formulas (Myers, 1993, p. 405).

Despite the issues some scholars have had with her methods, Densmore remains an important figure in the formation of ethnomusicology as an established field and in the Society for Ethnomusicology, North America's largest organization on the subject. Her field reports and bibliographies appeared in a number of the society's newsletters as well as its journal, *Ethnomusicology*. Densmore is noted as an integral early member of the society, and as the organization expanded, she served as the society's first Second Vice President. She took the position in name only, as she could no longer travel to attend meetings and died shortly after being named to the position. Much of her collection is now housed at the Library of Congress in Washington, D.C.

Justin R. Hunter

See also: Eastern Woodland Native American Music; Native American Flute; Native American Music

Further Reading

"Frances Densmore (1867–1957)." 2005. Smithsonian Institution Archives. http://siarchives.si.edu/research/sciservwomendensmore.html.

Frisbie, Charlotte J. 1991. "Women and the Society for Ethnomusicology: Roles and Contributions from Formation Through Incorporation (1952/53–1961)." In Bruno Nettl and P. V. Bohlman (eds.), *Comparative Musicology and Anthropology of Music: Essays on the History of Ethnomusicology*, 244–274. Chicago: University of Chicago Press.

Myers, Helen. 1993. "North America—1: Native American Music." In Helen Myers (ed.), *Ethnomusicology: Historical and Regional Studies*, 404–417. New York: Macmillan Press.

Rhodes, Willard. 2001. "Densmore, Frances." In Stanley Sadie and J. Tyrell (eds.), *The New Grove Dictionary of Music and Musicians,* vol. 7, 218. London: Macmillan.

Dhol

The *dhol*, also known as *dholak* in Hindi and Punjabi languages, is a musical instrument popular in India and in certain other countries of South Asia. The dhol, a hand drum beaten by both of the player's hands, is equally popular in folk and elite performances. A Punjabi dhol is larger. In north India and Maharashtra, smaller dhols, called *dholakis*, are also very popular.

A cotton rope is laced around the dhol, and tightened with a screw-turnbuckle. Being tensioned, the rope produces sound. Both the ends of the dhol are mounted with a membrane. The membrane used in the right-hand side of the hollow wooden trunk is a simple membrane, whereas the membrane mounted on the left-hand side is treated with a special coating on the inner surface. The coating is done for the specific purpose of lowering the tone and creating the intended rhythm, and is achieved with a specific mixture of clay, charcoal, and sand. Nut-and-bolt dhols are also made. A dhol is usually made of *sheesham* or mango wood. The wood of

The *dhol* is a double-headed drum used in a range of regional styles across the Indian subcontinent. Pictured is a musician performing Rajasthani folk music during Diwali, the Hindu festival of lights. (Rozenn Leard/Dreamstime.com)

the jackfruit tree is also used to make dhols, though it is costly. In some coastal areas, coconut palm stems are also used for making dhols.

There are generally two styles of playing dhol: either keeping it in the lap, or slinging it down the shoulder and beating up. In the second case, it is supported by pressure from one of the player's knees. The beating of dhol resembles that used to play *tabla* and *pakhawaj*. The high-pitched head of a dhol may also be played by striking it with a bamboo stick. Professional dhol players must also be good singers and performers, and blend their dhol rhythm skills with singing and acting for a better performance.

In performances of *Kirtan, Qawwali, Lavani,* and *Bhangra,* playing dhol is a must. Classical dance performances are also assisted by the playing of dholak. In folk culture, dholak is usually played by less skilled performers. In the *Banna-Banni geet* (marriage songs), *Sohar geet* (songs sung at childbirth), *Mundan* (a ritual), marriage *sangeet*, and many other Hindu rituals, the family members play dholaks. In the popular culture of India, especially in Bollywood cinema, many songs have been composed for dhol; a feature film entitled *Dhol* was released in 2007.

In northern India, almost every household keeps a dholak to be played on various occasions. The Indian diaspora to Fiji, Jamaica, Suriname, Guyana, Trinidad and Tobago of indentured immigrant laborers from colonial India has carried the tradition of dholak beating, and these drums are frequently used for various festivities and rituals.

The playing of dhols also has a long tradition in Asia, especially in the Indian subcontinent. These instruments have been quite popular in many Sufi ceremonies over the years. The beating of dhol is an integral part of the performances during celebrations in various parts of India, such as the Rongali Bihu festival in Assam, folk singing in Uttar Pradesh, the *shigmo* celebration in Goa, Bhangra in Punjab, *Garbha* during Navaratris in Gujrat, *Ganesha Utsav* celebration in Maharastra, *dollu kunitha* in Karnataka, *attan* dance performance by Pastuns, and many others. The Goans' *permom* blends the playing of dhol with *tasha* (cymbals). The

South Asian diaspora has carried the tradition of dhol playing to global culture, and has resulted in different versions fusing with different music cultures.

Ravindra Pratap Singh

See also: Karnatic Music

Further Reading

Kaufmann, Walter. 1961. "The Musical Instruments of the Hill Maria, Jhoria and Bastar Maria Gond Tribes." *Ethnomusicology* 5(1), 1–9.

Kothari, K. S. 1968. *Indian Folk Musical Instruments.* New Delhi: Sangeet Natak Akademi.

Singh, R. P. 2012. "Representative Folk Literature of Hindi Speaking North India." *Spark International Online Journal* 4(8) (August), 34–45. https://www.researchgate.net/profile/Azadeh_Mehrpouyan/publication/332381027_Developing_Teaching_Processes_and_Practices_in_the_Study_of_Poetry_at_Colleges/links/5cb0b8514585156cd792efc8/Developing-Teaching-Processes-and-Practices-in-the-Study-of-Poetry-at-Colleges.pdf.

Dhrupad

Dhrupad is a classical North Indian vocal style that is considered the oldest and most serious. The name *dhrupad* is derived from Sanskrit *Dhruva* (fixed) and *pad* (verse). It has had a strong influence on other vocal styles as well as on instrumental classical raga performance practice. While it is considered the oldest classical vocal style, it nearly died out before being revived in the 1960s and 1970s by performances from a few devoted artists.

Dhrupad developed from the ancient *prabandha* vocal style in the Gwalior region 200 miles south of Delhi in the early period of Muslim rule. Raja Mansingh (1486–1517) was the father of this style. Court musicians Swami Haridas and Tansen (both of the 16th century) were the most prominent dhrupad voices in the past.

The dhrupad text, in the Braj devotional dialect of Hindi, usually consists of two or four lines, in rhyming couplets, typically praising a Hindu God, talking about a king, or extolling romantic love, musicology, or philosophy. Traditionally, dhrupad has four sections: *asthayi, antara, sanchari,* and *abhog.* Modern performance practice usually omits the last two parts.

The *tala* or rhythmic cycle must be medium-slow to allow for rhythmic elaboration. The most common is *cautal* (12 beat). Other talas include *jhaptal* (10 beat), *dhamar* (14 beat), *surfak tala* (10 beat), *ada cautal* (14 beat), and *rupak* (7 beat).

Dhrupad singing is traditionally accompanied by a *tanpura* (plucked lute) providing the drone and *veena* (plucked zither). The *pakhawaj* barrel drum provides the rhythmic cycle and the *harmonium* (a small pump organ) and *bansuri* (bamboo flute) are sometimes used as well.

The *raga*, a framework for improvisation, is the essence of dhrupad. It begins with a long and leisurely free-rhythm *alap* section, accompanied only by tanpura drone. Here the vocalist introduces the tones of the raga mode one by one, beginning with the tonic, moving into the lower register, then into the higher register. In the next section, the *tom nom* alap, the singer introduces a rhythmic feel by singing groups of notes with a steady rhythm, with syllables such as "na." Then the fixed composition begins. The singer begins the composition in the middle of the rhythmic cycle, and the pakhawaj joins on the first beat of the cycle. The singer then sings the poem, and gradually elaborates with rhythmic improvisation. The tempo remains steady as the singer introduces complex rhythmic variations that are multiples of its basic pulse. The density is increased (*laya kari*) by doubling (*digun*), tripling (*trigun*), or quadrupling (*chaugun*) the pulse, along with more complex ratios such as *adi* (1 1/2), *kuari* (5/4) and *bewari* (3/4). There are also formulaic patterns for ending, which are observed by most performers and known to audience members.

Gharana are regional or family schools or lineages. The major dhrupad gharana are Gwalior gharana, Seni gharana, Timondo gharana, Betia gharana, Dagar/Udoipur gharana, Alladia gharana, Benaras gharana, and Bishnupur gharana. Schools recognize four *banis* (or *vani*, vocal styles) of dhrupad—*Gauri, Khandar, Nauhar,* and *Dagar*—and identify their vocal style with one or more of the banis.

In the late 19th and early 20th centuries, dhrupad performance nearly died out, but the Dagar and Mallick families helped to revive the style starting in the second half of the 20th century. The senior Dagar brothers, Ustad Nasir Moinuddin Dagar (1921–1966) and Ustad Nasir Aminuddin Dagar (1923–2000), toured Europe in the 1960s, and then the younger Dagar brothers, Ustad Nasir Zahiruddin (1933–1994) and Ustad Nasir Faiyazuddin (1934–1989) performed internationally in the 1970s and made many recordings. The Mallick brothers actively perform and record dhrupad of the Darbhanga gharana in India and abroad.

Many of the great Hindustani instrumentalists and vocalists are trained in dhrupad. *Khayal* singers are expected to study dhrupad in order to know the ragas more deeply. Tabla drum virtuoso Alla Rakha (1919–2000) was originally a pakhawaj player and singer of dhrupad. Ravi Shankar's (1920–2012) performances are highly influenced by the dhrupad form. Rabindranath Tagore (1861–1941), Bengali Nobel Laureate poet and songwriter, created a genre called *drupadanger gan* (songs based on dhrupad). The North American Dhrupad Association was founded in Los Angeles in 1996 to support the study and preservation of dhrupad in North America.

Abdur Rahman

See also: Harmonium; Rahka, Alla; Sitar; Tabla

Further Reading

Dastidar, Nitya Priya Ghosh. 1979. *Stepping Stone to Indian Music*. Calcutta: Sri J. B Ghosh Dastidar.

Dutta, Sunil. 2012. "Dhrupad: An Ancient Tradition." *Raga.com*. http://www.raga.com/text/dhrupad.html.

Hunt, Ken. 2000. "India: The Sacred and the Profane." In James McConnachie and Mark Ellingham (eds.), *World Music: The Rough Guide; Vol. 2*, 2nd ed. London: Rough Guides.

Lavezzoli, Peter. 2006. *The Dawn of Indian Music in the West*. New York: Continuum.

Mallick, Prashant Kumar, and Nishant Kumar Mallick. 2015. "Introduction and Brief Summary of Dhrupad." http://dhrupadmusic.org/dhrupadmusic.html.

Powers, Harold, and Richard Widdess. "Theory and Practice of Classical Music: Hindustani Vocal Genres." In Stanley Sadie (ed.), *New Grove Encyclopedia of Music and Musicians,* vol. 12.

Didgeridoo

The didgeridoo is a natural musical instrument of Aboriginal people living in the north of Australia. Mostly tubular in shape, and made from a piece of tree internally hollowed out by termites, the didgeridoo is classified as a reed aerophone. Researchers have established its origin at about 2,000 years ago, after the discovery of stone art and paintings on the walls of caves depicting images of humans playing the didgeridoo. In the oldest paintings (those more than 2,000 years old), scholars have never found depictions of didgeridoo or anthropomorphic creatures playing it.

The Aborigines use didgeridoos mainly during ceremonies (both sacred and otherwise), in the songs of the clan, and for lullabies, funerals, weddings, and celebrations that may last for weeks. On these occasions, the bodies of the participants are painted with ocher and the dances are accompanied by songs and beats to the rhythm of the hands from sticks and boomerangs. In addition, the didgeridoo is used by the elders of the tribe in the initiation or "passing" rites when young Aboriginals symbolically pass into adulthood. In these ceremonies, characterized by deep intensity, young people are also subjected to tests that include scarification, circumcision, and bloodletting.

Sounds, noises, songs, and dances have a particular meaning and an even more ancestral function that goes back to the timeless time of creation called the "Dreamtime." The term "didgeridoo" is an onomatopoeic interpretation given by the English settlers who landed on the continent at the end of the 18th century and heard the first performances. They interpreted the rhythmic timbre like a "did—ge - ridoo" word coming from some hollow eucalyptus branches played by the Aborigines. The instrument is originally from Arnhem Land, a region in the northeast of Australia, and is named in at least 50 different ways depending on the location and ethnic group: *djalupu, djubini, ganbag, gamalag, Maluk, yirdaki, yirago, yiraki*, and *yigi yigi* are but a few examples. According to some scholars, to some tribes the didgeridoo symbolizes the Rainbow Serpent known by such names as *Julunggul, Yurlunggur,* or *Julunggui*.

The traditional didgeridoo is made of eucalyptus and decorated with Aboriginal totemic motifs, although today there are instruments made of materials from teak to plastic, from metal to ceramic. The structure of the didgeridoo consists of three different parts: the mouthpiece, the instrument itself, and the bell.

The size of the didgeridoo may vary depending on the instrument. It can have a length that varies from less than one to four meters and an inner diameter that ranges from a minimum of 3 cm (mouthpiece) up to 30 cm or more (in the final part). To play the didgeridoo, the performer uses the technique of circular breathing (or continuous breath), in which one takes in air through the nose while exhaling the air contained in the mouth, thus allowing the creation of a continuous sound. The timbre of this instrument is bass, deep, and hypnotic.

There are several traditional styles of playing the didgeridoo, which differ slightly from place to place. In several areas, the way of playing differs in the use of accents, of *toot* (like a trumpet effect) as a rhythmic call, and the use of the voice. In any style, however, the listener can recognize common traits such as imitation of

Aboriginal didgeridoo player from the group Nunukul Yuggera Aboriginal Dancers. The didgeridoo is a long, end-blown instrument used by the indigenous people of Australia. (Rozenn Leard/Dreamstime.com)

animals' voices, the presence of harmonics, the pronunciation of words, and the use of sticks (*bilma*) or boomerangs that form the rhythmic accompaniment through strikes on the same instrument.

The didgeridoo is used both in sacred rituals and in everyday life. Some ethnic groups absolutely forbid women to use the didgeridoo, but, paradoxically, this is so in South Australia where it is not considered as a traditional instrument. Most Aborigines consider the instrument a phallic symbol and therefore appropriate only for male players. However, women are allowed to participate in decorating a ceremonial didgeridoo.

The didgeridoo is also used for therapeutic purposes. Despite the fact that academic music therapy has not yet fully recognized its therapeutic properties, various scholars argue that the sound massage helps relaxation of mind and body, a necessary condition for any kind of healing.

From the musical point of view, the didgeridoo has been used in a variety of languages, styles, and combinations with other modern genres such as rock, pop, jazz, and classical music. Among the recognized performers in the field of traditional music are David Blanasi and the White Cockatoo Performing Group, the maker and performer Djalu Gurruwiwi, and Milkay Munuggurr. It is also worth mentioning the Australian Charlie McMahon, the first non-Aboriginal musician to become a professional didgeridoo performer, and inventor of the "Didjeribone," a constructive variant of the instrument. Mark Atkins, an eclectic and international artist, was one of the first to include the didgeridoo in the orchestra and rock bands, collaborating with Robert Plant, Jimmy Page, and Philip Glass. European musicians who use or play the didgeridoo include the Swiss Willi Grimm and the English Stephen Kent. The aboriginal group Youth Yindi, probably the best-known worldwide group for its performances and record productions, were leaders in the combination of traditional music and rock.

Lorenzo Sorbo

See also: Carmody, Kevin Daniel "Kev"

Further Reading
Atkins, Mark. 1994. *Didgeridoo Concerto* [CD]. Larrikin 338.
Blanasi, David. 1998. *Didjeridu Master* [CD]. Big Bang Records.
Cawte, John. 1996. *Healers of Arnhem Land.* Sydney: University of New South Wales Press.
Gurruwiwi, Djalu. 2003. *Diltjimurru* [CD]. ON-Records & Djalu Gurruwiwi.
Lindner, David, ed. 2005. *The Didgeridoo Phenomenon: Ancient Times to Modern Age.* Schönau, Germany: Traumzeit-Verlag.
Mununggurr, Milkay. 2005. *Hard Tongue Didgeridoo: Exercises in Northeast Arnhem Land Yidaki Style* [CD]. Buku-Larrngay Mulka Centre, BLMD001.
Schellberg, Dirk. 1994. *Didgeridoo: Ritual Origins and Playing Techniques.* Diever, Germany: Binkey Kok.
Yindi Youth. 1991. *Tribal Voice* [CD]. Mushroom Records.

Dixieland

Dixieland is an early style of jazz which developed at the start of the 20th century in New Orleans and spread to Chicago and New York in the late 1910s. The term "Dixieland" makes reference to the southern states, known as "Dixie," and was popularized by the late 1917 release of the Original Dixieland Jazz Band's first recordings. Dixieland, though somewhat lesser known today, was an important style of jazz and presents cultural and racial issues through its derivation.

Dixieland is in fact one of the earliest styles of jazz music. Created by white musicians, and hence developing from New Orleans' white band culture, the style emulated the heritage of French military bands and combined the sounds of brass-band marches and French quadrilles, as well as ragtime and blues, with polyphonic improvisation. Instrumentation and the size of bands was not standardized, but a typical Dixieland band may have consisted of a "front line" of trumpet or cornet, trombone, and clarinet and a "rhythm section" of banjo or guitar, string bass or tuba, piano, and drums (usually the band would employ no more than two rhythm section instrumentalists). Jazz, instead of playing straight notes as written, allowed players to extemporize arrangements that distinguish one performer or performance from another through the anticipation of beats, swinging, grace notes, an enriched harmony, and the development of brief motivic units into a more continuous line. It is this improvisation around a short melody (usually beginning with the trumpet before being adopted by the other front-line instruments) and the polyphony created thereby that defines the Dixieland style. In its syncopation, timbre, and moderate tempo, Dixieland bore a similarity to the black New Orleans jazz alongside which it grew. Recordings from the 1910s demonstrate that the style was a syncopated modification of traditional two-step dance music. But Dixieland, with its accentuation of two beats per measure, as opposed to accenting four or eight beats as later quick jazz styles did, was much more of a marching music than a dance music.

Dixieland players and their black jazz counterparts were culturally very similar; like black jazz, Dixieland grew out of the working-class ideals of aspirational young men. Poor whites, as well as the European immigrants who had flooded into New Orleans since the 1890s, were an especially vulnerable social group, and Dixieland was an expression of the identity and pride of these people. Despite their cultural similarities with the black residents of New Orleans, Dixieland players were often dismissive toward the black jazz players who developed alongside Dixieland musicians. Racism had not prevented white musicians in New Orleans from encountering black syncopating bands, but the social distance between uptown black people and the skilled white working class which gave birth to Dixieland was unusually large. It is worth noting that up until the 1920s white musicians often had far greater access to performance opportunities than blacks did, something which is fundamental in understanding the reception and popularity of different genres of jazz during this time.

As jazz progressed throughout the 1920s and 1930s, Dixieland music failed to develop, and this stagnation resulted in the style being overlooked by the artists of the 1920s who created the more definitive styles of jazz that we appreciate today. Regardless, during its heyday in the late 1910s Dixieland was incredibly popular with white audiences. The Original Dixieland Jazz Band (among others), through their recordings and tours around America, made jazz accessible to the masses, which allows Dixieland to remain an important element in the history of jazz as the first genre of syncopated improvised jazz to gain widespread success.

C. M. Gregory-Thomas

See Also: Jazz; Joplin, Scott; Original Dixieland Jazz Band; Ragtime

Further Reading

Brunn, H. O. 1960. *The Story of the Original Dixieland Jazz Band.* Baton Rouge: Louisiana State University Press.

Peretti, B. W. 1992. *The Creation of Jazz: Music, Race, and Culture in Urban America.* Urbana: University of Illinois Press.

Suhor, C. 2001. *Jazz in New Orleans: The Post-War Years through 1970.* London: Scarecrow Press.

Djembe

The *djembe* (or *jembe*) is a hand drum that originated in West Africa during the period of the Malian Empire (approximately the early 13th century CE). This empire covered what is now portions of Mali, Senegal, Gambia, Guinea, and Mauritania to the north. The djembe's distinctive goblet shape serves to concentrate the volume of the strokes on the head, so that the drum works well as a loud solo instrument. The drum is used in ballet performances in present-day Mali and Guinea, but has spread throughout the world as a popular instrument in "drum circles." It is the best-known African drum outside of that continent.

Historically made with antelope-skin drumheads, djembe makers now use goat skin. The shell of the drum is usually carved out of a hardwood, and elaborate designs are etched into the exterior. The interior of the drum is also not smooth; even though this part of the instrument is invisible to the performer, the grooves created by the drum maker determine the sound and quality of the djembe. Some traditional djembes have metal plaques inserted into the side of the shell to create a jangly sound.

Djembe players use three basic strokes: (1) the slap, (2) the tone, and (3) the bass. These strokes are created by moving the hand further toward or away from the center of the head; the slap has the hand furthest away. Each stroke is produced by using a different hand shape and stroke location. Because the drum has only one head (the bottom is open), the fundamental "pitch" of the bass stroke is determined by the size and shape of the body of the instrument. The pitch of the other two strokes are determined by the tension of the head. The experienced player uses the hand shape to create higher overtones, audible above the normal "tone" stroke.

The drum is held between the legs with the drumhead facing away from the performer; the open bottom is thus facing the player. One can also play standing up with the help of a shoulder and waist strap.

In traditional West African performances, the djembe is often accompanied by at least one lower drum, the *dundun* (or *dunun*). This drum is not a hand drum; rather, it is played with a hooked wooden stick. The djembe is traditionally played by men only. Women take the role of dancers, or play handheld accompanying percussion instruments (shakers, rattles, and the like). As with many aspects of gender roles in traditional societies, the present century is seeing a lot of change. More and more women are becoming *djembefolas* (djembe players).

A typical village performance may involve two to five or six drummers, several onlookers, and improvising dancers. The onlookers may become dancers, and may even become drummers. The roles are not strictly defined, and they can change during an event. This type of social activity is quite fluid and is an example of "part-counterpart" interaction. The performance of the music is dependent on audience participation, and sometimes the line between performer and spectator gets blurred.

Djembe Shape

The goblet-shaped (sometimes described as hourglass-shaped) profile of the *darbuka* drum, though unusual, is shared by several indigenous drums found in the African continent, especially in the far west and coastal countries of Guinea, Mali, and Ghana. Here, the *djembe* drum—a cousin of the darbuka—shares the same goblet shape. The djembe, however, is typically two to three times larger than the darbuka and is made of wood, with the drumhead made of goat skin. The goblet-shaped darbuka likely predates the djembe and was brought to the west of Africa by Arab traders travelling along the Silk Road which spanned the African and Asian continents and connected them by the Middle East. African artisans and musicians modified the shape of the drum by adapting its construction using local materials; hence, wood replaced the metal/clay shell or drum and goat skin replaced the fish skin of the drumhead.

In the Western world, the djembe is a crucial part of the "drum circle" phenomenon. This is a relatively recent social activity which started as an outgrowth of hippie culture in the 1960s. Drumming together is used as a social bonding activity in some communities in the United States and Western Europe. Drum circles are sometimes associated with neopagans and other alternative spiritual seekers. The circle can be led by a master drummer, or it can be free-form and open to anyone. In all cases, the music played is extemporaneous and improvised.

Christopher Gable

See also: Darbuka; Gyil; Kora; Kuti, Fela

Further Reading

Diallo, Yaya, and Mitchell Hall. 1989. *The Healing Drum: African Wisdom Teachings.* Rochester, VT: Destiny Books.

Nketia, J. H. Kwabena. 1974. *The Music of Africa.* New York: W.W. Norton.

Dmitri Pokrovsky Ensemble

The Dmitri Pokrovsky Ensemble is a vocal ensemble best known for performing Russian folk songs in a highly original manner. The internationally acclaimed ensemble became a constituent part of the folk revival movement in Russia.

In 1973, Dmitri Pokrovsky (1944–1996), a graduate of the Gnessin Pedagogical Institute, formed a group of several nonprofessional singers to perform songs collected during folklore expeditions. A member of the Folklore Commission of the Union of Composers described the group's first performance as "hysterical, aggressive" and "completely engrossing." The group became affiliated with the commission as an experimental ensemble.

Trying to convey a feeling of authenticity, the Pokrovsky Ensemble avoided the authored repertoire of professional folk choirs (such as *Kalinka*). The ensemble's performances included lectures on folk music and appealed to intellectuals. The complexity of the village music and the diversity of regional singing traditions in Russia contrasted with the popular image of a homogeneous national culture. By singing not Russian, but Smolensk, Belgorod, or Don Cossack songs, the ensemble reimaged folk as a mash-up of regional styles.

The ensemble exaggerated distinctive elements of particular styles. Improvisation, which was central to many regional traditions, became the ensemble's major feature. Some critics reproached it for reinterpreting local music. Others praised the musical complexity, avant-gardism, and emotionality of its performances. The Pokrovsky Ensemble inspired a large number of revivalist groups and became part of the global roots revival featuring idealization of the authentic village in contrast with the artificial industrial city. In Russia, the village music performed by the Pokrovsky Ensemble contributed to national identity formation.

Despite some problems with the authorities, by the 1980s the Pokrovsky Ensemble had become widely known across the country. It cooperated with prominent contemporary composers, as well as theater and film directors. The ensemble met the emerging international interest in Russian culture. In 1986, it performed at Harvard University. Pokrovsky gave lectures on regional traditions and voice production mechanisms at the Library of Congress, the Smithsonian Institution, Dartmouth College, and elsewhere.

The Pokrovsky Ensemble toured the United States, Australia, Japan, and other countries and cooperated with international musicians. The joint recording with Paul Winter (1939–), *Earthbeat*, was nominated for a Grammy in 1988. That same year, Dmitri Pokrovsky was awarded the Soviet Union's State Prize. In 1994 the ensemble performed *Les Noces*, a folk-inspired stage piece by Igor Stravinsky (1882–1971).

After Dmitri Pokrovsky's demise in 1996, the ensemble experienced a crisis but decided to continue performances. Developing new concert numbers, contributing to theater and film soundtracks, cooperating with internationally acclaimed performers, and conducting folklore expeditions, the Pokrovsky Ensemble remains an important part of contemporary global music.

Ivan Sablin

See also: Cossacks, Music of; Russian Orthodox Church Music

Further Reading

Levin, Theodore. 1996. "Dmitri Pokrovsky and the Russian Folk Revival Movement." In Mark Slobin (ed.), *Retuning Culture: Musical Changes in Central and Eastern Europe*, 14–36. Durham, NC: Duke University Press.

Olson, Laura J. 2004. *Performing Russia: Folk Revival and Russian Identity*. New York: Routledge.

Dorsey, Thomas A. (1899–1993)

Thomas Andrew Dorsey (not to be confused with big band leader and trombonist Tommy Dorsey) was an American musician and composer known today as the "Father of Gospel Music." In his earlier life, he was a prominent blues piano player called "Georgia Tom" who performed with such singers as Ma Rainey. After devoting himself to sacred music, Dorsey became the music director at Chicago's Pilgrim Baptist Church, a post he held from 1932 through his retirement in 1983. He composed approximately one thousand songs, was the first African American to be inducted into the Nashville Songwriter's Hall of Fame, was featured in the movie *Say Amen, Somebody*, and was honored in a tribute by the Smithsonian Institution.

One of seven children, Thomas Andrew Dorsey was born on July 1, 1899, in Villa Rica, Georgia, to the Rev. Thomas Madison Dorsey and his wife, Etta. His father was a traveling Baptist preacher who delivered his message in a colorful style to appreciative gatherings. Rev. Dorsey always kept up a dapper appearance, though in reality he could barely support his family. Thomas Andrew's mother, a devoutly religious church organist, owned a piece of land, but they still could not make a living farming it even through backbreaking labor. They sold the land and moved to Atlanta, Georgia, where Dorsey's mother worked as a domestic servant while his father worked as a laborer. When they still struggled financially, the family returned to Villa Rica, where Dorsey's father tried to make a living as a sharecropper.

Singer and composer Thomas A. Dorsey, known as the "Father of Gospel Music," ushered in a new style of black religious expression during the 1920s and 1930s. (Michael Ochs Archives/Getty Images)

Dorsey recalls that his father was also able to preach from time to time. In a foretaste of the future, Dorsey noted the sharp contrast of two different lifestyles: arduous manual labor in the fields versus the pleasant diversion of preaching, which was often accompanied by attention and good food. Dorsey studied the organ with his mother and also learned piano, finding that he loved music. At age 11, Dorsey left school and worked for a time with a circus, then at a local theater where he played piano. He then traveled to Atlanta, where he sold concessions at a vaudeville theatre. It was there that he experienced the music of such blues artists as Ma Rainey and Bessie Smith.

At age 16, Dorsey left for Chicago, where he quickly found success in 1916. He was known as the "whispering piano player" who could play good music quietly enough at after-hours clubs to avoid attracting unwanted police attention. However, Dorsey was torn between playing the "lowdown" blues and serving the Lord. He was forced to work odd jobs during the day to survive, while playing blues for low pay at night, which took their toll on his physical health. Dorsey suffered a breakdown and returned to Georgia to recover. Though his mother urged him to devote himself to sacred music rather than secular, he returned to Chicago and the blues when he recovered.

Dorsey took formal music studies at the Chicago College of Composition and Arranging, and became an agent for Paramount Records. But his heart was in playing the blues, which he performed under the names "Barrelhouse Tom," "Texas Tommy," and "Georgia Tom." As the latter, he teamed up with slide guitarist Hudson "Tampa Red" Whittaker in writing and recording a raunchy 1928 hit "It's Tight Like That." The record ultimately sold 7 million copies and is said to be the forerunner of such rock songs as "Long Tall Sally" and many others.

Dorsey worked as a session pianist, a musician in speakeasies, and also as composer of more than 400 blues and jazz songs. In 1924, he joined Ma Rainey and Her Wild Cats Jazz Band as its bandleader. Dorsey married Nettie Harper, who was Rainey's wardrobe mistress. In 1925, a second breakdown left Dorsey unable to perform as a musician. It took more than two years for him to recover, at which point he was determined to dedicate himself to music of faith after allegedly being told by a minister that the Lord had work for Dorsey. However, after learning of his "unsavory" reputation as a bluesman, most houses of worship rejected his songs, leading Dorsey to claim, "I've been thrown out of some of the best churches in Chicago."

Dorsey developed music of faith that departed from traditional spirituals, which were often coded messages sung in the fields by enslaved workers. Wedding secular blues with sacred text, Dorsey's compositions were based on the musical styles of jazz and blues, featuring syncopated notes in an eight-bar blues structure. His music asked for divine guidance as well as carrying a message of hope, with songs of this type sometimes being called "Dorseys" in his honor well into the 1950s. He himself called his new songs of praise "Gospel music," referring to the first four books of the New Testament bringing the revelation, or good news, of Jesus Christ.

At first, Dorsey's gospel tunes met strong resistance from pastors of mainstream churches, who preferred worship to be restrained, though the National Baptist Convention of 1930 allowed two of his compositions to be performed. One of them, 'If You See My Savior, Tell Him That You Saw Me," received an especially warm reception. In 1931, Dorsey and Theodore Frye organized the first gospel choir at Chicago's Ebenezer Baptist Church. January of 1932 saw the first commercial recording of a Dorsey song when the Famous Blue Jays of Birmingham recorded "If You See My Savior" (under the title of "Standing by the Bedside of a Neighbor"). This was followed later that same month with the first performance of the Dorsey/Frye gospel chorus at Ebenezer Baptist Church. In 1932, Dorsey became choir director at Pilgrim Baptist Church, a position he held for the next 50 years.

Dorsey felt slighted by traditional music publishers and thus opened the Dorsey House of Music in 1932. It was the first music company created to sell black gospel music compositions. In August 1932, Dorsey traveled from Chicago to St. Louis to attend a Baptist revival when he received word that his wife and infant son, Thomas Jr., had died from complications of childbirth. In despair, he turned to the piano, and a tune emerged which he said came directly from God. It was "Take My Hand, Precious Lord," which was sung to great acclaim at Ebenezer Baptist Church and went on to become one of the most revered gospel songs of all time. Its earliest known recording was made by Emory Johnson in 1938.

From 1932 onward, Dorsey traveled to promote his music, sometimes accompanying noted gospel singers such as Sallie Martin and Mahalia Jackson. He also staged concerts for a small admission price called "Evenings with Dorsey," which were the first to feature black gospel music in a concert setting. Singers at these concerts often included Martin, Jackson, and Frye. With Martin, he founded the National Convention of Gospel Choirs and Choruses in 1933, a conference which meets annually to spotlight gospel music and musicians. Dorsey served as its first president. In 1937, Dorsey wrote "Peace in the Valley" for his friend Mahalia Jackson, a song that became a gospel standard and went on to become the most-recorded gospel song of all time.

Dorsey continued traveling, composing, and serving as musical director at Pilgrim Baptist Church for much of the remainder of his life. His songs were recorded by dozens of singers, both black and white. On Elvis Presley's historic 1957 appearance on the nationally televised *Ed Sullivan Show*, Presley chose to sing "Peace in the Valley," accompanied by a gospel group The Jordanaires as well as bewildered screams from the audience. Afterward, Sullivan praised the controversial Presley as a "real decent, fine boy."

In 1968, Dorsey was on a train traveling to Houston when the news arrived that the Rev. Martin Luther King had been killed in Memphis. "Take My Hand, Precious Lord" was known to be King's favorite gospel song. King was leaning down to talk to musician Ben Branch, who was in the parking lot of the Lorraine Motel, asking that "Precious Lord" be played at the rally that night. According to the *Chicago Sun-Times*, that was the last conversation King had before being assassinated moments later. King had previously asked that Dorsey's "Precious Lord" be sung at his funeral, a request honored by Mahalia Jackson.

Dorsey passed away in Chicago at the age of 93 of complications from Alzheimer's disease on January 23, 1993. He is buried at that city's Oak Woods Cemetery.

Nancy Hendricks

See also: Blues; Jackson, Mahalia; Jazz

Further Reading

Boyer, Horace Clarence. 2000. *The Golden Age of Gospel* (Music in American Life Series). Urbana: University of Illinois Press.

Darden, Robert. 2005. *People Get Ready!: A New History of Black Gospel Music.* New York: Bloomsbury Academic.

Harris, Michael W. 1994. *The Rise of Gospel Blues: The Music of Thomas Andrew Dorsey in the Urban Church.* New York: Oxford University Press.

Reagon, Bernice Johnson. 1992. *We'll Understand It Better By and By: Pioneering African American Gospel Composers* ("Wade in the Water" series). Washington, DC: Smithsonian Institution Scholarly Press.

Duduk

The *duduk* is a small, double-reed wind instrument that is capable of intense emotional expressiveness, despite its limited one-octave range. It is classified as an aerophone, a category of musical instruments that includes the bassoon, clarinet, flute, and oboe. Aerophones are played by blowing air from the mouth through a wooden reed into a wooden or metal pipe, and manipulating tone holes positioned at intervals along the length of the pipe to produce different notes or tones. The duduk may have seven to nine finger tone holes on the front or top side of the instrument and one thumb hole on the back or bottom. Duduks come in various sizes, with lengths ranging from approximately 10 to 16 inches, and an external diameter of about three-fourths of an inch. Duduks are available in several different keys, such as A, C, E, F, G, and others. The sound produced by the duduk often is compared to that of the oboe.

The duduk is believed to be indigenous to Armenia, where it is a revered symbol of the historical continuity of Armenian culture. Similar instruments, including some with the same name, such as the Turkish duduk or *mey*, are found throughout Central Asia, Eastern Europe, and the Middle East, but none has a cultural significance remotely comparable to the Armenian namesake. In recognition of the duduk's centrality to Armenian cultural heritage, the United Nations Educational, Scientific and Cultural Organization (UNESCO) designated the instrument, and its music, a Masterpiece of the Oral and Intangible Heritage of Humanity.

The duduk or *tsiranapogh* (its traditional Armenian name) is a centuries-old instrument that originated approximately 1,500 to 2,700 years ago, with a plausible mid-range date of origin corresponding to the 40-year reign (95–55 BCE) of the Armenian monarch Tigran or Tigranes II, a/k/a Tigran or Tigranes the Great (140–155 BCE). No instrument is as integral to Armenian culture as the duduk. Its capacity to evoke the collective spirit of the Armenian people is unrivaled. The foremost Armenian duduk master Jivan Gasparyan, Sr. (1928–) writes, "The Duduk is a unified symphony of the human spirit; it gives voice to the lament of our bitter past in one instance, the song of our present life in another and to the hymn of our faith and strength" (Gasparyan, 2018).

Duduks are constructed from fruit or nut tree woods, such as mulberry, plum, or walnut. The Armenian duduk typically is fashioned out of apricot wood. Duduks usually are played in tandem: one instrument plays a melody accompanied by a second instrument producing a sustained drone sound called a *dam*.

Duduk repertoire consists mostly of traditional folk music, some dating from ancient times. The duduk also is a featured instrument in some classical and contemporary music, including non-Armenian popular music. For example, the ex-Beatle Sir Paul McCartney (1942–) was so impressed when he heard a duduk solo, composed by Ravi Shankar (1920–2012), a renowned Indian classical musician, performed at a memorial concert for his former bandmate George Harrison (1943–2001), that he invited the Venezuelan musician, Pedro Eustache (1959–), to play the duduk on the recording of his English ballad "Jenny Wren." In addition to Jivan Gasparyan, Sr., and Pedro Eustache, other notable duduk musicians include Gasparyan's grandson, Jivan Gasparyan, Jr., Vatche Hovsepian, Levon Madoyan, and Margar Margaryan.

Greg A. Phelps

See also: Dastgah; Tar

Further Reading

Gasparyan, Jivan. 2018. *Yeraz*. Buda Musique B075ZDV63W [audio CD].

Karahasanoglu, Songül. 2008. "A Comparative View of the Mey, Balaban, and Duduk." *Journal of Academic Studies* 37, 129–142.

Mkrtchyan, Kamo. n.d. "About Duduk and the Armenian Duduk-Players." http://www.armenianduduk.am/about-duduk-and-the-armenian-duduk-players.html.

Nercessian, Andy. 2001. *The Duduk and National Identity in Armenia*. Lanham, MD: Scarecrow Press.

UNESCO. n.d. "Armenian Duduk Music." https://ich.unesco.org/en/projects/armenian-duduk-music-00024.

Dulcimer

The dulcimer and instruments of the dulcimer family are found throughout Europe, the Middle East, and Asia under a number of different names: *cimbalom* in Hungary, Czechoslovakia, Romania, and Poland; *Hackbrett* in Germany, Austria, and Switzerland; *santur/santir/santoor* in Iran and other Middle Eastern countries and India; *salterio* in Mexico, France, and Italy; *yang chin* (or *yang qin*) in China; *sandouri* in Greece; *tsimbaly* in Russia, Ukraine, and other Eastern European countries; *chang* in Uzbekistan; *khim* in Thailand; and *dan tam thap* in Vietnam. Although the dulcimer, or dulcimer-type instruments, appear to be found almost worldwide, no similar or analogous instruments have been found among the native peoples of, for example, Africa, South America, or Australia.

The dulcimer is a stringed instrument, classed as a struck chordophone, which is one of the precursors of the piano. It is shaped like a triangle with the top cut off and has groups of strings, or *courses*, with between two and four strings in a group (though five or six is not unusual), stretched laterally across the body. Each group of strings passes over a bridge: one set of bridges is positioned near, and almost parallel to, the right side of the soundboard and the other is toward the left side, approximately two-thirds of the way across. The bridges on the right side give the lower, bass notes, while the more central bridges yield the treble. The strings crossing the central bridges give two notes, one on each side of the bridge, usually a fifth apart. However, there are variations of these string/bridge arrangements: the yang qin, for example, may have five sets of bridges across the sound board giving a chromatic tuning of four octaves from G^0 to g^3. Similarly, the concert cimbalom also has five sets of bridges, but in a very different configuration.

There are also two different styles of bridge. With the fixed bridge, several sets (courses) of strings cross the continuous length of the bridge. The individual (sometimes called "chessman"), movable bridge which is crossed by a single course of strings is seen on East Anglian (and some other regional U.K.) dulcimers and santurs.

The instrument is usually played using two beaters made from wood or cane. Again, there are regional variations (and even personal variations) and variations in the way the beaters are held. In the United States, China, and the United Kingdom, players usually hold the beater between the thumb and forefinger, whereas cimbalom, Hackbrett, and santur players hold their beaters between the middle finger and index finger. In the United States and the UK, the instrument is often now called the "hammer" or "hammered" dulcimer to differentiate it from the Appalachian dulcimer, which is not actually a dulcimer but is related to the Norwegian *langolette* and the French *epinette de voges*.

However, though classified as a "struck chordophone," there are traditions of dulcimer playing where the strings are plucked instead of struck, notably in Birmingham, England. Some of the East Anglian (an area of Eastern England) traditional players sometimes plucked the strings as well as using cane beaters; the Mexican salterio is exclusively played by plucking the strings.

It is probable that the dulcimer was initially taken to the United States by British settlers, but it is clear that immigrants from other parts of Europe also took their own versions of the dulcimer. It has been suggested that the early dulcimer in Ireland was called the *timpan*; however, the description of the timpan in P. W. Joyce's 1906 *Social History of Ireland* suggests otherwise.

> The Irish had a small stringed instrument called a Timpan, which had only a few strings—from three to eight. The body was a small flat drum or *tympanum* (whence the name) with a short neck added; the strings were stretched across the flat face and along the neck, and were tuned and regulated by pins or keys and a bridge, something like the modern guitar, or banjo, but with the neck much shorter. It was played with a bow, or with both a bow and plectrum, or with the finger-nail; and the strings were probably stopped with the fingers of the left hand, like those of a violin. (Joyce, 1906)

Although there is a tradition of dulcimer playing in Ireland, specifically Northern Ireland, it is not as ubiquitous as the harp, fiddle, accordion, or uilleann pipes, and there are very few known players in the recent past. However, the dulcimer does seem to have been in Ireland in the 17th century, where it may have been played more in "art" or courtly music rather than in a folk tradition. In later years, specifically the 20th century, it was mostly found in County Antrim, but one or two players in the Dublin area have been identified.

The origins of the dulcimer are obscure; it is often said to have originated in Persia (modern-day Iran), but this is based on an indistinct and damaged Assyrian carving in the British Museum dating from around the seventh century BCE, which is now thought to depict a 10-string harp. Nevertheless, some still subscribe to the Persian-origin theory which the musical instrument historian, Francis Galpin, dismissed in 1937 (Galpin, 1937). In truth, it is difficult to say where the instrument originated, and even the concept of a single origin for the instrument is not now generally accepted. There may, however, have been several different routes for the instrument's development and its distribution around the world. For example, it is thought that the ubiquitous Chinese dulcimer—the yang qin, which translates as "foreign zither"—may have been introduced into South China by European traders or sailors in the 17th century.

Paul M. Gifford, in his comprehensive study of dulcimers worldwide, suggests that the dulcimer as it is known today originated in Europe, with the Hackbrett and dulcimer (or *doulcemèr*) developing independently across the European continent (Gifford, 2001), whereas the santur may have developed from a similar Arabic instrument, the *qaum*.

Whatever the origin of the instrument, it has obviously been part of the European musical tradition for hundreds of years. It is depicted in psalters and artworks from at least the 15th century, and one of the roof boss carvings in Manchester Cathedral depicts an angel playing a dulcimer.

Today the dulcimer is considered a "folk" instrument, although the cimbalom in Eastern Europe, the yang qin in China and other Far Eastern countries, and the santur in Iran and India are very much part of a classical music tradition. In 18th-century Europe, the dulcimer was one of the instruments used in art/court music. Music was composed for the dulcimer or salterio; unfortunately, most of this music has been lost, but in 1974, 14 of these pieces were published by Karl Heinz-Schickhause, a German Hackbrett player.

The best-known dulcimer player in Europe during the 18th century was Pantaleon Hebenstreit, who played a specially developed and designed dulcimer. Pantaleon was a dancing master and music teacher of violin and harpsichord who fell into debt while studying in Leipzig. Obviously inspired by the Hackbrett players he saw in the drinking houses in Leipzig, and with the help of a pastor who had woodworking skills, Hebenstreit developed a form of double-soundboard dulcimer with both gut and metal strings.

Hebenstreit became famous throughout the European aristocratic courts and played before many monarchs; indeed it was King Louis XIV of France, who, seeing and hearing him in 1705, christened his instrument the *pantaleon*. Several pantaleon players followed in his footsteps, but none seem to have been as celebrated as Pantaleon Hebenstreit himself. Unfortunately, none of his instruments have survived, so the knowledge of his instrument comes only through contemporary accounts and descriptions. However, around 1717 one of the inventors of piano-key mechanisms, Gottleib Schröter, developed an "over-striking" mechanism for his first instrument, which he called a *pantaleon*, indicating that he was most likely inspired by Pantaleon's instrument. Unfortunately, this mechanism was not a success (Galpin, 1937).

Although the dulcimer appears to have gone out of favor in art music circles thereafter, it continued to retain a place within traditional and popular music. In Eastern Europe, for example, the cimbalom became strongly associated with traditional gypsy music. The 17th-century London diarist, Samuel Pepys, noted that street musicians busked with a dulcimer. Writing on May 23, 1662, after attending a puppet show in Covent Garden, he noted that "here among the fiddlers, I first saw a dulcimere played with sticks knocking of the strings, and is very pretty." He saw, or rather heard, another being played in a tavern a month later. Indeed at this time the instrument seems to have been associated with taverns and houses of ill repute (Galpin, 1937).

By the middle of the 18th century, the instrument seems to have almost disappeared from art music, although there is some evidence that the dulcimer retained a place in the music-making and entertainment of middle-class households during this period. Also, a number of highly decorated dulcimers from this period have survived. The dulcimer does appear to have retained a place as a "folk" instrument in many parts of Europe, such as Austria, Switzerland, parts of Germany, Hungary, and Romania, although the number of players had apparently diminished enough so that an 1827 encyclopedia entry noted that the instrument was entirely out of use—but then immediately contradicted itself by adding "only perhaps with common people here and there" (Gifford, 2001, p. 71). Similarly, although apparently obscure in folk music-making in the United Kingdom by the 19th/20th century, recent research into the dulcimer playing traditions in the East Anglian region of the UK by John and Katie Howson, has revealed more and more players within the region during this time.

There has been a revival of interest in the dulcimer in the United Kingdom since the early 1970s, when collectors and folk music enthusiasts "discovered" such players as Billy Cooper and Billy Bennington in Norfolk, England; Jimmy Cooper in Glasgow, Scotland; Reg Reeder in Suffolk, England; John Rae in Northern Ireland;

Ted Carr in London, England; and Bill Fell, and later Fred Woodley, in Birmingham, England. However, the publication of David Kettlewell's influential book *All the Tunes That Ever There Were* in 1975 stimulated a much wider interest in the instrument. At around the same time, there was a revival of interest in the United States, with players such as Bill Spence, Malcolm Dalglish, John McCutcheon, Sam Rizzetta, and Howie Mitchell in the forefront of the revival (Hulan, 1977).

In countries such as Iran and India, the santur has been very much a continuing tradition; there does not seem to be a large divide between what could be termed a folk tradition and the Eastern classical music art form. In Eastern Europe, the cimbalom is closely associated with gypsy music, but is now a characteristic instrument in classical/art music; it is also extremely popular among classical music players in the Far East, despite the very strong yang qin tradition. The Hungarian concert cimbalom was developed in 1874 by József Shunda in Budapest, who set the cimbalom on legs, developed a pedal damping system, and increased the range of the instrument to be chromatic from C two octaves below middle C to two octaves above middle C. Schunda also established the current cimbalom tuning pattern. The design of the cimbalom was further elaborated in the 1920s by Bohak Lajos, who established his cimbalom-making company around 1900.

The increased size of the more modern cimbalom, along with its iron or steel internal bracings, makes the concert cimbalom much less portable than the traditional instrument. However, makers do produce a smaller, more portable version of the pedal cimbalom, with a three-octave chromatic starting at C below middle C.

The sound of the cimbalom has inspired several composers, including Kodály, who used it in his *Hary Janos Suite*, and Géva Allaga (1841–1913). Igor Stravinsky was so enamored of it that he had the Hungarian musician Aladár Rácz teach him to play it. He wrote a major part for the cimbalom in his chamber music piece *Ragtime* and in the score for the ballet *Renard*. Now many composers are writing new pieces for the cimbalom and the yang qin.

George Monger

See also: Bartók, Béla; Iranian Classical Music; Qānūn; Qin; Zither

Further Reading

Bandera, Mark Jorslav. 1991. *The Tsymbaly Maker and His Craft: The Ukrainian Hammer Dulcimer in Alberta*. Edmonton: Canadian Institute of Ukrainian Studies Press, University of Alberta.

Galpin, Francis W. 1937. *A Textbook of European Musial Instruments*. London: Williams & Norgate.

Gifford, Paul M. 2001. *The Hammered Dulcimer: A History*. Lanham, MD: Scarecrow Press.

Hulan, Richard H. 1977. *The Hammer Dulcimer Compendium*. Silver Springs, MD: MIH Publications.

Joyce, Patrick Weston. 1906. *A Smaller Social History of Ancient Ireland*. London: Longman and Green.

Kettlewell, David. 1975. *All the Tunes That Ever There Were*. Wiltshire, UK: Spoot Books.

Leach, John. 1972. "The Cimbalom." *Music & Letters* 53, 134–142.

Dylan, Bob (1941–)

An American musician, songwriter, visual artist, and writer, Bob Dylan is regarded as one of the most important musical figures of the 20th century. Throughout a career spanning more than six decades, Dylan has pioneered new musical conventions throughout the world of popular music while remaining dedicated to American roots traditions such as blues, country, gospel, and folk. Although Dylan's popularity peaked in the 1960s, his steady if unpredictable musical output and near-constant touring in subsequent decades have made him a prolific artist with enormous influence.

Dylan was born Robert Allen Zimmerman on May 24, 1941, in Duluth, Minnesota. When he was six, his parents, Abe and Beatty, moved the family to Hibbing, where his father ran a hardware store. Drawn at an early age to rock and roll, by age 10, he had learned to play harmonica, piano, and guitar, and in his high school years formed his first group, the Golden Chords. In 1960, after a brief enrollment at the University of Minnesota, where he began performing solo in coffeehouses as "Bob Dylan," he moved to New York City. Not coincidentally, one of his musical heroes, Woody Guthrie, was hospitalized for Huntington's disease there, and Dylan visited Guthrie in the hospital frequently. At the same time, Dylan was also becoming a recognized figure in coffeehouses and folk clubs throughout Greenwich Village.

Following a positive concert review by Robert Shelton in *The New York Times*, producer John Hammond signed Dylan to Columbia Records, the label that has since released nearly all of his albums. His first, *Bob Dylan*, was released in 1962. Though the album contains only two originals ("Talking New York" and "Song to Woody"), it reflects the breadth of his early influences, from blues (Bukka White's "Fixin' to Die") to standard spirituals ("Gospel Plow"). Dylan's formidable songwriting talents emerged on follow-up albums, *The Freewheelin' Bob Dylan* (1963) and *The Times They Are A-Changin'* (1964). With these efforts, Dylan remained committed to the folksong idiom, but also created new songs with pointed political commentary. Anthemic songs such as "Blowin' in the Wind," "Hard Rain," and "The Times They Are A-Changin'" were congruent with the goals of political activists and protest movements of the time.

Another Side of Bob Dylan (1964) signaled a turn away from the overt politicism that had marked Dylan's previous work and toward introspection and abstract imagery. Illustrative is "My Back Pages," which offered a rejection of his earlier protest-inspired idealism: "I was so much older then/I'm younger than that now." The album's follow-up, *Bringing It All Back Home* (1965), was also a stylistic departure for Dylan. Featuring electric instruments for the first time, the album reveals pop influences, particularly that of British Invasion groups such as the Beatles and the Animals, and folk-rock acts such as the Byrds, who had had a hit with "Mr. Tambourine Man" earlier that year. Dylan's decisive break with the folk community came at the Newport Folk Festival in 1965, where he performed with an electric guitar alongside members of the Paul Butterfield Blues Band. Although interpreted by many as a put-down of the folk music establishment that had nurtured his early career, Dylan's "going electric" at Newport reflected Dylan's evolving musical aesthetic: one that did not reject his roots in folk, but rather embraced the entire popular music spectrum of the time as a potential influence. *Highway 61 Revisited* (1965) and *Blonde on Blonde* (1966) continued the musical trajectory begun by *Bringing It All Back Home* and established the organ-driven "wild mercury sound" (Rosenbaum, 1978) defined by songs such as "Like a Rolling Stone" and "Visions of Johanna."

Following an exhausting British tour in the spring of 1966 and a motorcycle crash near his home in Woodstock, New York, in late July, Dylan retreated from the spotlight. Renting a house in West Saugerties dubbed "Big Pink," he and The Band recorded material that would eventually be released as *The Basement Tapes*

Bob Dylan in the recording studio, 1965. Dylan was a key figure in the 1960s counterculture movement and an influential singer-songwriter. (Library of Congress)

in 1975. These recordings, made in early 1967, reveal yet another shift in Dylan's songwriting, gesturing toward the country-tinged, acoustic textures and lyrical directness that would pervade *John Wesley Harding* (1967) and *Nashville Skyline* (1969) shortly thereafter.

Dylan released a number of albums in the early 1970s that were met with mixed reviews. However, in 1974, his career resurged with *Planet Waves* (1974), his first No. 1 record; and a successful tour, his first in eight years. This comeback continued with *Blood on the Tracks* (1975) and *Desire* (1976), each of which hit No. 1 and were hailed by critics as a return to form. At this stage, Dylan's penchant for spinning out lengthy narratives and rich character portrayals was manifested in songs such as "Idiot Wind" and "Hurricane," a protest song about the unjust imprisonment of boxer Rubin Carter.

Reinventing himself yet again, Dylan declared himself a born-again Christian in late 1978. To that end, his next three albums, beginning with *Slow Train Coming* (1979), evoked evangelical themes. 1983's *Infidels* marked a return to the secular and cultivation of a more polished sound. This was owed in large part to the efforts of producers such as Mark Knopfler (*Infidels*), Daniel Lanois (*Oh Mercy*), and Don and David Was (*Under the Red Sky*). This period during the 1980s and early 1990s was also punctuated by Dylan's touring and work with other artists, including the Grateful Dead and the Traveling Wilburys.

Like *Planet Waves*, the success of *Time Out of Mind* in 1997 sparked renewed interest in Dylan. As the first album of original material to be released in seven years, the album's mixture of blues, country, and folk styles harked back to the sound of his earliest influences, and re-established Dylan as a rock icon still capable of making interesting new music. Its follow-ups, *Love and Theft* (2001) and *Modern Times* (2006) fueled this renaissance and also showcased Dylan's stylistic scope and creativity. Both self-produced, *Through This Life* and an album of holiday songs, *Christmas in the Heart*, were released in 2009. *Tempest*, Dylan's 35th studio album, was released in September of 2012.

John Stanislawski

See also: Banjo; Guthrie, Woody; Rock and Roll

Further Reading

Cantwell, Robert. 1996. *When We Were Good: The Folk Revival.* Cambridge, MA: Harvard University Press.

Dylan, Bob. 2004. *Chronicles, Volume One.* New York: Simon & Schuster.

Filene, Benjamin. 2000. *Romancing the Folk: Public Memory & American Roots Music.* Chapel Hill: University of North Carolina Press.

Rosenbaum, Ron. 1978. "*Playboy* Interview: Bob Dylan." *Playboy* (March), p. 14.

Shelton, Robert, Elizabeth Thomson, and Patrick Humphries. 2011. *No Direction Home: The Life and Music of Bob Dylan*, rev. & updated ed. (originally published in 1986). Milwaukee, WI: Backbeat Books.

E

Eastern Woodland Native American Music

The Wabenaki (or Abenaki) are a group of semi-nomadic, patrilineal American Indian peoples speaking Eastern Algonquin languages, whose ancestral homeland stretches from Canada's Atlantic provinces and Gaspé Peninsula to the Merrimack and Connecticut River valleys in Massachusetts. The name derives from the word *wapánahki*, meaning "dawn land people" or "Easterners." At the time of the first contact with French in the 16th century, they were expanding westward into what became a hotly contested borderland between New England and French Acadia.

The earliest transcriptions of Native music from this region are three songs by *Sakmow* (grand chief) Henri Membertou of the Mi'kmaq (1607); they demonstrate parallels between Native and missionary music such as heightened speech/chant, use of words like "Alleluia" as vocables, and sung prayers for healing. The Franciscans translated special repertories of song used for rites of passage into French. L'Abbé Pierre Maillard (ca. 1710–1762), based at the Louisbourg Fortress, helped to establish a written form of Mi'kmaq and translated psalms for local use (1738). Conversion led to the replacement of Native music in religious ceremonies with Christian hymns and canticles. Ceremonial songs, however, were considered an individual's property and were thought to bring good luck in hunting, quiet rough waters, and strengthen canoe paddlers.

Accounts of 18th-century cultural practices among the five tribes—Abenaki, Penobscot, Maliseet (Malecite/Wolstoqiyik), Passamaquoddy, and Mi'kmaq (Micmac)—include English captive narratives by Elizabeth Hanson (1728), Susannah Johnson (1754), and Jemima Howe (1755). The Maliseet and Passamaquoddy remained in the border region of eastern Maine and southern New Brunswick; their language and song texts have recently been reconstructed.

Music and dance were central to public ceremonies for greeting, harvesting corn, "chief-making," and war, as well as for family feasts, weddings, and funerals. For the Snake Dance, as in the related Iroquois and Cherokee stomp dances, people gather in a line behind the leader and dance in a counterclockwise spiral. During contemporary reenactments of the Corn Ceremony by the Penobscot, the Legend of the First Mother and the origins of corn and tobacco are recounted, and a burial song is sung.

Percussive accompaniment, especially for the Snake Dance, can be provided by the *ji'kmaqn*, an ash slapstick approximately one foot in length. Mi'kmaq singers and shamans used bark drums, but that tradition was lost by the late 18th century. Gourd and birch bark rattles were common, along with the shot horn, a cow horn filled with buckshot. Recent adoptions are the double-headed frame drum and the single-headed frame drum, adopted from Plains practice.

Eastern Woodlands music (including that of the Iroquois) employs an undulating melodic contour, with more descent than ascent overall. Greeting songs begin high, or with an initial rapid rise through a broken triad. Solo songs usually span an octave, but antiphonal songs have a somewhat smaller range. Pentatonic scales are common, and internal melodic movement is generally in intervals of major seconds and major and minor thirds. Larger intervals are more typical of Paddling and War Dance songs. Songs are short, consisting of two or three themes repeated in various combinations, usually with minor variation (*AABB, ABA'B, ABAB'A'B*). Greeting and Death songs (especially in Mi'kmaq) have meaningful texts, but songs for dancing usually contain only vocables. Traditional Woodlands male vocal quality (before contact with Plains music) was comparable to European folk practice, with little vocal tension and an open and resonant tone.

Ceremonial songs and borrowings from other tribes have been performed by the Penobscot in summer pageants at Old Town, Maine, since the 1930s, and women have been encouraged to sing publicly since the pioneering efforts of Sarah Denny (an Eskasoni Mi'kmaq) in the 1960s. The Canadian Aboriginal Festival (Hamilton, Ontario) was established in 1996 to encourage traditional art forms and to award music prizes: groups have revived Woodland song forms, featured locally made instruments, and reinterpreted traditional stories through song and dance.

The largest collections of Eastern Woodland language and music are held by the Federal Cylinder Project (738 cylinders recorded from 1890–1930, at the Library of Congress); the Indiana University Archives of Traditional Music (78 cylinders recorded from 1905–1911); and Cornell University (manuscripts and hymnals in Eastern dialects from the early 19th century).

Laura Stanfield Prichard

See also: Densmore, Frances; Native American Church Music

Further Reading

Diamond, Beverley. 2007. *Native American Music in Eastern North America.* Oxford: Oxford University Press.

Diamond, Beverley, M. Sam Cronk, and Franziska von Rosen. 1994. *Visions of Sound: Musical Instruments of First Nations Communities in Northeastern America.* Chicago: University of Chicago.

Emmett, Dan (Daniel Decatur) (1815–1904)

Perhaps best known for compositions such "Old Dan Tucker" and "Dixie," Dan Emmett is a central figure in the American blackface minstrel tradition that flourished in the mid-19th century. As a songwriter, instrumentalist, entertainer, and founder of the Virginia Minstrels, Emmett helped establish early minstrel show conventions and repertoire.

Born in Mount Vernon, Ohio, Emmett received little formal training in music, instead learning popular songs from his mother before teaching himself to play the fiddle. Emmett worked in his father's blacksmith shop and as a printer's apprentice prior to enlisting in the United States Army in 1834. While stationed in Jefferson Barracks, Missouri, Emmett developed his musical skills, mastering the drum and fife. After being discharged from the army in 1835, Emmett relocated to Cincinnati, where he joined a circus and began performing as a blackface musician and entertainer and writing his own minstrel songs. Among the first of these was "Bill Crowder," written for blackface singer Frank Whitaker. Emmett learned to play the banjo from a man named "Ferguson" in 1840, and by the summer of 1841, was playing banjo for audiences along with Baltimore-born comedian, singer, dancer, and bones player Frank Brower (1823–1874).

In November of 1842, Emmett moved to New York, where he and Brower formed a fiddle and bones duo. Soon after, they were joined by banjoist Billy Whitlock and tambourine player Dick Pelham. Whitlock, like Emmett, had worked as a printer's apprentice before taking up the banjo in 1838, and Pelham had earned his reputation as a dancer prior to joining the group. Billing themselves as "the Virginia Minstrels," the group's first performance took place on February 6, 1843, at the Bowery Amphitheatre in New York City. A month later, the group staged their first full-length "Ethiopian Concert" at the Masonic Temple in Boston on March 7, 1843, before enthusiastic audiences. Unlike previous blackface acts, which were usually performed only during intermissions of a play or as one of many acts in a comic variety show, the Virginia Minstrels presented an entire evening of imitation black songs, dances, stump speeches, and parody skits.

Following their success in New York and Boston, the Virginia Minstrels embarked on a tour of the British Isles in the late spring of 1843. In the midst of mixed audience response and financial difficulty, the group disbanded. Emmett went on, traveling with a number of circuses and performing independently before rejoining Pelham and Brower in April of 1844. Upon returning to the United States in September of that year, Emmett published *Old Dan Emmitt's Original Banjo Melodies*, a collection of tunes that he may have partly composed or collected from other sources. In addition to songs like "Old Dan Tucker" (previously published in 1843), other songs attributed to Emmett, such as "Jim Crack Corn, or the Blue-Tail Fly," appeared in this publication.

To find footing amidst the avalanche of minstrel groups that emerged in the wake of the Virginia Minstrels' success, throughout the next few years, Emmett formed a number of his own troupes, sang and acted in "Ethiopian Burlettas" (musical farces), and even pioneered a new genre called "machine poetry" in which uneducated black characters assumed the innovative qualities of the Industrial Age. In November 1858, Emmett joined Dan Bryant's Minstrels, a popular minstrel troupe based in New York. With this group, Emmett not only performed, but also wrote songs and words for "walk-arounds," song-and-dance routines that closed each show. The most well-known of the "walk-arounds" attributed to Emmett is known today as "Dixie." Becoming popular almost immediately after its premiere at Mechanic's Hall on Broadway on April 4, 1859, the song offered a nostalgic, joyous vision of Southern plantation life that caught on with both Northern and Southern audiences.

Emmett moved to Chicago in 1867, where he began performing with Haverly's Minstrels. After losing his voice, however, Emmett was restricted to playing fiddle in various saloons throughout the city. By 1882, Emmett's commitment to crude representations of black culture and music were at odds with the more restrained kind of spectacles that came to characterize that time. Hence, Emmett struggled for recognition and financial security. Although Emmett's last performing years were punctuated by a successful tour through the South with Leavitt's Gigantean Minstrels (made possible, no doubt, by the previous success of "Dixie"), in 1888, Emmett retired to his hometown of Mount Vernon, Ohio. From 1893 to the end of his life, he was supported by a weekly allowance from the Actor's Fund of America.

John Stanislawski

See also: Virginia Minstrels

Further Reading

Crawford, Richard. 2001. *America's Musical Life: A History.* New York: Norton.

Nathan, Hans. 1962. *Dan Emmett and the Rise of American Negro Minstrelsy.* Norman: University of Oklahoma Press.

Sacks, Howard L., and Judith Rose Sacks. 1993. *Way Up North in Dixie: A Black Family's Claim to the Confederate Anthem.* Washington, DC: Smithsonian Institution Press.

Enka Music

Enka is one of the Japanese popular music genres, whose meaning has changed greatly since its inception during the Meiji era (1868–1912). Originally, *enka* meant "speech song" (half-sung and half-spoken), which was a form of protest in the street during the Freedom and People's Rights Movement from 1874 to 1890. An enka singer known as an *enkashi* sang without accompaniments by any musical instruments. After the establishment of the Imperial Diet under the Meiji Constitution, enka lost its immediate purpose and declined. However, around the end of the Meiji era, it resurfaced without its political implications, and regained popularity. The focus of enka shifted from speech to music, and the songs satirized contemporary life. The musical elements were influenced by *shoka* (school songs) and *gunka* (military songs), which had adopted Western music. As a result, enka songs started to sound more musical in the Western sense and started to include a few accompanying instruments, such as shamisen and violin. A representative enka song of this period is "Rappa Bushi" (Bugle Call Song, 1905) composed by Soeda Azembo (1872–1944), an enkashi in Tokyo. This song became extremely popular, spreading all over the country and inspiring numerous local renditions of the piece.

Today's enka is most closely related to the *ryukoka* (popular or fashionable song), which fully developed in the Taisho era (1912–1926). In the early 20th century, enka was a subgenre of ryukoka, and enkashi started to incorporate Western musical elements in their compositions during this period. Due to these influences, enka performances from this time period were often accompanied by a small ensemble. One of those compositions was Tottori Shunyo's "Kago no Tori" ("A Bird in a Cage," 1924), which was a huge hit. With the advent of new technology, the popular ryukoka songs were distributed through printed sheet music and recordings, and they were also used as background music for silent films.

Enka underwent various stages during the long Showa era (1926–1989). Record companies were established with the help of foreign investments, and they became central to producing and distributing ryukoka from the late 1920s to the 1930s. Although ryukoka songs around this time were not called enka, these songs, influenced by a wide range of genres from Japanese traditional music such as *naniwa-bushi/rokyoku* to American popular music, became a foundation of enka in later years. Although ryukoka continued to be synonymous with Japanese popular music after World War II (1939–1945), songs close to today's enka emerged in the late 1940s. Both Misora Hibari (1937–1989) and Kasuga Hachiro (1924–1991), who became the first enka stars, started their careers around the end of the 1940s. In the late 1950s, production companies, instead of record companies, started to have more important roles in producing recordings and managing singers.

Enka in the earlier period tends to employ a pentatonic major (1, 2, 3, 5, 6) and a pentatonic minor (1, 2, minor 3, 5, minor 6) scales. These scales differ from scales found in Japanese traditional music in that they lack the fourth degree but resemble the latter because both lack the seventh degree. In addition, enka melodies often consist of stepwise motion instead of the leaps that are found in Western popular songs. This is largely due to the fact that enka melodies, unlike Western popular songs, are not very closely related to underlying harmonies. Lacking a harmonic basis in melodies is characteristic of Japanese traditional music in general. Most enka songs, especially those with a slow tempo, feature a very characteristic vocal technique called *kobushi*, which is a type of melismatic singing.

The term "ryukoka" gradually disappeared and was replaced by different kinds of popular music genres during the 1960s. The term "enka" started to refer to *kayokyoku* (a generic term for Japanese popular music) that has Japanese elements rather than Western-influenced sounds. Enka's original function as social criticism is taken over by *foku* (folk) songs imported from the United States after the war. A number of enka singers emerged and produced hit songs during the 1960s and the 1970s. The themes of these songs varied, including but not limited to lost love, family love, and nostalgia for a hometown. The song titles often included words such as *sake* (alcohol), *namida* (teas), *ame* (rain), and *onna* (woman). Due to the popularity of karaoke since the late 1970s, songs that are easier for amateurs to sing became more popular than technically demanding songs. Competing with other popular genres such as foku, *nyuu mujikku* ("new music"; Western-influenced popular music), and *aidoru* (idol) *kayokyoku* (kayokyoku sung by good-looking teenage girls and boys), enka flourished in the 1970s and 80s.

Although there were many enka hits in the 1980s, people's musical tastes became more and more diverse. Enka's popularity declined among Japanese youth, who preferred Western-influenced *poppusu* (pops; pop music) and *rokku* (rock). In addition, these new genres also influenced enka, creating hybrid sounds. Therefore, the definition of enka in terms of musical characteristics was gradually broadened. Some songs sounding like pop and rock could be considered enka if they were sung by enka singers. In the mid-1990s, enka's popularity drastically declined. Some record companies discontinued the enka division and dropped their artists toward the end of the 1990s.

In the 2000s, enka made a small comeback with the emergence of a few notable singers and their hit songs. One is Hikawa Kiyoshi (1977–), who has released several hit songs and received a number of awards since his debut in 2000. His popularity depended in part on his fashionable and youthful appearance, which was unusual for enka singers. Another anomaly is a mixed-race (three-quarter African American and one-quarter Japanese) singer Jero (Jerome White, Jr., 1981–), who debuted in 2008. The mismatch of his hip-hop fashion and the mastery of traditional enka singing techniques (including *kobushi*) created a sensation in the enka world, earning him many awards, including best new artist, at the Gold Disc Awards in 2008.

Although Hikawa and Jero appealed to younger audiences, enka in general is often considered to be music for elderly people. There are some enka singers who sing pop-style songs, and non-enka singers who sing enka-style songs without traditional enka singing techniques. Although some of these nontraditional enka songs became small-scale hits, enka at large has been struggling to regain the popularity it once enjoyed. In Taiwan and Southeast Asian countries such as Singapore and Malaysia, however, enka songs—both cover versions of Japanese songs and the original songs—are still favorites among the mainly Chinese population.

Yoko Suzuki

See also: Japan, Music of; Kayokyoku

Further Reading

Okada, Maki. 1991. "Musical Characteristics of Enka." *Popular Music* 10(3), 283–303.

Wajima, Yosuke. 2014. "The Birth of Enka." In *Made in Japan: Studies in Popular Music*, 71–83. New York: Routledge.

Yano, Christine Reiko. 2002. *Tears of Longing: Nostalgia and the Nation in Japanese Popular Song*. Cambridge, MA: Harvard University Press.

Erhu

The *erhu* (*er*: "two" or "the second"; *hu*: "barbarian") is one of the instruments in the *huqin* ("barbarian-(bowed-string)-instrument") family, also known as *nanhu* ("southern-hu") in southern China and Taiwan. Despite the huqin's thousand-plus years of history, the modern standard erhu only gained popularity with the establishment of *guoyue* (national music) in the early 20th century.

The erhu consists of a vertical, stick-like neck rising out of a resonator body. There are two strings that run from pegs at the top of the neck to the base, and a taut loop of strings that holds the strings close to the neck and is similar to a nut on a violin fingerboard. The pressure from the strings holds a small bridge in place on the resonator, and a bow of bamboo stem and horsehair is inserted between the strings. The body is made of wood (often padauk, ebony, or red sandalwood). The resonator is usually hexagonal, octagonal, or round. The front of the resonator is covered with python or snakeskin, while the back is partially closed with wood or bone. The two strings, traditionally made of silk, though today steel strings are commonly used, are typically tuned to the interval of a fifth—d^1 and a^1—which can produce notes spanning three octaves. In performance, the erhu is held upright with the resonator resting on the performer's left thigh. The player's left-hand fingers apply pressure to both strings at the same time, while the right hand holds the frog end of the bow. The player switches from the outer or inner strings by manipulating the pressure applied to the bow hair.

The term "erhu" is a fairly recent derivation from the older name "huqin,: which can be traced back to the Tang dynasty (618–907 CE). Even though it is not certain when and how the term "erhu" emerged, both historical documents and folklore inform us that the term made its appearance no later than the Qing dynasty (1644–1911 CE). In an early document, *Qingchao xu wenxian tongkao* (*Encyclopedia of the Historical Records of the Qing Dynasty, Continued*), the author describes erhu as one accompanying instrument in local operas of the Qing dynasty.

Moreover, there are two stories circulating about how the term "erhu" came into being. One cites *er* as "two," representing the number of the strings on the instrument, a name used by folk musicians in southern China in the late Qing dynasty. The other story regards *er* as "the second," emphasizing it being the second highest huqin in pitch in the local operas. Whatever the actual derivation of the name, the erhu was used primarily to accompany various forms of Chinese operas and narratives, or associated with the people of low social status, such as beggars or street musicians. It was not standardized, but instead varied in size and form according to the needs of the performance.

The *erhu* is a two-string spike fiddle used in Chinese music. (Lembi Buchanan/Dreamstime.com)

From the early 1920s onward, inspired by the wave of nationalistic sentiment accompanying the May Fourth Movement, a small number of Chinese academics began to modernize and "improve" Chinese music. Several important characters in the first half of the 20th century made significant impact on the reformation of the "modern erhu." Three of the most influential are discussed here.

Zhou Shaomei (1885–1938) was a pioneer and explorer of the modern erhu. Zhou was a skilled erhu (and *pipa* [Chinese four-string lute]) player. During his time, the erhu was equated with the lower class. In order to raise its position, Zhou worked on developing the instrument, especially its physical structure. He enlarged the length of the neck, expanding the range of the instrument from slightly over one octave to two or more octaves. Zhou changed the size of the resonator; he made use of special kinds of snakeskin and strings, which increased the volume of the instrument, and he set the tuning of the two strings to d^1 and a^1. In 1912, Zhou introduced

Chinese music (including the erhu) into school. Moreover, he collected and rearranged folk music, and even wrote new solo pieces and etudes for the erhu.

Liu Tianhua (1895–1932) was a significant figure in the establishment of modern erhu playing and in elevating the instrument into the academy. Liu was a teacher trained in Western music who also had a strong background in *kunqu* opera, pipa, and the folk music of the Jiangsu area. In 1917, Liu visited Zhou Shaomei. Impressed by Zhou's works, Liu also devoted his efforts to raising the status of Chinese music. Furthering Zhou's reformation of the erhu, Liu standardized the erhu, including the size of the instrument and the materials of all parts. He also designed the bow after the violin bow. Aware of the lack of a systematic training method, Liu adopted Western classical playing skills to enhance the techniques in both left-hand movement and right-hand bowing styles, and he aided pedagogy for erhu playing by composing 10 solo pieces and 47 etudes.

Even though Liu transported many Western idea and techniques into the erhu realm, his music is in many respects Chinese. For example, Liu used a lot of harmonic and sliding techniques in his pieces, which were believed to imitate the sound of *guqin* (a seven-string zither), pipa, and the regional folk music. Liu taught at Peking University from 1922 until his death in 1932. During that time, he strived to include the erhu in the agenda of music education, and he successfully elevated the instrument (and Chinese folk music) into conservatories. His pupils Jiang Fengzhu (1908–1986) and Lu Xiutang (1911–1966) were all influential during the 1930s and 1940s.

Another musician who left his mark on the history of erhu playing is Blind Abing (originally named Hua Yanjun, 1893–1950). Unlike the previous figures, who worked in academia, Abing was a Daoist monk who later became a street musician after he lost his eyesight at the age of 35. The musicologist Yang Yinliu (1899–1984) discovered him, interviewed him, and documented Abing's performance in 1950. Since then, Abing has been lauded as an example of an oppressed revolutionary for the new China. His most famous piece, "Erquan Yingyue" ("The Moon Reflected on the Second Springs"), has become one of the most popular pieces in the erhu solo repertory. The song was improvisatory in nature, depicting Abing's life as an impoverished, blind musician. It has been recorded, notated, and presented in new musical and social contexts.

Since the 1950s, countless more Chinese musicians have been involved in developing the performing techniques and repertoires for the erhu, and have achieved significant results. Today, equated to violin, erhu has become a primary instrument for solos and concertos and the leading instrument in both regional ensembles and the modern Chinese orchestra. Moreover, erhu has become a popular instrument for contemporary musicians of diverse genres as a symbol of Chineseness and folk roots.

Chia-Yu Joy Lu

See also: Huqin

Further Reading

Chen Wei. 2007. *Erhu Yishushi* [The art history of the erhu]. Hefei, China: Anhui Renmin Chubanshe.

Lau, Frederick. 2008. *Music in China: Experiencing Music, Expressing Culture* (Global Music Series). New York: Oxford University Press.

Liu, Terence. 2002. "Instruments: Erhu." In Robert C. Provine, Yosihiko Tokumaru, and J. Lawrence Witzleben (eds.), *The Garland Encyclopedia of World Music; Vol. 7: East Asia: China, Japan, and Korea*, 175–178. New York: Routledge.

Stock, Jonathan. 1993. "A Historical Account of the Chinese Two-Stringed Fiddle Erhu." *The Galpin Society Journal* 46 (March), 83–113.

Stock, Jonathan. 1996. *Musical Creativity in Twentieth-Century China: Abing: His Music, and Its Changing Meanings*. Rochester, NY: University of Rochester Press.

Tan Yong, Bihai Xu, and Xiaoli Sun. 2011. *Xibu Minzu Yunei Huqin Yanbian Ronghelu* [An integrated record of the huqin's transformation among China's Western ethnic groups]. Beijing: Minzu Chubanshe.

Thrasher, Alan R. 2000. *Chinese Musical Instruments*. New York: Oxford University Press.

Yang Mu. 1993. *Chinese Musical Instruments: An Introduction*. Canberra: Coralie Rockwell Foundation, Australian National University.

Zhang Shao. 1989. *Erhu Guangbo Jiaoxue Jiangzuo* [A compiled lesson for erhu in broadcasting teaching program]. Shanghai: Shanghai Yinyue Chubanshe.

Eurovision Song Contest

The Eurovision Song Contest is an annual international music competition in which each competitor represents one nation with a musical performance. John Kennedy O'Connor, author of Eurovision's official history, described it starting as a small event in 1956 that has since grown into a 40-nation event with billions of people watching, legions of dedicated fans, and heavy influence on several other similar contests. Vocalists and bands perform original musical compositions which are aired on television, and audiences vote for their favorite performance; however, they cannot vote for their own country's performer. The contest has become one of the most-watched television events in the world and has ignited national debates about tradition and culture. This success has not been without controversy, including political tension between countries, debates about "Europeanness," criticism about Eurovision's "watered-down" pop music, and questions about the contest's voting methods.

Eurovision Song Contest

Although it may appear very unusual to many American audiences, the Eurovision song contest has grown into one of the largest global television events each year. The contest is not without its peculiarities: chief among these are the language choices of the songs and the artists chosen to sing them for each country. There are no rules requiring countries to field singers hailing from that sponsoring home country, so many smaller countries utilize up-and-coming or established American popular music stars to sing their contest entry songs. This includes Canadian Céline Dion, who sang "Ne partez pas sans moi" for Switzerland in 1988. The language of the song entries, too, is somewhat surprising, in that a majority of song entries are in English, despite the entrant's country speaking different native languages.

Following the Second World War (1939–1945), the nations of Europe started initiatives that would bring former enemies together. One of the earliest efforts to bridge economic and political problems was the creation of the European Coal and Steel Community in 1950, which established a common market for coal and steel and paved the way for European integration that culminated decades later with the European Union. That same year, the European Broadcasting Union (EBU) was created; later, in 1954, it developed broadcasting ideas, including a one-time music competition in 1956. The competition was intended to bring together European nations and allow countries to present their best new songs to an international audience. Eurovision's first contest, hosted by Switzerland, included seven nations (only one of which was EBU member), represented by vocalists from each nation performing two songs each. According to the competition's official history, no video of the inaugural contest survives, and it is not clear how the winner was selected. Nevertheless, Eurovision proved popular, and the next year a total of 10 countries joined for a live broadcast. Over the years, the show underwent stylistic changes, and its first color broadcast in 1967 (produced in London by the BBC) helped it gain the modernized style known today by contemporary Eurovision fans. The contest has grown to host artists from several non-European nations and has also spawned numerous imitators, including the Eastern Bloc's short-lived Intervision Song Contest.

The original rules established by the EBU have since been rewritten, including changes to time limits, language requirements, and expansion of the number of nations involved. The first year was the only time nations were allowed to enter more than one song, but the contest rules then required that at least one be sung in the official language of the country being represented. The language rule was subsequently altered; however, in 1977 the EBU again required that the song must be in an official language—only to have this rule once again abolished in 1999. The live musical performance was also originally an important part of the contest, but this, too, was subsequently changed. The first backing musicians made their appearance in 1957. Though the EBU initially required all music to be sung live, the rules were gradually changed to allow prerecorded backing vocals, then prerecorded orchestras, and finally in 1997 to allow any or all music to be prerecorded.

The number of countries taking part in Eurovision has consistently grown, causing the EBU to establish qualifying events and change the format of the television broadcast. The 10th anniversary marked the biggest event yet, with 18 participating countries and 150 million viewers, including Eastern European audiences. In 1987, the EBU limited the number of competing nations to 22, and in the early 1990s it instituted a prequalification round. Starting in 1993, competitors were not guaranteed a spot, as the 22 previously participating nations received automatic enrollment and the seven other nations interested competed for the other three positions. In 2004, Eurovision underwent a major format change when 36 performances were spread across two nights. The next year saw 39 nations compete, with 25 countries participating in a prequalification round.

The selection of the winner has been one of the most exciting and controversial parts of the contest. Due to criticisms and confusion, the rules have been constantly refined since the inception of the contest. In 1957, the winner was decided by a jury made up of 10 people (one from each participating nation) voting for their favorite act; no jurors could vote for their own country. In 1962, this was modified so that the juries ranked the performances and gave points to their top three choices, which resulted in four countries receiving no points that year. Changes were again made the next year by having the judges give points to their top five; initially the size of the jury was increased to 20, but the organizers then returned the number to 10. Some countries were unclear about having a jury of 10 or 20, which led to confusion in voting and caused the Swiss to complain that they were robbed of a victory over the Danish. Then, in 1969, there was a four-way tie for the winner, which caused the rules to be revamped and reestablished with a way to break any future ties.

The problems with picking a winner caused the EBU to reformulate the process so as to ensure public confidence in the results. The rules were changed in 1972 so there were only two judges, who ranked each song with five points, but a new method of voting was instituted in 1975. It used a jury of 11 people, with six individuals between ages 16 and 25 and five between 26 and 55, who awarded points for all the songs except that of their own country. The most popular selection received 12 points, followed by 10 and eight; the songs that ranked fourth to tenth earned seven through one point. While this proved to be more complicated than previous systems, it was considered fairer and more exciting for viewers. In 1997, the Austrians, British, Germans, Swiss, and Swedish viewers voted by telephone for their favorites, and this prompted other nations to follow. Another change occurred in 2009, when professional juries of five people, selected from each nation's music industry, were used as half of the total vote and televoters made up the other half.

Eurovision has hosted many notable artists and served as the launch pad for several acts. Several singers, such as Céline Dion, Julio Iglesias, and Olivia Newton-John, appeared early in their careers and found commercial success later. In contrast, Eurovision catapulted other acts to fame and commercial success almost immediately, most notably ABBA's performance of "Waterloo" in 1974. More recently, in 2006 Lordi, a Finnish heavy metal band, was a controversial selection, and accused of being "satanists" by critics. Ultimately, Lordi's "Hard Rock Hallelujah" won the competition with the highest score ever, which pushed the song to No. 1 in Finland as well as earning them praise from the Finnish press for being the country's only Eurovision win. However, not all Eurovision winners went on to successful careers, nor have all the songs withstood the test of time. Among those criticized, Herreys's 1984 "Diggi-Loo Diggi-Ley" has been consistently named an unpopular winning song.

Aside from music, the contest has been the site of political expositions such as boycotts and protests. In 1964, a man appeared on stage with a sign that read "Boycott Franco and Salazar," but was quickly rushed offstage as the cameras panned away. In 1969, the contest was held in Madrid and Austria did not participate, citing opposition to General Franco. When Israel appeared in 1973, it caused debate about whether a non-European nation should be involved in the contest. As an EBU member, Israel was allowed to compete, but its appearance provoked questions surrounding what it meant to be European. Israel's entrance also brought security concerns, especially since the previous year had seen the massacre of Israeli Olympians in Munich. Consequently, Eurovision made safety a priority. In 1978, Israel won the competition, causing broadcasters problems in the Arab world. During Israel's performance, several Arab broadcasters aired commercials and as results were read, showing that Israel would win, many cut the transmission feed. Jerusalem hosted the contest the following year and Turkey's Arab neighbors pressured the Turks to withdraw from the competition. When Russia hosted the contest in 2009, Latvia and Georgia said they would not compete, but eventually Stefane Da 3G of Georgia joined to perform a song "We Don't Wanna Put In," an overt criticism of Vladimir Putin. Russian television complained to the EBU, which in turn ruled that the lyrics were inflammatory and had to be changed. After refusing to alter the lyrics, the group was disqualified, but earned national praise and the song became popular due to the controversy.

Race and sexuality have also been part of the competition and have played a role in discussions about national identity. In 1966, the first non-white artist (Milly Scott for the Netherlands) performed, and in 1967 the first black male singer debuted. According to Eurovision's official history, "Black artists did not fare particularly well at Eurovision until Dave Benton broke through the barrier and won for Estonia in 2001" (O'Conner, 2010, p. 46). The first openly gay artist, Paul Oskar of Iceland, performed in 1997, and the next year Dana International, an Israeli transsexual singer, won the competition. This was noteworthy due to criticism about a transsexual representing a nation with many orthodox religious people. The questions about race and sexuality debated in the Israeli national press reflected consistent struggles about how people wanted their nation portrayed, not only through music, but also in imagery on international television. Scholars such as Robert Deam Tobin have argued that the contest has become increasingly popular with lesbian, gay, bisexual, transgender, and queer (LGBTQ) audiences due to the alternative, nonessential notion of European citizenship.

Eurovision is also involved in the larger debate about what countries are considered European, which took on gained greater significance in postcommunist Europe with the expansion of the European Union. Aside from Israel, there are many countries that have been controversial additions to the competition. In 1975, Turkey made its first appearance and used Middle Eastern style, which failed to resonate with the audience and earned them last place. Yugoslavia, the only Cold War communist country to compete, won the contest in 1989, which meant that Zagreb, Yugoslavia, was chosen to host the 1990 event. The cost to Yugoslavia of producing the contest caused worries about whether the country could afford to host it, and the money spent was criticized by citizens whose wages remained low. Despite the worries and a "near disaster" during the competition that was marred with technical problems, the event was not the failure some predicted. In 1992, Yugoslavia made its last Eurovision appearance and in the following year former Yugoslav territories Bosnia-Herzegovina, Croatia, and Slovenia debuted. The songs performed by Bosnia-Herzegovina and Croatia were about the Yugoslavian war, which received international media attention. Scholar Dean Vuletic has argued that Eurovision was a location where Yugoslav distinction and division played out in an international cultural contest. In the new millennium, many new Eastern European nations joined, including Belarus, Ukraine, Macedonia, and Moldova, as well as non-European countries, including Armenia in 2006, Georgia in 2007, and Azerbaijan in 2008 (which went on to win in 2011).

Ryan Shaffer

See also: Dmitri Pokrovsky Ensemble; Rock and Roll; Seeger, Peter

Further Reading

Fricker, Karen, and Milija Gluhovic, eds. 2013. *Performing the "New" Europe: Identities, Feelings and Politics in the Eurovision Song Contest*. Basingstoke, UK: Palgrave Macmillan.

O'Connor, John Kennedy. 2010. *The Eurovision Song Contest: The Official History*. London: Carlton Books.

Raykoff, Ivan, and Robert Deam Tobin, eds. 2007. *A Song for Europe: Popular Music and Politics in the Eurovision Song Contest*. Farnham, UK: Ashgate.

F

Fado

Fado is a traditional genre of Portuguese song, typically performed by a male or female solo vocalist (called a *fadista*) to guitar accompaniment. Originating in the 19th century, the genre rose to global popularity in the mid-20th century through the widespread fame of fado singer Amália Rodrigues. Today, the genre is a symbol of Portuguese national identity and remains one of Portugal's most distinctive musical and cultural legacies.

Fado songs are typically short works with Portuguese poetic texts structured as verses with a repeated refrain. The central figure in fado performance is the fadista—a role equally realized by males and females—who performs the songs, many of which form a standard central repertory. Two guitarists, one on the traditional Portuguese guitar (*guitarra portuguesa*, a small guitar with a distinctive rounded body) and one on a classical guitar, provide the traditional instrumental accompaniment. Singers will also occasionally accompany themselves on the Portuguese guitar. Fado performances usually take place in traditional venues called *casas do fado* (houses of fado) that also function as bars and restaurants. Depending on the nature of the event, fado performances in such venues might feature professional singers, who perform a predetermined list of songs (known as *fado profissional*, or professional fado); many fado houses, however, invite amateur singers to stand at will and to perform in an improvised and spontaneous manner (known as *fado vadio*, or amateur fado). In both cases, the patrons of the bar or restaurant are the typical audience and enjoy the entertainment over a meal and conversation. Given the deep integration of fado into Portuguese cultural life, many famous Portuguese singers get their professional start singing as children and young adults in amateur performance events, such as those regularly held in the casas do fado of Lisbon and cities throughout Portugal. Due to the widespread popularity of fado since the mid-20th century, fado performances have also adapted to larger, concert-type venues, and the typical fado instrumentation has been enlarged to embrace a wider variety of styles and instruments, including full orchestral accompaniment.

The word "fado" means "fate" or "destiny" in Portuguese, and the genre is characterized by its Portuguese poetic texts, which frequently assume a deeply sentimental, melancholic, and nostalgic tone. The consummate and untranslatable Portuguese term *saudade* encompasses many of these emotions and is frequently evoked in lyrics meditating on love, homesickness, loss, and the past—focuses often attributed to the country's nostalgic cultural memory of the Portuguese "Golden Age" (Age of Discoveries) in the 15th and 16th centuries. The more traditional repertoire often presents such themes through maritime metaphors and language related to Portuguese geography and cultural history. Though fado performances utilize many traditional poetic texts, passed down through generations and forming a central standard repertory, Portuguese poets frequently contribute new texts to this growing body of literature.

Throughout its history, two distinct fado traditions have emerged in Portugal around the geographical centers of Lisbon and Coimbra. In Lisbon fado, female singers and male guitarists predominate, and performances unfold in traditional venues, as described earlier. In Coimbra, however, male singers and instrumentalists prevail, and performances revolve around the culture and traditions of the city's famous medieval university (Universidade de Coimbra). Coimbra's male university students often organize fado performances, for instance, outside the windows of their current love interests, in the style of a serenade, and perform in traditional Coimbra academic uniform (all-black uniforms with a long cloak). Distinct features in the Portuguese guitar also differentiate the Lisbon and Coimbra fado traditions, with the two locations preferring slight differences in instrument length, shape, and timbre. Although Lisbon fado remains the standard for the genre in general, Coimbra fado continues to evolve around localized performance contexts and poetic themes.

Though the exact origins of the genre are difficult to place, scholars believe that fado originated in poor neighborhoods of Lisbon in the early 19th century. During that time, the Portuguese monarchy transferred to Brazil to evade French invasions (1808–1822), and the resulting integration of Portuguese and Brazilian society in this period encouraged the mixture of numerous song and dance styles from across the Portuguese transatlantic empire. Fado probably adopted elements from both Portugal and Brazil, and today bears resemblances to various Brazilian and European song and dance genres, such as the *modinha* (a 19th-century Portuguese salon song), the *lundu* (a Brazilian dance of African origin), and the *fandango* (an Iberian dance of Spanish origin).

The earliest known Portuguese singer to achieve widespread fame for fado singing was Maria Severa Onofriana (1820–1846, known popularly as "A Severa"), a prostitute who sang fado and accompanied herself on guitar in taverns in Lisbon's Mouraria neighborhood. Though Severa died young of tuberculosis and received little recognition during her lifetime, she achieved legendary status following the production of a novel and stage play about her life in the late 19th and early 20th centuries. The Mouraria area of Lisbon has remained a center for fado performance since Severa, and several other famous fadistas, such as Fernando Maurício (1933–2003) and Mariza (1973–), grew up and developed their early careers singing in casas do fado in the same neighborhood.

From about the 1950s to the 1970s, fado enjoyed a period of intense international recognition and interest, largely due to the popularization of the genre by an innovative generation of fado singers led by Amália Rodrigues (1920–1999). Known popularly as the "Queen of Fado," Rodrigues transformed fado performance through her strong and soulful vocal timbre, impassioned performance style, original poetry, and inventive artistic collaborations. Rodrigues's influence has in many ways defined the genre since the height of her career, and she remains the foremost symbol of fado in Portuguese cultural heritage. Other notable Lisbon fado singers also contributed to the popularization of the genre around the same time as Rodrigues, such as Carlos do Carmos (1939–, son of fado singer Lucília do Carmo [1919–1998]).

Despite the widespread global influence achieved by Rodrigues and her generation of fado singers in the 1960s, Portuguese national reception of the genre was deeply impacted by the complicated political environment and upheaval of Portugal's authoritarian regime in the mid-1970s. Under the long tenure of António de Oliveira Salazar (1889–1970), who a virtual dictatorship during time as prime minister of Portugal (1932–1968), the regime sometimes controlled fado's poetic content and utilized the genre for propaganda. While this partly contributed to the genre's national popularity in Portugal in the 1950s and 1960s, following the overthrow of the government in a bloodless coup on April 25, 1974 (the Carnation Revolution), the genre suffered a marked decline in popularity and experienced increasingly negative reception due to its association with the regime. After being falsely implicated in the actions of the deposed regime, Rodrigues and her generation of fado singers regained in popularity in the late 1970s, and the genre today remains one of the most widely recognized symbols of Portuguese musical culture.

Since Rodrigues, new generations of fado singers and guitarists have continued to transform fado to meet the needs of contemporary Portuguese and international audiences. A primary figure in this new generation is Mariza Nunes (1973–) (known simply as "Mariza"), who began singing fado in Lisbon's Mouraria neighborhood around age five and has drawn together various musical influences from Portugal, Brazil, and Portuguese-speaking Africa in her fado productions. Many consider her 2002 debut album, *Fado em Mim*, the beginning of a new wave of fado by a younger generation of fado singers—yet the album acts both as a symbol of the forward motion of the genre and an homage to its past. Six of the album's 12 songs are interpretations of classic fado songs popularized by Amália Rodrigues, including "Ó Gente da Minha Terra" ("Oh, People of My Land"). Mariza's interpretation of this classic song has become an anthem of the new fado generation; the remaining songs on the album expand the traditional repertoire through new stylistic explorations. Other contemporary Portuguese fado singers also continue to interlace typical fado poetry and music with a wide variety of traditional and contemporary musical styles: Ana Moura's (1979–) album *Desfado* (2012; the title translates to "Un-fado") exemplifies this trend, blending an Afro-Brazilian dance feel with Portuguese guitar and fado poetry in the song "Desfado." On the same album, Moura unites fado style with broader global folk music tradition in a cover of Joni Mitchell's "A Case of You." Speaking of her generation of fadistas, Moura stated in a *New York Times* interview: "We all have one thing in common, and that is the desire to renew the fado. The curiosity of young people for the fado is all very recent, and I think it can best be explained by this new approach to an old music that all of us have adopted" (Rohter, 2011, p. 1).

Named an Intangible Cultural Heritage of Humanity by UNESCO in 2011, fado has become a symbol of Portuguese culture and musical patrimony. Though the genre is still transmitted through amateur performance and at home in Portuguese culture, some Portuguese schools and cultural institutions now offer professional lessons and training as well. While still centered and developed largely in Portugal, the genre can be heard in fado houses across the Portuguese-speaking world.

Carlos Saura's 2007 documentary film *Fados* captures the contemporary variety of fado performances around the globe and unites many of fado's representative voices—from archival footage of Amália Rodrigues to new interpretations by Mariza—in a wide-ranging exploration of the genre.

Danielle M. Kuntz

See also: Brazil, Music of; Rodrigues, Amália

Further Reading

Brito, Joaquim Pais de, ed. 1994. *Fado: Voices and Shadows*, trans. James Ormiston. Lisbon: Museum of Ethnology.

Elliott, Richard. 2010. *Fado and the Place of Longing: Loss, Memory and the City*. Farnham, UK: Ashgate.

Gray, Lila Ellen. 2013. *Fado Resounding: Affective Politics and Urban Life*. Durham, NC: Duke University Press.

Rohter, Larry. 2011. "Carving Out a Bold Destiny for Fado." *New York Times*, March 25. http://www.nytimes.com/2011/03/27/arts/music/ana-moura-is-among-singers-reinvigorating-fado.html?pagewanted=1.

Saura, Carlos, dir. 2009. *Fados* [DVD]. New York: Zeitgeist Films.

Vernon, Paul. 1998. *A History of the Portuguese Fado*. Brookfield, VT: Ashgate.

Fairuz (1935–)

Born Nuhad Haddad, Fairuz (or Fairouz) is one of the most famous 20th-century female singers in Lebanon and the Arab world. The work she produced with the Rahbani brothers transformed the Lebanese music scene and theater in less than three decades and created a music genre that echoed and represented the national identity at the time. Fairuz became a symbol of the Lebanese nation, a national treasure and Lebanon's own "ambassador to the stars," as she was called by the famous Lebanese poet Said Akl.

In 1947, at the age of 14, Fairuz was discovered and trained by artist Mohammed Flayfel, one of the founders of the Lebanese Conservatory, who was looking in schools for talented singers to participate in his chorus. Her talent was also recognized by Halim el Roumi (1919–1983), composer and musical director of the Lebanese Radio, who gave her a soloist position and the stage name "Fairuz" (which means "turquoise" in Arabic); he also composed several songs for her. In 1951, el Roumi presented her to Assi and Mansour Rahbani, composers who were adamant supporters of Arab and Lebanese music modernization. Assi Rahbani (1923–1986), together with his brother Mansour (1925–2009), tried to impose new forms on the Lebanese song. Looking for a female voice to interpret their new ideas, the Rahbani brothers found Fairuz to be the perfect match for their project. Fairuz then became inseparable from the Rahbani brothers, especially after her marriage to Assi in 1954. Mansour wrote the lyrics, Assi composed the music, and Fairuz sang.

Their music and songs corresponded to the political and social context of the country and the region at the time. During the 1950s, the Middle East was undergoing a series of transformations due to urban development, increasing Western influence, and the explosive advancements in media technologies. New nationalist and independent movements were arising. Musical singers and popular folkloric songs and anthems were emerging and being disseminated for a new nationalist and modern audience. The Rahbani project followed these changes and reinforced existing nationalist ideologies and movements by modeling their songs according to this new and modern "Lebanese identity."

They created a popular and national art by mixing classical Western music and popular Levantine music. At the beginning of their career, they wrote songs based on Latin dance music that was popular in the West. Over time, they became associated more with the development of a new musical form called *fulklur* (folkloric music). With the publication of their first songs, the trio caused controversy because of their adaptation of Western-style music to present Arabic lyrics. Traditionalists were against this renovation of music, but supporters of the modernization of the "Lebanese folklore" defended the project. Fairuz and the Rahbani brothers were also criticized for their use of "Western" techniques, especially the harmony and the introduction of Western orchestral instruments that were incapable of playing the Arab quarter tone.

This project started to gradually impose itself on the Lebanese and Arabic music scene, and in 1957, the committee of the Baalbeck International Festival asked Fairuz and the Rahbani brothers to prepare a Lebanese evening for the occasion of the festival's first anniversary. Fairuz inaugurated the festival and it was there that she sang live for the first time. She was then given the title of "the seventh column," alluding to the magnificent six columns of the Baalbeck's Roman temple setting. Since then, Fairuz and the Rahbani brothers became associated with this festival, where they presented an annual musical theater production until the outbreak of the Lebanese civil war in 1975.

The songs of Fairuz were known for their simplicity, speed, and content that addressed themes such as village life, children's innocence, love, life, and nation. Many of these songs were presented in musical theater pieces expressing patriotism and nostalgia for the Lebanese country life. These plays were patrimonial in the sense that they praised the Lebanese cultural identity, centering on the solidarity and union of the Lebanese and the

Lebanese singer Fairuz (Nouhad Wadie' Haddad) performing in 1979. Fairuz is one of the most influential and successful Middle Eastern artists. (Jean-Claude Francolon/Gamma-Rapho via Getty Images)

beauty of their country, which was always represented as being strong, peaceful, and unified.

Many, including her own son Ziad Rahbani, criticized Fairuz and the Rahbani brothers for creating an imaginary Lebanon that did not resemble reality. Their plays never directly mentioned what was actually happening in Lebanon. Their speech was allusive, hiding the conflicts and violence then emerging among Lebanese. Some accused the trio of making songs and plays that represented a Christian and right-wing vision of Lebanon, as their plays referred many times to the triptych of "god, country, family." Moreover, Fairuz's representation of the Lebanese woman emphasized this social conservatism, as she always appeared as chaste, immaculate, and showing a strong sense of sacrifice for society.

By the end of the 1970s, the Rahbani project came to an end. Suffering from a stroke in 1972, Assi never recovered completely and died in 1986. Assi and Fairuz were separated in 1979, which also put an end to the collaboration between the two brothers. After the death of Assi, Fairuz worked only with her son, Ziad Rahbani, starting a new musical project that was more influenced by jazz music. However, the public, accustomed to the romantic and conservative lyrics of the Rahbani brothers, did not easily accept this musical style and at first rejected Ziad's bold, humorous, and youthful lyrics.

From the early 1950s until the Lebanese civil war, Fairuz and the Rahbani brothers caused a deep change in the musical history of the region. Performing in major Arab and international cities, Fairuz became a symbol of Lebanon. Singing for the Palestinian cause, she also became "the Arabs' Voice," like Umm Kalthoum. Today her work is recognized as a patriotic, cultural, and political symbol, and has attracted admirers from many different social, national, and ideological backgrounds.

Diana Abbani

See also: Arab Classical Music; Kalthoum, Umm

Further Reading

Asmar, Sami. 1999. "Fairouz: A Voice, a Star, a Mystery." *Al Jadid* 5(27), 14–16. http://www.aljadid.com/content/fairouz-voice-star-mystery.

Boullata, Kamal, and Boulos Sargon. 1981. *Fayruz, Legend and Legacy*. Washington, DC: Forum for International Art and Culture.

Frishkopf, Michael. 2010. *Music and Media in the Arab World*. Cairo, Egypt: American University in Cairo Press.

Salem, Elise. 1999. "Imagining Lebanon through Rahbani Musicals." *Al Jadid* 5(29), 4–6. http://www.aljadid.com/content/imagining-lebanon-through-rahbani-musicals.

Stone, Christopher. 2008. *Popular Culture and Nationalism in Lebanon: The Fairouz and Rahbani Nation* (Routledge Studies in Middle Eastern Literatures). London: Routledge.

Zuhur, Sherifa. 2001. *Colors of Enchantment: Theater, Dance, Music, and the Visual Arts of the Middle East*. Cairo, Egypt: American University in Cairo Press.

Fiddle

The *fiddle*, a bowed chordophone, traces its lineage back to medieval Europe. The North American fiddle is actually a violin, with a few structural modifications and an altered performance practice. Elements that separate the fiddle from the violin include construction materials, woodworking style, and varnish, all adapted to outdoor usage. To be heard by dancers, many fiddlers use metal strings. Bowing is often more rhythmic in fiddling, and the range of desired timbres is greater, sometimes even to the extent of allowing a nasal sound. Fiddlers during the early 20th century preferred instruments created during the previous century in Europe, but some violin makers modified the instrument to accommodate these desired qualities. The German family, Stainer, made what were called "fat" instruments, with a higher arch and belly for the instrument. Although many fiddlers have some level of musical literacy, most learn their music by rote and play by ear.

Tuning may be the same as the concert violin (G-D-A-E), or employ a scordatura pattern (A-E-A-E) that allows for more drones and double stops. Old-time fiddlers most frequently play in the keys of G, D, A, and C.

Immigrants to the United States, primarily from Ireland, Scotland, and England, brought many music traditions with them, including fiddling. Fiddles were played in Europe by people of varied economic classes, from peasants to nobles. In America, the demographics were similar: the instrument was played by both Thomas Jefferson and Davy Crockett. The repertoire consists of such genres as reels, jigs, schottisches, and hornpipes. In Revolutionary-era America, many fifers were also fiddlers; thus, military marches and dance forms used by military ensembles, such as waltzes and polkas, have also become part of the fiddlers' music. Two principal styles developed during the late 19th century: old-time music (square dance) and bluegrass.

As settlers expanded the zone of settlement, regional styles became distinctive. Fiddlers perform within a wide geographic area, reaching from Alaska to the Southern states. Those in New England tended to retain Irish genres and styles, and styles in upstate New York resembled this. Styles developed in southeastern Pennsylvania differed from those in southwestern Pennsylvania and northern West Virginia. The Appalachian Mountains in Virginia were the site of other regional developments. Southern styles resembled Scottish repertoires, but also utilized African American elements, such as syncopation, and often employed the drone.

In rural and mountainous New York, the fiddle and musical ensembles served a social function. Besides uniting people during winter months, fiddle music was often heard during housewarming parties for newly married couples. In such venues the ensemble employs mock serenades, in addition to reels, lanciers, quadrilles, jigs, and hornpipes.

During the emergence of black minstrelsy during the 19th century, ensembles consisted of a fiddle and banjo duet. Both the fiddle and banjo were interchanged between Southern whites and slaves prior to the American Civil War (1861–1865). Thus, a cultural exchange of ideas occurred during the antebellum period. Some slaveholders even provided musical training, including violin, to the African Americans they owned. This situation changed drastically when the idea of Celtic and African American musicians performing together became part of a contentious ideological battle.

Many of these minstrels borrowed melodies and rhythms from Scottish or British folk songs; for example, "Backside Albany" (1815) borrows a melody from the

British folk song "Boyne Water." Somewhat later, the rise of the new industry of mail-order catalogs increase the proliferation of these instruments.

In old-time fiddling for square dances, the fiddler and caller often coordinated rhythmically. Tunes played were nursery rhymes, polkas, schottisches, reels, ragtime music, and waltzes. In contrast, bluegrass music originated in Kentucky in the 1930s. Its name is derived from the Bluegrass Boys, a band led by mandolin player Bill Monroe (1911–1996) and fiddler Art Wooten. The typical bluegrass ensemble consisted of guitars, fiddles, a mandolin, banjo, bass, and Dobro guitar. Sound was produced acoustically, with the exception of an occasional electric bass.

Following the end of Prohibition in 1932 and throughout the Great Depression, musicians were in demand, so fiddlers and similar instrumentalists learned popular tunes such as "Tiger Rag" and "Alabama Jubilee." Performance styles also differed between old-time square-dance music and bluegrass music, though the line between them is not always clear. The Bluegrass Boys and Bill Monroe expanded the tonalities to include the keys of B, B-flat, and E, to supplement Monroe's high voice. While the guitar and banjo players could employ a capo to accommodate the key changes, the fiddle, mandolin, and bass players had to transpose their music, a much more intellectually challenging activity.

The fiddle has also found its way into Native American music. The fiddle and guitar are part of Choctaw instrumental ensembles in Appalachia and other regions. Their songs include "Sally Gooden," "Orange Blossom Special," and "Old Joe Clark" (Draper, 2009). Fiddling has been incorporated into the music of Athapaskan tribes of Alaska and the Yukon, distinguished as two styles, "upriver" and "downriver." The upriver style spans the Gwich'in territory between Fort Yukon, Alaska, and Fort McPherson, Yukon, and is used in communities of the Mackenzie River Delta. The Gwich'in utilize miners' tunes and contra dances, such as "Virginia Reel," and square dance music, but employ small ensembles (fiddle and guitar duets). Much of the old-time fiddle music of the Gwich'in was brought to the region by employees of Hudson's Bay Company during the middle and late 19th century. The "downriver style," found farther west, is more prevalent in Minto, Galena, and Koyukuk, Alaska. Their tunes and styles reveal more influence from gold rushes, with larger ensembles, often called *bands*. Tanana, at the confluence of the Tanana and Yukon Rivers, marks the site of the Athapaskan Old-Time Fiddling Festival, an important intertribal festival held each June since 1983.

The fiddle has been used in several cultural and political venues. In Louisiana, Huey Long hired Will Gilmer's Leake County Revelers during campaign events of the 1930s. Originally a fiddler, Roy Acuff was a one-time candidate for Tennessee governor. Senator Albert Gore, Sr., of Tennessee, performed "Soldier's Joy" on the floor of the United States Senate. Performance styles of the fiddle also pervaded the concert hall in 20th-century American classical music. Leroy Anderson's *Fiddle Faddle* (1947) exhibits the quick tempo and festive nature of fiddle music. Aaron Copland's "Hoe Down" from *Rodeo* (1942) employs an American fiddle tune called "Bonaparte's Retreat."

Ralph Hartsock

See also: Bluegrass; Country Music; Hardanger Fiddle

Further Reading

Bronner, Simon J. 1987. *Old-Time Music Makers of New York State*. Syracuse, NY: Syracuse University Press.

Draper, David E. 2009. "Identity, Retention, and Survival." In Tara Browner (ed.), *Music of the First Nations*, 67–91. Urbana: University of Illinois Press.

Guntharp, Matthew G. 1980. *Learning the Fiddler's Ways*. University Park: Pennsylvania State University Press.

Mishler, Craig. 1993. *The Crooked Stovepipe: Athapaskan Fiddle Music and Square Dancing in Northeast Alaska and Northwest Canada*. Urbana: University of Illinois Press.

Wolfe, Charles E. 1997. *The Devil's Box: Masters of Southern Fiddling*. Nashville, TN: Country Music Foundation Press.

Field Hollers

Field hollers are an improvised form of African American song, sung by Southern laborers to accompany their work. Although related to calls and shouts, a holler differs from collective work songs in that it was sung solo, though early observers noted that a holler, or "cry," might be echoed by other workers or passed from one to another. Though commonly associated with cotton cultivation, the field holler was also sung by levee workers, mule skinners, and field hands on rice and sugar plantations.

Field hollers served a dual purpose: Farmers and other workers involved in solitary work used them to communicate with fellow workers, but hollers also served as an important means of self-expression and became more prevalent after the Civil War (1861–1865). Frederick Law Olmsted described field hollers as a "long, loud, musical shout, rising and falling and breaking into falsetto," a description that remained pertinent to examples recorded a century later (Olmsted, 1856). Field hollers are expressions; they do not tell stories or form songs in the true sense of the term. However, they are by no means devoid of pattern, and rely heavily upon the techniques of repetition and variation.

A holler typically lasts as long as one breath; then another breath is taken and the holler is repeated, often in variation. This enables field hollers to function as continuous communications to other workers. Some hollers are wordless, consisting only of vocables, such as the "Field Call" by Annie Grace Horn Dodson (1950, on the Folkways record *Negro Folk Music of Alabama*). Others feature improvised lines concerning the singer's thoughts, with elaborated syllables and melismas, such as the long example recorded at the Parchman Farm penitentiary in Mississippi in 1947, by "Bama," of a "Levee Camp Holler" (1947, on *Negro Prison Songs* [Tradition]). An unidentified singer of a camp holler was urged on with shouts and comments by his friends, suggesting that the holler could also have a social role (1941, *Negro Blues and Hollers* [Library of Congress]).

Some street cries might be considered an urban form of holler, though they serve a different function. An example is the call of "The Blackberry Woman," Dora Bliggen, in New Orleans (1954, *Been Here and Gone* [Folkways]). It is believed that the holler foreshadowed the blues, though it may actually have been influenced by blues recordings.

No recorded examples of hollers exist from before the mid-1930s, but some blues recordings, such as *Mistreatin' Mama* (Black Patti, 1927) by the harmonica player Jaybird Coleman, exhibit strong relationships to the field holler tradition. Recordings of hollers were made in the 1930s for the Library of Congress. A white tradition of "hollerin'" may be of similar age, but has not been sufficiently researched. A 1942 recording of hollers by Son House stylistically foreshadows developments in blues singing. Since 1969, an annual hollerin' contest has been held in Sampson County, North Carolina. Several of the contest champions have appeared on national television talk shows, demonstrating and preserving the tradition.

Eldonna L. May

See also: Blues; Jazz; Vaudeville; Vocables

Further Reading

Botkin, B. A., and Alan Lomax, eds. 1999. *Negro Work Songs and Calls*. Library of Congress Archive of Folk Culture, Rounder Records.

Brown, Ray B. 1954. "Some Notes on the Southern 'Holler'." *Journal of American Folklore* lxvii: 73–77.

Epstein, Dena J. 1977. *Sinful Tunes and Spirituals: Black Folk Music to the Civil War*. Urbana: University of Illinois Press.

Hendson, S. F., M. Wilson, and the Rounder Collective. 1995. *Hollerin' [the Ceased Music]*. Cambridge, MA: Rounder Records Corp. CD 0071 [disc notes].

Lomax, Alan. 1957. "Murderer's Home." Negro Prison Songs, Tradition 1020 [disc notes].

Olmsted, Frederick L. 1856. *A Journey in the Seaboard Slave States in the Years 1853–1854*. New York: Dix and Edwards.

Southern, Eileen. 1973. "Afro-American Musical Materials." *Black Perspective in Music* (0090–7790), 1(1), 24.

Flamenco Music

Flamenco is often considered one of the most important music-dance traditions in Spain, and has gained immense popularity worldwide. Despite its global presence, flamenco is most commonly associated with the southern Spanish region of Andalusia. Flamenco consists of a "continuum of styles," from large-scale spectacles to intimate performances (Manuel, 1989, p. 47). Generally speaking, flamenco consists of a combination of three key elements: song (*cante*), guitar (*toque*), and dance (*baile*). Traditionally, the song has always occupied the most prestigious position in the flamenco world. Due to flamenco's international popularity, however, the guitar and dance have become the most famous features of the tradition. Since the 1970s, flamenco musicians have fused traditional styles with other musical traditions from around the world. Nowadays, flamenco is a truly global art form, while remaining firmly rooted to its Spanish/Andalusian origins.

HISTORY

According to most scholars, flamenco emerged in southern Spain under the influence of numerous groups, including Andalusians, Arabs, gypsies (*gitanos*), and

Jews. In particular, Spain's Islamic heritage (711–1492 CE) is viewed as a crucial factor in the emergence of early styles that would later form the basis for flamenco. Nonetheless, how flamenco developed as a cohesive tradition is often the subject of scholarly debate (Washabaugh, 1996). For some, flamenco is synonymous with gitano ethnicity, having allegedly developed exclusively amongst gitano families. Others place emphasis on the contributions of Andalusian lower classes (*payos*), who used flamenco to voice their social woes. What is clear is that flamenco as a consolidated tradition only appeared in the 19th century. Although earlier musical styles may have influenced the development of flamenco, its standardization as a recognizable tradition only occurred during this period. Historian Timothy Mitchell (1994) believes that flamenco began to form at the beginning of the 19th century, basing his research on historical accounts that depict flamenco performances and jam sessions (*juergas*) in gitano homes, bars, and taverns. According to Mitchell, flamenco was patronized by *señoritos* who were wealthy members of the upper class and who were attracted to the flamboyant and lower-class performance styles of flamenco. This interaction between lower-class musicians and upper-class patrons enabled flamenco to gain a place in the theater scene.

In the mid-19th century, a number of specialized venues called *cafés cantantes* opened across Spain, which were devoted to flamenco and offered artists a context in which they could earn money through performance. In these venues flamenco became more accessible to a larger audience, particularly the middle classes.

The increased popularity of flamenco during this time is partly due to the prominence of romanticism in 19th-century Europe. Many people were attracted by the exotic and the oriental. Flamenco's flamboyant dance style, its Arabic-sounding musical style, and its association with gypsies suited the tastes of the time, not only in Spain but also in other countries such as France. In addition to increasing the popularity of flamenco, the cafés cantantes also helped consolidate flamenco as a tradition. Many of the styles that are now associated with flamenco were standardized in the cafés cantantes. The guitarist was also emancipated from the traditional role as an accompanist for singers. The instrument began to feature in solo performances, with guitarists performing more complex techniques and compositions. Flamenco also became more commercialized during this time, with dance playing an important role in the popularization of the tradition.

This commercialization was not well received by everyone. In the late 1800s, Antonio Machado Álvarez (1848–1893), otherwise known as Demófilo, attempted to salvage the flamenco tradition by collecting lyrics from nonprofessionals (often gitanos). Demófilo viewed flamenco as an Andalusian-gitano folk tradition that was being tainted by theaters and that needed to return to its "pure" roots. Later intellectuals and composers followed a similar line, most notably the poet Frederico García Lorca (1898–1936) and the composer Manuel de Falla (1876–1946). They hoped to revive traditional flamenco by staging the *Concurso del cante jondo* (Competition of Deep Song) in 1922, a competition that attracted nonprofessional musicians who had grown up with flamenco in the family context. This competition occurred at a time when flamenco's commercialization in the theaters was becoming more prominent, particularly with the creation of *opera flamenca* (flamenco opera) during the 1920s. This theatrical genre was a more diluted form of traditional flamenco that drew influences from South American styles and was characterized by a highly ornamented vocal style.

During the early 20th century, flamenco was also closely tied to profound social and political changes in Spain. In the 1930s, intellectuals such as Blas Infante (1885–1936) tried to combine flamenco with Andalusian regionalist politics. At this time, some regions of Spain wanted their own autonomous powers and regional identities (regionalism). In Andalusia, Infante was considered the father of Andalusian regionalism and recognized flamenco as a powerful symbol of regional identity. However, in 1936 the Spanish Civil War broke out, and in 1939 the dictator Francisco Franco (1892–1975) came to power and implemented a suppressive and nationalist regime. During the regime, flamenco became a state-sponsored art form and was reconstructed as a distinctly national identity symbol. In particular, flamenco was utilized for the tourist industry as a display of exoticism. Therefore, during the 1950s a number of flamenco clubs (*tabalos*) opened up across Spain, catering almost exclusively to the tourist trade for which dance was the most important feature.

Traditional flamenco also went through somewhat of a revival during the Franco regime. In the 1950s, gitanos began to reclaim flamenco as a tradition unique to their ethnicity. Some scholars believe that this was allowed during the regime because it separated flamenco from politics and its association with regional identity. A number of developments happened during this time: flamenco scholarship developed (known as *flamencología*), artists began to salvage older styles, and a network of clubs (*peñas*) opened that were devoted to the performance of traditional flamenco. The gitano singer and scholar Antonio Mairena (1909–1983) helped consolidate the idea that flamenco was a purely gypsy art and that anything performed by payos was not "authentic." While often criticized for his biased view, Mairena's perspective is still upheld by some.

In the 1970s, flamenco began to diversify both politically and geographically. Some artists, such as the singer Manuel Gerena (1945–), used flamenco as a tool to express political messages, particularly as they related to social class and regional identity. Others, such as the renowned guitarist Paco de Lucía (1947–2014), helped globalize flamenco by adding new instruments and styles that brought the tradition to a fresh audience. The globalization of flamenco became more prominent following Franco's death in 1975, which enabled the creation of a modern and democratic Spain. In 1978, a new Spanish Constitution was created and 17 autonomous regions were recognized. These dramatic political changes in Spain encouraged flamenco to modernize and internationalize, allowing the tradition to enter the international market. The reclamation of regional identity following the dictatorship also meant that flamenco was used once again as a symbol of Andalusian identity.

FLAMENCO MUSIC AND DANCE

Flamenco is characterized by a number of mini-styles, referred to as *palos*, that consist of unique musical, lyrical, and dance-related features. According to the ethnomusicologist Peter Manuel (2010, p. 107), there are around 12 key palos that make up the classical repertoire. However, beyond these key styles there are many more palos that can be found in the flamenco tradition. Palos are often grouped into different categories. On one level, individual palos belong to a larger family that may be united by common musical features and lyrical themes. For example, the *soleá* (often considered the "mother" of flamenco) belongs to a larger group referred to as the *cante jondo* (deep song). This genre of palos is characterized by tragic lyrics and a modal tonality. At another level, individual palos may be broken down into different substyles (*estilos*). For example, a palo may be recognized by its geographical origin, such as the *soleá de Triana*—a soleá that originated in the Triana neighborhood of Seville (the capital of Andalusia). Most of the flamenco repertoire comes from different areas of Andalusia, with palos being found throughout the eight provinces of the region. However, there are some styles that show influences from other regions of Spain, or even other countries, such as the genre *ida y vuelta* ("round trip"), which draws influences from South America.

Musically, flamenco is characterized by a number of distinct features. Vocal and guitar music are often based on the Andalusian mode. This scale is equivalent to a major Phrygian mode in classical music (for example, in E the scale would be: E, F, G#, A, B, C, D). Using this mode, guitar music is often based on a chord sequence called the *Andalusian cadence* (again, using the Phrygian in E, the chords would be A minor, G major, F major, and E major). A number of the more festive and joyous palos use a major key with a typical I-IV-V chord sequence. Rhythmically, each palo uses a specific time cycle (*compás*), with many palos sharing the same cycle. Most *compás* cycles consist of 12 beats with accents on 3, 6, 8, 10, and 12. Depending on the palo, the starting point of each cycle will differ. For example, a soleá begins on beat one, whereas a *seguiriya* begins on beat eight. This means that many flamenco styles are based around the interaction between groups of 6/8 and 3/4. Some palos use simple 4/4 time, whereas others are unmetered with no strict rhythmic structure.

When people think of flamenco, they usually think of the dance, as it is the most recognizable aspect of the tradition. Traditionally, however, the song (*cante*) is considered the most important part. Some flamenco songs are very old, with the oldest palos often performed without accompaniment. Normally, though, the singer is accompanied by a guitarist who provides the rhythmic and harmonic framework. Flamenco lyrics normally consist of different verses (*coplas*) that contain three- to five-line stanzas. Thematically, these lyrics cover a range of emotions, from the tragic and profound (death, sadness, and loss) to the joyous. Lyrics are often anonymous and are passed down over generations. However, nowadays it is common for the *cantaor* (the word used for a flamenco singer) to sing lyrics based on the works of famous Andalusian poets such as Frederico García Lorca. While not a traditional practice, some artists will compose their own lyrics, particularly for political motives. One characteristic feature of flamenco lyrics is the strong Andalusian accent that is used, which is notoriously difficult to understand even for Spaniards.

Flamenco singing has a unique performance style that is peculiar to southern Spain, while retaining elements that are reminiscent of singing styles in the Middle East. The vocal style is highly melismatic (extending a single syllable over many notes) and ornamented with the use of microtones. This style is believed to be a remnant of Spain's Islamic heritage and is particularly pronounced in older song forms. Singers also adopt a very rough vocal style, often referred to as *voz ronca* (hoarse voice), a performance technique that is often linked to gitano identity. Along with this rough vocal production, singers often use vocal sobs and impassioned facial expressions. This uniquely flamenco style has a social significance, being viewed as a symbol of social hardship and inequality amongst the lower classes and gitanos in Andalusian history. If singers have reached an intense emotional connection with the audience, they are said to have achieved the state of *duende*. This term is used for great artists (usually singers) who have reached the pinnacle of their art, moving the audience in a profound way. This communication between artist and audience is usually heightened by the *jaleo*, which refers to the calls of encouragement and recognition from audience members during a performance (such as shouts of ¡*olé!*).

Arguably, it is the guitar (*toque*) that is at the forefront of innovation and creativity in flamenco. It is the international ambassador for the tradition, and flamenco guitarists perform in the most prestigious concert halls around the world. This is significant given the guitar's humble beginnings as an accompanying instrument for the cante. Although the guitar is still used in this capacity, it is also used as a solo instrument and can steal the show in group performances. Beginning with the technical advancements of guitarists such as Ramón Montoya (1880–1949) during the cafés cantantes period, the guitar has become a virtuosic instrument with new generations of guitarists constantly pushing the boundaries of technique and style.

In terms of construction, flamenco guitars are very similar to Spanish classical guitars. However, they often have lighter bodies to achieve a more percussive sound with a shorter sustain, preferable for accompanying song and dance. Traditionally, flamenco guitars had tuning pegs made of wood. Nowadays, however, most guitarists opt for guitars with typical machine heads. As in the cante, the construction of the guitar assists in the production of the rough and "unclean" timbre preferred in flamenco performance. Often flamenco guitars are built with a slight buzz which adds to the aesthetic soundworld.

Flamenco guitar technique also assists in the production of this particular timbre. Guitarists use a number of unique right-hand techniques that produce a rough sound that is enhanced by playing close to the bridge. Techniques include the characteristic strumming patterns (*rasgueado*) that consist of various permutations of the right-hand fingers and thumb. Additional techniques include the *alzapúa*, where the thumbnail is used in a rapid up-and-down motion (similar to the use of a plectrum), florid arpeggios, and tremolo. When accompanying a singer, the guitarist must retain the rhythmic framework of the compás (where necessary) and introduce rasgueado sections that mark the accents and outline the harmony. The guitarist will interject short melodic passages (*falsetas*) in between a singer's verses or a dancer's movements in a partly improvised fashion. Traditionally, these falsetas were anonymously passed down through the generations. More commonly now, guitarists compose their own falsetas, which are then passed onto other guitarists. In a solo context, the guitarist tries to evoke the whole flamenco soundworld through using strummed sections and falsetas to perform particular palos. Often these solo versions of palos became compositions in their own right, later performed in their entirety by subsequent guitarists.

Like the guitar and song, flamenco dance (*baile*) emerged in small, private contexts and was a source of cathartic expression. During the cafés cantantes era, dance became far more popular and exuberant, fulfilling the popular tastes of the day and giving birth to so-called "classical" dance. Nowadays, dance is perhaps the most common international representation of flamenco and many people are familiar with the stereotypical image of a dark-haired gypsy dancer wearing a polka-dotted red dress. Generally speaking, flamenco dance can be broken down into two key elements: the upper body and footwork. In terms of the upper body, dancers use florid arm and hand movements and graceful turns. The flamenco dress (*bata de cola*) usually has a long, ruffled tail that is used within dance movements. In terms of the footwork (*zapateo*), flamenco dancers adopt a very rough and percussive technique using rapid and rhythmic stamping of the feet. In the traditional gitano style, dancers use a less virtuosic technique and the routines are often improvised. "Classical" flamenco dancers, however, adopt a more virtuosic style, often adopting influence from ballet or contemporary dance. Modern dance is usually choreographed, with distinct sections and movements being performed in different palos. In both styles, flamenco dance is characterized by its intensity and emotional content. In any flamenco performance artists are usually accompanied by *palmas*, which refers to rhythmic clapping patterns that mark out the compás.

INTO THE FUTURE

In recent years, flamenco has seen a large increase in popularity both within Spain and globally. The cante, toque, and baile have expanded in terms of technique and style, and performers of all nationalities have become interested in the art. In part, this is due to the work of prolific artists such as Paco de Lucía and the cantaor Camarón de la Isla (1950–1992). Such artists have modernized the tradition, bringing it to new audiences and introducing new styles. In particular, Paco de Lucía is recognized as having created the genre *flamenco nuevo* (new flamenco) where traditional styles are mixed with other musical traditions such as jazz, Latin American music, and popular music. He also introduced other instruments, such as the *cajón* (a box-shaped percussion instrument), bass, and flute. This new fusion music has been continued and developed by a number of groups and artists, including Ketama and the singer Enrique Morente (1942–2010). Flamenco has now become a popular genre on the world music scene, and is featured at many international concerts and festivals. In recognition of its international popularity, flamenco was declared an Intangible Cultural Heritage of Humanity by UNESCO in 2010. This declaration means that the tradition will be preserved and developed for future generations, both in Spain and internationally.

As flamenco has become more global, it has also become more "regional," and is viewed as a powerful symbol of regional identity in Andalusia. In recent years, flamenco has become the object of great political interest and is used by the Andalusian government to express regional identity both in Andalusia and abroad (Washabaugh, 2012). This indicates a return to the politics of autonomy in Spain, where each of the

17 autonomous regions has been encouraged to represent and support its own regional culture. Even though flamenco is recognized as a Spanish music, its close historical links to Andalusia has meant that it is now representative of that region. As a result, the Andalusian government is developing the tradition within and outside of the region, investing heavily in flamenco performances and performers. This institutional development and the UNESCO declaration mean that flamenco will continue to thrive, delighting audiences in its homeland of Andalusia and around the globe.

Matthew Machin-Autenrieth

See also: Basque, Music of the; Fado

Further Reading

Chuse, Loren. 2003. *The Cantaoras: Music, Gender, and Identity in Flamenco Song.* London: Routledge.

Manuel, Peter. 1989. "Andalusian, Gypsy and Class Identity in the Contemporary Flamenco Complex." *Ethnomusicology* 33(1), 47–65.

Manuel, Peter. 2006. "Flamenco in Focus: An Analysis of a Performance of Soleares." In Michael Tenzer (ed.), *Analytical Studies in World Music*, 92–119. Oxford: Oxford University Press.

Manuel, Peter. 2010. "Composition, Authorship, and Ownership in Flamenco, Past and Present." *Ethnomusicology* 54(1), 106–135.

Miles, Elizabeth J., and Loren Chuse. 2000. "Spain." In Timothy Rice, James Porter, and Chris Goertzen (eds.), *The Garland Encyclopedia of World Music; Vol. 8: Europe*, 588–603. London: Routledge.

Mitchell, Timothy. 1994. *Flamenco Deep Song.* New Haven, CT: Yale University Press.

Washabaugh, William. 1996. *Flamenco: Passion, Politics, and Popular Culture.* Oxford: Berg.

Washabaugh, William. 2012. *Flamenco Music and National Identity in Spain.* Farnham, UK: Ashgate.

Woodall, James. 1992. *In Search of the Firedance: Spain through Flamenco.* London: Sinclair-Stevenson.

Folkways Records

Founded in 1948 by Moses Asch (1905–1986) and his former assistant Marian Distler (1919–1964), Folkways Records and Service Corporation was an innovative and influential record label based in New York City. The company's objective, according to Asch, was to document "all the sound of the world" (Carlin, 2008, p. xviii), and to this end the label issued everything from jazz, blues, folk music, and classical music, to recordings of nature sounds, spoken word, sound effects, and language instruction. The label is primarily known for its contributions to American folk music, having issued important recordings by Woody Guthrie, Pete Seeger, and Huddie "Lead Belly" Ledbetter, and for producing some of the earliest commercial recordings of world music. Under the direction of anthropologist Harold Courlander (1908–1996), Folkways Records established the "Ethnic Folkways Library" series which, by 1960, included field recordings of music from Haiti, Indonesia, India, Equatorial Guinea, Palestine, Ukraine, Romania, Korea, Spain, Pakistan, Ethiopia, Cuba, Japan, Norway, Myanmar, Ghana, and more.

Folkways Records was Moses Asch's third attempt at success in the record industry, following the earlier failure of his Asch Records (1939–1945) and Disc Records of America (1945–1947). Taking it as his mission to preserve the ethnic music and culture of people throughout the world, Asch adopted the name "Folkways" (coined by sociologist William Graham Sumner) to describe the specific type of material his company would produce: the sounds of "the folk." To further augment his emphasis on preservation and education, Asch also insisted that each Folkways release contain a separate booklet of thorough liner notes, which provided a general context for the album as well as specific information about each track.

Unlike most record companies at the time—whose financial security depended on massive sales of hit records—the Folkways business model was to sell smaller quantities of each record it produced, but make up the difference with a large catalog of titles, none of which were ever discontinued. Therefore, while Folkways had a few successful releases (the label's best-selling album was 1966's *You'll Sing a Song and I'll Sing a Song* by children's music singer Ella Jenkins), the majority of the label's output comprised niche albums with limited commercial appeal. The titles in the Ethnic Folkways Library, for example, were designed as archival material for anthropologists and musicologists; the few copies sold usually went to libraries and universities. By the time of Asch's death in 1986, the Folkways catalog contained 2,168 titles, nearly all of which had been kept in print continuously.

The Smithsonian Institution Center for Folklife and Cultural Heritage acquired Folkways Records in 1987 and established the Moses and Frances Asch Collection, which includes the company's master tapes, business papers, and album artwork. As part of the negotiations with Asch prior to his death, the Smithsonian agreed to keep the substantial Folkways catalog intact and to ensure each title's availability forever. In 1998, the Smithsonian relaunched Folkways Records as Smithsonian Folkways Recordings, which maintains the label's back catalog and issues new material in the spirit of the original Folkways recordings.

Brian F. Wright

See also: Guthrie, Woody; Lead Belly; Seeger, Peter

Further Reading

Carlin, Richard. 2008. *Worlds of Sound: The Story of Smithsonian Folkways.* New York: Smithsonian Books.

Goldsmith, Peter D. 1998. *Making People's Music: Moe Asch and Folkways Records.* Washington, DC: Smithsonian Institution Press.

Olmstead, Anthony. 2003. *Folkways Records: Moses Asch and his Encyclopedia of Sound.* New York: Routledge.

Smithsonian Folkways. n.d. "Folkways Records." http://www.folkways.si.edu/folkways-records/smithsonian.

Foster, Stephen Collins (1826–1864)

Stephen Foster was the first American composer ever to earn a living solely from the sale of his music. He published nearly 300 works, mostly songs. Though they form only a small percentage of his output, he is best known today for his plantation

Stephen Foster (1826–1864) is considered the father of American music. He was one of the earliest prominent American songwriters and composers. (Library of Congress)

songs or "Ethiopian Melodies." These often contain lyrics horribly racist by today's standards. They were considered suspect: "trashy and objectionable" in Foster's own words. His work evolved as he matured, and his legacy should today be viewed in its totality, rather than on the basis of a few early songs.

Foster was born in Pittsburgh, Pennsylvania, on July 4, 1826. He came from a nonmusical family and was never formally trained as a composer, nor did he have instruction on any the many instruments that he taught himself. He came from a businessman's family, and at the age of 20 did what was expected of him, moving to Cincinnati to work as a bookkeeper in his brother's steamboat company. While there, he sold his first great hit, "Susanna," for $100. He eventually left his brother's company, signed his first formal publishing contract, and entered the 1850s at the height of his creative powers (Root, 2014).

Marrying in 1851, Foster and his new wife took a steamboat trip to New Orleans on a belated honeymoon in 1852. Ironically, this was the only time the composer, so closely associated with the Old South, ever travelled there. His life, having started so well, turned bad very quickly. In 1854 he separated from his wife, and in 1855 both his parents died. He very nearly stopped composing, producing only one song each in 1856 and 1857. He went deeply into debt, borrowing money against future songs that he then struggled to compose. During this time he increasingly turned to alcohol to cope. After 1860, Foster lived in New York City, near to publishers and performers, where he produced well over a hundred songs, though only two were of any note: "Old Black Joe" in 1860, and "Beautiful Dreamer," written in 1862 and published after his death. In early 1864, weak from pneumonia, Foster fell in his unheated boarding-house room, severely cutting his neck on a washbasin. He died three days later in Bellevue Hospital at the age of 37 (Smolko and Saunders, 2009, pp. 3–7).

Foster was a master of assimilation. He was exposed not only to the Scots-English folk music of the region, but also to the music of immigrant Germans who made Pittsburgh their home. Additionally, in the polite parlor society, Foster learned the elegant vocalism of the Italian opera, which he used in "Ah, May the Red Rose," among others. In 1854 he published a series of instrumental arrangements in *The*

Social Orchestra that included five "Gems" by Gaetano Donizetti from *Lucia di Lammermoor* (Foster, 1974). Other songs echo Schubert *lieder*. "Sadly to Mine Heart Appealing" specifically quotes "Ständchen" (Smolko and Saunders, 2009, p. 6). The Scots-English tradition influenced Foster's "Gentle Annie" and many others (Jackson, 1936, pp. 154–169). The specific musical influence of black spirituals is more difficult to find, and remains elusive and unproven (Jackson, 1936, pp. 155–156).

Foster was generally his own lyricist. This created a close, powerful bond between words and music that possibly accounts for much of the music's visceral impact. The vast majority of his songs were for the parlor or salon. This intimate setting was a primary meeting place for middle-class society in both the United States and Europe in the 19th century. Partly as a response to the increased mechanization of society and industry, the 19th-century person of education and taste increasingly turned inward to poetry, novels, and songs of sentimentality. Foster understood this milieu, having grown up in it, and carefully tailored his creations to it. Songs of sentiment were sophisticated, genteel, and aimed for effect without requiring too much technical ability. His songs, though mostly written for amateur singers—the range is rarely more than an octave and a step—create seeming virtuosity by the careful arrangement of stepwise motion interrupted by a dramatic, upward leap. The accompaniments are easy to play but musically effective.

The most important aspect of his legacy, and the source of the majority of his earnings, the "Ethiopian Melodies" were often crude, comic songs with coarse lyrics and simple stepwise melodic movement. These were performed primarily in minstrel shows (theatrical productions with white performers in blackface) and played to the crudest racial stereotypes in text and music. Some of Foster's first songs, such as "Susanna," fall firmly into this category, but his later efforts are much more subtle and lyrical, incorporating more elements of his parlor style. Ironically, like his one trip to the South, Foster seems to have seen few, if any, of the minstrel shows during his busiest period composing for them (Root, 2014).

In 1850, Harriet Beecher Stowe (1811–1896) wrote the highly influential abolitionist novel *Uncle Tom's Cabin*. Around the same time, Foster's Ethiopian Melodies began to change. "Nelly Was a Lady" is apparently the first ever published song in which a black woman is described as a lady (Saunders, 2012, pp. 275–289) and her grieving husband is a figure of great dignity. "My Old Kentucky Home" was used in staged versions of *Uncle Tom's Cabin*; the interior verses speak movingly of the tragedy of families being torn apart and sold. Foster himself, in a letter to the leader of the most important minstrel group, E. P. Christy, asked to have his name reinstated as composer (Christy had been named composer in the first publications of the song "Old Folks at Home") and expressed his intention of elevating the genre. In another letter to Christy, he directed his songs be to be sung in a tragic, rather than comic, manner. In later versions of early songs, he removed exaggerated, mocking dialect and replaced it with standard English (replacing "ribber" with "river," for example). Foster's genius was, increasingly, to be able to infuse his songs for the minstrel shows with a transcendent humanity that spoke across class and race. Frederick Douglass (1818–1895), the escaped former slave and prominent abolitionist, in speaking about Foster's songs, said: "[We] have allies in the Ethiopian songs. They awaken sympathies for the slave in which anti-slavery principles take root and flourish" (Emerson, 2012, p. 403).

Foster's music never ceased to be popular, even if the composer himself was sometimes lost in the shuffle. It has been used in more than 600 films and television productions, becoming an inextricable part of the fabric of the American musical heritage (Haines, 2012, p. 306). Though not the first important American composer, he was the first to be heard internationally, and perhaps a dozen of his best songs remain instantly recognizable around the world.

Robert Crowe

See also: Virginia Minstrels

Further Reading

Emerson, Ken. 1998. *Doo Dah! Stephen Foster and the Rise of American Popular Culture.* New York: Da Capo Press.

Emerson, Ken. 2012. "Stephen Foster and American Popular Culture," *American Music* 30, 397–404.

Foster, Morrison. 1896. *Biography, Songs and Musical Compositions of Stephen C. Foster.* n.p.: Percy S. Smith Printing.

Foster, Stephen. 1973. *The Social Orchestra.* New York: Da Capo Press.

Haines, Kathy Miller. 2012. "Stephen Foster's Music in Motion Pictures and Television." *American Music* 30, 373–388.

Jackson, George Pullen. 1936. "Stephen Foster's Debt to American Folk-Song." *The Musical Quarterly* 22, 154–169.

Root, Deane. 2014. "Foster, Stephen C." *Grove Music Online.* http://www.oxfordmusiconline.com.

Saunders, Steven. 2012. "The Social Agenda of Stephen Foster's Plantation Melodies." *American Music* 30, 275–289.

Smolko, Joanna, and Stephen Saunders. 2009. *Stephen Collins Foster: Sixty Favorite Songs.* Pacific, MO: Mel Bay Productions.

French Folk Dances

Folk dancing in France began as medieval round dances, from which developed the *farandole* chain dance, the wild *carmagnole* of the French Revolution, and diverse regional *branles*. Most early branles (both line- and circle-dance forms) were accompanied by *a cappella* singing. When Catherine de Medici's luxury-loving court moved from Italy to France in 1547, the *branle de Poitou, branle des Brandons,* and *branles nimes* were in vogue. They brought with them the early *courante*, which passed through three distinct phases of development.

The first book on dance was written as a series of Socratic conversations by Jehan Tabourot under the pen name of Thoinot Arbeau (*Orchesographie*, 1587). Arm positions were shown as low and relaxed, with hands resting on hips, skirts, and swords. Fifteenth-century forms added specific steps and figures for couples, but did not yet require the toes and knees to be "turned out" in the manner of Baroque dance and ballet. The stately *basse danse* (including later courtly types such as the processional *pavane*) alternated with a variety of *haut danse* forms (incorporating leaps, jumps, and higher footwork). The pavane (from the Latin *pavo*, or peacock), was a stately figured dance of Spanish and Italian origin, notated by the letters "s" (for a simple step) and "d" (for a double step). Its basic step required the dancer to bend both knees, then step forward onto the ball of one foot, and bend both knees as the second foot slid forward. Double steps involved three steps forward before the *plié*.

Arbeau described the triple-time *galliard* as a series of four light jumps on alternating feet, with one leg suspended gently in front of the center of gravity. The fourth jump, called the *saut majeur*, took two pulses, followed by both feet coming together in a *posture*. The English sometimes referred to the dance as the "sink-a-pace" since there were *cinq pas* (five steps) per six-beat phrase. This partner dance involved more elaborate figuration and travel for male dancers, who were praised for the height of their leaps. The galliard rhythm provides one note for every jump or step and is recognizable in the current British national anthem (*God Save the Queen*), chosen by Elizabeth I of England. Both Sir John Davies (*Orchestra*, 1596) and composer Thomas Morley (*A Plaine and Easie Introduction to Practical Musicke*, 1597), described courantes, galliards, and *voltas* danced in the French style.

Figured dances of the French Baroque were incorporated in musical suites; they include the courante, the *sarabande*, the *menuet*, and the *gavotte*. This second courante, developed from the *branle de Poitou* in France, was the most popular dance from 1550 to 1700. A running (*courir*) couples dance characterized by short advances and retreats, the courante was a sprightly and vigorous dance in triple time. Its chief steps were *pas glissés*, and it included springing steps, turns, *coupé* and *jetté* steps, and short *pas de basque* circles.

By 1661, French folk and court dance had diverged, with Louis XIV establishing the first professional dance school in Europe (Académie Royale de Danse) with 13 experts in court, character, and folk dance. French courtiers at Versailles enjoyed opportunities to dress as country folk throughout the 18th century, and court fashion followed the fashion of peasant women shortening their dresses to the instep (for dancing). The stately French Baroque court menuet also developed from the bawdy branle de Pitou, but gradually slowed until each third beat in triple time could accommodate a graceful pose in plié. While a variety of figures (the Z-formation being the most common) were used, letters could be spelled out through the floor patterns of dancers, who proceeded in symmetrical opposition to each other, rather than as paired dancers throughout. The main step of the dance became highly stylized, with four of six beats in plié, extreme turnout of the toes, and a sideways grapevine step that mirrored the grace and artificiality of 18th-century French court life. Arm movements became much more elaborate, and ladies even manipulated fans in complex patterns while dancing.

In the French royal court, many of the *danses anglaises* were reworked with some of the Breton longways formations in opposite lines of alternating couples, and the French term *contredanse* (sometimes *contredanse française*) began to be used to denote those dances. By 1706, French dance master Feuillet's *Recueil de Contredanses* included more than 30 dances in the longways formation. In 1710, dance master John Essex translated Feuillet's book *For the Further Improvement of*

Dancing and described the contredanse as a specific "sequence of figures" arranged in combinations of "two-or four-bar step combinations"; interrupting the set figures of the dance was a series of 12 short "changes."

In colonial Virginia, Southern landowners patterned their social dancing after the aristocracy of England and France. Virginian aristocrat William Byrd noted that the governor's ball in Williamsburg on February 6, 1711, was officially opened "with a French dance" (most likely the minuet). The ball continued with "several more French dances" performed by the other invited guests. After the conclusion of the French dances, they "danced country dances for an hour." Plantation owner Robert Beverly had in his personal library a translated version of Pierre Rameau's *Le maître à danser* (1725). Charles and Mary Stagg established a theater and taught French dancing both at the College of William and Mary and in a private school (from 1716, until Charles's death in 1736, although Mary taught until 1745 and sponsored assembly balls). They owned copies of Raoul Feuillet's *Chorégraphie* and Rameau's *Le maître*, which were particularly valuable for teaching protocol, etiquette, five foot positions, and discipline.

During the years 1760 to 1785, French publishers Landrin and La Cuisse issued dance instruction manuals and annual "collections of dances." They included all sorts of contredanses and *cotillons*, including a series of 12 figured contredanses and English country dances. Most of the La Cuisse pamphlets were four pages long and featured step descriptions of a single dance, an illustration, and suggestions for music. La Cuisse also improved on Feuillet's dance notation system in an instructional manual that contained more than 85 contredanses and variations (*Le répertoire des bals*, 1762). When the popular French contredanse was danced in England, its name was translated into English as "Contra dancing." This involved many of the same figures and techniques, such as smooth interweaving figures and the camaraderie of couples. The French also adapted the round dances described in Playford's editions of *The Dancing-Master*; however, most French dances were limited to a "round for eight," with a maximum of four couples. Both the reworked Contra formation and the circle dances were grouped under the general title of *cotillon*. The French word was loosely translated as "petticoat" and was first popular in France around 1723. By the 1770s, the French cotillon and menuet were introduced in most French colonies (formal balls still opened with a minuet, followed by a long set of French cotillon folk dances, intermission, and then a second half of English country dances). Americans and Canadians still followed the European lead for new dances—especially the French.

The best-known French folk dance today is the *bourrée*, which is a direct descendant of the rustic branles danced with clogs in Auverne and Berry. The Bourbonnais style of bourrée (with partners facing each other, arranged in a longways set of couples) is commonly danced in urban "*bals folk*" throughout Europe. Local rural bourrée variants exist in Auvergne, Berry, Nivernais, and Moran. Although modern folk dancing includes players of the *vielle* (hurdy-gurdy) and *musette* (folk bagpipe), early bourrée accompaniments were mostly sung. Author George Sand described superstitions regarding such musicians in her writings, and a large society based in Nohant (Department of Indre) was founded in 1888 for the encouragement of such folk music and dance. Germain and Louise Hébert of Quebec,

Canada, are regarded as the finest French dance authorities in North America; they emphasized French bourrées. The Hébert's fieldwork took place from 1964 to 1972, and they studied with Pierre Panis, Paul Bouard, Geneviève His, Michel Piot, and Nicole Andrioli. The couple taught at the influential University of the Pacific Folk Dance Camps (Stockton, California) and the San Diego State University Folk Dance Conferences throughout the 1960s and 1970s.

Popular central French and Alsatian couple dances include bourrées (in duple and triple meter), *schottisches*, waltzes (following the Viennese model with regular turning throughout), mazurkas, polka, *zweifachers*, and contredanses in a variety of meters. Haute Bretagne (in the east) is home to the *rond de St. Vincent*, and Basse Bretagne (in the Breton-speaking west) preserves a variety of (mostly) line dances such as the *an dro, hanter dro, laridé, gavotte, plinn*, and *kost ar c'hoat*.

The Alps are home to the lively, hopping *rigaudon* (with links to English country dancing), whereas the southwestern regions of Béarn and the Basque country feature the *branle d'Ossau*, a variety of *sauts, rondeaux* in chains and couples, and *fandangos* from Spain. The *gavotte* come from the related *branles doubles* circle dances by the Gavots native to the upper Alpine province of Gap, in the ancient province of Dauphine. Genuine French folk bourrée, rigaudon, and gavotte have been incorporated into classical ballets such as *La Fille Mal Gardée* (Dauberval, 1789; Ashton, 1960), and *Coppélia* (Saint-Léon, 1870).

Although traditional music and movement fell out of popular favor in France by the late 19th century, the 1960s folk revival movement resulted in the modern *Mouvement Folk*. Singer Lionel Rocheman founded "le Hootenanny" at the Centre Américain d'Estudiants & d'Artistes in 1964, and other folk clubs followed (Le Bourdon and Le TMS in Paris, and La Chanterelle in Lyon), copying the British model of a casual atmosphere with admission fee and limiting performers to a few songs in an "open mike" atmosphere.

French folk festivals inspired by Woodstock sprang up, including Lambesc (1970), Malataverne (1971), and Pons (1973). Folk harpist Alan Stivell (Celtic Brittany) developed a new Breton pop hybrid sound. Stivell's guitarist, Gabriel Yacoub, released the first diverse French folk album (*Pierre Grenoble*, 1973), leading the way for other folk-pop groups such as Mélusine (a polyphonic trio), La Bamboche (Lyon), Tri Yann (Brittany), and Perlinpinpin Folc (Gascony). Field recordings were made of instrumentalists (especially bagpipe, accordion, and Alpine fiddlers such as Emile Escalle) and singers such as the Goadeg sisters (Brittany) and Louise Reichert (Cantal).

Regional music and dance were sometimes politically motivated, as they asserted local traditions over the hypercentralized French state. By 1981, the new Socialist government began to sponsor folk dance and music through the efforts of Maurice Fleuret, the new director for music and dance in the Ministry of Culture headed by Jack Lang. Several regional centers for *musique traditionnelle* were created (Dastum in Brittany, Conservatoire Occitan in Toulouse). Pioneering folk performers have become leaders of folk organizations including cornemuse player Jean Blanchard (co-founder of La Bamboche at CTM in the Rhône-Alpes), Eric Montbel (Provence-Alpes-Côte-d'Azur), and Jean-François Duterte (of Mélusine, national CIMT). Brittany is now an especially multicultural area, as many

Gypsy-Balkan-Breton and jazz-Breton musical combos have paved the way for the dance band Carré Manchot, which often plays with a West Indian ensemble. Most Breton towns host a summer *fest noz* (night dance) including the traditional *an dro, suite gavotte, suite plinn,* and *suite fiselš* accompanied by *bombarde* (an oboe), *biniou* (small bagpipe), and folk string band.

Leading folk dance gatherings include the Maison des Cultures des Mondes' *Festival de l'Imaginaire* (Spring), the CIMT's *Planète Musiques,* the Stade de France's Celtic Festival (March 17), the Festival Musiques & Danses du Monde (May, in Courcouronnes), the *Festival de Cornouaille* (early July, Quimper); the Arles World Music Festival (July, near Marseille); the Estivada Festival (late July, Rodez); the Saulieu Cajun Festival (early August, Burgundy); the *Festival Interceltique* (August, Lorient); and the *Festival des Panards* (October, West Yorkshire, England). From 1976 to 2014, the leading folk festival (featuring many forms of the bourrée) was the annual *Rencontres Internationales de Luthiers & Maîtres-Sonneurs.* The current *Trad Magazine* publishes a festival guide in its May/June issue, and contemporary "French folk dance" clubs exist in both France, England, and Canada.

Laura Stanfield Prichard

See also: Austro-German Dances; Quadrille; Schottische

Further Reading

Anthony, James R. 1997. *French Baroque Music from Beaujoyeulx to Rameau.* Portland, OR: Amadeus Press.

Hilton, Wendy, and Caroline Gaynor. *Dance of Court and Theater: The French Noble Style, 1690–1725.* Princeton, NJ: Princeton Book Co.

Little, Meredith Ellis, and Carol G. Marsh. 1992. *La Danse Noble: An Inventory of Dances and Sources.* New York: Broude Brothers.

Mather, Betty Bang. 1988. *Dance Rhythms of the French Baroque.* Bloomington: Indiana University Press.

Fujara

The *fujara* is a Slovakian flute traditionally used by shepherds from the mountainous Podpol'ani region for entertainment and for herding. The modern fujara originated at the end of the 17th century, but it has roots in medieval wind instruments of similar design. It has become an important symbol of Slovakia and Slovakia's historical shepherd culture, and it is frequently played at folk festivals and competitions. In 2005, the fujara was proclaimed a UNESCO Masterpiece of the Oral and Intangible Heritage of Humanity, and in 2008 it was inscribed on the Representative List of the Intangible Cultural Heritage of Humanity. In addition to its traditional uses, since the 20th century the fujara has also been used in orchestral arrangements, film scores, electronic music, and for meditation and therapy practices.

The overall length of the fujara is between 160 and 200 centimeters (approximately 63–78 inches). Fujaras are typically wooden, and black elder wood was the traditional choice of fujara makers. The fujara has two tubes, one that serves as the main body of the flute and another smaller tube that channels air from the player's mouth to the main tube where it passes over a fipple, or plug. Significantly, the fujara has only three finger holes. It relies on the harmonic series for tuning, so pitch is controlled by the amount and strength of the air blown through the instrument. The tone of the fujara is complex, ranging from gravelly low notes to sweet reedy high notes. Skilled players can produce multiphonics that utilize both ends of this sonic spectrum. The fujara can also be used to mimic natural sounds, such as bird cries or flowing water. Traditionally, the fujara was played as a solo instrument or as an accompaniment instrument for vocal songs describing shepherd life. Varying songs utilize different styles of playing and call for different timbres depending on the mood and setting of the described events.

Fujaras are known for their beautifully ornamented appearance as well as their characteristic sound. Historically, this would have elevated their status beyond simple objects of entertainment to valuable family heirlooms that could be passed from generation to generation as a symbol of a family's wealth and musical skill. The acoustical and artistic expertise necessary to craft a sonorous and beautiful fujara has created considerable interest in fujara makers, and some folk festivals have included competitions for fujara building. While traditional fujara designs are still prevalent, some makers have experimented with nontraditional kinds of wood and even the spacing between the finger holes, which affects tuning.

The fujara's multiphonic capabilities have made it attractive to 20th- and 21st-century composers, such as Maurice Jarre, Peter Breiner, and Juraj Kojs (among others). Jarre famously used the fujara in his film scores during the 1960s and 1970s, Breiner has experimented with the use of fujara in jazz pieces, and Kojs has integrated electronic music and fujara in his performance art pieces. Innovative uses of the fujara demonstrate its versatility as well as the continued interest in its cultural importance and musical applications.

Amelia Davidson

See also: Tin/Pennywhistle

Further Reading

"The Fujara and Its Music." 2009. UNESCO: Representative List of the Intangible Cultural Heritage of Humanity—2008. September 28. https://www.youtube.com/watch?v=8VFlS_dHWPA.

Garaj, Bernard. 2006. "The Fujara: A Symbol of Slovak Folk Music and New Ways of Its Usage." *Tautosakos Darbai* 32 (January 1), 86–94.

Pro Musica. n.d. "Fujara Musical Instrument and Its Music: Candidature for Its Proclamation as Masterpiece of the Oral and Intangible Heritage of Humanity." UNESCO Candidacy Proposal, Bratislava, Slovakia. http://ethnomusicology.eu/domains/9n3zqt3dno/my_files/Fujara/Book_UNESCO_min.pdf.

Funk

A term originally used by early jazz musicians to describe something dirty, nasty, and low-down, funk music is a style of African American popular music that developed from rhythm and blues (R & B), jazz, gospel, doo-wop, soul music, and rock and roll. Strongly associated with the Black Power movement of the late 1950s and 1960s, funk is generally characterized by highly complex, interconnected rhythms that emphasize a syncopated back beat in quadruple meter; simple forms built around melodic and/or rhythmic ostinatos, or "riffs"; extended instrumental solos performed over a simple vamp; prominent melodic bass lines; jazz-based harmonies; doo-wop and soul oriented vocals; and dynamic horn arrangements.

Heavily influenced by the big bands of the 1930s and 1940s, and the soul and R & B groups of the 1950s, the instrumentation of most funk bands consisted of two to three lead singers; two to three background vocalists; a horn section relying heavily on saxophones, trumpets, and trombones; and an expanded rhythm section, which featured electric guitars, bass guitar, and keyboards. The lyrical content of many funk songs focused on the trials and tribulations of the African American experience during the Civil Rights era, as well as touching on more taboo and recreational aspects of popular culture, such as dancing, drugs, and sex.

American musician James Brown played a key role in the development and popularity of many popular genres, especially soul and funk. (Michael Putland/Getty Images)

Considered the founder of the style, James Brown (1933–2006) established the polyrhythmic dance style in the mid-1960s, specifically with his post-soul album *Papa's Got a Brand New Bag* (1965) and with the singles "Cold Sweat" (1967), "Say It Loud—I'm Black and I'm Proud" (1968), "Get Up (I Feel Like Being a) Sex Machine" (1970), and "Make It Funky" (1971). Brown's gospel-influenced vocal style and high-energy dance grooves, combined with his flamboyant live performances, created a lasting legacy that had far-reaching effects on future pop, rock, disco, hip-hop, and jazz musicians.

In the late 1960s, Sly and the Family Stone, one of the first popular multiracial and multigender American rock bands (Rock and Roll Hall of Fame Museum, 2013), combined James Brown's funky new sound with soul and psychedelic rock. With such socially conscious hit singles as "Dance to the Music" (1968), "Everyday People" and "(I Want to Take You) Higher," both from their album *Stand!* (1969), Sly and the Family Stone created a polystylistic musical sound that epitomized the countercultural youth movement of the sixties.

In the early 1970s, George Clinton, along with his two bands, Parliament and Funkadelic, continued to explore and expand the sounds and concepts associated with funk. Experimenting with longer musical forms, intricate vocal arrangements, unconventional album designs, and outlandish stage shows, the two-band collective, later to be known as P-Funk, fused funk and psychedelic rock with the conceptual Afrofuturism of jazz composer Sun Ra, and released some of the most important albums in the genre, including *Funkadelic* (1970), *Maggot Brain* (1971), *One Nation Under a Groove* (1978), and *Up for the Down Stroke* (1974) and *Mothership Connection* (1975), respectively.

Other important songs and albums during this period include "Soul Finger" (1967) by The Bar-Kays, "It's Your Thing" (1969) by the Isley Brothers, "Superstition" (1972) by Stevie Wonder, Kool & The Gang's "Jungle Boogie" (1973), "Fire" (1974) by the Ohio Players, "Hang Loose" (1972) by Mandrill, Curtis Mayfield's soundtrack to the blaxploitation film *Super Fly* (1974), and *That's the Way of the World* (1975) by Earth Wind & Fire.

As funk began to fuse with soul and rock in the 1970s, rhythmic practices associated with the style—specifically, the use of a syncopated back beat—began to influence the music of several prominent jazz composers, including Miles Davis, Herbie Hancock, Stanley Clarke, and Joe Zawinul. This blending of styles was later named jazz-fusion (Vincent, 1996, pp. 137–152, 288–290). Furthermore, as elements of funk became a mainstay of pop, rock, and disco in the 1980s, samples from various important funk recordings—most notably "Funky Drummer" (1970) by James Brown and "Amen, Brother" (1969) by The Winstons—were used on numerous rap and hip-hop albums, including those by such artists as Public Enemy, LL Cool J, and N.W.A. Not surprisingly, the influence of funk can also be heard on recordings by such nineties hard rock, hardcore punk, and rap metal bands as Living Colour, Fishbone, the Red Hot Chili Peppers, Bad Brains, and Rage Against the Machine.

William Price

See also: Blues; Davis, Miles; Jazz; Rap/Hip-Hop; Rock and Roll; Soul

Further Reading

Brown, James. 1965. *Papa's Got a Brand New Bag.* King KS 938.

Brown, James. 1991. *20 All-Time Greatest Hits!* Polydor 314 511 326–2.

Funkadelic. 1970/2005. *Funkadelic.* Westbound CDSEW 210.

Funkadelic. 1978/2002. *One Nation Under a Groove.* Priority 72435-39378-2-9 (originally released by Warner Bros.).

Parliament. 1975/2003. *Mothership Connection.* Mercury 440 077 032–2 (originally released by Casablanca).

Parliament. 1977/1990. "Flash Light." On *Funkentelechy Vs. the Placebo Syndrome.* Casablanca 824 501–2.

Rock and Roll Hall of Fame Museum. 2013. "Sly and the Family Stone." Rockhall.com, December 1. https://www.rockhall.com/inductees/sly-and-the-family-stone/bio?name=sly+and+the+family+stone&field_inductee_induction_year=&field_induction_category=All.

Sly and the Family Stone. 1969/1993. *Stand!* Epic EK 53410.

Southgate, Darby E. 2010. "Funk." In Emmett George Price, III, Tammy L. Kernodle, and Horace J. Maxile, Jr. (eds.), *Encyclopedia of African American Music*, vol. 3, 338–346. Santa Barbara, CA: Greenwood.

Vincent, Rickey. 1996. *Funk: The Music, the People, and the Rhythm of The One*. New York: St. Martin's/Griffin.

Zuberi, Nabeel. 2004. "The Transmolecularisation of [Black] Folk: Space Is the Place, Sun Ra and Afrofuturism." In Phillip Hayward (ed.), *Off the Planet: Music, Sound and Science Fiction Cinema*, 77–95. Bloomington: Indiana University Press.

G

Gagaku

Gagaku, which means "elegant music," has been called the longest continuously surviving "orchestral" ensemble in the world. Influenced by foreign musics, which began to be imported to Japan in the sixth century CE, *gagaku* has had patronage in the Japanese court from at least 701 CE. Accordingly, gagaku is often described as the music of the imperial court, but it also serves Shinto shrines and Buddhist ritual contexts throughout Japan, and is even taught in community and student ensembles in Europe and the United States.

As a courtly tradition, gagaku took form in the imperial court starting in the Nara Period (710–794 CE) and was influenced by traditions of mainland Asia. The courtly traditions of the Táng Dynasty (618–907 CE) in China influenced much of Asia, and Táng courtly musics, known as *yayue*, spread to neighboring kingdoms including Korea, there known as *aak*, and Vietnam, there known as *nha nhac* (Terauchi, 2001, p. 619). In Japan, gagaku serves as a living testament to the tradition now long dead in China. Japan reached its imperial heights during the Heian period (794–1192 CE), a time when gagaku took on more Japanese aesthetics and musicians began to cultivate a music tradition quite unique to Japan. During the Edo Period (1601–1868 CE), when the emperor's power was greatly reduced, gagaku fell in prominence. However, with the Meiji Restoration of 1868 and the reinstatement of the emperor's power, the tradition began a new life as a symbol of both the emperor and Japan's rich history.

Gagaku, like many genres in Japan, is primarily an orally transmitted tradition, meaning the music is not taught through written notation. Scorebooks, which have a long history, do exist, but are typically used now only as a secondary source for professional and amateur musicians alike. As read today, these scorebooks do not provide complete melodies, exact pitches, or definite rhythms. Rather, they are shorthand abstractions of those musical elements; more accurately, they are representations of an oral mnemonic system known as *shôga*, literally "singing-song." Students learning in the traditional way will often never hold an instrument until the shôga are memorized. They are expected to learn the melodies from their teacher one line at a time and completely by memory. Teachers pass down the tradition based on a set style of shôga that was handed down to them through their lineage. This type of learning can be seen across Japanese traditional musics, but it is a crucial component in gagaku transmission. Each instrument in the gagaku ensemble will have a slightly different form of shôga to produce its melodies. Though the melody played by two instruments may be similar, the established shôga includes each instrument's particular melodic nuances and "hidden" motions not indicated in the abbreviated score. These hidden elements are only realized when learning through the shôga, as these are vocalizations of the played melody.

Gagaku can be divided into three categories based on origin, each with its own instrumentation, performance practice, and set of aesthetics: accompanied vocal music and dance originating in Japan, instrumental music and dance originating from mainland Asia, and accompanied vocal music of mixed origins.

There are a handful of musics surviving in gagaku that are said to have originated in Japan. The best known is called *mikagura*, which loosely means "music of the gods." This genre is associated with the Shinto *mikagura no gi* rite, from which it gets its name, and is said to entertain the gods on their invited trip back to the earth. The rite is held annually in mid-December in both the royal palace and a few select Shinto shrines around Kyoto. Other genres of musics originating in Japan are used in various ceremonies for the emperor and his ancestors. The *azuma asobi* is used to comfort imperial ancestral spirits; the *ônaobi uta*, or "purification song," is used to uplift the soul of the emperor during the *tinkon sai* rite held in November; the *ôuta*, or "big song," and the *kumeuta*, or "Kume clan song," are used in the coronation of a new emperor; and the *ruika* is a lament to honor the emperor upon his death (Terauchi, 2001, p. 620). Instruments of both foreign and native origins, discussed later, can accompany these genres.

The best-known repertory of the gagaku tradition is based on musics of the Asian mainland. Initially this category consisted of several separate genres based on place of origin, such as China, India, Korea, Southeast Asia, and so on. However, since the ninth century CE these have been simplified to two genres: *tôgaku* and *komagaku*, each with its own aesthetics, instrumentation, and performance styles. Tôgaku, also known as the "music of the left," is derived from traditions mainly of Chinese and Indian origins. The costuming for *bugaku* dance in tôgaku is ornamented in red to symbolized its origins in China. The stoic melodies of the repertory are said to directly correlate to ancient Táng melodies (Picken et al., 1981). Tôgaku comprises some 90 *kangen* instrumental pieces and roughly 30 bugaku pieces; many pieces can be used for either kangen or bugaku, though the style and tempo will vary depending on use (Terauchi, 2001, p. 621). Komagaku, also known as "music of the right," is quite small in comparison, with only two dozen bugaku pieces and no kangen examples. It consists of music derived from Korean and Manchurian origins, symbolized by green or blue embellishments in costuming.

The final category consists of vocal music of mixed origins. *Saibara*, a genre of courtly songs, developed in the ninth century CE and reached its height late in the Heian Period, from which several dozen examples survive. The earliest surviving musical manuscripts of the genre with melodic notation were compiled between 1171 and 1192 CE (Markham, 1983, p. 3). In the 16th century the tradition nearly died out, but today there remain 14 examples that were reconstructed during the Meiji Period (1868–1912 CE). The lyrics of saibara songs are based on "Japanese poetry depicting regional landscapes, lovers' feelings, and so on, and expressed in simple, direct language" (Terauchi, 2001, p. 625). *Rôei* is a separate court-song tradition of sung excerpts from Chinese-style poems by Chinese and Japanese poets. The tradition is said to have been formalized by Minamoto no Masanobu (920–923

CE), but it may have predated Masanobu as an improvised practice (Nelson, 2008, p. 42).

Instrumentation for the gagaku ensemble varies depending on context and tradition. As an "orchestral" ensemble, it employs an instrumentation similar to that of a Western orchestra: winds (flutes and reeds), strings (lutes and zithers), and percussion (drums and gongs). It is important to note, however, that the context of this genre is quite different from that of the Western orchestra, in both performance practice and cultural meaning.

The wind section is the center of the gagaku ensemble, as it carries the main melodic lines as well as the bulk of the harmonic development. The three horizontal flutes used in the gagaku ensemble are typically the main melodic instruments. Each is similarly constructed of bamboo and is wrapped with cherry or wisteria bark and lacquered on the inside. The *kagurabue* (also known as *yamatobue*) is used exclusively for the *mikagura* traditions. It is said to have originated in Japan and has six finger holes. Today, the *ryûteki* (literally, "dragon flute," also known as *yokobue*) from the tôgaku repertory is commonly substituted. The ryûteki has seven finger holes and is said to be of Chinese origin. It is also the largest of the gagaku flutes. The ryûteki has very large finger holes, which makes it difficult to play, but allows for greater access to the microtones which are distinctive to the gagaku sound. The third type, the *komabue*, is the smallest of these flutes and is used in the *komagaku* repertory. The komabue has six finger holes and is considered to be of Korean origin. All these flutes are known for their shrill and sharp sounds, especially in the upper registers.

The *hichiriki* is a small but loud double-reed instrument that probably originated in Central Asia but came to Japan via China. Its double reed is somewhat like the reed used on the Western oboe, but is much larger. Additionally, the hichiriki musician uses loose embouchure, or position of the mouth, which allows the musician to explore a wider range of microtones much like the ryûteki. These microtone variations enable expanded embellishments of the melodic line. The hichiriki has nine finger holes, seven on top and two on the underside. The windpipe is constructed of specially processed bamboo wrapped in cherry or wisteria bark. The double reed sits delicately at the head of the windpipe. The hichiriki often plays a similar, but not quite the same, melody as the ryûteki and is commonly used in both the tôgaku and komagaku repertories and occasionally in mikagura accompaniment.

Tradition claims that the *shô*, a mouth organ, is meant to imitate the cry of the phoenix, and its shape is modeled after that mythical bird's graceful wings (Malm, 2000, p. 110). The shô, which sounds somewhat like a pipe organ, is constructed of 17 reed pipes set in a cup-shaped chamber with a fixed mouthpiece. Inhaling or exhaling while covering certain finger holes on the pipes produces chord clusters. The harmonic structure for each line of the melody can be heard in these chord clusters, which act as a driving force moving the melody from one phrase the next. The shô is probably of South East Asian origins but was imported via China and is quite similar to the Chinese *sheng* still in use today.

The string instruments of the gagaku ensemble today play subdued roles compared to their possible origins in the repertory, and are not typically used to accompany dance. There are three surviving string instruments used in the contemporary gagaku ensemble. Typically these instruments serve as rhythm markers and play stereotyped patterns with few melodic lines. The *wagon* ("wa" rhyming with "spa") is a six-string zither used in mikagura. Though it may have origins in mainland Asia, its history dates back long enough to be considered as originating from Japan. The *gakusô* (also known as *sô*) is a zither with 13 strings, similar to the Japanese *koto*, both of which are indigenized forms of the Chinese *guzheng*. It is tuned by positioning the movable bridges up or down the string to create a shift in pitch. The musician uses both bare fingertips and finger plectrums to pluck the stings. The final string instrument is called the *biwa* or *gakubiwa*, and is related to the Chinese *pipa*. This pear-shaped lute has four strings and four frets that are plucked with a small paddle-like plectrum.

The percussion instruments of the gagaku ensemble can be quite grand. In the imperial gagaku room, there are two giant drums known as *dadaiko* (literally, "big drums"). Smaller versions, known generically as *taiko* (literally, "drum"), are much more common in smaller ensembles, but function the same. These drums serve as time markers and work with the bugaku dancers as a means to provide special effects accentuating the movements of the dance. The taiko is a barrel drum with two leather heads stretched over the body. The player uses two stick mallets, known as *bachi*, to percuss the resonant drums. The *shôko*, or metal gong, is a high-pitched gong struck with two thin sticks that create a metallic "tink" that marks time, typically sounding after strong taiko beats. The *kakko* is a small cylindrical drum with two laced leather heads. Unlike the taiko, the kakko is played on both drum heads with two thin drumsticks, one in each hand. This instrument drives the speed of the ensemble, pushing and slowing the tempo with drum rolls and quick strikes. Finally, there is the *san no tsuzumi*, which is used only in the komagaku repertory and resembles hourglass-shaped drums from Korea. This drum functions in the same way as the kakko to drive the ensemble, but is struck on one drum head, with one drum stick, similar to its Korean predecessors.

Justin R. Hunter

See also: Mikagura

Further Reading

Garfias, Robert. 1975. *Music of a Thousand Autumns: The Togaku Style of Japanese Court Music*. Berkeley: University of California Press.

Harich-Schneider, Eta. 1973. *A History of Japanese Music*. London: Oxford University Press.

Kishibe, Shigeo. 1982. *The Traditional Music of Japan*. Tokyo: Ongaku no Tomosha.

Malm, William P. 2000. *Traditional Japanese Music and Musical Instruments (The New Edition)*. Tokyo: Kodansha International.

Markham, Elizabeth J. 1983. *Saibara: Japanese Court Songs of the Heian Period*. London: Cambridge University Press.

Nelson, Steven G. 2008. "Court and Religious Music (1): History of Gagaku and Shōmyō." In Alison McQueen Tokita and David W. Hughes (eds.), *The Ashgate Research Companion to Japanese Music*, 35–48. Surrey, UK: Ashgate.

Nelson, Steven G. 2008. "Court and Religious Music (2): Music of Gagaku and Shōmyō." In Alison McQueen Tokita and David W. Hughes (eds.), *The Ashgate Research Companion to Japanese Music*, 49–76. Surrey, UK: Ashgate.

Picken, Laurence, et al. 1981. *Music from the Tang Court*, vol. 1. London: Oxford University Press.
Terauchi, Naoko. 2001. "Gagaku." In Robert Provine, Yosihiko Yokumaru, and Lawence Witzleben (eds.), *Garland Encyclopedia of World Music; Vol. 7: China, Japan, and Korea*, 619–628. New York: Routledge.
Tokumaru, Yoshiko, and Osamu Yamaguti, eds. 1986. *The Oral and the Literate in Music*. Tokyo: Academia Music.

Gamelan Orchestra (Balinese)

Balinese *gamelan* orchestras are traditional musical ensembles of the island of Bali, Indonesia, consisting primarily of a variety of instruments—including metallophones, xylophones, gongs, drums, and cymbals—as well as flutes, stringed instruments, and sometimes vocals. The word "gamelan" may refer to both a set of such instruments and an ensemble that plays gamelan. Gamelan music often accompanies other types of Balinese arts performances, including dance (*tari*) and puppetry (*wayang*), and is a central feature in Balinese Hindu ritual contexts as well as in social settings. Gamelan is also a central element in cultural tourism to the island, which comprises the majority of Bali's economy. There are approximately 40 distinct types of gamelan in Bali. Although Balinese gamelan is related to Javanese gamelan ensembles historically, culturally, and through shared playing technique, they are distinctive in compositional style, repertoire, and performance contexts. In addition to the thousands of active Balinese gamelans within Bali, hundreds also exist throughout other parts of Indonesia and the world, including in Australia, Europe, Japan, and the United States.

Balinese gamelan music is largely shaped by the cultural history of the island itself; many scholars divide the history of gamelan into three periods: *tua* (old), *madya* (middle), and *baru* (new). The first evidence of gamelan-like instruments on Bali dates back more than a thousand years, at a time when the roots of contemporary Balinese society were already beginning to take shape—a cooperative society that valued honoring ancestor and local spirits, and was in large part governed by cyclical rhythms of religious ritual that centered on the cultivation of rice and maintaining the systems of irrigation that distributed water from the mountains to the crops. This is the era of the tua gamelans. Two ensembles thought to date from this era are the *gamelan luang*, which contains a mix of bronze and bamboo instruments, and the *gamelan selonding*, which is the only gamelan to be composed of iron instruments. Only a few sets of each currently exist in Bali, and they are considered to be sacred and rare.

Starting at the beginning of the second millennium CE, these indigenous beliefs fused with Hindu ideals brought by missionaries, traders, and immigrants. By the time that the Javanese Hindu Majapahit empire fell in the 15th century CE and its royalty established a series of nine kingly courts in Bali, a distinctly Balinese style of Hindu society was developing: one with proscribed, highly stratified yet interdependent social roles, a focus on the temple and complex calendars of religious events as a central locus of social and spiritual activity, and the performing arts as an integral part of social, religious, and political life.

Musicians in a Balinese gamelan orchestra play traditional music, Bali, Indonesia. Gamelan orchestras are traditional Indonesian musical ensembles that consist largely of percussion instruments. (Saiko3p/Dreamstime.com)

The era of the post-Majapahit Balinese kingdoms, from approximately 1400–1908 CE, corresponds to the madya, or middle period, of the development of the Balinese performing arts. *Gamelan gambuh*—which features enormous *suling gambuh* (bamboo flutes), *rebab* (spike fiddle), gongs, drums, and tinkling bells, but no keyed instruments—may predate the madya era, but the stories of its accompanying dance-drama feature exploits of the Hindu-Javanese prince Panji were known to be popular during this era. The *gamelan gong gede*, a large ensemble with a full complement of gongs and gong chimes, keyed metallophones, and drums that required up to 50 musicians to play, was also favored at the courts at this time. Two related ensembles, *gamelan semar pegulingan* and *gamelan pelegongan*, were particularly popular at the courts; *semar pegulingan* was supposedly played exclusively outside the king's bedchambers at night. *Gamelan beleganjur*, a marching style of gamelan featuring drums, gongs, and cymbals, also developed during this time; it was traditionally used to accompany warriors into battle and guide cremation processions.

There are many prominent types of gamelan whose precise history is unknown, but that likely date to the madya era: *gamelan gambang*, whose wooden keyed xylophones (*gambang*) are similar to Javanese instruments of the same name, and may date back to the tua era; *gamelan gender wayang*, a small ensemble that accompanies shadow puppetry; *gamelan angklung*, the sound of whose tiny four- or five-keyed metallophones are synonymous with funerals; and *gamelan jegog*, a type of bamboo gamelan found only in the west of the island.

During the past hundred years, gamelan genres, playing styles, and repertoires in Bali have been developing rapidly. One critical moment for Balinese artistic developments was the colonization of Bali by the Dutch and the dissolution of the Balinese courts as centers of political and economic power. As social and political power shifted to the villages, new ensembles and genres emerged. Central among these ensembles was the *gamelan gong kebyar*, which was first created in the 1910s and came to dominate Balinese traditional music for the 20th century. Somewhat akin in instrumentation to a smaller *gong gede*, the gamelan gong kebyar represented a musical break from the previous court gamelans and featured a new, more virtuosic repertoire (*kebyar* means "flare") that was deemed more fitting for the new lifestyles of the Balinese.

Political transitions from a Dutch colony to part of the Indonesian nation, the development of regional and international cultural tourism, and the continued interexchange of ideas with other parts of the world through technology (particularly cell phones and the internet) have more recently shaped gamelan genres. In the 1930s, a style of vocal gamelan called *kecak* (*gamelan suara*), which originally accompanied trance-dances in the madya period, was repurposed into a popular dance-drama that is primarily performed for tourists. Another repurposing was that of *gamelan beleganjur* in the 1980s into a competitive style of gamelan.

While originally gong kebyar had constituted a significant artistic break from previous traditions, it maintained many of the core principles of instrumentation and instrument function found in earlier gamelan styles. With the development of *musik kontemporer* in the late 20th century, even these basic compositional principles were reconsidered. This move toward experimentation was matched by a concern for loss of older repertoires, and concentrated preservation efforts began. Sometimes, these seemingly contradictory impulses overlapped; the *gamelan semaradana*, popularized in the 1990s, contains seven keys and can play any of the older styles of repertoire as well as compositions unique to its particular design.

Gamelan instruments may be made of bamboo, wood, iron, or bronze. Each type of ensemble discussed earlier contains a unique and distinctive subset of the instruments listed here. One of the most common types of instruments in Balinese gamelan are keyed metallophones, which are struck with different types of mallets (*panggul*). Most of these metallophones are in the *gender* family, in which the keys are suspended above bamboo resonators that amplify the instruments' sound. This instrument family contains a number of instruments: the *jegogan*, the *calung* or *jublag*, the *penyacah*, the *gangsa*, and the *gender* (single instrument). Except for the instrument the gender, each of these instruments is the largest and is played by striking the center of the key with a padded panggul and then damping the pitch with the opposite hand; the gender is played with a mallet in each hand where each pitch is damped with the wrist of the striking hand. Although these descriptions apply primarily to metal-keyed rather than bamboo-keyed instruments, the bamboo ensembles are structured in a similar way, but long, rubber-headed mallets are used to strike carved bamboo keys.

An equally large variety of gongs is present in Balinese gamelan music. Most of the hanging gongs are struck with a padded mallet on a large, protruding boss in the center of the instrument. The largest of the hanging gongs, the *gong ageng*, may be almost three feet in diameter. The smaller *kempur* and *klentong* (also called *kemong*) are responsible for other metric divisions, while the *kempli*, *kajar*, or *tawa-tawa* are held in the musician's lap or a small stand and are often used to mark the beat. The flat-bossed hanging *bebende* may mark rhythmic accents. Some types of gamelan contain no gongs; bamboo-based varieties, such as the *gamelan jegog*, may use gigantic, low-pitched bamboo tubes instead. Many ensembles also contain gong-chimes, or sets of small gongs that are suspended on strings within frames, such as the *trompong* and the *reyong*.

The *kendang* (drums) are also central to many ensembles. Carved from wood and featuring a skin head on each side, the drums may be played by hand on both sides or with a mallet in the right hand. They may be played singly or in pairs, with a higher-pitched (*lanang*) and lower-pitched (*wadon*) instrument playing different, interlocking parts with different roles.

Many other instruments are also commonly found within Balinese gamelans. *Cengceng* (cymbals) may be found in both larger crash-cymbal and smaller mounted varieties. *Suling* (flutes) accompany or play a central role in a number of genres; they are uniformly carved from bamboo, may correspond to any number of melodic registers, and are played using a circular breathing technique. The rebab, a two-stringed bowed spiked fiddle, is associated with older repertoires. Some instruments, such as the wooden-keyed gambang, are unique to only one or two specific ensembles.

Creating instruments for any Balinese gamelan ensemble is a specialized task. While gongs are typically forged in Java, the other metal instruments are created in Bali by *pandé*, clans of metalsmiths. The keys and small gongs found in keyed metallophones and gong-chimes are housed within instrument cases, which are intricately carved. A gamelan is built and tuned as a single set; each gamelan has a distinct tuning and, with a few exceptions, instruments are generally not interchangeable between ensembles. Gamelan tunings are distinctive to the families of the pandé who make each set, but tunings of specific instruments tend to fall within a certain pitch range, and adhere to one of two tuning systems: *slendro* and *pelog*. The slendro tuning system contains five pitches; the pelog system contains seven. Different types of gamelans may be constructed using subsets of each system. Instruments in Balinese gamelans are also often tuned in gendered pairs, with one instrument tuned to a slightly higher frequency (*lanang*, male) and one instrument tuned to a slightly lower frequency (*wadon*, female). When the same note is struck on each instrument of the pair, the slight dissonance creates audible "waves" (*ombak*).

Compositional structures vary between different types of Balinese gamelan. However, compositions often contain multiple formal sections that are internally cyclical, or built upon on a gong cycle (*gongan*, or colotomic structure), which can last between two and more than 200 beats. A timekeeping instrument guides the tempo of the *pokok*, or core melody, which is played on the mid-range instruments and punctuated by different gongs. The pokok is elaborated upon by the higher-range instruments and the gong-chime instruments as well as suling and rebab, when present. The kendang serve in either in colotomic or leader role; in the latter capacity, they cue changes in tempo and dynamics within the ensemble and coordinate the ensemble with dancers or puppeteers (*dalang*). In musik kontemporar, it is common to invert or otherwise alter these instrumental roles.

Gamelan music and its associated performing arts function as an integral part of many facets of modern Balinese society. It is a foundation of religious ceremonies and can be considered a form of *ngayah*, voluntary religious service. It is performed in intraregional competitions and at political events, and is a central component of Balinese cultural tourism. Children and young adults often learn gamelan or dance in their villages, studying the music by rote through the *maguru panggul* (mallet-as-teacher) method in which a student imitates an instructor's playing until the piece is memorized. More serious students may pursue study with *seniman alam* (teachers with no institutional education) or at Institut Seni Indonesia, the Balinese arts conservatory. Although gamelan is traditionally a province only of Balinese men, women's gamelan ensembles have existed since the 1980s; gender-integrated groups are still rare. Due to foreign interest in Balinese gamelan since the mid-20th century, dozens of Balinese gamelans also exist outside of Bali (including approximately 80 in the United States) and are studied by musicians from all over the world.

Elizabeth A. Clendinning

See also: Gamelan Orchestra (Javanese); Gender Wayang; Kecak; Kendang; McPhee, Colin

Further Reading

Bakan, Michael. 1999. *Music of Death and New Creation: Experiences in the World of Balinese Gamelan Beleganjur*. Chicago: University of Chicago Press.

Dibia, I. Wayan, and Rucina Ballinger. 2004. *Balinese Dance, Drama and Music: A Guide to the Performing Arts of Bali*. Singapore: Periplus.

Gold, Lisa. 2005. *Music in Bali: Experiencing Music, Expressing Culture*. New York: Oxford University Press.

McGraw, Andrew C. 2013. *Radical Traditions: Reimagining Culture in Balinese Contemporary Music*. Oxford: Oxford University Press.

McPhee, Colin. 1966. *Music in Bali: A Study in Form and Instrumental Music in Bali*. New Haven: Yale University Press.

Stepputat, Kendra, ed. 2013. *Performing Arts in Bali: Changing Interpretations, Founding Traditions*. Grazer Beiträge zur Ethnomusikologie/Graz Studies in Ethnomusicology, vol. 24. Graz, Germany: Institute of Ethnomusicology, University of Music and Performing Arts.

Tenzer, Michael. 2000. *Gamelan Gong Kebyar: The Art of Twentieth-Century Balinese Music*. Chicago: University of Chicago Press.

Gamelan Orchestra (Javanese)

A large ensemble consisting mainly (but not exclusively) of knobbed gong and metal-keyed percussion instruments, the *gamelan* orchestra developed in the royal courts of Yogyakarta and Surakarta (Solo) in central Java starting around the eighth century CE (Lindsay, 1992). Evolving over the centuries to meet new conditions and needs, the gamelan has continued to be an important expression of Javanese culture and identity. Indicating Java's regional influence, the gamelan spread to neighboring areas, including western Java, eastern Java, Bali, Malaysia, and South and East Kalimantan, where local gamelan traditions developed (Kartomi and Mendonça, 2018). Other parts of Southeast Asia have related types of music. The gamelan tradition of central Java includes two styles of playing which correspond to the cities of Yogyakarta and Surakarta (Solo). Today a complete gamelan typically includes from 40 to 60 instruments (Sumarsam, 2013). The ensemble uses two different tuning systems (*slendro* and *pélog*). Gamelan music is integrated with other arts, especially dance and theater, which are performed for ceremony and entertainment. In contemporary Java, gamelan orchestras perform in a wide range of contexts, including coming-of-age celebrations, weddings, births, funerals, harvest rituals, exorcisms, public holidays, political campaigns and government advertising, anniversaries of institutions, public ceremonies and events, and radio and TV broadcasts. With its long and layered history of mutual influence and interaction with other cultures, the gamelan represents an ancient and dynamic tradition in the contemporary world.

GEOGRAPHY, HISTORY, AND CULTURE

Part of a densely populated and culturally diverse area, Java is located in the southwestern part of Indonesia. An archipelago between Asia and Australia, Indonesia is made up of approximately 17,000 islands extending across 3,400 miles of ocean. The region is home to hundreds of different ethnolinguistic groups, and its great cultural diversity is reflected in Indonesia's national motto: *Bhinneka Tunggal Ika*, an Old Javanese proverb, translated as "Unity in diversity." The island of Java is one of the oldest continually inhabited places in the world and has been a center of commerce and communication for centuries. The island's long history can be divided into four periods characterized by contact with foreign cultures that the Javanese people have used in developing their own culture (Sumarsam, 2013). Between the fifth and seventh centuries CE, the consolidation of Hindu/Buddhist kingdoms established the presence of tantric philosophies, styles of art, and literary works from India. Next, during the 14th century Islam arrived with Muslim traders and spread quickly, but did not eliminate or completely obscure existing elements of Hindu/Buddhist culture. Then, starting in the 16th century, European nations (Portugal, Britain, and the Netherlands) colonized Java, culminating in Dutch dominance for 350 years and catalyzing processes of Westernization. Indonesia declared its independence in 1945, and fought the Netherlands for recognition, which was granted after much international pressure in 1949. The influence of Westernization shifted in the modern era, but continues in some sense into the present day, as the gamelan has an established presence in many Western countries.

INSTRUMENTS AND ENSEMBLES

The name *gamelan* comes from the word *gamel*, which means to strike. It refers to the predominance of knobbed gongs and metal-keyed instruments which sound when struck with a wooden mallet. The metal instruments are usually made of bronze, but may also be made of iron. The gamelan orchestra is laid out in groups or families of instruments that can be usefully thought of as functional groups. Corresponding to how the music is organized and played, these functional groups include time-cycle instruments, skeletal melody instruments, melody-elaborating instruments, singers, and a drummer.

The time-cycle instruments include vertically hanging and horizontally suspended (also called kettle-shaped) gongs. There are three groups of vertically hanging gongs. The largest, lowest pitched, and most important gong is the *gong ageng*. Next are the *gongs suwukan* or *siyem*, which are higher in pitch than the gong ageng. The highest-pitched hanging gongs are the *kempul*. The time-cycle instruments also include two types of horizontal gongs. The *kenong* are the lowest pitched of the horizontal gongs. Finally, the *kethuk* and the *kempyang* are small horizontal gongs.

The next group of instruments is the skeletal melody instruments, which include all metal-keyed instruments with a range of one octave. Of this group, the *saron* family has thick, slab-like keys which sit over a trough-shaped resonator, and the *slenthem* have thinner keys, suspended above bamboo or metal tubes. The saron family includes three sizes of instruments, the *saron demung* (large and low-pitched), *saron barung* (medium and middle range), and *saron panerus* or *peking* (small and high-pitched). There is only one size of slenthem, although its construction is similar to that of the approximately two-octave *gendèr*.

The next group of instruments is made up of melody-elaborating instruments. This group is the most varied, including gongs, keyed percussion, string, wind, and voices. The *bonang barung* and the *bonang panerus* are sets of horizontal kettle gongs. These two instruments often play interlocking parts that elaborate the skeletal melody. The *gendèr barung* and *gendèr panerus* are keyed instruments similar to the slenthem in construction but wider in range and higher in pitch. Other elaborating instruments are the *rebab*, a two-sting spike fiddle; the *suling*, a bamboo flute; the *gambang*, a wooden xylophone; and the *celempung* or *siter*, a steel-stringed zither. In addition to musical instruments, some gamelan music includes female solo singers called *pesindhèn* and a male chorus called *gérong*.

The gamelan includes a set of three double-headed drums (small, medium, large) together called *kendhang*. The role of the drummer shares some similarities with that of the conductor in Western orchestras (Pickvance, 2005). For example, the drummer indicates when the music begins and ends, sets the tempo, leads transitions between sections, and indicates other changes such as volume level.

Note that some of the instruments of the gamelan ensemble, such as the suling or rebab, are much softer and quieter than others. At one time, there were probably two separate ensembles, one "loud" ensemble consisting of metal percussion instruments that was used for stately ceremonies, and a separate "soft" ensemble, including solo singing and quieter instruments, that was likely used for more intimate events. Today the loud and the soft instruments are combined into one large ensemble. The musical repertoire, however, maintains a distinction between loud- and soft-style pieces. Soft-style pieces include singers, rebab, suling, gambang, celempung, or sither and gendèr. The slenthem is the only soft-style instrument that has a permanent role in loud-style pieces (Pickvance, 2005). All of the gongs and metal-keyed instruments (the saron family) play in both loud- and soft-style groups.

TUNING

The gamelan ensemble is unified by its tuning but is not tuned to a set of absolute pitches. This means that the instruments are in tune with one another but are not interchangeable with instruments from other ensembles. Each ensemble has a set of pitches that follow the pattern of the tuning system, within an acceptable range of variation. The unique tuning of each set of instruments makes up part of the gamelan's individual identity and goes along with the belief that the ensemble is a living entity that must be treated with proper respect and etiquette. For this reason, gamelans are typically given proper names. Furthermore, the process of making gongs and other gamelan instruments is highly ritualized and requires both spiritual and technical knowledge.

For a gamelan to be complete—that is, to be able to play in either tuning—it must have two sets of instruments. This is because the two tuning systems have different types of intervals. The two sets of instruments that make up a complete gamelan will have one note common to both scales, referred to as *tumbuk*. This pitch provides a pivot point for compositions that use both tuning systems.

The two tuning systems used in gamelan music are called *slendro* and *pélog*. The slendro scale consists of five (more or less) equidistant tones. The intervals between the notes of the slendro scale are approximately the size of a half-step in Western scales. The pélog scale has seven tones in a combination of large and small intervals. The intervals between the notes in pélog range in size from approximately a half step to a little less than a minor third. Furthermore, the seven notes of the pélog tuning system are not used all at once. Rather, there are three different pélog modes made up of five notes each.

MUSICAL STRUCTURE

Gamelan music is a type of classical music that developed in temples and courts. For most of its history, the music was learned orally/aurally, with minimal or no use of notation. Notation came into widespread use in the 19th century (Lindsay, 1992). Notation traditionally recorded only the skeletal melody (*balungan*). From this central melody, the players derive the part appropriate to their instrument and build up the music in layers. As mentioned earlier, there are three basic roles: playing the skeletal melody, elaborating the melody, and organizing a sense of time by punctuating the phrases of the melody. The punctuating or time-cycle instruments play in a repeating cycle, called the gong cycle (*gongan*). Pieces are categorized by the length of the gong cycle and the way the gong cycle is divided among the punctuating instruments. The notes of the skeletal melody will coincide with the notes of the gong cycle. By speeding up and slowing down the melody in each section of a piece, the elaborating instruments are able to play different patterns that elaborate the skeletal melody.

A gong cycle can be thought of in terms of the clock face, with the gong ageng playing at 12, and each of the various gong-cycle instruments playing at different points in the cycle. For example, in a *lancaran* the kenong plays on the quarter hours, while the kempul plays on the cross-quarters. The kethuk plays between each of the beats of the other time-cycle instruments. Whereas Western music tends to accent the beginning of each phrase or measure (the downbeat), gamelan music places the biggest accent (the gong ageng) at the end of the time cycle. The time cycle, which defines the form of the piece, varies in length and can be as short as 16 beats and as long as 512 beats.

In performance, a piece will begin with an introduction by a solo instrument. The drums join in for a phrase that leads into the large gong stroke which ends the introduction and begins the piece. The drummer will signal section changes and lead the corresponding change in tempo. The sections of a piece are distinguished by the expansion and contraction of the melody in time. These time relations are called *irama* and can be conceptualized as a "gearbox" (Pickvance, 2005). The melody instruments will repeat the melody at different speeds, creating space for different patterns of elaboration based at different levels of density in relation to the skeletal melody. The drummer also signals the end of the piece with a phrase that speeds up the tempo and leads to the last large gong stroke, which is followed by the last note played by the other instrumentalists. A number of pieces may also be strung together to create an even larger composite form.

ASSOCIATED ARTS

Gamelan music can be presented as an instrumental concert, but is also performed with certain types of associated arts. These include rituals, dance, and different forms of drama. The main form of theater in central Java is the shadow puppet theater called *wayang kulit*, which is accompanied by a small gamelan ensemble and singers. The puppet master or *dalang* leads the performance of stories drawn from ancient Hindu epics, the *Mahabharata* and the *Ramayana*.

Other forms of drama accompanied by gamelan orchestras include other types of puppet theater, the Ramayana ballet (invented for the tourist trade during the 20th century), a variety of regional dance forms, and various types of popular drama.

Gamelan music also accompanies classical dance. Two important styles of dance from the central Javanese court tradition are *bedhaya* and *srimpi*. These dances were used in ceremonies and portray esoteric knowledge.

Elizabeth Kimzey Batiuk

See also: Gamelan Orchestra (Javanese); Gender Wayang; Kendang; Rebab; Zither

Further Reading

Becker, Judith. 1980. *Traditional Music in Modern Java*. Honolulu: University Press of Hawaii.

Becker, Judith. 2004. *Gamelan Stories: Tantrism, Islam, and Aesthetics in Central Java*. Tempe, AZ: Program for Southeast Asian Studies Monograph Series.

Becker, Judith, and Alton Becker. 1981. "A Musical Icon: Power and Meaning in Javanese Gamelan Music." In W. Steiner (ed.), *The Sign in Music and Literature*, 203–215. Austin: University of Texas Press.

Becker, Judith, and Alan H. Feinstein, eds. 1987. *Karawitan: Source Readings in Javanese Gamelan and Vocal Music*. Ann Arbor: Center for South East Asian Studies, The University of Michigan.

Brinner, Benjamin. 1995. *Knowing Music, Making Music: Javanese Gamelan and the Theory of Musical Competence and Interaction.* Chicago: Chicago University Press.

Kartomi, Margaret, and Maria Mendonça. 2018. "Gamelan." *Grove Music Online.* https://www.oxfordmusiconline.com.

Lindsay, Jennifer. 1992. *Javanese Gamelan: Traditional Orchestra of Indonesia.* Singapore: Oxford University Press.

Perlman, Marc. 2004. *Unplayed Melodies: Javanese Gamelan and the Genesis of Music Theory.* Berkeley: University of California Press.

Pickvance, Richard. 2005. *A Gamelan Manual: A Player's Guide to the Central Javanese Gamelan.* London: Jaman Mas Books.

Sorrell, Neil. 1990. *A Guide to the Gamelan.* Boston: Farber and Farber.

Spiller, Henry. 2004. *Gamelan Music of Indonesia.* New York: Routledge.

Sumarsam. 2013. *Javanese Gamelan and the West.* Rochester, NY: University of Rochester Press.

Ganga

Ganga, a cylindrical membranophone similar to a snare drum or military side drum, is popular in several locations around the world, especially in Africa. It normally has two membranes, or is two-headed with two snares on the top membrane and none on the lower one. The lower membrane has a higher sound that contrasts with the low sounds of the upper membrane. Because of the double membrane, the ganga is classified as a closed drum, which produces a clear, clean, transparent, and homogeneous sound.

The term "ganga" and its related translations are used by various cultural groups in West and North Africa for the double-membrane drum. These include the *batá, hausa, idoma, margi,* and *mbula* (Nigeria); the *dendi* (Benin); the *fulani,* the *kanuri songhai,* the *shlūh,* and *berbers* (Morocco); the *songhay* (Niger); the *tauregs*; and other groups. Other names for the ganga by African ethnic groups include *akangga, enyabo, gaga, gangado, ganggang, gangan, gangangu, gonga, gunguru, gungak, kangak,* and *oganga.*

The substance used to make the drum, its shape, and its size also play an important role in the timbre it produces. The shallow body of the ganga is usually made of various types of wood covered with animal skin (usually cow leather, but the skins of goat, sheep, and other animals are also used). In few locations, the body is made of metal. To increase the vibrations, shells may be inserted prior to covering with the membrane.

The ganga can range in size from 4 inches (10 cm) or smaller to as large 30 inches (75 cm) or larger in length or height. It can range from 16 to 20 inches in depth and diameter. The ganga is hung or thrown over the drummer's left shoulder and held around the neck by straps attached to the instrument. A curved or hooked drum stick and a straight stick or two curved sticks are often used to play the snare and upper membrane with the right hand, while the lower one is played by the left hand. The outer membrane is a little high, but both membranes are more or less parallel to the ground. Sometimes the ganga drummer wears a bracelet rattle on the right wrist while performing.

The repertoire ranges from solo to duets, trios, and other varied combinations of drums echoing and synchronizing rhythmic and melodic patterns of songs and dances. The rhythms can sometimes be complex when the ganga plays solo.

The ganga is often used to accompany singing and dance and in various ensembles with other instruments such as trumpets, oboes, horns, flutes, and sometimes a xylophone. Many times the ganga is played in ensemble with another ganga or with other drums and percussion ensembles. In some locations in Africa, it is only performed by professional musicians. This drum is also used in ritual ceremonies for healing the sick, in women's dance, with wedding songs, and in joyous celebrations. In performance, the ganga player usually also dances. Ganga players may even lift the instrument over the heads of the other performers while striking it.

Barbara Bonous-Smit

See also: Batá Drums

Further Reading
Blench, Roger. 1987. "Idoma Musical Instruments." *African Music* 6(4), 42–52.
Erlmann, Veit. 1983. "Notes on Musical Instruments among the Fulani of Diamare (North Cameroon)." *African Music* 6(3), 16–41.
Grame, Theodore C. 1970. "Music in the Jma al-Fna of Marrakesh." *The Musical Quarterly* 56(1, January), 74–87.
Harris, P. G. 1932. "Notes on Drums and Musical Instruments Seen in Sokoto Province, Nigeria." *Journal of the Royal Anthropological Institute of Great Britain and Ireland* 62 (January-June), 105–125.
Hause, H. E. 1948. "Terms for Musical Instruments in the Sudanic Languages: A Lexicographical Inquiry." *Journal of the American Oriental Society*, suppl. 7.

Ganga Singing

The *ganga*, an archaic polyphonic vocal genre, form, and style of traditional song is prevalent in Serbia, Croatia, Bosnia and Herzegovina (the former Yugoslavia). Its rural folk character is often lyrical, and diatonic with chromaticism. The melodic line employs unstable intervals such as seconds and nontempered modes and scales.

A typical ganga usually consists of two lines or (rarely) three. One part accompanies with nonsense syllables such as "Oo," "ah," and "r" while the lead voice sings the text, some of which is improvised. The accompanying or lowest voice can range from two to four vocalists who sing melismas and decorative phrases containing ornaments such as grace notes and trills. These are often sung in the upper or falsetto registers. Contrasting with this, the lead line has regular notes. Normally limited to a fourth or fifth, the melodic lines often have a rural folk quality. The phrases can range from short to long and extended; the rhythm tends to be more stable but independent of the text. An AB form is prevalent, with each section quite distinct from the other. The A section is sung homophonic or solo, whereas the B section is sung in polyphonic style. The voices in the polyphonic section are normally a second apart and the song frequently ends on the second. Some gangas contain refrains, where the voices tend to blend with each other and sound like one integrated whole.

The style of the ganga is basically the same even though it developed regionally. There was variety in the ganga depending on the region of its origin. The main ethnic groups of Bosnia-Herzgovina are Serbs (Orthodox Christians), Croats (Roman Catholics), and Muslims. There are also Sephardic Jews. The Turks, Lika, and Slavs, some of whom converted to Islam, settled in what is now Bosnia and Herzegovina. The area was ruled by Bosnian kings during the medieval era, followed by the Ottoman Empire from the 15th through the mid-19th centuries. The regions were eventually taken over by the Austro-Hungarian Empire. The ganga of each region acquired special characteristic sounds and stylistic features of the locale where it was performed. Gangas can express political, national, social, and cultural ideas.

Some performing and listening to the ganga often found it to be aesthetically beautiful. Even though the general spirit of the ganga is that of happiness, it can emotionally affect the listener to the point of tears. Some gangas are sung loudly and with vigor; others are more calm and quiet. For example, singers could be from regions where most worked as shepherds, so their gangas would sound like shepherd's music: "loud, outdoor, carrying over a distance" (Krader, 1987, p. 12). Nevertheless, the message and symbolism of all the ganga musics were similar and they are usually filled with emotions.

Groups of three to five singers (all-male or all-female) in close formation perform the ganga. Due to the separation of the sexes in Serbia, Croatia, and Bosnia and Herzegovina, the ganga was never sung by a mixed group of males and females. The styles of the male and female gangas were different despite the fact that they came from the same region. "Properly performed female ganga was always experienced as a powerful sexual sound symbol. . . . Male gangas also expressed ideas about sexuality, experienced as emphatic masculinity" (Petrovič, 1995, p. 67). The female ganga sounded more delicate and gentle, while the male ganga had a crude or harsh sound, "often provoked by over-consumption of alcohol" (Petrovič, 1995, p. 67). Many of the gangas are sung outdoors, though they are also performed indoors. Some are love songs and others are bold and heroic. The ganga was sung by both adults and children, so the skill level varied among those performing the ganga.

Rich in cultural heritage, the ganga had great aesthetic value and symbolism to the people of each region. One can also say that it was a uniting and defining force for the various ethnic and religious groups. It was also a means for them to socialize and communicate via these songs. Thus, the ganga was an important means of expression and a unifying force for those in the community: Muslims, Roman Catholics, and Orthodox Christians in Serbia, Croatia, and Bosnia and Herzegovina.

Barbara Bonous-Smit

See also: Bartók, Béla; Turbo-Folk

Further Reading

Krader, Barbara. 1987. "Slavic Folk Music: Forms of Singing and Self-Identity." *Ethnomusicology* 31(1, Winter), 9–17. http://www.jstor.org/stable/852288.

Perkowski, Jan L. 1978. *Gusle and Ganga among the Herzegovians of Toronto*. Ann Arbor, MI: University Microfilms International.

Petrovič, Ankica. 1977. "Ganga, a Form of Traditional Rural Singing in Yugoslavia." Doctoral diss., Queen's University of Belfast.

Petrovič, Ankica. 1991. "The Musical Form Ganga as a Multi-Channeled Cultural Symbol in the Rural Society of Central Yugoslavia." In *Tradition and Its Future in Music: Report of the SIMS 1990, Tokyo*, 283–286. Osaka, Japan: Mita Press.
Petrovič, Ankica. 1995. "Perceptions of 'Ganga.'" *The World of Music* 37(2), 60–71.
Vidic-Rasmussen, Ljerka. 1995. "From Source to Commodity: Newly-Composed Folk Music of Yugoslavia." *Popular Music* 14(2), 241–256.

Gender Wayang

Gender wayang is a genre of *gamelan* music from Bali, Indonesia. The term "gender wayang" refers not only to a type of instrument, but also to the ensemble itself, and the genre or repertory performed on these instruments and in that ensemble. It is most internationally recognized for its accompaniment of Balinese *wayang kulit*, a shadow-puppet theater. This genre of music is also reserved for very elite Balinese Hindu rituals, and it is its *wali* (sacredness) that many Balinese scholars attribute as a pre-Hindu and pre-Javanese, ancient gamelan genre (Gold, 2005, pp. 72–73).

The music is performed by four players (two of which double the others at the octave), and features the unique hocketing techniques employed by other gamelan genres. The music of gender wayang is regional, with disparities unique to village or location. The most notable style of gender wayang, and perhaps the most proliferated within the West, originates from the village of Sukawati in Central Bali, and was taught by I Wayan Loceng (1928?–2006).

The instruments of the gender wayang are similar to other keyed bronze metallophones of *gamelan* ensembles (known in Bali as *bilah*). The keys themselves are made from a bronze alloy, approximately three parts copper to 10 parts tin (Tenzer, 2011, p. 34). The alloy is melted down from raw materials and broken bronze objects, cast into a mold, and cooled slightly so as to remain pliable. The keys are then hammered into shape, filed, and polished to perfection. The pitch of the key is determined by two geometric factors: the length of the key and the thickness of the key. If the key is filed down lengthwise, it will rise in pitch; similarly, if the key is shaved thinner (done from the bottom of the key), the key becomes "longer in proportion to its diminishing thickness," and a lower pitch is the result (Tenzer, 2011, p. 35).

Gender wayang instruments feature the same tuning methods used in other gamelan ensembles. The tuning, not to be thought of as scalar, but as a relationship of rough intervals, is disparate from ensemble to ensemble. No two ensembles are tuned exactly alike, nor are the instruments within the ensemble; in fact, it is preferred as a Balinese aesthetic to have the instruments tuned slightly apart from one another, so as to create a shimmering or "beating" quality to the sound (Gold, 2005, pp. 31–34; McPhee, 1966, p. 36; Tenzer, 2011, p. 36). This is achieved by tuning one of the paired instruments several cents higher than the other. When the instruments are played together, the disparity between frequencies results in both constructive and destructive interference patterns. *Constructive interference* is where the two frequencies' waves align, and the wave is doubled; *destructive* is where the two frequencies' waves are exactly opposite one another, and they cancel one another out. By slightly raising one frequency in pitch, the frequency aligns itself with the other at specific temporal periods, and then disaligns itself. This results in a beating phenomenon, similar to an out-of-tune guitar or piano. In the context of the gender wayang ensemble, the result—perhaps due to its rich overtones and bell-like timbres—is astonishingly bright and shimmering, creating a light tremolo-like effect. In Bali, this phenomenon is referred to as *ombak* (waves).

The instruments themselves are tuned to the Balinese *slendro* scale, which is a pentatonic scale roughly equivalent to the Western pitches A-C-D-E-G. The Balinese use a solfége system unique to their five-tone scales, with the symbols *ding, dong, deng, dung,* and *dang* representing the five tones (Tenzer, 2011, p. 37). The ensemble is comprised of four players, each playing with two hands. Two players double the parts, except at one octave higher; this practice is less common in North Bali, where two players often suffice (Kartawan, 2014, p. 2). The lower-register instruments are known as *pemade*, and the higher-register instruments are referred to as *barangan*.

The instruments' keys are suspended above tuned bamboo resonators, called *bumbung*; bamboo is preferred for its porous qualities, allowing the instrument to resonate longer, although today PVC is often used. PVC replicates the effect of bamboo, but with less appealing visual aesthetics and a diminished sound quality and resonance, due to the lack of pores. Bamboo lasts longer in instruments *in* Bali, because of the humid weather; instruments in other, less humid areas of the world, such as the United States, tend to crack and break more easily, and thus the bumbung are replaced with PVC to prevent unwarranted and undesired cracking. The bumbung are fitted into a wooden case, called *pelawah*, which is elaborately carved with motifs derived from Hindu, Chinese, and (occasionally), Egyptian motifs (Kartawan, 2013, p. 16). These elaborate carvings are often adorned with gold leaf, or are in some cases painted red, black, or left naturally unfinished.

Balinese music is periodized into the three following categories: *tua*, or old; *madya*, or middle; and *baru*, or new. Typically, music that doesn't feature drum accompaniment—more specifically, the *kendang*—is considered tua. This is because of the history of the kendang (the double-headed barrel drum) in Bali. It is believed that this instrument made its way into Bali sometime during the Chola Dynasty of Southern India, approximately between the ninth and 13th centuries CE. Thus, the emergence of this drum in Balinese musical ensembles aids in dating the instruments, ensembles, and repertories, and gives credence to the notion that gender wayang pre-dates the influx of Javanese or Hindu culture in Bali. The gender wayang ensemble accompanies *wayang wong* (a masked dance originating from Java, based on Hindu epics and tales); *wayang kulit* (a sacred or secular form of shadow-puppet theater); and cremation and tooth-filing ceremonies. Since the enculturation of the tourism industry in the mid-20th century, the ensemble and repertory are also performed at hotel lobbies as background music for curious tourists.

"Wayang wong" (literally, "human theater") bases its stories upon the Hindu Ramayana and Mahabharata, both of which more than likely arrived during the influx of Hinduism into Bali around the ninth century CE. Wayang kulit, however, is believed to be a much earlier tradition, given its repertory of indigenous Javanese and Balinese tales from the *tantri* or *babad*. The tantri are stories based on animals, and derived from *gamboeh*, a type of dance-form or drama indigenous to Bali and Java. "Tantri is the name not of a dance-form but of an individual story within a dance-form, which has imposed its name and been accepted as a type" (Spies and Zoete, 2002, p. 149). Babad are "genealogical chronicles and dynastic histories" indigenous to Bali, based on high-caste, raja families (a ruling, elite family in Bali). These two terms—*babad* and *tantri*—are contested insofar as they have Indic roots; babads based on "raja" families can be Hindu in nature, given the fact that "raja" is a term derived from the Hindu *rigveda*. Likewise, tantri are believed to originate from the 14th-century Javanese interpretation of the *Panchatantra*, a five-volume series of Hindu animal tales. By the 14th century, Java was exposed to Hinduism and Islam, and several seminal texts were translated into the Javanese language.

Wayang kulit features the gender wayang instruments, the performers of which get their performance cues from the *dalang*, or master puppeteer. Performances of wayang kulit have their own specific repertories unique to each tale, and are also unique to the time of day for the performance. Performances during the day are considered sacred (*wayang lemah*); performances at night (*wayang peteng*) are more commonly associated with entertainment. Tooth filings and cremation ceremonies do not have specific repertories, but typically feature slower, softer music, "including compositions such as *Sekar Sungsang*, *Rebong*, or *Alas Arum*, as well as pieces from the various *wayang kulit* repertoires" (Kartawan, 2014, p. 4).

Although the Central-Bali village of Sukawati is the most recognized for its achievements in the development of a gender wayang repertory, other villages have made similar achievements and contribution to gender wayang. The villages of Munduk, in North Bali, and Kayumas, in South Bali, have both made significant strides in gender wayang performance. Most recognizable are tuning modes and slight variations in interval relationships (known as *saih*) for differentiating regional styles; however, some scholars believe that Northern "Buleleng" gender wayang can be recognized by its lack of *barangan* players (Kartawan, 2014, p. 36).

Most notable pieces for gender wayang include, but are not limited to the following: *merak ngelo, rebong, sekar gendot*, and *sekar sungsang* (all from the wayang kulit repertory). Current innovations in gender wayang repertory include adapting the *Pelog* scale (another Balinese pitch-interval set similar to Western notes C#-D#-E-G#-A) to *gender* instruments, and adapting instruments from different ensembles (*gong kebyar*, for example) to the wayang kulit repertory. The gender wayang is not an ensemble for which new material is often written (*kreasi baru*, in Indonesian), although the pre-existing musical traditions are constantly revised, restructured, and on some occasions, rewritten.

John Forrestal

See also: Colometry/Colometric; Gamelan Orchestra (Balinese); Gamelan Orchestra (Javanese); Kebyar; Kecak; Kendang; McPhee, Colin; Wayang Kulit

Further Reading

Gold, Lisa. 2005. *Music in Bali*. New York: Oxford University Press.

Gray, Nicholas. 2011. *Improvisation and Composition in Balinese Gendér Wayang: Music of the Moving Shadows*. Surrey, UK: Ashgate.

Kartawan, I Made. 2014. *Tuning in Gender Wayang: Voices, Concepts, and Analysis*. Master's thesis, University of British Columbia, Vancouver.

McPhee, Colin. 1966. *Music in Bali*. New Haven, CT: Yale University Press.

Spies, Walter, and Beryl de Zoete. 2002. *Dance and Drama in Bali*. Hong Kong: Periplus Editions.

Gimbri

The *gimbri* (also spelled *gunbri*, *guimbri*, *guenbri*, and in other ways) is a three-stringed instrument of West African origins. The gimbri seems to take its name from the Soninke term *gambare*. In Morocco, the instrument is seen as part of the Gnawa, a Sufi (Islamic mystical group) group composed mainly of those with West African slave origins, and is frequently called *gimbri gnawi*.

The gnawi version is a bit larger, with a deeper sound, and is more like the Mande hunters' harp or the *donso ngoni*; called a *hajhouj*, it has a large, rectangular wooden sound box that is covered in a leather sound board. Its strings are made of animal gut, the neck has no frets, and at the tip of the neck, there is a long piece of metal with small metal rings along the sides that provide a buzzing noise when the strings are plucked. The neck is long and can accommodate charms hung along its length as protection for the players in a Gnawa meeting where spirits are called. This is similar to the donso ngoni, which is a harp-like instrument found in Mali that has a calabash sound chamber and is topped with a piece of metal with small metal hoops attached to the sides. The sound is also similar, as both instruments are deep sounding with an after-resonance.

Different forms of the instrument under different names are found mainly in West Africa, but north to Morocco and east to Chad. There are numerous instruments with nearly the same construction techniques. Because it has no frets, the gimbri is the "art" instrument among the *griot* class in West Africa. Among the Wolof-speakers of Senegal, it is called the *xalam*; in Mauritania, it is called the *tindinit*. The idea that the instrument began as a type of long-necked lute in ancient Egypt, based on tomb paintings (part of the larger attempt to find the "cultural hearth" for those interested in diffusion theory), is tantalizing but so far has not been proven.

John A. Shoup

See also: Griot; Xalam

Further Reading

Aydoun, Ahmed. 2001. *Musiques du Maroc* [Music of Morocco]. Casablanca: EDDIF/Autres Temps.

Charry, Eric. 2000. *Mande Music*. Chicago: University of Chicago Press.

Rault, Christian, and Marc Loopuyt. 1999. "Les Cordophones." In Catherine Homo-Lechner and Christian Raukt (eds.), *Instruments de musique du Maroc et d'al-Andalus* [Musical instruments of Morocco and al-Andaluz], 35–36. Paris: Centre Européan de Recherche pour l'Interpretation des Musiques Médiévales.

Gospel Music

Gospel music is a vernacular, nonliturgical genre of music in the Protestant Christian religious tradition. It is characterized by an emphasis on vocals, often with a strong use of harmony. While it is an indigenous American musical tradition, gospel music spread worldwide during the 20th century. Gospel music is distinguished from hymnody by the strong influences of folk and popular music on gospel.

The roots of gospel music can be found in the oral tradition of the African American spirituals and the revival spirituals of the early 19th century. These two bodies of song share a number of common characteristics, including simple tunes, repetitive lyrics, a tendency toward verse-refrain structure, and the use of call-and-response singing.

The first known use of the term *gospel song* in association with a body of music came in 1874, with the publication of Philip Bliss's songbook *Gospel Songs: A Choice Collection of Hymns and Tunes* (1838–1876). The songs included were becoming common within the revival movement started by Dwight Moody (1837–1899) in the 1870s and have a different character than the traditional hymns that were used in American Protestant churches at the time. Traditional hymn-writers tended to write for a musically literate collection of trained singers, whereas the Bliss songs exhibited the influence of the spirituals with their simpler, more repetitive lyrics and melodies that were easier for untrained singers to sing. Many of these songs, such as "I Am So Glad that Jesus Loves Me" and "Sweet Hour of Prayer," also show the influence of the Holiness movement in their personal, experiential lyrics. Bliss's songs were only part of the new wave of sacred song during this era. Many revivalists employed popular singers to lead the singing during their meetings. The most famous of these, Ira D. Sankey (1840–1908), worked with Moody. In addition to Bliss, songwriters such as George F. Root (1820–1895), Fanny Crosby (1820–1915), and Charles H. Gabriel (1856–1932) provided new songs for the movement. Bliss and Sankey began compiling a collection of these songs under the title *Gospel Hymns and Sacred Songs* in 1875. In all, there were six volumes of *Gospel Hymns* containing more than 700 different songs.

The popularity of these songs carried over from the urban revivals into rural churches, which were open to the simpler style of the new gospel hymns. In the late 19th and early 20th centuries, several publishing houses opened with the purpose of publishing gospel songs. One of those was founded by the singer and songwriter Homer A. Rodeheaver (1880–1955), who started his career touring with evangelist Billy Sunday. Another was founded by singer Charles Tillman (1861–1943), who published original songs and adaptations of pre-existing songs that became the foundation of the style that came to be known as *Southern gospel*. Another well-known publisher of gospel songs was Charles Albert Tindley (1851–1933) who is regarded as the "father" of Black gospel music.

SOUTHERN GOSPEL

In the early 20th century, gospel music began to fragment stylistically into two basic styles and approaches: Southern gospel and Black gospel. *Southern gospel,* sometimes called "White gospel" or "quartet music," is so named because of its roots in the American Southeast. Singer and publisher James D. Vaughan from Tennessee is often credited with originating the style because he was responsible for establishing the first professional quartet for the purpose of singing gospel songs and selling the songbooks he published. Many of the songs that are considered staples of this genre, however, existed long before that time. For instance, Charles Tillman published a version of the spiritual "Old-Time Religion" and promoted it among white Southern churches almost 20 years earlier.

Musically, Southern gospel was heavily influenced by the barbershop singing tradition, with its use of all-male quartets featuring a tenor-lead-baritone-bass makeup. Initially these quartets sang a cappella or were accompanied only by piano or guitar. Over time, other musical styles that were popular in the South, such as shape-note singing, country, and bluegrass, also began to blend with this quartet singing. While all-male quartets, such as The Cathedral Quartet, the Florida Boys, and The Gaither Vocal Band, are the ensembles most commonly associated with Southern gospel, mixed groups of various sizes, such as The Bill Gaither Trio, The Crabb Family, The LeFevres, The Rambos, and Jeff and Sheri Easter, have also been popular. Many of these groups, as their names indicate, were created by or around families. From the 1970s, solo performers such as Squire Parsons, Janet Paschal, and Jason Crabb have also been common.

BLACK GOSPEL

Black gospel shares many commonalities with Southern gospel. Early Black gospel also centered around the all-male quartet, although Black gospel quartets were most often unaccompanied. Because this style of singing had been introduced into African American churches through groups like the Fisk Jubilee Singers, its close harmonies with bluesy inflections became known as the "jubilee" style. In the 1920s, elements of African American secular music began to be integrated into Black gospel. In 1922, a blind singer-pianist named Juanita "Arizona" Dranes (1889/1891–1963) joined the Church of God in Christ in Wichita Falls, Kansas, and became well-known for her ragtime and boogie-woogie piano accompaniment styles.

Many of the new Black gospel songs introduced into churches were penned by Charles Albert Tindley, a minister in the Methodist Episcopal Church. Tindley's songs include "A Better Day Is Coming By and By," "I Know the Lord Will Make a Way," "I'll Be Satisfied," and "I'll Overcome Some Day," which is believed to have been the basis for the 1960s civil rights anthem "We Shall Overcome."

In the 1930s, pianist Thomas A. Dorsey (1899–1993) changed the direction of gospel music through a number of innovations. Dorsey, the son of a Baptist minister, had made a career as a blues pianist under the names "Barrelhouse Tom" and (most famously) "Georgia Tom." He served as the musical director and pianist for Gertrude "Ma" Rainey's (1886–1939) Wild Cats Jazz Band for a time. In the late 1920s, Dorsey began to perform and record gospel songs as well as blues songs and dedicated himself completely to gospel following the deaths of his wife and newborn child in 1932. That tragedy also led Dorsey to pen his most famous song,

"Precious Lord, Take My Hand." Dorsey helped to legitimize gospel music in mainstream black churches when the National Baptist Convention programmed his song "If You See My Savior" during its 1930 national convention, which officially adopted gospel as the main musical expression for worship in the Convention.

Dorsey's approach to gospel music was heavily influenced by the blues in both its sound and its character. Most of his songs reflect personal sentiments, such as "Precious Lord, take my hand" and "If you see my Savior," rather than the sentiments of a group. This further connects Black gospel with the personal and experiential faith of the Holiness movement. In 1932, Dorsey founded Dorsey House of Music, a publishing house, to publish this new gospel style, and created the first organization dedicated to promoting and supporting gospel choirs. The organization was formalized the following year as the National Convention of Gospel Choirs and Choruses. Music published by Dorsey House was marketed like Dorsey's blues songs were, which meant they were published as individual sheet music rather than in songbook form, as had been common with previous gospel music.

Another impact Dorsey had on Black gospel was the development of solo artists such as Mahalia Jackson (1911–1972) and Willie Mae Ford (1904–1994). These artists not only created a public face for Black gospel in the 1930s and 1940s, they also served to promote Dorsey's songs. They were also a departure from the earlier gospel quartets and gospel choirs in that they performed in both churches and nightclubs. As a result, they tended to perform with a style more closely connected to the free and loose style of blues and jazz singers than to the stricter interpretations that were common in churches. These changes were not without controversy, as many congregations objected to singers bringing a nightclub act into the church, complete with sequined dresses in lieu of choir robes.

In the 1940s and 1950s, gospel quartets began to incorporate some of Dorsey's stylistic characteristics, moving away from the jubilee style and toward what became known as "hard gospel." Hard gospel emphasized the individual singers over the quartet sound. Quartets transformed from egalitarian ensembles into the lead singer/ backup singer model that was becoming popular in secular rhythm and blues and eventually in doo-wop groups. Each singer in the group was free to embellish his or her melody "as the Spirit moves," creating what the Dixie Hummingbirds called vocal "trickeration."

CONTEMPORARY GOSPEL

The developments in both Southern and Black gospel led to a greater mainstream presence of gospel music starting in the 1950s. In 1950, Joe Bostic created the first Negro Gospel and Religious Music Festival at Carnegie Hall in New York. Over the next decade, the festival grew in popularity and finally moved to Madison Square Garden in 1959. In 1967, Edwin Hawkins created a soul/funk-influenced arrangement of the 18th-century hymn "Oh Happy Day," and within two years, the recording had peaked at number four on the *Billboard* chart in the United States, reached number two on the UK pop charts, and won a Grammy award.

Since the 1970s, the lines between sacred and secular music have blurred even more. The "Jesus Movement," a Christianized segment of the youth counterculture

Gospel singer CeCe Winans is one of the best-selling female gospel artists of all time. (R. Diamond/WireImage/Getty Images)

in the late 1960s, led to the use of the rock styles that were common to that "hippie" culture in the context of gospel music. Solo performers such as Larry Norman, Barry McGuire, Randy Stonehill, Paul Stookey (of Peter, Paul, and Mary), Honeytree, and Keith Green; psychedelic groups such as Servant, Resurrection Band, Agape, and The All-Saved Freak Band; and mainstream rock bands such as Petra, DeGarmo & Key, and Daniel Amos laid the foundation for what would become known as "contemporary Christian music." In the mid-1980s, bands like Stryper, Saint, Bride, and Barren Cross brought heavy metal into the world of contemporary Christian music. In the late 1980s, Vengeance Rising, Deliverance, Tourniquet, and Believer introduced thrash and speed metal under the gospel music umbrella, and by the 1990s, bands such as Mortification, Horde, Crimson Moonlight, and Pantokrator were performing death metal and black metal music with Christian-oriented lyrics.

Meanwhile, the soulful style of Andrae Crouch and The Disciples in the 1970s laid the foundation for a brand of Black gospel known as "urban contemporary gospel." A more traditional approach to urban contemporary gospel reintroduced the gospel choir over a background of electric guitar, bass, drums, and keyboards. Other artists followed Crouch's example and created gospel music that blended soul and funk. In the 1980s and 1990s, a number of urban contemporary gospel artists, such as BeBe and CeCe Winans, Yolanda Adams, and Tramaine Hawkins, turned to rhythm and blues (R & B) and established themselves on both the inspirational and secular R & B charts. Other artists brought hip-hop and rap into gospel music. The earliest gospel rap recordings came from around 1982 and were essentially Sunday School teaching songs. Following the success of DC Talk, the world of "holy hip-hop" flourished in the 1990s and 2000s through artists such as T-Bone, Knowdaverbs, The Cross Movement, 116 Clique, Lecrae, and Trip Lee.

THE INDUSTRY

In 1964, the Gospel Music Association (GMA) was formed to support, promote, and cultivate the creation and performance of all forms of gospel music. In 1968, the National Academy of Recording Arts and Sciences awarded the first Grammy Award for Best Gospel Performance. In 1969, the GMA established the Dove Awards as a way for the Association to recognize outstanding achievements within the gospel music industry. The idea for the Dove Awards came from singer/songwriter Bill Gaither, and all artists whose music was sold in Christian Booksellers Association-affiliated stores were eligible. In 1971, the GMA created the Gospel Music Hall of Fame to further recognize significant contributions by individuals and groups to gospel music.

Eric S. Strother

See also: African Spirituals; Dorsey, Thomas A.; Jackson, Mahalia

Further Reading

Boyer, Horace Clarence. 2000. *The Golden Age of Gospel.* Champaign: University of Illinois Press.

Cusic, Don. 2012. *Saved by Song: A History of Gospel and Christian Music.* Oxford: University Press of Mississippi.

Cusic, Don. 1990. *The Sound of Light: A History of Gospel Music.* Milwaukee, WI: Popular Press.

Darden, Robert. 2005. *People Get Ready!: A New History of Black Gospel Music.* New York: Bloomsbury Academic.

Goff, James R., Jr. 2001. *Close Harmony: A History of Southern Gospel.* Chapel Hill: University of North Carolina Press.

Heilbut, Anthony. 2004. *The Gospel Sound: Good News and Bad Times.* New York: Limelight Editions.

Thompson, John J. 2000. *Raised by Wolves: The Story of Christian Rock & Roll.* Toronto: ECW Press.

Greek Popular Music

Greek popular music traces its roots to a variety of musical genres, including the music of Asian Minor Greeks, West European, Latin American, North American, Turkish, and Egyptian popular music, Indian film music, and Western classical music. Greek popular music offers a unique fusion of Eastern and Western musical elements and has had a profound influence on Mediterranean musical cultures. Some of the most popular indigenous genres include: *demotika, rebetika, laika, entehna,* political song, *neo kyma,* new-wave laika, and *skyladika.* There are also growing rock, rap, jazz, and electronic dance music scenes in Greece.

Greece, or the Hellenic Republic, is located in southeastern Europe and is a country located at the crossroads of Europe, Western Asia, and Africa. The modern Greek state dates back to 1830 and was formed after gaining independence from the Ottoman Empire. Treaties after the First and Second Balkan Wars almost doubled the area and population of Greece. After the Greco-Turkish War of 1921–1922, the population of Greece was further increased by 1.5 million people (mostly Christians) due to the influx of Asia Minor Greeks. The arrival and settlement of Asia Minor Greeks had a profound and long-lasting influence on Greek popular music.

In the 1920s, Asia Minor Greeks brought with them a long-established tradition of musical innovation and originality that blended Greek language with Eastern musical styles. The musical landscape of the time in Greece consisted of demotika (rural folk songs), songs from the 1821 revolution, Western-influenced operettas, Neapolitan-style Ionian island serenades called *kantades*, tangos and foxtrots (popular among the wealthier and elite classes), and songs about dislocation and drug dependency (popular among the poorer classes) played on stringed instruments similar to those of the Asia Minor Greeks (Pappas, 1999, p. 354). The music that Asia Minor Greeks brought with them was rebetika. Rebetika (known as the urban blues of Greece) is an urban folk style of music which originated at the start of the 20th century in Aegean ports and was originally a subculture associated with drugs, crime, and economic hardships. The roots of this music can be traced back to about the 1850s onwards, in Asia Minor's Smyrna (Izmir); in Istanbul, in the port of Syros; in the working-class areas of Athens, Pireaus, and Thessaloniki; and in the United States (Emery, 2000, p. 11). Rebetika is an urban musical form whose main instruments include the long-necked *bouzouki*, the *baglamas* (smaller versions of the bouzouki), and the guitar. The particular style of music the Asia Minor Greeks brought with them from the eastern Aegean was Greek-Ottoman café music, also known as the Smyrnaiko style of rebetika. Greek-Ottoman café music was dominant until the mid-1930s, when the Pireaus bouzouki style of rebetika gained popularity. However, rebetika did not gain a wide popular audience until the late 1940s.

During the fascist dictatorship of Ioannis Metaxas (1936–1941), the Axis Occupation (1941–1946), and the Greek Civil War (1946–1949), rebetika was censored by the Greek state. From the 1930s until the Greek Civil War in the late 1940s, rebetika was mostly defined in negative terms by the state. It was looked down upon as the song and culture of the "underworld" and of those not respectable enough to be members of the Greek middle classes. These associations began to change in the late 1940s once rebetika gained popularity among the Greek middle classes.

During the 1950s, rebetika provided the background for several new strands of Greek popular music: laika, entehna (art-popular song), and political song. The genre of neo kyma (new wave) also emerged during this time period. Laika, the "songs of the people," first emerged in Athens from rebetika in the 1950s. Laika is a broad-based genre of Greek popular music which originally emerged as a simplification of rebetika in order to make this type of music more broadly marketable. The influences of laika included rebetika, West European, Latin American, North American, Turkish, and Egyptian popular music and Indian film music (Pennanen, 2005, p. 116). From the 1960s and onwards, laika became fashionable among wealthier segments of Greek society and variations of the genre were produced to suit the tastes of the middle classes who frequented nightclubs and tavernas that featured these musical forms. At this time, laika also started to be performed in *bouzoukia* nightclubs, which to this day play a central role in Greek nightlife.

During the late 1950s and early 1960s, Greek composers created the genre of Greek popular music known as "entehna." The entehna musical genre combines elements of Western classical music, Greek popular music (including rebetika, laika, rural folk music, and the like) and poetry and is best exemplified by classically trained composers such as Mikis Theodorakis and Manos Hadjidakis. During this same time period, political song also emerged as a genre. Political songs were generally associated with broadly defined left-wing positions and sought to challenge the current status quo. This is not surprising given the political conditions of this time period. On April 21, 1967, Stylianos Pattakos, George Papadopoulos, and Nikolaos Makarezos seized power in a coup d'état. Their period of right-wing military rule was known as the Greek Military Junta of 1967–1974.

During the military junta, the music of Mikis Theodorakis (one of the main proponents of entehna and political song) and the poetry of Yiannis Ritsos were banned. Theodorakis spent the dictatorship in prison, under house arrest, and eventually in exile, while Ritsos remained under house arrest for the duration of the period. Rebetika were once again banned during this period. In the early 1960s, neo kyma emerged in the Athenian Plaka district. This genre was influenced by the politicized folk movements of Latin America and songs of the Greek left. Singer-songwriters such as Dionysis Savopoulos best exemplify the genre of neo kyma. Because his lyrics were not openly political in nature, Savopoulos was able to release records and perform publicly during the military junta.

In the 1970s and 1980s, after the fall of the military junta in Greece, there was a rebetika revival. Rebetika became widely popular, especially among leftist Athenian youth who had opposed the military dictatorship. The widespread popularity of rebetika both in Greece and among the Greek diaspora overseas was due in part to the anti-elitist cultural policy of the PaSoK party that came to power in 1981. PaSoK promoted the genre through state-sponsored stadium concerts and semi-fictional television shows.

During the 1980s, one of the new musical genres that emerged was new wave laika, a hybrid musical genre that merged laika and rebetika with Western pop music. One of the most popular, and simultaneously most denigrated, subgenres of new wave laika is disparagingly known as *skyladika* (dog music). Skyladika, also known as contemporary folk music, "started as fringe music addressing the alienated, nihilist and consumption ridden aspects of urban life" and drew upon Arabic and Asian musical forms while including elements of synthesizer and electric guitar (Papageorgiou, 2005, p. 121). Originally, skyladika addressed itself to alienated rural migrants who were unable to integrate into the city; it was a type of music popular in the working-class areas of Athens and it was released primarily through independent labels that charged performers to record and produce their records (Papageorgiou, 1997, p. 72). Skyladika have become increasingly popular and are performed in bouzoukia with great commercial success.

According to statistics, more popular music recordings were made in the 1990s in Greece than during all the other previous decades (Pennanen, 2005, p. 117). One of the genres that flourished during the 1990s was Greek pop music, which is sung mostly in Greek and modeled on international pop music. Greek pop offers an eclectic mix of Eastern and Western musical sounds and cultural elements. Longstanding artists such as George Dalaras, Eleftheria Arvanitaki, Glykeria, and Ana Vissi offer engaging mixes of Greek popular music, global pop, and world music. In addition, there are growing rock, rap, jazz, and electronic dance music scenes in Greece. For example, rap music in Greece began as a subculture in the late 1980s/early 1990s. By the middle of the 1990s, many of the founding hip-hop groups had signed with major labels, but by the early 2000s many of these hip-hop groups had been dropped from their major labels. From 2003 and thereafter, rap music and R & B gained large-scale commercial success (mainly through crossover collaborations between hip-hop artists and Greek popular artists, such as the popular rap group Goin' Through collaborating with artists such as Stelio Roko, George Mazonaki, David Lynch, and Peter Andre, among others). As a result of the strength of indigenous musical genres (such as rebetika, laika, etc.), localized forms of rock, rap, jazz, and electronic dance music have had a difficult time gaining legitimacy within the popular music industry in Greece. Though artists from these genres, such as rap artists, have gained commercial success, many of these genres are still seen as "foreign" musical forms.

Athena Elafros

See also: Cretan Lyra; Nisiotika

Further Reading

Dawe, Kevin. 2003. "Between East and West: Contemporary Grooves in Greek Popular Music (c. 1990–2000)." In Goffredo Plastino (ed.), *Mediterranean Mosaic: Popular Music and Global Sounds*, 221–240. New York: Routledge.

Elafros, Athena. 2013. "Greek Hip Hop: Local and Translocal Authentication in the Restricted Field of Production." *Poetics* 41, 75–95.

Emery, Ed. 2000. "Introduction." In E. Petropoulos, *Songs of the Greek Underworld: The Rebetika Tradition*, 11–39. London: Saki Books.

Papageorgiou, Fouli T. 1997. "Popular Music and the Music Industry in Greece." In A. J. Ewbank and F. T. Papageorgiou (eds.), *Whose Master's Voice? The Development of Popular Music in Thirteen Cultures*, 67–87. Westport, CT: Greenwood Press.

Papageorgiou, Fouli T. 2005. "Athina (Athens)." In John Shepherd, David Horn, and Dave Laing (eds.), *Continuum Encyclopedia of Popular Music of the World; Vol. 7: Europe*, 120–123. New York: Continuum.

Pappas, Nicholas G. 1999. "Concepts of Greekness: The Recorded Music of Anatolian Greeks after 1922." *Journal of Modern Greek Studies* 17, 353–373.

Pennanen, Risto Pekka. 2005. "Greece." In John Shepherd, David Horn and Dave Laing (eds.), *Continuum Encyclopedia of Popular Music of the World; Vol. 7: Europe*, 114–119. New York: Continuum.

Gregorian Chant

Conventionally, *Gregorian chant* refers to the vocal music of the Latin Liturgy of the Roman Catholic Church. This melodic repertoire accompanied the Catholic liturgy for more than a millennium; the Second Vatican Council (1962–1965) replaced the Latin service with local vernaculars. The songs comprising this repertoire were restored in the late 19th century by the monks of the Benedictine Abbey of Solesmes.

Gregorian chant is named after Pope Gregory I (ca. 540–604 CE), known as Saint Gregory the Great. Gregory I radically reformed the liturgy during his pontificate (590–604 CE). His *Antifonarium Cento* became the basis for the unified version of liturgical chant adopted by the entire Western Church. The traditional iconography pictures him on the papal throne, holding a stylus and a book while a dove (which symbolizes divine inspiration) dictates the songs for the liturgy to him. Recent theories claim that the repertory nowadays known as Gregorian chant derives from the unifying action of several local traditions carried on by Pope Gregory II (669–731 CE), and the Frankish kings Pippin the Younger (ca. 714–768 CE) and Charlemagne (ca. 742–814 CE) between the eighth and ninth centuries.

None of those local traditions still survive in Western Europe, with the exception of the Ambrosian chant, spread over *Mediolanum* (nowadays Milan, Italy) and its surroundings, due to the political and religious role played by Lombardy's capital between the late Roman Empire and the high Middle Ages. Other local traditions were extant in Europe in early medieval times. The Greco-Byzantine chant, which originated in Constantinople and the Middle East, is still used in today's Orthodox Church in the Christian East (for instance, Bulgaria, Romania, and Greece). Aquileian and the Beneventan chants were diffused respectively in today's Udine district (northern Italy) and Benevento, near Naples. Roman chant was diffused in Rome, while the so-called Gallican tradition spread over France. Finally, the Old Spanish chant, addressed as Mozarabic (among the Arabs), was strongly influenced by the culture of the Muslims, who ruled Spain until the Christian *reconquista* of Toledo in 1051.

The fusion between the Frankish Gallican chant and the Old Roman tradition spread all over Europe from the ninth century onward, replacing most of the local traditions and giving birth to Gregorian chant. The Gregorian chant repertoire concerns the two principal classes of services of the Christian liturgy: the Office and the Mass.

The chants of the Office, first codified by St. Benedict (ca. 480–ca. 546 CE) in his *Rule*, are sung every day at stated times by the clerics. Specifically, they are *Matins*, *Lauds*, *Prime*, *Terce*, *Sext*, *Nones*, *Vespers*, and *Compline*. The Office, the music for which is collected in the *Antiphonale* (Antiphoner), consists of prayers, psalms, canticles, antiphons, responses, hymns, and readings.

The *Antiphonale* derives its name from the *antiphon*, a short melody that precedes and follows the performance of a psalm. The chants of the Mass were grouped into two sections called *Ordinarium* (ordinary) and *Proprium* (proper). The first features chants whose texts do not change throughout the entire span of the liturgical year. The songs of the *Proprium* varied on a day-to-day basis, according to the current festivity. The *Ordinarium* included five chants, which appeared relatively late in the liturgy: *Kyrie*, *Gloria*, *Credo*, *Sanctus*, and *Agnus Dei*. Although their poems do not change, they are set to a large number of different melodies.

The *Kyrie*, used in every Mass, makes clear reference to the original liturgical language, Greek. Three simple invocations make up this relatively short piece: *Kyrie eleison; Christe eleison; Kyrie eleison* (Lord, have mercy; Christ, have mercy; Lord, have mercy). Prior to the 20th century, they were each repeated three times, but due to the new regulation enforced by the Second Vatican Council, the formula is now sung only once. The *Gloria* is a prayer to the glorification of Christ, and it is performed on festive days only—with the exception of Advent and Lent—as is the *Credo*, through which faithful Christians state the truth of their belief. The *Sanctus* and *Agnus Dei* are sung in every Mass.

The chants of the *Proprium* were *Introitus, Graduale, Alleluia* (replaced by *Tractus* on certain penitential festivals such as Easter and Lent), then *Offertorium* and *Communio*. This sequence had been added by the ninth century. The *Introitus* (introit) is the entry chant for the Mass. Originally a whole psalm was meant to be sung, where verses and antiphon alternated; later a single psalm verse survived, to be performed together with the *Gloria Patri*. The *Communio* (communion chant) is performed during the administration of the Eucharist. As with the *Introitus*, the earlier version of the *Communio* involved the alternation of verses and antiphon, while later it became a short song delivering the antiphon only.

The *Graduale* (gradual) is the oldest of these forms. It was likely named thus due to its being sung on the *gradus* (step) of the ambo. It is made of two sections, a solo part and a response by the choir. The same noun is used to denote a liturgical book, also called *Antiphonale missarum*, featuring the chants for the Proper for the whole liturgical year. Sometimes it contained the *ordinarium* as well, as an appendix. The *Alleluia* originated in the Judaic liturgy; in Hebrew it means "Praise Yahweh." It is an independent composition of joy in responsorial form, similar to the gradual. It alternates the alleluia itself, which is sung twice, and a versicle.

The *Offertorium* (offertory), so named because it was sung during the procession that brings bread, wine, and any sacrificial offerings to the altar, has a function similar to that of the Introit and Communion. It was first in antiphonal style but later developed a more embellished style. The *Proprium* was organized according to the Christian liturgical year, which starts on Easter Day (the Sunday immediately following the feast of the spring full moon); 50 days thereafter, Pentecost takes place. The number of weeks after Pentecost is variable in order to allow a four-week period of Advent before Christmas. After Epiphany (January 6), another further variable period leads to the *septuagesima*, comprised of the nine weeks prior to Easter.

Gregorian chant was mainly transmitted orally, but during the ninth century this repertoire witnessed the birth of a new musical notation. Such *neumatic* musical notation consisted of staffless signs in the shape of accents and punctuation marks. The etymology of the noun *neume* goes back to the Old Greek, either from *neuma*, which means "sign," or from *pneuma*, meaning "breath." *Neuma* refers not to a single note, but to the note, or notes, sung to a single syllable (thus a single breath). Neumes did not carry any rhythmic meaning, nor did they give any indication of pitch; they merely suggested the relation between two consecutive notes.

Neumatic notation was not meant to replace memory, but rather to be used alongside it. The monastery of St. Gall, located in today's Switzerland, played a remarkable role in the development of this notation, which reached a peak of complexity in the 10th century. Its notation is one of the earliest, and is renowned as being extraordinarily elaborate. Its use of *litterae significativae* (meaningful letters) significantly improved neumatic notation by indicating variations of rhythm (e.g., *c* standing for *celeriter*: "quicker"), and pitch (*e* standing for *equaliter*: "same as the previous note").

At the beginning of the 11th century, it became possible to indicate small intervals, such as semitones (diastematic notation), through the use of colored lines (initially just a red line for F and a yellow line for C). Progressively, more lines were added, hence establishing the tetragram (four-line stave). The invention of diastematic notation is ascribed to an Italian Benedictine monk, Guido d'Arezzo (ca. 992–1050 CE). Although his role in this has been relatively downplayed, he certainly brought together improvements from all over Europe to compile the *Micrologus*, a treatise which represents the most important musical achievement since Boethius (475/80–524 CE). He developed new techniques for teaching the monks how to sing Gregorian chant more quickly than ever before. His main mnemonic method used the first syllables of the hymn to St. John the Baptist written by Paul the Deacon, which started each line on a successively higher degree of the scale.

By memorizing this melodic scheme, the singer was able to calculate the position of the semitone, always occurring between *mi* and *fa*. Thanks to Guido's invention of the tetragram, from the beginning of the 12th century Gregorian chant became completely diatonic, as the semitone was now the smallest interval one could notate (it had been possible to represent microtones with the adiastematic notations). With the tetragram, neumes changed their shapes and became more quadrate, leading to the squared notation still in use today by the Vatican editions of the Catholic liturgy.

The rhythmic interpretation of neumes is intensely debated among scholars, but a main theory prevails, claiming that such music is organized through so-called "free rhythm." This does not mean absence of rhythm; rather, it indicates singing according to the length and stress of the syllable, where each *protasis* (forward movement) necessarily requires a sort of cadence (*apodosis*).

Unfortunately, contemporary theorists do not shed much light on the matter. Gregorian chant theory is based on early medieval treatises, where theorists mainly concentrated on analyzing prosody, metrics, and the nature of the intervals. They mostly repeated, more or less explicitly, concepts featured in the fundamental *De institutione musica* by Boethius. Boethius brought Greek musical tradition into Latin culture. Like him, other Latin authors (e.g., Cassiodorus, Isidore of Seville) borrowed music theory and terms from Greek culture. It is for this reason that the peculiarly Greek concept of *oktoechos* (eight sounds) is at the root of the eight modes theory used in Gregorian chant. The term *mode*, in this context, refers to a set of diatonic scales, characterized by their fundamental sound and the differing sequence of tones and semitones. Four basic modes—*protus, deuterus, tritus,* and *tetrardus*—are called "authentic" and start respectively on D, E, F, and G. Each of them is extended downwards in a series of four notes to obtain four additional plagal (oblique) modes. Together these constitute the eight ecclesiastical modes.

Although the main musical stress of the songs was on the *finalis* (first note of the mode), there was a secondary focus on the *repercussio* (repeated note), usually corresponding to the fifth grade in the case of authentic modes. The modal system was a great aid for the medieval performer, who could take advantage of it by memorizing the repertoire through melodic formulas arranged according to modes.

Jacopo Mazzeo

See also: Classical Music, European; Concerto; Medieval Secular Song; Psaltery

Further Reading
Apel, Willi. 1958. *Gregorian Chant*. Bloomington: Indiana University Press.
Cardine, Eugène. 1983. *Gregorian Semiology*. Solesmes, France: Abbaye Saint-Pierre de Solesmes.
Catholic Church, Abbaye Saint-Pierre de Solesmes Benedictines. 1979. *Graduale triplex: seu Graduale Romanum Pauli PP. VI cura recognitum & rhythmicis signis a Solesmensibus monachis ornatum* [Graduale Triplex: Roman graduale settings of Paul's letter to the Romans chapter 6 and recognized rhythmic standards of Solesmensibus monks]. Solesmes, France: Abbaye Saint-Pierre de Solesmes.
Guzasky, G. Fredrick. 2011. *Gregorian Chant Handbook*. Boston: FP Ltd.
Hesbert, René Jean. 1967. *Antiphonale Missarum Sextuplex*. Rome: Herder.
Hiley, David. 1995. *Western Plainchant: A Handbook*. Oxford: Clarendon Press.
Hiley, David. 2009. *Gregorian Chant*. Cambridge: Cambridge University Press.
Jones, Noel, and Ellen Doll Jones. 2010. *A Beginner's Guide to Singing Gregorian Chant, Notation, Rhythm and Solfeggio*. Englewood, TN: Frog Music Press.
Meconi, Honey. 2011. *Medieval Music*. Farnham, UK: Ashgate.

Griot

A *griot* (pronounced "gree-oh") is a West African professional musician, storyteller, and oral historian. As artisans who usually work in the service of noble or economically powerful patrons, griots are masters of several verbal art forms, especially epic historical narratives, praise-singing, recitation of genealogy, folktales, song lyrics, and proverbs. Griots also specialize in a number of song styles and musical instruments, which vary widely among ethnic groups. In addition to these central skills, griots often have other responsibilities, which may include serving as political advisers and spokespeople, conflict mediators, and teachers. The word "griot" is an umbrella term referring to similar social roles that exist in many cultures of the West African Sahel. Local terms include the Mande *jali* (primarily in Mali, Senegal, and The Gambia), Wolof *gewel* (primarily in Senegal and The Gambia), Moorish *iggio* (primarily in Mauritania), Soninke *gesere* (primarily in Mali, Senegal, The Gambia, and Guinea-Bissau), and Fula *gaulo* (a migratory ethnic group living throughout West Africa), among others.

Other cultures in Africa and around the world have positions similar to griots in their skillsets and social role. They may be called bards, praise-singers, court musicians, or storytellers, and there is often a specific word for them in the local language. In Africa, for example, the Ethiopian *azmari*, Yoruba *oniyalu*, Xhosa *imbongi*, and Fang *mvet* all have social roles and status similar to the West African griots. Because of this, scholars disagree about whether the term "griot" applies to a broad region of Africa, or only the smaller area of Senegambia and its neighbors. Most agree that the crucial identifying attributes of griots are their role as oral historians and musicians, their specific situation in the social hierarchy, their hereditary transmission of skills, and their connection to the historical and cultural nexus of the West African Sahel.

The word "griot" comes from the older term *guiriot*, which was first recorded by French colonists in the 17th century and seems to be based on a jumbling of local African words. The term is useful today because it emphasizes a point of unity among several different West African cultures, which share this similar social role. However, it is important to remember that West African music is characterized as much by its diversity as by its unity, and that each cultural community has its own distinct ways of making music and telling stories. Each of the local terms for griots refers to musicians who play different instruments, sing different songs, tell different stories and oral histories, and occupy specific positions within their society. Because the more general term "griot" does not encapsulate these specific cultural characteristics, West African musicians most often refer to themselves by the term specific to their cultural group, though they may also use "griot" when speaking with cultural outsiders.

Griots are professional musicians and literary artists found in West Africa. Pictured are griots in Cameroon. (Maurice Ascani/Gamma-Rapho via Getty Images)

The word "griot" was popularized in the United States by the 1976 novel *Roots*, written by African American author Alex Haley, and the hugely successful TV miniseries that was based on it. While doing research for the book, Haley met with a Gambian griot who helped him trace his genealogical lineage back to a Mandinka ancestor named Kunta Kinte. Since then, many African Americans have adopted the term to refer to storytellers, musicians, and keepers of cultural heritage. For example, numerous rappers, jazz musicians, and poets have been called griots, and the term lends its name to cultural institutions such as the Griot Institute for Africana Studies at Bucknell University and the Griot Museum of Black History in St. Louis. The city of Baltimore, Maryland, even appointed an "Official Griot" in 1983. This diasporic usage of the term celebrates the importance of African roots and modes of cultural expression, though it often omits the hereditary transmission and ambivalent social status that characterize traditional West African griots.

The griot position exists across so many cultures because of the common history that unites much of Sahelian West Africa. Complex societies have existed in the region since at least 1500 BCE. One of the first major civilizations that we know of is the empire of ancient Ghana (800 to 1235 CE), which covered a large region in what is now Mali and Mauritania (much further north than the present-day country of Ghana). This eventually became the empire of Mali (1235 to 1600 CE), which stretched into the present-day countries of Senegal, The Gambia, and Niger. Both of these early civilizations traded extensively across the Sahelian and Saharan regions, spreading their economic influence as well as cultural ideas, including the role of musicians in society. Both empires developed hierarchical social structures, which were similar in some ways to the feudal societies of medieval Europe. Villages reported to vassal states, which reported to larger kingdoms, which in turn paid homage to the central empire government. This hierarchy probably extended into everyday life as well, with different social positions ranked from indentured servants to artisans to nobility and royalty.

Islam has also been highly influential in West African social life for centuries. Islamic leaders and teachers, called *marabouts*, gained momentum by converting West African rulers and kings starting in the 10th century. Muslim religious ideas spread through the Ghanaian and Malian empires, including the use of singers to announce daily prayer times and to praise religious and political leaders. Contact with European traders (beginning in the 15th century) and formal colonization (beginning in the late 19th century) also had profound effects on West African societies. For example, Europeans supported large empires by utilizing their long-established trade routes and, later on, they sometimes encouraged and rigidified hierarchical social structures to facilitate the collection of taxes, the administration of laws, and the capture of slaves.

There are different ideas about how griots entered into this historical situation. Some scholars believe that griots originated in ancient hunter's cults, which used music to initiate new members and to praise the bravery and skill of their leaders. This practice would then have been adopted by leaders of the ancient Ghanaian empire, who employed griots to spread their renown and keep track of their family and political history. Many Mande griots trace their family lineage back hundreds of years to the historical figure Bala Faseke Kouyate, who served as a praise-singer and advisor to Sundiata Keita (ca. 1217–1255 CE), the founder of the ancient Malian empire and the heroic protagonist of an epic song cycle that is still sung by griots today. Islamic griots often trace their lineage even further back to a man named Surakata. In the Quran, Surakata is an infidel who tries to kill the prophet Mohammed (ca. 570–632 CE) but converts to Islam when he witnesses the prophet's power. Surakata then travels with Mohammed singing the praises of Allah to all who will listen, in a sense becoming the first griot. Which (if any) of these historical origins is really true remains in debate, though it is likely that multiple cultural and historical streams contributed to the present-day griot position. Griots themselves may emphasize one or another history to suit a specific situation or audience.

Griots occupy a specific position within the social hierarchies to which they belong. With a common legacy of regional empires, many West African cultures traditionally had a hierarchical social organization based on a tripartite division into freeborn or noble people, artisan classes, and serf or slave classes. The griot position is one of the artisan classes, which may also include leatherworkers, blacksmiths, potters, carpenters, and religious poets, among others. The specifics of these artisanal divisions vary depending on the social or ethnic group: in Mande society, the artisan classes are called *nyamakala*; in Wolof and Fulbe they are called *nyeenyo*; and in Mauritanian Hassanaya they are called *ma'allimin*. Typically, the artisanal occupations are hereditarily determined, meaning that only people born into griot families were allowed to serve as griots. In Mande cultures, the speech and music of griots is thought to unleash a potentially dangerous force called *nyama*, which can be safely controlled only by properly trained people from certain families. Although scholars have sometimes focused only on male griots, women also frequently serve as griots (or *griottes*), at times drawing from a specifically female verbal and musical repertoire. As with the other artisanal occupations, the skills necessary to serve as a griot are closely guarded within families. In addition to their primary occupation, each of the artisanal positions serves specific cultural functions which are their duty and sole privilege to fulfill. Griots are known not only as musicians, entertainers, and historians, but also as skilled conflict mediators and advisors to nobility and political leaders.

Within West African societies, the griot position is typically viewed with ambivalence. On the one hand, griots are vital bearers of culture and history, and they are known to be exceptional entertainers. Likewise, they can wield considerable power in their roles as mediators of conflicts and advisors to political leaders. On the other hand, griots are sometimes looked down on because they may be seen as sycophantic puppets of the wealthy and powerful, and they are also notorious for demanding money from audience members. The Malian novelist Manthia Diawara recounts his intense dislike of griots because, to him, their involvement in hierarchical social structures represents the opposite of an idealistically egalitarian, democratic society; and yet, when he attends a griot concert in a nightclub, he gets so caught up in the performance that he almost unwittingly gives the griot singer a crisp $100 bill. Likewise, the contemporary Malian singer Salif Keita, who was born into a noble family directly descended from the legendary founder of the Malian empire, has discussed the pressures he faced when he decided to pursue music, because the griot profession was considered below him and musicians were regarded as immoral and irresponsible. In the most extreme cases, griots are said to have been buried in trees rather than the ground to avoid polluting the earth, which reflects both their scorned social status and the fear inspired by their mastery of words.

Today, this hierarchical social structure has become much more fluid, though social stratification and inequality still remain. Rather than working in the patronage of noble-born families, griots have adapted to new social and economic environments by seeking out more diverse venues and audiences. Likewise, people from non-griot families may decide to pursue careers in music, whether it be local traditional music or regional and international popular musics. Even so, musicians from griot families continue to be prevalent in West African music scenes, national folkloric ensembles, and even international superstardom. Both traditional and popular musics in West Africa continue to be inspired by griot musical instruments, style, and repertoire.

Although griots are sometimes thought of only as verbal artisans, it is the combination of verbal and musical skills that gives griot performances their power. Music played by griots is extremely diverse. They may play stringed instruments, xylophones, or drums, and they may sing a cappella or with accompaniment. They may perform for private social events, public rituals, or political events, and they may perform in nightclubs, public gathering spaces, private homes, street corners, or international concert stadiums. They can be heard on the radio, on cassettes and CDs, on personal cellphone music collections, and of course on digital media. Griot music is always rooted in deep history and tradition, but griots may also create new popular musics that blend their family traditions with internationally popular music styles. Some griots have become nationally important cultural figures, and a small number have achieved the status of international superstardom.

In addition to their vocal skills, griots typically specialize in one musical instrument, either a plucked lute, a harp or harp-lute, a xylophone, or a drum. Griot plucked lutes go by a variety of names depending on the culture, including the Wolof *xalam*, Fulbe *hoddu*, Moorish *tidinit*, Mande *ngoni*, Songhay *molo*, and Soninke *gambare*. Although they may differ in playing style, repertoire, size, number of strings, decoration, and use of electric pick-ups, the basic format is very similar. Typically, the instrument's oval or boat-shaped resonator is carved from a single piece of hardwood covered in animal skin, with a round neck attaching to a fan-shaped bridge that supports three to five nylon strings. The strings are all different lengths, and they are played in a combination of up- and downpicking with the index finger and thumb. This family of plucked lutes may have originated in the Ghanaian empire or may date back to cultural contacts with the ancient Egyptian empire, which used similar instruments. Collectively, the West African griot lutes are considered to be prototypes of the American banjo, which was first built by enslaved African Americans in the Caribbean and the United States. Some of the best-known players today include Bassekou Kouyate (1966–) and Cheick Hamala Diabaté, among others.

Griots from Mande cultures (*jalis*) are famous for playing the *kora*, a large chordophone with 21 strings made from a large calabash gourd covered with cowskin and a hardwood neck. It is called a harp-lute or bridge-harp because, like a lute, the strings are supported by a bridge that sits perpendicular to the soundplane but, like a harp, the strings are arranged in a line that is perpendicular to the soundplane. The left hand plays short, repetitive patterns (called *kum-bengo*) while the right hand plays stock melodies and virtuosic improvised runs (called *birimintingo*). The unique kora likely originated in the Senegambian region and more recently spread to other Mande cultures in Mali and Guinea. It is played almost exclusively by men. The best-known living kora players are Malian Toumani Diabaté (1965–) and Gambian Foday Musa Suso (1950–), who both play in traditional, popular, and fusion styles.

Moorish women griots (*iggio*) play another harplike instrument called the *ardin*. Like the kora, it is built from a large calabash resonator covered with animal skin, but the ardin has 10 to 13 strings and does not have a perpendicular bridge.

Sometimes described as a link between West and North African styles, music played by Moorish iggios is based on a series of melodic modes which each have a color designation of black, white, or mixed. The two most famous iggios are Dimi Mint Abba (1958–2011) and Malouma Mint Moktar Ouid Meidah (1960–), both women with powerful voices who accompany themselves on the ardin.

Mande griots may also play a xylophone called the *balafon*. The balafon consists of a series of hardwood bars, each with a small calabash resonator underneath, which are struck with rubber-tipped playing sticks. It is mentioned prominently in the Sundiata epic. In this origin story, Sundiata's griot Bala Faseke Kouyate was captured by a rival king who owned the first balafon. When Sundiata conquered his rival, Kouyate took the balafon and spread its popularity throughout the Malian empire, becoming the first true jali in the process. This original balafon is supposedly kept today in Guinea by members of the Kouyate family.

Griots may also play drums. There are hourglass-shaped pressure drums, such as the *tama*, and the collection of tall cylindrical drums known as *sabar*. Pressure drums are held underneath the arm and played with one or two curved sticks. By squeezing the drum under the arm, the drummer can increase the tension on cords that tighten the head, thereby changing the pitch of the instrument. Using sequences of tones and rhythms, griot drummers can pronounce messages and proverbs with their drums. This is why they are sometimes called "talking drums." The sabar is a large drum played by Wolof and Serer griots, and increasingly by non-griot musicians. Typically played in an ensemble of five or more drummers along with other musicians, sabar music is the foundation of local dance circles (also called sabar) as well as the popular Senegambian dance music called *mbalax*. The sabar's best-known exponent is the Senegalese griot Doudou Ndiaye Rose (1930–) who, along with his 43 children, has brought the instrument and its complex rhythms into national and international settings.

West African popular music draws inspiration from griot music. Griot instruments such as koras and sabars can frequently be heard on tracks that also include synthesizers, electric guitars, and horn sections. Senegalese superstar Youssou N'Dour (1959–) was born into a griot family on his mother's side, and he drew on his family traditions in shaping the popular mbalax dance music. The Malians Salif Keita (1949–) and Ali Farka Touré (1939–2006) and Senegalese Baaba Maal (1953–) have no hereditary ties to griot lineages, but they learned to play music under the tutelage of griots. All three performers play guitar in a distinctive style that draws from the techniques and repertoire of griot instruments such as the kora and ngoni.

Scott V. Linford

See also: Kora; Mande Music; Xalam

Further Reading

Appert, Cathrine. 2011. "Rappin' Griots: Producing the Local in Senegalese Hip-Hop." In P. Khalil Saucier (ed.), *Native Tongues: An African Hip-hop Reader*, 3–22. Trenton, NJ: Africa World Press.

Austen, Ralph, ed. 1999. *In Search of Sunjata: The Mande Oral Epic as History, Literature, and Performance*. Bloomington: Indiana University Press.

Bebey, Francis. 1983. "Le Monde ambigu des griots [The ambiguous world of griots]." *Balafon* 58, 54–58.

Belcher, Stephen. 2004. "Studying Griots: Recent Work in Mande Studies." *African Studies Review* 47(3), 172–186.

Bird, Charles. 1976. "Poetry in the Mande: Its Form and Meaning." *Poetics* 5, 89–100.

Charry, Eric. 2000. *Mande Music: Traditional and Modern Music of the Maninka and Mandinka of Western Africa*. Chicago: University of Chicago Press. [Companion CD: *Mande Music*].

Conrad, David. 1999. *Epic Ancestors of the Sunjata Era: Oral Tradition of the Maninka of Guinea*. Madison: University of Wisconsin African Studies Program.

Coolen, Michael Theodore. 1991. "Senegambian Influences on Afro-American Musical Culture." *Black Music Research Journal* 11, 1–18.

DjeDje, Jacqueline Cogdell. 2008. *Fiddling in West Africa: Touching the Spirit in Fulbe, Hausa, and Dagbamba Cultures*. Bloomington: Indiana University Press.

Dramé, Adama, and Arlette Senn-Borloz. 1992. *Jeliya: être griot et musicien aujourd'hui* [Jeliya: Being a contemporary griot and a musician]. Paris: L'Harmattan.

Hale, Thomas. 2007. *Griots and Griottes: Masters of Words and Music (African Expressive Cultures)*. Bloomington: Indiana University Press.

Janson, Marloes. 2002. *The Best Hand Is the Hand that Always Gives: Griottes and Their Profession in Eastern Gambia*. Leiden, The Netherlands: Center for Non-Western Studies.

Moloney, Governor. 1889. "On the Melodies of the Volof, Mandingo, Ewe, Yoruba, and Houssa People of West Africa." *Journal of the Manchester Geographical Society* 5, 277–298.

Pfeiffer, Katrin, ed. 1997. *Mandinka Spoken Art: Folk-Tales, Griot Accounts, and Songs*. Köln, Germany: Rüdiger Köppe Verlag.

Smith, M. G. 1957. "The Social Functions and Meaning of Hausa Praise-singing." *Africa* 27(1), 26–45.

Tamari, Tal. 1991. "The Development of Caste Systems in West Africa." *Journal of African History* 32(2), 221–250.

Guitarrón Mexicano

The Mexican *guitarrón* is a very large acoustic bass with six strings; the Chilean type has 24 to 25 strings. Although its pear-shaped soundbox resembles a guitar, the guitarrón evolved from the 16th-century *bajo de uña*, and its use was first recorded in the Ameca-Cocula Valley in central Jalisco. Versions of the guitarrón made before 1900 usually had four or five gut strings (like the *vihuela*), rather than the modern six. It is used as the bass instrument in *trío, orquestra típica* (a late 19th-century mixed string ensemble of five to seven players), and mariachi, for which it had replaced the *arpa* (diatonic harp) in most regions of Mexico by the late 19th century.

The strings are arranged to facilitate playing in series of parallel octaves to increase volume (called "double-string" style in mariachi). Due to the high action and tension of the thick strings, *guitarróneros* (guitarrón players) develop strength and dexterity in both hands. The left quickly depresses octaves and makes rapid scalar flourishes. The right must "pull" the strings away from the instrument body to produce the proper tone. Strings are typically a combination of three heavy gauge metal and three plastic (originally gut). It is tuned A'-D-G-c-e-a.

The guitarrón is a unique type of folk bass due to its size and shape; it possesses a large, vaulted (convex) body topped by a comparatively short neck. Some folk instruments are fretless, but urban guitarróneros have gradually begun to prefer instruments with as many as eight widely spaced frets. The broad top of the body is usually made from spruce, *grenadillo*, or *tacote* (a light Mexican native wood similar to balsa), while the back and sides (usually 13 cm or five inches deep) are of walnut, cedar, or mahogany. Despite the large, slightly ungainly size of the instrument, it is very light and portable. The deep sides have a slight V shape, as does the back of the instrument. This high, ridged contour contributes to the guitarrón's characteristic deep cavity and produces a loud, full, resonant tone. Its sonorous sound carries easily and does not require electronic amplification.

The *mariachi* ensemble began as a Jaliscan string group typified by one or two violins, harp, and regional guitar. By the 1930s, it had developed into the urbanized form we currently recognize—violins, trumpets, Spanish guitar, vihuela, a guitarrón, and sometimes the Jaliscan diatonic harp. The rhythmic core, or *armonía*, of mariachi music consists of the vihuela, guitar, and guitarrón and must be coordinated and precise. Their parts interlock and provide syncopation over which the melodic instruments play contrasting melodies and improvisations.

Although the guitarrón may play parts of the melody, it only does so to support the harmony and rhythmic structure of a piece, rather than to deliver a complete melodic line. It is often referred to as the "heartbeat" of Mexican folk ensembles. In a *ranchera*, the rhythmic organizing principle as forwarded by the armonía often falls along a quadruple or triple meter with stresses on the first and third beats.

Mexican folk music's low-class origins and its association with drunkenness and machismo have caused composers such as José Luis Quiñones to use the figure of the guitarrón player as a symbol of traditional Mexican music and of its stigmatized status. His hit song "*Se fue con el mariachi*" ("She Took Off with the Mariachi") describes a woman abandoning her lover in favor of an old guitarrónero: "*Y la ingrate se ligó al viejo del guitarrón*" ("The ungrateful girl banded together with the old guitarrón player"), and "*El hijo de Garibaldi a mi mujer me quitó con su guitarra grandota todita la apantalló*" ("Garibaldi's son took away my wife: he conquered her with his giant guitar").

The guitarrón has been featured in visual art, popular music, and poetry of the 20th century. Pablo Picasso's first adult cardboard construction (1912) was titled *Guitarrón*. He built a Cubist version of a Spanish guitar, and surrounded it in his studio with drawings of expanding and contracting instruments. The guitarrón's sound on the track "New Kid in Town" on the Eagles' *Hotel California* album (1976) was contemporaneous with Ernie Ball's development of the acoustic bass guitar. Contemporary poet Gary Soto uses the guitarrón to evoke rejuvenation and freedom from modernity, and as a way to experience authentic pleasure in his 1992 "Ode to El Guitarrón."

Laura Stanfield Prichard

See also: Conjunto; Conjunto (Norteños); Mariachi; Mexican Regional Music; Polka

Further Reading

Santiago González, Natividad de. 1983. *Méthodo Práctico de Guitarrón* [Practical method for the guitarrón]. Mexico City: Author.

Shecter, John. 1999. *Music and Cultures of Latin America*. New York: Schirmer.

Sheehy, Daniel. 2006. *Mariachi Music in America: Experiencing Music, Expressing Culture*. New York: Oxford University Press.

Gumba

Gumbe (also spelled *goombay* and *gombey*) is a genre of music that has its origins in the traditional music of Guinea-Bissau and Sierra Leone. It is also the name of a square-frame drum that is played both in West Africa and certain islands of the Caribbean.

The instrument is normally played while sitting, with the drum in between the player's legs. The gumbe is a frame drum, which means it does not have a large resonating cavity, and the sound comes from the vibration of the head only. Often with a frame drum, the player increases the tension of the head by pressing on part of it to change the pitch. In this case, the head is tightened by using the foot. The drum is played by descendants of the Krio people from West Africa, and was supposedly used to warn of impending attacks of an enemy. It was also used as part of ceremonies to communicate with ancestors, and for predicting future events.

This instrument has an interesting history that is tied to the story of the slave trade in West Africa and the Caribbean. When Jamaica, originally colonized by Spain, was overtaken by the British in 1655, a group of freed slaves went into the rugged mountains of the island, fought off any white settlers that tried to come near them, and established their own culture, which lasted for more than 200 years. This ethnic group, which was partially descended from the Krio of West Africa, was called the Maroons (other Maroons fled to nearby Suriname and French Guiana, along the north coast of South America). They made gumbe drums out of simple materials such as wood and goatskin, and used them as part of ritual dance ceremonies.

Gumbe also refers to the music that was originally played on this instrument, but has evolved into a genre of Afropop in its own right. The West African version of the style is centered in Guinea-Bissau and Sierra Leone, and is primarily percussion and vocal-based. As is true of many of the music styles from the developing world, the history of Gumbe is inherently connected with the region's political history. (The former Portuguese colony Guinea-Bissau is not to be confused with the neighboring country of Guinea, also called Guinea-Conakry, which is a French-speaking former French colony.)

Guinea-Bissau and Sierra Leone are among the poorest countries in the world, and both have been wracked by ethnic violence, dictatorships, and civil wars throughout the 20th century. The general poverty of the area has forced musicians to make music out of whatever materials they can find, and the gumbe drum is no exception. The drum is traditionally played in an ensemble that also consists of shakers, bottle percussion, and musical saw (used as a scraped percussion instrument, not a melodic instrument as in Appalachian folk music). One significant type of shaker that was common in Sierra Leone was a "Milo" can, known by the name of a brand of a malt powder product made by Nestlé (similar to Ovaltine). When emptied of its contents and refilled with stones or beads, it gives the characteristic sound of a music genre called "Milo jazz." The foremost artist of Milo jazz was "Dr. Oloh" (Israel Olorunfeh Cole, 1944–2007) of Sierra Leone. He was active from the 1970s through the 1990s.

Gumbe is a combination of earlier styles of Guinea-Bissau, much of which was lost during the civil war of 1998–1999. Unlike some other African countries, Guinea-Bissau has several ethnicities living within its borders. It is a relatively small country, and ethnic conflict in an enclosed geographic space has been exacerbated by close proximity to a possible rival. Some earlier musical styles from which gumbe developed, such as Tinga, were largely acoustic, especially in the earlier decades of the 20th century. In addition, earlier styles were associated with ethnicities and even religions, as some were Christian and others were Muslim or linked with traditional belief systems. Guinea-Bissau is a former colony of Portugal (it gained its independence in 1973) and has several ties to that country and to Brazil, from which it derives some musical influence. However, for many years, Gumbe music was only recorded outside of the country, in Portuguese studios.

One of the most important performers of Gumbe was Zé Carlos (José Carlos Schwarz, 1949–1977), who formed a group called Cobiana Djazz. Although they only recorded one album, released in 1977, this group was at times persecuted by the government of Bissau, and became a voice of the opposition. Zé Carlos later became the Minister of Arts and Culture under the new government. Sadly, he died in a suspicious plane crash near Havana, Cuba, in 1977. Before he died, Carlos had the honor of performing and recording his song "Diju di Galinha" with South African singer Miriam Makeba, who was at the time exiled from her home country and living in Ghana.

Kaba Mané (1957–) is another Guinea-Bissauan artist, popular in the 1980s with a dance style called *kussundé,* named after the kora-like traditional harp of the region. Mané sings in the Balanta language and plays electric guitar, but his style is influenced by the kora. He has recorded most of his albums in Paris, where he still lives.

Other Guinea-Bissauan musicians immigrated to Portugal and recorded there also. Justino Delgado is a popular artist who sings in Portuguese and combines traditional rhythms with a healthy dose of synthesizers and energetic guitar work. Delgado has also become involved in the politics of his native country, and at one point considered a run for the presidency.

Gumbe may also be tangentially related to a genre of Bahamanian music called goombay. Much of the 20th-century Caribbean musical history is dominated by calypso and reggae and other styles that became successful on the United States mainland. Goombay was one of those styles, and is closely associated with tourism and performances at hotels in Nassau, even though the gumbe drum is only used occasionally. One of the most famous of these hotel performers was Blake Alphonso Higgs (1915–1986), known by his stage name of "Blind Blake" (not to be confused with an earlier American blues performer who also used that name). Blind Blake was a performer on guitar and banjo, and also a songwriter. In fact, the Beach Boys were inspired to adapt the Caribbean folk song "John B. Sail" into their hit "Sloop John B" after hearing Blind Blake's version.

Christopher Gable

See also: Kora; Mento; Rara; Riq; Tassa Drumming

Further Reading

Broughton, Simon, et al., eds. 2006. *The Rough Guide to World Music; Vol. 1: Africa and Middle East,* 3rd ed. London: Rough Guides.

Ellingham, Mark, et al., eds. 2000. *World Music: The Rough Guide; Vol. 2: Latin and North America, Caribbean, India, Asia and Pacific.* London: Rough Guides.

Guoyue

Guoyue literally means "national music" in Chinese. This term is used both in China and in Taiwan. In the broadest sense, it can be applied to any music composed for Chinese musical instruments and the format includes solo, ensemble, or large orchestra. Nowadays it is also referred to as *minyue* (which means "folk music") or *zhongyue* (which means "Chinese music").

The usage of guoyue can be traced back to the Sui-Tang period (581–907 CE), which refers to *yayue* (literally "court music"), but the term is not pervasively used until the beginning of the 20th century, when it was employed to distinguish between the Western music that was being newly imported to China, and traditional Chinese music, including Chinese instrumental music, opera, folk music, and so on. When the Communist Party of China took over mainland China and established the People's Republic of China in 1949, "guoyue" was used in Taiwan (Republic of China), while "minyue" and "zhongyue" were used in China.

Although "guoyue" can be used to refer to any Chinese music, this term is often applied to Chinese art music more than folk music. Under the influence of large orchestras from European countries, Chinese intellectuals became interested in modernizing and revitalizing the traditional Chinese music and proposed establishing a Chinese orchestra, a form that is based on the structure and principles of a Western symphony orchestra but using Chinese instruments instead. The Chinese orchestra consists of bowed strings, mainly the *huqin* family; plucked instruments, including *yangqin, pipa, liuqin, zhongruan, daruan, sanxian,* and *guzheng*; wind instruments, such as *dizi, sheng, suona*; and percussion instruments such as *luo* (gongs), *gu* (drums), *bo* (cymbals), *Tanggu, muyu,* and *qing.*

Famous guoyue pieces include "The Moon Mirrored in the Erquan Pool," which was composed for *erhu* solo first and later orchestrated; "Horse Racing," an erhu solo piece; "Suzhou Travel," for dizi solo; "Dance of the Yao People," which was originally composed for a Western orchestra; "Dance of the Yi People," for pipa; "Ambushed from Ten Sides," for pipa; and "Hundred Birds Pay Homage to Phoenix," and "Spring Flowers on Moonlit River," both for Chinese orchestras.

Besides of China and Taiwan, many Asian countries also have Chinese orchestras. Notable Chinese orchestras include the China Broadcasting Chinese Orchestra, China National Traditional Orchestra, Shanghai Chinese Orchestra, Hong Kong

Chinese Orchestra, Singapore Chinese Orchestra, Taipei Chinese Orchestra, National Chinese Orchestra (Taiwan), and Philippine Cultural College Chinese Orchestra.

Chloe Hsun Lin

See also: Erhu; Guzheng; Huqin; Pipa

Further Reading

Fung, Victor. 1995. "Chinese Music Journals Published in Chinese and Located in Selected Major U.S. Libraries." *ACMR Reports* 8(2), 52–70.

Liang Mingyue. 1985. *Music of the Billion: An Introduction to Chinese Musical Culture.* New York: C. F. Peters.

Moser, Leo. 1985. *The Chinese Mosaic: The Peoples and Provinces of China.* Boulder, CO: Westview Press.

Guthrie, Woody (1912–1967)

Woody Guthrie was a folksinger, songwriter, and author whose songs stand among the greatest testimonies to the Great Depression and the Dust Bowl era. He was also a prolific writer and cartoonist. With a playful, often ornery, hillbilly persona that he turned on and off at will, Guthrie accompanied himself on guitar and sang with a straightforward, penetrating tone. In the words of Guthrie, "Every folk song that I know tells how to fix something in this world to make it better, tell what is wrong with it, and what we've got to do to fix it better" (quoted in Cohen, 2012, p. 31). During the course of his life, Guthrie wrote the lyrics to more than a thousand songs, some of which have become an accepted part of the American folk canon, including "This Land Is Your Land" and "So Long, It's Been Good to Know You." "This Land Is Your Land" is arguably Guthrie's most famous song, and some have called it the unofficial national anthem of the United States.

Woodrow Wilson Guthrie was born on July 14, 1912, to parents Charley and Nora (Tanner) Guthrie in Okemah, Oklahoma. Guthrie was named after the Democratic presidential candidate, Woodrow Wilson, who had been nominated 12 days before the folksinger's birth. He enjoyed a comfortable, middle-class childhood, but his family experienced numerous tragedies during his teenage years. His father's real estate business struggled when Okemah's oil industry plummeted after the end of World War I, plunging the family into dire financial straits. Additionally, Guthrie's sister and father were seriously burned in two separate household fires, and his sister's injuries proved fatal; though accounts of the events differ depending upon the source, Nora Guthrie is known to have been involved on both occasions. Shortly thereafter, Guthrie's mother was committed to an asylum with undiagnosed Huntington's disease, the disease that would eventually afflict her son as well. Following his mother's committal and his father's convalescence, 15-year-old Guthrie was left to fend for himself, living with friends, neighbors, and on his own.

Guthrie moved to Pampa, Texas, in 1929 to join his father and extended family. Already proficient on the harmonica, he learned to play guitar and became a member of a local band, the Corncob Trio. Despite being a high school dropout,

American folk musician and political activist Woody Guthrie performing in 1943. (Eric Schaal/Time & Life Pictures/Getty Images)

Guthrie was an avid reader and continued to educate himself by means of the local library. He was remarkably well self-educated, though he often disguised it behind a hillbilly facade. In 1933 he married Mary Jennings, setting up residence in a shotgun shack in Pampa; together they had three children, Gwendolyn ("Teeny"), Sue, and Bill. During 1933 and 1934, major dust storms swept through the central United States, causing massive erosion and blackouts that lasted for entire days at a time. The hardships inflicted by the storms inspired some of Guthrie's earliest songs, including "So Long, It's Been Good to Know You" and "Dust Bowl Blues."

In 1937, Guthrie, who always had a tendency to wander, left his growing family and traveled west to Los Angeles. There he performed on a radio show called *The Oklahoma and Woody Show* with his cousin, Jack Guthrie, a moderately successful cowboy singer. The show, in its various manifestations (it later became *Woody and Lefty Lou*), met with sufficient success for Guthrie to send for Mary and the children.

While in California, Guthrie also met Ed Robbins and actor Will Geer, who introduced him to leftist politics. Through Robbins, Guthrie began writing the column "Woody Sez" in the Communist publication *People's World*. He wrote in an entertainingly exaggerated, folksy tone and often accompanied the column with a witty cartoon. Though never a member of the Communist Party, Guthrie became involved in many of its causes, most notably labor unions, having witnessed the poverty and mistreatment of "Okies" and other migrant workers in the California agriculture industry.

Never one to be stationary for long, Guthrie moved to New York City in 1939. He soon made a place for himself within the small folk music community there, which at the time included Lead Belly (Huddie Ledbetter, 1888–1949), Aunt Molly Jackson (1880–1960), and a young Pete Seeger (1919–), among others. Early on during his time in New York, Guthrie penned the words to "This Land Is Your Land." Originally titled "God Blessed America," the song contained several politically oriented verses and came as a direct response to Irving Berlin's recent hit, "God Bless America." In 1940, Guthrie spent three days in Washington, D.C., making extensive, and now historic, recordings of his stories and repertoire for the Library of Congress at the request of Alan Lomax (1915–2002), a friend and head of the Archive of American Folk Song.

Not long afterward, Guthrie set out on a cross-country road trip west with Pete Seeger, singing for a variety of union gatherings along the way and writing new union songs such as "Union Maid." Early 1941 saw Guthrie in Portland, Oregon, writing songs about the Grand Coolee Dam for the Bonneville Power Administration. The month spent in Portland was one of Guthrie's most productive and resulted in some of his most memorable songs, including "Roll On, Columbia, Roll On," "The Biggest Thing that Man Has Ever Done," and "Pastures of Plenty." In June, Guthrie returned to New York City and joined the Almanac Singers, a folk-singing group that had been recently formed by Pete Seeger, Lee Hays, and Millard Lampell. For the next few years Guthrie often performed with the group, and he contributed significantly to their material. During this time he also produced a creative autobiography, *Bound for Glory*, published in 1943.

In 1943, Guthrie joined the war effort and enlisted with the United States Merchant Marine alongside Gilbert "Cisco" Houston (a close friend and fellow folk-singer) and Vincent "Jim" Longhi, and together they served three tours. Following his discharge, Guthrie was drafted into the military for nine months in 1945 just as World War II was ending. Once released from duty, Guthrie returned to New York City to live with his new wife, Marjorie Mazia, with whom he had been living occasionally since 1942 and with whom he had a young daughter, Cathy Ann. Guthrie and Mary (née Jennings) divorced in 1943.

After the war, Guthrie became a part of People's Songs, an activist group organized by Pete Seeger. He also wrote a large number of children's songs, inspired by his own children, and recorded them for Disc Records. The albums that resulted, *Songs to Grow On: Nursery Days* and *Songs to Grow On: Work Songs for Nursery Days*, showcase Guthrie's childlike whimsy and his fascination with wordplay and rhyme. During the late 1940s, Marjorie and Guthrie had three more children: Arlo, Joady, and Nora. Sadly, Cathy Ann died after an accidental house fire in 1947—yet another incident of fiery tragedy in Guthrie's life.

Though little known outside of the New York folk sphere, Guthrie developed a number of relationships that eventually contributed to more widespread fame. One such friendship was with "Ramblin'" Jack Elliott (born Elliot Adnopoz, 1931–), who idolized and imitated Guthrie much as Bob Dylan would in the 1960s. Elliott toured extensively in England and performed much of Guthrie's repertoire. As a result, Guthrie became widely known in England before he did in the United States. Guthrie also began to accompany the Weavers (a folk group of which Pete Seeger and Lee Hays were members) to many of their engagements, and their recording of his song "So Long, It's Been Good to Know You" reached no. 4 on the pop charts in 1951 (Cohen, 2012, p. 38).

By the early 1950s, Guthrie's behavior was becoming even more erratic than usual. Though initially misdiagnosed with alcoholism, Guthrie was eventually diagnosed with Huntington's disease in late 1952. Despite his divorce from Marjorie in 1953 (and a short-lived third marriage that resulted in the birth of his last child, Lorina), Marjorie became Guthrie's caretaker as his disease progressed. In 1954, his hospitalization became permanent. During this time Guthrie was showered with visits by family, old friends, and new admirers and folksingers who came on pilgrimages to meet him. The most historic of these visitors was Bob Dylan, who first visited Guthrie in 1961 and included the "Song to Woody" on his first album. When Guthrie died on October 3, 1967, in the Creedmore State Hospital on Long Island, his fame and reputation exceeded any he had enjoyed during his active performing years.

The years following Guthrie's death saw a panoply of tribute concerts featuring the best-known names in folk music. Recently, a number of popular artists have produced albums using some of Guthrie's previously unset lyrics, including *Mermaid Avenue* and *Mermaid Avenue II* by British recording artist Billy Braggs and the band Wilco, as well as *Wonder Wheel* and *Woody Guthrie's Joyous Happy Hanukkah* by the Klezmatics. Most significantly, Guthrie's legacy continues in the music of those he influenced, such as Bob Dylan, Ramblin' Jack Elliott, Pete Seeger, and his son Arlo Guthrie.

Christy J. Miller

See also: Dylan, Bob; Folkways Records; Lomax, Alan and John; Seeger, Peter

Further Reading
Cohen, Ronald D. 2012. *Woody Guthrie: Writing America's Songs.* New York: Routledge.
Cray, Ed. 2004. *Ramblin' Man: The Life and Times of Woody Guthrie.* New York: W.W. Norton.
Edgmon, Mary Jo Guthrie, and Guy Logsdon. 2012. *Woody's Road: Woody Guthrie's Letters Home, Drawings, Photos, and Other Unburied Treasures.* Boulder, CO: Paradigm.
Guthrie, Woody. 1968. *Bound for Glory.* New York: E. P. Dutton.
Klein, Joe. 1980. *Woody Guthrie: A Life.* New York: Alfred A. Knopf.

Guzheng

Guzheng, or *zheng* (*gu* means "ancient"), is a Chinese plucked zither with movable bridges. It has a history extending over more than 2,500 years and is considered the ancestor of several Asian zither instruments. Guzheng originally had five strings and a bamboo body. In the Qin dynasty, general Meng Tian (d. 210 BCE) increased the number of strings to 12, altered the shape of the guzheng, and used wood instead of bamboo. In the Tang dynasty, it was further expanded to 13 strings. Today the size of guzheng varies from 120 to 170 cm long and 20 to 35 cm wide, depending on the number of strings, which ranges from 13 to 25. Today a guzheng usually has 21 strings and measure 65 inches (163 cm) in length.

According to *Shuowen Jiezi*, an early Chinese dictionary that was edited by Xu Shen from the Han Dynasty around 100 CE, guzheng originally was an instrument made of bamboo. Today, however, the soundboard is usually made of wutong wood or white pine wood, with the bottom being flat and the upper arched. A hardwood, such as red sandalwood, rosewood, or boxwood, is used for the sides. Traditionally strings are made of silk, but today they are commonly made of steel wound with nylon. The strings are tightened on pins at one end and stretched over individual, movable bridges, which helps to tune the instrument to a pentatonic scale according to the mode system, and then wound around tuning pegs at the other end.

There are some explanations of the origin of guzheng. One of the most famous is a story about two people who fought over the *se* (another bamboo zither) and broke it into two halves, which became guzheng. Indeed, the pronunciation of "zheng" is close to that of "fight" in Chinese, and some believe that this is where the name came from. Another story from *Shuowen Jiezi* is that the name of the zheng derived from its sound, which is more reliable, but does not explain the origins of the word. The character zheng has two parts: the radical *zhu*, meaning bamboo, which indicates the material; and the phonetic element *zheng* which implies the sound or "to quarrel." One thing of which we are sure is that guzheng was developed before the Qin dynasty. The music of guzheng is considered to be the music of Qin, which comes from an article by Li Si (280–208 BCE): "tapping and scrapping jars and instruments of baked earth, playing the zheng, slapping the thighs and singing a song pleasing to the ear—that is the true music of Qin" (Li Si, 1958).

There are many different schools of guzheng performance. They can be broadly identified as Northern and Southern, but they are varied from region to region. Northern style is associated with Henan, Shandong, and Shaanxi, whereas the Southern is associated with the Chaozhou and Hakka regions of eastern Guangdong, Hangzhou of Zhejiang, and Fujian.

Chloe Hsun Lin

See also: Huqin; Koto; Pipa; Qin; Zither

Further Reading

Cao Zheng, and Yohana Knobloch. 1983. "A Discussion of the History of the Guzheng." *Asian Music* 14(2), 1–16.

"*Li Si Liezhuan* [historical biography of Li Si, 237 BCE]." In Sima Qian (ed.), *Shiji* [Records of the grand historian], vol. 87. Beijing: Zhonghua Shuju.

Te-yuan Cheng. 1991. "Zheng, Tradition and Change." PhD diss., University of Maryland (Baltimore County).

Gyil

The *gyil* (plural, *gyile*) is a type of African xylophone from northwestern Ghana, northeastern Côte d'Ivoire, and southern Burkina Faso. Gyil music is played almost exclusively by the Dagara, Lobi, Dagaaba, Losaale, Birifor, and Sissala people. A regional iteration of the xylophone, gyile have between 12 and 14 keys, major or minor pentatonic tuning, wooden frames, and gourd resonators. They are played by a *gyilimbwere*, who sits on a short stool. The gyil is thought to be derived from the *kpan kpul* or pit xylophone, which is constructed with 14 keys strung together, placed over a shallow pit resonator, and played by a musician who sits on the ground. Today, kpan kpul is usually played by children learning traditional repertoire of the gyil.

The gyil is made from dry wood harvested from the *nega* tree during the dry season between October and February. The keyboard is attached to the frame using leather strips, and dried gourds of various sizes are hung beneath the bars in two

> **Gyil**
>
> Made from the wood of the nega or liga tree, the *gyil* (sometimes spelled *gyill*) has many similarities to its central and south American counterparts, the marimba and marimba del arco. The hardwoods used to make the instrument's keys (nega or liga for the gyil, rosewood, for the marimba) share similar acoustical properties. Interestingly, in both of these building traditions the instrument's keys must dry and age for a prescribed time after harvesting—the longer the better. High-quality gyil, for example, are often decades old before the instrument is considered to reach its peak. Famed gyil master the late Bernard Woma played an instrument that was nearly 100 years old.

rows. The gyil's highly desirable "buzzing" sound is created by small holes punctured in each gourd, covered by spider egg sac casings, and placed facing outward to project the buzzing sound. Xylophone beaters, called *gyilibie* ("child of the gyil"), are made of a hard wood and have rubber ends made from wrapped natural rubber or automobile tire tread. Held between the index and middle finger, the stick rests down the middle of the player's palm.

The gyil repertoire can be divided into two subcategories: (1) music for funerals, and (2) recreational music performed at festivals, naming ceremonies, weddings, and other more casual gatherings. Both funeral and recreational music employ the gyil ensemble, including a lead gyil part; a supporting gyil; and the *kuor*, *ganga*, and *lar* drums. The lead gyil plays the melody, which requires excellent hand independence as the part uses independent motions, forming a composite rhythm. The supporting gyil part is similar to the lead, except that the player's left hand frequently utilizes the wooden end of the mallet to tap a repeating rhythm (*kparo*) on the lowest key of the instrument.

Kuor is a drum made from a hollow calabash with the top removed and covered with the skin of a monitor lizard, which is stretched tightly over the opening and fastened in place with tacks. Played using fingers on the drum head, kuor produces two sounds: an open tone and a higher, sharp slapping sound. Ganga is a double-headed, cylindrical drum played with sticks. It is made with thick cowhide heads and produces a low sound to complement the gyil. Lar are a pair of smaller kettle drums with closed bottoms. They are carved from wood and have goatskin heads, thinner than those of the ganga, that are laced around the bottom of the drum and played with a thin branch. These drums are never heard within one ensemble at the same time and are used in different ways by the various ethnic groups that play gyil ensemble music.

At a young age, gyilimbwere begin learning the traditional repertoire unique to their culture through oral tradition. Scholarly attempts to transcribe gyil ensemble music in traditional Western notation have presented several issues. Highly syncopated and extra-metrical embellishments make it difficult to notate both the gyil parts and the dense drum parts. This music is a coded language, each song with distinct meaning and implications difficult to capture in Western notation. Additionally, gyile are not built using standard pitches or intervals between the bars.

Although gyil music is a geographically insular tradition, similar instruments called *balafons* and other xylophones are also found in Western Africa and throughout the African continent. It is important to note that these instruments have their own unique meanings and heritage separate from that of the gyil.

Phoebe E. Hughes

Further Reading

Mensah, Atta Anan. 1982. "Gyil: The Dagara-Lobi Xylophone." *Journal of African Studies* 9(3) (Fall), 139–154.

Strumpf, Mitchel. 1970. *Ghanaian Xylophone Studies*. Legon: Institute of African Studies, University of Ghana-Legon.